THE
AA
KEYGuide

CW00486965

KEYGuide

The **AA** **KEY**Guide
South Africa

Contents

KEY TO SYMBOLS

- Map reference
- Address
- Telephone number
- Opening times
- Admission prices
- Bus number
- Train station
- Ferry/boat
- Driving directions
- Tourist office
- Tours
- Guidebook
- Restaurant
- Café
- Shop
- Toilets
- Number of rooms
- No smoking
- Air conditioning
- Swimming pool
- Gym
- Other useful information
- Shopping
- Entertainment
- Nightlife
- Sports
- Activities
- Health and Beauty
- For Children
- Cross reference
- Walk/drive start point

HOW TO USE THIS BOOK

Understanding South Africa is an introduction to the country, its geography, economy and people. **Living South Africa** gives an insight into the country today, while **The Story of South Africa** takes you through the country's past.

For detailed advice on getting to South Africa—and getting around once you are there—turn to **On the Move**. For useful practical information, from weather forecasts to emergency services, turn to **Planning**.

Out and About gives you the chance to explore South Africa through walks and drives.

The Sights, What to Do and **Eating and Staying** sections are divided geographically into eight regions, which are shown on the map on the inside front cover. These regions always appear in the same order. Towns and places of interest are listed alphabetically within each region.

Map references for **The Sights** refer to the atlas section at the end of this book or to individual town plans. For example, Table Mountain has the reference ✚ 326 C11, indicating the page on which the map is found (326) and the grid square in which Table Mountain sits (C11).

UNDERSTANDING
SOUTH AFRICA

**South Africa has some of the most varied and extreme
environments in the world, from the tropical beaches of
KwaZulu-Natal to the rolling red sand dunes of the Kalahari Desert.
And roaming through these landscapes are the animals that
draw countless visitors eager to see charismatic creatures in the
country's world-class game reserves. But scratch the surface a
little and a further attraction becomes clear—the people.
South Africa's population is an incredible mix of races, religions
and identities, so that it truly merits the nickname
'Rainbow Nation'.**

Young fans supporting the Springboks, the country's rugby union team

LANDSCAPE
South Africa is a huge country. The total land
area is 1,219,912sq km (471,008sq miles)—
1,267,462sq km (489,367sq miles) including
Swaziland and Lesotho. These are independent
countries; Lesotho is completely surrounded by
South Africa, but Swaziland borders both South
Africa and Mozambique. Contained within the
country are tropical rainforest in the east, the
spectacular mountains of the Drakensberg, the
rolling grasslands of Kruger, temperate woodlands
along the Garden Route, cacti-studded plains in
the interior and the endless deserted beaches
fringing the entire coast.

CLIMATE
As a country in the southern hemisphere, South
Africa's seasons are the reverse of those in
the northern hemisphere, which means that
summer is from November to March, and the
coldest months are June to September. Summer
weather is generally hot and, in certain areas,
humid, and temperatures often soar above 30°C
(86°F). Winter days are often sunny and mild, but
don't be deceived—temperatures can drop below

freezing at night in some areas. Much of the
interior and the north of the country are dry
with sporadic rain, while areas like the Garden
Route have light rainfall all year round.

LANGUAGE
There are 11 official languages in South Africa,
but English is widely understood and spoken.
Before the end of apartheid, Afrikaans was the
other official language with English, and it is still
the most widely seen—many road signs, for
example, are in both languages. Many of the
African languages are more or less mutually
intelligible. The major distinction is between the
Nguni languages (isiXhosa, isiZulu, SiSwati and
isiNdebele) and those closely related to Sesotho
and Setswana.

ECONOMY
South Africa has for many years suffered from
having both a developed and a developing
economy within the same country. It is incredibly
rich in natural resources—the economy is dominated by mining—and while a small sector of the
population is affluent, the majority suffers from

The Big Five—South Africa is famous for its national parks, particularly Kruger. Heading off into the wilderness to spot lion, leopard, black rhino, buffalo and elephant (the 'Big Five') is an unforgettable experience.

Adrenalin sports—From the world's highest bungee jump to white-water rafting or great white shark diving, South Africa has an astounding range of heart-pumping activities.

The Drakensberg have majestic mountain landscapes and some of the best hiking in southern Africa.

The San legacy—Get to grips with South Africa's ancient history through the rock art of the San people, going back more than 20,000 years.

There's a whole range of experiences to be had in South Africa, such as abseiling (rappelling) down Table Mountain (left), spotting leopards (middle) or relaxing in Johannesburg (right)

The Two Oceans—South Africa's shores are washed by the Atlantic on one side and the Indian Ocean on the other, making it an unbeatable scuba diving destination.

Architecture—From traditional Cape Dutch homesteads to Zulu beehive huts, the country has astoundingly rich and varied architecture.

A *braai*—Don't miss out on this great South African institution, the traditional Afrikaner barbecue, best enjoyed at sunset with a cold beer.

The nightlife in cities like Johannesburg, Durban and Cape Town rivals that of Europe's clubbing capitals.

Beach life—The country's endless coastline is blessed with stunning beaches, from the wind-lashed expanses on the West Coast to the palm-fringed coves of the east.

Traditional culture—Take in some traditional African culture—dancing, singing or a festival—such as the remarkable Umhlanga Reed dance in Swaziland.

Tasting wine on one of the centuries-old estates in the Western Cape's verdant Winelands area.

poverty and high levels of unemployment. Agricultural production also makes a significant contribution to the economy; almost one third of the workforce is in agriculture, although employment in this sector is characterized by extremely low wages and seasonal unemployment. The government is doing much to redress the imbalance between rich and poor—which in effect still means between white and black. It has introduced empowerment legislation, which is designed to shift a percentage of ownership and management of businesses into black hands. Certainly, the last ten years have seen significant progress: The economy is the strongest in Africa and an affluent black middle class has emerged, something which was unthinkable in the years of apartheid. Tourism, meanwhile, has been the country's big success story, with South Africa having the fastest growing annual visitor numbers in the world.

DEMOGRAPHY
South Africa's population (a total of 42.7 million) consists of numerous races, religions, ethnicities and cultures, which can be bewildering for visitors. While many people today resent being classified in terms of race and ethnicity, it is impossible to discuss modern South Africa without touching on these terms.

Most of the population is black African, which makes up around 77 per cent of the total. About 11 per cent is white, while 9 per cent is referred to as 'coloured' (descendants of slaves, white settlers and Africans), the most contentious classification, but one that is still used. There are also many coloured people who are partially descended from the pre-colonial San and Khoi populations of the Cape. Around 80 per cent of the coloured population speaks Afrikaans.

The African population is further split into different ethnic groups, also known as tribes. The largest group is the Zulu, the majority of them living in KwaZulu-Natal or in the industrial areas of Gauteng. The second biggest ethnic group is the Xhosa, who live in the Eastern Cape province and in and around Cape Town. Many

There are three ethnic groups whose members are closely related to the populations of three of South Africa's neighbouring countries: the Tswana (Botswana), the Swazi (Swaziland) and the Southern Sotho (Lesotho). These three, along with four other ethnic groups—the Tsonga, the Ndebele, the Venda and the Northern Sotho— have populations that are dispersed in the old homeland areas, although many have gravitated to the cities.

South Africa's white population can be divided into two main groups: English speakers and Afrikaans speakers. The ancestors of English-speaking white South Africans first arrived in the

School children in KwaZulu-Natal (left); a bride in traditional Indian dress (middle); cricket fans (right)

of the leaders of the ruling African National Congress (ANC), including former president Nelson Mandela (1918–), are Xhosa from Eastern Cape, reflecting the area's long history of resistance politics.

country in 1820, while the Afrikaner population is descended from the original Dutch settlers.

South Africa has a small Asian population, accounting for about 3 per cent of the total, whose ancestors came from South Asia as indentured labourers.

RELIGION
Most South Africans are Christian, with large groups belonging to the Church of England, the Dutch Reformed Church and countless other denominations. A small proportion of Africans practise indigenous religions. There are also significant numbers of Hindus and Muslims, and a small Jewish population.

POLITICS
South Africa is a constitutional democracy with a three-tier system of government: national, provincial and local. All tiers have legislative and executive authority in their own areas. Parliament sits in Cape Town and national government ministries are in Pretoria. Parliament consists of two houses, the National Assembly and the National Council of Provinces. The National Assembly has 400 members, who are elected for a five-year term. The last general election was held in April 2004, which saw the ruling African National Congress (ANC) win an overwhelming 279 seats. Ten other parties joined the National Assembly, the majority of which went to the opposition Democratic Alliance (who have 50 seats). The country's constitution is one of the most progressive in the world, and forbids discrimination on any grounds.

Members of the Christian St. John's Church in Maseru, Lesotho

THE PROVINCES OF SOUTH AFRICA

South Africa is divided into nine provinces. In this book, some of them have been grouped together and are listed here. A chapter about the independent kingdoms of Lesotho and Swaziland has also been included.

The Cape Peninsula has South Africa's most agreeable city, Cape Town, characterized by Table Mountain and its magnificent bay.

Western Cape has a huge range of environments and sights, including the rolling vineyards of the Winelands, the forests and beaches of the Garden Route and the dry expanse of the Karoo.

Eastern Cape is a less visited area but is immensely rewarding for its beautifully preserved Cape Dutch towns, the deserted beaches of the Wild Coast, and the superb wildlife viewing at the Greater Addo National Elephant Park.

KwaZulu-Natal is a subtropical area with a magnificent stretch of coastline, the inland battlefield sites from the Zulu and Anglo-Boer wars, and the Drakensberg Mountains, a spectacular wilderness area ideal for hiking.

Limpopo and Mpumalanga have South Africa's premier attraction: the Kruger National Park, which has some of the best places to view game in southern Africa.

Gauteng and Free State hold the country's two most important cities—the metropolis of Johannesburg and the administrative capital, Pretoria—as well as the towns and parks of the Eastern Highlands.

Northern Cape and North West Province cover a vast area of the arid north, on the fringes of the Kalahari, and include excellent game parks and the diamond capital, Kimberley.

Lesotho and Swaziland are independent countries that border South Africa, respectively providing a chance to experience traditional Sesotho or Swazi culture as well as excellent game viewing.

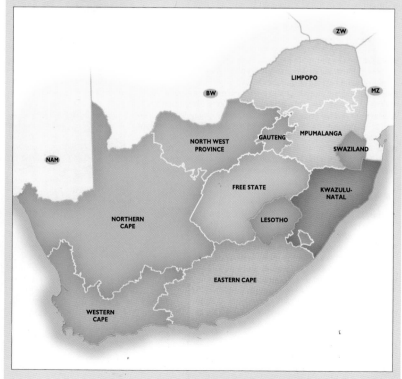

THE CAPE PENINSULA

Sunset The views from the top of Table Mountain (▷ 75) are superb at any time of day, but at sunset the panorama of the glittering ocean surrounding the city comes into its own.

History Grand colonial structures grace the wide streets in central Cape Town (▷ 64–69), not far from the brightly painted houses of Bo-Kaap, historically the city's Islamic district (▷ 65).

Beach Cape Town has some of South Africa's finest beaches; you can laze beneath palm trees on Camps Bay (▷ 61), or swim with penguins on Boulder's Beach (▷ 71).

Walk Stroll up to Cape Point (▷ 62), the stark promontory that straddles the Peninsula, with wide-reaching views of the Atlantic and False Bay.

Picnic Join the locals for a concert picnic at the lush Kirstenbosch Botanical Gardens (▷ 72), on the side of Table Mountain.

A view from Table Mountain

WESTERN CAPE

Wine On the old estates of the Winelands (▷ 90–95) you can enjoy world-class wine tasting in traditional Cape Dutch homesteads, amid surroundings of rolling mountains.

Nature The ancient forest giants of Tsitsikamma National Park (▷ 88) inhabit beautiful walking territory; or you can take a canopy tour for a birds'-eye view (▷ 196).

Beach Join the family throngs on one of the long, sandy stretches of the Garden Route (▷ 80, 228–229), or watch whales from Hermanus (▷ 89).

Wildlife Oudtshoorn (▷ 84), a quiet town in the Karoo, has 90 per cent of the world's ostrich population. You can see them at one of the many ostrich farms.

Eating The open-air seafood *braais* (barbecues) on the West Coast (▷ 262–264) serve huge portions in a beautiful beach setting.

A canopy tour at Tsitsikamma

EASTERN CAPE

Wildlife The Greater Addo Elephant National Park (▷ 101) is the best place in South Africa to see elephants, with enormous herds roving across its grasslands.

Beach Escape the crowds on the endless windswept beaches of the Wild Coast (▷ 104), backed by traditional Xhosa *kraals*.

Wilderness A drive to the viewpoint above the Valley of Desolation (▷ 98) reveals the vast expanse of the Eastern Karoo stretching to all horizons.

Walk The mystical Amatola Mountains (▷ 97) inspired J. R. R. Tolkien's *Lord of the Rings*; they make great walking country.

Surf Jeffreys Bay (▷ 97) is a top site for surfers, where you can learn how to ride the waves.

An ostrich at Oudtshoorn (above) Fun at the Wild Coast (below)

KWAZULU-NATAL

Wetlands A boat trip across the expansive wetlands of St. Lucia (▷ 112–113) gives you the chance to see many birds, plus hippos and crocodiles.

Tour Take a guided tour of historic battlefields (▷ 106–107) and let the rolling grasslands come alive with tales of bravery and loss.

Hiking The finest hiking in South Africa is in the magnificent Drakensberg mountain range (▷ 120–123).

Underwater Sodwana Bay (▷ 119) is famed for its scuba diving, and is one of the top places in the country for diving with sharks.

Culture Soak up some traditional Zulu culture, from tasting home-brewed beer to watching the time-honoured craft of basket weaving (▷ 119).

Stopping for a break while in the Drakensberg

A lioness in the Kruger Park

Plenty of shopping in Pretoria

Kgalagadi Transfrontier Park (top); flowers of the Namakwa (above)

Northern Mountains herdsman

LIMPOPO AND MPUMALANGA

Wildlife A tour with a ranger in Kruger National Park (▷ 128–135) is the best way of seeing the Big Five.

Walk Get up close and personal to Kruger's wildlife on a guided walk (▷ 134–135), and enjoy the park's flora.

Overnight Stay in one of the private or public camps in Kruger (▷ 290–291) and listen out for the roar of lions, or watch hungry hyenas prowling the perimeters at night.

Views Winding for 26km (16 miles) and dropping by as much as 750m (2,460ft), the Blyde River Canyon (▷ 126–127) is an impressive sight.

History A stroll among the perfectly preserved gold miners' houses in Pilgrim's Rest (▷ 137) gives an evocative insight into the harsh days of the gold rush.

GAUTENG AND FREE STATE

History A harrowing but ultimately inspiring account of the darkest days of apartheid is vividly told at Johannesburg's Apartheid Museum (▷ 142–143).

Nightlife Taste life in the fast lane and visit one of Johannesburg's cutting-edge clubs (▷ 212–213).

Shopping Gauteng has many shopping malls (▷ 211–215), each with hundreds of glitzy shops, restaurants, bars and cinemas.

Drive You'll find the Eastern Highlands in the spectacular Golden Gate National Park, where you can drive among the bizarre multi-hued rock formations (▷ 246–247).

Township The vast township of Soweto (▷ 151) was a hotbed of political resistance during apartheid, and is a fascinating mix of cultures.

NORTHERN CAPE AND NORTH WEST PROVINCE

Diamonds Take the plunge into one of Kimberley's diamond mines (▷ 158–159), and see the workings beneath the diamond capital.

Views The smoothly shaped rocks and shimmering desert around Augrabies Falls (▷ 153) supply an eerie backdrop to the magnificent waterfalls.

Wildlife Traverse the rolling red sand dunes of the Kgalagadi Transfrontier Park (▷ 156–157) and search for the Kalahari lion.

Adventure The finest way of experiencing the Gariep (Orange) River is on a white-water rafting trip (▷ 217).

Flowers An unexpected attraction of the arid Northern Cape is the colourful flowering of the desert in Namakwa every spring (▷ 160–163), when the rains bring a riot of wild flowers.

LESOTHO AND SWAZILAND

Adventure Lesotho's bleak and beautiful peaks and friendly Sesotho villages should be visited in the traditional way: on the back of a hardy Lesotho pony (▷ 219).

Views You'll find nothing better than the expansive panoramas which unfold from the top of the tortuous Sani Pass (▷ 170), accessible only by horse or 4WD.

Royalty Drive the length of the Ezulwini Valley (▷ 171), browse in its craft shops, and stop off at the royal Swazi household of Lobamba.

Wildlife Swaziland's biggest national park, Hlane Royal National Park (▷ 171), is a superb place to get close to rhino, lion and cheetah.

Nature Wander amid herds of zebra and antelope on a horseback ride across the savannah of Mlilwane Wildlife Sanctuary (▷ 173).

GAME PARKS

No trip to South Africa is complete without at least one visit to a major game park. The country has some of the best game viewing in Africa, with an excellent infrastructure that makes going on safari a hassle-free (and relatively affordable) undertaking. The main game parks are extremely well organized with good facilities for game viewing, including well-surfaced roads and excellent accommodation.

The actual game-viewing experience is a much more independent one than in other countries, with many visitors choosing to self-drive on the extensive network of roads found in parks such as Kruger.

It is worth considering taking a guided tour, however, as game rangers will be more adept at spotting wildlife and are an excellent source of information on flora and fauna.

WHEN TO GO

The optimum times of the day for game viewing are early in the morning and late in the afternoon. The best time of year is in winter, from July to September, when dry weather forces animals to congregate around waterholes; at this time vegetation is lower and less dense, making it easier to spot wildlife. Summer weather, from November to January, when rainfall is at its highest, has its advantages as animals will be in good condition after feeding on the new shoots, and there are chances of seeing mating displays and young animals. The landscape is green and lush in summer, but the thick vegetation and the wide availability of water means that wildlife is far more widespread and difficult to spot.

The map below shows only some of the country's parks. As many of them are so large, they are often subdivided into game or nature reserves

FIELD GUIDE

The 'Big Five' are fairly common in South Africa. The term was coined by hunters who wanted to take home trophies of the largest, most charismatic animals. So, in hunting parlance, the Big Five were elephant, black rhino, buffalo, lion and leopard. Nowadays this can also refer to hippos. Equally deserving of top status are the zebra, giraffe and cheetah. Whether they are the Big Five, or the Big Nine, these are the animals that most people come to South Africa to see; and with the possible exception of the leopard and the black rhino you have an excellent chance of seeing them all.

WHAT TO LOOK FOR

Common/Masai giraffe (*Giraffa camelopardalis*) **1**. Yellowish with patchwork of brown marks, usually two horns, sometimes three. Their long necks have the same number of vertebrae as in humans. Usually seen browsing around trees.

Buffalo (*Syncerus caffer*) **2**. Often found on open plains but also at home in dense forest, they have distinctive curving horns. Buffalo look docile but can be aggressive.

Cheetah (*Acinonyx jubatus*) **3**. Fastest land mammal, it can reach speeds of 90kph (55mph) over short distances. Often seen in family groups walking across the plain or resting in shade. Found in open, semi-arid savannah, rarely in forested country.

Lion (*Panthera leo*) **4**. Nearly always seen in a pride (group), lions hunt at night and sleep during the day, but are usually easy to spot.

Leopard (*Panthera pardus*) **5**. Found in varied habitats ranging from forest to open savannah. Generally nocturnal, and difficult to spot during the day; look for them resting in trees.

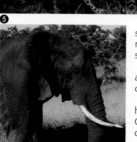

Black rhinoceros (*Diceros bicornis*) **6**. Long hooked upper lip. Prefers dry bush and thorn scrub habitat. Males are usually solitary, females in small groups. One of the most endangered animals in Africa because of poaching for its horn.

White rhinoceros (*Ceratotherium simum*). Square muzzle and bulkier than the black rhino. Found in open grassland, often in groups of five or more. Also endangered but less so than black rhino.

Elephant *(Loxodonta africana)* **7**. Often seen in large herds. Can be aggressive when there are young around.

Hippopotamus *(Hippopotamus amphibius)* **8**. Prefer shallow water, graze at night and have strong sense of territory, which they protect aggressively. Live in large families, or 'schools'.

Mountain zebra *(Equus zebra zebra)* **9**. Smallest of the two zebra sub species, with short mane and broad stripes (mix of dark and paler stripes).

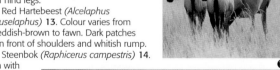

⑨   **⑩**

Common zebra/Burchell's *(Equus burchelli)* **10**. Broad stripes which cross the top of the hind leg in unbroken lines.

Blue wildebeest/gnu *(Connochaetes taurinus)* **11**. Often seen grazing in large herds.

Eland *(Traurotragus oryx)*. World's largest species of antelope, can grow to 1.80m (6ft). Grey to light brown; both sexes have spiral horns.

⑪

Impala *(Aepyceros melampus)* **12**. Very common in Kruger, rich light brown with white underbelly, long horns in males, and thick black tufts on heels of hind legs.

Red Hartebeest *(Alcelaphus buselaphus)* **13**. Colour varies from reddish-brown to fawn. Dark patches on front of shoulders and whitish rump.

Steenbok *(Raphicerus campestris)* **14**. An even brown with white underside and white ring around the eye. Prefers open plains; usually seen alone.

⑫

⑬

Oribi *(Ourebia ourebi)*. Slender with long neck, oval ears and short straight horns.

Reedbuck *(Redunca arundinum)*. Horns (males only) hook sharply forward. Brown to greyish-brown fawn with white underbelly and short bushy tails.

⑭   **⑮**

Springbok *(Antidorcas marsupialis)* **15**. Upper part of body is fawn, separated from white underbelly by dark brown lateral stripe. Reddish-brown stripe runs between the base of the horns and the mouth.

Bushbuck *(Tragelaphus scriptus)* **16**. Shaggy coat with variable pattern of white spots and stripes. High rump gives characteristic crouch. Often seen in thick bush.

Common duiker *(Sylvicapra grimmia)*. Grey-fawn with darker rump and pale underbelly. Small in stature, found in open grassland.

⑯

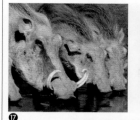

Warthog *(Phacochoerus aethiopicus)* **17**. Almost hairless and grey with very large head and curving tusks. Runs with tail sticking straight up in the air. Can often be seen in family groups near water.

African wild dog *(Lycaon pictus)* **18**. Large head and slender body; coat has mixed pattern of dark white and yellow. Rare and is threatened with extinction.

Dassie/rock hyrax *(Procavia Capensis)*. There are three main groups of these brown guinea pig-like mammals, but rock hyrax are most common. Live in colonies among boulders and on hillsides.

Bat-eared fox *(Otocyon megalotis)*. Distinctive large ears and short snout. Greyish-brown coat with bushy tail. Mainly nocturnal.

Civet *(Civetctictis civetta)*. Yellow-grey coat with black and white markings and black rings around eyes. Found in woody areas or thick bush. Shy and nocturnal.

Black-backed jackal *(Canis mesomelas)* **19**. Fox-like canine with red-fawn coat and black-grey area on its back.

Spotted hyena *(Crocuta crocuta)* **20**. High shoulders and low back with loping walk. Larger than related brown species, with dark spots and rounded ears.

Brown hyena *(Hyaena brunnea)*. Brown variety is smaller, with pointed ears and shaggy coat. Both species of hyena are nocturnal.

Serval *(Felis serval)* **21**. Narrow frame and long legs with small head and large ears. Similar coloration to cheetah but spots are more spread out.

Caracal *(Felis caracal)* **22**. Also known as African lynx. Small, reddish-sandy coat with paler belly. Distinctive tufted ears and black stripe from eye to nose. Nocturnal and rarely seen, but are found in hilly terrain.

Baboon *(Papio ursinus)* **23**. Live in large troops. Heavily built, with bright-pink buttocks. Males have manes and can be very aggressive. Opportunistic and can become pests in park camps.

Vervet monkey *(Cercopithecus aethiops)* **24**. Much smaller than baboon, with grey coat and small black face. Feet, hands and tip of tail are black. Treated as vermin in many locations.

Blue-headed Agama lizard (*Agama atricollis*) **25**. Grow to up to 20cm (8 inches) in length and can be seen scutttling over walls and rocks near camp sites. The orange-headed Agama lizard can also be seen, but is not as common.

Reed frog (*Hyperolius nastutus*) **26**. The male of this species has a distinctive call, sounding like a loud creak. Rests on branches that are overhanging water.

Crocodile (*Crocodylus niloticus*) **27**. Found throughout tropical and southern Africa in rivers, mangrove swamps and some lakes. Nile Crocodiles can weigh more than 1,000kg (2,200lb) and grow between 2.5m (8ft) and 5.5m (18ft) in length. Up to 70 per cent of their diet is fish but other prey includes zebra and migrating wildebeest.

Fish Eagle (*Haliaeetus vocifer*) **28**. Usually seen perched high up in a tree, with a good view of its territory. Large, white-breasted eagles have a distinctive call. Diet is mainly of live fish, although they do eat some water birds and their young. They can be found near lakes and rivers south of the Sahara.

Martial Eagle (*Polemaetus bellicosus*) **29**. This is the largest eagle in Africa, surviving on the open plains and semi-desert areas, down to the Cape. It soars to great heights and distances and swoops down to its prey of mammals such as lyrax and antelope.

Bataleur (*Terathopius ecaudatus*) **30**. This striking looking eagle spends most of its time on the wing and is part of the Snake eagle group.

Little Bee Eater (*Merops pusillus*) **31**. Vivid yellow and green plumage. Often found near woodland streams. Feeds on insects and butterflies and perches in groups at night or in cooler weather.

Marabou Stork (*Leptoptilos crumeniferus*) **32**. Grows to a height of 1.5m (5ft) with a wing span of 2.6m (8.5ft). It is a scavenger and exists on carrion and scraps.

Lilac Roller (*Coracias caudata*) **33**. So called due to bird's courtship flight (fast dive followed by a rocking and rolling motion). Highly territorial birds, they live in pairs or small groups and make their nests in tree-holes or termite hills.

Living South Africa

Showing off a bright headdress in Shakaland (left)

A Venda local (above); a fisherman from the Overberg (left); Angel Jones (below)

The Rainbow
Nation

In 2004 South Africa took to the streets to celebrate the 10th anniversary of the arrival of democracy. A decade had passed since the majority of South Africans voted for the first time in a general election. There was good reason to rejoice, as much has happened since Nelson Mandela's famous inauguration speech in 1994. Racial barriers have been demolished and there is a substantial black middle class, something unthinkable during the darkest days of apartheid. And South Africans have learned to revel in being the 'Rainbow Nation'. The term is a paraphrase of that coined by Desmond Tutu, the country's first black Anglican archbishop, during a speech in the last days of apartheid: 'We, the Rainbow People of God…'. This is an easily justifiable title as the country has the most diverse population in Africa, with far more complex distinctions than simply black and white. About 77 per cent of the population is African, 11 per cent white, 9 per cent 'coloured' (mixed race descendants of slaves, white settlers and Africans), and 3 per cent Indian. There are also numerous national languages and religions.

The Homecoming Revolution

It's been called South Africa's 'brain drain': Thousands of young, skilled South Africans emigrate every year. Most of them head to the UK and Australia, hoping to earn big bucks before returning. The First National Bank has seized upon this idea of the final return home and have sponsored the Homecoming Revolution (www.homecoming revolution.co.za). This non-profit online initiative is aimed at inspiring South African expatriates to return and contribute to their homeland's future. As founder Angel Jones, director of a South African advertising agency, puts it: 'Don't wait until it gets better, come home and make it better!' She returned after 10 years in London. The figures indicate that the tide may be turning; it's thought that for every person leaving, another is making that journey back home.

A man and his son in the Islamic district of Cape Town, known as Bo-Kaap (left)

A group of students in Johannesburg (right)

A Indian woman in a pretty yellow sari

Xhosa women, taking a break from working in the pastures of the Transkei, east of the Wild Coast

Festival of Lights

One of the highlights of Durban's events calendar is *Diwali* (or Deepavali), the Hindu Festival of Lights. Although the traditionally Zulu province of KwaZulu-Natal doesn't seem an obvious spot for a Hindu celebration, it is in fact home to the majority of South Africa's 1.2 million Indian population. *Diwali*, which occurs in October or November (the date falls according to the lunar calendar), symbolizes the triumph of good over evil. The shops in Durban's Indian district are illuminated by hundreds of tiny oil lamps in the days leading up to *Diwali*, with clothing and food sales taking place around the city. Other places across the country join in too, such as in the Indian township of Lenasia in Johannesburg, which holds a huge fireworks display.

Laughing at Racism

The comedy scene has become a platform for some of the most popular, and controversial, portrayals of modern South Africa. Few have made a bigger career out of it than Mark Lottering. Born in the townships of the Cape Flats outside Cape Town, Lottering defines himself as coloured. Much of his material focuses on how different races interact and the general absurdity of racism. He has been at the forefront of a shift on the comedy circuit; where once only whites stood, black and coloured comedians now talk about race issues in front of a mixed audience. Lottering's shows are both hilarious and shocking—and have landed him a TV show and several international tours.

Women on Top

Before South Africa's first democratic elections the country ranked 141st in the world for gender representation. In the space of a few years, the country has changed its rank to eighth in the world for the number of women in government. In 2004 women made up 30 per cent of South Africa's MPs, nine out of 27 Cabinet ministers and eight out of 14 deputy ministers. Although this is a step in the right direction, more needs to be done to encourage women to participate in the political life of the country. Laws on domestic violence and child maintenance are designed to have a positive impact on women's lives—some commentators say it won't be long before South Africa has a woman president.

Rise of Rosebank

As a free South Africa began to breathe, a new black middle class began to emerge. Research by a leading business magazine showed that about 300,000 black South Africans have became middle-income earners and about 500,000 upped their class status to the lower middle-income group since early 2000. When apartheid fell, educated black South Africans began to move into previously 'whites-only' suburbs. Nowhere in South Africa is there more evidence of this than in the Jo'burg suburb of Rosebank. A radio station called YFM established itself as the voice of this confident, young group and based itself in a Rosebank shopping mall. As black and white South Africans mix freely, this suburb has become a role model for integration for the rest of the country.

Johnny Clegg at a music festival
(above left)

Musicians in
Jo'burg (above) and
Cape Town (below)

Sound of
Music

The key to understanding South African music is in realizing where it comes from. Whether it's the adaptation of Dutch instruments in the 17th century by Indonesian slaves or the mutation of 1990s house music into township kwaito, home-grown and foreign influences mingle to produce a singularly South African sound. And like so much of the culture, music is inextricably linked with the political upheavals of the last century. From demonstrations against apartheid in the 1960s to the reflection of disillusioned white youth in the 1980s, music has a history of expressing social currents and it remains a powerful force.

Forums for hearing music are as variable as the styles, as diverse as catching a gospel choir in a church, squinting through the dense smoke of a Cape Jazz club while listening to the traditional music of Cape Town, or seeing a rock band at an open-air festival.

South African diva
Miriam Makeba

God's Music
Vocal harmony has its roots in communal dances accompanied by elaborate call-and-response patterns. This tradition has long been popular in South Africa, but it was the group Ladysmith Black Mambazo that first propelled it onto the international stage. The beginnings for the group were not easy; at their first concert in Soweto in the 1980s, they received R5.28 (£2–£3) each. But the group became a hit. When Paul Simon invited them to sing on his *Graceland* (1997) album, they were thrust into the limelight, and they remain the most popular South African group of all time. Made up of 10 male singers, including frontman and original founder, Joseph Shabalala, the group continues to tour, and has now recorded more than 40 albums.

Ladysmith Black
Mambazo (above);
music in all forms

God Bless *Afrika*

Few songs are as power-
ful as 'Nkosi Sikelel'
iAfrika' ('God Bless
Africa'), the national
anthem composed by
Sontonga in 1897. Sung
in rousing harmony, it
was originally a freedom
song, and its history
means it still packs an
emotional punch. It was
once the anti-apartheid
anthem, which led to
the singers sometimes
being dispelled with tear
gas. Today, it is sung at
most types of gathering.
However, the fact that
it is now combined with
the old apartheid-era
anthem, 'Die Stem' ('The
Call'), and has verses
in Zulu, Xhosa, Sotho,
Afrikaans and English,
means that much of the
population knows only
a small part. To combat
this, the First National
Bank launched an initia-
tive in 2004 to distribute
10 million leaflets to
schools across the coun-
try. The scheme, entitled
'Your Anthem Needs
You!', aims to encourage
people to learn all
verses, regardless of
ethnicity or language.

All That Jazz

Jazz has been hugely
influential in South
Africa since emerging
from the Johannesburg
slums in the 1920s.
There were turbulent
times when many of
the biggest stars left
due to apartheid, but the
jazz scene is once again
flourishing. It's best experienced at the annual
Cape Town International
Jazz Festival. Many of the
godfathers of Cape Jazz,
such as Abdullah Ibrahim
(aka Dollar Brand,
1934–) and Hugh
Masekela (1939–), can
be seen performing,
while newcomers, using
a range of influences
from the harmonica of
migrant west African
miners to drum 'n' bass,
are also making a big
impact. Every year
top international talent
perform—2004 saw
appearances by British
singer and pianist Jamie
Cullum and R & B soul
singer Alicia Keys from
New York.

Sound of the City

Zola, a young musician
from Soweto, encapsu-
lates South Africa's
biggest force in music
today. He has become
a national phenomenon
and recognized leader of
the latest music move-
ment, kwaito. This mix of
dance, hip-hop and rap
is the sound of young,
black Johannesburg, and
has a resolutely urban
feel, its deep beat over-
laid with chanted *tsotsi*
(township gangster)
slang. Born and bred in
Soweto, Zola raps about
guns and crime and his
music has a dark, angry
edge to it. But he is
also a TV presenter and
extols the importance of
kwaito's responsibility to
young people: 'Turn the
gun into a microphone'
is one of his mottos.
Ubiquitous in the clubs
of the black community,
kwaito is now also
popular in designer
nightclubs, until recently
the preserve of the white
and wealthy.

The White Zulu

No one better sums
up the white rebellious
musical force that
opposed the repressive
social laws of apartheid
in the 1980s than
Johnny Clegg. Clegg,
born in 1952 in England,
spent his first nine years
in Zimbabwe before
moving to South Africa.
In the 1970s, Clegg
began performing tradi-
tional Zulu material with
Sipho Mchunu, and later
added a mix of Western
rock to form the band
Juluka. Clegg remains
something of a South
African legend, and
still draws thousands of
fans when he performs.
Known affectionately as
the 'White Zulu', Clegg
challenged the racial
boundaries manifest in
music under apartheid,
and blazed a crossover
trail that survives to this
day. Although his popu-
larity is mainly among
white people, his tours
are sell-outs and he
remains a big influence
on the music scene.

A Mkhuze warden (left); the Skukuza camp (above) and elephants (below) in Kruger

FISH POACHING IS STRICTLY PROHIBITED

KEEP AWAY FROM WATERS EDGE-CROCODILES!

You can take a tour (top) or visit by yourself (right), but look out for warnings (above)

Park Life

Few people leave South Africa without visiting at least one of its parks. In contrast to many protected areas elsewhere in Africa, however, the parks are shared with residents, many of whom enjoy the outdoors lifestyle. During the school holidays, the parks and reserves become busy with South Africans; there are reductions on entry for citizens of the country, although the majority of those visiting the parks are still from the wealthier sections of society.

South Africa's protected parks have a considerable impact on the country, both in terms of revenue—an estimated one million people visit Kruger every year—and in terms of area. Kruger alone is slightly larger than many countries, and that's still considerably smaller than the new Great Limpopo Transfrontier Park, which from 2002 also incorporated Mozambique's Limpopo National Park and Zimbabwe's Gonarezhou park. It forms the largest wildlife reserve in Africa (although at the moment you can't cross from one country to another). South Africa's other national parks are also growing. For instance, the Greater Addo Elephant National Park in the Eastern Cape now encompasses five neighbouring game reserves, stretching from the Indian Ocean to the Little Karoo, and sheltering elephant, rhino, lion, buffalo, leopard, whales and great white sharks.

The Godfather of Camps

Skukuza is the biggest camp in Kruger National Park, and indeed in the whole of South Africa. It can accommodate an astonishing number of people—more than a thousand at full capacity—turning it into something like a small, bustling town. The facilities are impressive, but a sense of isolation and of the wilderness may be hard to come by. Hundreds of huts, *rondavels* (circular African-style thatched hits), campsites and family bungalows stretch through the straggling undergrowth. It has its own airport, a bank and post office, three swimming pools, an auditorium showing nature films, a cafeteria and restaurant, a church and a nursery selling indigenous plants. Finally, for those who can't leave their clubs behind, the camp has its own 18-hole golf course.

Animal welfare comes first (above right and below right) David Mabunda (below)

Elephants are one of the 'Big Five' you'll be able to see

The Speed Limit is

40

Please protect our Wildlife

Zulu & I Restaurant
Croc Centre / Snake Park

A Change in Direction

David Mabunda grew up just outside Nelspruit, close to Kruger, but as a 'non-white' was forbidden from entering the park under the apartheid government. He first experienced the magnificence of South Africa's animals when his parents' employers took his family with them on a visit to the park. Mabunda's passion for the great outdoors was born. Following several years of study abroad and stints in Sri Lanka, Tanzania and Zimbabwe, he returned to South Africa to work in land management. He became the first black director of Kruger National Park in the 1990s, and in 2003 was appointed Chief Executive Officer of South African National Parks, presiding over the country's most important natural means. Today he heads a 3,000-strong workforce and manages 20 national parks.

New Super Park

In early 2002, South Africa, Zimbabwe and Mozambique agreed to establish the Great Limpopo Transfrontier Park. It is a merger of the world-famous Kruger—with its extraordinary abundance of wildlife and stunning geological splendour—and two other game reserves in Mozambique and Zimbabwe. The park brings together some of the best and most established wildlife areas in southern Africa. The cross-border park, measuring 35,000sq km (13,650sq miles) is managed across an unprecedented three international boundaries. It contains the 'Big Five' animals and a huge variety of other game. It's also the place where tropical, moist, temperate and dry savannah climates all converge. The creation of the park is the first phase of the establishment of a bigger conservation area measuring a staggering 100,000sq km (39,000sq miles).

Displacement with a Happy Ending

The Makuleke region fell outside the borders of Kruger National Park until 1969, when the people of the clan were forcibly removed by the apartheid government so that the park could be extended. More than 24,000ha (60,000 acres) of land was taken. However, a historic decision by the Land Claims Court reinstated the land to the Makuleke in 1998. The clan chose not to challenge the conservation status of the area and reached an agreement with South Africa National Parks to bring in private sector support to assist with the management of the land. The deal was worth R45 million, and later that year the first luxury lodge was opened. The community is being trained to take over the entire business within 20 years. In the meantime, they earn a percentage of all takings and more than one hundred jobs are being created.

Tough Justice

By the end of the 20th century Swaziland's rhinos were in dire need of protection, with up to 45 being killed every year. The consequence has been the introduction of some of the most stringent anti-poaching laws in the world. The law stipulates that poachers face a minimum sentence of five years in prison, and that they must 'replace' the slain animal by paying to have another introduced to the reserve where it was poached, which can cost the equivalent of hundreds of thousands of South African rands. Anti-poaching game rangers have been armed with shotguns and have the right to shoot to kill if they need to protect themselves, a move which has been criticized outside Swaziland. While two poachers have been killed in the last 10 years, not a single rhino has been lost.

Herschelle Gibbs in action in a test match against England (right)

Riding the waves at Umhlanga Rocks

Adventure sports have become very big business

Lesley Manyathela of Orlando Pirates (above)

Serious About Sport

South Africans take their sport seriously. The entire country is sports mad, and playing and watching sport is very much part of the national lifestyle, be it watching a soccer match or surfing a wave. Who watches what, however, still largely depends on background and race. While soccer is hugely popular among black South Africans, cricket and rugby union remain largely the preserve of the white population. Rugby and cricket thus enjoyed impressive funding for many years, resulting in a number of world-class stadiums dotted around the country. Yet feelings run high no matter what sport is being watched, from the festive rivalry between the Johannesburg soccer teams Kaizer Chiefs and Orlando Pirates, to the emotional roars that accompany every match of the national rugby team, the Springboks.

The biggest growth industry in recent years has been adventure sports—South Africa's good climate and range of environments make it an ideal place to try adrenalin activities. It has the world's highest bungee jump, offers cage diving with great white sharks, and has some of the world's best paragliding in the Kalahari desert. Along with surfing, hiking and mountain biking, a popular activity with visitors is 'kloofing', which involves boulder-hopping (literally, leaping from boulder to boulder), hiking and swimming down kloofs (gorges).

World Cup Fever

The announcement that South Africa is to host the 2010 soccer World Cup was met with widespread jubilation by the soccer-mad nation. Recovering from its disappointment of losing out to Germany by just one vote in the contest to host the 2006 event, South Africa now has the job of preparing for an estimated 400,000-strong influx of visitors in 2010. South Africa has held both the rugby union and cricket world cups, but the soccer World Cup is in another league, being the second largest sporting event in the world after the Olympics. It means the economy will receive a huge boost, predicted to be around R21 billion, and the tourism industry is anticipating a huge surge in interest in the country. The issue of ticket prices has already been fiercely debated, and it has been decided to drop the price for South African nationals, to allow all soccer fans access to the matches.

Supporting the national soccer team, which is nicknamed Bafana Bafana (left) Kaizer Chiefs versus England's Tottenham Hotspur in a World Cup bid match (below)

Heptathlete Janice Josephs at Athens 2004

Boxing to Fight Crime

Cape Town police officer Paul 'Skollie' Manuel, a former Western Province boxer, has received widespread praise for setting up an after-school boxing club. His aim is to draw underprivileged children away from the streets and the temptations of crime, and he's had some considerable success. The Olympia Boxing Academy was launched in 1996 and now has 32 active members, both boys and girls, ranging in age from 9 to 19. Manuel's view is that sport can play a big role in empowering children, and gives them something to focus on when they're not at school. The club has produced two South African and 14 provincial champions on a shoestring budget, but Manuel insists that the real reward is in steering children away from crime.

Golf Studies

Proof that South Africans really do take their sport seriously can be found at Technikon Pretoria. The institute now offers degrees in Golf Studies, a four-year course accredited by the Professional Golf Association of South Africa. The degree prepares students to become professional golfers, coaches and managers, and is proving a huge hit with its 70-plus students. The course was first introduced as an incentive to keep young golfing talent in the country; many young hopefuls are lured to Europe and the US with generous scholarships. A key proportion of the Golfing Studies course involves practical golf sessions, with students spending much of their days on the greens. Golf has also been added to the curriculum of a handful of high schools, with pupils spending up to two hours a day practising.

Surf's Up

Jeffreys Bay, or 'J-Bay', as it's known to surfers, is South Africa's top surfing destination—and never more popular than during the annual Billabong Pro championship, one of the stops on the Association of Surfing Professionals World Championship Tour. The six-day competition, held every July, attracts more than 40 of the world's top surfers, who jet into the Eastern Cape town in the hope of winning the US$250,000 prize. J-Bay is said to have the world's most consistent right-hand break, and the aptly named Supertubes break is the venue for the contest. This seaside town, usually a sleepy resort popular with hippies and sandcastle-building families, comes to life during the festival, when surfers and backpackers swarm to the beach to watch the surfing events and take part in the ensuing all-night parties.

Paralympians Lead the Way

There were some who were disappointed at the performance of the country's Olympic team in the 2004 Athens games, where it finished 43rd with only five medals and one gold. So it was left to the country's Paralympians to restore national pride. And they did—with an outstanding performance, showing their counterparts how it should be done. At the Paralympics the South Africans notched up 25 medals, including 15 golds, to finish an impressive 13th. The star of the show was swimmer Natalie du Toit, who won four of her five gold medals with world records. Her times were so good that she has declared her intention to compete in the next able-bodied Olympics.

A Krugerrand gold bullion coin (far left)

Luxury camps at private game reserves have attracted tourists back to the country (right)

Red-hot molten gold being poured and shaped

Diamonds, cut and rough, are a huge part of the economy

Boom Time
South Africa

South Africa is the economic powerhouse of Africa, comprising of about one quarter of all Africa's gross domestic product (GDP). The country leads the continent in industrial output (40 per cent of Africa's total output) and mineral production (45 per cent of total mineral production) and generates more than 50 per cent of Africa's electricity. With low inflation, dropping interest rates and booming house prices, some commentators have proclaimed this period South Africa's 'golden era'. The currency, the rand—which is one of the most traded developing-world currencies—has recovered remarkably to become one of the world's top performers. Tourism remains one of the biggest boom industries, with impressive visitor numbers.

But the country still faces big challenges. It has a terrible record in terms of unequal distribution of income and an exaggerated divide between rich and poor. Unemployment sits worryingly at around 30 per cent, according to official figures. However, things are changing and there is action to redress the balance between rich and poor through 'empowerment'; more specifically, the Black Economic Empowerment (BEE), which means selling stakes in a company to black-owned and controlled companies, thus transferring some equity and control. The government is keen to spread the wealth derived from the country's incredibly rich mineral resources, and is implementing a range of initiatives and industrial charters.

Gold Changing Hands

South Africa is the world's largest gold producer, with an astonishing 40 per cent of global reserves. Mining—as one of the bedrocks of the economy—has spearheaded the country's Black Economic Empowerment (BEE) initiatives. BEE encourages the redistribution of wealth and opportunities to those who were disadvantaged by apartheid. Each sector of the economy has been drawing up voluntary BEE charters that outline policies and goals for more black participation in those sectors of the economy. A much celebrated example includes a deal in 2003 worth US$1.5 billion, between three corporations, creating the country's largest black-owned mining company, known as African Rainbow Minerals.

South African
Airways (above left); wine
has helped the economy and the
tourism industry (right)

There are many wine estates where
you can sample a variety of brands

The Mohair Route

For those who want a
slightly different itinerary
to follow, there's the
unusual Mohair Route,
named after the soft and
silky fleece of the angora
goat, an economic
backbone of the Karoo
region. South Africa is in
fact the world's largest
producer of mohair, with
a 60 per cent share of
the global market—an
impressive statistic given
that the industry began
with just 13 animals
imported from Turkey
in the mid-18th century.
The route starts in the
historic central Karoo
town of Graaff-Reinet
(▷ 98) and ends in
Uitenhage, taking in a
number of farms and
towns which depend
on the hardy goats. In
the Karoo, however,
you'll find that mohair
lacks the luxury status
it enjoys abroad and is
regarded as just a locally
produced staple.

Diamonds are Forever

De Beers, the world's
biggest diamond-mining
group, estimates that at
least 11 per cent of its
11,000 South African
employees are infected
with HIV/AIDS. Following
heavy criticism of the
government's stance
on the disease, the dia-
mond giant announced
that it would supply
its workers with anti-
retroviral drugs, following
a similar move by miner-
als giant Anglo-American
(which has a 45 per cent
stake in De Beers). The
group has since received
widespread acclaim
for its initiative, launched
in 2003, whereby
anti-retroviral drugs
are supplied free to its
infected workers, their
spouses or life partners,
and retired workers. The
scheme also involves
a system of education
for the entire workforce
on the prevention of
infection.

Tourists Flock to South Africa

Research by a major
bank in South Africa
showed that tourism had
replaced gold as the
country's top foreign
exchange earner. In
2003, foreign exchange
from tourism totalled
R53.9 billion, compared
to R35.3 billion from
gold exports. Since
1994, arrivals have
grown tenfold, from
640,000 to 6.5 million
in 2003. According to
the research, tourism
now contributes about
7 per cent to South
Africa's gross domestic
product. Despite a
global slump, the
country continued to
defy world tourism
trends, and in 2003
achieved a 4.2 per cent
increase in overseas
arrivals over the year
before. The 2010 soccer
World Cup, which South
Africa won the right to
host, is likely to see the
tourism boom reach
even further heights.

Grape Expectations

Wine is one area that
seems unstoppable in
the world market, and
the South African wine
industry has grown
phenomenally since
the lifting of apartheid-
era sanctions in 1994.
Between 1994 and
2000, South Africa's
exports rose from 50
million litres (11 million
gallons) to almost 140
million litres (31 million
gallons). In 2003, South
African producers sold
7.6 million cases world-
wide. This amounts to a
10 per cent global mar-
ket share, much of which
is enjoyed in the UK.
South African wines rep-
resent both excellent
value and high quality;
they are also in fashion,
with producers having
benefited considerably
from the decline in pop-
ularity of wines from
traditional producing
countries like France.
It remains to be seen
whether South African
wines can conquer the
US market.

Coetzee is one of South Africa's most famous writers (above); art galleries are helping to promote local talent

South African actress Charlize Theron at the Golden Globes in 2005

The Arts

J. M. Coetzee

South Africa has produced a number of internationally recognized and award-winning novelists, but the most celebrated must be John Coetzee. The author of nine novels, he is the only writer to have twice won the Booker Prize, the UK's most prestigious literary prize (first in 1983 for *The Life and Times of Michael K*, and again in 1999 for *Disgrace*). In 2003, he was awarded the Nobel Prize for Literature. He is a reclusive figure, never giving interviews, but is regarded as one of South Africa's most brilliant modern commentators on the lasting effects of apartheid. His fellow countrymen were understandably disappointed when, in 2002, he emigrated to Australia, where the heroine of his novel *Elizabeth Costello* (2003) is based.

South Africa's contemporary art scene is immensely exciting. Following years of neglect, it seems to be finding its feet, as artists respond to the changing cultural scene with imagination and flair. This certainly hasn't always been the case. During apartheid, simply owning a painting that was considered 'subversive' could have led to a jail sentence. Black artists were largely ignored and lacked the funds to promote their work. Since the advent of democracy, funding for the arts has been more equally distributed. This revival has also been driven by private enterprise, with new galleries opening up and showcasing contemporary artworks, including an exciting 'neo-tribal' art movement. Theatre, too, has come alive again; apartheid had been an abundant source for commentary, and now that it has passed, actors and playwrights have had to grapple with new subject matter. The film industry has been less successful, but is gaining some momentum. Literature, meanwhile, is perhaps South Africa's greatest cultural hotbed.

The Township Photographer

Zwelethu Mthethwa is one of the most successful artists on the contemporary scene, a photographer originally from Durban but now based in Cape Town. In the 1980s, he studied fine art at the University of Cape Town, but his real breakthrough came when he was awarded a Fulbright Scholarship to study at the Rochester Institute of Technology in the US. Here he first experimented with colour photography, and colour became a crucial component of his work. He is famous for his portrayals of township life, using large-format photography, pastels, paint and screen prints. Some of his best-known images focus on township interiors and sugar cane workers. He has exhibited throughout the world, including France, the US and Italy, and is celebrated as one of South Africa's success stories.

The Story of South Africa

The First People

South Africa is the self-proclaimed Cradle of Humankind, home to the oldest fossil human remains in the world. It is believed that our earliest ancestor, *Australopithecus africanus*, made its first tottering, bipedal steps on South African soil nearly three million years ago. Other ancestral species evolved and died out until, within the last 100,000 years, one of them developed still further into *Homo sapiens*, or modern humans. The earliest fossil remains of modern man anywhere in the world are thought to be those from the Klasies River mouth in the Eastern Cape and Border Cave on the KwaZulu-Natal border. They are dated as being more than 50,000 years old. The descendants of these Stone-Age people were the San (once known as Bushmen) and Khoi (originally called Hottentots by European settlers), who inhabited the Western Cape when the first Europeans arrived in the 15th century. The San were hunter-gatherers, living in small egalitarian communities. They were nomadic and moved with the seasonally migrating herds of wild game, carrying few personal possessions. They lived mostly in the dry interior. The Khoi, on the other hand, were pastoralists with a concept of ownership of property and a degree of social hierarchy, and occupied the coastal lands. The two groups, although distinct, had a certain level of interaction.

Footsteps from the Past

Although it's hard to picture it today, the parched expanse of baked red earth which makes up the Great Karoo in the Western Cape was once a vast lake surrounded by lush swampland. Around 300 million years ago, the lake was inhabited by invertebrates, and the shores were tramped by dinosaurs. Today, the area has revealed an exceptionally rich fossil record, from the aquatic creatures that perished in the lake to the footprints and tail-drag marks left behind by dinosaurs. The Karoo is now recognized as one of the world's most important palaeontological sites, not just for its number of fossils, but for the fact that the layers of rock contain a virtually unbroken record of species stretching back 50 million years.

Mrs Ples (above, left); a tableau showing the San at Cape Town's National Museum (bottom)

Before 1488

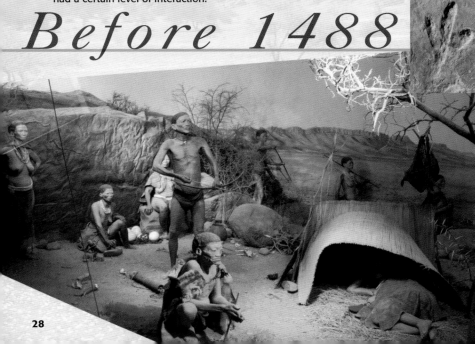

Enter Mrs Ples

The most famous of all hominid fossils in South Africa is the skull of an *Australopithecus africanus* discovered in 1947 at Sterkfontein Caves, near Krugersdorp. The skull, the most complete example of an Australopithecine skull found by archaeologists, is affectionately known as 'Mrs Ples', a nickname derived from the former species name, 'Plesianthropus', which means 'almost human'. *Australopithecus africanus* is believed to be a distant relative of mankind, and the discovery by Dr. Robert Broom received international publicity. Mrs Ples and her relatives lived in South Africa around 2.5 million years ago, sharing some of our traits such as walking upright. But 'Mrs' Ples is now known to be a 'Mr'—a CAT scan in 2002 revealed that the skull belonged to an adolescent male.

Dinosaur prints found on the outskirts of Moyeni, Lesotho

Art of the Past

The sandstone caves of the Drakensberg are some of the best places in the world to see rock art. Here the caves are covered with the intriguing shapes, images and depictions produced by the San, who were once prolific in the area but were driven out by European settlers. Most of the best preserved paintings are fairly recent, dating back some 200 to 300 years, but they form part of a long-standing tradition; some of the earliest cave paintings in southern Africa date from 28,000 years ago. There have been numerous attempts to interpret the meaning of the images, but the most popular theory maintains that they were a mix of scenes from daily life, such as hunting, and images used in magic and rituals.

A gold rhino from Mapungubwe

New Arrivals

The San and Khoi, regarded as the original, indigenous inhabitants of South Africa, were joined from about AD500 by peoples who had gradually migrated south, bringing with them new technologies such as iron smelting and crop cultivation. The ancestors of the vast majority of South Africa's present-day population, the newcomers spoke a number of languages known as the Bantu group. Like the Khoi, they were essentially herders, although it was their crop-raising and iron-smelting skills that brought about extensive trade networks. The large degree of contact between the different groups is reflected in the fact that some of the newer groups incorporated the Khoi-San clicks (characteristic of these tongues) into their language: today these clicks can be heard in both Xhosa and Zulu.

The Lost City of Gold

Mapungubwe formed the centre of the largest African civilisation and trade hub in the sub-continent between 1200AD and 1300AD. It was the home of a thriving, complex society that traded in gold and ivory with countries such as China, India and Egypt. Set in what is now South Africa's Limpopo Province, the Iron-Age site is evidence of African civilisation before colonisation and probably the earliest known site in southern Africa where evidence of a class-based society existed. At its height, the kingdom supported a population of 5,000 and was based on a successful agricultural industry. Mapungubwe was abandoned in the 14th century as a result of climate changes that resulted in the area becoming colder and drier, leading to migrations further north to Zimbabwe. The site was declared a World Heritage Site by the United Nations in 2003.

A delicate San painting in the Drakensberg (left); a guided tour of the San rock art sites at Giant's Castle in the Drakensberg (above)

Arrival of the Europeans

The first European to set foot on South African soil was Portuguese explorer Bartolomeu Dias, who landed at Mossel Bay in 1488 on his way to the spice islands of Asia. Over the next 200 years more Portuguese traders and their Dutch and British competitors made the journey to the east via the Cape of Good Hope. The hostile reception they received from the Khoi discouraged permanent settlers, but the Cape became an important restocking point. It was not until 1652 that the Dutch East India Company (the Vereenigde Oostindische Compagnie, or VOC) built a fort and established a supply station under the command of Jan van Riebeeck. A permanent settlement grew as workers completed their contracts and settled as farmers. As the settlers moved east and north they came into increasing contact with Bantu-speaking Africans, which prompted uneasy trading relations and a state of almost constant warfare. During the 18th century, Dutch power began to wane, and in 1795 the British sailed into False Bay and annexed the Dutch colony. Their sovereignty was finally accepted by other European powers in a peace settlement of 1816. The British set out to fund their expansion and, in 1834, to ban slavery—much to the chagrin of many Dutch settlers.

Eva or Krotoa?

In the late 1650s, Jan van Riebeeck took a young local girl into his household. Krotoa, or Eva as she became known by the Dutch, was from a local Khoi tribe but became completely assimilated in the van Riebeeck household. She was educated with his daughters, baptized and formally adopted by the family. Eva became an important link between the Dutch settlers and the local tribal groups, although she struggled with her identity from the start. In 1664, Eva married Pieter van Meerhof, the station's doctor, becoming the first indigenous person to marry a European. Her story has an unhappy ending: Her husband perished during a trip to Madagascar and she ended her years as an alcoholic, shunned by both European and Khoi society.

1488

A statue of Dias (top); the Dutch East India Company or VOC logo (above); Jan van Riebeeck with native Khois (inset); Cape Town harbour in 1675 (right)

Voices from the Past

In mid-2003, developers in the fashionable district of Green Point outside Cape Town unearthed a mass grave, thought to be more than 200 years old. Building was halted immediately; archaeologists were called in and they uncovered upwards of a thousand individual bodies. Most of these were thought to have been slaves, and the findings proved to be a shocking reminder of the city's past. The graves were shallow and disordered, most bodies were buried without coffins, and tests on bones and teeth revealed harsh living conditions, backbreaking work and a poor diet. When the slave trade was halted in the British Empire, around 63,000 slaves had been brought to the Cape.

The Great Trek

Having had enough of being told what to do by the British, scores of Dutch settlers (Boers) set out with their families and servants in search of new land beyond the British colonial boundaries. Between 1835 and 1840, around 5,000 people left the Cape colony and headed north and east in a movement that became known as the Great Trek. They were called the Voortrekkers, a hardy bunch who overcame harsh obstacles. Their experiences became fertile ground for 20th-century Afrikaner nationalism, and the Voortrekkers were used as a symbol of Afrikaner culture. One thing not often mentioned in the myths that grew up around the Trek is that a large number of Khoi servants and freed slaves also took part in the Trek alongside their masters or patrons.

International Language

Afrikaans is the language of around 60 per cent of the white population and 90 per cent of the coloured population, but it was recognized as a distinct language only in 1925. Originally spoken by Dutch settlers and the imported workforce of indentured labourers and slaves from Asia and East Africa, it was regarded as a dialect, and remains closely related to 17th-century Dutch. Cape Dutch (as it was known) had a gradually diverging vocabulary, absorbing words from various languages—those of European settlers (German, French and English), of slaves and workers from Indonesia and East Africa, and of the indigenous Khoi and San. Many Afrikaans words clearly indicate their exotic origins. One such is *piesang*, meaning banana, which comes from the Malay word *pisang*.

Shaka Zulu

The early 19th century heralded an era of radical change among Bantu-speaking Africans in the east. Under the command of the most famous pre-colonial African, Shaka Zulu, the Zulu nation was transformed into an enormously powerful political and military force. He set about raiding and defeating all surrounding chiefdoms using his *impis*, organized regiments of full-time soldiers. During the 1820s the *impis* (who amounted to a 40,000-strong army) became increasingly predatory, while at home Shaka's reign grew ever more autocratic; his punishments of any sign of opposition were notorious. This led to a period of unprecedented disruption, fighting and suffering throughout the region. Shaka's reign of terror eventually came to an end in 1828 when he was assassinated by one of his half brothers, Dingane.

A statue of King Shaka Zulu (left); a depiction of the Voortrekkers' Great Trek, when Boer farmers moved inland to escape British rule (below); a statue of a typical settler family (below right)

1855

Tapestry of an idealized view of the Great Trek, displayed next to the Voortrekker Monument, Pretoria (above); a statue of Jan van Riebeeck in Cape Town (left)

Getting Rich

In the mid-1800s, two separate republics, the Orange Free State and the Transvaal, were established by the Boers. The British meanwhile set up the new colony of Natal based around present-day Durban, but this and the Cape remained of little importance to the British Empire. This was all to change in 1867 when alluvial diamonds were discovered near the confluence of the Harts and Vaal rivers. By 1872, tens of thousands of fortune-hunters had converged on the site, which soon revealed itself as the world's richest diamond pipe. In 1886, there was a further mineral discovery: of gold on the Witwatersrand in the Transvaal Republic. Miners from across the world rushed to the new reef, and the main town on the Rand, Johannesburg, grew rapidly. Boer President Paul Kruger (1825–1904) saw a serious threat to Afrikaner independence as huge numbers of newcomers, mostly British, descended on the gold fields. The British demanded that voting rights be given to the 60,000 foreign whites on the Witwatersrand, but Kruger refused, and war broke out in October 1899. The Second Anglo-Boer War lasted until 1902, and included a series of humiliating defeats for the British, although the latter's scorched earth policy finally brought the Boers to surrender.

1855

Gandhi's Role

Mohandas Karamchand Gandhi, who arrived in Natal in 1893 to work as a lawyer, had his first taste of racial discrimination shortly after his arrival. During a train journey, he was thrown from the carriage at Pietermaritzburg station after refusing to move to a third-class carriage (car). During the Second Anglo-Boer war, he observed that the role of South African Indians was confined to bearing stretchers for the wounded—a duty which Gandhi undertook himself during the battle of Spioenkop. He took up the Indian cause and developed his philosophy of non-violent resistance. He led huge protest marches and sparked off strikes by Indian workers. When he returned to India in 1914, he was already being called the 'Great Soul' or Mahatma.

A young Gandhi (1869–1948)

Dressed for the gold mines (inset, above right); digging for diamonds at one of the many mines (right)

The Grand Imperialist

Cecil John Rhodes (1853–1902) played a central role in the history of southern Africa. Born in England, he moved to South Africa at the age of 17, and soon went to Kimberley to make his fortune—he slowly bought up shares in diamond-buying concerns. He spent a year at Oxford University, returning to South Africa in 1874, where he gained control of diamond-mining activities—by the late 1880s he had the monopoly. He then set his sights on a career in politics, and by 1890 he was prime minister of the Cape Colony. Rhodes continued to advocate British expansion, including the founding of the colony which took his name—Rhodesia (now Zimbabwe and Zambia). Rhodes remained hugely influential until his death in 1902.

Scorched Earth

During the Anglo-Boer war, the infamous scorched earth policy (burning farmhouses and flushing out Boer support) of the British commander Lord Kitchener (1850–1916) left much of the countryside a smouldering wasteland, and tens of thousands of Boer women and children were made homeless. The British decided to introduce 'concentration camps', to which these destitute people were brought. Poor administration meant that food and medical supplies in the camps ran out, leading to 26,000 deaths. Memories of the British scorched earth policy were often revived by Afrikaner politicians during the 20th century. Less widely known was the policy of rounding up African workers and placing them in similar concentration camps; at least 14,000 died.

Starving Out the Enemy

October 1899 to February 1900 saw the most famous of the Boer War sieges, that of the diamond capital Kimberley. Some 4,000 Boer soldiers marched on the town, hemming in 500 British troops and 50,000 civilians, including Cecil Rhodes. Although the Boers failed to break through the town's defences, they did their best to starve Kimberley into surrender. However, the extensive stores owned by the De Beers Diamond Mining Company meant that food never ran out. The inhabitants did suffer, however, and—inevitably—the African population suffered the most. There were widespread cases of scurvy and high infant mortality. The arrival of fresh British troops at nearby Modder River sparked an attack on the Boers and the town was finally relieved. With that, the whole impetus of the war turned against the Boers.

Britain's Worst Defeat

When Lord Chelmsford (1827–1905) invaded Zululand in January 1879, it was widely thought that the Zulus, armed only with their shields and spears, would suffer a swift defeat. In reality, the Anglo-Zulu War became one of the most documented wars in southern Africa, and brought about the worst defeat suffered in British colonial history. Isandlwana was the site of the first—and for Britain, the worst—battle of the war, when thousands of Zulu warriors, under the command of King Cetshwayo, advanced on the poorly prepared British troops. More than 1,300 British soldiers and their African allies were killed. It took another five months of fierce fighting for the British, under the command of Lord Chelmsford, finally to defeat the Zulus, at the battle at Ulundi.

Cecil Rhodes (left)

Paul Kruger (right)

The last stand at the battle of Isandlwana on 22 January 1879 (left)

1902

A tableau from Talana Museum, with soldiers in period dress

The battle of Spioenkop in 1900 during the Second Anglo-Boer War (above)

The Rise of Nationalism

Following the Boers' surrender to the British in 1902, the British and Boer territories moved towards union, and a unified South Africa came into being in 1910. The Act of Union and the entrenchment of voting arrangements in the Boer republics, by which Africans were denied any political rights, felt like a powerful slap in the face for many. Most had supported the British during the Anglo-Boer War and had assumed that their loyalty would be recognized in the post-war settlement. Black and coloured (mixed race; ▷ 6) people in the Cape had their voting rights embedded in the Constitution, but they feared that the Cape government's willingness to placate the two northern former republics was a very bad omen. In 1936 these voting rights were removed by law. There was also a rise in opposition movements at this time. Many of these were spurred on by the Land Act of 1913, which prohibited black people from buying or leasing land outside the designated 'native' reserves, effectively restricting black access to just 8 per cent of South Africa's land. Afrikaners, meanwhile, were also dissatisfied. In the early 20th century, many were forced to move to the cities. Caught between the British who dominated the economy, and black workers, who competed with them for jobs, their plight came to be known as the 'poor white problem'.

Birth of the ANC

The changing laws regarding voting rights began to stir up more opposition to white dominance. In 1911, Pixley ka Isaka Seme (1882–1951), a lawyer, called on Africans to forget the differences of the past and unite as one national organization. On 8 January 1912, more than one hundred chiefs and church and community leaders gathered in Bloemfontein and formed the South African Native National Congress, later renamed the African National Congress. Under Seme's leadership, the ANC was moderate and its most common form of protest was to make appeals to the Imperial authorities.

1902

Daniel François Malan (above left) was president from 1948 to 1954

The Boer Peace Treaty was signed in Pretoria in 1902 (above)

GREETINGS TO OUR BOYS
WELKOM AAN ONZE JONGENS

Champion of the Workers

The first few decades of the 20th century saw a burst of short-lived but radical opposition movements. The most successful of these was the Industrial and Commercial Union (ICU), led by the charismatic Clements Kadalie (1896–1951). A champion of farmers' and workers' rights, at just 23 he led a prominent dock strike in Cape Town, which forced managers to accede to demands for significant wage increases and better working conditions. By 1926, he had created a membership of more than 150,000 workers. His success did not last, however; internal rifts led to the eventual downfall of the ICU in 1928.

The Union Building in Pretoria has been the seat of the government since 1910

South Africa Gets its Call Up

White and black South Africans made contributions to the Allied effort during both World Wars. In 1917, during World War I, the sinking of the *SS Mendi* carrying about 850 South African troops from Cape Town to France bears witness to a remarkable tale of brotherhood and bravery in the face of death. About 805 black privates, five white officers and the ship's crew sang and danced together as the ship sank, with the loss of all still on board and many who leapt into the icy waters. South Africa's political involvement was at the highest level with the then Prime Minister General Jan Smuts serving as a member of British Prime Minister Lloyd George's war cabinet during 1917–18. Smuts was also a very good friend of British Prime Minister Winston Churchill. In fact, Churchill had such a high opinion of his old friend that he even toyed with the idea of leaving Smuts in charge of Britain when he went to the Teheran conference in 1943.

Celebrations with a Sting in the Tail

In 1938, D. F. Malan (1874–1959) and his colleagues at the right-wing Gesuiwerde Nationale Party, (GNP, or the Purified National Party) rallied the white Afrikaner population to take part in a commemorative celebration of the Great Trek. A team of ox wagons journeyed from Cape Town to Pretoria in a symbolic re-enactment of the trek, and by the time the wagons reached Pretoria, more than 200,000 Afrikaners had gathered in the city to welcome them and take part in the festival. Malan—who was soon to become the first leader of an apartheid government—succeeded in whipping up nationalistic fervour. The foundation stones were laid for the Voortrekker Monument (which today stands more as a monument to skewed interpretations of history) on 16 December. This happened to be the exact date when, a hundred years earlier, the Zulus had been defeated by the Boers at the Battle of Blood River.

A New Breed

The year 1944 saw the dawn of a new era in African nationalism, when a fiery idealist named Nelson Mandela (1918–) joined forces with Oliver Tambo (1917–1993), Walter Sisulu (1912–2003) and Anton Lembede (1914–47) to form the ANC Youth League. While the traditional ANC had limped along rather ineffectually, the Youth League injected a fierce Africanist ideology and refused to work with other organizations. These militant young activists revitalized the ANC, led by Lembede and his rejection of moderate opposition movements. Industrial strikes became a key weapon in the fight against oppression, and in 1946 the African Mineworkers' Union launched a crippling strike with more than 100,000 gold-mine workers laying down their tools.

Field Marshall Smuts, right, talking to a squadron leader of a SAAF (below left); the Voortrekker Monument built in 1940 (below)

1948

Troops returning to Cape Town in 1919 (left)

The Apartheid Era

Although the first apartheid government was voted in under D. F. Malan in 1948, the full agenda of legislation was not finalized until the mid-1950s. The term 'apartheid' simply means 'apart-ness', and the ruling Nationalist Party stated that their long-term aim was the total separation of races. In the meantime, they had to be practical and recognize that white industry relied upon African labour. In effect, apartheid became a way of ensuring a continuous supply of cheap labour while denying Africans any political rights.

Legislation such as the Group Areas Act tightened previous segregation regulations, and the government launched a massive national campaign to remove Africans from urban areas. Africans living in vibrant urban communities, such as Sophiatown in Johannesburg, were forcibly removed to bleak townships away from central city districts. The 1960s saw a huge upsurge of opposition from the ANC and the new, more militant Pan African Congress (PAC), particularly against the hated pass laws, which dictated that the black population carry identity documents at all times, severely restricting their movements. The government responded brutally: Violent suppression became the norm; both the ANC and PAC were banned; and forced removals increased as the government set about dividing the country into clear racial zones and 'homelands'.

The Sharpeville Massacre

In March 1960, the Pan African Congress called on all Africans to leave their passes at home and present themselves at the nearest police station. They hoped that the prison system would be swamped and the pass laws revoked.

On 21 March, large crowds gathered across the country, but these were dispersed by police. In the township of Sharpeville, however, the crowd stayed on the streets even when they were buzzed by jets. At 1.15pm there was a scuffle and the police panicked. They later claimed that they had come under attack but this has been denied by almost all eyewitness accounts. What is clear, however, is that the police suddenly opened fire on the crowd with sten guns. The terrified people ran for cover but the police continued to fire on the fleeing protesters. Most of the 69 dead and 180 wounded were shot in the back.

1948

A prison cell on Robben Island (above left); apartheid was enshrined in all aspects of life, including where you ate (below)

Hendrik F. Verwoerd on the cover of *Time* magazine in 1966

Architect of Apartheid

Hendrik Verwoerd (1901–66), prime minister from 1958 to 1966, did much to push through early segregationist legislation. He set up the system of independent homelands, where Africans were to govern themselves away from the white areas. In 1961, with growing friction between South Africa and Britain, he succeeded in creating the Republic of South Africa. The new republic was expelled from the British Commonwealth. Verwoerd appointed John Vorster as Justice Minister, in which post he passed a string of repressive laws. In 1966, Verwoerd was killed in a fatal stabbing. Ironically, the assassination was not racially motivated: Dimitri Tsafendas said that he had been ordered to assassinate Verwoerd by the tapeworm in his stomach.

The Soweto Uprising

A key turning point in protests against apartheid was the pupil protests of 1976, in which black school children took to the streets to protest against new rules enforcing the Afrikaans language in schools. On 16 June, a Soweto school pupils' committee organized a mass march to deliver their grievances to the authorities. This peaceful march was met with a brutal and shocking response. Police opened fire, killing 13-year-old Hector Peterson. After the Soweto Uprising, as the incident became known, rioting erupted around the country and a constant and violent level of unrest spread through the townships. By the following year, more than 500 protestors had been killed in the revolts.

Robert Sobukwe (1924–78), leader of PAC, was one of many held on Robben Island (left)

The World's First Heart Transplant

During the late 1960s, a virtually unknown South African surgeon by the name of Christiaan Barnard performed the world's first human heart transplant at Cape Town's Groote Schuur hospital. The operation turned Barnard into an instant celebrity and put South Africa on the medical map. The brilliant doctor travelled the world giving lectures and was celebrated wherever he went, including being received by the Pope in Rome and President Johnson in the US. Before performing the transplant, Barnard had spent years experimenting with the procedure. Barnard went on to pioneer other heart-related operations and devoted the last part of his career focusing on slowing the aging process. Arthritis forced Barnard to end his career in the 1980s. He died in 2001 of an asthma attack while on holiday in Cyprus at the age of 78.

Cry Freedom

One of the best-known names in the struggle against apartheid is Steve Biko (1946–77). He was co-founder and president of the Black Peoples Convention (BPC), the leading black consciousness movement in the 1970s. In 1973, Biko was banned as an individual by the government and suffered numerous arrests and interrogations. On 12 September 1977, he died in police custody. His death was blamed on a hunger strike, but the work of Donald Woods, the editor of the East London *Daily Dispatch*, put pressure on the government to open an inquest (this campaign was the subject of the movie *Cry Freedom*, 1987). The inquest revealed that Biko died of brain damage, but it was not until the 1990s that this was attributed to beatings while in custody.

Dr. Christiaan Barnard

NON-WHITES EATING HOUSE

An ANC supporter on a march

1988

ASPELING STREET

ASPELING STREET

CONSTITUTION ST

ST PHILLIP STREET

MBRIDGE STREET

STUCKERIS STREET

11 Feb

District Six Museum in Cape Town is committed to remembering the horrors of apartheid

Homage to Steve Biko by South African Willie Bester

SC300

*R*oad to Freedom

By the late 1980s, the government had more or less lost control of large portions of the townships. Growing unrest and international sanctions were hitting the economy hard. The government, fearing revolution, was forced to embark on a gradual series of reforms under the presidency of P. W. Botha (1916–), who set about dismantling some of the segregationist policies. However, this did nothing to assuage the unrest and was seen as little more than an attempt to hold off further sanctions. Following a stroke, Botha was replaced by F. W. de Klerk (1936–), who was handed the reins of a country in turmoil. He revoked the ban on the ANC and released Nelson Mandela in 1990, launching a new era of reform. De Klerk signed an agreement with Mandela in May 1990 to revoke repressive laws and release political prisoners. Mandela persuaded the ANC to stop armed resistance, and a fragile process of negotiation began.

The next four years saw escalating levels of violence and the negotiations repeatedly broke down, but on 27 April 1994 the first democratic elections passed peacefully.

The Bang-Bang Club

As violence rocketed in the townships in the early 1990s, a small team of photojournalists took to the streets to record what was going on. The foursome, made up of Ken Oosterbroek, Kevin Carter, Greg Marinovich and Joao Silva were nicknamed the 'Bang-Bang Club', a reference to the fighting (or the bang-bang of a gun) they witnessed. The name stuck and their images of the horrific violence, murders and gangland executions remain the most compelling record of the 'Hostel Wars'. The horror of their subject matter took its toll: Oosterbroek was killed in cross fire on 18 April 1994, and Kevin Carter committed suicide a few weeks after winning the Pulitzer Prize for a photograph of a starving child in the Sudan. The remaining members published their story, *The Bang-Bang Club*, in 2000.

1988

Mandela election poster (above);
the cover of a bestseller (below)

The First Elections

On 27 April 1994, Nelson Mandela, at the age of 76, voted for the first time in his country's elections. More than 19 million people, around 91 per cent of registered voters, joined him at the polls, most of them for the first time in their lives. Despite very long waits, voting was peaceful and the ANC won by a landslide. On 10 May, Mandela was inaugurated as South Africa's first black president in front of a crowd of 60,000 cheering supporters. His inauguration speech was watched by millions and his pledge stirred the nation: '...we shall build a society in which all South Africans, both black and white, will be able to walk tall, without any fear in their hearts, assured of their inalienable right to human dignity—a rainbow nation at peace with itself and the world.'

Mandela and de Klerk on the campaign trail

Namibia Leads the Way

South Africa's history has been intertwined in more ways than one with its northern, desert neighbour. Namibia, or South West Africa as it was then known, was effectively run as a South African province from 1920, when the former German colony was given to South Africa to administer as a mandate after World War I. Unlike other countries that were given mandates, South Africa refused to surrender control of Namibia to the United Nations, ignoring pressure from the world community. The apartheid regime proceeded to pursue its racist policies of homelands and segregation and it was only after decades of continuous pressure from the international community that negotiations in New York led to South Africa eventually granting Namibia independence in 1988. Free elections were held in the early 1990s and a majority government was voted into power.

One Street, Two Prizes

South Africa has the distinction of having the only street in the world that produced not one but two Nobel peace prize laureates. The famous Vilakazi Street in Soweto township was home to both former South African president Nelson Mandela and outspoken anti-apartheid cleric Desmond Tutu, who was awarded the prize in 1984 after being nominated for the third time, humbly declared at the ceremony that he was merely 'a little focus' of the stalwarts of the struggle for freedom from apartheid. Mandela received his Nobel peace prize in 1993 together with former president F. W. de Klerk as the country headed towards its first democratic election. The Nobel committee said the award was recognition of their work on 'the peaceful termination of the apartheid regime, and for laying the foundations for a new democratic South Africa'.

Pocket of the Past

Hidden in the dusty depths of the Northern Cape is the small town of Orania, unexceptional but for one thing: It is inhabited exclusively by whites. Founded in 1991 by Afrikaner professor Carel Boshoff, Orania is dedicated to white separatism and the creation of an Afrikaner Volkstaat, or 'people's state'. What was originally a community of just eight families has grown to more than 600 residents, drawn by a fear of crime and a longing for the return of apartheid. The village is guarded by a statue of Hendrik Verwoerd (1901–66), revered as the architect of apartheid, although the town is not actually closed to black visitors.

1994

Prince Buthelezi, leader of the opposition Inkatha Freedom Party (left); waiting to vote (below)

A New Era

Few envied Nelson Mandela (1918–) the task of dealing with the aftermath of apartheid, but then few could imagine any degree of meaningful progress without his leadership. Mandela commanded huge popular support among the African population and won the backing of much of South Africa's white population as well. During his presidency, he managed successful negotiations for a new constitution, launched a reconstruction plan that put housing, health and education at the forefront, and instigated the Truth and Reconciliation Commission (see below). Some areas experienced more success than others: The government failed to build its promised one million new houses by 2000, but it did introduce water and electricity to the majority of homes. President Thabo Mbeki (1942–) faces different problems. The divisions of apartheid still affect the country, but poverty, unemployment and HIV/AIDS are today's challenges.

Love Life

No issue is more important in South Africa today than that of HIV/AIDS. There are more people living with the disease here than in any other country, and an estimated 600 people die of it every single day. AIDS is the biggest killer in the country. It is also an issue that has landed the President Mbeki in hot water. His famous denial that HIV causes AIDS was followed by uproar and his reputation suffered considerably, not least because his controversial stance was preventing the free distribution of anti-retroviral drugs. This policy was reversed in 2003 and free anti-retroviral drugs are now available. National campaigns are also prominent, such as the hugely successful Love Life campaign, aimed at teenagers.

The Healing of Old Wounds

A crucial step in the healing process of post-apartheid South Africa was the creation of the Truth and Reconciliation Commission (TRC), headed by Archbishop Desmond Tutu. The aim of the commission was to uncover the atrocities of apartheid—but not to punish its perpetrators. The commission sat from April 1996 until July 1998, during which time it heard testimonies from more than 20,000 people, revealing harrowing stories of torture, disappearance and murder. Both victims and perpetrators could give their accounts, and those who confessed to their crimes could apply for amnesty from prosecution. The TRC became a vital component in the transition to full and free democracy, and despite some flaws, was lauded as an enormous success.

1994– today

truth & reconciliation commission

Bishop Tutu led the TRC (above and left); on a march for better HIV care (above right) Mbeki and Mandela (right); students enjoy a new-found confidence (below)

On the Move

ARRIVING

ARRIVING BY AIR

The three main international airports are Johannesburg, Cape Town and Durban. Johannesburg is the regional hub with numerous daily flights to Europe, North America, Asia and Australia. Although most flights arrive in Johannesburg, a fair number of carriers fly directly to Cape Town. There is a huge choice of routes and flights, but for the lowest fares you need to make reservations at least three to four months in advance, especially over Christmas.

AIRLINES

South Africa's national and international carrier is South African Airways (SAA), but most major international carriers fly here, including British Airways, Virgin Atlantic, KLM, Lufthansa, American Airways and Qantas (▷ 44).

AIRPORTS
Johannesburg International Airport (JNB), formerly known as Jan Smuts, is at Kempton Park on the R24, 24km (15 miles) northeast of central Jo'burg. There are six terminals, all in one long building. A new domestic

A South African Airways plane at Cape Town International Airport

terminal was opened here in 2003, and the airport now ranks as the major hub for air travel in southern Africa, with 53 airlines carrying 13 million passengers

TRANSFERS FROM AIRPORT TO CITY			
	JOHANNESBURG (JNB)	**CAPE TOWN (CPT)**	**DURBAN (DUR)**
Distance	24km (15 miles)	22km (13.5 miles)	16km (10 miles)
Taxi	Taxi rank outside main terminal building Price: around R180 Journey time: 20 min Airport Link Taxis: tel 011-7922017	Taxi rank outside International and Domestic terminals Price: around R200 Journey time: 20 min Touchdown Taxis (official operator)	Taxi rank outside Arrivals Terminal Price: around R150 Journey time: 30 min Aussie Taxis: tel 031-3010014
Shuttle Bus	Magic Bus: tel 011-5480822; www.magicbus.co.za Airport Link Shuttle: tel 011-7922017 Both drop off at the major hotels in Johannesburg and Pretoria. Reserve seats ahead. Price: R75–R150 A free shuttle bus connects hotels within the airport's environs. Some backpacker hostels provide free pick-up (arrange ahead).	Magic Bus: tel 021-5056300; www.magicbus.co.za Way 2 Go: tel 021-9346409 City Hopper: tel 021-9344440 Desks in Arrivals, but it's cheaper to reserve seats ahead: the bigger the group, the lower the fare per person.	Magic Bus: tel 031-2632647; www.magicbus.co.za Drops off at the major hotels in Durban. Desk in Arrivals, but it's cheaper to reserve seats ahead. Price: R75–R150 Airport Bus Service: tel 031-4651660 Leaves hourly 5.30am–8pm from outside the domestic terminal, to corner of Aliwal and Smith streets, next to the SAA building in central Durban.
Car Rental	Desks are in Parkade Centre, opposite main terminal building across from pick-up/drop-off zone. Avis: tel 011-3945433; Budget: tel 011-3313631; Europcar: tel 011-3948832, Hertz: tel 011-3909700; Imperial: tel 011-3903909	Desks are in the international arrivals hall. Avis: tel 021-9340330; Budget: tel 021-3803140; Europcar: tel 021-9342263; Hertz: tel 021-9353000	Desks are in the arrivals hall. Avis: tel 031-4081777; Budget: tel 031-4081809; Hertz: tel 031-4521500; Imperial: tel 031-4690066

AIRPORTS

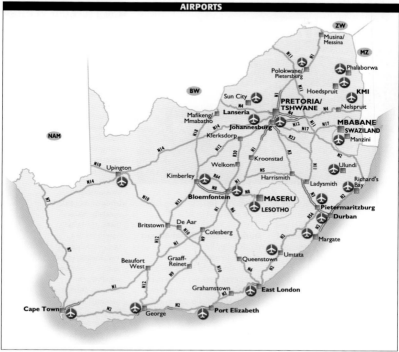

annually. International flights usually arrive early in the morning and depart in the late afternoon or evening.

Terminals 1 and 2 are for international arrivals; Terminal 3 handles South African Airways (SAA) and SA Express domestic arrivals; and Terminal 4 handles non-SAA domestic arrivals. Domestic departures for all airlines are from Terminal 5, while Terminal 6 handles international departures. There are information kiosks in International Arrivals and Departures, and Domestic Arrivals (tel 011-9216262). Baggage trolleys and porter services are available at designated areas in each terminal and at drop-off zones. There are also orange-uniformed porters (look for their ACSA permits) in all terminals; expect to pay around R5 per item. The VAT Refund desk is in the

lounge of International Departures in Terminal 6 (for information on VAT Refunds, ▷ 303). There are elevators in all terminals, suitable for wheelchair users (two are equipped with Braille).

Each terminal has a choice of restaurants and snack bars, shops selling newspapers, clothes and gifts, plus banks (see below). Terminals 1 and 2 have a desk each for rental of mobile phones (cell phones) and South African SIM cards (▷ 308), and a post office. There is a duty free shopping mall in International Departures, with an extensive range of shops including the second biggest duty free gift shop in the world. Internet access is available in International Departures. Left luggage (tel 011-3901804) is on the upper level of the parking area near International Arrivals, and costs R32 per item.

There are ATMs on the public concourse of International Arrivals (Terminal 2), Domestic Arrivals (Terminal 4) level 1, and the Domestic Departures public concourse and lounge (Terminal 5). Foreign currency exchange is available at branches of ABSA Bank, American Express, Rennies/Thomas Cook Foreign Exchange and Master Currency, all on the public concourse of the International Arrivals Hall (Terminal 2). ABSA Bank also has an exchange service for foreign nationals in the International Departures lounge (Terminal 6).

Cape Town International Airport (CPT), formerly known as D. F. Malan, has a large volume of international and domestic flights passing through every day. It's the second largest airport in South Africa, with an annual turnover of 6.5 million passengers. The airport is 22km

Car rental offices at Cape Town International Airport

(13.5 miles) from central Cape Town, a 20-minute drive on the N2. There is an International and a Domestic Terminal, connected via a walkway. The International Terminal was recently upgraded, and the Domestic Terminal is undergoing refurbishment. Long-haul flights arrive in the morning and depart in the late afternoon or evening.

International Departures has a public concourse filled with shops (selling newspapers, luggage, gifts) and cafés. There is a bank, an ATM and an ABSA bureau de change. International Arrivals has an ATM and a Master Currency bureau de change; a restaurant and bar are on the first floor. The arrivals hall also holds all the major car rental desks, as well as desks for rental of mobile phones (cell phones) and South African SIM cards (▷ 308). There is a tourist office desk in the middle of the hall. The VAT Refund desk is to the left of the check-in desks in the International Departures hall (for information on VAT Refunds, ▷ 303). The International Departures lounge has a string of mall-style duty free shops.

Domestic Arrivals has two ATMs, cafés and a post office. Domestic Departures has a bank, three ATMs and an ABSA bureau de change. Left luggage (tel 021-936 2884) is in the Domestic Arrivals Terminal, costing R15 per bag per day.

Durban International Airport
(DUR) is by far the smallest of the international airports in South Africa, and has a limited number of international arrivals (most are from within southern Africa). Most flights within Africa are connected via Johannesburg or Cape Town, although Durban does have a good selection of national connections. It is 16km (10 miles) from central Durban, and transport into town takes about 30 minutes. There is one terminal building, which holds the Arrivals and Departures terminals. There is a tourist information office in the domestic arrivals hall (tel 031-4081000; daily 6.30am–9pm).

The ground floor of the Arrivals Terminal has banks, an ATM and a bureau de change. There is a bureau de change in International Departures and a post office in the main concourse, where there are also shops, cafés and restaurants, internet access, and desk for rental of mobile phones (cell phones) and South African SIM cards (▷ 308). The arrivals hall has desks for the major car rental companies (see panel to the right).

The Transfers chart on page 42 has more information on getting from the airports to the cities, and car rental details.

CAR RENTAL
South Africa is best explored by road, and many visitors choose to rent a car on arrival. All the major airports have car rental desks, although it is wise to make an advance reservation, especially during high season.
● You will need a full driver's licence to rent a car, but it will be valid only if it is printed in English and has a photograph.

Otherwise, you should get an international driving permit, available in your home country.

● The minimum age for drivers is usually 21; those under 23 may have to pay an additional levy of R50.

● A credit card (or cash) deposit will be needed when you pick up your keys.

● Thoroughly check your rental car before you set off and point out any scratches or anomalies. These must be marked on the rental form, otherwise you may be charged for the damage.

● Most rental companies rent out cars with full tanks of petrol (gas). Be sure to fill up just before returning the car, or you risk being charged much more for fuel by the car rental firm.

● Given South Africa's size, it is a good idea to get an unlimited kilometre package, rather than being limited to a set distance per day.

● Check if there are any limits to taking the car off road. This is particularly important if you plan to drive yourself around one of the national parks, as some roads are unsurfaced.

● Particular hazards worth watching out for include stray animals in the countryside, and hijackers in and around the big cities and on quiet country roads. Never stop for anyone other than the police (cars are clearly marked).

● See pages 54–57 for more information on driving within South Africa.

ARRIVING OVERLAND

There are good roads between South Africa and Namibia, Botswana, Mozambique, Lesotho, Swaziland and Zimbabwe. The Department of Home Affairs in Pretoria (tel 012-3241860) can provide up-to-date details of the opening and closing times of border posts.

MAIN ENTRY POINTS

Botswana The main border crossings into South Africa are at Pioneer Gate, Ramatlabama and Tlokweng Gate. The crossing is usually swift and efficient. The R49 from Tlokweng connects with the N4 at Zeerust heading towards Johannesburg. From Ramatlabama there is a road leading to Mafikeng, which connects with the R52 to Jo'burg.

Lesotho From Lesotho, the main border crossings are Maseru Bridge, Maputsoe Bridge and Calendonspoort. There are several others, such as Sani Pass, that are open for limited periods and can be crossed only in a 4WD vehicle and, in some cases, on horseback or on foot.

Mozambique The journey by road between South Africa and Maputo has improved due to the completion of the section of toll road between Nelspruit and Maputo via the border at Komatipoort.

Namibia The main crossing point is Vioolsdrif, with less

frequently used border crossings at Ariamsvlei and Rietfontein.

Swaziland Crossings between South Africa and Swaziland are at Ngwenya/Oshoek, Lavumisa and Mahamba. The N17 then the R33 heads from Oshoek to Johannesburg via Carolina.

Zimbabwe The only border crossing between Zimbabwe and South Africa is at Beitbridge, a notoriously slow crossing during peak periods, with long waits and thorough searches.

ARRIVING BY LONG-DISTANCE BUS

Three main long-distance bus companies cover routes across South Africa's borders, and some services go as far as Malawi.

● Translux (tel 011-7743333; www.translux.co.za) runs buses from Johannesburg to Blantyre (Malawi), Bulawayo and Harare (Zimbabwe) and Lusaka (Zambia), and from Pretoria to Maputo (Mozambique).

● Intercape (tel 086-128728; www.intercape.co.za) runs buses from Johannesburg and Pretoria to Gaborone (Botswana), Windhoek (Namibia), Maputo (Mozambique) and Victoria Falls in Zimbabwe (via Namibia).

● Greyhound (tel 011-2768500; www.greyhound.co.za) runs buses from Pretoria to Maputo, Harare and Bulawayo.

ARRIVING BY CAR

If crossing any international borders in a private car, you must have a registration document, insurance and a driver's licence printed in English with a photograph. If you've rented a car, be sure to check with the rental company that you are permitted to take the car into another country.

If you are planning to drive around South Africa, remember distances are vast.

An Intercape bus waits at Port Elizabeth

GETTING AROUND

South Africa has an efficient transportation network with the best road system and flight network in Africa. Highways (motorways/expressways) are of a very good standard, comparable to those in Europe and the US. A well-developed fleet of private long-distance buses criss-crosses the country, and the train system (although painfully slow) provides another way of getting around. City transportation, on the other hand, is a problem. South Africa's cities lack safe and reliable urban public systems (the exception is Cape Town; ▷ 48), often making private transportation the only option for visitors. Safety is an issue throughout South Africa—see tips for each mode of transportation on the following pages.

BY ROAD

South Africans rely on their cars, and the road system is correspondingly excellent. A web of highways, known as N roads, stretches across the country linking the major cities. The N1 links Cape Town with Johannesburg and Pretoria; the N2 links Cape Town with Port Elizabeth and Durban. Various smaller highways connect towns in between. The main roads are largely toll free, although some short stretches have started to introduce tolls.

The real joy of driving in South Africa, however, is veering away from the major highways and exploring the countryside along the far reaches of the regional (R) roads. Although these tend to be slower, they are usually quieter and pass through some of the most spectacular scenery in the country. Many people also choose to self-drive through the

national parks, such as Kruger, and this can be a great way of going on safari. Here, roads tend to be well maintained and are usually tarred.

The good road system means that South Africa is also easily explored by bus, and there is a wide network of luxurious long-distance buses, although they are not as cheap as you might expect. Three major bus companies cover the country, and there is also a good value backpacker bus (▷ 51).

There is an enormous network of mini-buses, but these are best avoided because of high accident rates and security issues.

RAIL AND AIR

In contrast to the excellent roads, the rail system is relatively unreliable. Although comfortable, trains tend to be slow and inefficient. However, a splendid way of experiencing some

colonial style is by taking one of the luxury trains which are becoming increasingly popular with visitors.

Given the huge distances involved in exploring South Africa, domestic flights are perhaps the most practical option for getting about, particularly for those with limited time. The national carrier, South African Airways (SAA), has numerous daily flights connecting the major cities and towns. The last few years have also seen several 'no-frills' airlines springing up, offering low-fare flights between major airports.

The map opposite shows how to get around the country using air, rail and bus, and which cities have interconnections. Also see chart on page 53.

Stunning scenery along Katse Dam Road, Lesotho

Transportation Network

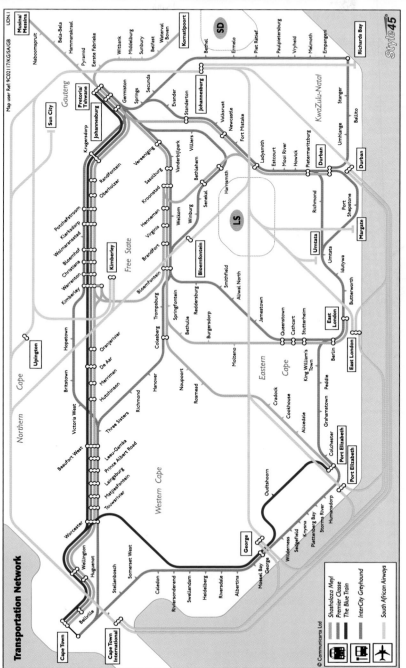

Map user Ref 9CO2|17/KG/SA/GB UDN.I

Style@45®

Musina/Messina
Beleba-Beleb
Naboomspruit
Hammanskraal.
Pyramid
Eerste Fabrieke
Witbank
Middelburg
Sunbury
Belfast
Waterval
Boven
Komatipoort

Gauteng
Sun City
Pretoria/Tshwane
Johannesburg
Krugersdorp
Germiston
Springs
Secunda
Evander
Johannesburg

Bethel
Ermelo
Piet Retief
Pauljpietersburg
Vryheid
Melmoth
Empangeni

SD

KwaZulu-Natal
Richards Bay

Randfontein
Oberholzer
Vereeniging
Vanderbijlpark
Villiers
Standerton
Volksrust
Newcastle
Fort Mistake
Ladysmith
Estcourt
Mooi River
Howick
Pietermaritzburg
Umhlange
Stanger
Ballito
Durban
Durban

Potchefstroom
Klerksdorp
Wolmaransstad
Bloemhof
Christiana
Warrenton
Kimberley
Kimberley

Sasolburg
Kroonstad
Henneman
Virginia
Brandfort
Welkom
Winburg
Senekal
Bethlehem
Harrismith

LS

Richmond
Port
Shepstone
Margate

Hopetown
Bloemfontein
Bloemfontein

Springfontein
Reddersburg
Smithfield
Aliwal North
Umtata
Umtata
Idutywa
Butterworth

Northern
Cape
Upington

Britstown
Oranjerivier
De Aar
Merriman
Hutchinson
Hanover
Colesberg
Trompsburg
Bethulie
Burgersdorp
Molteno
Rosmead
Noupoort
Jamestown
Queenstown
Cathcart
Stutterheim
East London
King William's Town
Berlin
East London

Victoria West
Beaufort West
Three Sisters
Richmond
Cradock
Cookhouse
Alicedale
Grahamstown
Peddie
Colchester
Port Elizabeth
Port Elizabeth

Eastern
Cape

Leeu-Gamka
Prince Albert Road
Laingsburg
Matjiesfontein
Touwsrivier
Worcester

Western Cape

Oudtshoorn
George
Wilderness
Sedgefield
Knysna
Plettenberg Bay
Storms River
Humansdorp
Mossel Bay
George

Wellington
Huguenot
Stellenbosch
Somerset West
Caledon
Riviersonderend
Swellendam
Heidelberg
Riversdale
Albertina
Bellville
Cape Town
Cape Town International

© Communicarta Ltd

Shosholoza Meyl
Premier Classe
The Blue Train
InterCity Greyhound
South African Airways

Getting Around in Cape Town

ON THE MOVE

Although the heart of Cape Town is easily explored on foot, there are also a number of sights stretched along the peninsula. The public transportation system is skeletal, and most visitors either rent a car or rely on taxis or organized tours to get out of town. It is worth noting, however, that Cape Town is the only large city in South Africa with any sort of reliable public transportation system.

BY BUS

The bus system in Cape Town covers the central area, the Southern Suburbs and the Atlantic seaboard. Buses run throughout the day, but they tend to be slow and inefficient and on the whole are best avoided. However there are two exceptions:

● The Waterfront bus is a useful service covering the short distance from Cape Town City Bowl to the Victoria and Alfred Waterfront. Buses leave from Cape Town rail station on Adderley Street every 15 minutes from 6am until 11.15pm, seven days a week. Buses from the Waterfront start at 6.20am and run until 11.45pm. Tickets are bought on the bus and cost R2.50 one-way.

● The other useful service runs from the City Bowl along the Atlantic seaboard. This route starts from the main bus station on Grand Parade and runs approximately every 15–30 minutes from 5.30am to 8.50pm (Mon–Fri) and from 6am to 6pm on Saturdays; three buses run on Sundays (last bus at 5.05pm). The bus stops at Sea Point and Camps Bay and ends in Hout Bay, taking about an hour (depending on traffic) to cover the whole seaboard. There is a useful information kiosk at the main bus terminal on Grand Parade (freephone 080-1212111; www.gabs.co.za).

BY METRO

The Metrorail train line serves the Southern Suburbs, running from the main train station on Adderley Street as far as Worcester (in the Winelands). This is mainly a commuter service, but the ride to Simon's Town on False Bay is a

worthwhile visitor excursion, with the train running alongside the crashing waves of False Bay for the last stretch. However, don't take the train any farther: Beyond Cape Town there's a risk of mugging.

● It is best to use the trains only during the rush hours (7–8am and 4–6pm) or in the middle of the day, as there is again some risk of mugging if the train is not busy. It is also a good idea to travel first class; each station has signs indicating where the first-class carriage (car) will be when the train comes in.

● The first train is around 5am, and they then run approximately every 15 minutes between the central station and Simon's Town, until around 7pm. Train times change seasonally, so be sure to check with Metrorail (tel 0800-656463) for the latest timetable information before setting out.

● Tickets, which can be bought from the kiosks at the main concourse in Cape Town station, cost R12 one-way between Cape Town and Simon's Town.

BY TAXI

Taxis are the safest way of getting around at night and convenient during the day. Cape Town has several different types. Metered taxis are regulated by the Cape Town Municipality and leave from taxi stands around town.

● The most useful taxi stands are: outside the train station at Adderley Street; at the Victoria and Alfred Waterfront; near the Park Inn hotel on Greenmarket Square; halfway along Long Street; and at the lower Table Mountain Cableway station. Expect to pay around R12 per kilometre (half mile). If you are outside central Cape Town, you will have to call a taxi in advance.

● Companies include Unicab (tel 021-4481720) and Marine Taxis (tel 021-4340434). Hotels and restaurants are usually happy to call one for you.

● Rikki taxis are an alternative to standard metered taxis. These shared people-carriers, recognizable by their bright purple and white paintwork, are good value and reliable; they pick up several people on each route, significantly bringing down fares. Rikkis must be called in advance (tel 021-4234888).

● Minibus taxis serve the city on fixed routes, but are best avoided by visitors for security reasons.

BY CAR

Many visitors choose to rent a car to give them the freedom to explore the peninsula without having to rely on taxis. Car rental prices should be lower at quiet times than at the peak time of December and January.

● Parking is generally not a problem. Most of central Cape Town has demarcated areas, costing R6 per hour. There are official parking attendants (in blue uniforms) who patrol the central area—they'll ask how long you want to stay and you hand them the coins. Hotels and guesthouses usually have secure parking, but call ahead to check.

● Fuel prices are reasonable and there are plenty of large petrol (gas) stations around the city. Note that none are self-service and they often accept only cash.

BY BICYCLE

Despite Cape Town's outdoors lifestyle, few people use bicycles to get around town and there are few bicycle lanes in the city. However, bicycling as a sport is very popular and mountain biking has taken off in a big way.

Domestic Flights

Because of the vast distances in South Africa, flying can be an excellent way of seeing as much of the country as possible in a short space of time. The main hub of South Africa's far-reaching and efficient domestic air services is Johannesburg. South African Airways (SAA) links it to just about anywhere in the country, including the Greater Kruger National Park.

ON THE MOVE

SAA has had to deal with an upsurge of competition in recent years, and prices have dropped correspondingly. Several no-frills carriers have started up following the example of Kulula, which launched in June 2001 (although some have closed down again). These carriers are very similar to the low-cost airlines found in Europe and North America, offering ticket-free no-frills flights; in effect, this means you have to pay extra for any snacks and refreshments,

there are no numbered tickets or designated seats, and extras such as in-flight magazines are limited. These flights can represent excellent value for money, often costing only a little more than a long-distance bus ticket for the same route—and taking a fraction of the time.

DOMESTIC AIRLINES
South African Airways (SAA) has the most comprehensive network. It works in conjunction with its subsidiaries SA Airlink

Arriving to blue skies at Ulundi Airport

and SA Express, making it the largest domestic carrier, with regular daily flights connecting Johannesburg with many towns and cities within South Africa.
● Central reservations: tel 011-9781111, freephone 0861359722; www.flysaa.com.

Checking the departures board at Cape Town International Airport

FLIGHT INFORMATION	
Johannesburg to Cape Town:	2 hr 10 min
Johannesburg to Durban:	1 hr 10 min
Johannesburg to East London:	1 hr 30 min
Johannesburg to George:	1 hr 50 min
Johannesburg to Kimberley:	1 hr 15 min
Johannesburg to Port Elizabeth:	1 hr 40 min

Baggage allowance for SAA domestic flights

Hold luggage:	First Class, 40kg (88lb); Business Class, 30kg (66lb); Economy Class 20kg (44lb)
Hand luggage:	7kg (15.5lb) per bag (2 bags allowed per passenger in First and Business classes; 1 bag in Economy Class).

British Airways Comair

operates several flights each day between Cape Town, Durban, Johannesburg and Port Elizabeth. Comair is basically a domestic subsidiary of British Airways, and has been running in South Africa for more than 50 years.

- British Airways Comair: tel 011-9210222; www.ba.co.za.

Kulula

is the most successful no-frills airline in South Africa and remains the most reliable. It has daily services between Cape Town, Durban, Johannesburg, Port Elizabeth and George. The cheapest fares are available through its website.

- Kulula: tel 0861-585852; www.kulula.com.

1 Time

is a newer no-frills airline with services between Johannesburg and Cape Town, Durban and East London.

- 1 Time: tel 0861 345345; www.1time.co.za.

PRICES

Return fares from Johannesburg to Cape Town with standard carriers are in the region of

R950–R1,200. No-frills carriers are slightly cheaper, and have the advantage of offering one-way tickets (as opposed to return/round-trip tickets). Expect to pay in the region of R300 for a one-way fare from Cape Town to Johannesburg.

BUYING TICKETS

The method of buying your ticket depends on which airline you choose to fly with. The no-frills domestic airlines offer their cheapest fares online; standard

Cape Town's airport is the second largest in the country

carriers may have online offers, but over-the-phone fares should be similar to online prices. Whatever the carrier, it's worth making reservations as far in advance as possible, as prices fluctuate considerably—although you may find some good deals on last-minute flights: Check with travel agents, as they often have the best access to the cheapest deals.

DOMESTIC AIRPORTS AND SERVICES				
	SAA	BA COMAIR	KULULA	1 TIME
Bloemfontein	✔	–	–	–
Cape Town	✔	✔	✔	✔
Durban	✔	✔	✔	✔
George	✔	–	–	✔
East London	✔	–	✔	–
Hoedspruit	✔	–	–	–
Johannesburg	✔	✔	✔	✔
Kimberley	✔	–	–	–
Kruger Mpumalanga Int	✔	–	–	–
Lanseria	✔	–	–	–
Manzini	✔	–	–	–
Margate	✔	–	–	–
Nelspruit	✔	–	–	–
Phalaborwa	✔	–	–	–
Pietermaritzburg	✔	–	–	–
Port Elizabeth	✔	✔	✔	✔
Richard's Bay	✔	–	–	–
Sun City	✔	–	–	–
Ulundi	✔	–	–	–
Umtata	✔	–	–	–
Upington	–	✔	–	–
Maseru (Lesotho)	✔	–	–	–

Long-Distance Buses

There are three main bus operators running luxury services—known as coaches—and between them they cover just about every visitor hub, town and city in South Africa. Buses tend to be the most popular way of covering long distances: They are well maintained and comfortable, the roads are excellent and it's a safe mode of transportation.

PRICES

Coaches are cheaper than flying, and are far more efficient than trains. If you're on a budget, note that prices for short-distance trips are relatively expensive; they become better value for longer trips. Sample fares include:
- Johannesburg to Durban (8 hours, costing R190).
- Cape Town to Port Elizabeth (12 hours, costing R210).
- Cape Town to Pretoria (18.5 hours, costing R350).

MAIN BUS OPERATORS

Greyhound (tel 083-9159000; www.greyhound.co.za) runs services around much of the country, including popular routes from Cape Town to Port Elizabeth (via the Garden Route) and from Johannesburg to Durban. The website has online reservations; tickets must be picked up at a Greyhound office or Computicket outlet (see Tickets) at least four hours before departure. Passengers must be at the bus departure point half an hour before departure. If you're planning to spend some time on the road, Greyhound's bus passes are good value: 7 days' unlimited travel (within 30 days) R1,400; 15 days' unlimited travel (within 30 days) R2,700; 30 days' unlimited travel (within 60 days) R4,500.

Intercape (tel 086-1287287; www.intercape.co.za) covers an extensive network around the country, and has similar luxurious coaches, with air conditioning and reclining seats; some have televisions on board and hostesses handing out snacks and drinks. There are good year-round discounts, including family deals (up to 50 per cent off for children) and a standard 5 per cent discount for students.

Intercape also has a range of passes, including the 30-day Garden Route pass (Cape Town to East London) for R499.

Translux (tel 0861-589282; www.translux.co.za) has an extensive 24-hour network and comfortable double-decker coaches. Although it does not offer online reservations, it has a range of special seasonal offers. Timetable information is available on its website.

INTERNATIONAL ROUTES

All three of the main bus service providers include some routes across international borders, and between them cover Maputo (Mozambique), Windhoek and Walvis Bay (Namibia), Victoria Falls and Bulawayo (Zimbabwe), and Gaborone (Botswana).

TICKETS

As well as individual companies, Computicket (tel 083-9158000; www.computicket.co.za) sells tickets for all national bus services. However, for phone and internet reservations it accepts only credit cards issued in South Africa. You can pay in person with foreign-issued credit cards if you visit a Computicket outlet, found in all major shopping malls in the big cities.

BAZ BUS

Baz Bus (tel 021-4392323; www.bazbus.com) is probably the most popular bus service with visitors and is specifically designed for backpackers: It is a good way to see the country on a budget. One of the best aspects of the service is that, with a few exceptions, the bus collects and drops off passengers at their chosen backpacker hostel. When you are moving on, it is important to remember to call the Baz Bus to arrange to be collected; during busy times of the year it is advisable to call as soon as you have decided what your next move will be.

Tickets are priced per segment (see table). You are allowed to hop off and on the bus as many times as you like along the given segment, but must not backtrack (unless you buy a return ticket). This is where the savings are made, since other commercial buses such as Translux and Greyhound charge high prices for short trips. However, note that for long distances without stops, the mainline buses provide better value.

Baz Bus vehicles are fairly cramped, particularly at busy times, but a trailer at the back has space for large items such as rucksacks and surfboards.

BAZ BUS	
ROUTE	PRICE
Cape Town to Durban	R1,600
Durban to Cape Town	R1,600
Cape Town to Port Elizabeth, via the Garden Route	R810
Port Elizabeth to Cape Town, via the Garden Route	R810
Cape Town to Johannesburg, via the Drakensberg	R1,900
Johannesburg to Cape Town, via the Drakensberg	R1,900
Cape Town to Johannesburg, via Swaziland	R2,300
Johannesburg to Cape Town, via Swaziland	R2,300
Johannesburg to Durban, and back to Johannesburg via Swaziland and the Drakensberg	R1,010

Trains

Unlike the domestic air and bus network, train travel is relatively inefficient. Although most of the major cities are linked by rail, services are slow and some routes are poorly covered, with only one or two trains a week running along certain stretches. However, many visitors choose to take one of the luxury trains, such as the Blue Train.

ON THE MOVE

SHOSHOLOZA MEYL
The most frequent services are the named trains run by Shosholoza Meyl, part of the national network Spoornet (tel 086-0008888; www.spoornet. co.za). These trains, with names such as Trans Oranje and the Komati, run most days, and while they are fairly comfortable and inexpensive, travel times are intimidating. Reservations must be made at least 24 hours in advance at most stations, or you can make them through the national reservations telephone number above.

Named trains are split into three classes (no longer officially called 1st, 2nd and 3rd, but effectively just that). The 'sitter' class is made up of rows of plastic seats; the 'six-sleeper' has cabins with six fold-down beds and shared washing facilities in each carriage (car); and the 'four-sleeper' (the most comfortable option) has four fold-down beds in each cabin and shared washing facilities in each carriage (car). 'Coupés' are also available in four-sleeper class, sleeping two people at a slightly higher price. Some services offer 'Premier class' with an air-conditioned lounge and a restaurant car. Accompanied children under the age of five travel free; children between 5 and 11 pay half price.

All trains have a problem with security: If you leave your compartment, make sure a train official locks it after you. The four-sleeper is the most secure, as you can lock yourself into the cabin during the night. Refreshments are available on all trains, with either a dining car or a trolley selling snacks.

LUXURY TRAINS
The Blue Train This service, operated by Rovos Rail (tel 012-3348459; www.bluetrain.co.za), is the ultimate in luxury train travel. It has two routes—between Pretoria and Cape Town, and between Port Elizabeth and Cape Town.

TRANSPORTATION NETWORK

As well as highlighting the rail network, the places on this map correspond to the Transportation Network chart opposite

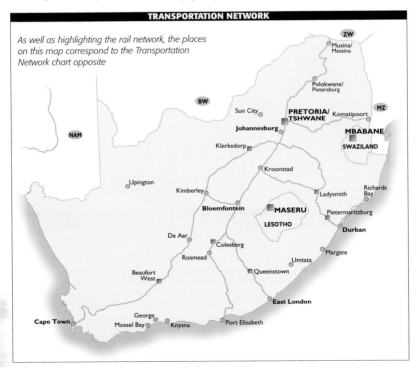

SHOSHOLOZA MEYL JOURNEY TIMES AND FARES

ROUTE	TIME	PRICE
Johannesburg to Durban	12.5 hours	R100 (sitter class)
		R165 (six-sleeper)
		R250 (four-sleeper)
Cape Town to Pretoria	25 hours	R210 (sitter class)
		R350 (six-sleeper)
		R520 (four-sleeper)

Passengers travel in beautifully designed compartments with a distinct colonial theme, equipped with either twin or double beds, private bathrooms with shower and bath, air conditioning, TV, and large windows to show off the passing landscapes. Meals are served in an elegant dining car. Expect to pay for the privilege though: A one-way fare from Pretoria to Cape Town, taking one day and one night, is R19,215 for two people sharing. A one-way trip from Port Elizabeth to Cape Town, the most popular route, as it passes along the Garden Route (taking two nights and one day), costs R22,745 for two people sharing.

Union Limited A slightly less expensive company operating 'historical' train trips is the Union Limited (tel 021-4494391; www.transnetheritagefoundation.co.za). The appeal of these trips is that much of the journey is under steam. The train is the original Blue Train, and the route, from Cape Town along the Garden Route and through the Little Karoo, is split between traditional steam engine and modern diesel.

The compartments have twin or double beds, mock-1940s decoration and private bathrooms, and there is a renovated wood-panelled dining car, where meals are silver service. The price for the round-trip from Cape Town, taking five days, is R18,250 for two people sharing, including all meals, drinks and excursions.

TRANSPORTATION NETWORK JOURNEY TIMES

This chart gives the journey times (hours in larger number) between major hubs. As it is not always possible to travel using one single mode of transport, the chart highlights which other modes should be used. The chart assumes that domestic flight is the best travel option. See transport map on page 47 for more details.

Journeys other than by air:
A = Bus
B = Rail
C = Air and Bus
D = Air and Rail
E = Air, Bus and Rail
F = Bus and Rail
* = change at Port Shepstone

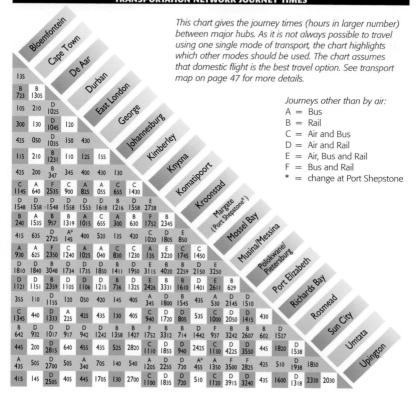

Driving

South Africa's excellent infrastructure makes driving an efficient and straightforward way of getting around the country. Roads are generally well maintained, although the more rural the road, the more likely you are to come across potholes and poor surfaces. South Africans rely heavily on their cars, partly because of the lack of a viable public transport system. In the cities, certainly, there is very little choice of transportation other than driving (the exception is Cape Town), while long-distance trips are facilitated by the excellent system of highways (motorways/expressways). Bear in mind, however, that South Africa is a very large country, so always plan your itinerary carefully, make sure you have water with you and leave plenty of time to get to your destination.

ON THE MOVE

WHAT TO BRING
● You must have either an International Driving Permit, available from your own country, or a foreign driver's licence printed in English, with a photo, and it must be valid for at least 6 months.
● A credit card is advisable for the deposit on a rental car (cash is usually also accepted, but amounts required are high).

Road signs often appear in a number of languages

Geen Swaar Voertuie
en Woonwaens
No Heavy Vehicles
and Caravans
Akufuneki Nqwelo
Zinzima Nekaraveni

HIGHWAY NETWORK

Towns and cities marked with a red square correspond to the Road Distances chart opposite

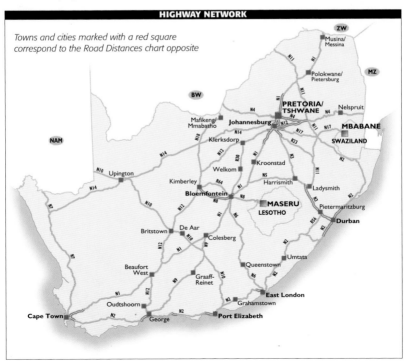

ROADS
- Main roads are identified by a number. National highways linking the major cities have the prefix 'N' followed by a number.
- The country's main artery, the N1, starts in Cape Town and passes through Johannesburg and Pretoria, ending at the Zimbabwe border.
- The N2 from Cape Town passes along the Garden Route to Port Elizabeth and Durban, and ends at the border with Mozambique.
- Regional highways and roads (sometimes two-lane highways) have the prefix 'R'.
- Major urban roads and ring-roads carry the prefix 'M', followed by a number.
- There are a few toll roads in South Africa. These accept cash only, so always keep some coins in the car.

BASIC RULES OF THE ROAD
- Driving is on the left.
- At roundabouts (traffic cirlces), unless otherwise indicated, traffic coming from the right has right of way.
- Overtaking is on the right.

SPEED LIMITS
- All distances and speed limits are measured in kilometres.
- Urban areas, towns and cities: 60kph (35mph).
- Secondary (rural) roads: 100kph (60mph).
- National highways and urban freeways: 120kph (75mph).

OVERTAKING
- Look out for 'No Overtaking' signs and adhere to them.
- On minor roads, South African drivers will often veer into the hard shoulder to let others overtake, particularly on blind corners. This is not advised.
- If you allow someone to overtake, they may flash their hazard lights as a means of thanking you.
- Rural roads are often straight and flat, but watch for hidden dips, which are particularly well camouflaged in hot conditions.

FOUR-WAY STOPS
South African roads have four-way stops, a crossroad or intersection where each approach road has a stop sign.
- Always come to a complete stop when approaching a four-way stop.
- If you are the only vehicle at the intersection, stop, look left and right and then proceed if the road is clear.
- If another vehicle has already stopped at one of the other stop signs, it has the right of way, so stop and give way.

ROAD DISTANCES										
	Bloemfontein	Cape Town	Durban	East London	Grahamstown	Johannesburg	Kimberley	Port Elizabeth	Pretoria/Tshwane	Welkom
Beaufort West	544	460	1178	605	492	942	504	501	1000	697
Bloemfontein		1004	634	584	601	398	177	677	456	153
Britstown	398	710	1032	609	496	725	253	572	783	551
Cape Town	1004		1753	1099	899	1402	962	769	1460	1156
Colesberg	226	778	860	488	375	624	292	451	682	379
De Aar	346	762	980	557	444	744	305	520	802	499
Durban	634	1753		674	854	588	811	984	646	564
East London	584	1079	674		180	982	780	310	1040	737
George	773	438	1319	645	465	1171	762	335	1229	926
Graaff-Reinet	424	787	942	395	282	822	490	291	880	577
Grahamstown	601	899	854	180		999	667	130	1057	754
Harrismith	328	1331	306	822	929	282	505	1068	332	258
Johannesburg	398	1402	588	982	999		472	1075	58	258
Kimberley	177	962	811	780	667	472		743	530	294
Klerksdorp	288	1271	645	872	889	164	308	1009	222	145
Kroonstad	211	1214	537	795	812	187	339	888	245	71
Ladysmith	410	1413	236	752	932	364	587	1062	422	340
Mafikeng/Mmabatho	464	1343	821	1048	1065	287	380	1141	294	321
Musina/Messina	928	1932	1118	1512	1529	530	1071	1605	472	788
Nelspruit	757	1762	707	1226	1358	355	827	1434	322	639
Oudtshoorn	743	506	1294	704	532	1141	703	394	1199	896
Pietermaritzburg	555	1674	79	595	775	509	732	905	567	485
Polokwane/Pietersburg	717	1721	907	1301	1318	319	791	1394	261	577
Port Elizabeth	677	769	984	310	130	1075	743		1133	830
Pretoria/Tshwane	456	1460	646	1040	1057	58	530	1133		316
Queenstown	377	1069	676	207	269	775	554	399	833	525
Umtata	570	1314	439	235	415	869	747	545	928	718
Upington	588	894	1222	982	851	796	411	945	854	669
Welkom	153	1156	564	737	754	258	294	830	316	

- If you stop at the intersection at the same time as another vehicle, it is a matter of common courtesy and either vehicle may proceed.

DRIVING IN RURAL AREAS

- Watch for stray animals. Some rural areas have no fences, so cows and goats often wander into the road. This is a particular problem in the Eastern Cape.
- While the rural roads in areas popular with visitors, such as the Western Cape, are well maintained, farther afield you may find poorly surfaced and potholed roads. Drive slowly and keep a lookout for hazards.
- More remote areas like the Northern Cape or the Great Karoo have long, deserted stretches of road between towns or villages, so always make sure you have plenty of fuel and a good map, and carry 2 litres (4pt) of water per passenger (this is particularly important in the scorching summer months).
- There is a small risk of hijacking in South Africa, and visitors can be vulnerable on quiet rural roads. Various scams have been used in the past to

One of the more unusual road signs that you're likely to see

lure cars to stop, such as staging accidents and waving at passing drivers for help.
- Never pull over for anyone other than the police (cars are well marked), and never pick up hitchhikers.

ROAD SIGNS AND TERMS

- Traffic lights are called 'robots' in South Africa.
- Street names are often in English and Afrikaans. Those in Afrikaans are usually recognizable, and don't vary significantly from the English.

AFRIKAANS ROAD SIGNS	
doeane	customs
dorp	village
geen ingang	no entry
gevaar!	danger!
grens	border
inligting	information
links	left
lughawe	airport
ompad	detour
pad	road
padwerke voor	road works ahead
poskantoor	post office
regs	right
sentrum	centre
stadig	slow
stad	town/city
stad sentrum	city centre
strand	beach
verbode	forbidden
verkeer	traffic

- Road signs are generally bilingual, but are sometimes in Afrikaans only, particularly in rural Afrikaner areas such as the Winelands. See the box above for some common Afrikaans signs.

PARKING

- Designated parking areas are indicated with a large white 'P' on a blue background, found in central parts of all cities and towns.
- Payment is usually a system of pay-and-display tickets or parking meters; these are often serviced by (uniformed) parking attendants whom you pay on arrival. Expect to pay around R5 per hour.
- Be sure to note the time limit on parking—it is often a maximum of two hours.
- Away from central areas parking is usually free, but unofficial parking attendants will often watch your car for a small fee (R3–R5), which you pay on your return. Expect to find these unofficial attendants also in (free) parking areas belonging to shopping malls, restaurants and visitor sights.

A main road in rural Venda

Some are employed by local businesses but many are casual opportunists. As they make their living from watching cars, they can usually be trusted to keep an eye on your vehicle.

● Watch for parking restriction signs. Traffic wardens will fine you if you fall foul of restrictions.
● It is illegal to park facing oncoming traffic, that is on the right-hand side of the road.

FUEL

● Petrol (gas) stations are not self-service. You will be assisted by an attendant. Make sure you stipulate what fuel your car takes (unleaded, super, diesel, etc).
● Attendants will expect a small tip (around R3–R5). They may also wash your windscreens and check oil and water (a good idea if you've been driving for a long stretch).
● Many petrol stations accept only cash, so always carry enough with you. Do not rely on credit cards.
● Large petrol stations are modern and usually have small shops selling magazines, snacks and drinks. Most have toilets, and some have ATMs.

SAFETY

● Lock all your doors while you're driving in built-up areas.
● Keep windows rolled up enough to prevent people from reaching into your car.
● Keep valuables out of sight while driving in built-up areas.
● Never leave anything valuable in your car when leaving it unattended. If you must, store items out of sight.
● Avoid driving at night, particularly along the beachfront area of Durban and in downtown Johannesburg.
● Townships are best avoided if you are driving without a guide, as it is easy to get lost and to become vulnerable.
● Don't stop at remote, isolated picnic spots.
● Don't pick up hitchhikers and be very wary of people flagging you down on the road. Stop

only for the police (cars are easily identified).
● Hijacking hotspots include northern KwaZulu-Natal and approach roads to Kruger National Park.
● Some urban areas, mostly in Johannesburg, have 'Hijacking Hotspot' signs. These mean that you can drive over a red traffic light (checking both ways before you do so) if you feel at risk.
● Carry a mobile phone (cell phone) with you at all times in case of emergency (but note that it is illegal to use a hand-held phone while driving).
● If you break down or are involved in an accident, call the appropriate emergency services as soon as possible (Police: 10111; Ambulance: 10177).
● Major routes have yellow SOS phones set at 2km (1.2 miles) intervals along the road, or call the South African AA emergency rescue number (freephone 0800 010101).
● Check with your car rental company before you set off, as some provide their own SOS emergency telephone numbers.
● South African drivers often drive fast. Do not feel pressured into joining them, but be aware of what the traffic around you is doing at all times.
● As in many other western countries, drinking and driving is

Friendly roadside services

a problem. The maximum allowable alcohol blood content is 0.05 per cent, but you should never drive under the influence of alcohol. Drivers face penalties and may lose their licence if they fail a breath test.
● Be especially wary on the roads over Christmas when the number of road deaths soars dramatically.

TAXIS

● In the major cities, metered taxis are run by the municipality.
● They are found at taxi stands, usually outside airports and train stations and at key visitor sights in central city areas.
● Always check to see that the meter is working and is set to the minimum fare when you set off.
● If there is no meter, or it is not working, agree a fare before setting off.
● You can't usually hail a taxi in the street, although in some towns taxis may stop for you.
● Taxi drivers are usually tipped up to 10 per cent of the fare.
● You can phone for a metered taxi. Ask your hotel or restaurant to call one for you, or ask at the local tourist office for reputable companies. You should check fares before departing.

VISITORS WITH A DISABILITY

Although the idea of easy access to museums, hotels and restaurants for visitors with a disability only recently began to take hold in South Africa, things are developing quickly, and a number of places to stay advertise facilities with wheelchair access. Some attractions now have amenities specifically for visitors with a disability.

The fact that South Africa is a very car-friendly country should make getting to the major sites relatively easy, and most places have disabled parking near the entrances. Getting around game parks should not prove too difficult, although park accommodation and washing facilities are rarely wheelchair friendly. However, the situation is gradually improving within the parks.

AIR TRAVEL

The international airports are all well equipped for passengers with a disability, having elevators to all floors and wheelchair access to most toilets. The airport in Johannesburg is particularly disability friendly, with wheelchair access to all toilets and a large number of elevators, some equipped with Braille.

Domestic airlines provide assistance and seating for all wheelchair users, but you should notify your carrier before you travel. No-frills carriers have limited space for wheelchair users, so it is essential to telephone ahead.

If you have a visual or hearing impairment and have a guide dog, you are permitted to bring the dog into the cabin with you on SAA flights, provided the airline is given notice in advance. Guide dogs travel free of charge.

TRAINS

Shosholoza Meyl trains are wheelchair accessible, but you must phone ahead to request a ramp to board the trains. Doorways to individual compartments and communal washing facilities are wide enough for wheelchairs, although conditions are cramped and you may find that turning is a problem.

BUSES

Mainline buses are not easily accessible by wheelchair. The main companies offer assistance from the driver or hostess, which in effect means that passengers with limited mobility will be assisted onto the buses and to their seats.

AROUND TOWN

The wide pavements (sidewalks) and colonial layout of many towns make moving around in a wheelchair fairly easy, although many pavements are still not ramped. Some older quarters, such as Bo-Kaap in Cape Town

City Bowl, are cobbled and hilly, making access difficult. The government has introduced legislation concerning access for people with disabilities, with the result that many museums and other visitor sights are now wheelchair friendly. You can expect ramps, elevators and equipped toilets in the main cities, but there are often no facilities whatsoever in more rural areas or in the older museums.

HOTELS AND GAME PARKS

Large hotels will have some rooms suitable for guests with disabilities, and some guesthouses may have wheelchair access (usually advertised on their websites).

Game parks are adding to their facilities to make their various types of accommodation more accessible. Many sites have introduced short Braille Trails for visitors with a visual impairment, such as the Kirstenbosch Botanical Gardens in Cape Town.

SOURCES OF TRAVEL INFORMATION

Disabled People South Africa
tel 021-4220357; www.dpsa.org.za
A national body representing people with disabilities; they have contact details about transport and accessibility.

Epic Enabled
tel 021-7829575;
www.epic-enabled.com
Their excellent range of tours for people with disabilities uses fully modified overland trucks, camp assistants and wheelchair friendly accommodation.

Flamingo Tours
tel 021-5574496;
www.flamingotours.co.za
Arranges tailor-made tours and fly-drive holidays for visitors with disabilities.

National Council for Persons with Physical Disabilities in South Africa
tel 011-7268040; www.ncppdsa.co.za
Provides advice about renting wheelchairs and other services for people with disabilities.

Rolling SA
tel 033-3304214; www.rollingsa.co.za
Organizes South African holidays for wheelchair users.

South African National Parks
tel 012-3431991; www.sanparks.org
Up-to-date information about access to South Africa's national parks for people with disabilities.

This chapter is divided into eight regions (see pages 6–7) and includes a section on Lesotho and Swaziland. Places of interest are listed alphabetically in each region. Major sights are listed at the front of each section.

The Sights

CAPE PENINSULA

The Cape Peninsula has such a mixture of environments and communities that it is an instantly likeable and captivating place. It is also home to Cape Town, South Africa's 'Mother City', which is dominated by the iconic Table Mountain. Few places in the world can offer wide open spaces, mountain hiking, lazing on a beach and tasting world-class wines all in one day.

MAJOR SIGHTS

Camps Bay, backed by the Twelve Apostles (above); keeping out of the hot sun at Clifton Beach (inset)

CAMPS BAY AND THE ATLANTIC SEABOARD

The Cape's most exclusive beaches are found along the Atlantic seaboard: Perfect arches of powder-white sand slope into the chilly turquoise waters.

Just along the coast from Cape Town are the famous beaches of Clifton and Camps Bay. The closest seaside residential areas to Cape Town City Bowl are Green Point and Sea Point, but these lack the beaches—as well as the charm and character—of other Atlantic seaboard areas. Both are a mixture of high-rise apartment blocks lining the rocky waterfront and more attractive bungalows creeping up the mountain. Green Point and the brightly painted Victorian bungalows known as De Waterkant Village are the focus of Cape Town's gay scene, with a correspondingly lively nightlife. To explore the Atlantic seaboard, your best means of transport is a rental car or taxi.

CLIFTON

The Cape's best-known beaches stretch along Clifton, and are renowned as the playground of the young and wealthy: This is the place to see and be seen. Clifton's four sheltered beaches are stunning, but the water is very cold—usually around 12°C (54°F). The beaches, reached by a series of winding footpaths, are divided by rocky outcrops and are named First, Second, Third and Fourth. Each has a distinct character. If you're bronzed and beautiful, head for First Beach. More demure visitors may prefer Fourth, which is popular with families. Most of the relatively small-scale development has been behind the beaches, against the cliff face (some grand houses can be glimpsed from the winding steps leading down).

CAMPS BAY

Following the coast south, you soon skirt around a hill and come out above Camps Bay, a long arc of sand backed by the series of hills known as the Twelve Apostles. This has to be one of the most beautiful beaches in the world, but the calm cobalt water belies its chilliness. The sand is also less sheltered than at Clifton, and sunbathing here on a windy day can be quite painful. But there are other distractions as the beachfront is lined with a number of excellent seafood restaurants.

RATINGS					
Good for food	●	●	●	●	●
Good for kids	●	●	●		
Photo stops	●	●	●	●	●

BASICS

✚ 326 B11

🛈 The Pinnacle, corner of Burg and Castle streets, tel 021-4264260; Mon–Fri 8–6, Sat 8.30–2, Sun 9–1

🍽 Selection of restaurants, bars and cafés in Camps Bay, Sea Point and Green Point

🛍 Camps Bay and Sea Point have seaside shops selling towels, swimsuits and sunscreen

🚻 On Fourth Beach at Clifton

🅿 For beaches, parking along the main road, Victoria Road, is free. Also one or two small parking areas off this road (small fee for attendant)

www.cape-town.org

TIPS

● If you have the time, carry on past Camps Bay towards Hout Bay. The road is spectacular, clinging between the slopes of the Twelve Apostles and the crashing ocean.
● There is limited parking along the seaboard in high season, but you'll usually find a space before 11am.
● Although there are no snack bars on the beaches, vendors march up and down selling cold drinks and ice creams.

Overlooking the coast at the Cape's Diaz Beach (above); you'll find baboons around the nature reserve (inset)

RATINGS

Good for kids	● ● ●
Outdoor pursuits	● ● ● ●
Photo stops	● ● ● ● ●
Walkability	● ● ● ● ●

BASICS

➕ 326 C11
☎ 021-7018692
🕐 Apr–end Sep daily 7–5; Oct–end Mar daily 6–6
💶 Reserve: adult R35, child (under 12) R10. Funicular (runs 8–5): adult round-trip ticket R31, one-way R20
🍴 Two Oceans Restaurant and kiosk
❓ Information office has hiking maps of the area
🎁 Curio shop
🚻 At bottom of funicular
🅿 Main parking at bottom of funicular
www.tmnp.co.za

TIPS

● Take a hat and plenty of sunscreen, as the Point is fully exposed to the sun.
● If you have brought a picnic, make sure it is out of sight of the baboons that stalk around the parking area.
● When driving along the approach road to the main parking area near the funicular, stop at the point where the road first joins the coast. A five-minute walk across some smooth rocks brings you to Platboom Bay, one of the least visited and most beautiful beaches in the reserve.

CAPE OF GOOD HOPE NATURE RESERVE

Cape Point's towering cliffs straddle the ground between the Atlantic seaboard and False Bay, giving astonishing ocean views. Beyond the tip are plains and deserted beaches with excellent hiking trails.

The Cape of Good Hope Nature Reserve, part of the Table Mountain National Park, is one of the area's highlights, and sits astride the tip of the peninsula south of Cape Town. The reserve was established in 1939 to protect the unique flora and fauna of this stretch of coast. It is an integral part of the Cape Floristic Kingdom, the smallest but richest of the world's six floral kingdoms, with as many different plant species within its boundaries as there are in the whole of the British Isles. You may also spot several species of antelope: eland, bontebok, springbok, Cape grysbok, red hartebeest and grey rhebok, as well as the elusive Cape mountain zebra.

CAPE POINT

Cape Point Lighthouse is nothing special in itself, but the climb up from the parking area is worth the effort for the spectacular views of the peninsula: On a clear day, the ocean views stretching as far as the eye can see are incredible—as are the winds, so be sure to hold on to hats and sunglasses. You can take the funicular to the top, but the 20-minute walk gives you better views of the coast. There are a number of viewpoints, linked by a jumble of footpaths. If you have a good head for heights, there is a dramatic walk along the left side of the cliff to the modern lighthouse at Diaz Point. The round trip takes about 30 minutes, but do not attempt it if it is windy.

AROUND THE RESERVE

The treacherous waters around Cape Point have taken their fair share of ships; five wrecks can be seen offshore when walking in the reserve. There are several marked hiking paths, including the spectacular route along the coast from Rooikrans towards Buffels Bay. The most popular walk is from the main parking area, down a steep set of steps to Diaz Beach. See pages 226–227 for details of a walk around the Silvermine Nature Reserve, one of the key places in the Cape Floristic Kingdom.

The pleasant surroundings of Groot Constantia, one of the oldest wine estates in Constantia

Rock formations looking out over Hout Bay

CAPE FLATS

⊞ Off 326 C11 🔸 The Pinnacle, corner of Burg and Castle streets, tel 021-4264260; Mon–Fri 8–6, Sat 8.30–1, Sun 9–1

Cape Flats, an area inland from Table Mountain and close to the airport, is home to Cape Town's main exposed high-density townships. The first township in the country was built just outside Cape Town in 1901, but was thought to be too close to the heart of the city (▷ 69). It, and its people, were moved to Langa, which is still there today. Other areas include Crossroads, which had very poor living conditions for many years, Guguletu, Mitchells Plain and Khayelitsha, which at one point had more than one million residents. An organized tour is the recommended way to visit the townships of Cape Flats. Contact the tourist office in the City Bowl for more information.

CAPE TOWN CITY BOWL

See pages 64–69.

CONSTANTIA

⊞ 326 C11

To the south of Table Mountain is Cape Town's most elegant suburb, the verdant area of Constantia with its wine estates. This district was South Africa's first wine-making site, and it provides an attractive introduction both to Cape Dutch architecture and to the country's wines.

There are five estates here, including Groot Constantia (tel 021-7945128; www.groot constantia.co.za) with its own fine Cape Dutch architecture, rolling vineyards and wine tastings. This is a delightful place to spend a few hours, although it does get swamped with tour buses in high season. The main house was originally home to Cape Governor Simon van der

Stel between 1699 and 1712. By the time of his death, he had planted most of the vines, but it was not until 1778 that the estate became famous for its wines. The main house is now a museum full of period furniture. Wine tasting takes place in the sales area near the main entrance (R20 for five wines).

Another estate worth visiting is Klein Constantia (tel 021-7945188; www.kleinconstantia. com), a hilly estate that is known for its dessert wine Vin de Constance, allegedly Napoleon's wine of choice.

FALSE BAY

See pages 70–71.

HOUT BAY

⊞ 326 B11

The view of this deep bay is frequently photographed from Chapman's Peak Drive (▷ 223), and deservedly so: Hout Bay, a half-hour drive from the City Bowl, is a perfect cove with a white sandy beach, clear blue waters and a busy fishing port. Activity is focused around the port, at the western end of the bay, and the collection of shops and restaurants at the other end. Next to the port is a commercial complex known as Mariners Wharf, the first of its kind in South Africa and popular with domestic visitors. It is based on Fisherman's Wharf in San Francisco, with a string of fish 'n' chip kiosks, gift shops, boats for rent and a fish market. Several boat charter companies organize trips from here to nearby Duiker Island. Another reason for coming here is the World of Birds on Valley Road, which has more than 400 bird species in a series of walk-through aviaries (tel 021-7902730; daily 9–5).

IRMA STERN MUSEUM

⊞ 326 C11 • Cecil Road, Rosebank, 7700 ☎ 021-6855686 🕙 Tue–Sat 10–5 💷 Adult R10, child (2–12) R1.50 🖼
www.irmastern.co.za

Irma Stern (1894–1966) was one of South Africa's pioneering artists in the mid-20th century. Her handsome house displays a mixture of her own works, a collection of objects from across Africa, and some fine pieces of antique furniture from overseas—17th-century Spanish chairs, 19th-century German oak furniture—and Swiss Mardi Gras masks. Stern's portraits are particularly poignant and those of her close friends are superb; her religious art is rather more disturbing. The studio, complete with paintbrushes and palettes, has been left as it was when she died. The kitchen houses a collection of Chinese ceramics including two fine Ming celadon dishes, with a characteristic greenish glaze.

KIRSTENBOSCH BOTANICAL GARDENS

See page 72.

Roza Van Gelderen *was painted in 1929 by Stern and is now on display at the Stern Museum*

Cape Town City Bowl

Cradled by the Cape Peninsula and bounded by the Atlantic Ocean, the 'Mother City' has a stunning setting. It's a diverse city, where grand colonial buildings stand side by side with architectural designs from the 1960s.

Brightly painted houses in the Islamic quarter of Bo-Kaap

A man dressed up for a day at Greenmarket Square

City Hall, where Mandela made his first speech as a free man in 1994

RATINGS

Good for kids	● ● ●
Historic interest	● ● ● ●
Photo stops	● ● ●
Walkability	● ● ● ● ●

BASICS

✚ 326 C11

ℹ The Pinnacle, corner of Burg and Castle streets, tel 021-4264260; Mon–Fri 8–6, Sat 8.30–1, Sun 9–1 www.cape-town.org

TIP

● If you want to shop for antiques, walk past the Methodist church on Greenmarket Square onto Church Street. A daily antiques market is held in the area between Burg and Long streets.

Market stands laid out in front of City Hall (opposite)

SEEING CAPE TOWN CITY BOWL

The area between the sea and the mountainous horseshoe formed by Signal Hill, Table Mountain and Devil's Peak is known as Cape Town City Bowl. Closest to Table Mountain are the residential suburbs of Tamboerskloof, Gardens, Oranjezicht and Vredehoek, attractive and wealthy Victorian suburbs with a good selection of hotels and restaurants. At the heart of the area are the high-rise blocks of the Central Business District (CBD), with Bo-Kaap rolling up the eastern slopes of Signal Hill and Company's Garden cutting a small green swathe in the middle.

It is easy to get around on foot as most of the major sights and historic buildings are concentrated within this compact area. The main rail station and long-distance bus station are both on Adderley Street, one of the city's main arteries and home to many examples of the elegant colonial buildings that character- ize the city's past. To explore more of the city and to visit Table Mountain, the suburbs or the beaches, it's a good idea to rent a car; otherwise taxis are quite affordable.

HIGHLIGHTS

BO-KAAP

✚ 66 A2

Bo-Kaap, to the west of the City Bowl, is Cape Town's old Islamic quarter and one of the city's most individual residential areas. It was developed in the 1760s and today feels a world away from the nearby CBD. Here the cobbled streets form a tight web across the slopes of Signal Hill, the closely packed houses painted in bright greens, pinks and blues. Most visitors come for the Bo-Kaap Museum (tel 021-4813939; Mon–Sat 9–4), in an 18th-century house on Wale Street and dedicated to the Cape's Muslim community. The house itself is one of the oldest in Cape Town to survive in its original form. It was built for artisans in 1763 and it was here that the Turkish scholar Abu Bakr Effendi started the first Arabic school. Effendi origi- nally came to Cape Town as a guest of the British government to try to settle religious differences among the Cape Muslims. Inside the house are furnishings from a wealthy 19th-century Muslim family,

MORE TO SEE

GOLD OF AFRICA MUSEUM

⊞ 66 A1 • 96 Strand Street, 8001
☎ 021-4051540 ⏰ Mon–Sat 9.30–5
🎧 Adult R20, child (under 16) R10
🍴 ♿

www.goldofafrica.com

The museum presents the history of gold mining, outlining the first mining by Egyptians in 2400BC and the subsequent development of trade networks across Africa. There are comprehensive displays of 19th- and 20th-century gold artworks from Mali, Ghana and Senegal. Downstairs you can watch goldsmiths at work.

and the back room has displays dedicated to the contribution made by slaves to the economy and development of Cape Town. The photographs are the best exhibits, giving a fascinating glimpse of life in Bo-Kaap in the early 20th century.

ADDERLEY STREET

⊞ 66 B1–B2

Adderley Street is one of the city's busiest shopping areas, running through the heart of town between Government Avenue and the foreshore. It's an odd mixture of impressive 19th-century bank buildings and more modern but less attractive buildings. Look out for the Standard Bank Building on the corner of Darling Street, a grand structure built in 1880, shortly after the diamond wealth from Kimberley reached Cape Town. Diagonally across from it is the equally impressive Barclays Building (1933), made of sandstone from Ceres to the northwest of Cape Town. At the northern end of Adderley Street is a large roundabout (traffic circle) with a bronze statue of Jan van Riebeeck, the first commander of the Cape settlement, which was given to the city by Cecil Rhodes in 1899.

CITY HALL AND GRAND PARADE

⊞ 66 B2 and 66 B1

From Adderley Street, a short walk down Darling Street will take you to the City Hall and the Grand Parade. The latter is the largest open space in Cape Town and was used for garrison parades before the Castle (▷ 68) was completed. Twice a week the oak-lined parade is

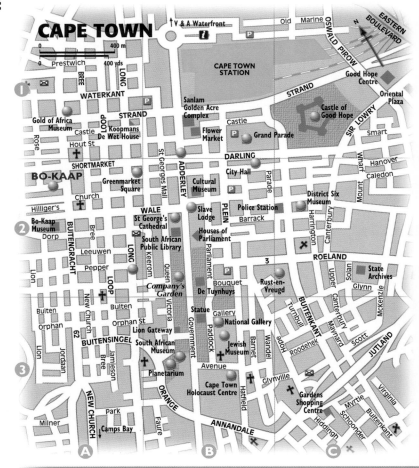

taken over by a lively market; otherwise it is used for car parking. The neoclassical City Hall, built in 1905, overlooks the parade. Nelson Mandela made his first speech here after his release from prison in 1994 to more than 100,000 people. City Hall's clock tower is a half-size replica of Big Ben in London. In 1979, the municipal government moved to a new Civic Centre on the Foreshore and the hall is now headquarters of the Cape Town Symphony Orchestra and houses the City Library.

COMPANY'S GARDEN

⊞ 66 B2 • Government Avenue, 8001 ☉ Dawn–dusk 🎫 Free 🍴

Running alongside Government Avenue is the peaceful Company's Garden, on the site of the original vegetable garden created by Jan van Riebeeck (▷ 69) in 1652 to grow produce for settlers and ships

JEWISH MUSEUM AND HOLOCAUST CENTRE

⊞ 66 B3 • 88 Hatfield Street, 8001 ☎ 021-4651546 ☉ Jewish Museum: Sun–Thu 10–5, Fri 10–2; Holocaust Centre: Sun–Thu 10–5, Fri 10–1 🎫 Adult R50, child (4–18) R15 🍴 ♿ www.sajewishmuseum.co.za

The Jewish Museum has a rich and rare collection of items depicting the history of the Cape Town Hebrew Congregation. There are displays of bronze Sabbath oil lamps, Chanukkah

The horrors of apartheid are displayed at District Six Museum

A statue at the Gold of Africa Museum

Company's Garden—a green space at the heart of the city

bound for the east. It is now a small botanical garden, with lawns, a variety of trees and ponds filled with Japanese koi. The grey squirrels living among the oak trees were introduced by Cecil Rhodes (Cape Prime Minister from 1890 to 1896) from America. There is a statue of him in the gardens, close to the oldest statue in Cape Town, that of Sir George Grey, Governor of the Cape from 1854 to 1862. At the northern end of the gardens are the gleaming white, colonnaded Houses of Parliament (for tours tel 021-4032537).

DISTRICT SIX MUSEUM

⊞ 66 C2 • 25A Buitenkant Street, 8001 ☎ 021-4618745 ☉ Tue–Sat 9–4, Mon 9–3 🎫 Adult R10, child (under 12) R5 🍴 ♿ www.districtsix.co.za

Housed in an old Methodist church, this is one of Cape Town's most powerful museums, providing a fascinating glimpse of the stupidity and horror of apartheid. District Six was once the vibrant, cosmopolitan heart of Cape Town, an inner city suburb with a population of many races and renowned for its jazz scene. In 1966, P. W. Botha, then Minister of Community Development, proclaimed District Six a white group area. Over the next 15 years, an estimated 60,000 people were given notice to give up their homes and move to the new townships on the Cape Flats (▷ 63). The area was razed, and to this day remains largely undeveloped, although the government has handed over the first pocket of redeveloped land to a small group of ex-residents. The museum contains a collection of photographs, articles and personal accounts depicting life before and after the removals. Often there are musicians at the back, playing guitars and tin pipes and adding immeasurably to the atmosphere of the place.

GREENMARKET SQUARE

⊞ 66 A2

In the middle of the CBD is Greenmarket Square, the old heart of Cape Town and the second oldest square in the city. For long a meeting place, it became a vegetable market during the 19th century, taking on a more significant role in 1834 as the site where the freeing of all slaves was declared. It is still a popular meeting place today, lined with outdoor cafés and restaurants. A busy daily market sprawls

lamps, Bessamin spice containers, Torah scrolls, Kiddush cups and candlesticks. Another section of the museum is devoted to the history of Jewish immigration to the Cape, mainly from Lithuania. Displays include photographs, immigration certificates, videos and a full reconstruction of a Lithuanian *shtetl* (village). On the opposite side of the courtyard is the Holocaust Centre (tel 021-4625553), Cape Town's newest museum, comprising an intelligent and shocking examination of the Holocaust.

LONG STREET

⊞ 66 A2

Slicing through the middle of town, Long Street is lined with street cafés, fashionable shops, bars, clubs and backpacker lodges. It has a distinctly youthful feel about it, but it also contains some fine old city buildings. Among its more interesting ones is the Slave Church Museum at No. 40 (tel 021-4236755; Mon–Fri 9–4). The oldest mission church in South Africa, built between 1802 and 1804 as the mother church for missionary work carried out in rural areas, it was used for religious and literacy instruction of slaves in Cape Town.

NATIONAL GALLERY

✚ 66 B3 • Government Avenue, 8001
☎ 021-4674660 🕐 Tue–Sun 10–5
👤 Adult R10, child (under 18) R5,
Sat free to all 🍴 🏛

The National Gallery houses a
mixture of local and international
art. There's a collection of
18th- and 19th-century British
sporting paintings donated by
Sir Abe Bailey, and changing
exhibitions of contemporary
South African art.

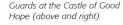

*Guards at the Castle of Good
Hope (above and right)*

RUST EN VREUGD

✚ 66 C2 • 78 Buitenkant Street,
8001 ☎ 021-4643280 🕐 Tue–Thu
8.30–4.30 👤 Adult R5, child (under
12) R2

This 18th-century building, just
off Government Avenue and
hidden behind a high whitewashed wall, was declared a
national monument in 1940
and subsequently restored.
Today it houses six galleries,
which display a unique collection
of watercolours, engravings and
lithographs depicting the history
of the Cape. Of particular note
are watercolours of ascents of
Table Mountain by Thomas
Baines (a British artist who
made journeys throughout
South Africa), lithographs showing Khoi and Zulu people, and a
collection of cartoons by leading
18th-century British cartoonist
George Cruikshank, depicting the
first British settlers arriving in the
Cape. Commercial exhibitions
are held in the galleries upstairs.

across the cobbles, with stands selling African crafts, accessories
and clothes. On one side is the Old Town House, built in 1751 to
house the town guard. It was made the first town hall in 1840 when
Cape Town became a municipality. Much of the exterior remains
unchanged, and with its decorative plaster mouldings and fine curved
fanlights it is one of the best preserved Cape baroque exteriors in the
city. Inside is the Michaelis Collection of Flemish and Dutch paintings
(tel 021-4813933; Mon–Fri 10–5, Sat 10–4; entry by donation).

CASTLE OF GOOD HOPE

✚ 66 C1 • Grand Parade, Darling Street, 8001 ☎ 021-7871082 🕐 Daily 9–4
👤 Adult R18, child (2–16) R8 🍴 Free guided tours at 11, 12 and 2 🍴
www.castleofgoodhope.co.za

This is South Africa's oldest colonial building, finished in 1679. Its original purpose was to defend the Dutch East India Company from rival
European powers. Under the British the Castle served as government
headquarters, and since 1917 it has been the headquarters of the
regional South African Defence Force. The castle is home to three
museums. The William Fehr Collection is one of South Africa's finest
displays of furnishings reflecting the social and political history of the
Cape. There are landscapes by Thomas Baines, an English painter
who lived in Cape Town in the mid-19th century, as well as 17th-
century Japanese porcelain and 18th-century Indonesian furniture.
The Secunde's House re-creates the conditions under which an

THE SIGHTS

official for the Dutch East India Company would have lived in the 17th, 18th and early 19th centuries. The third museum is the Military Museum, with absorbing displays of regimental uniforms and medals and a collection illustrating the conflicts of early settlers. The informative free tours take in the torture chambers, cells and the battlements.

SOUTH AFRICAN MUSEUM AND PLANETARIUM
✚ 66 B3 • 25 Queen Victoria Street, 8001 ☎ Museum: 021-4813800; Planetarium: 021-4813900 ⏰ Museum: daily 10–5; planetarium show times: Mon–Fri 2 (also Tue at 8), Sat–Sun 1 💰 Adult R20, child (under 18) R5, Sun free to all; planetarium shows: adult R20, child R6 ▣ ♿
This is the city's most established museum, covering natural history, ethnography and archaeology. There are extensive displays of the flora and fauna of southern Africa, including the 'Whale Well', where

ST. GEORGE'S CATHEDRAL
✚ 66 B2 • Wale Street, 8001 ♿
The cathedral is best known as the seat of Archbishop Desmond Tutu's diocese from 1986 until 1996. It is from here that he led more than 30,000 people to City Hall to mark the end of apartheid, and where he first gave voice to the notion of the 'rainbow nation'. Inside, the Great North window is a fine piece of stained glass dedicated to the pioneers of the Anglican Church.

You'll find dinosaurs (left) and the Linton panel (right) at the South African Museum

The exterior of the city's Slave Lodge

you can listen to the sound of whale song, but the highlight is the 'IQe—the Power of Rock Art' exhibition. The exhibits focus on the significance and symbolism of San rock art, with some fascinating examples including the beautifully preserved Linton panel, which depicts the trance experiences of shamans. The exhibition is beautifully arranged and is accompanied by the haunting sound of San singing. Nearby are the ethnographic galleries, with displays about the San, Khoi and Xhosa, among others, as well as the original sixth-century clay Lydenburg Heads.

Shark World, in the natural history section, is an interactive multi-media area exploring sharks and their environment. At the Planetarium next door, presentations change every few months, but a view of the current night sky is shown on the first weekend of each month. Shows last an hour.

BACKGROUND

Rock art by the San people is evidence that human life in the Cape dates back some 30,000 years. The first move to settle the Cape by Europeans wasn't until 1652. The Dutchman Jan van Riebeeck arrived on 6 April at Table Bay and erected a small fort—the site of which is where Grand Parade now stands. The settlement grew and towards the end on the 17th century the area was developing as an agricultural region. It was around this time that the first vines were planted that would produce Cape Town's famous wines.

Ownership passed from Dutch to British hands at the beginning of the 19th century and the city's growth followed that of the industrializing European cities, changing the face of Cape Town beyond recognition. The city's docks were very busy once gold and diamonds had been discovered in South Africa.

Apartheid urban planning forced many of the descendants of the slave population out from the heart of the city and the poorer African population were only allowed to settle on the outskirts and in surrounding townships, many of which still exist (▷ 63). Today, Cape Town has regained its racial mix and is the most cosmopolitan city in the country.

SLAVE LODGE
✚ 66 B2 • Corner of Adderley and Wale streets, 8001 ☎ 021-4608242 ⏰ Mon–Fri 10–4.30, Sat 9–1 💰 Adult R10, child (under 18) R5; Sat free to all
Slave Lodge is the second oldest building in Cape Town. It has had a varied history, but its most significant role was as a slave lodge for the Dutch East India Company (VOC). Between 1679 and 1811, the building housed up to 1,000 slaves at a time; conditions at the lodge were terrible and up to 20 per cent of the slaves died every year. At present, only a glimpse of this history is displayed by the museum. Instead, there are changing temporary exhibitions on the ground floor, focusing on the culture and history of the VOC. There are plans to restructure the museum to better reflect its history.

False Bay

False Bay is a popular stretch of coast with beautiful sandy beaches, family-friendly resorts and quirky fishing villages, with chances of whale watching in spring.

The busy little harbour at Kalk Bay

SEEING FALSE BAY

False Bay is on the other side of the peninsula from Cape Town, where its warmer waters can be as much as 8°C (14°F) higher than elsewhere on the Atlantic seaboard. The area is sheltered and well developed for visitors with a string of seaside resorts and villages, and some excellent beaches that get busy with domestic visitors in summer. In spring, False Bay is the haunt of calving whales, and there are excellent opportunities for seeing southern right, humpback and Bryde's whales. The bay is easily reached from central Cape Town by the M3, which runs around the mountain and along the coast.

Brightly painted beach huts at Muizenberg

RATINGS	
Good for kids	●●●●●
Historic interest	●●●
Outdoor pursuits	●●●●●

BASICS

➕ 326 C11 🛈 Publicity Association, 111 St. George's Street, Simon's Town 7995, tel 021-7865798; Nov–end Mar Mon–Fri 9–5.30, Sat 9.30–1, Sun 10–1; Apr–end Oct Mon–Fr 9–5, Sat 9.30–1 **www.**simonstown.com

At play along Muizenberg's lovely beach

HIGHLIGHTS

MUIZENBERG

Muizenberg has long been a popular local swimming spot. Today the town and its waterfront are rather run down, but the beach itself is still excellent: a vast stretch of powdery white sand sloping gently to the water. The town has a handful of historic buildings, including Het Post Huijs on the main road, thought to be the oldest building in False Bay, dating back to 1673. Farther along is Rhodes Cottage, the summer retreat of Cecil Rhodes and where he died in 1902.

KALK BAY

Kalk Bay is one of the most attractive settlements in False Bay, with a bustling fishing harbour, a number of antiques shops and an appealing bohemian character. Watch for the returning fishing boats at the harbour around noon. Their arrival is followed by a daily impromptu quayside auction, where you can buy a variety of fresh fish at the counters. Main Road is an attractive spot for a stroll, lined with antiques and bric-a-brac shops and a handful of arty cafés. Behind Kalk Bay is the beginning of Boyes Drive, a scenic route to Muizenberg. It's a spectacular road with sweeping views of False Bay and the Atlantic, and takes just 10 minutes to complete. Look for the signs from Main Road as you head out of Kalk Bay towards Simon's Town.

SIMON'S TOWN

This is the most popular town on False Bay, with a family-friendly atmosphere and numerous Victorian buildings lining Main Street. There are a few small museums, including Simon's Town Museum (Court Road, tel 021-7863046; Mon–Fri 9–4, Sat 10–1, Sun 11–1) in the 18th-century Governor's residence, an informative local history museum and the Heritage Museum (King George Way, tel 021-7862302; Tue–Fri 11–4, Sat 11–1), which charts the history of the

Muslim community in Simon's Town and the 7,000 people who were classified as coloured and relocated to the Cape Flats townships. But most people come here for a swim, a stroll along the main road, and a seafood lunch overlooking the harbour. Also take some time to wander up the hill away from the main road—the quiet, bougainvillaea-bedecked houses and cobbled streets are a welcome retreat from the bustle below. The main beach, Seaforth, is a short drive to the south of town.

BOULDER'S BEACH

About 2km (1.2 miles) south of Simon's Town is a delightful series of small sandy coves surrounded by huge boulders (hence the name). The beach is safe for swimming and gently shelving, making it good for children, but the main attraction is the colony of African penguins that live and nest between the boulders. The area, part of the Table Mountain National Park (tel 021-7862329; daily 8–5), has been created to protect the birds, and their numbers have flourished. This is one of only a few colonies on the mainland. The first cove tends to be packed with families on weekends and during school holidays; to find a more peaceful spot, walk along the boardwalk or crawl under the rocks on one side of the beach. Avoid the nesting areas at all times.

BACKGROUND

Simon's Town, the chief settlement on False Bay, is named after Governor Simon van der Stel, who decided in 1687 that an alternative, more protected port was needed in winter when Table Bay suffered from northwesterly winds. It was not until 1743 that the Dutch East India Company built a pier and barracks. In 1795, the town transferred to British hands, and following the end of the Napoleonic Wars in Europe, the British turned Simon's Town into a naval base, which it remained until 1957. The area was first propelled to the forefront of popularity as a holiday resort when Cecil Rhodes bought a cottage in Muizenberg in 1899. Many other wealthy people followed, including authors Agatha Christie and Rudyard Kipling. Although a significant coloured population lived in False Bay, much of the area was designated 'white' under the Group Areas Act in the 1960s. Today, Kalk Bay has one of the few remaining coloured populations on the coast.

African penguins at Boulder's Beach are also known as jackass penguins due to their braying call

TIPS

● In high season (mid-December to early February) drivers can avoid the traffic along the coast by taking the M65 from the Atlantic seaboard side, which crosses the mountains from Noordhoek to Fish Hoek.
● If you stop off for a meal in the resort of Fish Hoek, bear in mind that the town prohibits the sale of alcohol.
● Ask at Simon's Town harbour about boat trips to the Cape of Good Hope and Seal Island.

Checking the catch at Kalk Bay Harbour

Kirstenbosch Gardens was officially established in 1913

KIRSTENBOSCH BOTANICAL GARDENS

One of the finest botanical gardens in the world is spread spectacularly on the slopes of Table Mountain displaying a fascinating cross-section of southern African flora.

The biggest attraction in the Southern Suburbs is Kirstenbosch, South Africa's oldest, largest and most exquisite botanical gardens. It is one of the finest such gardens in the world, and its position and surroundings alone are incomparable. The gardens stretch up the eastern slopes of Table Mountain, merging seamlessly with the fynbos (indigenous woody plants) of the steep slopes above.

Although it is a joy to wander aimlessly in the gardens, it is worth seeking out some of the smaller specialist sections. The Fragrance garden, for example, is set out so that visitors can fully appreciate the scents of the herbs and flowers. The Dell is one of the most enjoyable sections, following a beautifully shaded path snaking beneath ferns and along a stream.

Indigenous South African herbs can be inspected in the Medicinal Plants garden, each one identified and used by the Khoi and San peoples in the treatment of a variety of ailments. For a sense of the past, visit Jan van Riebeeck's Hedge, which was planted by the first Governor of the Cape in 1660 to keep out the Khoi.

One of the most enjoyable ways of experiencing the gardens is at a Sunset Concert, held throughout summer. Every Sunday, a lower section of the gardens is transformed into an open-air concert venue, with the slopes above acting as seating. Hundreds of Capetonians spread out blankets on the grass and relax with wine and a picnic, while international artists play classical concerts, jazz, fusion-rock or pop. It's great fun and should not be missed if you're here in summer. Concerts are held every Sunday from November to March from 5pm.

RATINGS	
Outdoor pursuits	● ● ● ● ●
Photo stops	● ● ● ● ●
Walkability	● ● ● ●

BASICS

326 C11 • Rhodes Drive, Newlands 7700 ☎ 021-7998800
Sep–end Mar daily 8–7; Apr–end Aug daily 8–6 Adult R22, child (6–18) R5 Golden Arrow service from Adderley Street to Kirstenbosch, takes around 40min 'Eco-tours', or tours by motorized golf cart (reserve in advance)
www.nbi.ac.za

The Rhodes Memorial is made from rock from Table Mountain

RHODES MEMORIAL

326 C11 • Off Rhodes Drive, Rondebosch 7707 ☎ 021-6899151
Daily 9–5 Free

The Rhodes Memorial towers grandly on the slopes of Devil's Peak. This extravagant granite memorial to Cecil John Rhodes (Cape Prime Minister 1890–96) is made up of eight bronze lions flanking a wide flight of steps, which lead up to a Greek Temple. Inside is an immense bronze head of Rhodes, above which is inscribed: 'To the spirit and life work of Cecil John Rhodes who loved and served South Africa'. There is also a magnificent view of the Cape Flats and the Southern Suburbs, best enjoyed from the little tea house set in a garden of hydrangeas.

SOUTHERN SUBURBS

326 C11 The Pinnacle, corner of Burg and Castle streets ☎ 021-4264260 Mon–Fri 8–6, Sat 8.30–1, Sun 9–1
www.cape-town.org

Cape Town's affluent suburbs stretch around Table Mountain, starting in the north with Woodstock. Observatory is an appealing area of tightly packed Victorian bungalows and student hangouts. Mowbray, Rosebank and Rondebosch lie just below the University of Cape Town, and are popular with students. Newlands backs right up to the slopes of Table Mountain and is best known for its beautiful test cricket ground. On Boundary Road is Josephine Mill, the only surviving watermill in Cape Town. In summer, concerts are held in its grounds. Claremont has little of interest other than the Cavendish Square shopping mall. A little farther along is Wynberg, then Little Chelsea. To the west lie the prosperous valleys of Constantia (▷ 63) and Tokai.

Robben Island is an evocative and moving place (above) and its most famous inmate was Mandela (inset)

ROBBEN ISLAND

This is the notorious isolated prison in which Nelson Mandela was held for 18 years. A visit here gives a fascinating insight into the workings of apartheid, with informative tours led by former political prisoners.

Lying 13km (8 miles) offshore from Cape Town's Victoria and Alfred Waterfront (▷ 76), Robben Island is best known as the prison that held many of the ANC's most prominent members during the years of the struggle against apartheid, including Nelson Mandela and Walter Sisulu. It was originally named by the Dutch after the word for seals, 'robben', which used to be found here. The island functioned as a leper colony and then a military base until 1960, when it was handed over to the Department of Prisons. It was declared a UNESCO World Heritage Site in 1999.

ISLAND TOURS

The island can be visited only on a tour organized by the Robben Island Museum. They run throughout the day, and passengers are ferried to the island by catamaran. All tours are led by former political prisoners, who paint a vivid picture of prison life. Lasting two-and-a-half hours, it begins with a drive around the key sites on the island, including the lime quarry where Mandela was forced to work, the leper cemetery and the houses of former warders.

BACKGROUND

Robben Island's effectiveness as a prison did not rest simply with the fact that escape was virtually impossible. The authorities anticipated that the concept of 'out of sight, out of mind' would be particularly applicable here, and to a certain extent they were correct. Its isolation did much to try to break the spirit of political prisoners, not least that of Robert Sobukwe, leader of the Pan African Congress (▷ 36), who was kept in solitary confinement for nine years. Other political prisoners were spared that at least, but conditions were harsh, with forced hard labour and routine beatings. Contact with the outside world was virtually non-existent: Newspapers were banned, and letters were limited to one every six months. Yet despite (or perhaps because of) these measures, the B-Section, which housed Mandela and other major political prisoners, became the international focus of the fight against apartheid. The last political prisoners left the island in 1991.

RATINGS	
Historic interest	●●●●●
Photo stops	●●●●
Outdoor pursuits	●●●

BASICS

✚ 326 B11
☎ 021-4134200 (Robben Island Museum)
◉ Tours: daily departures, on the hour between 9 and 3
💰 Adult R150, child (under 17) R75
🚌 Golden Arrow bus runs from Adderley Street to the V & A Waterfront
⛴ Boat crossing lasts half an hour
🍴 Restaurant in the Nelson Mandela Gateway
🛍 Small shop on the island selling postcards and books
🚻 At the Nelson Mandela Gateway, and the pier on Robben Island
🅿 Parking in the Clock Tower Centre, attached to the Nelson Mandela Gateway
www.robben-island.org.za

TIPS

● If you have to wait for the catamaran crossing, check out the small museum upstairs in the Nelson Mandela Gateway, which has good interactive displays.
● Tickets sell out, so make reservations a day in advance (or two days in high season).
● Don't drink any tap water on the island.

Table Mountain

One of the world's most famous city backdrops, **Table Mountain** is a towering wilderness in the middle of Cape Town. From its summit there are unforgettable views stretching over the ocean and the peninsula below.

RATINGS	
Outdoor pursuits	● ● ● ● ●
Photo stops	● ● ● ● ●
Walkability	● ● ● ● ●

BASICS

✚ 326 C11
🛈 The Pinnacle, corner of Burg and Castle streets
☎ 021-4264260
🕐 Mon–Fri 8–6, Sat 8.30–1, Sun 9–1
www.cape-town.org
www.tablemountain.net
www.cpnp.co.za

SEEING TABLE MOUNTAIN

Rising a sheer 1,086m (3,563ft) from the coastal plain, Table Mountain dominates almost every view of Cape Town. For centuries, it was the first sight afforded to seafarers, its looming presence visible for hundreds of kilometres. Its size still astonishes visitors today, but it is the mountain's wilderness, bang in the middle of a bustling conurbation, that makes the biggest impression. Table Mountain, managed by Table Mountain National Park, sustains more than 1,400 species of flora, as well as baboons, dassies (hyraxes) and countless birds.

HIGHLIGHTS

THE CABLEWAY

✉ Lower Cableway station, off Kloof Nek Road, 8001 ☎ 021-4248181 🕐 Daylight hours—phone ahead for details 💷 Adult round-trip ticket R110, child (4–17) R58, family R280 🚐 Shuttle service from main tourist office on Burg Street, every half hour, R40 🍴 🖺 🏧 🚻 🅿 At bottom station and Tafelberg Road
The dizzying trip to the top of the mountain in the Aerial Cableway takes around three minutes. There are two cars, each carrying up to 65 passengers; as you ride up, the floor rotates allowing a full 360-degree view. At the top, paths criss-cross the area around the station, with numerous viewpoints giving astounding panoramas. From here you can also pick out the other formations that flank the main flat-topped massif: Signal Hill and Lions Head to the west, Devil's Peak to the east, and the spine of the Twelve Apostles stretching south.

The views of and from Table Mountain are extraordinary, here from Signal Hill (above) and from the summit (left) The cableway is not for the faint-hearted (inset)

TIPS

● Look for dassies (rock hyraxes), rodent-like small mammals which scamper about the rocks. Bizarrely, their closest genetic relative is the elephant.
● The cableway stops operating in poor weather or high winds. Conditions can change with little warning, so do not rely on taking a cablecar back down after climbing up.
● The restaurant sells cold drinks and beers, which you can take to the nearest viewpoints to enjoy with the sunset—better value than the cocktail bar in the station.
● Signal Hill's summit at 350m (1,150ft) also has spectacular views. You can drive up, and it is a popular spot at sunset. The two-hour hike up Lion's Head is equally popular and provides 360-degree views.
● For Metro Rescue tel 021-9489900; for weather reports tel 021-4248181.

CLIMBING THE MOUNTAIN

Much of the area is a nature reserve and a delightful wilderness to hike through. There are an estimated 100 paths to the top, but one of the easier routes starts from Kirstenbosch Botanical Gardens (▷ 72), taking about three hours to the top. Even the most used routes should not be taken lightly: Conditions can change alarmingly quickly, and fog (the famous 'Table Cloth' that flows from the top) and rain often descend without warning. Numerous people have been caught off guard and the mountain has claimed its fair share of lives. Be sure to buy a detailed map (from the tourist office or lower Cableway station) and follow the mountain code—ask about it at the tourist office.

BACKGROUND

Table Mountain started to form around 700 million years ago when mud and sand deposits were laid on the seabed, and it was still under water until 160 to 300 million years ago. It was pushed further upwards about 70 million years ago, when exposure to the elements helped shape the mountain.

There are many restaurants at the Waterfront (above); the Time Ball tower was a signalling device used by ships in the harbour (inset)

RATINGS

Chainstore shopping	●●●●●
Good for food	●●●●○
Good for kids	●●●●○

BASICS

➕ 326 C11 • Foreshore 8001
🛈 Clocktower Centre, tel 021-4054500; daily 9am–9pm
🚌 Waterfront bus, run by Golden Arrow, runs every 15 min between rail station on Adderley Street and Waterfront, R2.50 one-way
🍴 Huge selection of restaurants, cafés and bars
🛍 Large shopping mall, plus smaller boutiques and markets
🚻 In mall and Clocktower Centre
🅿 Main parking outside mall is free; three covered parking areas charge fees
www.waterfront.co.za

TIPS

● The outdoor amphitheatre in the middle of the Waterfront is a great place to catch live jazz at the weekend and during the annual Cape Town International Jazz Festival (▷ 190).
● Look for frolicking Cape Fur seals as you cross the swing bridge from the Clock Tower.
● Behind the main shopping malls are a couple of indoor markets selling local arts and crafts.

VICTORIA AND ALFRED WATERFRONT

The city's renovated harbour is a popular place for both visitors and locals and has numerous shops, restaurants and cinemas.

Cape Town's original Victorian harbour is the city's most popular attraction. The whole area was completely restored in the early 1990s, and today it is a lively district. At the same time, it remains a working harbour, and this provides much of the area's true charm. Original buildings stand shoulder to shoulder with mock-Victorian shopping malls, boutiques and alfresco restaurants, all crowding along a waterside walkway, with Table Mountain looming in the background. A recent addition, which has done much to raise the cultural profile of the area, is the Nelson Mandela Gateway to Robben Island (▷ 73).

THE CLOCK TOWER

At the narrow entrance to the Alfred Basin is the original Clock Tower, a red, octagonal Gothic-style tower built in 1882 to house the Port Captain's office. It stands in front of the Clock Tower Centre, the newest collection of shops, offices and restaurants along the Waterfront, with a helpful tourist office upstairs.

TWO OCEANS AQUARIUM

✉ Dock Road ☎ 021-4183823 ⏰ Daily 9.30–6 💲 Adult R60, child (4–17) R28 www.aquarium.co.za
A top attraction along the Waterfront is this aquarium, which focuses on the Cape marine environment created by the merging of the Atlantic and Indian oceans. The display begins with a walk through the Indian Ocean, where visitors follow a route past tanks filled with a multitude of brilliantly hued fish, giant spider crabs and phosphorescent jellyfish, floating in a mesmerizing circular current. Children are well served, with touch pools and the Alpha Activity Centre where they can enjoy free puppet shows and face painting. The top draw is the predators exhibit, an enormous tank complete with glass tunnel, holding ragged-tooth sharks, eagle rays, turtles, and some impressively large hunting fish. There are daily feeding sessions at noon, 3pm and 3.30pm; the sharks are fed on Sundays at 3.30pm.

WESTERN CAPE

The Western Cape is arguably the most beautiful and varied of South Africa's provinces. It has just about everything that the entire country has to offer, from endless beaches and indigenous forests to the historic wine estates at Stellenbosch, Franschhoek and Paarl, and the scorched semi-desert of the Karoo.

MAJOR SIGHTS

Vineyards around the Breede River Valley

The Victorian lighthouse in Cape Agulhas National Park

An exhibit at the Togryers' Museum in Ceres

BREDASDORP

⊞ 327 D11 🅘 Cape Agulhas Tourism Bureau, Long Street, Bredasdorp 7280, tel 028-4242584; Mon–Fri 8–5, Sat 9–12.30
www.capeagulhas.info

This old Overberg (▷ 86) town is South Africa's first village. It was founded in 1837 by local farmer Michiel van Breda, who built a church around which the village grew. The small Shipwreck Museum (Mon–Fri 9–4.45, Sat–Sun 11–4) on Independent Street houses a collection of oddments salvaged from along the coast. The whole display is greatly enhanced by sound effects: for example in the Shipwreck Hall you hear the distinct shrieks of seagulls and the thunderous sound of waves on a stormy night.

BREEDE RIVER VALLEY

⊞ 327 D11 🅘 Cape Winelands Regional Tourism, 29 Du Toit Street, Stellenbosch 7600, tel 0861-265263; Mon–Fri 8–4.30
www.tourismcapewinelands.co.za

A mere 310km (192 miles) long, the Breede River (also known as the Breë, meaning 'broad') is one of the most important rivers in the Cape. Leaving the mountains behind at Swellendam (▷ 86), the river flows across an undulating coastal terrace, meandering through the wheat fields of the Overberg (▷ 86) before entering the Indian Ocean at St. Sebastian Bay. Worcester (▷ 87) is the main town in the region, but along the broad valley are important agricultural market towns such as Prince Alfred Hamlet, Ashton and Bonnievale, as well as the attractive villages of Tulbagh (▷ 87), McGregor and Montagu (▷ 83). These old towns and villages are surrounded by vineyards and fruit farms that display wonderful variations in colours through the seasons. Mountains rise to 2,000m (6,560ft) behind the farms and their peaks are capped with snow in the winter. They also have challenging hiking trails and hidden valleys. The valley acts as the dividing line between two contrasting regions. To the southwest are the verdant Winelands and populous Cape Town. To the northeast is the start of the Karoo, a vast expanse of semi-desert.

CALEDON

⊞ 327 C11 🅘 Caledon Tourist Bureau, 22 Plein Street, Caledon 7230, tel 028-2121511; Mon–Fri 8–5, Sat 8–12.30
www.tourismcaledon.co.za

The regional capital of the Overberg lies just off the N2 at the foot of the Swartberg Mountains and is known for its naturally occurring hot springs (▷ 192). Caledon is a typical rural town—small and quiet, with a couple of sights. If you are planning an overnight stay, you should carry on to Swellendam. The House Museum (Mon–Fri 8–1, 2–5, Sat 9–1) can be found at 11 Constitution Street, in a Victorian building, originally the Freemasons' Lodge. It has displays about local history, domestic items and crafts, and there is a working kitchen where bread is baked every few days. Mill Street has a collection of historical buildings that have been declared national monuments, and Holy Trinity Church (ask for key at the House Museum) on Prince Alfred Drive is a small, neat church dating from 1855.

CAPE AGULHAS

⊞ 327 D12 🅘 Cape Agulhas Tourism Bureau, Long Street, Bredasdorp 7280, tel 028-4242584; Mon–Fri 8–5, Sat 9–12.30
www.capeagulhas.info

Cape Agulhas is the southernmost point in Africa and forms part of the Agulhas National Park, one of South Africa's newest parks. This is where the warm waters of the Indian Ocean meet the cooler waters of the Atlantic Ocean, and while the beach is rocky this is a good area for fishing. The Cape's scenery may lack the grandeur and drama that might be expected of such a significant spot, but a trip to the top of the attractive Victorian lighthouse has good views of the unforgiving ocean that has claimed many ships and lives. There are limited visitor facilities in the park (a couple of toilets), but there are ongoing plans to build a museum, lay out nature trails along the coastline and to build a tarred road. The closest accommodation for the Cape and Park is in the fishing village of Struisbaai.

CERES

⊞ 326 C10 🅘 Ceres Tourism, in the town library on Owen Street, Ceres 6835, tel 023-3161287; Mon–Fri 9–5, Sat 9–12
www.ceres.org.za

Ceres is famous for its fruit and, more specifically, its fruit juice—namely the Liquifruit and Ceres brands, both of which are packed here. Surrounded by the harsh and rugged Skurweberg Mountains (which see snowfall in the winter), this attractive farming town was founded in 1854 and aptly named after the Roman goddess of agriculture. The heart of town is characterized by the shady trees lining the winding Dwars River, which passes through Ceres. The Togryers' (Transport Riders') Museum (tel 023-3122045; Mon–Fri 9–1, 2–5), at 8 Oranje Street, is worth a quick visit for its fine collection of horse-drawn vehicles.

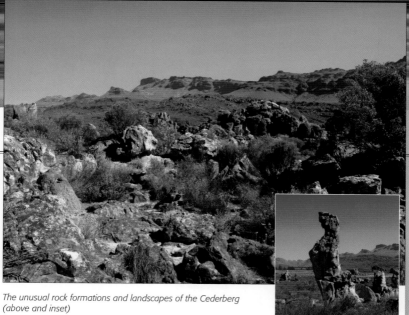

The unusual rock formations and landscapes of the Cederberg (above and inset)

THE CEDERBERG

A striking mountain area of strangely formed sandstone, sleepy rural towns and ancient rock art, the Cederberg is also home to some of the best hiking in the Western Cape.

The Cederberg, the mountain range north of the Cape Peninsula, is celebrated for its rugged scenery, stunning rock formations and centuries-old rock paintings produced by the native San people of the region. There are more than 250km (155 miles) of paths in the mountains, passing bizarre sandstone features like the Wolfberg Arch and the Maltese Cross. Other trails focus on San rock art, usually found in caves or under overhangs (See pages 230–231 for details of a rock art walk). The main administrative focus for the wilderness is the Forestry Station at Algeria.

The roads into the Cederberg are gravel, with steep and twisting sections; some of the steepest stretches have been covered with tarmac. There are two roads from which you can access the main trails. The most popular runs south from Clanwilliam along the Rondegat River Valley to Algeria, and then on to the small towns of Cederberg and Uitsig. The second road is the route serving the remote mission station at Wuppertal, in parts requiring a 4WD vehicle.

CLANWILLIAM

Clanwilliam, on the northern edge of the Cederberg, is a peaceful agricultural town that makes a good base for exploring the mountains. During the spring, the profusion of wild flowers that blankets the area attracts a large number of visitors. There is a handful of sights in town, including the Old Jail (Mon–Fri 8–1) built in 1808, a stocky, white, fortress-like building overlooking the main street, with a small collection of local history items.

CITRUSDAL

Another good base is Citrusdal. As the name implies, it is the focus for the local citrus industry, nestling in a valley filled with lush citrus orchards. During spring, the air is heavy with the scent of orange blossom. Even more impressive is the town's striking setting at the southern edge of the Cederberg. There are some intriguing San paintings on the Hex River farm, 20km (12 miles) north of Citrusdal, and the oldest orange tree in South Africa, a national monument that still bears fruit.

RATINGS	
Cultural interest	●●●○
Outdoor pursuits	●●●●●
Walkability	●●●●●

BASICS

⊞ 326 C10

ℹ Cape Nature Conservation, Algeria, issues hiking permits and maps, tel 027-4822812; Mon–Fri 7.30–4

ℹ Clanwilliam Tourism Bureau, Main Street, Clanwilliam 8135, tel 027-4822024; Mon–Fri 8–5, Sat–Sun 8.30–12.30

ℹ Citrusdal Tourist Office, 39 Voortrekker Street, Citrusdal 7340, tel 022-9213210; Mon–Fri 8.30–12.30, 1–5, Sat 9–1
www.cederberg.co.za

TIP

● The region is known for its excellent Goue Valley wines; you can try them at the Goue Valley shop on Vortrekker Street in Citrusdal, near the tourist office, with sales and tastings.

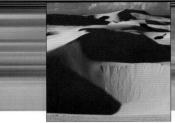
The sand dunes in De Hoop Nature Reserve

The Outeniqua steam train that runs from George to Knysna has impressive coast views

DE HOOP NATURE RESERVE

✚ 327 D11 ☎ 028-5421253
◉ Office: daily 7am–5.30pm; gate: daily 7am–6pm 🚗 From Bredasdorp, follow the R319 towards Swellendam. After 8km (5 miles) take a signposted right turn onto a gravel road. After 40km (25 miles) you reach Ouplaas—take a right for the western sector of the reserve or continue straight on for another 10km (6 miles) for the entrance to the eastern sector. The office and parking are at Potberg
www.capenature.org.za

This important coastal reserve extends 5km (3 miles) out to sea, protecting the shoreline and marine life. It is divided into two sectors: The western region is for hiking, game viewing and birdwatching, while the eastern section is for mountain biking. The reserve covers an exceptionally varied and rich environment within its 34,000ha (84,000 acres). There is a large fresh-water *vlei* (a hollow where water collects in the wet season) surrounded by marshlands; the coastline is made up of sandy beaches and rocky headlands; and inland are giant sand dunes backed by the Potberg Mountains. With such a variety of terrain crammed into a relatively small area, the region supports a great range of wildlife. More than 250 bird species have been recorded here, while elusive leopard, bontebok (a large antelope) and Cape mountain zebra share

Bonteboks can be seen at De Hoop

the land with the more common eland, baboon and two more—smaller—antelopes, the grey rhebok and klipspringer. There is also a chance of seeing southern right whales, which calve in the shallow waters between July and December. See page 192 for details of mountain biking.

GANSBAAI

✚ 326 C12 ⚕ Gansbaai Tourism Bureau, corner of Berg and Main streets, Gansbaai 7220, tel 028-3841439; Mon–Fri 9–5, Sat 9–2
www.gansbaaiinfo.com

This small, modern town is a prosperous fishing port with a deepwater wharf and several fish canning factories. Like Hermanus at the other end of Walker Bay, it has some excellent vantage points for whale watching, but most visitors come here to see Dyer Island or go cage diving with great white sharks. Dyer Island is an important breeding place for African penguins, and nearby Geyser Island has a breeding seal population. The area between the two islands is known as Shark Alley, as great white sharks are attracted to the breeding seals. See page 192 for details of shark viewing.

GARDEN ROUTE

✚ 328 F11
www.gardenroute.co.za

The Garden Route is a 200km (125-mile) stretch of the south coast extending from Mossel Bay in the west to Plettenberg Bay in the east. Its high level of exposure has made it hugely popular, and few visitors to the Cape miss it. Though some maintain that its appeal is overstated, few can deny the beauty of the rugged coast backed by lush mountains. The region is separated from the interior by the Tsitsikamma and Outeniqua

mountain ranges. In contrast to the dry area of the Karoo on the other side of the mountains, rain falls all year round on the Garden Route and the ocean-facing mountain slopes are covered with luxuriant forests.

The most popular stretch of the route follows the coast from Mossel Bay to Storms River in Tsitsikamma National Park. The larger towns, such as George (below) and Knysna (▷ 82), are highly developed resorts, while in other areas you can experience untouched wilderness and wonderful hikes, including one of the most famous in the country, the Otter Trail. This runs along the coast in Tsitsikamma National Park (▷ 88), among the most popular parks in South Africa. A second national park, Wilderness (▷ 87), is also very popular. If your preference is for the beach life, there's a choice of peaceful seaside villages or livelier surf spots.

GEORGE

✚ 327 E11 ⚕ 124 York Street, George 6529, tel 044-8019295/7; Mon–Fri 8–5.30, Sat 9–1 ⚕ Cape Nature Conservation at York Street, tel 044-8742160, issues permits for hikes in the area
www.georgetourism.co.za

Often referred to as the gateway to, or the capital of, the Garden Route, George lies in the shadow of the Outeniqua Mountains, but unlike the majority of towns along the Garden Route, it is not on the sea. It owes its status to the fact that it has an airport, and it is also an important intersection between the N2 coastal highway and the N9 running through the Outeniqua Pass into the Karoo. The main reason overseas visitors come to George is to play golf, but the town itself—largely a modern grid of streets interspersed with some attractive

Windmills are a feature of the Great Karoo landscape

Horseback riding is a popular activity in Grootbos

A Cape Dutch homestead in the Hex River Valley

old buildings—repays a short visit. St. Mark's Cathedral (daily 9.30–4.30), on the corner of Cathedral and York streets, is unusual for its large number of stained-glass windows. The Drostdy Museum (Mon–Fri 9–4.30, Sat 9–12.30), on Courtenay Street, has displays about the timber industry, as well as musical instruments and a collection of old printing presses. The exhibition at the Transport Museum (Mon–Sat 8–5) outlines the history of steam train travel. You'll find it adjacent to the platform from which the Outeniqua steam train departs (▷ 193), on Mission Street, just off Knysna Road.

GREAT KAROO

➕ 327 E10

The Groot Karoo, which is known as the Great Karoo in English, is a vast, ancient plateau making up nearly a third of the total area of the country. Endless plains stretch between stark mountain ranges, with little but characteristic steel windmills peppering the horizons. The landscape is a parched expanse of baked red earth inhabited by tough merino sheep and their even tougher owners. The sheer scale of the Great Karoo is remarkable—the average farm covers more than 20,000ha (50,000 acres). Hundreds of millions of years ago this whole area was an enormous swamp inhabited by dinosaurs, making it a key palaeontological site.

In the 19th century, the region played a significant historical role, as the Voortrekkers—Boer farmers seeking to escape British domination—penetrated the interior with their ox wagons. The southern districts of the Great Karoo are traversed today by the N1 highway between Cape Town and Johannesburg.

GROOTBOS

➕ 327 C11 ☎ 028-3840381 ⓘ Open to overnight guests only 🚗 From Hermanus, follow the R43 through Stanford and continue for 13km (8 miles). Grootbos is clearly signposted on the left www.grootbos.com

This private nature reserve and luxury camp, inland from Walker Bay, covers more than 1,000ha (2,500 acres) of fynbos-clad hills. Almost all of the fynbos (or woody plants) can be spotted by their small leaves, which are hard and leathery. The reserve, which has won several conservation and eco-tourism awards, lies inland from Gansbaai, with stunning views of Walker Bay and the surrounding countryside. This semi-wilderness is an ideal place to gain an impression of the variety and brilliance of the native Cape flora—fynbos. There are also milkwood forests and a collection of ponds that attract a variety of bird life. Activities include horseback riding and mountain biking trails through the hills, boat trips to Dyer Island and trips to the De Kelders caves.

HEX RIVER VALLEY

➕ 327 C10 ℹ Hex River Tourism, corner of the N1 and Voortrekker Road, tel 023-3562041; Mon–Fri 8–12.30, 1.30–5 www.grapeescape.co.za

Approaching from the arid landscapes of the east, this is the first glimpse you get of the fertility and glory of the Cape. The soils of the Hex River Valley are naturally productive and this has long been an important grape growing region. More than 60 of the table wines produced in South Africa for export originate from here, and there are an estimated eight million vines growing in the valley and on the mountain slopes. This multitude of vines provides a vibrant backdrop:

bright greens in summer; rich bronzes and reds in autumn; and snow-capped peaks setting off the leafless plants in winter.

To complement the natural beauty of the valley, the long history of farming here has left many fine examples of early Cape Dutch homesteads, built between 1768 and 1815. Some of these have been restored and turned into superior guesthouses. A one-time coach house known as Die Monitor has been turned into Die Vlei Country Inn, which is a popular overnight or lunch stop.

KAROO NATIONAL PARK

➕ 327 F9 ☎ 023-4152828 ⓘ Gates: 5am–10pm; park office: 7am–8pm 💵 All visitors R15 ❓ Trail and park maps available at park office 🚗 Main entrance is signposted off the N1, 5km (3 miles) southwest of Beaufort West www.sanparks.org

This National Park was created to conserve a representative area of the unique Karoo environment. The current boundaries of the park encompass an area of Karoo plains that merge into mountain slopes and a high-lying plateau. The park is accessible via one of its hiking trails, by 4WD vehicle or on a guided tour arranged at the office.

There is a surprisingly diverse range of game and smaller wildlife in the park, mostly small mammals, birds and reptiles—including five different species of tortoise (this is the largest number in a conservation area in the world). Look for the tent tortoise: Well camouflaged, it looks like an inverted egg box. The reserve is also home to two endangered species: the black rhino and the riverine rabbit. While the statistics are impressive, actually spotting these animals requires a degree of patience, effort—and luck.

The entry to the lagoon at Knysna (above) is guarded by The Heads promontories (inset)

RATINGS

Good for food	●●●●○
Good for kids	●●●○○
Outdoor pursuits	●●●●○

BASICS

🗺 328 F11
🛈 Knysna Tourism, 40 Main Street, Knysna 6571, tel 044-3825510; Mon–Fri 8–5, Sat 8.30–1
www.tourismknysna.co.za

TIPS

● A great day trip is the Outeniqua Choo-Tjoe steam train to George (▷ 193).
● Be prepared for crowds and/or long waits at restaurants during busy times, as the area is very popular.

The quayside at Knysna

KNYSNA

Knysna is the hub of the Garden Route, with a stunning lagoon, noble forests and plenty of accommodation and restaurants.

Many artists and craftspeople have gravitated to Knysna (the 'K' is silent) and it is a pleasant spot to spend a day or two. The lagoon-side town is fully geared up for visitors—its restaurants serve Knysna's famous seafood, especially its oysters, which are cultivated in the lagoon. Development is booming, with a waterfront complex known as the Knysna Quays setting the pace. The heart of town is a grid of leafy streets lined with Victorian bungalows, bed-and-breakfasts, craft shops and coffee shops. Don't come here for the beaches. For that you should travel 20km (12 miles) to Brenton-on-Sea.

THE LAGOON

Much of Knysna's life revolves around the lagoon. The Heads, the rocky promontories that lead from the lagoon to the open sea, are dramatic, and there's some good scuba diving (▷ 193). The Knysna National Lakes, more than 15,000ha (37,000 acres) of protected area, are also wonderful to explore, especially by kayak. Featherbed Nature Reserve is the unspoilt western side of The Heads. This is a private nature reserve that can be reached only by taking the Featherbed Co. Ferry (tel 044-3821693; www.featherbed.co.za), which runs from the John Benn Jetty, 400m (440 yards) west of the rail station. It's home to South Africa's largest breeding herd of blue duiker (*Cephalophus monticola*), an endangered species of antelope. There's also a cave once inhabited by the Khoi (original inhabitants of the region), which has been declared a National Heritage Site.

KNYSNA FOREST

On the southern slopes of the Outeniqua Mountains, behind Knysna, are the remnants of the grand forests that first attracted white settlers to the region. Although much of the game that once thrived here has vanished, there is an impressive variety of bird life, including the vivid Knysna lourie with its red wing feathers. Various short walks have been laid out in the forests, focusing on magnificent trees. East of here and of Knysna is Diepwalle Forest, which has an excellent elephant walk. However, don't expect to see any—the Knysna elephants are extremely rare and only two are on record at present.

Gannets on Bird Island,
Lambert's Bay

The exterior of the Lord Milner
Hotel, Matjiesfontein

Attractively painted houses in
Montagu

THE SIGHTS

LAMBERT'S BAY

🚩 326 B9 🛈 5 Medical Centre, Main
Road, tel 027-4321000; Mon–Fri 9–5,
Sat 9–12.30 🐦 Bird Island: adult R10,
child (under 12) R5
www.lambertsbay.com

Once just a small fishing village,
Lambert's Bay on the west coast
has become a popular holiday
town and gets busy in summer.
The famous Muisbosskerm
restaurant (▷ 262) has played
an important role in drawing visitors to the region, but the bay
has in fact appeared on maps
for many years—this was the
last point at which Portuguese
explorer Bartolomeu Dias went
ashore, before sailing around the
Cape for the first time in 1487.
Today, this modern town has one
absorbing, if pungent, attraction:
Bird Island. This rock outcrop of
just 3ha (7.5 acres) is now joined
to the land by a concrete jetty.
It is an important breeding
ground for African penguins,
Cape gannets and cormorants,
and also attracts Cape fur seals.
Early morning and evening are
the best times to see the birds,
but be warned: unless you are a
dedicated ornithologist, you may
find the screeching and overpow-
ering smell of the birds leaves a
longer-lasting impression than
the extraordinary sight of them.

LITTLE KAROO

See pages 84–85.

MATJIESFONTEIN

🚩 327 D10

In 1975, the entire village of
Matjiesfontein was declared
a national monument—little
surprise considering its excellent
Victorian houses. The town
itself consists of not much more
than a couple of dusty streets,
but these are lined with perfectly
preserved period houses. The
highlight is the Lord Milner Hotel,

resplendent with turrets and
adorned balconies. It was built
by a Scot, Jimmy Logan, an
official working for the Cape
Government Railways in the
1890s, who originally came here
hoping that the dry air would
cure a chest complaint. He settled in the area where he made
a fortune, and the history of the
town is a reflection of his life.
His hotel became fashionable,
attracting rich and influential
guests who, like him, suffered
from lung complaints. These
included Cecil Rhodes and the
Sultan of Zanzibar.
    Another famous resident was
the writer and feminist Olive
Schreiner, whose first novel, The
Story of an African Farm (1883),
was set in the Karoo. Today the
town is a popular stopover on
the route between Johannesburg
and the Cape.

MONTAGU

🚩 327 D11 🛈 Montagu Tourism
Bureau, 24 Bath Street, Montagu 6720,
tel 023-6142471; Mon–Fri 8.45–4.45,
Sat 9–5, Sun 9.30–12.30, 3–5
www.tourismmontagu.co.za

The long, oak-lined streets of
this delightful Karoo town are
full of whitewashed Cape Dutch
houses sitting beneath jagged
mountain peaks. Founded in
1851, the settlement was named
after John Montagu who, as the
colonial secretary from 1843 to
1853, had been responsible
for the first major road-building
scheme in the Cape. Long Street
has 14 national monuments
along its length, and with so
many well-preserved buildings,
it is easy to get a vivid impression
of how the settlement would
have looked in its early days.
Joubert House (Mon–Fri 9–1,
2–5), the oldest building in the
town, is now part of the museum
(the main museum building is
farther along Long Street). It has

a collection of late 19th-century
furnishings and ornaments, and
part of the garden is devoted
to a collection of indigenous
medicinal plants.

MOSSEL BAY

🚩 327 E11 🛈 Mossel Bay Tourism
Bureau, corner of Church and Market
streets, Mossel Bay 6506, tel 044-691
2202; Mon–Fri 8–6, Sat–Sun 9–4
www.visitmosselbay.co.za

Built along a rocky peninsula
providing sheltered swimming
and mooring in the bay, Mossel
Bay is one of the larger seaside
towns along the Garden Route.
During school vacations the town
is packed—it receives one million
domestic visitors in December
alone. For the rest of the year
it is just another coastal town,
its appeal not enhanced by the
fact that, since the discovery of
offshore oil deposits, Mossel
Bay is also the home of the
Mossgas natural gas refinery
and a multitude of oil storage
tanks, visible from any approach
into town.
    You may notice a number of
Portuguese flags and names
around the town. These relate to
the first European to anchor in
the bay—Bartolomeu Dias, who
landed in February 1488. All the
museums in town are on one
site known as the Bartolomeu
Dias Museum Complex. Here
you'll find the Culture Museum,
the Shell Museum, the Aquarium
and the Maritime Museum (all
are open Mon–Fri 9–5).
    In the middle of the bay is Seal
Island, which can be visited by
cruises departing from the harbour. The island is inhabited by
colonies of African penguins and
Cape fur seals (the best month
to see seal pups is November).
It's also possible to see great
white sharks and small hammerhead sharks, which prey upon
the seals.

Little Karoo

Valleys, rural towns, the fascinating caves at Cango and the world's largest ostrich population all make up a rewarding visit to the region.

Stalactites in one of the network of Cango Caves

You will see proteas around the Swartberg Pass

SEEING THE LITTLE KAROO

Unlike the stark Great Karoo to the north, the Little (or Klein) Karoo is made up of a series of parallel fertile valleys enclosed by the Swartberg Mountains to the north and the Langeberg and Outeniqua mountains to the south. In addition to the Cango Caves and the ostrich farms of Oudtshoorn, farther afield lies spectacular and peaceful countryside, dotted with attractive villages. Here too are some of South Africa's most dramatic kloofs (gorges) and passes—14 in all. Another incentive is Route 62, a fine stretch of road following the R62 and marketed as the 'longest wine route in the world'.

HIGHLIGHTS

OUDTSHOORN

➕ 327 E11 ℹ️ Oudtshoorn Tourist Bureau, Baron van Reede Street, Oudtshoorn 6625, tel 044-2792532; Mon–Fri 8–6, Sat 8.30–1
www.oudtshoorn.com

By far the largest town in the Little Karoo, the regional capital is a major visitor attraction, thanks to the nearby Cango Caves and the countless ostrich farms surrounding it. The town itself is appealing, with broad streets, smart sandstone Victorian houses and a good choice of restaurants. There are several 'ostrich palaces' built by the town's 'feather barons' in the 19th century (see Background) which, although not open to the public, are still worth a look since their ornate exteriors were an important part of their design. Most examples are in the old part of town along the west bank of the Grobbelaars River. In the heart of town, next to the old Queen's Hotel on Baron van Rheede Street, is the C. P. Nel Museum (Mon–Fri 8–5, Sat 9–5) with displays about the ostrich feather boom.

OSTRICH FARMS

Visiting an ostrich farm in the area can be great fun, although the appeal of all things ostrichey can fade quickly. To keep visitors interested, some farms have introduced different species. Opinions vary as to which farm is the least commercialized, but Highgate Ostrich Farm (tel 044-2727115, daily 8–5; www.highgate.co.za), 10km (6 miles) from Oudtshoorn off the R328 towards Mossel Bay, is perhaps the best organized. It's a very popular show farm and has won prizes for its high standards.

CANGO CAVES

➕ 327 E10 ☎ 044-2727410 🕐 By guided tour only: daily and hourly 9–4 and lasting 1 hour or 90 min 💷 R40–R55, depending on tour 🍴 🚻 ❓ Child day care and money exchange available 🚗 28km (17 miles) north of Oudtshoorn along the R328, signposted from town
www.cangocaves.co.za

Tucked away in the foothills of the Swartberg Mountains are the Cango Caves, a magnificent network of calcite caverns, recognized as among the world's finest dripstone cave systems. The only access is on a guided tour, the most popular of which takes in six caves and gives you a good overview. The caves contain an

extraordinary series of bizarre formations, including incredible stalagmites, stalactites and flowstone (thin layers of rock deposited by the flow of water). The timescale of some of the formations is hard to comprehend; many of the pillars took hundreds of thousands of years to form, while the oldest flowstone is more than a million years old.

Money from ostrich farming helped build 'palaces' around Oudtshoorn (inset); tourism is now the main source of income (above)

SWARTBERG PASS
✚ 327 E10
One of the most spectacular passes in South Africa, the Swartberg Pass is a national monument in recognition of the engineering genius of Thomas Bain, who built it in the 1880s. It is 24km (15 miles) long and rises to 1,585m (5,200ft) with a number of sharp, blind hairpins. As you descend towards Prince Albert, there are plenty of shaded picnic sites to pause at and enjoy the views.

CALITZDORP
✚ 327 E11 🛈 Voortrekker Street, Calitzdorp 6660, tel 044-2133775; Mon–Fri 9–5, Sat 9–12
www.calitzdorp.co.za
This attractive Victorian village is a successful agricultural hub and an important area for port wine production in South Africa. It is possible to visit a couple of port farms (ask at the tourist office), and a port festival is held on the last weekend of every July (tel 044-2133314). At harvest time, fresh fruit is sold along the wide roads of the village.

BACKGROUND
The Karoo was for centuries impassable thanks to its series of peaks and valleys. However, in the 19th century, dozens of passes were built across the Cape's mountains, effectively opening up the area. The history of the largest town in the Karoo, Oudtshoorn, goes back to around this time. It was settled by British farmers in the mid-19th century, but it was the advent of two fashion booms for ostrich feathers (1865–70 and 1900–14) that truly established the town. For a period of almost 40 years it was the most important town east of Cape Town. At the peak of its fortunes, ostrich feathers were selling for more than their weight in gold. While ostrich farming no longer brings in as much wealth, it remains an important business and visitor attraction.

TIPS

● Tours of the Cango Caves take limited numbers, so you may have to wait more than an hour to get in. Try to arrive early to avoid this.
● Wear shoes with good grip when visiting the caves as the ground can be slippery.
● There are no tour companies that organize daily trips to the ostrich farms or the caves, although it is possible to arrange a guide through the tourist office. The best alternative is to rent a car for the day.

MORE TO SEE

PRINCE ALBERT
✚ 327 E10
This village on the edge of the Swartberg Mountains, just 2km (1.2 miles) from the Swartberg Pass, feels remote and rural. Canals from these hills bring water to the gardens, helping to give an oasis feel to the settlement. As you walk about the old streets between houses of the Victorian era, you quickly gain an impression of Karoo life at the end of the 1800s.

Central Beach is one of three beaches at Plettenberg Bay

Grain silos in Malmesbury, Swartland

The Drostdy Museum in Swellendam

THE OVERBERG

⊞ 327 D11 🛈 Cape Overberg Tourism Association, Church Street, Caledon 7230, tel 028-2141466; Mon–Fri 8–4.30
www.capeoverberg.org

The Overberg, roughly the area to the east of the Hottentots Holland Mountains, extends as far as Mossel Bay on the Garden Route. To the north are the Langeberg Mountains and to the south the ocean. In the early days of settlement, people would refer to the area as 'over the berg'. It was not until the construction of Sir Lowry's Pass that the region began to be cultivated. Most visitors pass through on their way to the Garden Route and it has a handful of interesting towns that are enjoyable stop-off points. Swellendam (▷ 86), Caledon and Bredasdorp (▷ 78) all have examples of early Cape Dutch buildings. But the big draw is the Whale Coast and the whale-watching hot-spot of Hermanus (▷ 89).

PLETTENBERG BAY

⊞ 328 F11 🛈 Plettenberg Bay Tourism, Melville's Corner, Main Street, Plettenberg Bay 6600, tel 044-5334065; Mon–Fri 9–5, Sat 9–2, Sun 9–1
www.plettenbergbay.co.za

'Plett', as it is commonly known, is one of the most appealing resorts along the Garden Route and has particularly fine beaches. It has become fashionable in recent years, and during the busy Christmas season the town is transformed. Families descend on it and the pace can get quite frenetic. For the rest of the year the pace is more sedate. There are three beaches—Robberg, Central and Lookout—all good for swimming, but Lookout is the most attractive. There is also excellent deep-sea fishing and, in season, good whale and dolphin

spotting. The nearby Keurbooms River lagoon is a safe area for swimming and watersports.

ROBERTSON

⊞ 327 D11 🛈 Robertson Tourism Bureau, corner of Voortrekker and Reitz streets, Robertson 6705, tel 023-6264437; Mon–Fri 9–5, Sat 9–4, Sun 10–2
www.robertson.org.za

This small, prosperous town, with its tidy jacaranda-lined streets, orderly church squares and neat rose gardens, could be in a time warp. Stay to explore the heart of town and the nearby vineyards, one of which is the Robertson Valley Wine Route (tel 023-6263167; www.robert sonwinevalley.co.za) that follows the Breede River Valley (▷ 78). One of the most welcoming estates is Van Loveren (Mon–Fri 8.30–5, Sat 9.30–1). Tastings are conducted in a restored *rondavel* (round hut with a conical roof) in the middle of a garden. Robertson Winery (Mon–Thu 8–5, Fri 8–5.30, Sat 9–3), on Voortrekker Road, is the oldest winery in the area and has tastings and cellar tours (by prior arrangement). Nearby, the village of McGregor is made up of a collection of perfectly preserved, whitewashed thatched cottages radiating out from the Dutch Reformed Church (not open to the public).

SWARTLAND

⊞ 326 C10 🛈 De Bron Centre, Malmesbury, tel 022-4879400; Mon–Fri 8–5, Sat 8.30–12

North of Cape Town, following the N7 towards the Northern Cape, the landscape is made up of rolling wheat country known as the Swartland, or 'Black Country', after the dark rhinoceros bush which once covered the area. Most of the towns in

the region are small, prosperous farming communities; the main towns of the wheat industry are Malmesbury and Moorreesburg. The area contains the Olifants River valley, the eastern boundary of which is made up of the spectacular Cederberg Mountains (▷ 79). The Olifants River is named after the elephants that were spotted here by the first European explorers more than 300 years ago.

SWELLENDAM

⊞ 327 D11 🛈 Swellendam Tourism, Oefeningshuis, Voortrek Street, Swellendam 6740, tel 028-5142770; Mon–Fri 8–5, Sat 9–noon
www.swellendamtourism.co.za

Founded in 1745, Swellendam is the third oldest European town in South Africa, and one of the most attractive. The heart of town bears testament to its age with an avenue of mature oak trees and whitewashed Cape Dutch homesteads. Many of the original houses were destroyed in a fire in 1865, and more were pulled down in 1974 when the main street was widened. Despite all this, Swellendam has retained its appeal and it makes a pleasant base for exploring the region—the Breede River Valley and the Little Karoo are all within easy reach.

The Drostdy Museum (Mon–Fri 9–4.45, Sat–Sun 10–3.45) on Swellengrebel Street is often described as one of the country's great architectural treasures. The main H-shaped building dates from 1747, when it was built as the official residence and seat for the local magistrate, the *landdrost*. Inside, the displays concentrate on local history.

TSITSIKAMMA NATIONAL PARK

See page 88.

Pretty Cape Dutch architecture in Tulbagh

Swartvlei lagoon, part of Wilderness National Park

Kleinplasie Museum, Worcester, has exhibits on pioneer farmers

TULBAGH

🔲 326 C10 🚹 4 Church Street, Tulbagh 6820, tel 023-2301348; Mon–Fri 9–5, Sat 10–4, Sun 11–4 www.tulbaghtourism.org.za

Tucked away in the Tulbagh Valley and surrounded by mountains is this prosperous and peaceful village, with small wine estates and fruit farms. At its heart is a fine collection of traditional Cape buildings; it rates as one of the best examples of a rural Victorian settlement in South Africa.

However, the apparent preservation of the buildings is somewhat artificial. Much of Tulbagh was destroyed by a sudden earthquake in 1969, after which the buildings underwent heavy restoration, giving the village its present-day pristine appearance. The main attraction is delightful, tree-lined Church Street. The majority of the buildings are in private ownership, but three are part of the Town Museum (Mon–Fri 9–5, Sat 10–4, Sun 11–4). At No. 4 there is an excellent photographic display tracing the history of Tulbagh's houses. Number 22 has been furnished with 19th-century items and No. 14 is now a guesthouse, restaurant and shop.

WEST COAST NATIONAL PARK

🔲 326 B10 • Off R27, north of Cape Town ☎ 022-7722144 ⏰ Apr–end Sep daily 7am–7.30pm; Oct–end Mar daily 6am–8pm 💰 R15 for all (prices quadruple in flower season) 🚤 Daily guided boat tours to Malgas Island and around lagoon; reservations essential 🏪❓ There are two entrances: if approaching from the south on the R27, look out for signs on the left. The main entrance is accessed from the main road leading south from Langebaan town; it also houses the information office

Although it may not seem remarkable at first sight, West Coast National Park, stretching from the southern side of the natural harbour formed by Saldanha Bay, remains unmatched in South Africa. Covering 30,000ha (75,000 acres), it protects the rich marine life in Langebaan lagoon and the rare coastal wetlands surrounding it. The attraction is the varied and impressive bird life, and there are several hides allowing good viewing. Almost 250 bird species have been recorded here and the variety is quite remarkable, from flamingos and black oystercatchers to swift terns and Cape gannets. Apart from the prolific bird life, wild flowers are a big draw when they bloom after the first spring rains (Aug, Sep). Postberg Nature Reserve (open Aug, Sep only), within the park, holds the majority of blooms. The main towns near the national park are Langebaan, a modern holiday resort on the lagoon, and the industrial town of Saldanha.

WHALE COAST

See page 89.

WILDERNESS NATIONAL PARK

🔲 328 F11 • 4km (2.5 miles) east of Wilderness off N2 ☎ 044-8771197 ⏰ Reception open 24 hours 💰 R15 for all 📧 www.sanparks.org

This is one of the most relaxing places to stay along the Garden Route. The park covers 2,612ha (6,450 acres) and incorporates five rivers and four lakes as well as a length of coastline stretching 28km (17 miles). The series of freshwater lakes is between the Outeniqua foothills and sand dunes at the back of a fine, long, sandy beach. You can explore the park either on foot or by kayak.

The latter is perhaps the most enjoyable, and is ideal for spotting birds. The main camp has canoes and other boats for rent—a small fee is payable at reception, where you can also pick up a map of the park and useful information about the countryside. Accommodation in the park is good value, but the nearby holiday resort of Wilderness has a wider choice and a selection of restaurants.

WINELANDS

See pages 90–95.

WORCESTER

🔲 327 C11 🚹 Worcester Tourism Bureau, 23 Baring Street, Worcester 6850, tel 023-3482795; Mon–Fri 8–5, Sat 8.30–12.30

Worcester, the capital of the Breede River Valley (▷ 78), has a number of interesting buildings and some good museums. Worcester's most famous son is artist Hugo Naudé (1868–1941), and Hugo Naudé House, a gallery filled with his and other South African artists' work, is at 113 Russell Street (Mon–Fri 8.30–4.30, Sat 9–12). The giant KWV brandy cellar on Church Street is the largest in the world, with 120 copper pot stills producing 10- and 20-year-old brandies (Mon–Fri 8–4.30, tours at 10am and 2pm). The excellent Kleinplasie Museum (Mon–Sat 9–4.30), on Robertson Road, is an open-air museum depicting the lifestyle of the early pioneer farmers.

Also worth a visit is the Karoo National Botanical Garden (daily dawn–dusk), off Roux Street, which combines semi-desert plants with landscaped gardens filled with plants from arid regions. The area bursts into bloom after the spring rains, and there are several short trails in the gardens.

Dramatic scenery is everywhere in the park (above) and hiking through it will give you the best views (inset)

TSITSIKAMMA NATIONAL PARK

An amazing ancient rainforest that runs along a wild stretch of coast, making this the most spectacular part of the Garden Route.

This is one of the most popular national parks in the country, second only to Kruger. It consists of a stretch of lush, coastal forest extending for 80km (50 miles), and protects an area of 5km (3 miles) out to sea. The Tsitsikamma rainforest is the last remnant of what once covered this coast, the narrow strip of towering hardwoods combining with a haze of climbing vegetation to create an unforgettable forest scene. The coast is rocky and wild, and the deep river gorges and spectacular Storms River Mouth make this area the Garden Route's most entrancing section.

THE PARK
The park is split into two sections, both accessible only from the N2: There is no access by road between one section and the other. In the west is De Vasselot, including the resort of Nature's Valley, with a number of short walks through the forest and across rivers, as well as a lovely stretch of sandy beach. In the east is Storms River Mouth, where the wild Storms River surges into the frothy sea through a deep gorge. Again, walking is the main pastime here, with a number of enjoyable hikes across the forested cliffs. There is a huge variety of bird life in the park, the brightest of which is the Knysna lourie that can be spotted by the flash of red in its wings when it takes flight. You might also spot the rare African black oystercatcher, with black plumage and red eyes, beak and legs. Animals that you might see include the blue duiker, the smallest antelope in the country—the adult male stands less than 30cm (12 inches) high.

HIKING
There are a number of short hikes from both Storms River and De Vasselot; detailed maps are available at both camps. West from Storms River camp is one of South Africa's best-known treks, the Otter Hiking Trail (reservations must be made up to a year in advance, tel 012-4289111), a five-day hike which follows the coastline all the way to De Vasselot, crossing rivers, traversing forests and passing waterfalls. The Tsitsikamma Trail is an inland trail run by South African Forestry (tel 012-4265111).

RATINGS

Outdoor pursuits	● ● ● ● ○
Photo stops	● ● ● ● ○
Walkability	● ● ● ● ○

BASICS

✚ 328 F11
☎ 042-2811607
◉ Storms River Mouth Gate: daily 5.30am–9.30pm; reception: daily 7.30–4.30
💳 Adult R80, child (under 12) R40
🍴 Jabulani Restaurant open for breakfast, lunch and dinner
🏪 Shop stocks groceries, wine and beer
🛏 Range of accommodation in two main camps
🚗 Off the N2, 4km (2.5 miles) after the Storms River Bridge
www.sanparks.org

TIPS

● Don't miss the short boardwalk stroll from the restaurant at Storms River Mouth camp to the suspension bridge over the gorge, as the views are incredible.
● The best time to visit is between November and February, but bear in mind that it rains year round.

As the name of this stretch of coast implies, seeing whales is not a problem here

WHALE COAST

This is one of the best areas in the world for land-based whale watching, with guaranteed sightings during the calving season.

The evocatively named Whale Coast lives up to its title from July to November, when large numbers of whales visit the sheltered bays along the coast of Walker Bay to breed. They can be seen close to the shore from Cape Town's False Bay all the way east to Mossel Bay on the Garden Route. The most exhilarating stretch of the coast is along the R44 between Gordon's Bay and Hermanus (far more enjoyable than the faster R45), where the mountains plunge straight into the ocean forming a coastline of steep cliffs, sandy coves, dangerous headlands and natural harbours. There is a string of small seaside resorts along here, starting with Gordon's Bay and passing through Betty's Bay (known for its botanical gardens and colony of African penguins), Kleinmond, Onrus and Vermont. But most visitors go straight to Hermanus—and with good reason.

HERMANUS

Hermanus has grown from a rustic fishing village to a much-loved visitor resort. It is the self-proclaimed world's best land-based whale-watching site, and indeed its waters are host to impressive numbers of southern right whales during calving season. But don't expect any private viewings—Hermanus is popular and has a steady flow of visitors throughout the season. While this means it can get very busy, there is also a good selection of accommodation and restaurants.

The best months to see whales are September and October, when you're virtually guaranteed to see them breaching and lobtailing (the action of a whale's tail slapping the surface of the water) close to the shore. For the best sites, head along the Cliff Path that starts at the new harbour in Westcliff and follows the shore all the way round Walker Bay to Grotto Beach, a distance of slightly more than 15km (9 miles). Grotto Beach, with fine white sand, is the largest of a number of good beaches just a short distance in either direction from central Hermanus.

The Old Harbour in the heart of town is a national monument and a focal point of visitor activities. A ramp leads down the cliff to the attractive old jetty and a group of restored fishermen's cottages, including a tiny local history museum (Mon–Sat 9–4.30, Sun 12–4).

RATINGS	
Good for kids	●●●○
Outdoor pursuits	●●●○
Photo stops	●●●●

BASICS

✚ 326 C11

ℹ Greater Hermanus Tourism Bureau, Old Station Building, Mitchell Street, Hermanus 7200, tel 028-3122629; Mon–Fri 8–6, Sat 9–5, Sun 9–3
www.hermanus.co.za

TIPS

● Watch for the town's Whale Crier, who wanders along the coast blowing a kelp horn to alert visitors to where the whales are.

● Stanford, a sleepy Victorian village, is a pleasant trip from Hermanus and has the popular Birkenhead Brewery (daily 10–6) just outside it.

The Whale Crier is said to be the only such crier in the world

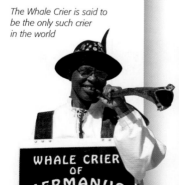

The Winelands

South Africa's oldest and loveliest wine-producing area offers the chance to sample several hundred different wines in a superbly scenic setting.

Picking grapes in the vineyards around Franschhoek

Stellenbosch's history is on display at the Village Museum

The porticoed entrance of a house in Stellenbosch

RATINGS	
Good for food	●●●●
Historical interest	●●●
Photo stops	●●●●
Outdoor pursuits	●●

TIPS

● If you are in the car, make sure one of the drivers stays off the wine. You should never drive under the influence of alcohol and South Africa's drink driving laws are stringent.
● The wine estates have some of the best restaurants in the Western Cape, so be sure to stop off for lunch.

Chamonix estate, Franschhoek (below); Zevenwacht estate, Stellenbosch (opposite)

SEEING THE WINELANDS

This series of fertile valleys is quite different from the rest of the Western Cape and was among the first areas to be settled after Cape Town. The best itinerary would involve a night in either Stellenbosch or Franschhoek, with a day to explore the towns and some of the surroundings, followed by a night on a wine estate. Alternatively, any one of the towns makes an easy day trip from Cape Town when combined with a couple of wine estates, although it's worth staying longer to appreciate the area fully.

HIGHLIGHTS

STELLENBOSCH

✚ 326 C11 🚇 36 Market Street, Stellenbosch 7600, tel 021-8833584; Mon–Fri 8–6, Sat 9–5, Sun 10–4
www.stellenboschtourism.co.za

The hub of the Winelands, Stellenbosch is the oldest and most attractive town in the region, with a handful of good museums and a large university, giving it a lively atmosphere and a fun nightlife. It's a fairly large place and makes a perfect base for visiting the wine estates. The old town has a pleasing mix of architectural styles: Cape Dutch, Georgian, Regency and Victorian. No other town in South Africa has such an impressive concentration of early Cape buildings. However, as in Swellendam (▷ 86) many of the earliest buildings were lost to fires in the 18th and 19th centuries; what you see today is a collection of well-restored buildings. Houses line broad streets, dappled with shade from avenues of centuries-old oak trees, and ditches still carry running water to the town gardens. With its carefully restored white-walled buildings, Dorp Street, which runs east–west in the southern part of town, is one of the finest of these classic Stellenbosch streets.

The most engaging museum in town is the Village Museum (tel 021-8872948; Mon–Sat 9.30–5, Sun 2–5) at 18 Ryneveld Street, a fascinating tour through four houses, each representing a different period of the town's history. West of here is the Braak, at the western end of Church Street, the original village green and a one-time military parade ground.

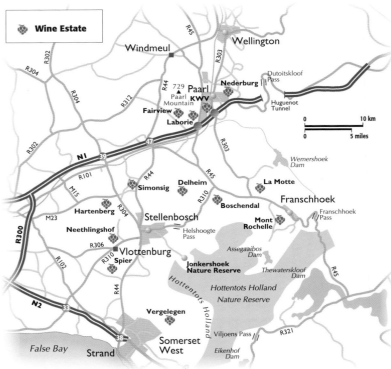

STELLENBOSCH WINE ROUTE
www.wineroute.co.za
When it opened in April 1971, this was South Africa's first wine route. It has been hugely successful, attracting tens of thousands of visitors every year, and today the membership is made up of around one hundred private cellars. It's possible to taste and buy wines at all of them, and the cellars can arrange for your purchases to be delivered internationally. Many of the estates have developed excellent restaurants as well as providing popular picnic lunches. The estates listed below are just a tiny selection of the total.

STELLENBOSCH WINE ESTATES
Delheim (tel 021-8884600; sales and tastings: Oct–end Apr Mon–Fri 9–5, Sat 9–3.30, Sun 10.30–3.30; www.delheim.com) is a large estate with a restaurant providing good views towards Cape Town and Table Mountain. Tastings are conducted in a cool downstairs cellar.

Hartenberg (tel 021-8652541; sales and tastings: Mon–Fri 9–5, Sat 9–3; www.hartenberg estate.com), a privately owned estate founded in 1692, is off the Bottelary Road, 10km (6 miles) north of Stellenbosch. In summer, lunches are served in the shady peaceful gardens; in winter, the tasting room doubles as a restaurant with warming log fires. A variety of red and white wines are produced, but reds seem the most successful: Winners of national awards include their 2000 Shiraz and the 2001 Merlot.

The long pine-lined avenue and cluster of Cape Dutch buildings of Neethlingshof (tel 021-8838988; sales and tastings: Mon–Fri 9–5, Sat–Sun 10–4; www.neethlingshof.co.za) make this a pleasant estate to visit, and there are two fine restaurants on site. The first vines were planted here in 1692 by a German, Barend Lubbe, and the manor house was built in 1814 in traditional Cape Dutch H-style. Today this has been converted into the Lord Neethling restaurant. Not only has Neethlingshof many award-winning wines, it was also named South African Wine Producer of the Year at the International Wine and Spirits Competition in 2002.

Spier estate (tel 021-8091100; sales and tastings: daily 9–5; www.spier.co.za) is the Winelands' most commercial wine estate with a vast array of activities in addition to tastings of their own wines and those of other Stellenbosch estates. Spier wines are well regarded, and their Private Collection Chenin Blanc '01 is especially good. Other attractions are a cheetah park, a birds of prey area, horseback riding, fishing, golf and a spa. An annual open-air music and arts festival is held in summer.

The large Simonsig estate (tel 021-8884900; sales and tastings: Mon–Fri 8.30–5, Sat 8.30–4; www.simonsig.co.za) has been in the Malan family for 10 generations, and in recent years has produced some exceptionally fine wines. There is an attractive outdoor tasting area with grand views of the mountains. One wine worth looking out for is Kaapse Vonkel, a sparkling white considered the best of its kind in South Africa. Their Chardonnay is consistently excellent.

FRANSCHHOEK
➕ 326 C11 ⓘ 29a Huguenot Road, Franschhoek 7690, tel 021-8763603; Mon–Fri 9–6, Sat–Sun 9–4
www.franschhoek.org.za
With its Victorian whitewashed houses backed by rolling vineyards and the soaring slopes of the Franschhoek Mountains, this is the most pleasant of the Wineland villages. Franschhoek is famed for its cuisine, so a visit here should guarantee an excellent meal. On the culture front, the Huguenot Memorial Museum (Mon–Sat 9–5) is housed in two buildings either side of Lambrecht Street, with displays tracing the history of the Huguenots in South Africa. Huguenots—Protestants fleeing persecution in France—arrived in the Franschhoek Valley in 1688. Next to the museum is the rather stark Huguenot Monument dating from 1938.

MORE TO SEE

THE BRANDY ROUTE
The Brandy Route (South African Brandy Foundation, tel 021-8873157; www.sabrandy.co.za) has been running for some years, touring 10 cellars. The route starts at the Van Ryn Brandy Cellar at Vlottenburg, 8km (5 miles) from Stellenbosch, and continues through Franschhoek and Paarl, finishing in the KWV Brandy Cellar (▷ 87), the largest brandy cellar in the world.

VERGELEGEN ESTATE
☎ 021-8471344 ⓘ Daily 9.30–4
🅿 R10, fee includes wine tasting and a cellar tour 🍴 🅿 Turn off N2 at exit 43, signposted Somerset West, and then turn left onto R44. Turn right at traffic lights and after 1km (0.6 miles) turn left into Lourensford Road. After 4km (2.5 miles) look for estate signpost on the right side of the road
www.vergelegen.co.za
This is one of the Cape's finest estates, with a superb manor house stocked with antiques and historical paintings. It has formal gardens, and the surrounding parkland is open for exploration. The modern cellars are buried on Rondekop Hill, overlooking the estate—there are good views of the mountains and False Bay from here.

AFRIKAANS LANGUAGE MUSEUM
✉ Gideon Malherbe House, Pastorie Street, Paarl 7625 ☎ 021-8723441
ⓘ Mon–Fri 9–5 🅿 Adult R10, child (under 12) R2
This small museum in Paarl gives a detailed chronicle of the development of the Afrikaans language and the people involved.

The Vergelegen wine estate (opposite) has a beautiful manor house (above)

BUTTERFLY WORLD

✉ Klapmuts, Paarl 7625 ☎ 021-8755628 ⏰ Daily 9–5 💷 Adult R25, child (3–18) R12.50 🅿 ♿

If you have children in tow, a good place to visit is Butterfly World at Paarl, the largest such park in South Africa, where butterflies fly freely in flower-filled landscaped gardens.

FRANSCHHOEK WINE ROUTE

All the vineyards lie along the Franschhoek Valley, so it is one of the most compact wine routes in the region. What makes it such a rewarding route is that many estates have opened their own excellent restaurants and several also provide luxury accommodation. Note that there are now 26 wine estates along the route, with more being added every year; below is a selection. All the valley's wines can be tasted at the Franschhoek Vineyards Co-operative (Mon–Fri 9.30–5, Sat 10–4, Sun 11–3).

FRANSCHHOEK WINE ESTATES

Boschendal estate (tel 021-8704210; sales and tastings: May–end Oct Mon–Sat 8.30–4.30; Nov–end Apr Mon–Sat 8.30–4.30, Sun 9.30–12.30; www.boschendal.com) has been growing vines for 300

The Huguenot Museum (left) and Monument (middle) in Franschhoek recognise Huguenot contribution to the wine industry

The wine cellars at the Chamonix estate

WELLINGTON

➕ 326 C11 ℹ Old Market Building, Main Road, Wellington 7655, tel 021-8734604; Mon–Fri 8–5, Sat 9–2, Sun 10–1
www.visitwellington.com

Wellington, like the other Winelands towns, stands amid pleasing countryside and has a number of fine old buildings, with the added bonus of far fewer visitors thronging the streets. There are several wine estates in the environs, but the town is best known for its dried fruit.

JONKERSHOEK NATURE RESERVE

☎ 021-8661560 ⏰ Daily 7.30–5 💷 Adult R20, child (3–18) R10

Some 12 km (7 miles) out of Stellenbosch, beyond the Lanzerac Hotel, is this forestry plantation, open to the public for hiking, fishing and mountain biking, with a choice of five self-guided trails. If you prefer the view from a car, you can follow a gravel road through the forest for 12km (7 miles).

years; today a third of the estate is owned by a black empowerment consortium (▷ 24, 25). It is one of the most popular estates in the region, not least for its excellent food and agreeable wine-tasting area beneath a giant oak. Much of the wine produced on the estate is white; their sparkling wines are highly regarded. The main manor house (1812) is open to the public as a museum.

Mont Rochelle (tel 021-8763000; sales and tastings: daily 10–6; www.montrochelle.co.za) has one of the most attractive setting in the region with splendid views of the valley. Owner Miko Rwayitare has doubled the area under vines in the last two years and completely redeveloped the estate, now offering three white and four red wines. Tastings are informal and friendly.

The original manor house and cellars of La Motte estate (tel 021-8763119; sales and tastings: Mon–Fri 9–4.30, Sat 10–3; www.la-motte.com) were built in 1752, and the grand old cellars (worth a visit alone) are now used as a classical concert venue in the evenings. Wine tasting takes place in an area overlooking the cellars.

PAARL

➕ 326 C11 ℹ 216 Main Street, Paarl 7646, tel 021-8723829; Mon–Fri 9–5, Sat 9–1, Sun 10–1
www.paarlonline.com

Like much of the Winelands, Paarl has a strong Afrikaner identity, encapsulated by the Taal Monument (daily 8–5), which celebrates the Afrikaans language. This controversial but striking monument, inaugurated in October 1975, stands outside the town on the slopes of Paarl Mountain. It is made up of three concrete columns linked by a low curved wall, with each column representing different influences felt in the language. The relative heights of each column and the negative connotations associated with them have been the subject of fierce debate.

PAARL WINE ROUTE

www.paarlwine.co.za

The Paarl Wine Route has 29 members, including two of South Africa's better known wine estates, KWV and Nederburg. However, only the largest estates conduct regular cellar tours.

PAARL WINE ESTATES

Fairview Estate (tel 021-8632450; wine and cheese sales and tastings: Mon–Fri 8.30–5, Sat 8.30–1; www.fairview.co.za) has the rather unusual attraction of a goat tower—a spiral structure that is home to two pairs of goats. In addition to a variety of good wines (look for the popular Goats do Roam blend), visitors can taste delicious goat's and Jersey milk cheeses.

The Laborie vineyard (tel 021-8073390; sales and tastings: Nov–end Apr daily 9–5; May–end Oct Mon–Sat 9–5; www.kwv-international.com), part of KWV (see below), is a carefully restored original Cape Dutch homestead, in many ways the archetypal wine estate, and has been developed with tourism firmly in mind. It's an attractive spot, with a tasting area overlooking rolling lawns and vineyards, and a highly rated restaurant.

BOTANICAL GARDENS

✉ Neethling Street, Stellenbosch 7600
☎ 021-8083054 🕐 Daily 8–5 💷 Free
The Botanical Gardens are part of the University of Stellenbosch, with a fine collection of ferns, orchids and bonsai trees. One of the more unusual plants to look for is the welwitschia from the Namib Desert.

Vineyards form a backdrop to all the wine routes, as here at Paarl

The Botanical Gardens at Stellenbosch

Block House, Wellington was a British defence against the Boers

A short distance from the Laborie estate is the KWV Cellar Complex (tel 021-8073900; sales and tastings: Mon–Sat 9–4.30; www.kwv-international.com), which contains the five largest vats in the world. The Kooperatieve Wijnbouwers Vereniging van Zuid-Afrika (Co-operative Wine Growers' Association) was established in Paarl in 1918 and is responsible for exporting many of South Africa's best-known wines. They are also known for their brandy (Worcester, ▷ 87).

The annual production at the Nederburg estate (tel 021-8623104; sales and tastings: Mon–Fri 8.30–5, Sat 10–4, Sun 11–4; www.nederburg.co.za) exceeds 650,000 cases. Every April the Nederburg Auction attracts international buyers and is considered one of the top five wine auctions in the world. Nederburg wines win countless annual awards—the 2003 Sauvignon Blanc and the 2001 Petit Verdot are more recent award-winners.

The contentious Taal Monument in Paarl

BACKGROUND

The Cape's wine industry was started by Governor Simon van der Stel in 1679. Previously, vines had been grown in Company's Garden (▷ 67) and in the area known today as the Cape Town suburb of Wynberg. The first wine was produced in 1652, and there was soon a great demand from the crews of ships when they arrived in Table Bay. As the early settlers moved inland and farms were opened up, more vines were planted. Stellenbosch became the first settlement to be established outside Cape Town in 1680. It flourished rapidly as a market town, and by chance the soils and climate proved to be ideal for grape growing.

The industry received its first real boost between 1688 and 1720 with the influx of Huguenot settlers from France, who brought their wine-making skills with them. A further boost came in 1806 when the English, at war with France, started to import South African wines. In the 20th century, under apartheid, sanctions hindered exports. Farm workers, mostly 'coloureds' (people of mixed race), suffered under the 'tot' system, when part of their wages were paid in wine. The inequality in the wine industry is very slowly changing, and some farms are now partially owned by black empowerment consortiums.

EASTERN CAPE

The Eastern Cape, although far less visited than many parts of South Africa, is a fascinating region of wild, empty beaches, forested mountains and the sun-baked plains of the Karoo. To the north is the Greater Addo Elephant National Park, now the third largest game reserve in the country, and the only place in South Africa where you can see the Big Seven.

MAJOR SIGHTS

Amatola Mountains, as seen from outside Hogsback

The dodo and its egg at the East London Museum

Deep valleys in the Langkloof mountain range

AMATOLA MOUNTAINS

⊞ 329 J10 ⚑ Fort Beaufort Museum, Durban Street, Fort Beaufort 5720 tel 046-6451555; Mon–Fri 8–5, Sat 8.30–12.30

The region of the Amatola Mountains, between Stutterheim and Fort Beaufort, is of rolling hills, lush indigenous forests and waterfalls. Some areas have been replaced with pine plantations, but there remains an abundance of untouched forest, criss-crossed with trails and perfect for hiking. Hogsback (see below) is the main hub, but there are also several nature reserves, including Tsolwana Game Park (tel 040-6352115).

EASTERN CAPE KAROO

See pages 98–99.

EAST LONDON

⊞ 329 K10 ⚑ Buffalo City Tourism, King's Entertainment Centre, Esplanade, East London 5201, tel 043-7226015; Mon–Fri 8.15–4.30, Sat 9–2, Sun 9–1 www.visitbuffalocity.co.za

East London is South Africa's only river port and a major industrial city, with an economy based on motor assembly plants and textile and electronics industries. This may seem unpromising, but the central part of the city has a certain energetic appeal to it, as well as a handful of attractive old buildings. There are also fine beaches, which throng with visitors over Christmas.

The Ann Bryant Art Gallery (tel 043-7264356; Mon–Fri 9–5, Sat 9.30–12), on St. Marks Road, contains many good contemporary South African works, while the East London Museum (Mon–Fri 9.30–5, Sat 2–5, Sun 11–4), on Oxford Street, has a range of natural history exhibits. The highlights of the museum include the world's only dodo egg and a coelacanth, which was

netted by a trawler off the coast near East London in 1938. The coelacanth, known as the 'fossil fish', was thought to have been extinct for 80 million years until it was rediscovered in the 20th century. Outside on Oxford Street is a monument to Steve Bantu Biko, the anti-apartheid activist who died in police custody in 1977 (▷ 37).

GRAHAMSTOWN

See page 100.

GREATER ADDO ELEPHANT NATIONAL PARK

See page 101.

HOGSBACK

⊞ 329 J10 ⚑ Nina's Deli, Main Road, Hogsback 5721, tel 045-9621326; Fri–Wed 9–8.30 www.hogsbackinfo.co.za

The quiet village of Hogsback lies in the heart of the Amatola Mountains, surrounded by rolling hills covered in forest reserves. The village itself is made up of a string of cottages, hotels, tea gardens and craft shops dotted along several kilometres of gravel road. Tucked away down the side lanes are some glorious gardens, more reminiscent of rural England than inland Africa. The beauty of the surroundings and the slow pace of life make this a perfect spot to relax for a few days and explore the forests.

JEFFREYS BAY

⊞ 328 G11 ⚑ Jeffreys Bay Tourism, corner Da Gama and Drommedaris roads, Jeffreys Bay 6330, tel 042-2932588; Mon–Fri 8.30–5, Sat 9–12

Surf is king at Jeffreys Bay, or J-Bay as it's known locally. Home to the perfect wave, this is an internationally acclaimed surfing spot and a major playground for self-respecting surfers. In the

evenings, the local bars buzz with talk of 'supertubes' and 'perfect breaks'. Waves can be big—sometimes as high as 3m (10ft)—but J-Bay is renowned for its safety. There are numerous surf shops selling a wide range of boards and wetsuits, as well as Billabong and Quiksilver factory outlets, but when surf's up don't be surprised to find many of the local businesses closed. See page 199 for details on surfing schools.

THE LANGKLOOF

⊞ 328 G10

Three mountain ranges lie to the north of the N2 and Jeffreys Bay: the Kougaberge, the Baviaanskloofberge and the Grootwinterhoekberge, known collectively as the Langkloof. The valleys of the Langkloof, referred to as 'the Kouga', are where modern man is thought to have first emerged some time in the last 100,000 years. The region became the meeting point of San hunter-gatherers and Khoi pastoralists (▷ 28), known collectively as the Khoisan, and their rock art stands as testament to this in overhangs and caves throughout the area. One of the most scenic routes through the Langkloof is the gravel road along the Baviaanskloof River valley between Patensie and Willowmore. The road meanders through a landscape dominated by red sandstone hills on either side.

Eastern Cape Karoo

This area of vast open spaces and craggy mountains has some of the country's most dramatic scenery, as well as a number of Victorian towns.

Valley of Desolation in the Karoo Nature Reserve

A sheep farmer in Somerset East, in the Karoo

Mountain Zebra National Park was proclaimed in 1937

RATINGS	
Historic interest	● ● ●
Outdoor pursuits	● ● ●
Photo stops	● ● ● ● ●

TIP

● Make sure your rental car has air-conditioning: You'll be covered in dust if you keep your windows open for long.

MORE TO SEE

KALKKOP IMPACT CRATER

⊞ Follow N9 in the direction of Aberdeen for about 30km (19 miles); at Aberdeen, turn left onto R338 and continue to a right turn marked as Aberdeen Road. From here a dirt road leads to the crater—it should be signposted
This giant crater was created by a meteorite more than 200,000 years ago. Research has shown that the original hole was several hundred metres deep. Over time the crater has filled, but the ridge, 640m (2,100ft) in diameter, is still visible.

A statue on display at the Owl House, Nieu Bethesda

SEEING THE EASTERN CAPE KAROO

The surreal Karoo landscape, clear air and desert sunsets are evocative of the very heart of South Africa. The archaic landscape, created from sedimentary rock around 250 million years ago, is rich in fossils and San paintings, studded with scrub and cacti. The climate is one of extremes: In summer, temperatures are blindingly hot and towns uncomfortably dusty, while in winter the night-time temperatures drop below 0°C (32°F), so come in the spring or autumn if you can. However, if you are here in summer, make sure you have a jacket or sweater for the evenings, when temperatures drop considerably.

HIGHLIGHTS

GRAAFF-REINET

⊞ 328 G9 🚹 Graaff-Reinet Publicity Association, 13a Church Street, Graaff-Reinet 6280, tel 049-8924248; Mon–Fri 8–5, Sat–Sun 9–12
www.graaffreinet.co.za
Founded in 1786, Graaff-Reinet is the oldest town of the Eastern Cape, lying between the Sneeuberg Mountains and the Sundays River. Years of prosperity derived from farming are reflected in the excellent local architecture—more than 220 of the town's old buildings have been declared national monuments. Today, Graaff-Reinet is a smart town, with row upon row of perfectly restored houses, leafy streets and a quiet, yet bustling atmosphere. See pages 236–237 for details of a walk past the sights and museums in Graaff-Reinet.

KAROO NATURE RESERVE AND THE VALLEY OF DESOLATION

⊞ 328 G9 ☎ 049-8923453 ◉ Daily 6am–8pm 🎫 Free
The Karoo Nature Reserve surrounds Graaff-Reinet, and the Valley of Desolation is the best place to appreciate the vastness of the Karoo. The stark rock formations and precariously balanced dolerite columns tower 120m (390ft) above the valley floor, giving stunning views stretching to the horizon. If you just drive up to the first viewpoint you'll see fine views, but continue for another few kilometres and you come to a parking area from where there's a short walk to even better vistas. Elsewhere in the park there are walking trails and 4WD routes.

CRADOCK

🕂 328 H9 ℹ️ Cradock Tourism, Market Square, Cradock 5880, tel 048-8812383; Mon–Fri 8.30–12.30, 2–4 www.cradock.co.za

This small Karoo town is made up of an attractive grid of wide roads lined with Victorian bungalows and a clutch of churches. It's a pleasant, sleepy place to wander around. The town is known for its connections with the author Olive Schreiner, who wrote *The Story of an African Farm* (published 1883). The Olive Schreiner House at 9 Cross Street illustrates aspects of her life (tel 048-8815251, Mon–Fri 8–12.45, 2–4.30). The nearby Fish River is one of the top white-water rivers in the world.

MOUNTAIN ZEBRA NATIONAL PARK

🕂 328 H9 ☎️ Reservations: 012-4289111/021-5520008; park: 048-8812427 🕐 Gates: Oct–end Apr 7–7; May–end Sep 7–6 💵 Adult R60, child (under 12) R30 🍴 🏧 🅿️ 25km (15.5 miles) west of Cradock, signposted from the town www.sanparks.org

The plains and mountains of this Karoo park support more than 280 mountain zebras, the largest group in the world. A wide variety of other mammals includes black wildebeest, kudu, springbok, buffalo and black rhino. The park is also the home of the giant earthworm. Game viewing is by car—there are 37km (23 miles) of rough roads crossing the reserve.

NIEU BETHESDA

🕂 328 G9 ℹ️ Municipality, Muller Street, Nieu-Bethesda, tel 049-8411659; Mon–Fri 7.30–4.30

This small village has become famous through the work of artist Helen Martins (1897–1976). Helen lived a hermit-like existence, devoting her time to her art and the study of Eastern philosophies. Her legacy is the Owl House, the home she decorated with motifs in finely ground glass of every colour, so that the whole interior glitters. It is now a museum (tel 049-8411603; daily 9–6), crammed with her art and ideas. There is a collection of other artists' galleries and a few little shops in the village, but not much else.

BACKGROUND

Despite its barren appearance, the Eastern Karoo is mainly a farming area, known for its sheep, cattle, Angora goats and horses, and has been such since the arrival of the Voortrekkers (▷ 30–31). Prior to this, the area was inhabited by pastoral Khoi people and San hunter-gatherers, who were brutally subjugated by the new arrivals—a process that has had far-reaching effects on today's Xhosa people, who live in the region. The area was one of significant political activism during the 20th century, and was home to a number of important anti-apartheid activists, most famously Matthew Goniwe and three of his colleagues who were killed in 1985. Although poverty has overshadowed the lives of the local Xhosa, things have begun to improve since the fall of apartheid.

The sheer scale of the Valley of Desolation gives you some idea of what the Voortrekkers had to overcome to penetrate the country's interior

MIDDELBURG

ℹ️ Middelburg Karoo Tourism, 8 Meintjies Street, Middelburg 5900, tel 049-8422188; Mon–Fri 8–1, 2–4.30 www.middelburgec.co.za

Middelburg is a good base for a hike on the Compassberg, the highest peak in the Sneeuberg mountain range. The main route is a 3-day circular trail of 48km (30 miles) around the Kompasberg foothills. For reservations, tel 049-8422418.

SOMERSET EAST

ℹ️ Blue Crane Tourism, 88 Njoli Road, Somerset East 5850, tel 042-2431448; Mon–Fri 7.45–4.30 www.somerseteast.co.za

This neat agricultural town is home to the Somerset museum (Mon–Fri 8–5), which re-creates the atmosphere and lifestyle of a Victorian parsonage set among rose gardens. The Walter Battiss Art Museum (Mon–Fri 9–5) has the world's largest collection of work by this South African artist (1906–82).

Shopfronts in Grahamstown (above); the camera obscura at the Observatory Museum (inset)

GRAHAMSTOWN

This is a lively student town with good museums, nightlife and a selection of old buildings that give the place a colonial feel.

RATINGS		
Cultural interest	● ● ●	
Historic interest	● ● ●	
Walkability	● ● ●	

BASICS

✚ 329 J10

ℹ Makana Tourism, 63 High Street, Grahamstown 6139, tel 046-6223241; Mon–Fri 8.30–5

www.grahamstown.co.za

TIPS

● The Grahamstown Festival in July is the largest arts festival in Africa.

● The ugly 1820 Settlers Monument is worth visiting only for the panoramic views of the area.

Views of the town from Fort Selwyn

Grahamstown is, first and foremost, a student town, home to one of the country's most important places of learning, Rhodes University. During term time the town is lively, its pubs and bars packed with students. Grahamstown was founded as military headquarters in 1812, but within two years it was a busy border settlement. It evolved into the second largest town in the whole of southern Africa by 1836, although today it feels more like a small country town, pleasant to wander around.

MUSEUMS

The Albany Museum comprises several town museums including the Observatory Museum, Natural Science Museum and History Museum, along with Fort Selwyn and the Provost. The highlight of the Observatory Museum (Mon–Fri 8–1, 2–5, Sat 9–1) is the entertaining camera obscura. This rare specimen, which claims to be the only Victorian camera obscura in the southern hemisphere, projects an image of Grahamstown onto a screen. In the Natural Science Museum (Mon–Fri 8–1, 2–5, Sat 9–1) most of the displays are aimed at children. Among the more intriguing exhibits are a large iron meteorite that came down in a meteorite shower over Namibia, a Foucault Pendulum (which demonstrates the rotation of the earth), and some dinosaur fossils. The History Museum (Mon–Fri 8–1, 2–5, Sat 9–1) has a collection outlining the area's history, including beadwork displays from the Eastern Cape and traditional Xhosa dress. Off Somerset Street is the Provost (Mon–Fri 8–1, 2–5, Sat 9–1), built in 1837 by the Royal Engineers as a military prison. Fort Selwyn (open by appointment only), on Fort Selwyn Drive, dates from the sixth Frontier War in 1834.

TOWNSHIP

Grahamstown's large township, to the east of the town across the river, is known as Rhini or Grahamstown East. It's a good idea to choose a walking tour, rather than one in a mini-bus, as this allows a greater degree of interaction with people. Mbuleli Mpokela organizes half-day tours (tel 046-6370630 or 082-97959061).

Elephants have complex social structures, with a herd usually ruled by a matriarch

GREATER ADDO ELEPHANT NATIONAL PARK

The Park is the best place in South Africa to see elephants, plus it's a chance to view the 'Big Seven' in a malaria-free environment.

The original elephant park at Addo covered 12,000ha (30,000 acres) and was proclaimed in 1931, when only 11 elephants remained in the area. Today, it is the third largest conservation area in South Africa, encompassing five contiguous game reserves and stretching from the Indian Ocean to the Little Karoo. It is a hugely rewarding park, thanks to the large herds of elephant and the relative ease of seeing them. With the reintroduction of lions in October 2003 and the expansion to include a marine reserve, it is now possible to see the 'Big Seven'—the original 'Big Five' of elephant, rhino, lion, buffalo and leopard, plus whales and great white sharks. At the smaller end of the scale, the park is also home to the unique flightless dung beetle.

WATERHOLES
The relative flatness of the low-lying indigenous bush and the large number of elephants present—around 350—means that the great animals are easily seen. The best places are the waterholes, which are accessible by car. There are lookout points above them, from where you can often see several herds drinking at one time. This can mean watching more than a hundred elephants splashing about in the water, a truly awe-inspiring experience.

GETTING AROUND
A network of gravel roads is open to the public from sunrise to sunset for game viewing, although some become impassable in a standard car if there's a lot of rain. Convenient as it is to explore in your own car, it's worth taking a tour in one of the park's 4WD vehicles, as the guides are highly knowledgeable about where the animals are best found.

There are two hides, one of which overlooks a floodlit water hole and can be reserved for the night. The other hide tends to be busier as it is near the main camp's restaurant, but it is good for bird-watching. Night drives, game walks and horseback rides can all be reserved through reception.

RATINGS	
Good for kids	●●●○
Outdoor pursuits	●●●○
Value for money	●●●○

BASICS

🔢 328 H10

☎ 042-2330556

🕐 Gates and office: daily 7–7

💰 Adult R80, child (under 12) R40

🍴 Restaurant serves breakfast, lunch and dinner

🏪 Shop sells a selection of groceries, meat, bread and wines; fuel (no diesel), laundry, telephone and mail services also available

❓ Range of SANParks chalet and camping accommodation (reservations: tel 012-4289111, www.sanparks.org), plus luxury private camp (▷ 283)

🚗 The main park entrance is 72km (45 miles) from Port Elizabeth, along R335

TIPS
● One of the best times to visit is in January or February, when many of the female elephants will have recently calved.

● Visitors are prohibited from bringing citrus fruits into the reserve, as the older elephants have a taste for them following a shortsighted feeding schedule in the 1970s. They were fed citrus fruits, which resulted in all the animals feeding in one place, causing overgrazing and aggressive behaviour.

● It is illegal to leave your vehicle anywhere other than at signposted climb-out points.

● The speed limit is 40kph (25mph).

The smart Royal Alfred Marina and the Kowie River play a big role in the water-based activities in Port Alfred

Shamwari Game Reserve is the best in the Eastern Cape

THE SIGHTS

PORT ALFRED

➕ 329 J11 🛈 Port Alfred Tourism, Info Centre, Causeway Street, Port Alfred 6170, tel 046-6241235; Mon–Fri 8.30–4.30, Sat 8.30–12.30
www.portalfred.net

Port Alfred, east of Port Elizabeth, consists almost entirely of summer homes and bungalows nestling among dunes. One of the largest holiday resorts along this stretch of coastline, it overlooks large expanses of water in all directions—the Kowie River estuary, the lagoon and the chic Royal Alfred Marina. The town's history is closely linked to the settlers of 1820 and there is a small Methodist church 1km (0.5 miles) out of town. Many of the names on the gravestones in its cemetery are those of settlers.

The weather on this coast is mild all year round, making it a popular spot with South Africans, who are drawn by the good watersports facilities. Surfing, canoeing, scuba diving and fishing are big business along the Kowie River and West Beach, which is also good for swimming. There are some interesting trails through the nearby dune forests.

SHAMWARI GAME RESERVE

➕ 329 H10 ☎ 042-2031111 ⏱ Day visits by reservation only 🚗 From Port Elizabeth, follow the signs for the N2, Grahamstown. After 65km (40 miles), the park is signposted off to the left
www.shamwari.com

This privately owned reserve, the winner of many international conservation awards, provides the best game viewing in this part of the country. The park covers an area of 20,000ha (50,000 acres) and has been well stocked with game from all over the region, including black rhino, elephant, buffalo, leopard, lion and antelope of all sizes. Wild dogs have also been introduced, last seen in the area more than 200 years ago. The reserve has four lodges within its boundaries, all of them expensive. Day visitors are welcome, but must make advance reservations for the half-day tour, which includes a game drive, lunch at the Shamwari/Born Free Conservation Centre overlooking the Bushman's River and a visit to the Kaya Lendaba, a traditional African healing village. If you stay overnight, all game drives are included, and you can also go on a walking safari.

UMTATA

➕ 330 K9 🛈 64 Owen Street, Umtata 5100, tel 047-5315290; Mon–Fri 8.30–4.30
www.ectourism.co.za

Umtata is a sprawling modern town with a small grid of early buildings at its core. Founded in 1871, it was the capital of Transkei from 1976 to 1994 and has grown into a busy administrative city. The main reason for coming here is the illuminating Nelson Mandela Museum (Owen Street; tel 047-5325110; Mon–Fri 9–4, Sat 9–12.30), officially opened by Mandela himself in 2000. The Museum is split across three sites with branches here, at Mvezo, where Mandela was born, and at Qunu, the village where he grew up. All three are dedicated to South Africa's first post-apartheid president, and provide a moving and insightful look at Mandela's life and his struggles. The displays focus on his autobiography, *Long Walk to Freedom* (1994), with extracts complemented by photographs, personal items, letters and video footage, including a short excerpt from an interview he gave in 1961. Although the displays are rather confusing from a chronological point of view, they give a good overview of his life. Another component of the museum is Mandela's primary school in the tiny rural village of Qunu (30km/19 miles west of Umtata), where he lived in his youth. Here, too, are the graves of some of his relatives, as well as his mansion, which can be photographed but not visited. The final element is Mandela's birthplace in the former Transkei village of Mvezo (to the west of Umtata).

WILD COAST

See page 104.

WITTEBERGE

➕ 329 J8

The Witteberge Mountains form part of the southernmost limits of the Drakensberg (▷ 120–123) and is the heart of South Africa's skiing industry.

The road heading into the Witteberge passes through the small towns of Elliot, Lady Grey and Rhodes, the last being a peaceful mountain village with a scattering of Victorian buildings. If you visit here in winter bring plenty of warm clothes: electricity did arrive a few years ago, but there is still no central heating. From Rhodes it is a one-hour drive through scenic mountain passes (passable by 4WD vehicles only) to the ski resort at Tiffindell, the most popular ski area in South Africa (for information tel 045-9749004; www.snow.co.za).

The resort has a ski lift, snow-making machines and ski rental, but be aware that the skiing here does not match the quality found elsewhere in the world. In summer, Tiffindell is popular with flyfishing enthusiasts, mountain bikers, grass skiers and horseback riders.

Algoa Beach (above); the Donkin reserve and memorial form part of the Heritage Trail (inset)

PORT ELIZABETH

Port Elizabeth is a large, vibrant city with good nightlife and long, sandy beaches.

PE, as it's often called, is a major port and industrial town, and the biggest coastal city between Cape Town and Durban. The heart of town, known as Central, is a grid of Victorian houses and green spaces, and is the most pleasant part of the city. Port Elizabeth is celebrated for its long hours of sunshine and for the warm waters of Algoa Bay, whose beaches form the main attraction for visitors. The city also has a large student population, lending the city a lively edge, with a vibrant bar and clubbing scene.

MARKET SQUARE AND AROUND

Market Square, in Central, is PE's most attractive corner, with a couple of fine buildings. City Hall was built between 1858 and 1862; the clock tower was added in 1883. The Main Public Library, shipped out from the UK, dates from 1837 and started life as a courthouse. Outside is a marble statue of Queen Victoria, erected in 1903.

BAYWORLD

Southeast of Central, off Marine Drive in Humewood, is Bayworld, a museum complex. There are three attractions: the Main Museum, the Oceanarium and the Snake Park. The Main Museum (daily 9–4.30) is a mix of natural and cultural history. The Oceanarium (daily 9–1, 2–5) has displays of more than 40 species of fish, with seal and dolphin presentations daily at 11 and 3. The Snake Park (daily 9–5) houses a collection of exotic reptiles, including some rare and endangered species.

BEACHES

Algoa Bay is one of the most visited stretches of coast in South Africa. The water is warm and calm for most of the year, making it ideal for watersports. The two main northern beaches are New Brighton, good for swimming and fishing, and Bluewater Bay, a long stretch of white sand. King's Beach, the closest to the city, between the harbour and quieter Humewood, is heavily developed. Hobie Beach is popular in the evenings thanks to the nearby Boardwalk entertainment area, filled with bars, clubs and restaurants. Sardinia Bay is a marine reserve with good snorkelling and scuba diving.

RATINGS	
Cultural interest	●●
Good for kids	●●●
Outdoor pursuits	●●●

BASICS

➕ 328 H11

ℹ Nelson Mandela Bay, Donkin Lighthouse Building, Belmont Terrace, Port Elizabeth 6001, tel 041-5858884; Mon–Fri, 8–4.30, Sat–Sun 9.30–3.30 www.nelsonmandelatourism.com

ℹ Eastern Cape Tourist Board, Allier Terrace, Port Elizabeth 6001, tel 041-5857761; daily 8–7 www.ectourism.org.za

TIPS

• The Donkin Heritage Trail is an enjoyable self-guided tour around Central. An excellent guidebook available from the tourist office lists 47 places of historical interest.
• The Algoa Bus Company runs a service between downtown PE and the beaches.
• Look for the pyramid near the tourist office, a memorial erected by Sir Rufane Donkin in memory of his wife Elizabeth, after whom the city was named. Local folklore is rather more gory and suggests that her heart was buried under the pyramid.

A beach at Haga-Haga (above); the jetty at the mouth of the River Kei (inset)

RATINGS

Outdoor pursuits	● ● ● ● ●
Photo stops	● ● ●
Walkability	● ● ●

BASICS

➕ 330 L9

ℹ Eastern Cape Tourism Board, King's Entertainment Centre, Esplanade, East London 5201, tel 043-7019600; Mon–Fri 9–5
www.ectourism.co.za

TIPS

● Many of the roads in the area are not surfaced, but they are usually passable by car.
● Always give yourself plenty of time to arrive at your accommodation before dark, as road safety is a serious issue after nightfall. Cattle straying onto roads and large potholes are two common problems.
● Learn a few words of Xhosa, as many people here speak nothing else.
● It is possible to walk from Coffee Bay to Port St. Johns along the Wild Coast Hiking Trail (for reservations, tel 043-7436181).

WILD COAST

The country's least developed coast has beautiful deserted beaches, tropical forest and nature reserves.

The Wild Coast stretches for about 280km (175 miles) from East London north to the Umtamvuna Nature Reserve next to Port Edward in KwaZulu-Natal. Its inland borders are the Drakensberg and Stormberg mountain ranges, and dotted between are small villages, brightly painted *kraals* (a traditional village of huts, often enclosed by a fence), and endless pastureland. It remains a traditional area, with most people speaking only Xhosa, and there is widespread poverty. During apartheid the Great Kei River was the border between South Africa and the so-called independent homeland of Transkei. Even today, the difference in the standard of living between the two areas is striking. Nevertheless, the Wild Coast has some of the finest and least developed beaches in South Africa and a handful of small nature reserves. The main resorts are close to East London, but Cintsa is much quieter. The best surf in the area is at Coffee Bay.

CINTSA

➕ 329 K10

The combined villages of Cintsa East and Cintsa West nestle among lush hills rolling down to a lagoon and a wide stretch of deserted beach. Although popular during the Christmas holidays with South Africans, the resort is blessedly isolated for the rest of the year and has relaxing outdoor activities such as canoeing and horseback riding. There are a couple of backpacker hostels which organize more adventurous pursuits, including kloofing (which is hiking, swimming and boulder-hopping down a 'kloof' or canyon) and surfing, but the main appeal here is the lazy exploration of the shell-strewn beach, forests and tranquil lagoon.

PORT ST. JOHNS

➕ 330 L9

This small, peaceful town along the banks of the Mzimvubu River has a laid-back atmosphere. Its bohemian air has attracted many artists and, more recently, backpackers, drawn by the stunning beaches. Second Beach is the most attractive, a stretch of soft sand, backed by smooth, forested hills. There are two nature reserves within easy reach of town: Silaka (tel 040-6352115), with great walks through tropical forest, and Mount Thesiger, which has a small herd of wildebeest belonging to an unusual sub-species which has no mane. The warm, sulphurous springs at Isinuka are just outside town.

KWAZULU-NATAL

KwaZulu-Natal is one of South Africa's most popular destinations and its game reserves are among the country's finest. It extends from the Drakensberg Mountains in the northwest to the humid sub-tropical coast in the southeast. The landscape of the central region has seen some bloody conflicts between the Zulus, Boers and British.

MAJOR SIGHTS

The Battlefields Route

The grassy landscape and rocky plains of this northwestern part of KwaZulu-Natal show little evidence of the fierce battles fought here between the Boers, Zulus and British during the 19th century.

A tableau at Talana Museum depicting battle scenes

RATINGS

Cultural interest	●	●	●	●
Historic interest	●	●	●	●
Photo stops	●	●	●	

BASICS

✚ 331 M6
ℹ Tourism Dundee, Civic Gardens, Victoria Street, Dundee, tel: 034-2122121 ext 2262; Mon–Fri 9–4.45, Sat 9–12
www.tourdundee.co.za

TIP

• If you drive yourself, note that access to the sites is along dirt roads. Allow enough time to return in daylight, as the bad roads and wandering cattle are dangerous at night.

A memorial to officers who died at the battle of Spioenkop in 1900

SEEING THE BATTLEFIELDS ROUTE

This area of vast open landscape in northern KwaZulu-Natal is the stage on which major wars between the Boers, British and Zulus were fought. The route covers 11 towns and more than 50 evocative battle sites, all of which can be visited. To the uninitiated there is often little to see other than landscape, so taking an organized tour is the best way of experiencing the sites. The tourist information offices in Dundee and Ladysmith have advice on how best to view the battlefields and can arrange tours. If you decide to tour them yourself, the major sites are signposted and can be reached from Dundee or Ulundi.

HIGHLIGHTS

ISANDLWANA

✚ 331 M6 ☎ Museum: 034-2718165 ⊙ Daily 8–4 💰 Adult R15, child (under 12) R5 🚗 80km (50 miles) from Dundee, west along R68, signposted south of Nqutu
Early in 1879 British troops entered Zululand to destroy the strongest independent African state in southern Africa. The Zulu king Cetshwayo immediately rallied his troops, stopping south of Isandlwana. The British, confident of their superiority, had not constructed any defensive positions to protect their camp. On 22 January, a small British cavalry unit was scouring the land to the south of their camp when they spotted some cattle being herded by Zulus and gave chase. Within moments, they reached the lip of a valley to see the entire Zulu army seated in complete silence. The Zulu force advanced: The British were outnumbered, suffering a humiliating defeat.

RORKE'S DRIFT

✚ 331 M6 ☎ Museum: 034-6421687 ⊙ Daily 9–4 💰 Adult R15, child (under 12) R5 🚗 42km (26 miles) from Dundee, off R68 between Dundee and Nqutu
Rorke's Drift is across the Buffalo River from Isandlwana. It was the site of a Swedish mission that had been commandeered by the British and converted into a hospital and a supply depot. Only 110 men were stationed there when two survivors of Isandlwana arrived to warn of an imminent attack. Four thousand Zulus appeared 90 minutes later. The ferocious attack was resisted for 12 hours before the Zulu soldiers withdrew, having lost some 400 men; 17 officers were among the British dead. The defence of Rorke's Drift is one of the epic tales of British military history and was immortalized in the 1964 movie *Zulu*. The mission station has been converted into a small museum, which illustrates scenes from the battle.

BLOOD RIVER

✚ 331 M6 ☎ Museum: 034-2718121 ⊙ Daily 8–5 💰 Adult R15, child (under 12) R5 🚻 🚗 48 km (30 miles) from Dundee, along R33 towards Dejagersdrif
Blood River is the site of the crushing defeat suffered by Zulus defending their territory against advancing Boers on 16 December 1838. Their short spears were no match for the Boers' rifles, and more than 3,000 Zulus were killed. The Boers, led by Andries Pretorius, did not lose a single man. The battle is commemorated on the site by a circle of 64 full-sized wagons.

SIEGE MUSEUM

330 L6 ⓘ Ladysmith Information Bureau, Murchison Street, Ladysmith 3379, tel 036-6372992; Mon–Fri 9–4, Sat 9–1 Adult R2, child (under 12) R1 www.ladysmith.co.za

This fascinating museum in Ladysmith reconstructs scenes from the Siege of Ladysmith, which lasted 118 days from October 1899, early in the Second Anglo-Boer War, until February 1900. There are displays of weapons and uniforms that were used during the siege.

TALANA MUSEUM

331 M6 • Vryheid Road 034-2122654 Mon–Fri 8–4.30, Sat–Sun 10–4.30 Adult R15, child (under 18) R2 1km (0.6 miles) north of Dundee

The Battle of Talana Hill near Dundee took place on 20 October 1899 and was the first major battle of the Second Anglo-Boer War. Talana Museum has been built on the site of the battle, with a self-guided trail that visits the remains of two British forts. The main building has good displays on the Zulu War and the Anglo-Boer Wars, while Talana House has historical displays on the lifestyles of the Zulus and the early settlers in Dundee.

A memorial at Spioenkop, one of the many battles in the Anglo-Boer War (top); the Isandlwana battle field (above)

BACKGROUND

The wars fought in the latter half of the 19th century and at the start of the 20th century were mostly about land and who owned or didn't own it. Tension was further increased by the discovery of diamonds and gold in other parts of the country (▷ 32–33).

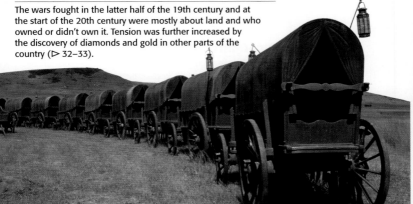

Durban

This tropical seaside city has a striking mix of architectural styles and excellent beaches. It is home to South Africa's largest Indian population, so you will find bustling Indian markets, hot curries and rickshaws.

Surfing the waves just outside Durban

Bright ceramics at the African Art Centre in Durban

Various curry and chilli powders on sale at Victoria Street Market

RATINGS	
Cultural interest	●●●●
Good for food	●●●
Specialist shopping	●●●

The impressive dome of City Hall, set in Church Square

SEEING DURBAN

The sprawling conurbation of Durban is Africa's largest port, and although its appeal is not immediately apparent—few original buildings survive and it can feel hectic and over-crowded—it possesses wide beaches, an extensive beachfront and a steamy tropical climate. Today, Durban has South Africa's largest Indian population, giving the city a mix of English, African and Indian cultures. As with all South African cities, the best way of getting about is by car, and there is a good system of highways and plenty of paying parking places. Durban also has a good, frequently running local bus service called Mynah that runs between the city centre, the beachfront and Berea and Morningside suburbs (information office on corner of Aliwal Street and Pine Street, Durban 4001, tel 031-3095942; average fare is R3). For daily guided walking tours of the city, contact the tourist office (see Basics), who offer either the Oriental Walkabout or the Historical Walkabout; both cost R50 per person and must be booked a day in advance. Minibus tours of the city and its surrounds are run by Strelitzia Tours (tel 031-2669480; www.strelitziatours.com), with a comprehensive range of daily city tours and trips to the townships.

HIGHLIGHTS

CENTRAL DURBAN

Palm-lined Francis Farewell Square is the hub of the colonial heart of Durban, with a bustling street market and commemorative statues, including the art deco Cenotaph monument. City Hall, on Smith Street, is one of Durban's grandest buildings. Built in 1910, it was lauded as one of the British Empire's finest colonial town halls. The nearby Natural Science Museum (tel 031-3112256; Mon–Sat 8.30–4, Sun 11–4), has a grand colonial entrance adorned with palm trees. Inside is a large collection of stuffed African mammals; more interestingly, the museum also houses an extremely rare dodo skeleton and South Africa's only Egyptian mummy. The KwaZuzulwazi Science Centre here has an excellent series of displays dedicated to the Zulu culture.

The Durban Art Gallery (tel 031-3112265; Mon–Sat 8.30–5, Sun 11–5) was one of the first galleries in South Africa to collect black South African art, and today has a mix of collections of work by local artists and superb displays of indigenous arts and crafts. Other buildings worth noting include the old Post Office; Tourist Junction, housed in the 19th-century train station; and the KwaMuhle Museum (Mon–Sat 8–4), a fascinating and moving exhibition of life as an African under the old regime—a must if you've missed the Apartheid Museum in Johannesburg (▷ 142–143). The collection includes waxworks of figures in hostels, a series of photographs of protest and riots, and displays of the Indian merchants of Grey Street and the Grey Street mosque. Nearby, at 160 Pine Street, is the African Art Centre (Mon–Fri 8.30–5, Sat 9–1), a showcase for rural artists, with a gallery and shop.

A rickshaw driver at the Waterfront, reflecting the city's Indian influences

BASICS

⊞ 331 M7

🛈 Station Building, 160 Pine Street, Durban 4001, tel 031-3044934; Mon–Fri 8–5, Sat 9–2
www.durbanexperience.co.za
www.zulu.org.za

- Do not walk around downtown Durban or along the waterfront after dark, as there is a serious risk of mugging.
- Avoid the area around Point Road and Gillespie Street at any time of the day.
- KwaZulu-Natal Tourism operates a Telitourist cellphone service (tel 082-2392400) with themed recorded visitor information.

Gift items for sale on Durban beachfront (above)
Addington beach (opposite, above)

The Madressa shopping arcade, next to the Victoria Street market

THE INDIAN DISTRICT

The area around Victoria, Queen and Grey streets is one of the oldest in Durban. The shopping arcades painted in pastel shades were built in the 1920s by Indian traders, although residents were evicted in the 1970s. Thankfully, the shops remained and today still sell spices, saris and other Indian goods.

Visitors come for the Victoria Street Market (Mon–Sat 6–6, Sun 10–4) on the corner of Queen and Victoria streets, where curios, fabrics and spices are sold from the stands. Upstairs, don't miss trying a local *bunny chow* curry, a Durban speciality, where a small loaf of bread is hollowed out and filled with spicy curry. Look too for the Jumma Muslim Mosque on Queen and Grey streets. It was built in 1927 and is the largest mosque in the southern hemisphere. If you visit, make sure you are wearing either a long skirt or trousers.

VICTORIA EMBANKMENT

The Victoria Embankment was originally built in 1897 as a grand and desirable residential area facing a stretch of splendid beach. Little of this grandeur remains today, although the high-rise blocks are still interspersed with a few sights of interest. At the eastern end is the ornate late Victorian Da Gama Clock. Nearby, at the intersection of Gardiner Street and the Victoria Embankment, the Dick King Statue commemorates the 1842 epic 10-day ride of local hero Dick King to Grahamstown, to alert British troops there to the plight of Durban, under siege by Voortrekkers opposing British ambitions. The Durban Club, on the opposite side of the embankment, was built in 1904 and is one of the few original buildings surviving. Coming up to date, the restaurant and shopping development of Wilson's Wharf overlooks the harbour, with shops, restaurants, a theatre and a fish market. The Natal Maritime Museum (daily 8.30–3.30), on the docks opposite the junction of Aliwal Street and the Victoria Embankment, offers access to a minesweeper, the SAS *Durban*, and two tugs, the *Ulundi* and the *J R More*. Just beyond the Maritime Museum is BAT (Bartle Arts Trust) Centre (▷ 203).

THE GOLDEN MILE

Traditionally known as the Golden Mile, the waterfront stretching along Marine Drive feels like a seaside resort, with high-rise hotels lining the promenade and beaches. The flea market at the northern end of Lower Marine Parade bustles with stalls selling Indian snacks and curios, while extravagantly dressed rickshaw drivers wait to pick up visitors. The beaches are divided into areas designated for surfing, body boarding and swimming; all are protected with shark nets.

BEREA

This residential district, to the west of the City Centre, is one of Durban's oldest and most prosperous. On Sydenham Road, in Upper Berea, are the Botanic Gardens (tel 031-3091170; daily 7.30–5), founded in 1849, supposedly the oldest botanical gardens in Africa. They cover almost 15ha (37 acres) and are a classic example of a Victorian botanical garden. There are some impressive avenues of palms crossing the park, an ornamental lake, and good displays of orchids and cycads. The tea garden (daily 9.30–4.15) is a pleasant place to relax. The KwaZulu-Natal Philharmonic Orchestra performs by the lake on Sundays during the summer.

USHAKA MARINE WORLD

✉ 1 Bell Street, Point, 4001 ☎ 031-3288001 🕐 Daily 9–5 💧 Wet 'n' Wild: adult R55, child (4–12) R40. Sea World: adult R80, child (4–12) R50
www.ushakamarineworld.co.za
Opened in 2004, the newest attraction in Durban is this enormous water park, with a wide selection of exhibits and rides. The park is split into three areas: uShaka Sea World is an impressive underground aquarium; uShaka Wet 'n' Wild World has waterslides and rides; and uShaka Village walk is a retail village filled with shops and restaurants.

The highlight is the Phantom Ship, where visitors walk through glass tunnels surrounded by ragged-tooth sharks and game fish. Each corridor has a different theme, and there are various presentations throughout the day in pools surrounding the ship.

The Da Gama Clock, built in 1897 to mark the 400th anniversary of the discovery of the sea route to India (below)

BACKGROUND

The earliest inhabitants of the area were members of the Lala tribe who fished in the estuary and hunted and grew crops in the fertile tropical forests along the coast. The first Europeans to land here were Portuguese explorers led by Vasco da Gama in 1497, en route to the east, but it was nearly 200 years before any Europeans settled. The first British traders arrived in 1823, spurred on by news of Shaka, the powerful chief of the Zulus, and his empire. The trader Henry Fynn made initial contact with Shaka. He ingratiated himself with the royal household and Shaka eventually granted him a tract of land covering more than 9,000sq km (3,500sq miles).

Fynn and his colleague Nathaniel Isaacs ran this area as their own personal fiefdom, taking many Zulu wives and fathering dozens of children. Fynn even declared himself King of Natal.

With the establishment of the Voortrekker republic of Natalia in 1838, the British saw their interests coming under threat. An expeditionary force was sent to Durban from the Cape in 1842; they were besieged by Voortrekkers on arrival, but by June the parliament in Pietermaritzburg had accepted British rule. The development of the sugarcane industry in the 1860s encouraged the growth of Durban as a port and gave the city one of its most distinctive characteristics when the planters imported a large number of indentured workers from India. Many remained in Natal, and soon dominated the local fruit and vegetable market or set up businesses. With the development of the Golden Mile in the 1970s, Durban was promoted as a seaside resort for white holidaymakers. Blacks were permitted to walk the length of the whole beach but, on the whites-only Addington Beach, were not allowed to sit down or enter the sea. In the last decade, Durban has taken on a more African feel.

Greater St. Lucia Wetland Park

A vast area of wetlands, beaches and sand dunes, this is the best site in the country for seeing hippos, crocodiles and a huge range of bird life.

SEEING GREATER ST. LUCIA WETLAND PARK

The protected area of the St. Lucia Wetland Park is the largest estuarine lake system in Africa, with a great variety of flora and fauna. It covers a number of formerly separate nature reserves and state forests, still referred to locally under a collection of old and new names. The entire reserve covering 3,280sq km (1,280sq miles) starts south of the St. Lucia Estuary and stretches north to the border with Mozambique, and includes ecosystems ranging from vegetated sand dunes and papyrus wetlands to sandy beaches and dry savannah. Most people come to see hippos and Nile crocodiles, and a good base for this is the town of St. Lucia itself. A great way of taking in the reserve and spotting wildlife is actually on the waters of the estuary, aboard a launch (see below). Cape Vidal, 32km (20 miles) north of St. Lucia town, is a particularly rewarding area (note that there is a daily limit of cars for Cape Vidal). It is possible to stay overnight at a number of camps throughout the park (no meals), including Cape Vidal, Charter's Creek and Fanies Island, but reservations must be made in advance (several months in high season).

HIGHLIGHTS

BIRDS GALORE

A staggering 420 bird species have been recorded in the reserve. As well as the species found year round in the dune forests and grasslands, there are also many unusual migrant birds. The most commonly seen include pink-backed and white pelicans, greater and lesser flamingos, ducks, spoonbills and ibises. The pelicans arrive every autumn to feed on migrating mullet in the Narrows, north of St. Lucia. At any one time, you might see 6,000 pelicans nesting at the northern end of the lake.

ST. LUCIA RESORT AND ESTUARY NATIONAL PARKS

St. Lucia Estuary, next to the town of St. Lucia, is the gateway to the eastern shores of Lake St. Lucia, with extensive wetland systems and coastal grasslands. There are 12km (7 miles) of self-guided trails, a network extending from the Indian Ocean to the estuary and crossing various habitats—dune forest, grasslands, mangrove swamps. The trail leading from the Crocodile Centre to the estuary takes in some good hippo-viewing spots. The Crocodile Centre (tel 035-5901368; Mon–Fri 8–4.30, Sat 8.30–5, Sun 9–4) is next to the entrance gate to Cape Vidal where displays highlight the important role crocodiles play in the ecosystem.

LAUNCH TOURS

☎ 035-5901340 ◷ Daily tours at 8.30, 10.30, 2.30 💷 R75

You can spot wildlife in comfort aboard the *Santa Lucia*, an 80-seater launch which departs from next to the bridge on the west side of the

Looking out for hippos from a 4WD

RATINGS

Good for kids	● ● ●
Outdoor pursuits	● ● ● ● ●
Photo stops	● ● ● ●
Walkability	● ● ● ●

BASICS

➕ 331 N6

ℹ St. Lucia office of KZN Wildlife, Mckenzie Street, St. Lucia, tel: 035 590 1340; daily 8–4.30
www.stlucia.co.za
www.kznwildlife.com

TIPS

● The turtle season runs from November to March. Tours to see the protected loggerhead and leatherback turtles laying their eggs are run by Shaka Barker Tours (tel 035-5901162; www.shakabarker.co.za).

● Keep an eye out for smaller mammals like duiker, warthog, and dassies (rock hyraxes), which are easily missed.

● While hiking around the lake watch out for hippos, snakes and crocodiles.

● When swimming stay away from the estuary, which is inhabited by crocodiles and Zambezi sharks. Watch for no-swimming signs.

● St. Lucia is a malarial area and preventive medication must be taken.

A tour boat coming in to the jetty on Lake St. Lucia

The beautiful beaches of Cape Vidal

The park is an ideal place for watching hippos (above)

A preening spoonbill on the edge of the lake (right)

St. Lucia Estuary. The tours last for 90 minutes and travel up the estuary past thick banks of vegetation as far as the Narrows, allowing plenty of chances to see hippos and crocodiles.

CAPE VIDAL

☎ 035-5909012 ◷ Gates open Oct–end Mar 5am–7pm, Apr–end Sep 6–6; office hours 7–6 ⛿ Adult R20, child (3–16) R15, plus R35 per vehicle ⊞

Cape Vidal, 33km (20 miles) north of St. Lucia town, is the most striking zone in the reserve. It is an area of vegetated dunes along what must be one of the most spectacular beaches in KwaZulu-Natal, with pure white sand lapped by the warm Indian Ocean. The rocks just off the beach teem with tropical fish and the shallow water is safe to snorkel in. In winter, look for humpback whales, which breed to the north. Thanks to the daily limit on cars that can enter Cape Vidal, the beach is never crowded, and although the area is popular with anglers, this too is restricted. There are a couple of self-guided trails across the dunes.

BACKGROUND

St. Lucia was named by the Portuguese explorer Manuel Perestrello in 1575, although European influence in the area was minimal until the 1850s. Up to that time the area was inhabited by a relatively large population of Thongas and Zulus who herded cattle and cultivated the land. Professional hunters began visiting the lake in the 1850s in search of ivory, hides and horns. So successful were they that within 50 years the last elephant in this region had been shot. However, Lake St. Lucia, along with Hluhluwe and Imfolozi was one of the first game reserves to be established in Africa, in 1895. In 1975, the Greater St. Lucia Wetland region was declared, and many conservation initiatives were introduced when St. Lucia won World Heritage status in 1999. In spite of ongoing measures to protect the area, the survival of the lake system has been under constant threat, both from agriculture and the planting of pine forests. The latter are slowly being removed to allow indigenous trees to regrow, and the lake is regularly dredged to prevent it from silting up.

MORE TO SEE

CHARTER'S CREEK

☎ 035-5509000 ◷ Sat–Thu 6–6, Fri 6–9 ⛿ Adult R20, child (2–16) R10, plus R35 per vehicle ⊞ 🅿 Access via N2, north of St. Lucia

This creek, on the Western Shores, is less visited than St. Lucia, with a boat launching area popular with fishermen who come here in search of kob, which can grow up to 20kg (44lb) in weight.

White pelicans are a common sight

Bottlenose dolphins at Margate, on the Hibiscus Coast

The Banana Express runs along the Hibiscus Coast and then on into the plantations

DOLPHIN COAST

✚ 331 M7 ℹ Dolphin Coast Publicity Association, corner of Ballito Drive and Link Road, Ballito, tel 032-9461997; Mon–Fri 8–5, Sat 9–1
www.thedolphincoast.co.za

The area north of Durban, between Umhlanga and Tugela Mouth, is known as the Dolphin Coast. It's famous for its stunning beaches, stylish resorts and the bottlenose dolphins that give it its name. The N2 highway bypasses most of the towns, so stick instead to the original main road, which runs through the resorts. After Umhlanga Rocks (▷ 119) come Ballito, Shaka's Rock (where Zulu warriors once leaped into the sea as a test of their manhood), Umhlali, Salt Rock and Sheffield Beach, forming a more or less continuous stretch. All the beaches are excellent, but bear in mind that there are sharks along the coast: Always ask whether the beach is protected by shark nets.

DURBAN

See pages 108–111.

GREATER ST. LUCIA WETLAND PARK

See pages 112–113.

HIBISCUS COAST

✚ 331 M8 ℹ Hibiscus Coast Publicity Association, Panorama Parade, Margate Beachfront, tel 039-3174630; Mon–Fri 8–4.30, Sat 9–12
www.hibiscuscoast.kzn.org.za

The overall impression of the coast south of Durban—the Hibiscus Coast—is of a long line of holiday homes set in a lush subtropical strip of forest. But it is the sea that deserves your attention. During the winter months millions of sardines travel close to the beaches attracting dolphins, sharks and birds, and the ocean teems with life.

Port Shepstone is the largest town on the south coast, but is more geared to industry than the holiday trade. However, the Banana Express vintage steam train runs from here to Paddock, following the coast for 6km (4 miles) before winding into green hills covered with banana and sugarcane plantations (for reservations, tel 039-6824821). The other main town on the coast is Margate, a developed family beach resort.

Attractive accommodation at Itala Game Reserve

ITALA GAME RESERVE

✚ 331 M5 ☎ 034-9832540
🕐 Oct–end Mar 5am–7pm; Apr–end Sep 6–6 💵 R30 per vehicle 🚩 Guided day hikes can be reserved at reception 🍴 At Ntshondwe Camp 🏪 Camp shop. Petrol (gas) is on sale next to the main gates 🚗 Along R66 from Pongola, then R69 for 73km (45 miles); entrance near the village of Louwsburg

Itala, although small and not very well known, is one of KwaZulu-Natal's most spectacular reserves, and game viewing feels much less crowded and more relaxed than in many other reserves. Itala's landscapes are stunning, with large areas of low-lying grassland, steep-sided forested valleys and granite cliffs reaching 1,450m (4,756ft). The steeply rising terrain has created several different ecosystems with an interesting diversity of wildlife. Twenty species have

been reintroduced into the reserve including a herd of young elephants and the only herd of tsessebi (a large antelope) in Natal. You can see three of the Big Five—elephant, leopard and black rhino—as well as cheetah, eland, giraffe, kudu, white rhino, blue wildebeest and zebra. Birdwatching is another important attraction, and some 320 species have been recorded in the reserve, including black eagle, bald ibis, martial eagle and brown-necked parrot. In June and July the flowering aloe trees come into bloom; their unmistakable large orange flowers are an important source of nectar at this time of year, attracting birds and insects.

KOSI BAY NATURE RESERVE

✚ 331 P5 ☎ 033-8451000
🕐 Oct–end Mar daily 5am–7pm; Mar daily 6–6 💵 Adult R20, child (3–15) R10, plus R15 per vehicle 🚗 Turn off the N2 at the Jozini turning
www.kznwildlife.com

Kosi Bay, north of Sodwana Bay, is one of South Africa's most popular wilderness destinations. The protected area is more than 25km (15 miles) long and consists of four lakes separated from the sea by a long strip of forest-covered dunes. The lakes are part of a fascinating tropical wetland environment, their shores bordered with reed-beds, ferns, swamp figs and umdoni trees. Five species of mangrove thrive in the estuary, where local fishermen have built traditional fishing traps.

There are also pristine beaches fringed with a stunning coral reef, perfect for snorkelling. The Kosi Bay Hiking Trail, 34km (21 miles) long, is popular and places can get fully reserved six months in advance.

A white rhino with calf (above); small-eared Burchell's zebra alongside a waterhole (inset)

HLUHLUWE-IMFOLOZI GAME RESERVE

Once two separate parks, the Hluhluwe-Imfolozi has a variety of landscapes that are home to numerous species of wildlife. The wilderness areas are superb and the guided walks with rangers should not be missed.

This is one of Africa's oldest game reserves. The landscapes encompass thick forests, dry bushveld and open savannah. What is unusual about the park is its hilly terrain, which provides great vantage points for game viewing. An extensive network of dirt roads can easily be negotiated in a standard rented car. There are hides at Mphafa and Thiyeni waterholes, but much of the best game viewing is from the road. Good areas are the Sontuli Loop, the corridor connecting Imfolozi to Hluhluwe and the areas around the Hluhluwe River. There are several camps within the park, with a mix of accommodation.

WILDLIFE
The wide range of habitats supports numbers of big game, with large populations of both white and black rhino and nyala (a large antelope). Hluhluwe is the northern sector of the reserve, with a hilly and wooded landscape where elephants are often seen around the dam. There are some areas of savannah in this sector where white rhino and giraffe may be spotted feeding. The park was the birthplace of 'Operation Rhino' in the 1960s, set up to save the endangered white rhino. There has been a growth in the population from around 500 in the 1950s to 6,000 today. Imfolozi, in the south, is characterized by thornveld, savannah areas of thorny bush and acacia trees, and semi-desert, and the grasslands here support impala, kudu, waterbuck, giraffe, blue wildebeest and zebra. Predators are rarely seen but cheetah, lion, leopard and wild dog are all present.

HIKING IN THE RESERVE
One of the most exciting ways to see wildlife here is on foot. Places on guided walks can be reserved at the camp offices; there are two daily walks with a game guard from Hilltop and Mpila camps lasting 2 to 3 hours; children are not allowed. There are also two self-guided walks, and three overnight wilderness trails (in the company of guides) in the southern section of the park.

RATINGS
Outdoor pursuits	●●●●
Photo stops	●●●●
Value for money	●●●●

BASICS
✚ 331 N6
☎ 033-8451000
🕐 Oct–end Mar daily 5am–7pm; Apr–end Sep daily 6–6
🎟 Adult R70, child (3–15) R35
🏪 Souvenir shops selling gifts and books about natural history at Masinda and Mpila Camps; small supermarket near Hluhluwe gates
🍴 Restaurant in Hluhluwe section
📷 Night drives R150; guided game walks R100; river boat trips from Maphumulo Picnic Site R85
🚌 Turning off N2, at Mtubatuba leading west on the R618 (50km/30 miles) to the Imfolozi entrance, or turning opposite the exit to Hluhluwe village which leads (14km/8.5 miles) to the northern Memorial Gate entrance
www.kznwildlife.com

TIPS
● The best time to see the reserve is between March and November, when the climate is cool and dry and it's easier to spot game around waterholes and rivers.
● The park makes an easy day trip from Maputaland or the St. Lucia region.
● There are two entrances, one at Imfolozi and the other at Hluhluwe.

Diving is a popular activity at Lala Neck

Nyala antelope, with their distinctive white stripes, grazing in the long grasses of Mkhuze Game Reserve

LALA NECK

➕ 331 P5 ℹ️ Rocktail Bay Lodge, tel 011-2575200 💲 R20 per vehicle plus R15 per person

In the northern reaches of the KwaZulu-Natal coast are these secluded beaches, only accessible by 4WD vehicles. They are renowned for being the ultimate game fishing destinations, but also have clear waters that offer spectacular snorkelling and diving, with good chances of seeing turtles and sharks as well as hundreds of tropical fish. There are no facilities and the only viable way of visiting is by staying at the lodge.

LAKE SIBAYA

➕ 331 N5

Lake Sibaya is the largest freshwater lake in South Africa and was previously connected to the sea. A long strip of thickly forested dunes now runs between the lake and the Indian Ocean. The tropical bird life is Lake Sibaya's main attraction, with swampy reed-beds and patches of forest providing varied habitats for the many species. Kingfishers, cormorants and fish eagles hunt in the lake, and hippos and crocodiles can also be seen.

MAPUTALAND

➕ 331 N5 ℹ️ Engen Garage, Hluhluwe 3960, tel 035-5620353; Mon–Fri 8.30–5, Sat9–1, Sun 10–12 www.elephantcoast.kzn.org.za

The region of Maputaland, named after the Maputa River, which flows through southern Mozambique, covers an area of 9,000sq km (3,500sq miles) stretching from Lake St. Lucia to the Mozambique border, and west from the Indian Ocean to the Lebombo Mountains. One of South Africa's least developed

Fish eagles live near water, such as Lake Sibaya, for feeding

regions, Maputaland still seems traditionally African. The land is unsuitable for intensive modern agriculture and the small farmsteads dotting the landscape are connected by a rough network of roads. The region is part of the huge St. Lucia-Maputaland Biosphere covering 13,000sq km (5,000sq miles) and encompassing the Greater St. Lucia Wetland Park (▷ 112–113) and a number of smaller regional game reserves up to and including Hluhluwe-Imfolozi (▷ 115). The climate varies from tropical in the north to subtropical in the south and this has created a diverse range of ecosystems, from the forested Lebombo Mountains to the low-lying expanses of the coastal plain. Maputaland's features include South Africa's largest freshwater lake (see Lake Sibaya, above), mangrove swamps, coral reefs, dune forest, riverine forest and savannah. Seeing Maputaland's last wild elephants from a 4WD vehicle in Tembe Elephant Park or diving on the reefs at Sodwana Bay (▷ 119) are among the country's ultimate wilderness experiences.

MKHUZE GAME RESERVE

➕ 331 N6 ☎ 035-5739001 🕐 Oct–end Mar daily 5am–7pm; Apr–end Sep daily 6–6 💲 Adult R35, child (under 12) R18, plus R35 per vehicle 🛍️ Curio shop selling books, postcards and some food 🚗 20km (12 miles) along a dirt road from Mkuze, or off N2 (clearly signposted)

This reserve, covering an area of 36,000ha (89,000 acres), has landscapes of open grasslands, dense forests, coastal dunes and pans. The area to the north is tropical, whereas the southern part is temperate. Not visited as often as Hluhluwe-Imfolozi, because it has fewer rhinos, Mkhuze has the advantage of being less crowded, and there are good opportunities to see some of Maputaland's more unusual animals, such as the shy nyala antelope. It is also an excellent place to see big game—elephant, giraffe, blue wildebeest, eland, kudu, both black and white rhino, cheetah, leopard and hyena are all present in the reserve. As part of the Mozambique coastal plain, Mkhuze attracts many tropical birds that are usually only seen farther north: More than 450 species have been recorded here, from sunbirds to flamingos and pelicans.

A network of roads totalling about 100km (60 miles) crosses the reserve. The best game viewing areas are the Loop Road, the Nsumo Pan and the airstrip. The Fig Forest Trail (3km/5 miles long, and next to Nsumo Pan) is a self-guided trail traversing one of the last surviving areas of fig tree forest in South Africa. The atmosphere of the forest is magical, as you pass between trees reaching 25m (82ft), with girths of 12m (40ft). There is a luxury lodge as well as several camps within the reserve.

The drop at Howick Falls in the Natal Midlands is 100m (328ft)

You will get into more remote sections of the Ndumo Game Reserve if you take a 4WD tour

THE NATAL MIDLANDS

✚ 330 L7

In the region encompassing the towns of Greytown, Richmond, Pietermaritzburg and Estcourt, the many rivers flowing off the Drakensberg escarpment have created a well-watered fertile landscape. It originally supported a large population of Zulu cattle herders and farmers in the lowlands. San migrated between here and the Drakensberg, following the herds of eland according to the changes of the seasons.

Later the fertile territory attracted first the Voortrekkers and then British immigrants in the 1850s, who all fought for control of the land. It is still predominantly a rural, agricultural area; there are farms cultivating wattle for tanning and paper pulp, cattle and sheep ranches, and studs for horse breeding.

The N3 bisects the Midlands and the majority of traffic passes through on its way between Gauteng and Durban. However, by taking the alternative R103, the Midlands towns and countryside can be explored at leisure. This is the Midlands Meander route, a visitor initiative highlighting the multitude of craft outlets, country restaurants and rural retreats in the region. For information about the Meander, tel 033-3308195 or visit www.midlandsmeander.co.za.

NDUMO GAME RESERVE

✚ 331 N5 ☎ 033-8451000 ◷ Gates: Apr–end Sep 6–6; Oct–end Mar 5am–7pm; office: 8–1, 2–4 ⬛ Adult R35, child (under 12) R18, plus R35 per vehicle ⬛ ⬛ 14km (8.5 miles) beyond the village of Ndumo on a rough dirt road www.kznwildlife.com

Ndumo, hugging the Usutu River along the Mozambique border, is a low-lying, humid, tropical floodplain renowned for its magnificent bird life and large numbers of crocodiles and hippos. It is one of the wildest reserves in South Africa and its verdant wetlands have been compared with the Okavango Delta in Botswana.

The pans at Nyamithi and Banzi are great areas to experience an African tropical swamp. Thousands of birds congregate here in the evenings and it is possible to see flocks of flamingos, geese, pelicans and storks. Buffalo are also occasionally seen in the swampy areas of the reserve, but nyala, hippos and crocodiles are present in large numbers. Black and white rhino, leopard and suni antelope thrive in these thickets, but you would be lucky to see them.

The reserve's roads are in good condition and you can drive around in your own car, or travel by 4WD with a guide. A good way to see Ndumo is on one of the tours organized by the reserve. You can go on five different guided walks with a game ranger. There is a private luxury camp and a KZN camp within the reserve.

ORIBI GORGE NATURE RESERVE

✚ 330 L8 ☎ 039-6791644 ◷ Reserve: 24 hours; camp office: daily 8–12.30, 2–4.30 ⬛ Adult R10, child (under 12) R5 ⬛ Camp shop sells wildlife books, souvenirs, charcoal, firewood and a limited range of food ⬛ 21km (13.5 miles) west of Port Shepstone via N2

This reserve was established in 1950 to protect an area of thick woodland and towering cliffs where the Umzimkulu and Umzimkulweni rivers meet. It's a popular spot for forest walks, and the ravines and waterfalls are good places for adrenalin-pumping sports activities such as abseiling or white-water rafting (▷ 204). The most spectacular waterfalls within the park are the Samango Falls, Hoopoe Falls and Lehr's Falls.

There are impressive views from the top of the sandstone cliffs, some of which are as much as 280m (920ft) high, and they provide nesting sites for birds of prey. The forest is home to the African python. It is so dense that although leopards are thought to live here they are never seen, but you can sometimes glimpse small groups of one of the animals on which they prey, the Samango monkey. Bird life is prolific and this is a good place to see forest species such as the Knysna lourie, grass owl and five different species of kingfisher. There are several clearly marked hikes and paths lead to viewpoints above the gorge. Do not swim in the river as there is bilharzia present in the water.

You may see malachite kingfishers around Oribi

A statue of Gandhi commemorates his arrival in 1893 in South Africa (above); Harwin's Arcade, built in 1904 (inset)

PIETERMARITZBURG

There is a lively atmosphere in this Victorian town due to its mix of Zulu, Indian, British and student populations.

Pietermaritzburg is the joint capital, with Ulundi, of KwaZulu-Natal. This attractive city dates from the late 19th century when it was the capital of the Colony of Natal and was named after the Voortrekker leaders Piet Retief and Gert Maritz. Today, Pietermaritzburg's red-brick buildings and town parks evoke many an English provincial city and it's a pleasant place to stroll around. It is an important trading hub for the local farming industry and is home to a campus of the University of KwaZulu-Natal and many other technical colleges. During the school term, the city has a bustling, youthful feel with a lively nightlife.

COLONIAL PIETERMARITZBURG

In the heart of the city are its finest Victorian buildings, civic gardens and war memorials. The City Hall, on the corner of Commercial Road and Church Street, was built in 1900 and is said to be the largest all-brick building in the southern hemisphere. Opposite is the Tatham Art Gallery (tel 033-3421804; Tue–Sun 10–6), which has exhibitions of French and British 19th-century art as well as an innovative collection of contemporary art. On the same block are the Supreme Court Gardens, filled with war memorials. The old Colonial Building, 100m (110 yards) farther on, was built in 1899; in front of it is a statue of Mahatma Gandhi, commemorating his arrival in South Africa in 1893. The Presbyterian Church (1852), opposite the Colonial Building, was the first British church in Pietermaritzburg. The Lanes, a network of alleyways between Longmarket Street and Church Street, are lined with small shops and cafés.

THE MUSEUMS

The Voortrekker Museum (tel 033-3946834; Mon–Fri 9–4, Sat 9–1) on Church Street, has a collection of period farm machinery, furniture and other everyday objects. There are also newer and more culturally significant exhibitions about Zulu heritage. The Natal Museum (tel 033-3451494; Mon–Fri 9–4.30, Sat 10–4, Sun 11–3) in Loop Street has a natural history gallery that includes the last wild elephant shot in Natal, in 1911. Also in Loop Street, at No. 11, is the Macrorie House Museum (tel 033-3942161; Mon 11–4, Tue–Sat 9–1), with period furniture and a collection of Victorian costumes.

RATINGS

Cultural interest	●●●○
Historic interest	●●●○
Walkability	●●●●●

BASICS

✚ 331 M7
ℹ Pietermaritzburg Tourism, Publicity House, 177 Commercial Road, Pietermaritzburg 3201, tel 033-3451348; Mon–Fri 8–5, Sat 8–3
www.pmbtourism.co.za

TIPS

● Cricket fans and Anglophiles may want to visit Alexandra Park for its splendid Victorian cricket pavilion dating from 1898.
● The warm, dry climate is more pleasant than Durban's humidity, but note that there is heavy rainfall from December to February.

The seafront at Umhlanga Rocks, which means 'Place of Reeds' in Zulu, after the reeds that are washed downriver north of town

The gateway at Shakaland in Zululand

SODWANA BAY

➕ 331 P5 ☎ 033-8451000 🕐 Gates open 24 hours 👤 Adult R20, child (3–15) R10 ⚡ KZN Wildlife turtle viewing trips held nightly Dec, Jan, R70 per person; must be reserved at reception the day before 🏧 🚗 On N2 from the south, take Ngwenya/Sodwana Bay exit. From the north, take the turning to Jozini and Mbazana. Follow the dirt road to Sodwana Bay (120km/75 miles)

Sodwana Bay is South Africa's premier scuba diving destination. It has the world's southernmost tropical reefs, and around 80 per cent of South Africa's 1,200 species of fish can be found here. Ragged-tooth and whale sharks, humpback whales, dolphins and turtles are other major attractions. Although Sodwana is popular with visitors all year round, divers prefer April to September, while fishermen congregate here in November and December. December and January are the best times to see turtles laying their eggs. Bear in mind that Sodwana is excessively busy during the school holidays (December and January).

TEMBE ELEPHANT PARK

➕ 331 N5 ☎ 035-5920001 🕐 Apr–end Sep 6–6, Oct–end Mar 5am–7pm 👤 Adult R35, child (under 12) R18, plus R35 per vehicle 🚗 72km (45 miles) from Jozini, off N2

Tembe was established in 1983 to protect the area's elephants. The present herd of 140 is thought to be the only indigenous elephant herd in KwaZulu-Natal. Other species in the park include lion, giraffe, black rhino, white rhino and buffalo. In addition to those who stay, a further five groups of day visitors in 4WD vehicles are allowed in daily. All groups must be accompanied by a ranger, but there is a self-guided walk within the Ngobazane enclosure area.

UKHAHLAMBA-DRAKENSBERG PARK

See pages 120–123.

UMHLANGA ROCKS

➕ 331 M7 ℹ️ Sugar Coast Tourism, Chartwell Drive, Umhlanga Rocks 4319, tel 031-5614257; Mon–Fri 8–4.30, Sat 8–1
www.sugarcoast.kzn.org.za

This classy resort lies a short drive north of Durban and is now virtually a suburb. There is a good beach, and Umhlanga Rocks' main attraction is the beach's relative safety and lower crime rate compared to Durban's waterfront. Also worth a visit is the Sharks Board (Mon–Fri 8–4), on Herrwood Drive, which studies the life cycles of local sharks and investigates how best to protect both them and swimmers. Umhlanga Rocks became the first beach in South Africa to have shark nets erected in 1962 following a series of attacks along the coast. Today the Board is responsible for looking after more than 400 nets, protecting nearly 50 beaches. Tours at the Sharks Board begin with a 25-minute video followed by a shark dissection (held on Tue, Wed, Thu at 9 and 2, Sun at 2).

UMTAMVUNA NATURE RESERVE

➕ 330 L8 ☎ 039-3112383 🕐 Daily 7–5 👤 R10 per person ❓ Map, bird checklist and information leaflets available at the entrance

Lying 8km (5 miles) north of Port Edward on the road to Izingolweni, this is the southernmost and one of the less visited reserves in KwaZulu-Natal, but has great day-long hikes down into a sandstone gorge. The sheer walls of lichen-covered rock, dropping down into thick rainforest, are the focal point of this dramatic landscape. There is

no big game here: The reserve is known best for its wild flowers in spring and is regarded as one of the world's top plant spots. One particular shrub, the *Raspalia trigyna*, is very rare and unique to the reserve. Look out, too, for the colony of Cape vultures that inhabit the area.

ZULULAND

➕ 331 N6
www.zululand.kzn.org.za

For many visitors, Zululand—homeland of King Shaka early in the 19th century—is South Africa's most evocative area. It certainly attracts a huge number of visitors. The region, extending from the northern bank of the Tugela River up to Mkuze and Maputaland, holds some of the country's most popular reserves, including Greater St. Lucia Wetland Park (▷ 112–113) and Hluhluwe-Imfolozi (▷ 115).

The gateway to the heart of Zululand is the town of Eshowe, which originally surrounded the *kraal* (huts) of the Zulu king Cetshwayo (▷ 33). Look for the Zululand Historical Museum on Fort Nongqai Road (tel 035-4742419; Mon–Fri 7.30–4, Sat–Sun 9–4), and the excellent Vukani Collection Museum (tel 035-4745274; daily 7–4), one of the largest collections of Zulu art in existence. Shakaland theme park is 14km (9 miles) north of here, providing a (perhaps not thoroughly authentic) glimpse of Zulu culture. To the west lies the Battlefields Route. On the coast is Mtunzini, a pleasant smart resort, once home to John Dunn who, in the 19th century, became a Zulu chief in his own right—he had 49 wives and fathered 117 children. The second largest town in the state is Richard's Bay, an industrial port. To its north is St. Lucia.

uKhahlamba-Drakensberg Park

South Africa's most spectacular mountain range offers superb hiking and fishing through its green wilderness areas. This is also the best part of the country to see examples of ancient San rock art.

RATINGS	
Outdoor pursuits	●●●●●
Photo stops	●●●●●
Walkability	●●●●●

TIPS

● Carry your passport with you at all times; in the High Berg it is easy to stray into Lesotho and guards patrol the border area.

● Entry fees are included in the cost of accommodation within the parks; only day visitors will have to pay fees at the gate.

● The Drakensberg peaks are becoming a top draw for mountain climbers. For information about climbing here, contact the Mountain Club of South Africa (tel 082-9905877, www.kzn.mcsa.org.za).

● Although there are some shops within camps, supplies are limited and expensive: It's best to stock up beforehand in one of the surrounding towns.

Taking a rest (below); the Amphitheatre at the Royal Natal National Park (opposite)

SEEING THE UKHAHLAMBA-DRAKENSBERG PARK

The Drakensberg Mountains rise to more than 3,000m (10,000ft) and extend 180km (112 miles) along the western edge of KwaZulu-Natal, forming the backbone of what is today known as the uKhahlamba-Drakensberg Park (and also part of South Africa's border with Lesotho). The main reason for coming to the Drakensberg is for its superb walking. Almost the entire range falls within protected reserves managed by the conservation body KZN Wildlife. They have a series of comprehensive maps, available from KZN Wildlife offices. Overnight hikers should read KZN Wildlife's brochure, *It's Tough at the Top—Hiking Safely in the Drakensberg.*

If you are visiting the Central Drakensberg (the Cathedral Peak or Monk's Cowl areas), the village of Winterton is your last chance to pick up supplies. The small market town of Underberg is the main service point for the southern Drakensberg, and visitors will find it an ideal base from which to plan trips into the mountains.

May to September is the best time to visit, as the weather is dry and still fairly warm (although there is snow on the highest peaks). Summers are wet and hot. There is no proper public transport network, so you will need to rent a car to get the most out of the area. For those on a budget, the Baz Bus (▷ 51) runs through the Drakensberg three times a week.

HIGHLIGHTS

ROYAL NATAL NATIONAL PARK

✚ 330 K6 ☎ 036-4386411 ◎ Office and Visitor Centre daily 8–4.30 🏛 Adult R25, child (3–15) R15 📖 KZN Visitor Centre sells hiking maps and a leaflet describing walks around the park 🏕 🚗 Access via N2

The Royal Natal National Park is the most popular of all the resorts in the Drakensberg, and is famous for its exceptionally grand scenery: You'll remember your first view of the massive rock walls that form the Amphitheatre, a cliff face arching northwards for 4km (2.5 miles) from the Eastern Buttress (3,009m/9,870ft) towards the Sentinel (3,165m/10,381ft). On the plateau behind the Amphitheatre is Mont-aux-Sources (3,299m/10,821ft). This mountain is the source of five rivers, the most impressive of which is the Tugela, which plunges over the edge of the Amphitheatre wall, dropping about 800m (2,500ft) through a series of five falls. The gorge created by the falls is a steep-sided tangle of boulders and trees; at one point it bores straight through the sandstone to form a long tunnel.

There are more than 130km (80 miles) of walking trails around the park, many of which are easy half-day strolls. Hikes are either climbs to the top of the escarpment or meanders through countryside of grassland dotted with yellowwood forests, set against the stunning backdrop of the Amphitheatre. The most popular hikes include the

➕ 330 L7
ℹ️ Drakensberg Tourism Association, library building on Thatham Road, Bergville, tel 036-4481244; Mon–Fri 7.30–4, Sat 9–12
www.drakensberg.za.org
www.kznwildlife.com

On the Giant's Cup hiking trial in the southern Drakensberg

HIKING

Hiking in the High Berg, which contains all the great peaks, requires a high degree of fitness; exploring the equally remote and empty Little Berg requires only average levels of fitness. For longer hikes, it is essential to plan ahead, as you have to be completely self-sufficient, and places in overnight caves (a popular accommodation choice) and mountain huts must be reserved in advance. Guided hikes are a good idea for the less experienced. Permits are necessary on all but the shortest walks and are available from camp offices for a small fee.

MORE TO SEE

DRAKENSBERG BOYS' CHOIR

The Drakensberg Boys' Choir, based at a school on the R600 towards Monk's Cowl, is Africa's best-known choir. It has sung all over the world in the last three decades, including in front of 25,000 people at the Vatican City. It is possible to see the Choir perform during term time on Wednesdays at 3.30 in the school auditorium. Reservations are essential (tel 036-4681012).

climb to Mont-aux-Sources (20km/12 miles), a round-trip in Tugela Gorge and a hike to Cannibal Cave (8km/5 miles). There's one camp with huts and two campsites within the park (▷ 288).

CATHEDRAL PEAK

➕ 330 L7 ☎ 036-4888000 🕐 Reception office at Mike's Pass: 7–7 💲 Adult R20, child (under 15) R10; vehicles to Mike's Pass R35 🍴 🚌 Signposted from Bergville and Winterton; some of the road is unsurfaced
www.cathedralpeak.co.za
Cathedral Peak is the main point of access to some of the wildest areas of the Central Drakensberg. It's a peaceful yet dramatic spot, with views of soaring peaks. The sheltered valleys are thought to have been one of the last refuges of the San in the Drakensberg, with large numbers of cave painting sites in the area (guided tours only, arranged from Cathedral Peak Hotel, ▷ 288). Leopards Cave and Poachers Cave in the Ndedema Gorge have especially good galleries of paintings. There is a good network of paths heading up the Mlambonja Valley to the escarpment, from where there are trails going south to Monk's Cowl and Injasuti or north to Royal Natal National Park. The hike of 10km (6 miles) to the top of Cathedral Peak (3,004m/9,853ft) is one of the most exciting and strenuous in the area—the views of the Drakensberg stretching out to the north and south are unforgettable. The campsite at Mike's Pass, or the two hotels there, are excellent bases for exploring the area. An alternative to hiking is to drive along the road heading up Mike's Pass, from where there are views of the Little Berg.

MONK'S COWL

➕ 330 L7 ☎ 036-4681103 🕐 Park gates: daily 6–6; office: daily 8–4 💲 Adult R20, child (under 3–15) R10 🚌 End of R600 from Winterton
The road to Monk's Cowl, in the Central Berg, passes through one of the most developed areas just outside the Drakensberg, peppered with hotels, golf courses and timeshare developments, and locally dubbed 'Champagne Valley'. Champagne Castle, Monk's Cowl and Cathkin Peak are impressive features in the landscape, and several superb long-distance hikes begin from here (including the two-day hike up to Champagne Castle). The short hikes around here get relatively busy, as there are many day-trippers. A map is available from the office and the paths are clear and well signposted.

GIANT'S CASTLE

➕ 330 L7 ☎ 036-3533718 🕐 Park gates: Oct–end Mar 5am–7pm, Apr–end Sep 6–6; camp office: daily 8–4 📖 Hiking trail details available from camp office
🍴 🚌 Signposted from Estcourt (65km/40 miles) on N3
The camp here has one of the most spectacular settings in the region, with the Drakensberg escarpment towering above it. A wall of basalt cliffs rises higher than 3,000m (10,000ft), and the peaks of Giant's Castle (3,314m/10,870ft), Champagne Castle (3,248m/10,653ft) and Cathkin Peak (3,149m/10,329ft) can be seen on the skyline. The grasslands below the cliffs roll out in a series of massive hills, which give rise to the Bushman's River and the Little Tugela River. The area around the camp has a network of short paths through riverine forest, but there are also numerous interconnected hikes of up to three days crossing the reserve.

SANI PASS

➕ 330 L7 🕐 South African border post: daily 8–4; Lesotho border post: daily 8–4
🅿️ At South African border post
The road from Himeville to Sani Pass rises steadily through rolling hills until it passes the Sani Top Chalet hotel (▷ 219), when the towering peaks on the escarpment come into view. This is the only road leading into Lesotho on its eastern border with South Africa, and a 4WD vehicle is needed to make the ascent. The road is one of the most dramatic in Africa, and the top of the pass is so high that it has a distinct alpine climate. The most rewarding hike in this area is the one-day climb up to the top of Sani Pass at 2,874m (9,427ft), but there are also shorter hikes. There are full border formalities when you cross into Lesotho, so don't forget your passport.

SAN ROCK PAINTINGS

⊙ Park gates: Oct–end Mar 5am–7pm, Apr–end Sep 6–6; office: daily 8–12.30, 2–4.30 🖐 Adult R20, child (under 12) R10 🚌 Guided tours to Game Pass shelter cost R40 per person and depart at 8.30 and 1.30 🚗 Turn off the N3 highway towards Nottingham Road and follow signposts to Kamberg (48km/30 miles) along the Loteni road). The last 19km (12 miles) are on a gravel road

The sandstone caves and rock shelters of the Drakensberg are among the best places to see San rock art. Hundreds of individual sites have been identified, but Kamberg and Giant's Castle have the most accessible caves. Although the majority of surviving paintings are fairly recent—some 200 to 300 years old—they form part of an ancient tradition and some of the earliest cave paintings in southern Africa date from 28,000 years ago. Kamberg's San Rock Art Centre gives visitors an insight into the lifestyle of the San. There's a guided walk of two to three hours to the Game Pass Shelter and its impressive array of paintings. Tours must be reserved in advance (tel 033-2677251).

SPIOENKOP DAM NATURE RESERVE

➕ 330 L6 ☎ 036-4881578 ⊙ Oct–end Mar 6am–7pm, Apr–end Sep 6–6 🖐 R10 🚗 14km (8.5 miles) north of Winterton on R600

This game park focuses on the site of the Spioenkop battlefield, where the British were defeated by the Boers on 23 January 1900. The battlefield overlooks the dam and there is a self-guided trail to the site. You will have a good chance of seeing white rhino, buffalo, giraffe, kudu, impala and zebra.

BACKGROUND

The earliest human inhabitants of the Drakensberg were the hunter-gatherers, the San. They left their imprint on the landscape in numerous rock shelters and paintings of hunting scenes, but came under increasing pressure towards the end of the 18th century as new settlers established themselves. Their numbers declined dramatically, and the last records of San being seen in the Drakensberg date from 1878. The Drakensberg's natural resources were exploited by the settlers, which had terrible long-term effects on the delicate ecosystem. This gave the impetus for the creation of the National Park. In 2001, it became a UNESCO World Heritage Site in recognition of its universal environmental value to mankind.

The view from the 3165m (10,381ft) Sentinel Peak (above); horse riding in front of Champagne Castle (inset)

HIMEVILLE

➕ 330 L7

Himeville, north of Underberg, is a small, prosperous village with an English air to it. Arbuckle Street runs through its heart, and there's a small museum in the old fort and prison (Tue–Sun 8.30–12.30).

A bearded vulture

LIMPOPO AND MPUMALANGA

Limpopo and Mpumalanga is home to the Kruger National Park, which gives visitors some truly spectacular game viewing moments. The provinces' many nature reserves and private game farms sustain intricate African ecosystems, including dry bushveld, waterfalls and forest.

MAJOR SIGHTS

There are watersports as well as spa treatments at Bela-Bela

At the top of the Zipliner, just outside Graskop

A sangoma or traditional healer at Shangana Cultural Village

BARBERTON

⊞ 325 M4 ⓘ Market Square, Barberton 1300, tel 013-7122121; Mon–Fri 7.30–4.30, Sat–Sun 9–4 www.barberton.info

There is a surprising amount to do in this quiet colonial town, much of it connected to the town's gold-mining past. Barberton is famous for being the site of one of South Africa's first large-scale gold rushes. Pioneer Reef was discovered in 1883 and by 1886 more than 4,000 claims were being worked, turning it into a wild frontier town of shacks, gambling dens and whisky bars. Wealth quickly followed, and South Africa's first gold stock exchange opened here in 1887. The gold rush lasted only a few years, and by the outbreak of the Boer War Barberton had been virtually abandoned. However, in recent years the industry has been revived and four gold mines operate within the area.

BELA-BELA/ WARMBATHS

⊞ 324 K3 ⓘ Corner of Old Pretoria and Voortrekker streets in the Waterfront development, 0480, tel 014-7364328; Mon–Fri 8–5, Sat 8–1 www.belabelatourism.co.za

Warmbaths is one of a number of towns in Limpopo that is undergoing a name change. The resort exists because of the natural hot springs 'discovered' in the 1860s by Jan Grobler and Carl van Heerden while hunting in the region; Bela-Bela, 'he who boils his own', was the name used by the local Tswana people. The springs bubble out of the earth at a temperature of 50°C (122°F), producing about 22,000 litres (4,840 gallons) per hour. The principal springs now lie within the massive Aventura Resort where visitors

can enrol in a whole variety of treatments at the spa (▷ 208). Bela-Bela is less than one hour's drive from Pretoria and the mild climate in winter ensures an average of 286 sunny days a year. All this leads to a staggering 2 million visitors annually.

BLYDE RIVER CANYON

See pages 126–127.

GRASKOP

⊞ 325 M3 ⓘ Panorama Tourist Association, Louis Trichardt Street, Graskop 1270, tel 013-7671377; Mon–Fri 8–5, Sat–Sun 8–1 www.panoramainfo.co.za

The small mountain resort of Graskop in Mpumalanga is just south of the Blyde River Canyon (▷ 126–127), and is the most convenient base for exploring the canyon. Graskop is best known in South Africa as the home of the pancake. The legendary Harrie's restaurant (▷ 268) started it all, and now the stuffed sweet and savoury pancakes are renowned throughout the land.

There are several hikes from Graskop, including the circular trail of 8km (5 miles) known as Jock of the Bushveld Trail. Other attractions include the Big Swing, which is similar to a bungee jump, and the hair-raising Zipliner (▷ 208).

The road to Hazyview (see below) goes over Kowyn's Pass a few kilometres from Graskop. Before descending towards the Lowveld it passes Graskop Gorge and waterfall and there are views looking up to the viewpoint known as God's Window (▷ 240).

HAZYVIEW

⊞ 325 M3 ⓘ Rendezvous Tourism Centre, Main Street, Hazyview 1242, tel 013-7377414; Mon–Fri 9–5, Sat 9–3, Sun 10–1 www.rendez.co.za

Hazyview lies on the banks of the Sabie River on the south-western edge of the Kruger National Park, surrounded by a large area of banana plantations. Because of its convenient position, facilities for visitors have been growing since the 1920s, and there is now a wide range of accommodation. Five kilometres (3 miles) from Hazyview is the Shangana Cultural Village, home of a Shangana family descended from Chief Shoshangana, an important tribal leader of the region at the end of the 19th centuries. Tours include a lesson in traditional medicine, historical explanations and a traditional meal (lunchtime and dinner only). Tours by arrangement only (tel 013-7377000).

HOEDSPRUIT

⊞ 325 M3 ⓘ Footprint Information Centre, corner of Kerk and Grobler streets, Hoedspruit 1380, tel 015-7932996; Mon–Fri 8–5

Hoedspruit is a busy little town at the extreme south of the Limpopo Province, surrounded by game-rich country and with ever-present views of the Drakensberg escarpment. Its main attractions are outside the town, along the R531 towards Blyde River Canyon. They include the Bombyx Mori Silk Farm (Mon–Sat 9–4, Sun in summer only 11–2; 5 tours daily), the only such farm in South Africa, and a series of wildlife rehabilitation establishments. One of these is Moholoio, 31km (19 miles) from Hoedspruit (Mon–Sat, guided tours at 9.30 and 3, Sun at 3), where orphaned, injured and poisoned animals are cared for. The Swadini Reptile Park (daily 9–5) is also worth a visit, with an extensive enclosure housing a huge range of reptiles.

Low cloud hanging over the Three Rondavels (above); a view from God's Window (opposite)

BLYDE RIVER CANYON

This spectacular canyon winds for 26km (16 miles) and its forested slopes drop to 750m (2,460ft) in depth in places.

Some 60 million years ago this deep gash in the landscape was created by the forces of the meandering Blyde River. It was in 1844 that a group of Voortrekkers named the river Blyde (meaning joy). Today it tumbles down from the Drakensberg escarpment over a series of waterfalls and cascades that spill into the Blydepoort Dam at the bottom. The canyon is one of the largest in the world and the Blyde River Canyon Nature Reserve extends for 27,000ha (66,500 acres) from God's Window viewpoint down to the far side of the Blyde River dam.

The best views are easily accessible as the R532 passes along the lip of the canyon, past dramatic viewpoints. There is also a drive to the base of the canyon (▷ 240–241).

VIEWPOINTS

The most famous of the viewpoints is God's Window, right on the edge of the escarpment, overlooking an almost sheer drop of 300m (1,000ft) into the tangle of forest below. The views through the heat haze stretch as far as Kruger. At 1,730m (5,675ft), Wonder View is the highest viewpoint accessible from the road, and Pinnacle Rock is a high quartzite 'needle' that rises dramatically 30m (100ft) out of the fern-clad ravine. From here it is possible to see the tops of the eight waterfalls that take the Blyde River down 450m (1,500ft) in a series of falls and cascades to the bottom.

The viewpoint at the Three Rondavels is by far the most dramatic, with the canyon opening up before you and the Blydespoort Dam shimmering intensely blue at the bottom. These circular rocky peaks capped with grass and vegetation look distinctly like traditional *rondavels* (huts with thatched roofs).

BOURKE'S LUCK POTHOLES

At the confluence of the Treur and Blyde rivers are these unusual rock formations, resembling Swiss cheese and formed by the swirling action of whirlpools. The smooth cylindrical holes are 15 million years old and are carved out of quartzite. The deepest part of the ravine created by the holes is 30m (100ft).

Looking down into Bourke's Luck Potholes

RATINGS				
Outdoor pursuits	●	●	●	●	●
Photo stops	●	●	●	●	●
Walkability	●	●	●	●	●

BASICS

🔲 325 M3

🈯 Panorama Tourist Association, Louis Trichardt Street, Graskop 1270, tel 013-7671377; Mon–Fri 8–5, Sat–Sun 8–1

🔲 Kiosk at Bourke's Luck Potholes

🎫 Craft stalls around God's Window

🍴 At Bourke's Luck and God's Window

❓ Visitor centre at Bourke's Luck Potholes

www.panoramainfo.co.za

TIPS

● There is a good visitor centre at Bourke's Luck Potholes (tel 013-7616019; daily 7–5, ▷ 240) with displays about the canyon.

● For accommodation, the canyon is close to Graskop, Sabie and Pilgrim's Rest.

● North on the R532 takes you to the R36 and the nearby Echo Caves (▷ 240).

Kruger National Park

The king of South African game parks, and one of the best game-viewing areas in southern Africa, the Kruger stretches across the Limpopo Province and Mpumalanga and along the border with Mozambique.

RATINGS	
Good for kids	● ● ● ●
Outdoor pursuits	● ● ● ● ●
Photo stops	● ● ● ● ●
Value for money	● ● ● ●

A family group of elephants, which is a common sight in the Kruger

SEEING KRUGER NATIONAL PARK

Kruger's figures speak for themselves: 500 species of bird, 114 of reptile, 49 of fish, 33 amphibians, 146 mammals and more than 23,000 plant species have been recorded here. The park measures 60km (37 miles) wide and more than 350km (217 miles) long, conserving 21,497sq km (8,384sq miles), an area the size of Israel. It certainly fulfils most visitors' fantasies of seeing magnificent herds of game roaming across acacia-studded stretches of savannah, and it's home to the Big Five (elephant, leopard, lion, black rhino and buffalo).

Despite its size, the park is well developed, with a good network of roads and numerous camps. There is no local public transport. Most people arrive in Kruger by road on a tour or in their own vehicle. If you are driving yourself and break down,

Kruger Emergency Road Services (tel 0800-030666) will tow you to the nearest garage outside the park (the service is not equipped to do any major repairs). While much of the park is designed for self-driving and renting simple accommodation with no meals provided, it is also possible to stay in a clutch of top-end private reserves. These are often more popular with first-timers as all game drives are led by rangers, leaving the animal spotting to the experts.

Don't expect to have Kruger to yourself. The park receives 1.5 million visitors a year and the camps cater to up to 5,000 visitors a day. Despite the huge number of people passing through, Kruger has managed to keep its magic. Only 5 per cent of the park is affected by the activities of the visitors and few areas in the south come close to the overcrowding seen in east Africa's game parks.

WHEN TO VISIT

The park looks its best after the summer rains when the new shoots and lush vegetation provide a surplus of food for the grazers. As the animals put on fat and become healthier, the females give birth to their young. Migratory birds are attracted to the area at this time of year and display their vivid breeding plumage. On the downside, the thick foliage and tall grasses make it harder to spot animals. In winter the dry weather forces them to congregate around waterholes and

BASICS

✚ 325 N2

☎ SANParks reservations, tel 012-4289111

◷ Reception and gate: Nov–end Feb daily 8–7; Mar, Sep and Oct daily 8–6.30; Apr–end Jun daily 8–6

💰 Daily conservation fee: adult R120, child (under 12) R60

🚗 Most camps have guided day drives and night drives (reservations essential)

🍴 Most camps have restaurants open for breakfast, lunch and dinner. Some also have a bar

🏬 All larger camps have shops selling foodstuffs, firewood, petrol (gas) and field guides

📖 Many identification guides for wildlife. Kruger map, travel guide and comprehensive 'Find it' guide
www.sanparks.org
www.greatlimpopopark.com

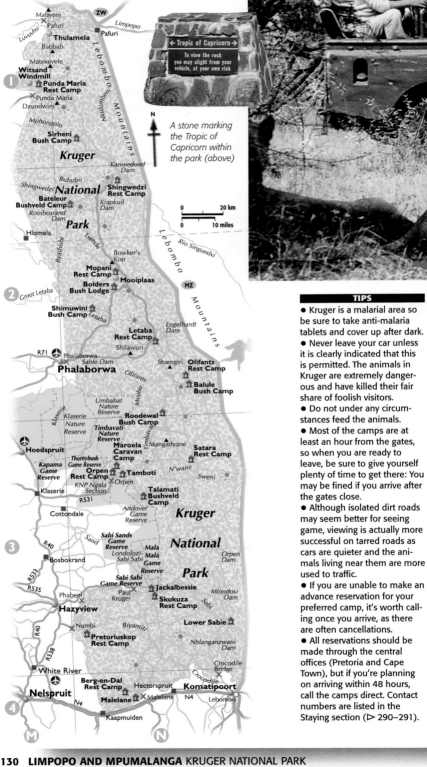

A stone marking the Tropic of Capricorn within the park (above)

◄ Tropic of Capricorn ►
To view the rock
you may alight from your
vehicle, at your own risk

Map labels

Mabyeni
Pafuri
ZW
Limpopo
Pafuri
Luvuvhu
Thulamela
Baobab
Matekevele
Witsand
Windmill
Punda Maria
Rest Camp
Punda Maria
Dzundwini
Mphongolo
Sirheni
Bush Camp

Nkumbeni Mountains

Kruger
Kanniedood
Dam
Bububu
Shingwedzi
National
Shingwedzi
Rest Camp
Bateleur
Bushveld Camp
Krapkuil
Dam
Rooibosrand
Dam
Park
Hlomela
Brashishi
Tsende
Bowker's
Kop
Mopani
Rest Camp
Bolders
Bush Lodge
Mooiplaas
MZ
Groot Letaba
Shimuwini
Bush Camp
Letaba
Engelhardt
Dam
Letaba
Rest Camp
Shilawuri
R71
Phalaborwa
Sable Dam
Shamgiri
Olifants
Rest Camp
Phalaborwa
Olifants
Balule
Bush Camp
Mvubu

Rio Singuedxi
Lebombo Mountains

Umbabat
Nature
Reserve
Klaserie
Roodewal
Bush Camp
Klaserie
Nature
Reserve
Timbavati
Nature
Reserve
Maroela
Caravan
Camp
Mangadyane
Satara
Rest Camp
Hoedspruit
Thornybush
Game Reserve
Orpen
Rest Camp
Tamboti
N'wane
Sweni
Kapama
Game
Reserve
KNP Ngala
Section
Orpen
Talamati
Bushveld
Camp
Klaserie
R531
Cottondale
Andover
Game
Reserve
Kruger
Sabi Sands
Game Reserve
Sand
Londolozi-
Sabi Sabi
Mala
Mala
Game
Reserve
National
Orpen
Dam
R40
Bosbokrand
Sabi Sabi
Game Reserve
R533
R535
Park
Phabeni
Paul
Kruger
Jackalbessie
Mlondosi
Dam
Skukuza
Rest Camp
Hazyview
Numbi
Biyamiti
Sabi
Lower Sabie
Pretoriuskop
Rest Camp
Nhlanganzwani
Dam
R40
White River
R538
Berg-en-Dal
Rest Camp
Hectorspruit
Crocodile
Bridge
Nelspruit
Malelane
Malelane
Komatipoort
Crocodile
N4
N4
Lebombo
Kaapmuiden
M
N

0   20 km
0   10 miles
N

TIPS
● Kruger is a malarial area so be sure to take anti-malaria tablets and cover up after dark.
● Never leave your car unless it is clearly indicated that this is permitted. The animals in Kruger are extremely dangerous and have killed their fair share of foolish visitors.
● Do not under any circumstances feed the animals.
● Most of the camps are at least an hour from the gates, so when you are ready to leave, be sure to give yourself plenty of time to get there: You may be fined if you arrive after the gates close.
● Although isolated dirt roads may seem better for seeing game, viewing is actually more successful on tarred roads as cars are quieter and the animals living near them are more used to traffic.
● If you are unable to make an advance reservation for your preferred camp, it's worth calling once you arrive, as there are often cancellations.
● All reservations should be made through the central offices (Pretoria and Cape Town), but if you're planning on arriving within 48 hours, call the camps direct. Contact numbers are listed in the Staying section (▷ 290–291).

the thinner foliage means you can spot more animals. However, they tend not to be in the best condition.

From the point of view of comfort, summer daytime temperatures can rise to a sweltering 40°C (104°F), and afternoon rains are common. The winter months of June, July and August are more comfortable, with daytime temperatures of around 30°C (86°F). Nights can be surprisingly cold at this time of year and temperatures drop to 0°C (32°F). Kruger is at its most crowded during the South African school holidays (Jun, Jul, Dec and Jan). Accommodation within the park will be completely full and the heavy traffic on the roads can mar the 'wilderness' experience.

GAME VIEWING

The highest concentrations and variety of game are around Lower Sabie, Satara and Skukuza. The best times for viewing are after dawn and just before dusk, as animals tend to rest during the heat of the day. The network of roads linking the camps outlined below is open to the public only during daylight hours, and the roads are subject to speed limits (monitored by radar). Game viewing takes patience, so do not travel faster than 20kph (12mph) or the chances are you'll have passed the animals before you've spotted them. Hours spent driving around Kruger in a car can be exhausting, so break your journey by stopping at one of the get-out points where you can watch the comings and goings at a waterhole.

HIGHLIGHTS

SOUTHERN KRUGER

The greatest concentrations of wildlife are in southern Kruger and many visitors only see this section. The landscape is more varied than elsewhere and supports a wider range of animals. The black and white rhinos, wild dogs and lions, as well as large numbers of giraffe, impala, wildebeest and zebra attract the greatest interest, and most of Kruger's large camps are here. Near the entrance at Malelane Gate is Berg-en-Dal, a large, modern camp with a rather austere institutional feel to it. It is set in a hilly landscape overlooking the Matjulu Dam. Game seen here includes giraffe, kudu, white rhino, zebra and wild dog. Malelane, a luxury private camp set in a rugged area of mountain bushveld (open bush country) along the banks of the Crocodile River, is also reached from Berg-en-Dal.

Getting close to the lions (above); a blackboard shows which tours around the Olifants area of the park are available for the day (inset)

PRIVATE GAME RESERVES

There are a number of private game reserves along the western border of Kruger, with some of the most exclusive game viewing opportunities in the world. Here you have the chance to see the Big Five in their natural environment and at the end of the day enjoy five-star luxury and cuisine. These include Kapama, Timbavati, Thornybush, Mala Mala, Sabi Sabi and Sabi Sands.

PROSPECTORS MUSEUM

✚ 130 M2 (Letaba) ✉ Letaba Camp
☎ 013-7356664 ◷ Mon–Sat 8–8, Sun
8–6 ⏻ Free

The air-conditioned museum at
Letaba has an excellent display
about elephants. There is a small
cinema showing wildlife videos
and a large hall dedicated to the
life cycle of the elephant.

*A night drive will give you a
different viewing experience*

THULAMELA

✚ 130 N1

Thulamela, in the northern corner
of Kruger Park close to the
Levuvhu River, is an important
late Iron Age site. Reservations
from Sirheni, Shingwedzi, Punda
Maria and Pafuri Gate.

*Don't be fooled by the docile
look of the buffalo, as they can
be very aggressive*

There is a hippo pool close to Crocodile Bridge camp, a small camp
in acacia woodland next to the park's southern gate. The area from
here to Lower Sabie is good for seeing large herds of buffalo, kudu,
impala, wildebeest and zebra. Lion and cheetah can sometimes be
spotted tracking the large herds.

The region around Lower Sabie is part of a classic African savannah
landscape, with grasslands, umbrella thorn and round-leaf teak
stretching off into the distance. This is regarded as a good area for
rhino and is generally one of the best regions for seeing game, which
is attracted by water at the Mlondozi and Nhlanganzwane dams. The
camp overlooks the Sabie River; accommodation is impersonal but
the camp itself is fairly peaceful. The oldest camp in Kruger—and the
third largest—is Pretoriuskop, near Numbi Gate. The game drives
around here pass through woodland and tall grassland, with good
game viewing areas to the north along the Sabie River and to the
south along the Voortrekker Road.

Kruger's largest camp is Skukuza, on the south bank of the Sabie
River, from where the park is controlled and administered. The camp
has grown to such an extent that it's possible to forget where you
are—it can accommodate more than 1,000 people—but it is still a
prime game viewing area and a good base for game drives.

The road heading northeast towards Satara has a lot of game and is
said to have one of the densest concentrations of lion in Africa (leading to the densest population of cars in Kruger). Some 8km (5 miles)
from here is Jackalbessie, the largest of Kruger's private camps. It is
on the Sabie River and has excellent game viewing opportunities,
with impressive numbers of animals passing through the thorn
thickets to the river.

CENTRAL KRUGER

The central area of Kruger is quieter than the south, with smaller
camps and fewer cars. There are large areas of flat mopane woodland
inhabited by herds of buffalo, elephant, wildebeest and zebra. In the
east, Olifants camp has one of Kruger's most spectacular settings,
high on a hill overlooking the fever trees and wild figs lining the banks
of the Olifants River. The thatched veranda perched on the edge of
the camp looks down into the river valley and is a superb place for
viewing game. Balule, also on the banks of the Olifants River, is one
of Kruger's wildest camps. It is little more than a patch of cleared bush
surrounded by an electrified chain-link fence; you can watch animals

wandering past just a few metres away. It's a thrill to see hyenas patrol the fence at night, drawn by the smell of *braais* (the traditional Afrikaner barbecues).

In the northern area of the central section, Boulders is an unfenced private camp in an area of woodland. The camp blends in beautifully with its environment and is set among massive granite boulders. One of Kruger's largest camps is Mopani, on a rocky hill overlooking the Pioneer Dam just a few kilometres south of the Tropic of Capricorn. The chalets at Mopani have been made from natural materials and it is more pleasant than some of the older camps. Shimuwini ('the place of the baobab'), farther west, has less game than you will see in the south of Kruger, but the private access road leading to the camp follows the Letaba River, where elephants can sometimes be seen bathing. The riverine forest around the camp is good for birdwatching.

Shingwedzi
You may alight from your vehicle on this bridge at your own risk. Stay between the yellow marks.

Blue wildebeest are only found in southern Africa

A greater kudu, one of the larger antelope species

The Niamanzi viewpoint on the Olifants River

Letaba, one of the larger public camps in Central Kruger, is a pleasant, neatly laid-out camp on the banks of the Letaba River. Animals to be seen here include, most notably, the large herds of elephant, but the list also contains cheetah, lion, ostrich, sable, steenbok and tsessebe antelopes. There is good game viewing to the east of Letaba along the river and at Engelhardt Dam. Roodewal is a private bush lodge on the Timbavati River, 29km (18 miles) from Olifants and 42km (26 miles) from Satara. Its unusual feature is a platform built around a nyala tree that overlooks a waterhole. Kruger's second largest camp is Satara, rather too developed for most people's liking, although the functional feeling is softened by trees and lawns. Satara is set in the flat grasslands of the eastern region, which attract large herds of wildebeest, buffalo, kudu, impala, zebra and elephant. There is good game viewing on the road to Orpen.

Giraffes will be easy to spot in the park

Maroela and Tamboti are both campsites close to Orpen Gate on the south bank of the Timbavati River; the latter is smaller and you do not need to bring any equipment. Orpen, also nearby, is a small camp just past the entrance gate. The area around the camp is known for its leopard, lion and cheetah. A little to the south is Talamati, set on the banks of the N'waswitsontso River which is normally dry. The grassland and acacia woodland along the western boundary attract kudu, giraffe, sable and white rhino.

NORTHERN KRUGER

The northern sector of Kruger is a relatively little visited, dry and remote region. As there is no year-round water supply, there isn't the same density of animals as in the south, but the area does support rare antelopes like Sharpe's grysbok, tsessebe, sable and nyala, as well as leopard. The Luvuvhu River, lined with ironwood and ebony, has some of the best wildlife viewing. Huge pythons thrive in the thick forests and some of the largest crocodiles in Kruger can be seen here. The bridge crossing is an excellent spot for birdwatchers after heavy rains—look for the cape parrot, Basra reedwarbler, tropical boubou and

A scops owl

yellowbellied sunbird. The picnic site at Mooiplaas, between Letaba and Shingwedzi, overlooks a waterhole on the Tsende River where game can often be seen.

The most southerly camp is Bateleur, an isolated bushveld camp surrounded by a vast area of woodland. Visitors have exclusive access to the two nearby dams, both of which are good areas for game watching. Further east is Shingwedzi, a large chalet camp. The best game viewing in this area is around Kanniedood Dam and the riverine forest along the banks of the Shingwedzi. In the middle of the northern section is Sirheni, a bushveld camp overlooking a dam. Although game is present, it is known mainly for its birdwatching.

Punda Maria, a peaceful rest camp hidden by dense woodland, is the northernmost large public camp in Kruger. It is in a unique area of sandveld (sandy grasslands) dotted with baobabs (a tree with a thick

Cheetahs can reach speeds of up to 90kph (56mph)

Eye to eye wiith a female warthog

A yellow-billed hornbill

A chameleon (above); an eland antelope, with distinctive spiral antlers (below)

trunk), white lilacs and pod mahogany. There are spectacular views of the surrounding landscapes from the top of the hill called Dzundwini, and good game viewing near the camp on the Mahonie Loop and up near the Witsand windmill. The bridge over the Luvuvhu River is a top place for birdwatchers.

WILDERNESS TRAILS

Seeing the park on foot is the most exciting way to experience Kruger's wilderness, although places are limited and usually fully reserved months in advance. A maximum of eight people are allowed on each of the seven trails and they are accompanied by an armed ranger. Hikers spend each night at the same bush camp and go out on day walks. The trails are up to 15km (9 miles) long, giving hikers ample time for game viewing. Food, water bottles, sleeping bags, rucksacks and cutlery are all provided.

The wilderness trails are run twice a week on Sunday and Wednesday and last for two days and three nights (tel 012-4265111; R2,150 per person). The best time of year for hiking is from March to July when the weather is dry and daytime temperatures are cooler.

The Bushman Trail is good for seeing white rhino and wild dogs; the hikes also take you to nearby San rock paintings. The camp is in a region of mountain bushveld in the southwest of the park, in an isolated valley surrounded by koppies (small hills). You check in at Berg-en-Dal near Malelane Gate, from where it's an hour's drive by Land Rover to the trail camp. Accommodation is in thatched bush huts.

The Napi Trail passes through a variety of habitats following the banks of the Biyamiti River through thick riverine bush and crossing mixed woodlands. Here you should be able to see both black and white rhino, duiker, jackal, kudu and giraffe. Check in at Pretoriuskop.

The Metsi-Metsi Trail camp is in an area of mountain bushveld near the N'waswitsontso River. The trail also visits areas of marula savannah where there are many plains animals. Check in at Skukuza.

The Nyalaland Trail passes through a vast expanse of mopane scrub, dotted with baobabs, aloes and koppies. The wildlife here is

unique to this sector of the park and nyala are often seen. The bird life is spectacular. The hutted camp is shaded by kuduberry trees next to the Madzaringwe Stream. Check in at Punda Maria.

The Olifants Trail crosses through classic African plain. There are excellent chances of seeing large herds of buffalo, wildebeest and zebra. The hutted camp overlooks the Olifants River and is 90 minutes by Land Rover from Letaba, where you check in.

The Sweni Trail is southeast of Satara overlooking the Sweni River and crosses through knobthorn and marula savannah where large herds of buffalo, wildebeest and zebra can be seen. Other species to spot include cheetah, lion, sable and steenbok. Check in at Satara.

The Wolhuter Trail passes through lowveld savannah where you might see lion, cheetah, black and white rhino, roan, sable and wild dog. The trail is named after the park ranger Harry Wolhuter, who killed a lion with his knife in 1903. The bush camp has wooden huts and is near the Mlambane River. Check in at Berg-en-Dal.

BACKGROUND

The first section of what was to become the National Park was officially formed in 1898 by Paul Kruger. Major James Stevenson-Hamilton, during his 44 years in charge, worked tirelessly to protect and extend the area, until it reached almost its current size. It was also under his care that the area was declared the Kruger National Park in 1926. The next phase in the park's life is for it to become part of the Great Limpopo Transfrontier Park (GLTP). This is a joint initiative between South Africa and the countries that border the Kruger. The GLTP links the Kruger with the Limpopo National Park in Mozambique, plus a number of parks in Zimbabwe. The first step was taken in 2002, when heads of state signed an agreement to establish the GLTP and part of the fence between the Kruger and the Limpopo was symbolically removed.

Leopards are generally noctural, but you may see one during the day in the trees

Baobab trees form part of the Kruger landscape

Picking tea leaves at an enormous tea plantation set in the Magoebaskloof

A wooden carving found near Makhado

KOMATIPOORT

➕ 325 N4

This is the last town in South Africa before the main road enters Mozambique at Lebombo. Being so close to the border, it has grown over the years with the increase in trade. Not far from here, on the Komati flats, is the Marehall Memorial, a national monument marking the site where Mozambique's President Samora Machel tragically died in a plane crash in 1986 (his widow Graça Machel went on to marry Nelson Mandela in 1998). These days the town is a popular place to pick up supplies for visitors to Kruger National Park—Crocodile Gate is only 9km (6 miles) away. There are a number of supermarkets along Rissik Street.

KRUGER NATIONAL PARK

See pages 128–135.

LYDENBURG

➕ 325 M3 ℹ Lydenburg Tourism, Viljoen Street, Lydenburg 1120, tel 083-3306267; Mon–Fri 7–5, Sat–Sun 7–3 www.lydenburg.co.za

The descent from Long Tom Pass west to Lydenburg, a quiet agricultural town, opens up vistas of rolling grasslands, cattle ranches and wheat-growing country. In 1957 seven clay heads were found on a farm near the town. The so-called Lydenburg Heads date from AD590 and are some of the earliest southern African depictions of the human form. The Lydenburg Museum (Mon–Fri 8–1, 2–4, Sat–Sun 8–5) is fascinating, with well-presented displays about the history of the Lydenburg region. It was the first home of the Heads; today they are in the South African Museum in Cape Town (▷ 69).

MAGOEBASKLOOF

➕ 325 M2 ℹ Rissik Street, behind the Elms Gift Shop, Haenertsburg 0730, tel 015-2764972; Mon–Fri 9–5, Sat 9–12 www.magoebaskloof.com

This beautiful mountainous area is good both for walking and exploring by car. The helpful tourist office has information about these excellent hikes, including the Magoebaskloof Hiking Trail and the easier one-day Rooikat Hiking Trail. One of the best times of the year to visit is in the spring (although many country hotels will be fully reserved), when the area becomes vivid with wild flowers and cherry blossoms. During December and January you can expect to see bright pink and mauve 'pride of India' trees. More than 200 species of orchid have been identified, and there are several yearly flower festivals. The lower slopes are verdant with tea and banana plantations and gum tree forests, and the image is of a rolling, green patchwork quilt.

MAKHADO/ LOUIS TRICHARDT

➕ 325 M1 ℹ Soutpansberg Tourism, corner of Old Trichardt Street and the N1, Makhado 0920, tel 015-5160040; Mon–Fri 8–4.30, Sat 8–1 www.golimpopo.com

Now renamed Makhado after a famous VhaVenda chief, this town was formerly known as Louis Trichardt, named after the Voortrekker leader who set up his camp near here in May 1836. The town is the hub of an agricultural area producing tea, coffee, timber and subtropical fruits. It's a sleepy backwater, disturbed only by the trucks rumbling through on the N1. The Indigenous Tree Sanctuary at the intersection of the N1 and Old Trichardt Street has 145 species of indigenous trees and some Voortrekker graves. Makhado has a small Swiss community, which was established through the Swiss Elim missionary hospital.

MALA MALA GAME RESERVE

➕ 325 N3 ☎ 031-7163500 🚗 Approach is from the R536, the Hazyview to Skukuza road www.malamala.com

Mala Mala, part of Greater Kruger National Park, was established as a safari lodge more than 40 years ago. It was one of the first private reserves to cater to the luxury market and has one of the most expensive private lodges with an excellent reputation for luxury service and game viewing. Guests have exclusive access to more than 50km (30 miles) of riverfront on the Sand River, as well as lands within Sabie Sands Game Reserve. The game and vegetation along the river are superb. Seeing the Big Five is a central part of the Mala Mala experience and guests get a 'Big Five' certificate to authenticate their sightings.

MUSINA

➕ 325 M1 ℹ Limpopo Valley Tourism, National Road, Musina 0900, tel 015-5343500; Mon–Fri 8–5

Musina, formerly known as Messina, is the northernmost town in South Africa, close to the border with Zimbabwe. It was originally a mining camp set up around copper mines, but today the local workforce is employed in the third biggest diamond mine in the world, which is owned by De Beers and is South Africa's biggest producer of diamonds. The town itself, however, is little more than a small *dorp* (the Afrikaner term for village).

Viewing an open cast mine in Phalaborwa

Carved animals and masks for sale in Pilgrim's Rest

Traditional craft at the Bakone Malapa Museum, Polokwane

This is also the access area to the Mapungubwe National Park, which, although open to the public, is still in the process of being developed—it will eventually cover 28,000ha (69,000 acres). It is set on the banks of the Limpopo River 70km (44 miles) northwest of Musina. The reserve forms part of the Transfrontier Conservation area, which covers South Africa, Zimbabwe and Botswana. It protects some San rock art sites as well as the Mapungubwe Hill, which researchers believe was the site of the first capital of the ancient kingdom of Great Zimbabwe between AD900 and 1300. Finds unearthed here include objects made from gold and ivory, as well as items of Arab, Chinese, Indonesian and Indian origin.

NELSPRUIT

🚹 325 M4 ℹ️ Lowveld Tourism Association, Crossing Centre, Nelspruit 1201, tel 013-7551988; Mon–Fri 8–4.30, Sat 8–1
www.lowveldinfo.com

Nelspruit is above all a town for shoppers. It's a good place to stock up with supplies if you are going to the Kruger, the Eastern Drakensberg, or over the border to Swaziland or Mozambique.

Mpumalanga's largest casino and shopping mall have been built 5km (3 miles) away on the road to White River.

Nearby are the small but important Lowveld National Botanical Gardens (9–5 in winter, 9–6 in summer) and the Croc River Reptile Park (daily 9–5), which claims to be the largest of its type in the whole continent and is a good attraction for children. The Botanical Gardens and the Croc River Park are both north of Nelspruit on the R40 heading towards White River.

PHALABORWA

🚹 325 M2 ℹ️ BaPhalaborwa Tourism Centre, Wildevy Street (opposite Spar supermarket), Phalaborwa 1389, tel 015-7816770; Mon–Fri 8–5

This quiet Afrikaner town is known for being the home of South Africa's Amarula Cream liqueur, made from the fruit of the marula tree and distilled here. Phalaborwa is a young town, established in 1958 when mining for minerals and copper began. With a width of 2km (1.2 miles), the open-cast mine is thought to be the widest man-made hole in Africa. At only 2km (1.2 miles) from Kruger's Phalaborwa Gate (for central and northern Kruger), the town is a convenient base for visiting the National Park and the luxury private game reserves. The airport has daily flights to Johannesburg and there are good facilities for visitors, including a variety of accommodation and restaurants, plus several car rental outlets. But as the red triangle signs in town will warn you: watch out for the hippos.

PILGRIM'S REST

🚹 325 M3 ℹ️ Main Street, Upper Town, Pilgrim's Rest 1290, tel 013-7681060; daily 9–12.45, 1.15–4.30
www.pilgrimsrest.co.za

Since the last gold mines of Pilgrim's Rest closed in 1972, the town has been completely reconstructed as a living museum to preserve a fascinating part of South Africa's cultural heritage. The restored miners' cottages, with their corrugated iron roofs and wooden walls, are evocative of gold-rush days, although today they are filled with gift shops, restaurants and hotels, turning the place into something of a theme park. Busloads of visitors come to spend the day here, so the best time to see Pilgrim's Rest is early in the morning or in the late afternoon after the day-trippers have gone. Although most of the buildings are strung out along one long street, the town has a clear division between the smart and prosperous Uppertown and the plainer Downtown.

POLOKWANE/ PIETERSBURG

🚹 325 L2 ℹ️ Limpopo Tourism Board, corner of Grobler and Kerk streets, Polokwane 0699, tel 015-2907300; Mon–Fri 8–4.30
www.golimpopo.com

The capital of Limpopo Province is a large modern city that has changed its name from Pietersburg to Polokwane, meaning 'place of safety'. As well as being a good base for exploring the relatively undiscovered Limpopo region, it has a few sights of its own. Irish House, on the corner of Thabo Mbeki and Market streets, is home to the Polokwane Museum (tel 015-2902182 for details), which traces the history of the region from the Stone Age to modern times. On the other side of Thabo Mbeki Street is the fascinating Hugh Exton Photographic Museum (Mon–Fri 9–4, Sun 3–5). This is a superb collection of prints and negatives that trace the first 50 years of Pietersburg; few towns have such a record of their past. Another museum well worth a visit is the Bakone Malapa Northern Sotho Open-Air Museum (tel 015-2952432; Mon–Fri 8.30–12.30, 1.30–3.30), which lies 9km (6 miles) from the middle of town on the R37 and celebrates the life and traditions of the Bakone tribe. The Polokwane Art Museum (tel 015-2902177; Mon–Fri 9–4, Sat 9–12) has a fine collection of South African paintings and sculptures.

The twin cascades of the Mac-Mac Falls, outside Sabie

A dirt track through a banana plantation near Tzaneen

A Venda villager carving a log in the Soutpansberg Mountains

SABIE

🕂 325 M3 ℹ Panorama Tourist Information, in the Sabie Market Mall, Main Street, Sabie 1260, tel 013-7671377; Mon–Fri 9–5, Sat–Sun 9–1 **www.panoramainfo.co.za**

Sabie, in a valley ringed by mountains and dominated by eucalyptus plantations and pine, lies within one of the largest man-made forests in the world. Once a gold mining town, it has little left to show of the glittering gold-rush era, and is now a prosaic timber-processing town. However, it is one of the more attractive towns in the region, its main road lined with pleasant craft and coffee shops. The Forestry Museum on Ford Street (tel 013-7641056; Mon–Fri 9–4) has displays of the development of South Africa's plantations and the timber industry. Refurbished during 1997, the museum's buildings also contain a satellite office of SAFCOL (the Forestry Department), which has information about hiking and mountain bike trails in the region, both very popular activities.

SOUTPANSBERG MOUNTAINS

🕂 325 L1 ℹ Soutpansberg Tourism, corner of Old Trichardt Street and the N1, Makhado 0920, tel 015-5160040; Mon–Fri 8–4.30, Sat 8–1 **www.golimpopo.com**

The Soutpansberg mountain range extends for 130km (80 miles) and reaches 1,753m

A handmade carving of a man's head, traditionally created by the people of the Venda

(5,750ft). Along the high plateau are a number of villages of the Venda people (see below) where many of their traditions have been preserved. Some of the valleys and lakes are considered to be sacred sights, including Phiphidi Falls, Lwamomdo Hill and the Thathe Vondo Forest. Many of these are difficult to find and you should enlist the services of a registered guide if you wish to visit them. This will also help ensure that you approach and treat the sights sensitively. You can pick up the Soutpansberg Mountain Meander map, a self-drive guide to day trips in the area, at the tourist office.

The Hangklip Forest Reserve is 3km (2 miles) west of Makhado and is signposted off the N1. This is an area of indigenous forest around the base of the Hangklip, 1,719m (5,638ft), a wall of rock rising over the forest. The tops of the cliffs are some of the highest points of the Soutpansberg. There are a number of one-day hikes here through spectacular mountain scenery.

TZANEEN

🕂 325 M2 ℹ Shop 13, Oasis Mall, Aqua Park, Tzaneen 0850, tel 015-3071294; Mon–Fri 8–5, Sat 9–noon **www.tzaneen.com**

Tzaneen lies on the eastern side of the Magoebaskloof Mountains, at the heart of a prosperous agricultural region which is the biggest producer of avocados, mangoes, tea and tomatoes in South Africa. Much of the countryside looks considerably greener than many other parts of South Africa, and the palm trees and banana plantations add to a sense of tropical lushness. If you're in the area, don't miss the Tzaneen Museum on Agatha Street (Mon–Fri 9–5, Sat 9–1), one of the best museums in the

region. The private collection of ethnological objects is crammed into three small rooms, forming an amazing display of pottery, pole carvings, drums, books, beadwork and other domestic items. Ask to be shown around by the owner, Jurgen Witt, and allow plenty of time for the tour.

VENDA

🕂 325 M1

Most visitors pass through this former tribal homeland region without stopping. This is a pity, as the Venda region looks and feels more like the 'real' Africa than any other part of South Africa. The lush, green land produces tea, bananas and mangoes, but despite this and the efforts towards improvement made by the ANC government, Venda's infrastructure and housing are still poor, the roads are badly maintained, and most people rely on subsistence farming to make a living.

This is the land of the VhaVenda people, whose culture is steeped in the spirit world; there are many important sacred sites in the region. Originally from Zimbabwe, the VhaVenda people are thought to have migrated here at the beginning of the 18th century. They are regarded as some of the finest artists in South Africa, and are particularly renowned for their pottery and drum-making. Thohoyandou is the former capital of the independent homeland and is the commercial and administrative hub of the district. Its name means 'head of the elephant' in the tshiVenda language. The town has a vibrant African atmosphere, with much of life carried on outdoors—local produce is sold from roadside stands and the people are extraordinarily friendly.

GAUTENG AND FREE STATE

Gauteng, Sotho for 'place of gold', and its two principal cities of Johannesburg and Pretoria have undergone a change of identity since the fall of apartheid and now have a distinctive cultural feel. The scenery of Free State is of sparsely populated prairie, scattered with dams and mountain rivers, and connected by pretty rural villages.

MAJOR SIGHTS

A fishing tackle shop, built in 1894 in Bethlehem

A restored wagon on display at Bloemfontein

Two men in traditional dress at Basotho Cultural Village

THE SIGHTS

BETHLEHEM

➕ 330 K6 ℹ️ Metropolitan Centre, 22 Muller Street, Bethlehem 9701, tel 058-3035792; Mon–Fri 7.30–1, 2–4.30
www.dihlabeng.org.za

Bethlehem is the principal town of the Eastern Free State, an important wheat growing area and one of South Africa's biggest exporters of roses. F. P. Naude, a local church minister, named the settlement Bethlehem ('house of bread'), inspired by the wheat that flourished in the valley. It is a large town with a good range of restaurants and some fine examples of Victorian sandstone buildings. The best way to explore these is to follow the Sandstone Walking Tour; there's a map tracing the walk, which takes about 90 minutes. The most interesting buildings are the Methodist Church (1911), the Strapp Building (1894), the Wooden Spoon (late 1870s), one of the oldest buildings still standing, and the Baartman Coach House (1894). The museum (Mon–Fri 10–12.30), at the top end of Muller Street, has a collection covering the region's local history; there's an early steam locomotive in the grounds.

BETHULIE

➕ 329 H8

Bethulie is a typically pleasant rural Free State town with a history closely related to the development of South Africa. The original settlement, called Heidelberg, consisted of a mission station founded in 1829 by the London Missionary Society. It was taken over by the French Missionary Society in 1833 and renamed Bethulia–'chosen by God'. A few of the original mission buildings still exist and are thought to be some of the oldest

European-built houses in the Free State. The local museum is housed in Pellissier House.

Just outside the town is a spectacular concrete viaduct across the Gariep (Orange) River (the railway is part of the main line to the port of East London). At 1,150m (1,260 yards), the road-rail bridge is the longest of its kind in the country.

BLOEMFONTEIN

➕ 323 H7 ℹ️ Tourist Office, 60 Park Road, Bloemfontein 9301, tel 051-4058490/8489; Mon–Fri 8–4.15, Sat 8–12
www.mangaung.co.za

The provincial capital of the Free State is the sixth biggest city in the country and the judicial capital of South Africa. Central Bloemfontein is a mix of modern tower blocks dating from the 1960s and 1970s and fine sandstone buildings from the late 19th century, when Bloemfontein was the capital of the small independent Orange Free State Republic.

Its central position in South Africa makes it an important transport hub and a popular overnight stop for motorists driving between Gauteng and the Cape. Few people actually spend time here, however, and like much of the Free State it has yet to figure on the tourist map (although fans of *The Lord of the Rings* should note that J. R. R. Tolkien was born here in 1892, moving to England when he was four years old). The city feels friendly, and a large youthful contingent has led to the appearance of a number of trendy bars and nightclubs.

The Tourist Office produces a useful self-guided walking map, known as the Rose Walk, which takes in all the best sandstone buildings in town. Most of note

are within easy walking distance of each other along President Brand Street.

CLARENS

➕ 330 K6 ℹ️ Clarens Information, Market Street, Clarens 9797, tel 058-2561189; Mon–Fri 9–5, Sat 9–1

Clarens was established in 1912 and named after the Swiss resort along the shore of Lake Geneva where President Paul Kruger died in 1904. This attractive small village is a relaxing place, an ideal spot to make your base while exploring the Eastern Highlands. Its charm has made it popular with visitors, and a number of galleries, craft shops and tea rooms surround a grassy square with a few sandstone buildings and shady trees. The natural beauty of the area has also attracted artists to the region. Clarens is the closest village to the Golden Gate National Park (▷ 141) when approaching from the west.

There is white-water rafting on the Ash River, and five reasonably preserved cave paintings can be seen on a farm called Schaapplaats, 15 minutes' drive from the village (call in at the Clarens Tourist Office and they will let the farm owners know you are coming). If you are heading for Golden Gate National Park, the Basotho Cultural Village (Mon–Fri 9–4, Sat–Sun 9–5) is 44km (27 miles) beyond the park gate. It provides an insight into the lives of the Basotho people of the region, whose traditions are similar to those of the people living over the border in Lesotho. Guided tours take you around a scattering of *bomas* (covered outdoor eating areas) and huts where traditional crafts are demonstrated, local beer can be sampled, and a lively band provides entertainment.

A hazy sunset silhouettes the hills of the Eastern Highlands

The blue waters of the Gariep Dam are edged by flat-top hills, and are a great spot for watersports

EASTERN HIGHLANDS

323 J7 Clarens Information, Market Street, Clarens 9997, tel 058-2561189; Mon–Fri 9–5, Sat 9–1

The countryside neighbouring the Lesotho border, dominated by sandstone outcrops and eroded river valleys, is the most dramatic in the Free State. The hills once provided shelter for the early San hunters who lived in the region and there are some fine examples of cave paintings. The best way to appreciate the countryside is on horseback: The highlands are perfect hiking country and ideal for pony trekking, and there is some great accommodation out of town on farms and in secluded valleys. Running parallel to the Lesotho border, the R26 passes through all the main towns in this region.

FICKSBURG

330 K6 In the Highlands Hotel, 37 Vootrekker Street, next to the town hall, Ficksburg 9730, tel 051-9332214; daily 8–8

Named after General Johan Fick, a hero of the Basotho Wars between the Boers and the Basotho people, the town was founded in 1867 to occupy what was known as the Conquered Territory after those wars. Its role was to prevent cattle rustlers coming over from Lesotho and to strengthen the Boers' general control over the area. Curiously, even today cattle rustling still occasionally occurs in this region. A Cherry Festival is held here during the third week of November each year, when you can indulge in cherry liqueur, maraschino, schnapps and brandied cherries in syrup.

These days the small town has important trade links with Lesotho, but there is little to interest casual visitors unless they are seeking basic supplies.

GARIEP DAM

329 H8

The mighty Gariep Dam on the Gariep (Orange) and Caledon rivers, in the Trans Gariep southwest of Bloemfontein, is the largest dam in South Africa. At the lake's western end is the town also known as Gariep Dam, which has evolved since the completion of the dam wall in 1971 and is now a quiet little Afrikaner town. It's worth going up to the top of town for commanding views of the lake and surrounding farmlands. It hosts an annual International Gliding Championship in December, which has quickly gained a reputation for being the place to try to break world records. At the eastern end of the lake is the Gariep Dam Nature Reserve (tel 051-7540108; daily 7am–6pm), primarily a watersports complex with excellent sailing and fishing.

GOLDEN GATE NATIONAL PARK

330 K6 058-2550012 24 hours Free Glen Reenen Shop, selling limited groceries, fuel, beer and wine, firewood, maps 15km (9 miles) along a tarred road from Clarens
www.sanparks.org

A small (11,600ha/28,600 acres) national park on the edge of the Drakensberg and Maluti mountains, the Golden Gate National Park is in an area of massive cliffs and rocky outcrops. The eroded valleys have produced spectacular golden sandstone rock formations, caves and cliffs set against a backdrop of green grasslands. This is a particularly extraordinary place at sunset when the tones of the rocks are at their most intense. Its proximity to Johannesburg (3 hours by car) makes it a popular park and many daily

visitors come to hike and climb the rock formations, or to go horseback riding.

The grasslands that dominate the sandstone slopes are known for their wide variety of wild flowers in summer. You are unlikely to see much wildlife from your car, but once you get up into the wooded valleys and the quiet hills you may see black wildebeest, Burchell's zebra, mountain reedbuck, blesbok, eland and grey rhebok. The larger raptors inhabit the high rocky cliff faces; look for bearded vultures, jackal buzzards and black eagles. The most popular hike here is the two-day Rhebok Hiking Trail (places must be reserved in advance).

Sandstone layers can be seen in the rocks at Golden Gate

Johannesburg

Johannesburg is South Africa's biggest and wealthiest city and is home to the Apartheid Museum, one of the country's finest museums. The city has a great nightlife, a diverse selection of restaurants and excellent shopping outlets.

Serving cakes and pastries in a local bakery

A street artist adding the finishing touches

Johannesburg's Stock Exchange on Diagonal Street

RATINGS	
Chain store shopping	●●●●●
Cultural interest	●●●●●
Historic interest	●●●●

Statue of Mandela at Nelson Mandela Square, Sandton

SEEING JOHANNESBURG

Johannesburg is the largest financial, commercial and industrial city in South Africa. However, the once-prosperous central business district is now an area of abandoned office blocks and overpasses, where very few of the original buildings are left standing. It is worth visiting the central area for an insight into how Johannesburg has developed over the decades, but because of safety concerns, it is essential that you go only on an organized tour.

The city's thriving suburbs are clustered around the main highway (motorway/freeway) to Pretoria, the M1. The hills to the north of downtown Johannesburg are where you'll find large residential areas with rows of mansions, well-tended gardens and shopping malls. What is unusual is the amount of protection around the properties—razor wire, guard dogs and armed response warnings are the norm. These suburbs are in fact far safer than central Johannesburg and have a good choice of visitor accommodation, particularly in Rosebank and Sandton. Many of the sights, shopping malls and entertainment complexes are in the suburbs, so there is little reason to venture right into the city to find facilities. To the east of Rosebank are the trendy suburbs of Melville, Parkhurst and Parktown, where most of Johannesburg's more popular restaurants and nightlife are to be found.

The rail station and main bus terminal are at the Park City Transit Centre, but on the whole it is safer to stick to radio taxis for transport or to rent a car: Johannesburg is a city where you really do need a car to get around.

HIGHLIGHTS

APARTHEID MUSEUM

✉ Next to Gold Reef City, Northern Parkway and Gold Reef Road, Ormonde 2091
☎ 011-3904700 🕐 Tue–Sun 10–5 💷 Adult R25, child (under 6) R12
www.apartheidmuseum.org

One of the finest museums in the country, the Apartheid Museum provides an excellent insight into what South Africa—past and

present—is all about. This extraordinarily powerful museum was officially opened by Nelson Mandela in April 2002 and it has already become the city's leading visitor attraction. It is divided into 'spaces', which highlight aspects of South Africa's recent history. When paying your entry fee you are issued with a random white or non-white ticket that takes you through one of two different entry points to symbolize segregation. The building itself has an innovative design to reflect the museum's chilling theme, using harsh concrete, raw brick, steel bars and barbed wire.

The museum begins with a 15-minute video, taking you briefly through Voortrekker history to the Afrikaner government of 1948, which implemented apartheid. The 'spaces' are dedicated to the rise of nationalism in 1948, pass laws, segregation, the first response from townships such as Sharpeville and Langa, the forced removals and the implementation of the Group Areas Act. From here, exhibits cover the rise of Black Consciousness, the student uprisings in Soweto in 1976, and political prisoners and executions.

The reforms during the 1980s and 1990s are well documented, including President F. W. de Klerk's unbanning of political parties, Mandela's release, the first democratic elections in 1994, the lifting of sanctions and the new constitution. The exhibitions effectively use multimedia, such as television screens, recorded interviews and news footage, all providing a startlingly clear picture of the harshness and tragedy of the apartheid years. You should allow several hours for a visit here.

The rebirth of Jo'burg is evident in smart hotels such as the Sandton Sun

BASICS

🔢 324 K4

ℹ️ Johannesburg Tourism, 195 Jan Smuts Avenue, Johannesburg 2001, tel 011-3278001; Mon–Fri 8–5, Sat 9–1
www.joburg.org.za
www.gauteng.net

TIP

● Despite (very successful) efforts in recent years to make downtown Jo'burg safer, it is still not wise to go anywhere on foot; visit this part of the city on an organized tour only. Outlying sights such as the Apartheid Museum can easily be visited by car.

*The bright lights of night-time
Jo'burg (above)
The New Mall building (below)*

MUSEUM AFRICA

✉ 121 Bree Street, 2001 ☎ 011-8335624 🕐 Tue–Sun 9–5 💵 Adult R10, child (2–16) free

This museum is housed in the city's former fruit and vegetable market. It focuses on the black experience of living in Johannesburg, with displays about the struggle for democracy and about life in the goldmines and the townships; there are mock-ups of both a mine shaft and an informal settlement to give you a sense of these environments. Other sections include a gallery dedicated to San rock art and a display about the life of Mahatma Gandhi. The photographic gallery on the fourth floor has a collection of early photographs of Soweto. Most Johannesburg city tours allow at least a couple of hours in this rewarding museum.

KWAZULU MUTI SHOP (MUSEUM OF MAN AND SCIENCE)

✉ Corner of Diagonal and President streets, 2001 ☎ 011-8364470 🕐 Mon–Fri 7.30–5, Sat 7.30–1 💵 Free

This is actually a shop, rather than a museum. It has been here since 1897 selling products used in 'muti', traditional medicines used by indigenous healers to treat physical ailments—as well as for rather more sinister undertakings. While largely misunderstood by white South Africans, their mystical powers are highly revered among much of the African community. The ingredients on sale include leaves, seeds and bark, as well as the rather more specialized items, such as ostrich feet. City tours usually stop here.

GOLD REEF CITY

✉ Northern Parkway and Gold Reef Road, Ormonde 2091 ☎ 011-2485152 🕐 Tue–Sun 9.30–5. Mine tours: 9.30 and 1.30 💵 Adult R70 for entrance to rides, child (under 1.2m/4ft tall) R35.50 📷 Mine tours R45 www.goldreefcity.co.za

Gold Reef City is built on the site of one of Johannesburg's gold mining areas, but today has developed into a garish theme park with rides, amusement arcades and a gaudy casino. Of greater interest are the original miners' cottages and the tour of the gold mine, which drops to a depth of about 220m (720ft), taking you down No. 14 Shaft, one of the richest deposits of gold in its day.

JOHANNESBURG ZOO
✉ Jan Smuts Avenue, Parktown 2193 ☎ 011-6462000 🕐 Daily 8.30–5.30 💷 Adult R30, child (3–12) R18 🍴
www.jhbzoo.org.za
The city zoo was established in 1904. It has around 400 different species housed in an area of parkland and gardens covering 54ha (133 acres). The ponds attract free-ranging aquatic birds, which come here to breed. All the enclosures have been upgraded, and the night tours to see the nocturnal animals are fun, ending with marshmallows and a hot chocolate around a bonfire.

BACKGROUND
The high plateau on which Johannesburg was built was formerly an arid place sparsely inhabited by Boer farmers grazing cattle and cultivating maize and wheat. In little over 100 years, Johannesburg has grown into the wealthiest city in Africa. Settlers from all over the world poured in from the first weeks of the gold rush in the 1880s, producing a vibrant and cosmopolitan town. Apartheid changed all that, creating deep divisions in society that remain evident today. During its height, the African population was evicted to new townships, such as Soweto (▷ 151), 20km (12 miles) to the southwest of the city. The most infamous forced removal was the bulldozing of an area to the west of Johannesburg called Sophiatown. During the 1940s and 1950s there was a huge outburst of a new African urban culture in Sophiatown, based largely on the influence of American jazz musicians. This cultural explosion attracted Bohemian whites and many African writers, journalists and politicians. To the apartheid planners the area stood for everything they opposed; in the mid-1950s the entire population was removed and the bulldozers were sent in. However, since the mid-1980s the movement of Africans from the city to the townships has been reversed and this trend has continued and been bolstered by the arrival of new immigrants.

Despite apartheid's demise, Johannesburg is still on the whole a segregated city with its heart and neighbouring suburbs, such as Hillbrow, largely home to a black urban population who inhabit a condensed area of overcrowded high-rise apartments where poverty and crime are rife. Today, downtown Johannesburg feels much like an authentic African city to rival, for instance, Nairobi in Kenya or Dar es Salaam in Tanzania, though sadly not without its own new set of problems.

Two gates symbolize division at the Apartheid Museum

MORE TO SEE
THE MARKET THEATRE COMPLEX
✉ Bree Street, 2001
This complex, next to Museum Africa, was once a busy area of street cafés, restaurants and shops. With the decline of this part of the city over the past decade, the complex has struggled to attract visitors, but revitalizing efforts have tidied up the area and provided safe parking and security patrols. The theatre is one of the best and most established in Gauteng and there are a number of places where you can eat and drink.

WORLD OF BEER
✉ 15 President Street, 2001 ☎ 011-8364900 🕐 Tue–Sat 10–6 💷 R10 including two complimentary beers
Lovers of the amber nectar will appreciate the South African Breweries (SAB) World of Beer. SAB dominate the African beer industry, and their Castle Lager is probably the most popular beer between Cape Town and Cairo. The 90-minute tour covers the brewing process and a variety of mock-up bars.

SOUTH AFRICAN NATIONAL MUSEUM OF MILITARY HISTORY
✉ 20 Erlswold Way, Saxonwold 2196 ☎ 011-6465513 🕐 Tue–Sun 9–4.30 💷 Free
This museum has exhibits about the role South African forces played in World War II including artillery pieces, aircraft and tanks. There is a more up-to-date section illustrating the war in Angola, with displays of modern armaments, such as captured Soviet tanks and French Mirage fighter planes.

THE SIGHTS

Wine tasting at Landzicht cellar in Jacobsdal

A detail of the coffee pot fountain at Koffiefontein

A San painting of a hunting scene close to Ladybrand

HARRISMITH

330 L6 Harrismith Tourist Information, Montrose Country Cell Complex, Harrismith, tel 082-4578166; Mon–Fri 8–5, Sat 9.30–12.30

Founded in 1849 and named after Sir Harry Smith, Cape Colony's belligerent governor, Harrismith lies on the N3 and is a popular stop en route between Gauteng and Durban. The Platberg, a long, flat mountain of 2,377m (7,798ft), dominates the town, and a race is held along the 5km (3-mile) top every year in October.

JACOBSDAL

323 G7 1 Andries Pretorius Street, Jacobsdal, tel 053-5910164

This small town is known for the Landzicht Wine Cellar, where the first wine grapes to be grown outside the Cape Province were cultivated in 1969. Cellar tours and tastings are possible on request (tel 053-5910164) and there is an annual wine festival in February. The Dutch Reformed Church, consecrated in 1879, enlarged in 1930 and now

The local bank at Koffiefontein

a national monument, was used as a hospital during the Anglo-Boer War—look for the bullet holes in the front door. There are two well-known Anglo-Boer battle sites just outside Jacobsdal: Magersfontein (▷ 164) and Paardeberg. The Battle of Paardeberg took place between 18 and 27 February 1900. Although it ended with the surrender of the Boers, and more than 4,000 prisoners of war were taken, the losses on the first day proved to be the greatest suffered by the British for any day during the whole war. More than 300 British troops were killed and around 900 wounded.

JOHANNESBURG

See pages 142–145.

KOFFIEFONTEIN

323 G7 Koffiefontein Tourist Office, Municipality, tel 053-2050147, Mon–Fri 9.30–1, 3–5.30

The name of this small sheep farming town on the Riet River originates from the days when the settlement was on the transport route to Kimberley: Whenever riders passed through they

stopped to make coffee by the town fountain. Today there is an ornamental fountain in the form of a pouring coffee pot to commemorate this. In June 1870 a transport rider picked up a diamond near the fountain and the town enjoyed a boom. By 1882 there were four mining companies operating here. The legacy of the boom is a few fine old buildings, including the Central Hotel in Groot Trek Street. The open part of the diamond mine can be viewed from a lookout tower. The Blue Diamond Tavern is a well-preserved old building still in use.

LADYBRAND

323 J7 Maloti Route Tourism Office, in the Catharina Brand Museum, Kerk Street, Ladybrand 9745, tel 051-9245131; Mon–Fri 8–5

The pleasant country town of Ladybrand is only 15km (9 miles) from Lesotho's capital, Maseru. Along with Ficksburg, the town was founded in 1867, following the war between the Boers and the Basotho people, to help guarantee peace in the so-called Conquered Territory. Ladybrand was named after Lady Catharina Brand, the mother of President Brand of the Orange Free State Republic. The small Catharina Brand Museum on Kerk Street has an exhibit about the huge and influential Lesotho Highlands

Karoo-style house along the main street in Philippolis

Sterkfontein Caves is a World Heritage Site

Water Project (▷ 168). Today, Ladybrand's best-known resident is Bev Missing, proprietor of the shop called Rain in the Cranberry Cottage. Her home-made linen sprays, body lotions and soaps are sold in New York under the Donna Karan label.

There are two major San rock painting sites nearby, with paintings ranging in age from 5,000 to 250 years old; you can visit them with a guide from the tourist office. It is thought that these sites have the highest concentration of San paintings in South Africa.

LESEDI CULTURAL VILLAGE

🚩 324 K4 ☎ 012-2051394 📷 Tours at 11.30 and 4.30 🍴 Adult R260, child (under 12) R130; includes a meal 🚗 On R512, 12km (7.5 miles) north of Lanseria Airport www.lesedi.com

The Cultural Village includes four African villages representing Xhosa, Zulu, Pedi and Sotho peoples, with two-hour tours taking in all four. The tours include an audio-visual presentation covering aspects of tribal life of the 11 ethnic groups that live in South Africa, There's also music, singing and traditional dancing by more than 60 performers around a large fire in an amphitheatre. The morning tour includes lunch; afternoon visitors are given a dinner of game meat such as impala or crocodile. The Village makes an easy day trip from Johannesburg or Pretoria.

LION PARK

🚩 324 K4 ☎ 011-4601814 ⏰ Mon–Fri 8.30–5, Sat–Sun 8.30–6 🍴 R100 for a car including 4 passengers; extra R10 for cub enclosure 🍴🚌🚗 30 min drive from Johannesburg on the Old Pretoria–Krugersdorp road www.lion-park.co.za

If your ambition is to photograph lions, you are unlikely to get any closer to them than here: There are more than 50 in the park, including many cubs (with which you can have close encounters) and a rare male white lion. Although the animals are bred in captivity, they are well cared for and have ample space in the drive-through enclosures. The lions are accustomed to vehicles and don't think twice about strolling right up to a car, so keep windows closed and adhere to any safety notices. The Lion Park is on the way to Lesedi (see left).

PHILIPPOLIS

🚩 328 H8 ℹ️ 25 Kok Street, Philippolis 9970, tel 051-7730006; Mon–Fri 8–5

The town of Philippolis is the oldest in the Free State, founded in 1823 as a station of the London Missionary Society. It has a number of attractive old buildings that have been declared national monuments; they are all found along the one main street. Look out for the Dutch Reformed Church, which has a pulpit carved from olive wood, and examples of Karoo-style houses. The tiny Transgariep Museum (Mon–Fri 10–noon), in a typical Griqua cottage, is where you can find out about the history of the region. There is an informative display about the Griqua—a people of mixed race, former slaves, who settled in the area seeking independence. The ashes of author Sir Laurens van der Post are kept in the memorial gardens named in his memory.

PRETORIA

See pages 148–150.

SOWETO

See page 151.

STERKFONTEIN CAVES

🚩 324 K4 ☎ 011-3551400 ⏰ Tue–Sun 9–4 🍴 Adult R20, child (under 12) R10 📷 Tours every hour, departing on the half-hour 🚗🚌 Off N14 from Randburg towards Hartbeetspoort Dam www.cradleofhumankind.co.za

Dubbed the Cradle of Humankind, the area around the Sterkfontein Caves holds some of the world's most important archaeological sites, where more than 40 per cent of all hominid fossils have been discovered. Although the dolomite hill holding the caves was discovered in the late 19th century, it was not until 1936 that the most important find was made, the first adult skull of the ape-man *Australopithecus africanus*—nicknamed 'Mrs Ples'. The skull, found by Dr. Robert Broom, is estimated to be more than 2.6 million years old (▷ 29).

The caves have six chambers connected by passages. Tours take in some of the archaeological sites, as well as a lake and some stalactite formations.

XHARIEP

🚩 323 H7

Xhariep is the region to the southwest of Bloemfontein. This is cattle and sheep ranch country, and is a quiet, seldom-visited corner of the Free State. The region has a handful of towns, including Koffiefontein (▷ 146) and Philippolis (see above). At the start of the 19th century this was classic big game country—in 1848, mail could not be despatched after 4pm because of the danger posed by animals. In 1860, a hunt organized for Prince Alfred, the second son of Queen Victoria, killed nearly 5,000 animals on a single day. Little wildlife remains today.

Pretoria

Pretoria is South Africa's administrative capital and a leading academic centre. The compact city has good museums, elegant buildings, leafy city parks and avenues lined with jacaranda trees.

SEEING PRETORIA

Pretoria, also known as Tshwane, is the administrative capital of South Africa and the third largest city in the country. Despite almost merging into Johannesburg 56km (35 miles) to the south, the two cities couldn't be more different in atmosphere. Like most major cities in South Africa, Pretoria has gone through a transformation in recent years. With the demise of apartheid, black South Africans are again permitted to live and work freely in central Pretoria, with the result that it feels much livelier and more African than before.

Most of the historic and interesting sights are outside the city, dotted around the surrounding hills, as the heart of the city was designed with corporate and governmental bodies in mind. This necessitates the use of a rental car or taking a half-day tour with a guide.

There is a metro commuter train between Pretoria and Johannesburg but it is not a safe option. It is better to take a bus; Greyhound and Intercape run a regular service between the cities each day. Although Pretoria has a fairly good local bus service (in contrast to many South African cities), it does not cover all the main sights, so it is still best to rent a car. It is also a good idea if you want to venture into the suburbs, where there is an excellent choice of accommodation and restaurants, plus some lively student-driven nightlife. The best suburbs for nightlife are Hatfield and Brooklyn.

HIGHLIGHTS

CHURCH SQUARE

The oldest buildings in Pretoria are in Church Square, which was once a Voortrekker marketplace. Today it is the focus of the city and a popular meeting spot for locals. A rather unattractive statue of Afrikaner political hero Paul Kruger stands in the middle, surrounded by fluttering flocks of pigeons and flanked by late 19th-century banks and government offices. The most interesting of these is the Palace of Justice, where Nelson Mandela and other leaders of the ANC were tried during the Treason Trials of 1963–64. On the southwest side is the Raadsaal, or Parliament; the Old Netherlands Bank building now houses the tourist office.

Jacaranda in full bloom (left)
One of the reception rooms inside President Kruger House (middle)
Strijdom Square is an open space in the central city (right)

RATINGS	
Good for food	● ● ● ●
Historic interest	● ● ● ●
Walkability	● ● ●

BASICS

✚ 324 K4

ℹ️ Pretoria Tourist Rendezvous Centre (also home to Tshwane Tourism Information Bureau), in The Old Netherlands Bank, Church Square, City Centre 0002, tel 012-3581430; Mon–Fri 8–5
www.tshwane.gov.za

❓ The main office of South African National Parks (SANParks) is at 643 Leyds Street, Muckleneuk 0002, tel 012-4289111 (open for telephone reservations Mon–Fri 8–5, Sat 9–1) www.sanparks.org

TIPS

● The best time to visit is in spring, when the city is transformed by 60,000 purple-flowering jacaranda trees.
● It is safe to walk around central Pretoria and the suburbs during the day, but avoid walking there at night.

TRANSVAAL MUSEUM

✉ Paul Kruger Street, 0002 ☎ 012-3227632 ⏰ Mon–Sat 9–5, Sun 11–5 💷 Adult R10, child (under 18) R8 ♿

This natural history museum is famous for holding the original hominid *Australopithecus africanus* fossil, known as 'Mrs Ples' (▷ 29), but you must get special permission to view it.

PRESIDENT KRUGER HOUSE

✉ Church Street West, 0002 ☎ 012-3269172 ⏰ Tue–Sat 8.30–4, Sun 11–4 💷 Adult R16, child (under 18) R7

The unpretentious house where President Kruger lived between 1884 and 1900 is now a museum, with a collection of his possessions, as well as objects relating to the Anglo-Boer War. At the back of the house is the state coach and his private rail carriage (car).

MELROSE HOUSE

✉ 275 Jacob Maré Street, 0002 ☎ 012-3222805 ⏰ Tue–Sun 10–5 💷 Adult R5, child (2–12) R3 🖳
www.melrosehouse.co.za

The Treaty of Vereeniging, ending the Anglo-Boer War (1899–1902), was signed in Melrose House on 31 May. The house was originally built in 1886 for George Heys, who made his fortune from trade and a stagecoach service to the Transvaal. It is regarded as one of the finest examples of Victorian domestic architecture in South Africa. The marble columns, stained-glass windows and mosaic floors all help to create a feeling of serene style and wealth. The house was restored after it was bombed by right-wingers in 1990. Today you might be lucky to catch the occasional classical concerts in the grounds.

Melrose House with a fountain outside

Relaxing on the grass at the city's Burgers Park

UNION BUILDINGS

✉ Arcadia 0083 ☎ 012-3005200 🎫 Garden tours by prior arrangement

The magnificent red sandstone complex of the Union Buildings, designed in grand imperial style by the British architect Herbert Baker and completed in 1913, overlooks the heart of the city. Today it is the administrative headquarters of the South African Presidency and was famously the site of Nelson Mandela's inauguration as first black president on 10 May 1994. Note that the interior is not open to the public.

PRETORIA ART MUSEUM

✉ Arcadia Park, Arcadia 0083 ☎ 012-3441807 ⏰ Tue–Sat 10–5 (also Wed 5–8), Sun 2–6 💷 Adult R5, child (under 18) R3
www.pretoriaartmuseum.co.za

The city's main art museum houses a fine collection of South African art and 17th-century paintings, including works by Pierneef, Frans Oerder and Anton van Wou.

BURGERS PARK

✉ Van der Walt and Andries streets ⏰ Summer 6am–10pm, winter 6–6

Pretoria's most central city park is between Van der Walt and Andries streets, and is a popular meeting place where visitors relax in the shade of rubber trees, palms and jacarandas. The 'florarium' houses a collection of exotic plants shown in contrasting environments, ranging from subtropical flowers to succulents from the arid Karoo and Kalahari regions. Elsewhere in the garden is a memorial to the officers and men of the South African Scottish Regiment who were killed during World War I.

BACKGROUND

Pretoria has always been closely involved with political upheaval and change in South Africa, culminating in the inauguration of President Nelson Mandela at the Union Buildings in 1994.

The town was founded in 1855, having developed slowly around a Boer farming community. In 1877, the British annexed the Transvaal, and their first action was to establish a garrison, which in turn attracted a large number of immigrants. They brought money with them, and new buildings were erected. The fortunes of the city began to look promising. However, during the Transvaal War of Independence, the British withdrew and the city was taken over by the Boers' leader Paul Kruger. At the end of the Anglo-Boer War (1902) Pretoria became the capital of the British colony, and after the creation of the Union of South Africa, in 1910, it was made the administrative capital of the new state. The growth of the city became closely related to the expanding civil service and it has remained the hub of government, with most overseas diplomats based in Pretoria. The city is also the headquarters of the defence forces and home to the University of South Africa (UNISA).

Like Johannesburg, Pretoria has large township areas, to the northwest and northeast of the city. The greater Pretoria area, now called Tshwane (meaning 'we are the same'), covers some 1,630sq km (630sq miles) and the population is estimated at 1.3 million. Tshwane is to become the new name for the city too.

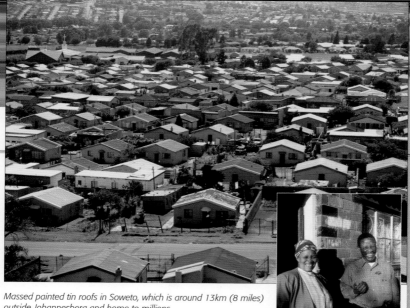

Massed painted tin roofs in Soweto, which is around 13km (8 miles) outside Johannesberg and home to millions

SOWETO

South Africa's most famous township is now a city in its own right—and the only place in the world with a street on which two winners of the Nobel Peace Prize have lived.

One of the country's highlights, Soweto (short for South Western Townships), is famous as a hotbed of political struggle, the powerhouse of the country's black urban culture. People first moved here in 1904 from Sophiatown, where there was an outbreak of plague. The township grew dramatically in the 1950s and 1960s when black people were forced to relocate from central Johannesburg. Since then the population has mushroomed as people from rural areas have flooded into Johannesburg in search of work. Today, Soweto is South Africa's largest urban living space, with an estimated population of around 4.2 million. In reality, the population is much bigger, swollen by an influx of immigrants from Nigeria, Mozambique, Zimbabwe and other parts of Africa.

SUBURB AND SLUM

Visitors are often surprised to see that much of Soweto is made up of tidy rows of houses, inhabited by aspiring professionals. Indeed, the township has the highest concentration of millionaires in the country. On the downside, there are also swathes of poverty-stricken squatter camps and rudimentary government housing, where unemployment is as high as 90 per cent. Many of these dwellings still lack basic amenities such as running water, electricity and sanitation, problems heightened by the estimated 20,000 people who pour into Soweto each month.

MANDELA'S HOME

The most popular sight in Soweto is the house where Nelson and Winnie Mandela lived before he was imprisoned in 1962. The tiny three-room house was rebuilt after being bombed several times by the South African security forces. Today it houses a small museum. On his release from prison, Mandela insisted on moving back into this house, but its small size and problems of security put too much of a strain on him and he moved out of Soweto. On the same road is the former home of Mandela's fellow Nobel Peace Prize winner, Archbishop Desmond Tutu.

RATINGS	
Cultural interest	●●●●○
Historical interest	●●●●○

BASICS

✚ 324 K4
www.soweto.co.za

TIPS

● It is not safe to visit Soweto on your own, but there are a number of excellent tours run here by reputable operators.
● Choose a tour that includes a walk: Chatting to local Sowetans can be the most enjoyable part of the experience.
● Don't expect many 'sights'—Soweto's main appeal is its atmosphere.

Gas chimneys are a feature of Soweto's skyline

NORTHERN CAPE AND NORTH WEST PROVINCE

This part of the country is where the rock-strewn semi-desert of Namakwa merges with the red dunes of the Kalahari. It has a stark beauty, with endless shimmering plains, hazy saltpans and a real sense of isolation. In complete contrast, Sun City is the amazingly extravagant gambling resort built to entertain.

MAJOR SIGHTS

The striking Augrabies Falls (above); canoeing along the Gariep River (inset)

AUGRABIES FALLS NATIONAL PARK

The Augrabies Falls are the sixth largest in the world, set in an equally impressive landscape.

The remote location of the Augrabies Falls park, not far from the Namibian border, has saved it from mass development, and it remains one of the highlights of the north. The falls are the main reason for coming here—but the landscape is equally striking, a bizarre moonscape of curious rock formations surrounded by shimmering semi-desert. The park was created in 1966 to protect the waterfall and the seemingly arid and barren ecosystem, but one that is rich in wild plants. There is good hiking here, and the Gariep (Orange) River above and below the falls has some excellent white-water rafting (▷ 217).

THE WATERFALL
The focus of the park is the waterfall. Above the falls, the Gariep (Orange) River drops over a series of cataracts, descending about 100m (300ft). From this point, the main channel passes over a drop of 56m (184ft) into a narrow gorge of steep, smooth rock, the water churning below like melted milk chocolate. The name Augrabies is derived from the Khoi term *!oukurubes*, 'Place of Great Noise'. The falls can be seen from viewpoints along the southern side of the gorge. Following heavy rains, a number of smaller water-falls drop into the main gorge along the sides of the main fall—a tremendous sight, but fairly rare.

FLORA AND FAUNA
Walking along the cliffs above the river, you pass a number of unusual plants that have adapted to the harsh desert environment. Some of the more notable trees are the quiver tree, camel thorn, tree fuchsia and wild olive; there are some informative displays about these next to reception. There is also a fair range of wildlife, including various antelope—klipspringer, eland, kudu, gemsbok—and springbok, although these all tend to be elusive. You are more likely to see ground squirrels foraging between the rocks. There are several short game drives (map available from reception) around the park, as well as walks including the popular two-day Klipspringer Trail.

RATINGS

Outdoor pursuits	●●●●●
Photo stops	●●●●●
Walkability	●●●●●

BASICS

✛ 321 D6
☎ 054-4529200
🕐 Gates: daily 24 hours; office: 7am–7pm
💷 Adult R60, child (2–11) R30
🍴 Restaurant with views of the falls
🏪 Large shop selling selection of groceries including meat and fresh vegetables, plus beer and wine
❓ Fuel available next to entrance; public telephones (cards only) next to reception desk. Reservations for Klipspringer Trail, tel 012-4289111
🚗 From Upington, take N14 and turn onto R359 at Alheit. From Springbok, there is a left turning before you reach Alheit. All clearly signposted
www.sanparks.org

TIPS
● A good time of day to visit is around sunset, when the swallows flitting through the gorge are slowly replaced by bats.
● There are some dangerously slippery spots at the edge of the gorge. Although there are fences, take care.
● March through to October is the best time to visit, as temperatures are not too high and there is limited rainfall. However, nights can be extremely cold.

Hartbeespoort Dam was created in 1923

The presence of the water at The Eye, a natural spring, in Kuruman is the main reason the town could develop

COLESBERG

➕ 328 H8 ℹ Tourist Information Centre, Colesberg Kemper Museum, Private Bag X6, Colesberg 9795, tel 051-7530678 (after hours 051-7530390); Mon–Fri 9–5

Colesberg lies at the base of a distinctive landmark, Cole's Kop, visible from 40km (25 miles) away. This rounded rock outcrop is 1,700m (5,570ft) high and was an important landmark for early settlers, who moved inland across a largely featureless region. The town established here was named after Sir Lowry Cole, Cape Governor in 1830. In its early days, it was a classic frontier town with illicit trade in a wide range of commodities, especially gunpowder and liquor. During the Anglo-Boer War it was close to the front. The surrounding hills are named after the British regiments that held them: Suffolk, New Zealand, Worcester and Gibraltar.

Today Colesberg is the focus for two successful activities: horse breeding and sheep farming. Most visitors just stop off for a night as they pass through along the busy Cape road (N1). The town springs to life in the early evening as people arrive to perform errands, and then Colesberg reverts to a peaceful farming town for the rest of the day.

HARTBEESPOORT DAM

➕ 324 K4 ℹ Hartbeespoort Dam Information Shop, Damdoryn Crossroad, Hartbeespoort 0216, tel 012-2535003; daily 8–5 www.hartbeespoortdam.com

The proximity of Johannesburg and of Pretoria has made this dam in the Magaliesberg Mountains (▷ 155) a popular watersports resort and weekend retreat. Around the shoreline are smart marinas and large private homes overlooking the lake. This is a popular site for a variety of sports including hang-gliding and paragliding, as well as watersports on the lake. The dam waters and some of the surrounding land form a designated nature reserve; birds are the main feature of the Oberon section, and there's game to see in the Kommandonek portion. There's also a snake park, a zoo and an aquarium.

KAKAMAS

➕ 321 D6 ℹ Tourist information Office, 19 Voortrekker Road, Kakamas 8870, tel 054-4310838; daily 7am–10pm www.kalaharigateway.co.za

The second most important agricultural town after Upington along this stretch of the Gariep (Orange) River is Kakamas. The meaning of the town's name is 'vicious, charging ox'. Legend has it that the pasture was so poor in this region that cattle often attacked their herders. The town, most of which is strung out along the main road running parallel to the southern canal, has a pleasantly relaxed, rural atmosphere. Driving along Voortrekker Road, in the middle of town, look for the set of giant waterwheels, part of an old irrigation system. The main industry today is raisins, which are exported around the world. There are a number of wine cellars and dried fruit co-operatives that you can visit for tours and tastings, including Orange River Wine Cellars Co-Op, off the N14 (tel 054-3378800).

KAMFERS DAM

➕ 323 G6

Kamfers Dam is a natural heritage site and an important area for greater and lesser flamingos. It lies 5km (3 miles) out of Kimberley (▷ 158–159) on the N12 heading for Johannesburg, partially hidden from the road by the raised rail line. Merely driving past the dam will give you views of the carpet of pink created by the resident flamingos, but to see them closer, look for a gravel track leading from the road under the railway line, where there is a small parking area. The waters are under threat from continual agricultural pollution, and it has been predicted that all the flamingos will one day disappear from here.

KGALAGADI TRANSFRONTIER PARK

See pages 156–157.

KGASWANE MOUNTAIN RESERVE

➕ 324 J4 ☎ 014-5332050 🕐 Sep–end Mar 5.30am–7pm, Apr–end Aug 6am–6.30pm 💰 Adult R10, child (6–16) R5, plus R10 per vehicle 🚗 Clearly signposted from the middle of Rustenburg

This is a popular mountain reserve (previously called Rustenburg Nature Reserve) along the northern slopes of the Magaliesberg range, 400m (1,300ft) above Rustenburg. The reserve is regarded as an important recreational area and a valuable educational environment for visitors from Johannesburg and Pretoria, a little more than 100km (60 miles) away; school buses are a regular sight. The reserve consists of a mix of grassland and a lush valley basin which acts as a natural catchment area. Some antelope live in the park, but most visitors come for the walking—there are currently three marked trails, two of which are open to day visitors (overnight trails must be reserved up to six months in advance).

The cemetery at Mafikeng has graves from the Anglo-Boer War

A stand selling wooden carved figures and masks at the roadside in the Magaliesberg

KIMBERLEY

See pages 158–159.

KURUMAN

322 F5 Tourist Office, 14 Federale, Mynbou Street, Kuruman 8460, tel 053-7121001; Mon–Fri 8–4.30 www.kalahari.org.za

There are two reasons why this isolated town is on the visitor map: the Moffat Mission and a natural spring known as The Eye. Robert Moffat (his daughter was to marry the missionary-explorer David Livingstone) set up the mission in 1821 and it can be visited just outside town, a series of restored buildings (Mon–Sat 8–5, Sun 3–5). The Eye, or 'die oog' in Afrikaans, on Main Street, is an extraordinary spring which continuously produces almost 20 million litres (94 million gallons) of fresh water per day, with little variation between the wet and dry seasons—a miracle in this arid region. The giant koi carp gliding through the pond created by the spring are a lovely sight. The gardens around the pond (daily 8–5) are a popular picnic spot—as the large goldfish in the pond, fattened by breadcrumbs, bear witness. Half a day should be more than enough to see Kuruman, although once you've made it this far north it is worth exploring the surrounding area.

MADIKWE GAME RESERVE

324 J3 Reservations: tel 011-3156194; park office: tel 083-6298282 Off N4, on R49 following signs to Gaborone; 100km (60 miles) from Zeerust, just before the border crossing, turn right on to a sand road for 12km (7.5 miles) to the Tau Gate. There are other gates at Derdepoort and Abjaterskop

Madikwe is the fourth largest game reserve in South Africa. Covering more than 75,000ha

(185,250 acres), it lies within a malaria-free zone and has the country's second largest elephant population, yet few people have heard of it. Madikwe is not open to passing day visitors; you need to stay in one of its luxury lodges.

The reserve lies entirely within South Africa, but it is only 35km (22 miles) from the Botswana capital, Gaborone. The northern limits are marked by the international border, while the park's southern limits coincide with the Dwarsberg Mountains. One of the best aspects of the reserve is its diverse geology, which has resulted in a broad mix of habitats suitable for a wide range of animals. Thanks to Operation Phoenix, one of the largest game translocation operations in the world, the park is well stocked and is an excellent place to see the Big Five. Visitors are taken on game drives and walks from their lodges, and thanks to the wide dispersal of the camps it is easy to feel as if you have the whole reserve to yourself.

MAFIKENG AND MMABATHO

323 H4 Mafikeng Tourist Information and Development Centre, just off Mandela Drive near the entrance to Cooke's Lake, tel 018-3813155/6, Mon–Fri 8.30–5, Sat 8–1

Before free elections were held in South Africa and the new political boundaries came into effect, Mafikeng was in the old Western Transvaal, while its satellite town of Mmabatho was the capital of the homeland known as Bophuthatswana. When the North West Province was created, it was decided to retain Mmabatho as the regional capital. However, there has been a gradual shift of power back to the principal town in the region, Rustenburg (▷ 164).

As a rather garish concrete town, Mmabatho is best bypassed for Mafikeng. At the turn of the 20th century this hot, dusty town—then called Mafeking—captured the imagination of the British public. In 1899, shortly after the outbreak of the Second Anglo-Boer War, the British-held town was besieged by a Boer force. The siege of Mafeking lasted 217 days, until 17 May 1900, when a combined force of Rhodesian troops from the north and Imperial troops from the south relieved the town. The British public were intrigued, their interest in the incident having been fired by the press: The Anglo-Boer War was the first war to be reported in detail. The Mafikeng Museum (Mon–Sat 8–5), on the corner of Martin and Robinson streets, has an excellent series of displays outlining the events of the siege.

MAGALIESBERG

324 J4

The Magaliesberg is a range of flat-topped quartzite mountains extending roughly from Pretoria to just beyond Rustenburg. In 1977, the area was declared a Natural Heritage Site and, along with the Hartbeespoort Dam (▷ 154), it is an important recreational area for the residents of Pretoria and Johannesburg. The region witnessed a number of bloody battles during the 19th century. The first major conflicts were between the Ndebele, who arrived in the area from modern day KwaZulu-Natal, led by their chief Mzilikazi, and the local peoples. At a later date the mountains were the scene of several important battles during the Anglo-Boer War, including the Battle of Nooitgedacht in 1900. Today the slopes are dotted with holiday resorts and are popular for hiking.

Kgalagadi Transfrontier Park

•

The Kgalagadi has some of the finest game viewing in South Africa, even though it is one of the least visited national parks in the country.

A gemsbok, one of the larger species of antelope

The rolling red dunes of the Kalahari desert

A ground squirrel, camouflaged by sand

BASICS

✚ 321 D4

☎ Park office: 054-5612000

◉ Twee Rivieren: Jan, Feb 6am–7.30pm; Mar 6.30am–7pm; Apr 7am–6.30pm; May 7am–6pm; Jun, Jul 7.30am–6pm; Aug 7am–6.30pm; Sep 6.30am–6.30pm; Oct 6am–7pm; Nov, Dec 5.30am–7.30pm

💷 Adult R120, child (under 12) R60 for day visitors

🏪 The three main camps all have small shops selling basic groceries, firewood and field guides

❓ Reservations from SANParks; tel 012-4289111. On the Botswana side of the park there are 3 campsites (reservations must be made through the Botswana parks authority: tel 09267-3180774)

🚗 From Upington, the first 190km (120 miles) are on an excellent tarred road followed by 61km (38 miles) of gravel. Allow 3 to 4 hours to the park gates
www.sanparks.org

Visitor information at the park gates

SEEING THE KGALAGADI TRANSFRONTIER PARK

The park is remote and relatively undeveloped and suffers uncomfortably high summer temperatures, but few visitors complain about the hot dusty roads once they've glimpsed their first lion. The roads follow the scrubby valleys of two seasonal rivers and cut across red sand dunes typical of the Kalahari. The park shares a border with Botswana, but Twee Rivieren is the only entrance on the South African side. Visitors wishing to visit the Botswana side do not need a passport as long as entry and exit is made through the same gate. As with many of the parks and reserves, you can choose to visit for the day in your own vehicle or stay at one of the camps, renting a 4WD when you are there. Do bear in mind when driving that the distances in the park are huge and you will be even longer with game viewing. For example, it takes around 2.5 hours to drive from Twee Rivieren to Mata Mata, one of the main camps, so plan carefully.

The nearest town of any size is Upington where you can buy supplies and visit the Green Kalahari Information Centre (Siyanda District Building, corner of Rivier and Le Roux streets, tel 054-3372826; www.greenkalahari.co.za). The office can supply you with information on the park and on the Kalahari area. See page 294 for information about accommodation within the park.

HIGHLIGHTS

WILDLIFE

The park is celebrated for its predators, particularly the dark-maned Kalahari lion,

which can sometimes be spotted lazing in the shade of trees along the river beds. Other predators to look for include cheetah, wild dog, spotted hyena, bat-eared fox, black-backed jackal and honey badger. Leopards are (as always) elusive, but they are seen relatively regularly in the park. Kgalagadi's prize antelope is the gemsbok, which has a dark glossy coat, strong frame and characteristic long, straight horns. You should also see giraffe, red hartebeest, Burchell's zebra and huge herds of wildebeest and springbok. The bird life, too, is remarkable. More than 200 species have been recorded in the park, and it is known for its birds of prey.

LANDSCAPE

The aridity of the region means that vegetation is sparse, which is why game viewing is so good here. Watch for the windmills that pump the boreholes, as these waterholes are usually frequented by some form of wildlife.

The two seasonal rivers of Auob and Nossob rarely flow now, but the great width of their valleys in some parts proves that they were once thundering waterways. Between the rivers stretch mighty red dunes, aligned from north to south and covered in yellow grass following good rains. These are fossil dunes, and their red tint is produced by an iron oxide coating on the white grains of sand. Two roads cross the dunes; never venture off them or you will get stuck in sand.

BACKGROUND

The area was declared a national park in 1931 as part of an initiative to tackle the problem of poaching. The first visitor camp was built in 1940 near the confluence of the Auob and Nossob rivers. Known previously as the Kalahari Gemsbok National Park, the area merged with the adjacent Gemsbok National Park in Botswana in 1999.

A lone tree sharply etched against blue skies

TIPS

● Although the park authorities insist that 4WD vehicles are not necessary, saloon (sedan) cars can be uncomfortable on the gravel roads and are quite likely to get flat tyres.
● The best time to visit is between February and May. In summer the heat is intense and you should carry at least 10 litres (20 pints) of drinking water in your vehicle.
● If you're camping in winter you'll need a warm sleeping bag as temperatures fall below 0°C (32°F).
● Always check accommodation availability in advance: This is the end of the road, and even space for tents gets fully reserved.
● A major advantage is that Kgalagadi is malaria free.

Kimberley

South Africa's diamond capital has an enthralling history and there are plenty of places to see, including the largest man-made excavation in the world.

A detail from an old wheel tower

RATINGS	
Historical interest	● ● ● ● ○
Photo stops	● ● ● ○ ○
Walkability	● ● ● ○ ○

MORE TO SEE

GALESHEWE

Galeshewe township was second only to Soweto as a hub of political activism during apartheid. It was home to Robert Sobukwe, the leader of the Pan African Congress (PAC), who spent the last days of his life, following his imprisonment on Robben Island, under house arrest in Galeshewe. For township tours, contact the Diamond Fields Tourist Information Centre (see Basics).

MCGREGOR MUSEUM

✉ 2 Egerton Road, Kimberley 8300 ☎ 053-8420099 🕐 Mon–Sat 9–5, Sun 2–5 💵 Adult R12, child (2–12) R5 www.museumsnc.co.za

The collection in this Kimberley house is a mix of objects depicting the history of Kimberley and standard displays of natural history. Downstairs are a couple of rooms devoted to the Siege of Kimberley (1899–1900), including two small rooms occupied by Cecil Rhodes during the siege.

SEEING KIMBERLEY

Kimberley, the capital of the Northern Cape, is famous for its diamonds, and the flat land surrounding the town is pockmarked with mines. No longer the fortune-seeker's frontier town that it once was, Kimberley is now a bustling commercial place. Most of the sights are in some way connected to the diamond industry, although the town itself displays little evidence of this wealth. The suburb of Belgravia is the only area of fine Victorian houses; central Kimberley is made up of modern shops and office blocks, dominated by the Telkom Tower and the De Beers headquarters. The town can be seen on foot, and there is a tram that runs from City Hall to the Mine Museum—the only working tram in South Africa.

HIGHLIGHTS

KIMBERLEY MINE MUSEUM AND THE BIG HOLE

✉ Tucker Street, Kimberley 8301 ☎ 053-8394902 🕐 Daily 8–6 💵 Adult R20, child (under 16) R15 ☐ 🏛

The Mine Museum is a collection of 40 original and model buildings dating from the late 19th century. They have been arranged to form a jumble of streets, with sound effects such as singing or snatches of conversation. In the Mining Hall, there are early photographs of the diggings that show the Big Hole gradually starting to take shape and provide a vivid impression of life during that time. To see what it was all about, have a look at the diamonds in the De Beers Hall.

The whole complex lies alongside the Big Hole—well named as it measures 1.6km (1 mile) around and covers more than 13ha (32 acres). There are two caged viewing platforms projecting over its rim with views down into the vast hole, most of which is filled with murky green water. It is an astounding sight, especially when you remember that the excavation goes down 800m (2,600ft) and that every piece of earth and rock was removed by hand.

DIAMOND MINE TOUR

✉ Molyneux Road, Kimberley 8301 ☎ 053-8421321 🕐 4-hour underground tours Mon, Tue and Thu–Fri at 7.45am (must be reserved a day in advance; no children under 16) 💵 Adult R90

On the other side of town from the Kimberley Mine Museum is the operational Bultfontein mine, at which you can take an underground tour. It begins with a safety video, and you are given protective overalls, hard hat, special shoes and head torch. You then take an elevator down to 820m (2,700ft) below the surface. Once down, the guide walks you around key areas of the mine, including the main retrieval areas and conveyor belts transporting kimberlite (a rare igneous rock that can contain diamonds). The most exciting part of the tour is when the miners are blasting—the ground and air shakes with the force of the explosion. Overground tours are also available.

THE SIGHTS

WILLIAM HUMPHREYS ART GALLERY

✉ Civic Centre, Cullinan Crescent, Kimberley 8300 ☎ 053-8311724 🕐 Mon–Fri 8–5, Sat 10–5, Sun 2–5 💰 Adult R5, child (under 12) R2

For a break from the diamond world, head to this excellent gallery, one of the most important art collections in South Africa. There are fine examples of 16th- and 17th-century art by British, Flemish and Dutch Old Masters, but of greater interest is the newer collection of contemporary South African art. There is the work of South African Impressionists, an excellent graphics and prints display and a few individual highlights such as the portraits by the artist Irma Stern (1894–1966).

BACKGROUND

The early history of Kimberley is also the tale of the discovery of diamonds. The first significant find was in 1866 on a farm called De Kalk, owned by Daniel Jacobs, near modern-day Hopetown. News soon spread and interest began to grow. Prospectors arrived quickly and, in 1870, more diamonds were found near Dorstfontein farm. The area was immediately flooded with fortune-seekers; within just a few months 50,000 diggers had turned the hill into a hole—today's 'Big Hole'.

As the miners delved deeper, it became clear that individual claims would have to merge: At one point there were 1,600 separate claims in the Kimberley mine. In addition to this, the price of diamonds started falling because of overproduction. It was at this point that Cecil John Rhodes and his partner Charles Dunell Rudd entered the scene. Together they began buying up claims in the mine, and in 1880 they founded the De Beers Mining Company. As Rhodes and Rudd expanded their operation, they came up against a man with similar ideas, Barney Barnato. This led to an infamous power struggle, resolved only when Rhodes paid Barnato a colossal payoff for his Kimberley Central Mining Company. The Big Hole stopped producing diamonds in 1914, but three mines remain productive in the area today: Dutoitspan, Bultfontein and Wesselton.

The deep turquoise lake at the bottom of the Big Hole (above)

An old tram car forms part of the exhibits (inset left)

You can try your hand at prospecting (inset right)

BASICS

➕ 323 G6
ℹ Diamond Fields Tourist Information Centre, corner of Bultfontein and Lyndhurst streets, Kimberley 8300, tel 053-8327298; Mon–Fri 8–5, Sat 8–12
www.kimberley.co.za
www.northerncape.org.za

Barney Barnato was the principal shareholder at Kimberley before being bought out by Rhodes

Namakwa

Namakwa is a striking semi-desert landscape that explodes into a carpet of wild flowers following the spring rains.

The town of Springbok is at the heart of Namakwa

It's not just flowers that define the landscape

A quiver tree in the Ai-Ais/ Richtersveld Park

RATINGS	
Historical interest	●●
Outdoor pursuits	●●●●
Photo stops	●●●●●
Walkability	●●●

BASICS

✚ 320 C8

ℹ Namakwa Tourism Information, Voortrekker Street, Springbok 8240, tel 027-7128035; Mon–Fri 7.30–4.15, and (flower season only) Sat–Sun 9–noon

www.northerncape.org.za

TIPS

● For up-to-date information about where the best flower displays are, call the Flower Hotline (tel 027-7182985).

● Namakwa has a fierce desert climate, so always carry several litres of water per person with you when driving.

● From Springbok, it is only another 118km (73 miles) on the N7 to the Namibian border, a popular crossing between the two countries.

● See pages 250–251 for a drive through Namakwa.

SEEING NAMAKWA

Namakwa ('land of the Nama people'), formerly called Namaqualand, is the arid northwest corner of the Northern Cape, starting in the south at the Doorn River bridge near Klawer, and extending north to the Namibian border. The region is best known for its flowers and they have become a major visitor attraction—during flower season the still valleys and sleepy towns are transformed into busy places crowded with tour buses. However, the interaction between light, temperature, and the timing and intensity of rainfall all affect the occurrence and distribution of the flowers. The very fact that the flowers appear in different locations from year to year means that the flower-viewing industry has remained relatively low key. The town of Springbok, capital of Namakwa, is the most viable base for exploring the area.

HIGHLIGHTS

THE PLANTS

More than 4,000 species have been identifed in the area, the most common of which is the orange and black gousblom, a large daisy. These flowers look their best when they occupy a valley floor, forming a stunning carpet of orange. On the mountainsides or rocky hills you will see *mesembryanthemums*, commonly known as vygies or Livingstone daisies. Their blossoms can be pink, scarlet, blue or yellow. Closer to Springbok are quiver trees *(Aloe dichotoma)*, from which the San people made their quivers. Another interesting plant to look out for is the halfmens *(Pachypodium namaquanum)*, a strange looking succulent which has a long spine with a clump of leaves at the top—some specimens are thought to be several hundred years old.

SPRINGBOK

✚ 320 B7 ℹ Namakwa Tourism Information, Voortrekker Street, Springbok 8240, tel 027-7128035; Mon–Fri 7.30–4.15, and (flower season only) Sat–Sun 9–noon

Springbok sits in a narrow valley surrounded by the Klein Koperberge (Small Copper Mountains) and hemmed in by *koppies* (small hills)

littered with rough yellow-gold rocks. It is a modern town with little of interest within its confines, but from it you can explore the country-side north to the Namibian border, and west to the Atlantic coast.

AI–AIS/RICHTERSVELD TRANSFRONTIER PARK

✚ 320 A6 ☎ 027-8311506 ⏰ Daily 7.30–6 💷 Adult R80, child (2–15) R40
❓ Reservations from SANParks: tel 012-4289111 🚌 North from Springbok on N7 towards Steinkopf; take Port Nolloth turning and follow R382 to the coast via Annienous Pass. In Port Nolloth take the coast road north towards Alexander Bay. The park is signposted from Alexander Bay
www.sanparks.org

The park of Ai-Ais/Richtersveld covers some of the most remote and starkly beautiful scenery in Namakwa. The park is both isolated and inaccessible, but that is much of its appeal. This is rough country, most of which can be reached only in a 4WD vehicle. Ai-Ais/Richtersveld encompasses a mountainous desert, seemingly barren but full of sturdy succulents, many of them endemic. This makes the park particularly appealing to botany enthusiasts, but the surreal, rugged terrain is another great attraction. A 4WD is essential in the park, and it's worth renting one in Springbok to explore this fascinating wilderness area. After much negotiation, the Richtersveld became part of a trans-frontier park in 2003, joining it with Namibia's Ai-Ais Hot Springs and Fish River Canyon over the border. You can stay in the park, which is camping only.

GOEGAP NATURE RESERVE

✚ 320 B7 ☎ 027-7121880 ⏰ Daily 7.30–7 💷 Adult R10, child (6–16) R5
🏢 🚌 From Springbok, pass under N7 towards the airport and turn right. Just before the airport, take a left turn; from here it's 15km (9 miles) to the reserve gates

The reserve is a mix of granite *koppies* (small hills) and dry valleys, with a good cross-section of typical Namakwa vegetation. Although the area looks parched and barren, it supports a surprising number of plant species—581 have been recorded in the reserve. The area is classified as semi-desert, with rain usually falling in winter; in summer

Orange and purple flowers contrast with the rocky, barren koppies *in the Goegap Nature Reserve (top)*

Driving through the Ai-Ais/ Richtersveld Park (above)

A spectacular mass of vygies and other wild flowers appear in the spring (above)
A 4WD is the only way to get around the park (inset)

temperatures soar and it is unwise to move around on foot under these conditions. The Hester Malan Wild Flower Garden is a highlight in spring.

PORT NOLLOTH

320 A7　Municipality, Main Road, Port Nolloth, tel 027-851111; Mon–Fri 8–12, 12.45–4.30

Port Nolloth is a little town on the windswept West Coast, important for fishing, but more intriguingly an area renowned for attracting fortune-seekers who trade (often, it is said, illegally) in diamonds. The town was established as a harbour and railway junction for the copper industry; today it has developed into a small holiday resort—the only one along this stretch of the coast. The beaches have a wild, desolate beauty, although the long stretches of sun-bleached sand can appear rather bleak.

ALEXANDER BAY

320 A6　Alexkor Ltd conduct 3-hour tours on Thu at 8am, booking is essential, tel 027-8311330

The diamond industry becomes apparent in Alexander Bay, in the far north of the region, near the Namibian border. Diamonds were first

found here in 1925, and today the town is run by the mining company Alexkor Ltd. Alexander Bay was closed to visitors until a few years ago, but now you can take part in diamond mine tours. It also has easy access to the Ai-Ais/Richtersveld Transfrontier Park. The Gariep (Orange) River estuary, at the Bay, is an important wetland area for birds.

BACKGROUND

In the past, the fortunes of Namakwa were closely linked with the copper industry. In 1852 copper production started in Springbok; this was the first commercial mining operation of any type in South Africa. Despite several other discoveries farther north, Springbok was able to develop into an important regional hub because of its abundant supply of drinking water from a spring, a rare and valuable commodity in the region before dams and pipelines were built.

Port Nolloth was established as a harbour and railway junction for the copper industry in 1854, but it proved too shallow for the bulk ore carriers, and the trade moved north to Alexander Bay, which today bases much of its industry on diamonds.

The exterior of the Paul Kruger Country House Museum, which has period displays

An elephant walking through the bush at Pilanesberg

MAGERSFONTEIN BATTLEFIELD

⊞ 323 G6 ☎ 053-8337115
🅿 🅱 32km (20 miles) from Kimberley; from Kimberley take the new road to Bloemfontein, following the signs to Modder River

On 11 December 1899, one of the most famous battles of the Anglo-Boer War took place here. The British force, under the command of General Lord Methuen, was defeated by a Boer force under General Piet Cronje, while attempting to come to the aid of besieged Kimberley (▷ 158–159). This was the first appearance of trench warfare, and the first major defeat suffered by the British (in the initial encounter, 239 British were killed and 663 wounded). The Boer trenches can still be seen from the hilltop. There are nine memorials commemorating the dead, including a Celtic cross in memory of the Highland Regiment, a granite memorial to the Scandinavians who fought with the Boers, and a marble cross in memory of the Guards Brigade. In 1971, the area was declared a national monument. There is a small museum containing weapons, uniforms and photographs.

NOOITGEDACHT ROCK ART CENTRE

⊞ 322 G6 ⏰ Daily 10–4.30 🎫 Adult R15, child (under 12) R10 🚗 24km (15 miles) from Kimberley on the Barkly West road, followed by 8km (5 miles) on gravel

This open-air site displays San rock engravings, thought to

be 1,500 years old. It is an important engravings site, with a number of displays. For those interested in the modern-day San, there is a local community of !Xu and Khwe people who were granted 1,200ha (3,000 acres) of land under the Land Reform Programme. The community shares this land, from where they produce traditional and progressive arts and crafts.

PAUL KRUGER COUNTRY HOUSE MUSEUM

⊞ 324 J4 ☎ 014-5733218 ⏰ Tue–Fri 10–4, Sat–Sun 10–2 🎫 Adult R15, child (2–12) R8 🚗 18km (11 miles) northwest of Rustenburg, off R565, en route to Sun City

The farm where Paul Kruger lived as a farmer before becoming president of the Transvaal Republic from 1883 until the end of the Anglo-Boer War is at Boekenhoutfontein. The Paul Kruger Country House is actually a hotel, but buildings have been preserved and restored as a museum dedicated to the life of Kruger and the earliest farmers in the Transvaal.

The main homestead contains many of Kruger's possessions, along with an assortment of period furniture from other homes. There is also a small but interesting collection of local historical items. Look for the statue of Paul Kruger by French sculptor Jean Archand, discovered in Paris in 1919 by generals Louis Botha and Jan Smuts. It depicts the president sitting grumpily in his armchair during his last days while in exile in France.

PILANESBERG NATIONAL PARK

⊞ 324 J3 ☎ 014-5555351
⏰ Nov–end Feb 5.30am–7pm; Mar, Apr 6am–6.30pm; May–end Aug 6.30am–6pm; Sep, Oct 6am–6.30pm
🎫 Adult R20, child (6–17) R15
🚗 Follow signs to Sun City, R510 north from Rustenburg
www.parksnorthwest.co.za

This is the fourth largest national park in South Africa, spread around an extinct volcanic crater. Although you can see all South Africa's big game here, the park itself is artificial, having been stocked with game from around the country in the 1970s. It's best to take a guided safari, as the rangers are in constant radio contact and monitor the movements of the Big Five (safaris can be arranged in Sun City). There are several camps within the park.

RUSTENBURG

⊞ 324 J4 🛈 Rustenburg Tourism Information and Development Centre, corner of Nelson Mandela Drive and Kloof Street, Rustenburg 0300, tel 014-5970904; Mon–Fri 8–5, Sat 8–noon
www.rustenburgtourism.co.za

Rustenburg ('castle of rest') is one of the oldest towns in the region and was important under the Transvaal Republic. Today it is a busy administrative hub for the many mining companies here, and sees many weekenders from Johannesburg and Pretoria, who come to enjoy the nearby Magaliesberg Mountains (▷ 155). It is also a useful stop en route to Sun City and the camps of the Pilanesberg National Park.

A gun exhibited in the study at the Kruger House Museum

The artificial beach, complete with wave machine, at the Valley of the Waves (above); slot machines in the casino (inset)

SUN CITY

One of the most luxurious resorts in the country creates a fantasy world with superb recreational facilities.

Tucked away on the fringes of the Kalahari desert is Sun City, a neon-lit extravaganza of kitsch surrounded by bush. It is South Africa's third most visited attraction, along with nearby Pilanesberg National Park, after Soweto and the Kruger National Park. While it may not appeal to everyone, if you're in the area it is worth a visit just to experience the sheer indulgence of the place.

Sun City opened its doors in 1979, with the focus on the Sun City Hotel and a golf course designed by the South African golfer Gary Player. Within months it had become a huge success. Much emphasis was placed on the gambling element, as the hotel was in the home-land of Bophuthatswana where gambling was legal, unlike the rest of South Africa at the time. However, the resort has experienced a drop in visitors since the first free elections were held in 1994. Gaming is now legal throughout South Africa, so the initial main appeal of Sun City has gone. The resort is working hard to attract overseas visitors, and by closing all but one of its casinos is changing its image from a 24-hour gamblers' paradise to an international leisure, entertainment and conference destination.

SIGHTS AND ACTIVITIES

Most people are likely to recognize the Palace of the Lost City, a magnificent hotel decorated with animal sculptures, mosaics, frescoes and hand-painted ceilings. Surrounding the hotel is a remarkable man-made forest, all 25ha (62 acres) of it, made up of 1.6 million separate plants.

The Valley of the Waves is a sandy beach complete with palm trees and a wave machine—all set in the arid bush landscape. You can even go surfing on the waves. There is an extra fee to enter the Valley for day visitors (adult R25, child (2–16) R10).

You'll find all sorts of sports here, including golf, horseback riding, squash, tennis, mountain biking and ten-pin bowling. There's also a whole host of watersports available at Waterworld: jet-skiing, para-sailing, canoeing, sailing, water-skiing and windsurfing to name a few. If these don't appeal, you can go shopping, see a film or a show, visit the slot machines or the crocodile farm, with its 7,000 animals (adult R50, child (3–12) R25).

RATINGS			
Good for food	●	●	● ●
Outdoor pursuits	●	●	●
Shopping	●	●	● ●

BASICS

➕ 324 J3 • Sun City, 0316 North West Province

☎ 014-5571000

🎫 Daily entrance fee: R60 per person, including R30 spending voucher; child (under 2) free

🍴 Numerous restaurants, fast food outlets and bars around the complex

❓ The Welcome Centre, in the middle of the complex, provides maps of Sun City. A 'Sky Train' runs throughout the whole vast complex

www.suninternational.co.za

A sculpture outside the complex's Palace Hotel

A bridge that takes you over the Gariep (Orange) River at Upington

A rock structure in the Wonderwerk Cave

UPINGTON

321 D6 Upington Tourist Office, in the Kalahari Oranje Museum, Schröder Street, Upington 8801, tel 054-3326064; Mon–Thu 8–5.30, Fri 8–5, Sat 9–12
www.upington.co.za

Upington is a modern town with attractive surroundings along the banks of the Gariep (Orange) River. It has searing summer temperatures, but is the largest town in this part of the Northern Cape, making it a welcome stop if you have been off the beaten track for a while. All the major South African shops and chains stores are here, making the town an excellent place to restock your supplies. As a major entry point to the Kalahari, Upington is also a good spot to organize trips to the Kgalagadi Transfrontier Park (▷ 156–157) and Augrabies Falls National Park (▷ 153).

The origin of the town is rather more disreputable than one might expect. In the mid-19th century, the northern reaches of the Cape Colony were home to a variety of outlaws and rustlers—there were no settlements, making it impossible for the police to track people into the uncharted wilderness. By 1879, the Cape government had had enough and founded a small settlement on the Gariep (Orange) River to try and exercise some control over the area. In 1884, Sir Thomas Upington, the new Prime Minister of the colony, visited the settlement, which was renamed in his honour.

VAALBOS NATIONAL PARK

322 G6 Park office: 053-5610088 Daily 7–7 Adult R60, child (under 12) R30
www.sanparks.org

This park, along the Vaal River, is known for its herbivores, including rhino (both black and white), giraffe and a range of antelope. There is a gravel road providing access to the farther reaches of the park, as well as several picnic spots. Overnight camping is available, but many visitors come on a day trip from Kimberley, 52km (32 miles) away. Vaalbos National Park has been under international scrutiny in recent years, as permission has been given for diamond mining activities to begin within the park boundaries.

VAN ZYLSRUS

322 E5 Tourist Office, 14 Federale, Mynbou Street, Kuruman 8460, tel 053-7121001; Mon–Fri 8–4.30

Van Zylsrus is a typical Kalahari town—one dusty street is lined with all of its shops. Although there is little of interest here, it is a sensible place to stop for the night if en route to Kgalagadi. The Oasis Café is famous for its 'fairy garden', a glorious patch of shady green, a welcome spot in the heat of the day. If you don't stop for the night, have a snack here and fill up with fuel before pushing on.

VRYBURG

323 G5 Municipality, Market Street, Vryburg 8600, tel 053-9282200; Mon–Fri 7.30–4

No matter from which direction you approach the town, the size of Vryburg comes as a surprise. After miles of flat dry savannah, you suddenly find yourself in busy urban surroundings. There are few sights in town, but the Leon Taljaardt Nature Reserve (Ganesa Road;

daily 7–6), 5km (3 miles) away, is a pleasant little reserve stocked with game. Access is by car (walking is not permitted) and you may see white rhino, buffalo, wildebeest and zebra, among other wildlife.

WONDERWERK CAVE

322 F6 053-3840680 Adult R25, child (2–16) R10 Access is with a guide only, by appointment Signposted 42km (26 miles) before Kuruman on the Kimberley Road
www.museumsnc.co.za

The Cave is an important archaeological site on a private farm, set back from the road in the Kuruman Hills. The vast cave contains a collection of rock paintings and evidence of early human habitation, including fire. The cave itself has been extensively examined by experts from the McGregor Museum in Kimberley (▷ 158), where most of the discoveries from the excavations are now displayed. It stretches back 139m (456ft) into the hillside, with a level path leading into it; the rock paintings are near the entrance. The grandparents of the current owners lived in the cave when they first settled in the region and started farming.

A memorial to the camel mounted police, Upington

LESOTHO AND SWAZILAND

Lesotho and Swaziland are independent countries
that share much of their border with South Africa.
Both are characterized by their friendly and welcoming
people, and are particularly great places if you are
looking for a more active holiday: trout fishing in clear
mountain streams, pony trekking through remote
mountain valleys and hiking with no fences.

MAJOR SIGHT

Looking down from the viewing platform at the Visitor Centre at the Bokong Nature Reserve

The busy streeets of Butha-Buthe

LESOTHO

BOKONG NATURE RESERVE AND TS'EHLANYANE NATIONAL PARK

330 K7 Lesotho Highlands: 266-22460723 Daily 8–5 Adult M5, child (under 12) M3

The establishment of this new national park and reserve, both north of the Katse Dam, is part of the Lesotho Highlands Water Project (see below). Bokong Nature Reserve covers 1,970ha (4,870 acres) and straddles the main road from Hlotse to Katse Dam at the Mafika Lisiu Pass, at 3,000m (10,000ft). It claims to be one of the highest nature reserves in Africa and has outstanding views across the highlands. There is an exciting information centre (daily 8–5) perched on the edge of a cliff, with exhibits about the local ecology. Given the reserve's alpine altitude, there are few animals other than large colonies of ice rats, found only above 2,000m (6,500ft). Nevertheless, it is the scenery that makes a visit worthwhile.

Ts'ehlanyane National Park covers some 5,600ha (13,800 acres) and lies where the Ts'ehlanyane and Holomo rivers join, on the western range of the Maluti Mountains. The park has extensive tracts of woodlands and is full of rivers and streams bordered by bamboo. Again there are few animals but it's a haven for butterflies and birds.

BUTHA-BUTHE

330 K6 Ministry of Tourism, 7th Floor, Post Office Building, Kingsway, Maseru, tel 266-22312427; Mon–Fri 8–4

Butha-Buthe is the most northerly town in the lowlands. It's a busy place with a number of supermarkets and stores where people from the highlands come every few weeks to stock up with provisions. You may notice the large suburb known as Likileng, which was built to provide accommodation for the workforce engaged on the tunnelling and hydropower components of the Lesotho Highlands Water Project. Butha-Buthe gets its name from the mountain that towers above the town; the name means 'place of lying down' or 'place of security', and it was here that Moshoeshoe (the early 19th-century chief of the Koena clan of the Sotho people) had his first mountain stronghold. The walk to the top of the mountain is fairly strenuous, but has fine views across the surrounding countryside.

The scenic Moteng Pass lies between Butha-Buthe and Oxbow (68km/42 miles). This tightly twisting road goes northeast—for much of the way at an altitude of more than 2,500m (8,200ft)—climbing up gradients of more than 35 per cent to the summit, where there are excellent views of the Basotho homesteads in the valley below. This is the original route of the 'Roof of Africa' motor rally, which takes place annually at the start of summer.

HLOTSE

330 K6

This town, known as both Hlotse and Leribe, is the administrative hub of Leribe district. Founded in 1876, it was also an administrative town for the British— you can still see the remains of a British fort and a statue of a kneeling British soldier. The Anglican Church dates from 1877 and is the oldest building in town. If you go some 8km (5 miles) north on the old Butha-Buthe road, and look in the Subeng stream about 400m (1,300ft) downstream from the bridge, you can see three- and five-toed dinosaur tracks estimated to be 108 to 200 million years old. Ask for directions in the village.

KATSE DAM

330 K7

Katse Dam in the Central Mountains (the most accessible highland region in Lesotho) is part of the massive Lesotho Highlands Water Project, one of the biggest such schemes in the world. It will not be finished until the 2020s, but when it is, it should provide the whole of Lesotho with electricity. South Africa has been the main financier and it maintains a large degree of control over the project's administration (much of the water is pumped to Gauteng). The first stage of the project, the Katse Dam, has been completed. The second phase, the construction of the Mohole Dam farther upstream, is largely finished and once it is operational it will double the water supply to South Africa through an interconnecting tunnel into Katse reservoir. The Lesotho Highlands Development Authority (LHDA) has stressed the importance of tourism development and has promised water-based recreational facilities, campsites and new lodges. The LHDA is in the process of establishing the Ts'ehlanyane National Park and Bokong Nature Reserve (see above), both north of the Katse Dam.

MAFETENG

323 J7

This is the main commercial and administrative town for the southern lowlands. It is 15 minutes' drive from Van Rooyens border post, so this will be the

Street vendors selling corn on the cob in Maseru

The dramatic outline of Mount Moorosi, the backdrop of a battle in the late 19th century

first place you get to if you cross from Wepner in South Africa's Free State. The town suffered considerably during riots in 1998, and some of the derelict shops and damaged buildings are still to be restored, but there are pleasant views across the lowlands towards the Thaba-Putsoa range of mountains. The British War Memorial, erected in memory of members of the Cape Mounted Rifles who died during the Gun War of 1880, stands near St. John's Primary School on the road going towards the Van Rooyens border post.

MASERU

➕ 330 J7　ℹ️ Ministry of Tourism, 7th Floor, Post Office Building, Kingsway, Maseru, tel 266-22312427; Mon–Fri 8–4

Maseru must be one of the world's sleepiest capital cities, although in comparison to the rest of the country, life here seems almost frantic. The heart of the city is along the Caledon River, and most shops, offices, hotels and restaurants are on the one long central street called Kingsway. This main road is choked with minibus taxis and busy with people milling in and out of the shops and offices. Many of the buildings are unfinished and the city still bears some scars from the riots that occurred here in 1998.

Maseru was founded in 1869 when Lesotho's second colonial leader, Commandant J. H. Bowker, sited his headquarters here. The city grew slowly and it was not until the 1960s that the town began to expand into a city. It is a good place for a wander, and the Basotho people are outstandingly friendly; it's not uncommon for people to approach you in the street to ask how you are and where you come from. Unlike many South

African downtown areas, where safety is in question, Maseru is safe to walk around and great for appreciating the vibrant African city street atmosphere.

MOKHOTLONG

➕ 330 L7

Mokhotlong Town or Camp is one of Lesotho's most remote towns; it is the administrative and economic hub of the northern mountain area. The name means 'the place of the bald ibis', and these birds can be seen along the river and in the surrounding valleys. Mokhotlong was established as a police post in 1905 and grew as a trading place supplied by pack ponies coming over the Drakensberg from KwaZulu-Natal. Until 1947, when radio contact was established with Maseru, it had no connections with the rest of the country, and it was not until the 1950s that it had a road connection. For the most part, the town is used by visitors simply as a base for buying supplies before heading into the remote north, but it retains something of an isolated outpost atmosphere and is worth a few hours of your time. You could happily while away a morning or afternoon watching the activities and interaction of local Basotho people who come into the town from the surrounding villages.

MORIJA

➕ 330 J7

Morija is the site of Lesotho's oldest church and the country's only museum. The French Protestant missionaries who established the church, on the main street, named the town after Mount Moriah in Palestine. Lesotho's first printing press was established here and the village is still important for culture,

theology and printing. Books in more than 50 languages have been printed here for export to other African countries.

The museum (Mon–Fri 8–5, Sun 2–5), also on the main street, has a number of important historic and prehistoric exhibits, and a well-organized archive of personal and church papers. There is a large fossil collection and a good display about the dinosaur relics found throughout the country. The annual Morija Arts and Cultural Festival takes place here in the first week of October, with concerts, traditional dance, choirs, horse racing and craft fairs (▷ 220).

MOUNT MOOROSI

➕ 329 K8

About 40km (25 miles) beyond Moyeni (Quthing), towards Qacha's Nek in the Southern Mountains, is Mount Moorosi along with the village of the same name, which has an important—if grim—history. In the mid-19th century it was the home of Chief Moorosi of the Baphuthi clan, who carried out raids against white settlers in nearby areas. After the British made Moyeni the district capital in 1877, they tried to subdue Moorosi by taking his son captive, but the chief resisted and managed to free his son. The British then spent more than two years trying to eliminate the threat posed by the chief, eventually capturing his mountain stronghold and massacring him and about 500 of his followers.

Nearby is Letsa-la-letsie (better known as Letsie) Lake, a reed-filled wetlands area which attracts water birds. A wildlife conservation project has been set up here involving the local people in the protection of the bearded vulture.

The bleak beauty of the Northern Mountains, as seen from the road that runs between Oxbow and Mokhotlong

MOYENI

329 J8

Moyeni (meaning 'place of the wind') is the administrative hub of Quthing district; the town itself is often also called Quthing (*Qu* means river in the San language). Central Moyeni straggles along one main street running uphill from the Main South Road. On the northern outskirts there are some sets of dinosaur footprints along the riverbank, and some farther up the Qomoqomong valley, although these are difficult to find without a guide. The valley is also home to some of the best preserved San cave paintings in Lesotho; follow the small road east out of Moyeni towards the village of Qomoqomong, where the road ends. The caves are in the hills to the southwest.

NORTHERN MOUNTAINS

330 L7

Commonly referred to as The Roof of Africa, the Northern Mountains are the highest in southern Africa. The high summits, unpopulated except for the occasional youth following his family herds in summer, have a harsh beauty. In winter the peaks are frequently under snow. There is one main road that runs across the area, from Butha-Buthe to Sani Pass, the highest road in all Africa. This road has recently been upgraded and the 200km (125 miles) between Butha-Buthe and Mokhotlong has been tarred. About 30km (20 miles) from Butha-Buthe (▷ 168) is the new Liphofung Cave Cultural and Historical Site (Mon–Fri 9–4.30), an initiative of the Lesotho Highlands Water Project to promote tourism in the region. There are some San rock paintings under and around a large overhang of rock that was once used as a hideout by Moshoeshoe, the 19th-century Basotho chief who fled to the area in the 1820s. A new walkway, a small visitor centre, shop and a rock art museum have been added to the site, and guides are available to tell you about the paintings and a little of Moshoeshoe's history.

Oxbow is the heart of the southern African ski industry, and while this may sound grand, the resort actually consists of one lodge. Hardy skiers still turn up occasionally, but there are no ski lifts or facilities. However, this may change as the skiing concession is up for sale, with the chance that an international company may move in and build a resort.

QACHA'S NEK

330 K8

This border town in the southeastern corner of Lesotho is on the only road pass from the southern mountain area into South Africa's Eastern Cape. This means it has residents from a number of southern African ethnic groups and you are as likely to hear Xhosa being spoken as Sesotho. Right up to 1970, Qacha's Nek had no direct road communication with the rest of Lesotho, and depended on the town of Matatiele in the Eastern Cape for supplies. Qacha, meaning 'hideaway', was the name of a local 19th-century chief who was apparently able to disappear into the mountains for months at a time. The British established an administrative settlement here in 1888 in an attempt to maintain control of the region. Today, this is one of the few areas in Lesotho that is heavily forested—look for the giant California redwood trees, which are as tall as 25m (80ft).

SANI PASS

330 L7

This steep, tortuously corkscrewing road is the only road from the Northern Mountains into South Africa and is passable only in a 4WD vehicle. The Sani Pass, originally a bridleway for packhorses, was opened to vehicular transport in the 1950s. The views across the mountains of KwaZulu-Natal (▷ 122) from here are awe-inspiring. About 12km (7.5 miles) from the pass is Thabana-Ntlenyana, the highest mountain in southern Africa at 3,482m (11,424ft). The name means 'pretty little mountain', hardly fitting for what is the second tallest mountain in Africa after Kilimanjaro in Tanzania. There are some magnificent hikes in this rugged area (▷ 122), but most people prefer to stop off for a meal in the Sani Top Chalet (▷ 219).

SEHLABATHEBE NATIONAL PARK

330 L7 ☎ 223-23600 ❷ Access is by 4WD vehicle only. There are two routes, one via Sehlabathebe village and one across the border from South Africa (by foot or horseback only)

Lesotho's only fully established national park is isolated, inaccessible and rugged, but all this represents much of its appeal. In the far east of Lesotho on the border with South Africa, it is covered in sub-alpine grasslands at an average height of 2,400m (7,900ft). There is little large game, except for the occasional hardy eland or baboon, but plenty of bird life, including the rare bearded vulture and black eagle. The park has excellent trout fishing, and is home to the Sehlabathebe water lily and the tiny Maluti minnow—a flower and a fish believed for many years to be extinct.

The Tintsab craft stalls are among many dotted along the roads in the Ezulwini Valley that sell locally made goods

SWAZILAND

EZULWINI VALLEY

⊞ 325 M4

The Ezulwini Valley ('Valley of Heaven'), clearly signposted from Mbabane, is the hub of most visitor activity in Swaziland. The area is also known as the Royal Valley as it is home to the Royal Village of Lobamba (see below). The valley itself has no real focus, but dotted along the road are craft shops, markets, hotels and restaurants; on weekends everyone in Swaziland seems to come here to play. The valley runs east for 30km (18.5 miles), ending at Lobamba. Here you'll see a service station, and just past it is the entrance to Mlilwane Wildlife Sanctuary (▷ 173).

HLANE ROYAL NATIONAL PARK

⊞ 325 N4 ☎ Office: 528-3943
🕐 Daily dawn–dusk 🛂 Adult E25, child (under 13) E12.50 🚗 2-hour game drive costs E130 per person; guided walks cost E25 for an hour 🚌 67km (42 miles) from Manzini along the road to Simunye. Turn left into the Ngongoni Gate, where all arrivals need to report www.biggameparks.org/hlane.html

Formerly a royal hunting ground, Hlane was declared a protected area in 1967 by King Sobhuza II. Following heavy poaching in the 1960s, the park has been restocked with wildlife and at 30,000ha (74,000 acres) is the kingdom's largest wildlife area. A number of predators have been reintroduced and lion, cheetah

and leopard are already evident, as well as elephant, zebra, giraffe, impala, hyena, white rhino and herds of wildebeest. Sadly the rhinos have had to have their horns removed to protect them from poachers. Hlane supports the densest population of raptors in Swaziland; the nesting density for the white-backed vulture is the highest in the whole of Africa, and the most southerly nesting colony of the marabou stork is found here.

The western area of the park has a network of roads that visitors can drive along to view the animals. The area around the Black Mbuluzi River attracts animals during the dry winter season. Close to Ndlovu camp is an Endangered Species Area, where elephant and rhino have been concentrated for security reasons. The Mahlindza waterhole, with its hippo, crocodile and water bird population, is one of the most peaceful picnic sites in the country.

LOBAMBA

⊞ 325 M4

The royal village of Lobamba, at the eastern end of the Ezulwini Valley, is set amid open bush countryside. This is where the present king, Mswati III lives, and from where he rules Swaziland with the Queen Mother, whose title is Ndlovukazi (meaning 'she-elephant'). Every August the king adds to his growing harem of wives at the Umhlanga ('Reed') Dance (▷ 220). All the royal buildings are closed to the public,

and it is strictly forbidden to take photographs. However, the National Museum in the village (Mon–Fri 8–1, 2–3.45, Sat–Sun 10–1, 2–3.45) has excellent displays relating to Swazi life throughout history, with old photographs, traditional dress and Stone Age implements.

Opposite the museum is a memorial to King Sobhuza II and a small museum depicting his life. His statue stands under a domed cover with open arches and a white tiled floor.

MALKERNS VALLEY

⊞ 325 M5

About 5km (3 miles) beyond Lobamba is a right turn for the Malkerns Valley, which is less geared to tourism than the Ezulwini Valley. But this does mean you get more of a feel for a typical Swazi lifestyle. There are restaurants and shops along the M13, including the well-known shop Swazi Candles (▷ 220). Items here are not all that cheap, but if you are on a budget, there are lower-price seconds with barely visible flaws.

South from Malkerns, the road continues towards Bhunya, which is 26km (16 miles) away. As the road climbs up into the highlands the forest closes in and it feels cool out of the sunlight. For part of this route the road follows the Great Usutu River, passing through rolling farmland.

Candles on display at the Swazi Candles shop, Malkerns Valley

A dry track leading through the Malolotja Nature Reserve

A group of traditionally dressed villagers performing a dance at the Swazi Cultural Village

THE SIGHTS

MALOLOTJA NATURE RESERVE

⊞ 325 M4 ☎ Swaziland National Trust Commission: 416-1179 🎫 Adult E22, child (under 12) E11 🚻 🚗 From MR3 turn, at Motjane, on to MR1; turn off after 7km (4 miles) and continue for another 18km (11 miles) to the reserve www.sntc.org.sz

Malolotja is a wild region of mountains and forest along Swaziland's northwestern border with South Africa. This reserve has been designed as a wilderness area, with most of the park accessible only on foot. There's a network of gravel roads, covering 25km (15.5 miles), for self-guided game drives, but the best way to see the park is on foot along one of the hiking trails.

Mgwayiza, Ngwenya and Silotfwane are three of Swaziland's highest peaks, and the hikes around these ranges cross deep, forested ravines, high plateaux and grasslands. Archaeological remains show that this region has been inhabited for thousands of years. The site of the world's oldest mine, thought to be 43,000 years old, is within the park; the diggings were used to excavate red and black earth, possibly for use as pigments.

A Swazi beehive hut in the Cultural Village

MANTENGA NATURE RESERVE

⊞ 325 M5 ☎ 416-1179 ⏰ Daily dawn to dusk 🎫 Adult E22, child (under 12) E11 🍴 🚗 Just past Lobamba in the Ezulwini Valley www.sntc.org.sz

This area of outstanding beauty and mature patches of forest between the main road and the Mantenga Falls (a walk of 2km/1.2 miles) is best known for the Swazi Cultural Village. This 'show' village is based upon traditional building methods and sells itself as a living cultural museum: This is exactly how a medium-sized Swazi homestead would have looked 100 years ago. There are 16 beehive-shaped huts built from local materials. As the guides show you around, the complex comes to life, with people performing traditional dances and songs. You will also see food being prepared and clothes and household objects being made. The set-up is both informative and informal—you can turn up at any time.

MANZINI

⊞ 325 N5

This industrial town has a good market, held on the corner of Mhlakuvane Street and Mancishane Road on Friday and Saturday mornings, and is worth a browse. It's one of the busiest local markets in Swaziland, bringing people from the local farming communities into town to sell fresh fruit and vegetables, clothes, a good selection of curios and freshly cooked snacks. The Bhunu Mall on Ngwane Street and The Hub on Mhlakuzane

Street are Manzini's newest shopping malls. Tiger-City on Villiers Street is a small complex where you'll find the cinema and a couple of restaurants.

The first trading station was opened here in 1885 and was originally run from a tent. The plot was later sold on to Alfred Bremer, who built a hotel and a shop. Manzini was originally known as Bremersdorp after Alfred Bremer, but was renamed Manzini after the Boers burnt the settlement to the ground during the Anglo–Boer War. The administrative focus then moved to Mbabane. While Swaziland was being administered by a provisional government composed of representatives of the Transvaal, the British government and the king during 1894, the headquarters were in the local hotel.

MBABANE

⊞ 325 M4 ℹ Swaziland Information Office, Swazi Plaza, tel 404-2531; Mon–Thu 8–4.45, Fri 8–4, Sat 9–1

Mbabane, the capital of Swaziland, is a small modern town built on the site of a trading station on the busy route between Mozambique and the Transvaal. After the Boer War, the British established their administrative headquarters here and the town grew up around it. Over the last few decades, the town hasn't developed well; there's a snarled traffic system, and just a handful of shopping malls and hotels. But do have a look at the Swazi market, which is near the central roundabout (traffic circle). It has an excellent display of fresh produce and you can engage in some good-natured bartering with the stallholders. The town also has useful amenities before you move onto the attractive Ezulwini Valley to the south (▷ 171).

*An antelope dashing out from the cover of the grass (above);
a warthog (inset)*

MLILWANE WILDLIFE SANCTUARY

**This unusual reserve is best explored on horseback or on
foot, which gives you close encounters with the animals.**

Mlilwane, stretching along a section of the Ezulwini Valley, is one of
the most popular of Swaziland's nature reserves. The land, originally
a ruined area of abandoned tin mines, is now filled with a variety
of game including hippo, giraffe, crocodile, eland, zebra, kudu and
the purple-crested lourie, the brilliantly plumaged national bird of
Swaziland. There are more than 100km (60 miles) of dirt roads
criss-crossing the reserve; some are for 4WDs only. There are several
choices of accommodation, but places on all guided walks and rides
can be reserved from the main camp.

ACTIVITIES IN THE RESERVE

As there are no big cats or rhino in Mlilwane, you can explore the
reserve on horseback, by mountain bike or on foot, peaceful ways
of experiencing the glorious landscape. The animals in the reserve
are pretty docile, allowing close viewings; horseback riding among
herds of zebra is an unforgettable experience. There is an extensive
system of self-guided walking trails including the Hippo, Macobane,
Sondzela and Mhlambanyatsi trails, each looping around the reserve
and taking in a variety of environments. The Macobane Trail, which
runs for 8km (5 miles), has an easy gradient and provides particularly
spectacular views of the Ezulwini Valley as it winds its way along the
contours of an old aqueduct on the Nyonyane Mountain.

RATINGS	
Cultural interest	● ● ●
Outdoor pursuits	● ● ● ● ●
Value for money	● ● ● ● ●
Walkability	● ● ● ● ●

BASICS

✚ 325 M4

☎ 528-3943

🕐 Gates: daily 24 hours

💷 Adult E25, child (under 13) E12.50

🐎 Horseback riding: E100 per person
per hour; guided walks: E25 per hour;
guided mountain biking: E85 per hour;
2-hour game drives day or night E130;
90-min sunset drives with drinks: E130;
village visits: E40

🍴 Restaurant in main camp overlooking a hippo pool

❓ Displays about conservation and
poaching at Sangweni Gate

🚗 The reserve is signposted from
Lobamba in the Ezulwini Valley
www.mlilwane.com

TIPS

● There are nightly performances of traditional Swazi
dancing in the main camp;
try to catch one, even if you're
staying elsewhere.
● The reserve arranges visits
to local villages which offer a
valuable insight into local life.

*An information board at
Mlilwane, with press cuttings
about the area*

The python pool in Mlawula Nature Reserve

A selection of soapstone carvings on the road to Pigg's Peak from Mbabane

MKHAYA GAME RESERVE

✚ 325 N5 ☎ 528-3943 ⊙ Daily 10–4 by pre-arranged tour only 👤 Adult E330, child (under 16) E165; prices include lunch 🚗 From Manzini, follow signs to Siteki for 8km (5 miles) and take a right turn and continue towards Big Bend (MR8); the reserve is signposted to the left after about 44km (27 miles) www.biggameparks.org/mkhaya.html

This small reserve, Swaziland's most exclusive, is now one of the best places in southern Africa to see black rhino. It is in an area of acacia lowveld southeast of Manzini. In 1995, the park received six black rhino from South Africa, a project funded, rather oddly, by the Taiwanese Government. During 1997, the first two baby elephants to be born in Swaziland in 100 years were born at Mkhaya. At present the only large cat you might see is the leopard. This is a private reserve and staying guests must arrange to arrive at either 10am or 4pm when the rangers will pick you up from the (locked) main gates. Day visits are allowed between these hours.

MLAWULA NATURE RESERVE

✚ 325 N4 ☎ Swaziland National Trust Commission: 416-1179 👤 Adult E22, child (under 13) E11 🎫 🚗 67km (42 miles) from Manzini along the road to Simunye, signposted after Simunye www.sntc.org.sz

Mlawula is part of the new greater Lubombo Conservancy. The Siphiso Valley and the Mbuluzi Gorge are good areas for game viewing on hiking trails or game drives. The main appeal of Mlawula is the variety of landscapes, from forests to dry thorn savannah. More than 1,000 species of plant have been identified here and the region is famed for its bird life—350 species have been recorded, such as African fin foot, crested guinea fowl and yellow spotted nicator. The good facilities include a vulture feeding area and a bird-watching hide. You can also see a range of antelope. Early traces of man dating back 100,000 years have been found in the riverbeds of the Mbuluzi and Mlawula rivers, which are also good places to spot crocodiles. The interesting plantlife includes the rare Lebombo ironwood and the *Encephalartos umeluziensis*, a cycad that only grows in the deep mountain valleys of the reserve.

Visitors are encouraged to hike on the network of trails, which pass through beautiful gorges, pools, waterfalls and rapids with views over Mozambique from the top of the escarpment. A leaflet on the trails and the reserve is available from the camp shop where you can also organize a guide to go with you.

PHOPHONYANE NATURE RESERVE

✚ 325 N4 ☎ 437-1429 ⊙ Daily 7.30–5 👤 Adult E30, child (under 12) E20 🚗 Signposted 14km (8.5 miles) north of Pigg's Peak www.phophonyane.co.sz

Close to the mountain community of Pigg's Peak is this small reserve in an extensive tract of natural vegetation full of bird and animal life. It lies on an escarpment, where the environment changes dramatically over a relatively small area. The dense riverine forest is home to small mammals such as duiker, bushbuck and the clawless otter, while in the mountains, the air is filled with the sound of waterfalls and there are more than 200 species of bird. The Phophonyane Falls, some of the best known falls in Swaziland, are here. You can explore the forest and mountains on foot or by 4WD vehicle.

PIGG'S PEAK

✚ 325 M4

This small town was named after William Pigg, a French gold prospector who came here in 1884. There was a working gold mine here until 1954, although no great fortunes were ever made. Today the town consists of little more than a string of shops along the main road. The principal industry here now is logging (as well as the huge Havelock asbestos mine). If you are going to and from South Africa through Jeppe's Reef border post, you are bound to pass through.

SHEWULA NATURE RESERVE

✚ 325 N4 🚗 10km (6 miles) south of the Lomahasha/Namaacha border with Mozambique; the camp is a further 30 minutes' drive

The community-owned Shewula Nature Reserve is just north of Mlawula. It is also part of the Lebombo Conservancy, straddling the Lebombo Mountains on the border with Mozambique and covering an escarpment of ancient ironwood mountain forest stretching down the Mbuluzi River. The views from the Shewula Mountain Camp, perched on top of a mountain, are incredible. On a clear day the ocean and Maputo can be seen to the east, and there is an uninterrupted view of 100km (62 miles) across Swaziland. Apart from during heavy rains (December to February), the camp is accessible by ordinary saloon (sedan) cars. When the road is too muddy, it is possible to leave your vehicle at the chief's office in the village, and be transported in a 4WD.

This chapter gives information on things to do in South Africa, Lesotho and Swaziland other than sightseeing. South Africa's best shops, arts venues, nightlife, activities and events are listed region by region.

What to Do

SHOPPING

Johannesburg, Durban and Cape Town have the country's largest shopping malls—slick complexes with a mix of chain stores and exclusive boutiques. At the other end of the scale there are the street vendors and African markets, great trawling grounds for excellent gifts. But wherever you shop, prices should be lower than in Europe and the US. Although the rand is no longer as weak as it was a few years ago, prices are still very reasonable and it's always possible to find a bargain.

SHOPPING MALLS

South Africans love shopping malls, and in Johannesburg affluent locals won't shop anywhere else. Many of the country's smarter malls are like self-contained towns, with

Little Karoo ostrich-skin handbags

alfresco restaurants, bars and cinemas all within one complex. Most cater to a mix of locals and visitors, with popular clothing, household and book shops interspersed with smart African curio shops. The Victoria and Alfred Waterfront in Cape Town is one of the most popular, while Johannesburg's enormous malls are some of the best places to seek out designer bargains. They are also good for slightly less expensive versions of international chains such as Guess or Quiksilver. The Gateway Shopping Mall, just outside Durban, claims to be the largest mall in the southern hemisphere—'Shoppertainment' is

beginning to feature in the South African vocabulary.

MARKETS

Craft and curio markets can be an excellent introduction to African souvenirs, as they are often manned by people from across the continent who import a range of crafts—from soapstone carvings from Zimbabwe to masks from Mali. Prices here tend to be slightly lower than in shops, and you can generally bring prices down further with a bit of friendly bartering, although you need to know your stuff if you're looking for genuine antiques or works of art. Bear in mind that local crafts and curios are significantly cheaper in neighbouring countries such as Lesotho and Swaziland.

OPENING TIMES
● Large shops and malls tend to stay open all day, seven days a week, usually until around 10pm.
● Smaller shops usually open around 9am and close at 5pm, although on Saturdays they will open later and close earlier (often as early as 1pm).
● Even in the big cities, most shops close on Sundays, and in rural areas you won't find anything open.

METHODS OF PAYMENT
South African services and shops have very similar methods of payment to those available in Europe and the US. Credit and debit cards

are widely accepted in shops, restaurants and hotels (notable exceptions are petrol/gas stations, where you need to pay in cash). In more rural or remote locations, cash may be the only accepted form of payment.

VAT REFUNDS
Value Added Tax (VAT) of 14 per cent is levied on goods and services, but foreign visitors can get a refund on goods over R250. You can do this at the airport before checking in when departing, or at some of the bigger shopping malls. To get the refund, present a full receipt (which acts as a tax invoice), a non-South African passport and the goods purchased. The procedure is simple enough at the airport, but allow plenty of time, especially if your flight is at night. At the border crossings, such as Beitbridge (Zimbabwe) or Ramotswa (Botswana), the procedure is very slow, as there are few officials to check goods against receipts.

WHAT TO BUY

Animal products
Animal products made from ivory and reptile skins are on sale in some areas, but if you take them back home you could well fall foul of the Convention on International Trade in Endangered Species of Wild Fauna and Flora (CITES) regulations. A more popular, and acceptable, animal product is an ostrich egg (painted, carved or plain, but empty), which you can find in most curio shops.

Basketwork
The majority of baskets in craft markets and gift shops are made by the Zulus. They have traditional functions, and most are decorated with distinctive

triangular patterns (denoting femininity), or diamonds or zig-zags (masculinity or warfare). The baskets are usually crafted from ilala palm fronds and grass, and dyed with natural tones—muted browns, beiges and greys—but you'll also see unusual baskets made out of telephone wire.

Beadwork
Zulu beadwork was always far more than the decorative art of weaving small glass beads into attractive patterns. Instead, the designs were a form of communication, with different colours representing different emotions—known popularly as Zulu 'love letters'. Today, most beadwork is decorative, and you'll see plenty of examples of *umgexo*—small rectangular shapes attached to a safety pin—as well as necklaces, ankle bracelets and head adornments.

Clothes and jewellery
Clothes and jewellery are good buys, with a number of South African designers making it big both at home and abroad. Traditional African jewellery can be bought in most curio shops; the bigger shops in the malls stock interesting pieces from across Africa.

Pottery
South Africa's best-known potters are the VhaVenda from Limpopo province, and their pots are sold throughout the country. All traditional clay pots are made by women and fired in grass-filled holes in the ground. The pots, which vary in size, have specific functions, such as storing traditional beer or maize flour, and their characteristic rough-hewed surfaces are glazed with silvery-grey graphite stripes or patterns.

Township crafts
Some of the most interesting contemporary purchases are arts and crafts produced in the townships. These include wire sculptures—anything from toy cars and key rings to candle-sticks—paper lampshades and sculptures made from recycled cans. In the major cities, these

Bright Zulu beadwork, in a variety of designs

are often sold at busy intersections and most markets.

Wine
Individual wine estates are the best places to buy wine and most will be able to ship abroad as part of their service. Transport and taxes can be expensive (expect to pay from R1,500 for the transport of 12 bottles to Europe), although the good value for money of the actual wines makes it quite tempting. Larger supermarkets and bottle stores also stock most good South African wines. See page 257 for more details on what to buy.

Wood carvings
The Venda men, from the Venda region in Limpopo province, are traditionally known as carvers, although women, too, have more recently taken up the craft. Venda carving has gained in popularity, with a range of interesting figures being produced by craftsmen, as well as practical items such as walking sticks or bowls. Craftsmen use traditional carving methods and work with local woods such as the strong *muhiri* (leadwood).

CHAIN STORES			
NAME	**DESCRIPTION OF GOODS**	**CONTACT NUMBER**	**WEBSITE**
Clicks	Cosmetics, photographic equipment, household goods	0860-254257	www.clicks.co.za
CNA	Books, magazines	0860-000262	www.cna.co.za
Edgars	Department store	0860-112468	wwwedgars.co.za
Exclusive Books	Coffee-table books, paperbacks, travel guides	011-7973888	www.exclusive books.com
Musica	CDs, DVDs	0860-687422	www.musica.co.za
Pick 'n' Pay	Food, household goods	011-8567000	www.picknpay.co.za
Woolworths	Fashion, household goods, food	0860-100987	www.woolworths.co.za

ENTERTAINMENT 🎵

South Africa's cultural scene has flourished in recent years, and the cities in particular will give you a good choice of theatre, musical performances and nightlife.

CINEMA
For many years there was little in the way of local South African cinema. The only exception to this had been the films by Leon Schuster, South Africa's best-known slapstick comic director and actor, responsible for the country's highest earning films. He plays on insecurities and comments on political currents through the unlikely medium of toilet gags and stereotyping.

Cinema Nouveau at the V & A Waterfront

However, this is all beginning to change. South Africa is a major film location—Cape Town in particular has acted as a set for an impressive range of movies in recent years. A new studio is under contruction in Cape Town and a number of independent films have made an impact (▷ 313).

There is a popular annual gay and lesbian film festival held in Cape Town, known as *Out in Africa*. Contact the local tourist office for more details.

CLASSICAL MUSIC, OPERA AND DANCE
The main cities have well-established classical music, opera and dance companies, although these have been radically modernized in the last decade—the whites-only scene is becoming far more inclusive and experimental—and much more interesting. Classical music and opera are becoming increasingly accessible, thanks in part to outdoor festivals like the summer concerts held at the Kirstenbosch Botanical Gardens in Cape Peninsula (▷ 72).

Ballet is no longer the prominent dance form, but you will find examples of interesting modern dance, especially when it incorporates aspects of African dance. Traditional tribal dance performances are very popular with visitors, but these vary widely in authenticity.

CONTEMPORARY MUSIC
Music is the cultural focal point of South Africa's arts scene, with live music—particularly jazz—remaining hugely popular. In and around Cape Town, you'll hear Cape Jazz, while Johannesburg offers cutting-edge and traditional sounds in its many jazz bars. There are several jazz festivals around the country; the most popular is the International Jazz Festival in Cape Town (▷ 190).

Live pop and rock concerts have boomed since the end of the apartheid era, when the cultural boycott was lifted and international artists began to tour here.

THEATRE
South Africa's theatre scene has rediscovered its feet following a tricky few years of freezes on government funds. Political theatre, once a pivotal genre during apartheid, is again proving popular.

Cutting-edge productions are also on the up and there remains a good selection of arts theatres around the country, but large-scale musicals are very popular.

INFORMATION AND TICKETING
Tourist offices will have the latest information on which companies and performers are coming to the local area. Drop in, or visit their websites (▷ 311). Computicket (tel 083-9158000; www. computicket.com) sells tickets for theatre, concerts and sports

Spier Music Festival held in the Western Cape

events across the country. Although this is the best source for tickets, it only accepts South Africa-issued credit cards for phone and internet bookings, so visitors have to go to a Computicket outlet to purchase tickets (you can pay with foreign-issued credit cards in person). You will be able to find these in major shopping malls in the big cities.

Foreign visitors can also book tickets in advance from home by faxing an international order form accompanied by copies of their credit cards and passports. To get hold of an order form, you can email info@computicket.com.

NIGHTLIFE

Nightlife is at its best in the cities. Johannesburg is renowned for its cutting-edge bars and clubs, while Pretoria, Port Elizabeth and Cape Town have more laid-back, studenty scenes. Although Saturday nights are the main event, Wednesdays are also popular. Opening hours are fairly flexible. Bars tend to fill up from around 6pm, clubs are virtually deserted before midnight, and some stay open until well into the next morning. Away from the biggest cities, things are much more sedate: Don't expect much more than a local pub in small towns. In major tourist areas, however, lively nightlife scenes have developed. On the Garden Route, for example, bars get busy most nights in high season, while backpacker areas such as the Wild Coast or KwaZulu-Natal have busy bars popular with a surfer crowd.

CLUBS

Music is central to a night out. You'll mostly hear mainstream house, but hip-hop and techno are popular, as are drum 'n' bass, Latin and home-grown rock. You should also listen to some kwaito (▷ 19), a relaxed form of house with booming bass—it is the sound of a young, confident and black Johannesburg. There are a number of large-scale dance events held around the country. Popular nights include Vortex and Alien Safari, both of which are all-night techno parties held at outdoor venues around the country.

Clubs usually charge you an entry fee—from about R20 up to R60.

BARS

Nightlife in big cities is usually focused on particular areas, making bar-hopping popular. Away from the larger cities, though, sophisticated bars are few and far between. Instead, small towns have traditional pubs, often with a 'ladies bar'—in some places women still avoid the 'saloon' section.

GAY AND LESBIAN

The South African constitution is one of the most gay-friendly and progressive in the world. This has enabled Cape Town to become the self-proclaimed 'Gay Capital' of Africa and it promotes itself as such. The city has a flourishing scene that draws visitors from across the country and continent.

Cape Town has a good range of bars, clubs and events aimed specifically at a gay crowd. The area around Green Point, known as De Waterkant Village, is the gay and lesbian hotspot, and all the main bars and clubs are found along Somerset and Main Road.

There is a Pride March (www.capetownpride.co.za, ▷ 190) held every February, but the main gay event is the Mother City Queer Project (www.mcqp.co.za, ▷ 190), a fantastically extravagant costume party and rave—not to be missed if you're in town in December: It is a highlight of the city's social calendar.

For more information, pick up the free Pink Map, available at tourist offices, and *detail* magazine, for listings.

However, away from the cities, South Africa remains deeply conservative and overtly affectionate behaviour between gay and lesbian couples may elicit a disapproving response—from both black and white communities—particularly in more remote rural parts.

HOW TO FIND OUT MORE

The best source of information on nightlife is the local newspapers, which have daily, up-to-the-minute listings on clubs, bars and events. Tourist offices, particularly in the cities, are also good sources of information. For venue information in Johannesburg, Pretoria, Cape Town and the East Coast, visit www.clubbersguide.co.za.

Cape Town

● *The Cape Times* and *Cape Argus* have good listings sections, as does *Cape Review* magazine. The tourist office

The Boardwalk bar in Port Elizabeth

also hands out the free Pink Map, with useful gay and lesbian listings, and the *Cape Gay Guide*, an annual booklet with information on nightlife and accommodation. *detail* is a free monthly gay lifestyle paper distributed in gay-friendly bars, clubs and shops.

Johannesburg and Pretoria

● Listings are published in the local papers *The Star* and *The Citizen*, as well as in the national *Mail and Guardian* and the bi-monthly magazine, *SA City Life*.

Durban

● Check listings in *The Daily News* and *The Natal Mercury*.

SPORTS AND ACTIVITIES

South Africans love watching sport, although racial divisions continue to play a role in who watches what. Cricket and rugby are largely the preserve of white South Africans, while soccer is hugely popular among the black population. Facilities, at least for the former two, are often excellent, with first-class stadiums in Bloemfontein (Springbok Park), Johannesburg (Ellis Park), Durban (Kings Park) and Cape Town (Newlands).

The country has an outdoors, get-fit lifestyle, and hiking, jogging and surfing are all very popular. But the real attraction in South Africa is the adventure sports (such as bungee jumping or kitesurfing) in more rural areas. Surfing and scuba diving are big business along the Garden Route and in KwaZulu-Natal. Hiking is the most popular activity overall and every national park and game reserve is crisscrossed with trails, some of which take more than a week to complete.

Cricket at Pretoria

BIRD WATCHING
With more than 700 species of bird recorded, bird watching has grown into a popular activity. The country has such diverse landscapes that many of the breeds are rare and specific to South Africa. For details contact Southern African Birding (tel 031-2665948, www.sabirding.co.za).

BUNGEE JUMPING
The most popular place in the country for bungee also claims to be the biggest jump in the world. The drop at the Bloukrans River Bridge (▷ 195) between Plettenberg Bay and Tsitsikamma is approximately 200m (655ft). The first rebound is higher

than the full descent at the famous drop in Victoria Falls. Another popular jump (60m/197ft) is at the Gouritz River Bridge (▷ 194) on the Cape Town side of Mossel Bay.

CRICKET
South Africa hosted the 2003 Cricket World Cup, with more than 54 matches being played, and its international team is well respected. Cricketing facilities are therefore excellent. It has also been acknowledged that the sport has done the most to become inclusive of all South Africans. The domestic season runs from October to April. Tickets for matches can be bought online with non-South African credit cards at www.sacrickettickets.co.za.

FISHING
Deep-sea fishing is big business, as is shore-fishing. Some of the most common catches are mako shark, long fin tuna and yellowtail, but there are strict rules governing all types of fishing. The simplest way of dealing with permits and regulations is to make a reservation through a charter company. Fly-fishing for trout is also popular, particularly in the Drakensberg and around the Western Cape.

GOLF
South Africa has some wonderful golf courses, such as the championship course at Milnerton in Cape Town, the Fancourt Country Club in George or Houghton in Johannesburg, venue for the South African Open. The most famous South African golfer is probably Gary Player, although Ernie Els is one of the most successful today.

HIKING
There is an enormous number of well-developed hiking trails across the country, many of

Hiking in the Drakensberg

which go through spectacular areas of natural beauty. These range from pleasant afternoon strolls through nature reserves to challenging hikes in wilderness regions. Hiking in South Africa involves some forward planning and permits, but the rewards and the choice of trails are well worth the effort. Opportunities begin in Cape Town on Table Mountain and the coastal trails around Cape Point, with a number of longer trails along the Garden Route. Inland, the Cederberg is an excellent and isolated hiking area, but the most popular and best-known region is the uKhahlamba-Drakensberg National Park, bordering Lesotho. The park, nearly

300km (186 miles) long, with a network of trails (some climbing to more than 3,000m/9,845ft) offers hikers a vast mountain region with undiscovered hiking possibilities comparable to regions of the Himalayas.

Day hikes are very popular, and well-signposted trails can be found in most nature reserves—ask at the park or reserve office. Longer trails involve at least one night in the wild, and you will need to bring a sleeping bag, tent, water, food and cooking equipment.

Some reserves and national parks have overnight huts, or if not, there will be campsites.

Wilderness trekking, available in the Cederberg and the Drakensberg, involves hiking away from designated footpaths. There is usually no specific overnight accommodation—you sleep in rock shelters or pitch a tent wherever possible. Hikers should have a good experience of map-reading and dealing with extreme weather conditions. Some national parks have guided wilderness trails which concentrate on game viewing and are accompanied by rangers.

HORSEBACK-RIDING
Horseback-riding is a popular activity among farming communities and in the mountains, particularly in the kingdom of Lesotho. The Drakensberg is a good place, and hotels can organize anything from a short morning trot to a six-day mountain safari. Longer treks are available in Lesotho, where ponies are the main form of transport in rural areas. On the Garden Route you can ride in the forests close to Knysna, and on the beaches in the Western Cape.

KLOOFING
Kloofing (also known as canyoning) is a popular adrenalin activity, especially with backpackers. It involves hiking, boulder-hopping (literally, jumping from boulder to boulder) and swimming along mountain rivers, and is available around Table Mountain in Cape Town, along the Garden Route and in the Drakensberg.

MOUNTAIN BIKING
Many nature reserves and wilderness areas have increased their accessibility for mountain bikes, and many routes have been planned to suit all levels of fitness. Some of the best organized regions include: De Hoop Nature Reserve, in the Overberg; Tulbagh Valley; Kamiesberg, close to Garies in Namakwa; Goegap Nature Reserve, outside Springbok; and the mountains around Citrusdal.

PARAGLIDING
South Africa has several world-renowned paragliding locations. Leaping from Lions Head in Cape Town, or wafting above the Kalahari are two of the most exhilarating options. Most of the action is around Kuruman in the Northern Cape and Barberton in Mpumalanga. Climatic conditions in South Africa are ideal—good thermal activity allows paragliders to climb between 6m and 8m (20ft and 26ft) per second and the cloud base is usually at 5,000m (16,400ft). The best season is between November and February.

RUGBY
South Africa's rugby team, nicknamed the Springboks, won the Rugby World Cup in 1995 and then-president Nelson Mandela memorably awarded the trophy to the winning captain in a Springbok jersey. Nevertheless, rugby remains the sport of choice for the white community and is yet to become truly popular in the black population, although the introduction of quotas has meant that the racial balance has changed to some extent. The most popular tournament is known as the Super 12, where teams from South Africa, Australia and New Zealand compete.

Divers can get a close-up look at the country's marine life

SCUBA DIVING
The South African coastline has particularly rich and diverse marine flora and fauna. The Agulhas current continually sweeps warm water down from the subtropical Indian Ocean and meets the cold nutrient-rich waters of the Atlantic. This mixing of water temperatures has created an incredible selection of marine ecosystems, from the tropical coral reefs of KwaZulu-Natal through to the temperate kelp forests around Cape Point. The diving community in South Africa is widespread and the facilities are generally excellent—but see Responsible Tourism on page 182.

SPORTS AND ACTIVITIES 181

SOCCER

Soccer is the country's most popular sport; the Premier Soccer League is the most important league, but there are a number of knock-out competitions. The season runs from August to May. The national team is known as Bafana Bafana (roughly meaning 'our boys'), and the best-known local teams include Kaizer Chiefs and Orlando Pirates, both from Johannesburg. A cause of much excitement has been the announcement that South Africa will host the 2010 World Cup, the first time that the championship has come to an African nation.

South Africa has great surfing for beginners and experienced alike

SURFING

South Africa has established itself as a major surfing hotspot, and has some of the best waves in the world. Jeffreys Bay on the south coast of the Eastern Cape is undoubtedly South Africa's surfing captial, known for its consistently good surf and host to the annual Billabong surf championships in July. This is also a good place to learn to surf, with a number of courses available and areas of reliable, small breaks, perfect for learning. The whole southern coast is dotted with good breaks, particularly around Port Elizabeth and East London. Cape Town, too, has some excellent, reliable breaks on

the Atlantic and False Bay beaches. The Golden Mile on Durban's beachfront has good surf, well protected by lifeguards and equipped with shark nets.

SWIMMING

Given South Africa's extensive coastline and beautiful beaches, swimming is often a top priority for visitors. The beaches of KwaZulu-Natal and the Garden Route have well-established swimming beaches catering to the domestic family market, which means patrolling lifeguards, changing facilities, toilets, picnic areas and kiosks selling cool drinks. In KwaZulu-Natal,

the biggest beaches also have shark nets to protect swimmers. Less tourist-orientated areas are obviously much less developed, and bathers must take extreme care. The seas around South Africa are renowned for their strong rips and swimmers should never venture out farther than they can stand. Although shark attacks are rare, it is worth bearing in mind that South Africa's waters are home to a variety of the creatures. Note, too, that the sea around Cape Town and the west coast is very cold and only really warms up towards the Garden Route (as the waters here come from the Indian Ocean, not the Atlantic).

WHALE WATCHING

The Whale Coast in the Cape Peninsula is one of the best places in the world to see whales. Between July and November, southern right and humpback whales mass to calve. You can also whale watch in the sheltered bays on the west coast and from boats on the KwaZulu-Natal coast, especially between June and October.

WHITEWATER RAFTING

Rafting is popular for visitors and is generally very well organized, with a high degree of safety. There are several excellent rapids: the Umzimvubu Falls in Transkei; along the Umzimkulu River in KwaZulu-Natal; on the Gariep River by the Augrabies Falls or near Kimberley; on the Great Usutu River in Swaziland; and on the Sabie, Olifants and Blyde rivers in Mpumalanga.

WINE TASTING

Wine tasting is big business. The Winelands in the Western Cape has several routes that take you through beautiful valleys and hundreds of estates. Look out for more unusual routes, such as along the Gariep (Orange) River. But be sensible if you are driving—one of you should stay off the alcohol.

RESPONSIBLE TOURISM

If you take part in any of these activities, especially scuba diving, you will come into close contact with South African ecosystems. Some of them, such as the coral reefs, are particularly sensitive. Please be sure to follow any instructions given to you on a tour or trip by your instructor or guide, which will help protect the landscape for future visitors. Local tourist boards will be able to recommend responsible operators.

HEALTH AND BEAUTY

The outdoors lifestyle in South Africa means that the health-conscious are well served, although spas and beauty treatments are only really just breaking into the mainstream. Thermal baths have long been popular, with well-established bases around the country. Beauty and wellness spas are, however, becoming more popular and the cities, in particular, have a handful of fashionable spas. Many hotels are also opening spas, especially trendier boutique hotels.

You can expect standards, and the range of treatments on offer, to be very similar to those found in Europe and the US. However, prices are considerably lower and you are likely to pay about half of what you would pay at home.

FOR CHILDREN

South Africa is a great place to bring the kids, with plenty of sights that interest adults while at the same time keeping children busy. Outdoors activities such as game walks, safaris or simply spending a day at the beach are very much part of a holiday in South Africa, with excellent facilities, particularly along the Western Cape and KwaZulu-Natal coasts. These areas have long been popular for domestic family holidays, so overseas visitors will find family-friendly hotels and restaurants, kids' clubs and plenty of child-orientated entertainment.

In the cities, museums and more traditional sights are starting to catch on to the importance of the family market, with some introducing fun interactive displays and special exhibits aimed at children.

There are a handful of theme parks around the country, including Ratanga Junction in Cape Town, Gold Reef City in Johannesburg and the new uShaka Marine World water park in Durban.

TAKING YOUR KIDS
● Most hotels and restaurants are family-orientated, so extra beds in rooms are rarely a problem, and smaller family-run bed-and-breakfasts will let you use the kitchen to prepare baby food.
● Only the larger hotels have babysitting services; you'll find most South African families bring their children out to restaurants with them.
● Restaurants in tourist areas and big cities often have children's menus.
● Central heating is a rarity in much of South Africa; bear this in mind if you're visiting in winter.
● Most attractions will offer some form of discount for children, with free entrance for the very young.

● The sun is extremely strong, so be sure to cover up children and use high-factor sun protection. Avoid the sun between 11 and 3.

Younger visitors will enjoy their time in South Africa

● Bear in mind that some wildlife safaris involve a lot of driving; smaller private reserves or animal sanctuaries may be more entertaining for small children.

WHAT TO DO

FESTIVALS AND EVENTS

Festivals and events are a relatively new concept in South Africa, but they are catching on fast, even in smaller towns. There is a wide range held throughout the year, from traditional carnivals and sports events to sophisticated arts festivals and music concerts. Perhaps the most important festival is the Grahamstown Arts Festival, where the country's actors, playwrights, musicians and comedians congregate to present the newest in South African arts. Other major festivals include Karnaval in Cape Town, the Rustler's Valley rock festival and the Umhlanga Reed Dance held in Swaziland.

Sports events are particularly popular, with a number of large-scale races, timed events and marathons taking place in Cape Town every year. Christmas is also well observed—a time when there is plenty going on.

CAPE PENINSULA

The Cape has just about everything you could want to do on holiday, much of which is focused around Cape Town and the Victoria and Alfred Waterfront (above): good shopping, entertaiment and nightlife that rivals Johannesburg, and beaches and mountains that give you the chance to get out and about.

Cape Town is good value for money for shoppers, and many visitors come here for little else. The main shopping area is the Victoria and Alfred Waterfront, which is crammed with clothes, gift, music and crafts shops, but prices are above the average. Central Cape Town also has a good range, with a couple of craft markets, some great second-hand book, antiques and bric-à-brac shops and a few fashionable clothes stores. Long Street and Kloof Street are good bets for alternative clothes and accessories.

The region is gaining a solid reputation for having a vibrant arts scene. Music, as always, is the focus, with live music—particularly jazz—hugely popular and culminating in the yearly International Jazz Festival. The comedy circuit, too, is booming, attracting talent from around South Africa and overseas. Cape Town is proud of its well-established

classical music, opera and dance companies, but is best-known for its nightlife, and it's a very gay- and lesbian-friendly city.

The area's temperate climate and excellent facilities make the Cape a great destination for adventure sports, as well as more sedate pursuits such as watching a cricket match or playing a round of golf. There are also a number of marathons and cycle races held during summer, although the most popular sport with young locals is surfing.

The beaches on the Atlantic Seaboard are almost always too cold to swim in—even during the hottest months, the water temperatures rarely creep above 14°C (57°F). False Bay, however, is always 5°C (9°F) warmer, and is perfectly pleasant for a dip during summer. A number of beaches have artificial rock pools built near the water, which, although rather murky, can be

perfect for children to paddle in. There are some very good municipal swimming pools in Cape Town, the best of which is the outdoor pool in Sea Point known as the Pavilion, which has spectacular views of Table Mountain.

Cape Town holds more events than anywhere else in the country, with a number of street festivals, such as the Karnaval, taking place throughout the year. Large-scale sports events, like the Two Ocean Marathon, are also extremely popular, and during the summer the city often comes to a standstill for timed walks or races.

KEY TO SYMBOLS	
⊕	Shopping
♬	Entertainment
♥	Nightlife
⚽	Sports
✪	Activities
♡	Health and Beauty
✹	For Children

CAMPS BAY AND ATLANTIC SEABOARD

🎭 GREEN POINT MARKET
Beside Green Point Stadium,
Green Point 8005
This large curio market is a good bet for African crafts, usually sold at cheaper prices than elsewhere. There are also food stalls, and buskers to entertain the crowds.
🕐 Sun 8–5

🍷 DIZZY JAZZ CAFÉ
41 The Drive, Camps Bay 8005
Tel 021-4382686
The busy Dizzy hosts nightly live jazz and is popular with locals due to its fairly small size, giving it a more intimate feel than many other bars. Its friendly crowd gives the place an appealingly down-to-earth atmosphere. Good food is served and the most popular nights are Thursday to Sunday. The music usually starts around 8.30pm.
🕐 Wed–Mon 5pm–late 🎫 From R20

🍷 THE BRONX
35 Somerset Road, corner of Napier Street, Green Point 8005
Tel 021-4199216
www.bronx.co.za
Cape Town's best-known and most popular gay bar and club gets packed out at weekends. The clientele is mostly men here, but women are more than welcome. DJs play techno every night, and there is karaoke on Monday.
🕐 Daily 8–late 🎫 Free

🍷 BUDDHA BAR
Main Road, Green Point 8005
Tel 021-4344010
www.buddhabar.co.za
The sophisticated Buddha Bar has a large balcony overlooking all the action in Green Point. The bar is tastefully decorated with a subtle Asian feel and is popular with a trendy media and model crowd. Wednesday is the biggest night here.
🕐 Mon–Sat noon–late 🎫 From R20 after 9pm

🍷 BUENA VISTA SOCIAL CAFÉ
Main Road, Green Point 8005
Tel 021-4330611
This Cuban-themed bar and restaurant caters to an affluent crowd. The music is a hot mix of live Cuban bands and a DJ playing Latin sounds. There's a pleasant loungey interior, although the broad balcony is the best place for cocktails on a hot evening.
🕐 Daily noon–late 🎫 Free

🍷 CAFÉ CAPRICE
Victoria Road, Camps Bay 8005
Tel 021-4388315
This is one of the most popular cafés and bars on the main road along Camps Bay Beach.

Taking to the skies with Para-Pax around Camps Bay

There are outdoor seats overlooking the sand, good snacks and great fresh-fruit cocktails. The crowd is beautiful and congregates here from sunset.
🕐 Daily 9am–late 🎫 Free

🍷 LA MED
Glen Country Club, 2a Victoria Road, Clifton 8005
Tel 021-4385600
www.lamed.co.za
La Med is a hugely popular meeting place for locals, with a busy bar overlooking the sea. There's a good choice of pub food, but the reason to come here is its legendary sundowners, though it will be hard to find a seat at sunset. The bar

turns into a raucous club later in the evening.
🕐 Daily 11am–late 🎫 From R20

🍷 SLIVER
27 Somerset Road, Green Point 8005
Tel 021-4215798
Sliver's stylish lounge bar has a mostly gay clientele, but is also very popular with a trendy, mixed crowd. There's a relaxed atmosphere that heats up later in the evening, and it is connected to the much more raucous Confession club in same complex.
🕐 Wed–Sun 10pm–4am 🎫 From R20

⭐ NOORDHOEK BEACH HORSE RIDES
Noordhoek Beach 9301
Tel 082-7741191
www.horseriding.co.za
Noordhoek Beach is a popular spot for horse rides: the long, hard-packed sand is perfect for galloping, and more sedate sunset rides are also available. Booking is essential.
🎫 From R170

⭐ PARA-PAX
Tel 021-4617070/082-8814724
www.parapax.com
Paragliding from Lions Head is very popular, with gliders landing by the sea between Clifton and Camps Bay. Para-Pax can also organize tandem paragliding sessions.
🎫 Single tandem paragliding session R750

CAPE TOWN

🎭 AFRICAN IMAGE
52 Burg Street, City Centre 8001
Tel 021-4238385
African Image is a bright and interesting curio shop with a far greater selection than most craft shops in town. It has a wide range of tribal art and crafts from across Africa. It's also worth visiting for its quirky gifts such as bags made from cola bottle tops and decorative chickens made from plastic bags.
🕐 Daily 9–5

AFRICAN MUSIC STORE
90a Long Street, City Centre 8001
Tel 021-4260857
This lively little shop sells a comprehensive choice of albums by major southern African artists, as well as compilations and reggae. The staff are incredibly helpful and will happily let you listen to any number of CDs before making your choice.
🕓 Mon–Fri 9–6, Sat 9–2

GREENMARKET SQUARE MARKET
Greenmarket Square, City Centre 8001
Cape Town's best-known and liveliest market sells arts, crafts and curios from across Africa. There is a pleasant, bustling atmosphere, helped by the buskers and entertainers who line the cobbles, and the cafés and restaurants flanking the stalls.
🕓 Mon–Fri 8–5, Sat 9–2

JEWEL AFRICA
170 Buitengracht Street, Bo-Kaap 8001
Tel 021-4245141
www.jewelafrica.com
You'll find a wide range of good quality gold, silver, platinum and precious stones here. The shop claims to be Africa's largest jewellery showroom, and specializes in personal designs (which can be completed in 24 hours).
🕓 Mon–Fri 8.30–5, Sat 9–5.30, Sun 11–4

MEMEME
279 Long Street, City Centre 8001
Tel 021-4240001
Mememe is one of many tiny boutiques on Long Street. It sells a good selection of clothes and accessories, most created by local designers.
🕓 Mon–Fri 10–6, Sat 10–3

MONKEYBIZ
The Pinnacle, corner of Burg and Castle streets, City Centre 8001
Tel 021-4260145
www.monkeybiz.co.za
Monkeybiz, something of a local sensation, creates

employment for Township women, who make beautiful and quirky one-off bead works, including figures, animals and accessories. Their work is also sold at the tourist office.
🕓 Mon–Thu 8–5, Fri 8–2

PAN AFRICAN MARKET
Long Street, City Centre 8001
Tel 021-4264478
Occupying a whole building, this 'market' is actually more like a set of shops, each selling arts and crafts from across the continent. It has a range of good-value jewellery, including Zulu beadwork and Masai necklaces, as well as a vast choice of masks, sculptures

Browsing in Greenmarket Square Market

and gifts. There is also a small restaurant serving traditional African dishes.
🕓 Mon–Sat 8.30–5

SCAR
22 Kloof Street, City Centre 8001
Tel 021-4225085
This is the place to come for eccentric one-off designs. The clothes at Scar are aimed at a young fashion-conscious clientele, with lots of 1980s-inspired skirts, tube tops, bikinis, oversized bags and perspex jewellery.
🕓 Mon–Fri 9–7, Sat 9–4, Sun 11–4

STREETWIRES
77 Shortmarket Street, City Centre 8001
Tel 021-4262475
www.streetwires.co.za
This wire sculpture co-operative is a great place to find interesting Township craftwork without feeling under pressure to buy. Look out for the key rings and sculptures.
🕓 Mon–Fri 8.30–5

UWE KOETTER
4th Floor, Amway House, Dock Road, City Centre 8001
Tel 021-4257770
www.uwekoetter.co.za
This shop sells traditional, high-quality, exclusive pieces from one of the country's best-known designers. It proudly claims that no piece is made twice. The emphasis is on diamonds, but there are some less expensive options. Tours of the workshop are available.
🕓 Mon–Fri 9–6.30, Sat 9–3.30

ARTSCAPE THEATRE CENTRE
10 DF Malan Street, Foreshore 8001
Tel 021-4217839
www.artscape.co.za
The Artscape is Cape Town's major art complex hosting opera, theatre and classical music concerts. There are three stages—the Main Theatre, the Arena and the Opera House—which show a mix of classical concerts, musicals and dance, as well as new experimental theatre.
💷 From R50

CAPE TOWN OPERA
Artscape Theatre Centre, 10 DF Malan Street, Foreshore 8001
Tel 021-4109800
www.capetownopera.co.za
The city's opera company stages regular performances, mostly the classics, and has a reputation for developing singers from different racial backgrounds—opera is no longer the reserve of the white and wealthy. Performances are usually held at the Artscape complex.
💷 From R85

CAPE TOWN PHILHARMONIC ORCHESTRA
City Hall, Darling Street,
City Centre 8001
Tel 021-4109809
Cape Town has a well-respected Philharmonic Orchestra based at the former City Hall. The 80 musicians are under the direction of conductor Bernhard Gueller and visiting guest conductors; they also perform regularly in the Artscape and at Kirstenbosch Botanical Gardens (▷ 72).
From R55

DRUM CAFÉ
32 Glyn Street, Gardens 8001
Tel 021-4611305
www.drumcafe.co.za
This huge venue has become something of a Cape Town institution, and hosts nightly drum sessions. The communal sessions are the most popular, where customers can grab a drum and join in, and there are professional sessions on Friday and Saturday nights.
Mon, Wed, Fri 8pm–late From R50

JAZZART
Artscape Theatre Centre, 10 DF Malan Street, Foreshore 8001
Tel 021-4109848
This is the oldest modern dance company in South Africa, founded in 1975. Jazzart has a history of cultural involvement and multiracial performances, and the company continues to be actively involved with disadvantaged communities, working as a racially mixed group and creating a fusion of Western and African dance styles.
From R35

LABIA
68 Orange Street, Gardens 8001
Tel 021-4245927
This is Cape Town's most enjoyable cinema, showing independent international films and hosting the Out in Africa film festival. A café serves good pre-movie snacks, and the whole cinema is licensed, so you can take your glass of wine into the movie.
Daily 1.45–11 From R25

169
169 Long Street, City Centre 8001
Tel 021-4261107
This R&B club has a lively, mixed crowd. The music is a blend of R&B, hip-hop and funk, but you may also hear some kwaito (▷ 19). It's a fairly small venue, but very popular so it's almost always packed (particularly on Fridays). There's a balcony overlooking busy Long Street.
Wed, Fri, Sat 10pm–late From R40

The Jo'burg bar on the city's Long Street

JO'BURG
218 Long Street, City Centre 8001
Tel 021-4220142
One of the city's most popular and best-established bars is trendy Jo'burg, serving pints and cocktails. Early evenings are relaxed, but the pace picks up from around 9pm when DJs play funky house and drum 'n' bass. The interior is eclectic and the crowd fashionably scruffy.
Daily 5pm–3am Free

PERSEVERANCE TAVERN
83 Buitenkant Street, City Centre 8001
Tel 021-4612440
The Perseverance is famed for being Cape Town's oldest pub, serving a range of bottled and draught beers and good pub food. There's a beer garden and plenty of little drinking corners. The pub gets full at the weekend, and is especially popular for its Sunday roasts.
10am–2am Free

POO NA NA SOUK BAR
Heritage Square, 100 Shortmarket Street, City Centre 8001
Tel 021-4234889
The ultra-fashionable Poo Na Na Souk, decked out in Moroccan lanterns and exotic fabrics, has lovely balconies overlooking the even trendier Moja restaurant downstairs. The bar usually has a relaxed atmosphere, but it sometimes hosts big-name international DJs, so expect a big crowd on these nights.
Mon–Fri 11am–1.30am, Sat–Sun 6pm–1.30am Free

THE ADVENTURE VILLAGE
295 Long Street, City Centre 8001
Tel 021-4241580
www.adventure-village.co.za
Surfing is serious business in Cape Town, and there are excellent breaks catering for learners right through to experienced surfers. The Adventure Village arranges lessons and surfing outings to some of the best breaks on Kommetjie, Noordhoek, Llandudno, Muizenberg and Bloubergstrand. For a daily surf report call 021-7881350.
R500 for a full-day, dropping to R350 for each consecutive day

CAPE SPORTS CENTRE
Langebaan Lagoon, Langebaan 7357
Tel 022-7721114
www.capesport.co.za
The Cape's strong winds have made it a great place for kitesurfing. The best spot is Dolphin Beach at Table View, north of central Cape Town, where winds are strong and waves perfect for jumping. Cape Sports rents equipment and organizes tuition.
Three-hour lesson R500

WHAT TO DO

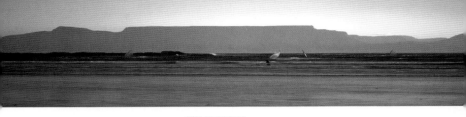

⊕ DOWNHILL ADVENTURES
Overbeek Building, corner of
Kloof, Long and Orange streets,
City Centre 8001
Tel 021-4220388
www.downhilladventures.com
The city's best-known biking
operator organizes a range of
mountain biking excursions,
including the popular Table
Mountain double descent
(90 per cent downhill) and
rides around Cape Point.
You can also rent bicycles.
🕓 Day trips of Cape Point and the
Winelands R500

⊕ SCUBA SHACK
289 Long Street, City Centre 8001
Tel 021-4249368
www.scubashack.co.za
The Cape waters are cold
but are often very clear and
good for wreck and reef
diving. Scuba Shack offers a
full range of PADI-recognized
instruction and equipment
rental, as well as organized
tours to the best dive sites and
great white shark cage dives.
There's also an office at False
Bay (tel 021-7827358).
💶 A single dive R120 (excluding
equipment); a PADI Open Water
course from R1,995

FALSE BAY

⊕ INDIA JANE
Station Road, Kalk Bay 7945
Tel 021-7883020
One of a small Cape Peninsula
boutique chain selling high
fashion items, India Jane has
a good choice of clothes from
South African designers and
some one-off pieces.
🕓 Daily 9.30–5.30

⊙ THE BRASS BELL
Next to rail station, Kalk Bay 7975
Tel 021-7885456
The celebrated Brass Bell is the
best known pub in False Bay,
with a spectacular setting right
on the waves. It's a great spot
for a cold beer while watching
the sunset, and serves pub
meals to a young, noisy crowd.
Expect live music at weekends.
🕓 Daily 11am–late 💶 Free

MILNERTON

⊛ MILNERTON GOLF CLUB
Bridge Road, Milnerton 7741
Tel 021-5521047
This is a true links course in
a beautiful setting in the
shadow of Table Mountain.
It is 6,011m (6,552 yards),
par 72, but watch your shots
when the wind blows.
💶 R290

⊛ MTN SCIENCENTRE
Century City, Milnerton 7446
Tel 021-5298100
www.mtnsciencentre.org.za
This is South Africa's only
interactive science museum,
aimed at helping children learn
about scientific discoveries and

The Brass Bell pub at False Bay

technological innovations.
There are more than 280 displays, most of them interactive,
as well as an auditorium and
an exhibition hall.
🕓 Daily 9.30–6, until 8pm Fri–Sat
💶 Adult R24, child R20

⊛ RATANGA JUNCTION
Century City, Milnerton 7441
Tel 0861-200300
www.ratanga.co.za
South Africa's largest theme
park is a re-creation of a
19th-century mining town,
crammed with impressive
thrill rides, roller-coasters and
family rides. Tickets allow as
many rides as you want. Some
have a height restriction.

🕓 Wed–Fri, Sun 10–5, Sat 10–6
(extended during school holidays)
💶 Adult R100, child R50

SOUTHERN SUBURBS

⊞ CAVENDISH SQUARE
Main Road, Claremont 7708
Tel 021-6575600
Trendy Cavendish Square mall
has clothes, household and
book stores, as well as a range
of restaurants and a cinema
complex. It's very popular with
the younger generation and
the fashion-conscious.
🕓 Mon–Sat 9–6, Sun 10–4

⊙ BAXTER
Main Road, Rondebosch 7700
Tel 021-6857880
www.baxter.co.za
This is Cape Town's more
alternative theatre complex,
with a long-term involvement
in black theatre and with a
good reputation for supporting
community theatre. As well
as small, independent plays, it
hosts international productions
and musicals.
💶 From R55

⊙ CAPE TOWN CITY BALLET
Cottage 3, Lover's Walk, Rosebank 7700
Tel 021-6502399
www.capetowncityballet.org.za
A small, tightly-knit company
without state sponsorship,
the Cape Town City Ballet
maintains a high standard.
The company performs well-
known classics such as *Giselle*
and *Cinderella*, as well as
modern works.
💶 From R65

⊙ INDEPENDENT ARMCHAIR THEATRE
135 Lower Main Road,
Observatory 7925
Tel 021-4471514
The Armchair, as it's known by
students, is a great little venue
where you can catch some
local rock, hip-hop and folk
acts. There are live bands on
most nights, but the venue
also hosts stand-up comedy
nights and screens movies.
🕓 Daily 8pm–late 💶 From R10

KIRSTENBOSCH SUMMER CONCERTS

Kirstenbosch Botanical Gardens, Rhodes Drive, Newlands 7708
Tel 021-7998899
www.sanbi.org
The summer concerts held in the idyllic setting of Gardens are a highlight of the Cape's arts calendar. Music varies from jazz and classical to pop. People spread out on the lawns, unpack picnics and enjoy the music with views of the mountain.
🕒 Nov–end Mar Sun from 5pm
💷 From R55

DAY TRIPPERS

Santos Park Unit 8, Voortrekker Road, Maitland 7405
Tel 021-5114766
www.daytrippers.co.za
This operator is one of the most popular for arranging all-round active tours and is popular with backpackers. A number of their trips include kloofing (canyoning).
💷 Full-day Cape Point trip R350, including lunch

MOWBRAY GOLF CLUB

Raapenberg Road, Mowbray 7700
Tel 021-6853018
www.mowbraygolfclub.co.za
Mowbray is one of the oldest clubs in Cape Town and hosts the national championships. It's a par 74 course with plenty of trees and water holes.
💷 R395

NEWLANDS CRICKET GROUND

Campground Road, Newlands 7700
Tel 021-6572003
www.wpca.cricket.org; tickets from www.sacricketttickets.co.za
Despite redevelopment, this famous test match ground still has a few of its famous old oak trees, and it is still possible to watch a game from a grassy bank with Table Mountain as a backdrop.
🕒 Cricket season: Nov–end Mar
💷 From R60

WESTERN PROVINCE RUGBY FOOTBALL UNION GROUND

Boundary Road, Newlands 7700
Tel 021-6594500
This is the city's main rugby ground and international games are played here. Be sure to wear a hat and bring plenty of sunscreen as shade is limited.
🕒 Rugby season: Apr–end Oct
💷 From R60

TABLE MOUNTAIN

ABSEIL AFRICA

Top Cableway station, Table Mountain
Tel 021-4241580
Abseil Africa operates what it claims is the world's highest and longest commercial abseil

Newlands Cricket Ground

(rappell)—a 112m (367ft) drop down the face of Table Mountain.
💷 R250, weather permitting—phone ahead for details

VICTORIA AND ALFRED WATERFRONT

TRAVELLER'S BOOKSHOP

King's Warehouse, Victoria and Alfred Waterfront 8001
Tel 021-4256880
This small bookshop stocks an excellent selection of travel literature, with a good section on South Africa, plus a range of guidebooks and maps.
🕒 Daily 9am–9.30pm

VAUGHAN JOHNSON'S WINE SHOP

Victoria and Alfred Waterfront 8001
Tel 021-4192121
Johnson's is one of the best-stocked wine merchants in the area, selling an exhaustive range from the Winelands and across the country. The staff here are knowledgeable and can arrange a shipping service.
🕒 Mon–Sat 9–5, Sun 10–5

VICTORIA WHARF

Victoria and Alfred Waterfront 8001
Tel 021-4087600
www.waterfront.co.za
The area's best known shopping mall is also its most central. Clothes shops (including international labels such as Levis and Diesel) sell their wares at marginally cheaper prices than back home.
🕒 Mon–Sat 9–9, Sun 10–6

CINEMA NOUVEAU

Victoria and Alfred Waterfront 8001
Tel 021-4258223
Cinema Nouveau is the alternative arm of the mainstream complex—Nu Metro—upstairs, and screens a good range of foreign films and small-budget, independent American films. Tickets half-price on Tuesdays.
🕒 Daily 11–9 💷 From R35

QUAY FOUR

Victoria and Alfred Waterfront 8001
Tel 021-4192008
Quay Four's large, shady deck overlooking the water is the perfect place for a cool early evening drink. The bar is popular with locals and visitors, who come here for the views and the good-value meals, draught beer and cocktails.
🕒 11am–midnight 💷 Free

TABLE BAY DIVING

Victoria and Alfred Waterfront 8001
Tel 021-4198822
This operator organizes dive charters and a full range of PADI courses, as well as selling scuba and snorkelling gear.
💷 From R450

JANUARY

KARNAVAL

Tel 021-4264260

Popularly known as the Coon Carnival (despite its derogatory connotations), Karnaval begins in the Bo-Kaap district and ends up at the Green Point Stadium. The procession of competing minstrel bands, complete with straw boaters and bright satin suits, is quite a spectacle.

◉ 2 January

FEBRUARY

CAPE TOWN PRIDE

www.capetownpride.co.za

Cape Town Pride starts with a gay pride parade touring central Cape Town and culminates in a street party which goes on until the early hours in Green Point.

◉ Last weekend of February

MARCH/APRIL

CAPE TOWN FESTIVAL

www.capetownfestival.co.za

This week-long arts and cultural festival is held at various venues throughout the city. A music stage is set up in Company's Garden, showcasing bands, singers and dancers, with special youth and children's events being held on one day of the week.

◉ End of March

CAPE TOWN INTERNATIONAL JAZZ FESTIVAL

Tel 083-1235299

www.capetownjazzfest.com

This is the city's biggest annual jazz event, taking place in the Convention Centre. There are usually four stages featuring a weekend's worth of performances by local and international jazz artists, from local legends like Hugh Masekela to international acts like Elvis Costello and Jamie Cullum.

◉ Last weekend of March

Minstrels at the Cape's Karnaval festival

CAPE ARGUS CYCLE TOUR

www.cycletour.co.za

A huge timed cycling event follows a gruelling circuit around Table Mountain to False Bay, across the mountains and along Chapman's Peak Drive to the Atlantic Seaboard and back into central Cape Town. Much of the city is out of bounds to motorists for the day.

◉ One Saturday in mid-March

TWO OCEANS MARATHON

www.twooceansmarathon.org.za

The popular Two Oceans Marathon covers 56km (35 miles) and follows a similar course to the Cape Argus Cycle Tour. It gets its name because the race route goes from one coastline of the Peninsula to the other. Nearly 10,000 competitors take part, many of them running for charity, so expect the usual wacky costumes. Again, much of the city is closed to motorists.

◉ Last weekend of March

OUT IN AFRICA

www.oia.co.za

The South African Gay and Lesbian Film Festival, known as Out in Africa, has been running for more than 10 years. One part of the festival is held at the Victoria and Alfred Waterfront, but there are also satellite events in other cities, such as Johannesburg.

◉ End of March into April

OCTOBER

CAPE TIMES/FNB BIG WALK

www.bigwalk.co.za

This is the world's largest timed walk, with an estimated 20,000 people taking part. Walkers, who are sponsored to raise money for various charities, can choose one of eight routes of varying lengths, the longest passing through the Southern Suburbs and along False Bay.

◉ One weekend in mid-October

DECEMBER

MOTHER CITY QUEER PROJECT

www.mcqp.co.za

This vast costume party is the biggest gay event in town. The annual theme guarantees outrageous costumes and an upbeat atmosphere. The venue changes every year so visit the website for details.

◉ Saturday night at beginning of the month

LONG STREET CARNIVAL

This is another street party, held on buzzing Long Street. Several stages are set up along the road and down some of the side streets, featuring live music (mostly rock bands and techno music) and stand-up comedy. Check with the tourist office for more information.

◉ One weekend in mid-December

WHAT TO DO

WESTERN CAPE

The Western Cape is a largely agricultural area and is a good place to stock up on fresh country produce. It's home to the Winelands, so buying wine should be at the top of your purchasing list. You'll also see people working in the vineyards, such as those in Franschhoek (above). Although the region's nightlife is much quieter than in Cape Town or Jo'burg, it's one of the best places in the country for outdoor activities.

Most towns in the region have small markets or stalls selling fresh fruit and vegetables along the roadside that are good for picnics. The Winelands are, of course, the best place for buying excellent-value South African wines. Most wine estates have sales and tastings: you simply turn up, taste what's on offer and buy what you like. Elsewhere, specialist leather items are a good buy. The Garden Route is popular with artists and craftsmen, and Knysna has a good selection of arts shops.

Other than a few cinemas, there is little in the way of entertainment. Stellenbosch has a local theatre and the nearby Spier wine estate has an attractive open-air amphitheatre which hosts most of the area's top shows.

Much of the rural Western Cape is fairly conservative, and you won't find many bars and clubs (although some of the larger settlements have a local pub). Along the Garden Route, resorts focus more on restaurants and nightlife tends to be

a good meal accompanied by fine wines. Stellenbosch, with its student population, has the liveliest nightlife, with a good selection of bars, also popular with backpackers. However, the gay and lesbian scene is somewhat limited in the Cape.

The Garden Route (and the coast in general) is one of the country's premier activity destinations. Just about everything is on offer here. Some of the highlights include whale-watching in Hermanus, scuba diving wrecks, kayaking and bungee jumping the world's highest jump at Bloukrans River Bridge. You will find some of the finest hiking in the forests of Tsitsikamma National Park, where the impressive Storms River Gorge is a must-see. Away from the coast, there is excellent hiking in the Cederberg and several areas have mountain biking.

The family-friendly resorts of the Garden Route make this an ideal area to bring children to. There are fabulous beaches with safe rock pools and on-duty life-guards, restaurants

with children's menus, and accommodation choices for families. The Winelands, although limited in sights for children, is also family friendly and many of the best restaurants on wine estates have play areas and children's menus. South Africans enjoy visiting the national parks during school holidays, so expect all the camps to be busy with young children.

Some of the large hotels in the region have on-site spas, usually offering a range of beauty treatments and massages. There are also a couple of older spas, with hot natural springs, where facilities range from basic swimming pools to a variety of indoor and outdoor treatments.

KEY TO SYMBOLS	
⊕	Shopping
🎭	Entertainment
▽	Nightlife
⚅	Sports
✪	Activities
♡	Health and Beauty
✵	For Children

CALEDON

⑦ THE CALEDON HOTEL & SPA
Nerina Street, Caledon 7230
Tel 028-2145100
www.thecaledon.co.za
Caledon's hot springs can be accessed through this modern complex (also known for its casino). The springs produce more than 800,000 litres (176,000 gallons) per day. Day visitors can use the spa's facilities, including a waterfall tumbling down the hillside that collects into a series of pools. There are additional saunas, gym, cold pool and steam room, and treatments such as massages and facials.
💷 A seaweed wrap R520; a deep-tissue hour-long massage R290 🚗 1km (0.5 miles) out of town, just off the N2

CITRUSDAL

⑦ THE BATHS
Citrusdal 7140
Tel 022-9218026
www.thebaths.co.za
A popular and long established natural hot water spring, sur-rounded by citrus groves. The first resort was established here in 1739 and the main Victorian stone buildings sur-vive. There are individual spa baths and Jacuzzis (guests keep the keys overnight if stay-ing here), all set in woodland.
💷 R45 per day for day visitors
🚗 18km (11 miles) south of Citrusdal, well-signposted between the N7 and the town

DARLING

⑨ EVITA SE PERRON
Darling Station, Darling 7345
Tel 022-4922831
www.evita.co.za
Drag-queen Evita is a South African institution, hosting lively cabaret events at this venue, 55 minutes' drive from Cape Town. It includes Bambi's Berlin Bar, a shop, restaurant and gallery.
🕐 Restaurant and bar: Tue–Sun 9am–5pm; shows on Fri 8pm, Sat 2pm and 8pm, Sun 2pm and 4.30pm
💷 Shows: Adult R85, child (under 11) free

DE HOOP NATURE RESERVE

✪ MOUNTAIN BIKING
The Reservation Office, De Hoop Nature Reserve, PO Box 66, Bredasdorp 7280
Tel 028-4255020
www.capenature.co.za
Cyclists are permitted to use the management roads in the western sector of the reserve. There is also the De Hoop Mountain Bike Trail, in the eastern sector (reservations essential). The trail varies in difficulty and you will need to allow two to three days to complete it. Note this is a self-guided trail within the park.
💷 Adult R20, child (2–18) R10 per day

Hats at El Sole, George

FRANSCHHOEK

🎨 BORDEAUX STREET GALLERY
Huguenot Road, Franschhoek 7690
Tel 021-8762165
A good selection of curios is sold in this series of rooms. It's great for local arts and crafts, including antique furniture, Masai jewellery, fabrics, woven baskets and batiks.
🕐 Mon–Sat 9–6, Sun 10–6

🎨 DELICIOUS!
Huguenot Road, Franschhoek 7690
Tel 021-8764004
This deli sells fresh produce from two well-known local restaurants—an ideal place to pick up items for a great picnic.
🕐 Mon–Fri 8–5, Sat 9–4.30

✪ DEWDALE FISHERIES
Off the Robertsvlei Road, Franschhoek 7690
Tel 021-8762755
www.dewdale.com
The Dewdale Fisheries has a number of trout-stocked pools in a beautiful leafy setting, with fly-fishing equipment rental.
💷 Daily rate R100, plus R50 for rod rental

✪ PARADISE STABLES
Franschhoek 7690
Tel 021-8762160
These stables have a range of guided trails throughout the vineyards. The most popular routes have stops at wine estates, with wine-tasting and lunch included.
💷 From R90 per hour

GANSBAAI

✪ WHITE SHARK ADVENTURES
Gansbaai 7220
Tel 028-3841380
www.whitesharkdiving.com
One of the most popular activities along the coast is cage diving to view great white sharks. Those with a diving certificate can view them from an underwater cage, but if you prefer to stay dry you can also see the sharks from the surface. Trips last between 3 and 7 hours.
💷 Around R1,200, including use of all diving equipment

GEORGE

🎨 EL SOLE
81 Market Street, George 6529
Tel 044-8735758
George is known for its good-quality leather goods. El Sole sells a selection of shoes, belts and bags in a variety of leathers, including ostrich and buffalo.
🕐 Mon–Fri 9–5.30, Sat 9–1

🎨 MARKLAAN CENTRE
Between Market and Meade streets, George 6529
The Marklaan Centre is a set of converted store rooms arranged around an open square, with several art

galleries and curio shops. A farmers' market is held here on Fridays from 7am to 10am.
⊙ Mon–Sat 7am–7pm

🔴 STEAM TRAIN
Outeniqua Choo-Tjoe
Tel 044-8018288
One of the most enjoyable day trips from George is a ride on this picturesque steam train to Knysna. The 67km (42-mile) journey has extraordinary views of coastal scenery and forests, passing through Wilderness National Park and along the Goukamma Valley.
⊙ May–end Aug Mon, Wed, Fri depart 9.30, arrive noon; Sep–end Apr Mon–Sat depart 9.30 and 2.15, arrive noon and 5 💲 Adult (round-trip) R80, child R55, child under 6 free

🔵 FANCOURT HOTEL AND COUNTRY CLUB
George 6529
Tel 044-8040000
www.fancourt.com
The Fancourt Hotel has a health and beauty spa with Roman-style baths and a mix of treatments, including a stress-reducing back treatment and a detoxifying seaweed wrap, as well as hydro-treatments and a hair salon.
💲 From R250

HERMANUS

🏛 CURIO MARKET
Market Square, Hermanus 7200
Market Square, in the middle of town just above Old Harbour, holds a craft, curio and clothes market, selling souvenirs and practical clothing such as lightweight linen trousers and shirts.
⊙ Daily 8–5

🔴 SCUBA AFRICA
New Harbour, Hermanus 7200
Tel 028-3162362
www.scubaafrica.com
This scuba company has equipment rental, runs dive courses (NAUI) and organizes daily dives. In addition to coral reef and kelp forest dives, there are three good wreck

dives between here and Arniston, which is 50km (31 miles) east of Hermanus.
🤿 Scuba Diver 6-day course R1,500

🔴 SOUTHERN RIGHT CHARTERS
Whale Shack, New Harbour, Hermanus 7200
Tel 028-3163154/082-3530550
For a water-based view of the southern right whales around Hermanus, take a boat trip, run daily by this company based in the New Harbour. Boats are prevented from getting too close to the whales, but views of them are exhilarating nevertheless.
💲 From R400

Stopping for a break at the Knysna Quays

🔴 WALKER BAY ADVENTURES
Tel 028-3140925
Fishing is a big draw in Hermanus, but there are strict regulations concerning what you can catch. Rock angling is popular with local fishermen, and deep sea fishing is most popular with foreign visitors. Walker Bay Adventures rents out fishing equipment and can organize charters.
💲 Two-hour cruise R250 📍 Just out of town, towards Gansbaai at Prawn Flats

KNYSNA

🏛 AFRICAN MARKET
There is a good African craft market set up on the side of the road as you enter Knysna on the N2 from George, with an extensive range of carvings, baskets, drums and curios.
⊙ Daily 8–5 📍 On N2, entrance to Knysna from west

🏛 KNYSNA QUAYS
Knysna 6571
Tel 044-3820955
This modern waterfront development is a mini version of the V & A Waterfront in Cape Town, with a range of clothes shops, curio shops, outdoor stalls and arts and crafts shops.
⊙ Mon–Sat 8am–7pm

🏛 METAMORPHOSIS
12 Main Road, Knysna 6571
Tel 044-3825889
There are a number of craft shops around Knysna, but this is one of the most intriguing, with a good line in artworks made from recycled cans and other unusual materials.
⊙ Mon–Fri 9.30–5.30, Sat 9.30–2

🔴 KNYSNA MOVIE HOUSE
Pledge Square, Main Street, Knysna 6571
Tel 044-3827812
This modern cinema has daily shows of new international and South African releases, in comfortable air-conditioned theatres. There are also art-house and subtitled releases.
⊙ Mon–Sat 11.30am–10.30pm, Sun 2–10 💲 From R25

🔴 HEADS ADVENTURE CENTRE
Bottom Car Park, Knysna Heads, Knysna 6571
Tel 044-3840831
This sports centre organizes a full range of PADI courses, as well as equipment rental. For qualified divers, there are trips to reefs outside the Heads and to a wreck in the lagoon.
💲 Single dive from R300, including equipment

⊕ MOUNTAIN BIKING AFRICA
Tel 044-3820260/082-7838392
Guided mountain bike trails take you around the remaining tracts of indigenous forest in the area. The rides are quite easy, with lots of down-hill sections. Bike rental and refreshments are included.
🚵 From R250

LANGEBAAN

⊕ CAPE SPORTS CENTRE
On the northern beach,
Langebaan 7357
Tel 022-7721114
www.capesport.co.za
Langebaan lagoon is known for its excellent watersports. Cape Sports organizes wind-surfing, kitesurfing and other watersports, with full instruc-tion, by the hour or by the day.
🚵 Three-hour lesson R500

LITTLE KAROO

✪ The ostrich farms around
Oudtshoorn are good places to pick up ostrich-related items, from empty egg shells to ostrich leather purses and bags. They include the Wilgewandel Holiday Farm, in the Shoemanshoek Valley 2km (1.2 miles) before the Cango Caves (daily 8–5, tel 044-2720878; www.wilge wandel.co.za); Highgate Ostrich Farm, 10km (6 miles) from Oudtshoorn, off the R328 towards Mossel Bay (daily 8–5, tel 044-2727115; www.high gate.co.za); and Safari Ostrich Farm, 6km (4 miles) from Oudtshoorn, on the R328 to Mossel Bay (daily 7.30–5, tel 044-2727311; www.safari ostrich.co.za).

MONTAGU

◉ AVALON SPRINGS
Uitvlucht Street, Montagu 6720
Tel 023-6141150
www.avalonsprings.co.za
This well-developed resort is focused on a set of hot springs that have been used for more than 200 years for their heal-ing powers. The waters are radioactive and have a steady

temperature of 43°C (109°F). There are two indoor pools and five outdoor pools, all at different temperatures.
🚵 Indian head massages R120, manicure R100 🚌 3km (2 miles) from central Montagu

MOSSEL BAY

⊕ DIVING ACADEMY
Tel 082-8965649
The best time for diving is between December and the end of April when the sea is at its calmest and conditions in the bay are clear and safe. Close to Santos Beach are four recognized dive sites, but none could be considered spectacu-lar. For experienced divers, the

Avalon Springs, Montagu

Windvogel Reef, 800m (0.5 miles) off Cape St. Blaize (13.5km/8 miles from Mossel Bay), is highly recommended, with drop-offs, a few caves, interesting soft corals and sponges.
🚵 Single boat dive from R250

✪ GOURITZ RIVER BRIDGE
Tel 044-6977001
www.faceadrenalin.com
This is a popular bungee jump from the road bridge into the 65m (213ft) deep river gorge. There's also a bridge swing, similar to a bungee, but with an outward swing as opposed to a downward jump. Reservations are not necessary.

◉ Daily 9–5 🚵 Bungee R175, bridge swing R160 🚌 Just outside Mossel Bay on the N2

✪ SHARK AFRICA
Corner Church and Market streets
Tel 044-6913796
www.sharkafrica.co.za
This company offers cage diving and snorkelling to view great white sharks on a 15m (50ft) catamaran aptly named *Shark*. You do not have to be a qualified diver and this trip is open to anyone. It lasts between 4 and 5 hours and includes lunch and drinks.
🚵 Dive R1,200; to view sharks R900

PAARL

⊗ BOLAND BANK PARK
Langenhoven Street, Paarl 7620
Tel 021-8624580
This is a delightful place to watch an international cricket match in a peaceful rural set-ting. The ground is the home of the Boland Cricket Board.
◉ Cricket season: Dec–end Mar
🚵 From R40

◉ THE WINELANDS
Klapmuts, Paarl 7625
Tel 021-8755357
www.santewellness.co.za
This working wine estate has a new luxury wellness spa and hotel. A huge range of 'Vinotherapy' treatments are available, which are massages and facial with a wine theme, like the 'Chardonnay Cocoon Wrap'. It also has several pools, lots of sporting activities and a yoga pavilion.
🚵 A full package Vinotherapy R1,240

✪ BUTTERFLY WORLD
Klapmuts, Paarl 7625
Tel 021-8755628
Those with kids in tow should visit Butterfly World, the largest park of its kind in South Africa, with butterflies flying freely in beautiful landscaped gardens. There is also a craft shop and tea garden on site.
◉ Daily 9–5 🚵 Adult R25, child R12.50 🚌 On the R44, just off the N1 by Klapmuts

PLETTENBERG BAY

✪ BLOUKRANS BUNGEE JUMP
Bloukrans River Bridge
Tel 042-2811458
www.faceadrenalin.com
At 216m (708ft), this claims
to be the highest commercial
bungee in the world. The first
rebound is longer than the
previous holder of the record,
the 111m (364ft) bungee
jump at Victoria Falls. Those
who'd rather not jump can
go on a guided bridge walk—
definitely not for anyone with
vertigo. Reservations are not
necessary.
🕘 Daily 9–5 💷 Bungee jump R580,
bridge walk R50 🚗 40km (25 miles)
from Plettenberg Bay

✪ DIVING INTERNATIONAL
Central Beach, Plettenberg Bay 6600
Tel 044-5330381/082-4906226
This scuba diving operator
runs daily dives in the area,
and offers a full range of PADI
courses. One of the more
exciting dive sites here is
Groot Bank, about 12km
(7.5 miles) northeast of
Hobie Beach, with a variety of
rock formations to explore,
including tunnels and caves.
💷 PADI courses from R2,000

✪ PLETT ANGLING CLUB
Tel 044-5359740
There are several recognized
rock angling sites along the
coast, including Beacon Island,
Robberg Beach, Lookout Rocks
and Nature's Valley. Local
South African fish, such as elf,
galjoen and steenbras, are the
most frequent catch. Deep-sea
fishing is also possible.
💷 River trips R240 per boat (5 people
per boat)

✪ PLETTENBERG BAY COUNTRY CLUB
Piesang Valley
Tel 044-5332132
www.plettgolf.co.za
This lush 18-hole course is
set in the middle of a private
nature reserve.
💷 R280

ROBERTSON

✪ WINE VALLEY TOURS
Tel 023-6251682
For a good overview of the
area's wine estates and to
buy some of the best wines
on offer, this operator runs
daily wine-tasting tours from
Robertson (and McGregor).
Tours usually take in up to
seven estates.
🕘 Tours start at 9 and return at 4.30
💷 R450

STELLENBOSCH

🏛 OOM SAMIE SE WINKEL
Tel 021-8870797
84 Dorp Street, Stellenbosch 7600
This famous shop has been
trading since 1791, and today

The Bohemia Pub, Stellenbosch

sells a wide range of goods,
such as home-made jams,
locally produced baskets and
hardware items. It has retained
its pre-war character and has
all the makings of a tourist
trap, but unlike many others
it is genuine.
🕘 Mon–Fri 8.30–5.30, Sat 8.30–5

🎭 DORP STREET THEATRE
Dorp Street, Stellenbosch 7600
Tel 021-8866107
The popular little Dorp Street
Theatre hosts a range of
local productions, with plays
(that are mostly in Afrikaans)
and popular live jazz nights
on Sundays.
🕘 Mon–Sat 10pm–late 💷 From R30

🎭 SPIER AMPHITHEATRE
Spier Wine Estate, Stellenbosch
Tel 021-8091100
www.spier.co.za
This is perhaps the area's most
appealing venue—an open-
air amphitheatre hosting a
summer festival (▷ 197), with
classical concerts, jazz events,
plays and comedy.
🕘 Mon–Sat 4.30–10.30 💷 From
R40 🚗 South of Stellenbosch on
the R44

🍷 BOHEMIA PUB
Corner of Andringa and Victoria streets,
Stellenbosch 7600
Tel 021-8828375
One of the main student
haunts in Stellenbosch with
an eccentric, vibrant interior
and attractive wraparound
veranda. This is one of the
most popular and busiest
bars in town, always lively
with a young clientele who
come for the cold beers,
relaxed atmosphere and
occasional live music.
🕘 Daily 9pm–2am 💷 Free

🍷 DROS
Corner of Bird and Alexander streets,
Stellenbosch 7600
Tel 021-8864856
This restaurant turns into a
noisy bar later at night. Tables
spill out on to the square and
get packed with backpackers
and students.
🕘 Daily 8pm–midnight 💷 Free

🍷 NU BAR
51 Plein Street, Stellenbosch 7600
Tel 021-8868998
This central venue is a
crowded bar and club
with a tiny dance floor at
the back. A nightly DJ plays
hip-hop and house tunes
to a young crowd. A good
place to come for a raucous
late night.
🕘 Mon–Sat 7pm–3am 💷 Free

TOLLIE'S
Drostdy Centre, Plein Street,
Stellenbosch 7600
Tel 021-8865497
Tollie's is a popular nightclub
which gets packed with
students on weekend nights.
The music is dance and pop,
with occasional live bands.
Daily 9pm–late Free

ADVENTURE CENTRE
Tourist Office, 36 Market Street,
Stellenbosch 7600
Tel 021-8828112
www.adventureshop.co.za
Adventure Centre can arrange
tours and rents out bicycles,
along with helmets and maps
of the area.
R70 for a day, R20 per hour

EASY RIDER WINE TOURS
Stumble Inn Backpackers, 12 Market
Street, Stellenbosch 7600
Tel 021-8864651
Easy Rider's hugely popular
day-long wine tours are
aimed at backpackers. These
well-organized tours take in
five estates, with five tastings
in each, including lunch and
cheese tasting.
Adult R250

VINE HOPPER
Adventure Centre, Tourist Office,
36 Market Street, Stellenbosch 7600
Tel 021-8828112
This is a useful hop-on hop-off
bus that runs between five
estates and the Stellenbosch
tourist office in town.
R135

TOY AND MINIATURE MUSEUM
Market Street, Stellenbosch 7600
Tel 021-8867888
Behind the tourist office is this
small but diverting collection
of antique toys and displays
of miniatures. There's also a
small workshop where you can
observe the painstaking work
of an expert craftsman producing tiny replicas of furniture,
clothes and household items.
Mon–Sat 10–5, Sun 2–5 Adult
R5, child (2–12) R1

TSITSIKAMMA NATIONAL PARK

STORMSRIVER ADVENTURES
Darnelle Street, Stormsriver 6308
Tel 042-2811836
www.stormsriver.com
The team at Stormsriver
Adventures organizes a
staggering number of tours
in the Tsitsikamma region,
including guided hikes, tubing,
abseiling (rappelling), mountain bike trails, boat cruises,
scuba diving, fishing and
dolphin-watching. One of the
most popular activities is the
canopy tour, which involves
climbing up to a platform in
the trees from where you are
attached to a steel rope

Canopy tours at Tsitsikamma National Park

(there's plenty of safety
equipment to prevent falls).
From here you glide between
different platforms attached
to forest giants, giving extraordinary views from high
above the ground.
Three-hour canopy tour R395

WILDERNESS

EDEN ADVENTURES
Tel 044-8770179
www.eden.co.za
This good-value adventure
tour operator organizes daily
trips to Wilderness National
Park. Activities include kayaking, kloofing (canyoning),
mountain biking, abseiling
(rappelling), canoe rental and

walking tours. The guides are
very knowledgeable about the
environment and are happy to
answer questions.
Half-day tour from R200

WINELANDS

SPIER WINE ESTATE
Tel 021-8091100
www.spier.co.za
The large, modern Spier wine
estate has a state-of-the-art
spa in its grounds, open to
hotel guests and day visitors.
There is a range of treatments,
including facials, wraps and
massage.
From R200 South of
Stellenbosch on the R44

WORCESTER

FLEA MARKET
Church Square, Worcester 6850
There is a weekly flea market
held on Saturday mornings
in the central Church Square,
with stalls selling a mix of
curios and local arts and crafts.
Saturday morning

WORCESTER WINELANDS
Robertson Road, Worcester 6850
Tel 023-3428710
www.worcesterwinelands.co.za
Housed within the Kleinplasie
Museum complex, this shop
has information on the surrounding wine farms and
offers tastings and sales of
local wines and brandies.
Four tastings R10

WORCESTER AIRFIELD
Tel 023-3432904
Local conditions round
Worcester are ideal for gliding
and it is not uncommon to
record flights of up to 6 hours.
This is the most stunning way
to appreciate the mountains
and valleys which surround
Cape Town.
Half-hour gliding R500

WHAT TO DO

FESTIVALS AND EVENTS

MARCH

CRAYFISH FESTIVAL
Lambert's Bay
Tourist Office, Church Street
Tel 027-4321000
www.lambertsbay.info
Lambert's Bay celebrates its famous crayfish and lobsters every March, when all the restaurants are given over to a feast of crayfish.
◉ End of March

JULY

PORT FESTIVAL
Calitzdorp
Tel 044-2133314
www.calitzdorp.co.za
A Port Festival is celebrated in the port capital of Calitzdorp every July, with tastings and sales throughout the village.
◉ End of July

SEPTEMBER

STELLENBOSCH FESTIVAL
Stellenbosch Tourist Office,
36 Market Street
Tel 021-8833584
www.stellenboschtourism.co.za
Not to be confused with the wine festival, this is a 3-day music and arts event concentrating on chamber music and art exhibitions.

WILD FLOWER FESTIVAL
Caledon
Caledon Tourist Bureau,
22 Plein Street Caledon 7230
Tel 028-2121511
www.capeoverberg.org
To coincide with the annual bloom of wild flowers each spring, Caledon holds a festival that celebrates the diversity of the flowers and promotes further research and conservation. It is an excellent opportunity to see many of the plants that make up the Cape flora. The principal display hall is in Hope Street, a short walk from the town museum.
◉ Second weekend of September

HERMANUS WHALE FESTIVAL
Hermanus
www.whalefestival.co.za
This festival marks the beginning of the calving season of southern right whales. In essence it is a community festival, but it attracts visitors from all around the Cape. The festivities kick off with an open-air concert at the Old Harbour, and continue with theatre, comedy, live music and sporting events (including a mini-marathon) held throughout the week.
◉ Last week of September

Southern right whales' calving season is celebrated in Hermanus

TULBAGH AGRICULTURAL SHOW
14 Church Street
Tel 023-2301348
www.tulbaghtourism.org.za
The local agricultural show is held on the banks of the Kliprivier and is the oldest of its kind in South Africa. There is also a Visual Arts Show held in October where many of the historical houses on Church Street open up as art and crafts galleries.

OCTOBER

SIMON VAN DER STEL FESTIVAL
Stellenbosch
Tel 021-8097216
This festival commemorates the establishment of Stellenbosch by van der Stel at the end of the 17th century—14 October was his birthday. Horsemen parade in traditional dress and other activities depicting the era are acted out.
◉ Fri and Sat nearest to 14 October

STELLENBOSCH WINE FESTIVAL
Stellenbosch
Tel 086-1222335
This wine festival is an annual event to promote local award-winning wines, along with traditional rural cuisine.
◉ Last week of October

DECEMBER–APRIL

SPIER MUSIC FESTIVAL
Spier Wine Estate
Tel 021-8091100
www.spier.co.za
The Spier wine estate hosts this summer festival, with a range of acts taking to the stage, from opera to stand-up comedy and rock concerts.
▣ South of Stellenbosch on the R44

EASTERN CAPE

Port Elizabeth is the main focus for things to do in the Eastern Cape, with its laid back nightlife and its beach, which is popular with windsurfers (above). It's not, however, the region to come to for shopping.

Few visitors come to the Eastern Cape to shop, and away from the cities there isn't much on offer other than the usual holiday gifts. Most of Port Elizabeth's shops are in large shopping malls and there is a popular outdoors art market held in St. George's Park in the middle of town. East London has a couple of shopping areas (one in an interesting historic building) with a good selection of shops. Hogsback is famed for its berries, so jam and preserved fruits are popular here, as are the arts and crafts produced by local Xhosa people, some of which you won't see in other parts of the country.

Port Elizabeth has two good theatres, offering a range of recitals and plays. However, the best time to see performances is during the National Arts Festival, held every July in Grahamstown (▷ 201), when lots of theatre troupes, orchestras and stand-up comedians come to town to perform.

The relaxed feeling to the nightlife in Port Elizabeth's bars and clubs, of which there are plenty, is thanks to the large student contingent. East London's importance as a surfing spot and its popularity with backpackers has given it a lively nightlife, with a bar scene based by the beach. A similarly young scene is found in the university town of Grahamstown.

Port Elizabeth is famous for its beach and has a correspondingly wide range of watersports. Surfing is the most popular pastime, but windsurfing and scuba diving are also good. East London is even more popular with surfers and has some of the most reliable breaks in the country. Jeffreys Bay, however, is the real surfing hotspot—it has what is said to be one of the best and most reliable 'right-hander' breaks in the world. You can also learn to surf here. The Fish River, near Cradock, is a good place to go whitewater-rafting.

The beaches and nature reserves, particularly Addo Elephant Park, make the Eastern Cape a good location to take the children. Port Elizabeth and East London have particularly family-friendly beaches, but the relatively undeveloped Wild Coast is probably not suitable for young children. Avoid the Karoo in summer, when conditions are hot and dusty.

Grahamstown is host to South Africa's most important arts festival, the Standard Bank National Arts Festival. The town is transformed, with a huge variety of plays, concerts and opera, and shouldn't be missed if you're in the area at the time.

KEY TO SYMBOLS	
⊞	Shopping
⊘	Entertainment
♡	Nightlife
⊗	Sports
✪	Activities
♡	Health and Beauty
✦	For Children

EAST LONDON

🔵 LOCK STREET GAOL
Fleet Street, East London 5201
The original structure of this unusual shopping mall was built as a prison in 1880, and the cells were transformed into shops in 1979, which includes antiques and African curio shops.
🕐 Mon–Sat 9.30–5.30

🔵 VINCENT PARK CENTRE
Devreux Avenue, East London 5247
This standard modern South African shopping mall has a wide selection of shops, as well as banks, a post office, a multiscreen cinema and restaurants. It holds an arts and crafts market every Sunday from 9 to 1.
🕐 Daily 9–6

🔵 BUCCANEERS
Eastern Beach, Esplanade 5201
Tel 043-7435171
Buccaneers is a popular pub and grill house that gets very busy at night, when it stages live music. This is a very popular venue for surfers and backpackers, with a great setting on the beach.
🕐 Daily 10am–late 🎫 Free

🔵 BUFFALO PARK
East London 5201
Tel 043-7437757 (ticket enquiries)
www.sacrickettickets.co.za
(on-line booking)
The East London cricket ground in Buffalo Park is South Africa's newest international venue. It is a short distance from the beach and is the smallest of the current test match grounds in the country, with a capacity of 15,000. The first international cricket match played here was during the Indian tour of 1992/93, and South Africa beat Canada here during the 2003 Cricket World Cup.
🕐 Cricket season: Dec–end Mar
🎫 From R20

🔵 SUGAR SHACK
Esplanade Road, Eastern Beach 5201
Tel 043-7228240
This friendly backpacker hostel is the best source of local information on surfing in East London. It can organize surfing lessons and has surfboards for rent. Easterns, in front of the Sugar Shack, is the most consistent beach break in the area, with regular tubes.
🕐 Daily 8–8

GRAHAMSTOWN

🔵 RAT & PARROT
59 New Street, Grahamstown 6139
Tel 046-6225002
A popular bar with students, which gets quite rowdy late at

Waiting for surfers at Jeffreys Bay

night once a few rounds of shooters have been passed around, the Rat & Parrot has a wide range of beers and other drinks on offer, and good potjies (hearty stews served in 3-legged cast-iron pots).
🕐 Daily noon–late 🎫 Free

HOGSBACK

🔵
Main Road is lined with little craft shops selling gifts as well as delicious locally made jams (the area is famous for its berries). Look out for Storm Haven and Arminel Crafts. At the entrance to the village you will also see local people selling their crafts, in particular clay animals: kudu, horses and

hogs are the most common, but these figures are rarely seen elsewhere.

JEFFREYS BAY

🔵 JEFFREYS BAY SURF SCHOOL
Island Vibe Backpackers, 10 Dageraad Street, Jeffreys Bay 6300
Tel 042-2934214
Most people come to Jeffreys Bay to surf, and this is one of the best places for beginners. Lessons run daily, year-round, and include wetsuits, beginners' boards and tuition. There are also seven-day learn-to-surf packages which include accommodation and meals.
🎫 2-hour lesson R180

PORT ELIZABETH

🔵 ART IN THE PARK
St. George's Park, Park Drive, Central 6001
You will find some good gifts at this open-air exhibition of craft stalls and local art.
🕐 First Sun of every month 10am–1pm

🔵 THE BRIDGE MALL
Cape Road, 6001
Tel 041-3638914
Port Elizabeth's biggest mall is a giant, trendy affair, built over a main road and with great views from its elevated position. There are banks, restaurants, coffee shops and fast food outlets, plus a smart fashion mall.
🕐 Daily 9–5

🔵 CINEMA
All the latest releases from Europe and the US are shown at two cinema complexes: Ster-Kinekor at The Bridge Mall, Cape Road 6001 (tel 041-3630577) is the largest; Nu-Metro in the Walmer Park Shopping Complex, Walmer 6070 (tel 041-3671102) shows similar films. Both are open from 11am and close after the last show, usually around 11pm. Tickets cost from R27.

🎭 THE FEATHER MARKET HALL

1 Baakens Street, Central 6001
Tel 041-5855514
www.feathermarket.co.za
This renovated Victorian
market hosts a wide range of
recitals, performances and
concerts. Drop by the tourist
office (Donkin Lighthouse
Building, Belmont Terrace,
tel 041-5858884;
www.nmbaytourism.co.za)
for listings and tickets.
🎟 Adult R5, child (2–11) R3

🎭 OPERA HOUSE

Whites Road, Central 6001
Tel 041-5862256
An annual Shakespearean
Festival takes place at this
delightful venue, where a
selection of the Bard's plays
is performed. The tourist
office in Belmont Terrace
(see above) is the best place
for listings.
🎟 From R25

🍸 52

52 Parliament Street, Central 6001
Tel 083-2485852 (mobile)
52 is a hugely fashionable bar
with attached restaurant. It
has an ultra-stylish interior
and expensive drinks. Its main
appeal is its relaxed ambience
and DJs—check out the funk
night on Saturdays.
🕐 Daily 5pm–late 🎟 Free

🍸 BARNEY'S TAVERN

The Boardwalk, Marine Drive, 6001
Tel 041-5834500
This is just one of the many
bars and clubs in The
Boardwalk, which is popular
as it is one of the safest areas
to walk around at night. It's
an atmospheric bar with live
music every night as well as
on Saturday and Sunday afternoons on The Deck–a decking
area that overlooks the beach.
🕐 Mon–Sat 10am–late, Sun
10am–8pm 🎟 Free

🍸 KWAITO HOUSE

Parliament Street, Central 6001
This three-floor club is a great
place to dance to kwaito (the

biggest movement in South
African dance music, ▷ 19).
There are pool tables and a
great atmosphere, but you
should expect to attract some
attention if you're white.
🕐 Wed–Sat 8pm–late 🎟 Free

🍸 TAPAS AL SOL

Brookes Hill Pavilion, 6001
Tel 041-5840660
A bustling tapas bar and pub,
this place has a popular
extended happy hour on
Thursdays, DJs on Friday and
Saturday, and occasional live
rock bands.
🕐 Daily 10am–11pm (later on Thu, Fri,
Sat) 🎟 Free

The Bridge Mall, Port Elizabeth

⭐ MCARTHUR BATHS

King's Beach Promenade,
Humewood 6001
Tel 041-5822282
Away from the large hotels
there are a couple of excellent
municipal swimming pools,
including the McArthur Baths,
which has a tidal pool, freshwater pool, children's water
chute and a restaurant.
🕐 Daily Nov–end Mar 8.30–6; Sep,
Oct, Mar, Apr 9.30–4.30; May–end Aug
closed 🎟 R20

⭐ OCEAN DIVERS INTERNATIONAL

10 Albert Raod, Walmer 6070
Tel 041-5815121
www.odipe.co.za

There are a number of good
dive sites around Port
Elizabeth and the best time
for diving is during the winter
months when average visibility
is between 8m and 15m (25ft
and 50ft). The best diving is
around St. Croix Islands, a protected set of islands. Ocean
Divers runs daily dives to the
area's major sites and offers
a full set of courses.
🎟 Courses from R1,300

⚫ ST. GEORGE'S PARK CRICKET OVAL

St. George's Park, Central 6001
Tel 041-5851646 (ticket enquiries)
www.sacrickettickets.co.za (on-line
bookings)
Set in the middle of town,
in the city park, this is South
Africa's oldest cricket ground
and was the site of the first
test match to be played in
Africa, in 1889. St. George's
is a pleasant old stadium
and an enjoyable venue to
watch cricket.
🕐 Cricket season: Dec–end Mar
🎟 From R22

⚫ TELKOM PARK

Port Elizabeth
Tel 041-5087700
Port Elizabeth is home to the
Eastern Province Rugby Union,
founded in 1888. Matches are
played at Telkom Park (formally known as Boet Erasmus
Rugby Stadium), which has
a capacity of around 34,000.
A unique feature is the steam
train which has been placed
on top of an open stand
overlooking the field, and
converted into a bar.
🕐 Rugby season: Apr–end Aug
🎟 From R20

⚙ OCEANARIUM

Bayworld, Marine Drive,
Humewood 6001
Tel 041-5840650
This is Port Elizabeth's aquarium, with displays of more
than 40 species of fish, as well
as a ragged tooth shark tank,
African penguins, rays and
turtles. The most interesting

WHAT TO DO

FESTIVALS AND EVENTS

The vibrant Grahamstown National Arts Festival encompasses all forms of the arts

FEBRUARY

PRICKLY PEAR FESTIVAL
Cuyler Hofstede farm museum,
Uitenhage
Port Elizabeth Tourism, Donkin
Lighthouse Building, Belmont Terrace,
Port Elizabeth
Tel 041-5858884
www.nmbaytourism.co.za
With more than 250 products
of this fruit on sale, crowds
of over 25,000 turn up each
year to enjoy traditional food
such as pancakes, ginger
beer, jam and fish barbecues.
It's not to be missed if you
are in the area, as this is a
golden opportunity to try real
South African cooking. Look
out for the local beer tent.
🕐 Last Saturday in February
🚗 34km (21 miles) northwest of
Port Elizabeth

EASTER

SPLASH FESTIVAL
Port Elizabeth Tourism, Donkin
Lighthouse Building, Belmont Terrace,
Port Elizabeth
Tel 041-5858884
www.splashfestival.com
Port Elizabeth hosts the
Splash Festival, a four-day
beach festival focusing
on watersports, surfing
competitions, live music
and fireworks.

JULY

NATIONAL ARTS FESTIVAL
Grahamstown
Tel 046-6031103
www.nafest.co.za
Grahamstown hosts this
famous 11-day festival, South
Africa's premier arts festival
and one of the top cultural

events in the country. More
than 50,000 visitors pour into
town to watch a selection
of performances, including
theatre, dance, fine art, films,
music, opera and an increasing variety of traditional crafts
and art, plus a huge range of
fringe shows.
🕐 Early July

**BILLABONG COUNTRY FEELING
SURF COMPETITION**
Jeffreys Bay
www.billabongpro.com
In winter (from April to
September), when the waves
are at their best, Jeffreys Bay
comes to life and in July it
holds this professional competition. This draws surfers
from across the globe and
the town gets packed out.

---

part of the complex is the
dolphin research centre, which
stages seal and dolphin presentations daily at 11 and 3.
🕐 Daily 9–4.30 💷 Adult R33,
child (under 13) R16; ticket covers
entry to Oceanarium and Snake Park
(see below)

✪ SNAKE PARK
Bayworld, Marine Drive,
Humewood 6001
The Snake Park houses a
collection of exotic reptiles in
realistically landscaped glass

enclosures, including some
rare and endangered species.
Inside the Tropical House you
follow a path through woodlands with bridges, waterfalls
and streams. Birds are free
to fly around within the giant
enclosure.
🕐 Daily 9–4.30 💷 Adult R33,
child (under 13) R16; ticket covers
entry to Oceanarium and Snake Park
(see above)

WILD COAST

✪ ACTIVE AFRICA
Tel 021-4616658
www.active-africa.com
Active Africa organizes a
number of different multi-day
treks and escorted walking
tours, including a walking tour
along the Wild Coast, starting
in East London. There is also a
6-day hiking trip that crosses
the border between the
Eastern and Western Capes.
💷 R600 per day; contact for more
details

KWAZULU-NATAL

WHAT TO DO

KwaZulu-Natal is the place to soak up Zulu and Asian culture in a variety of forms, from dancing to craftwork. Most of the activities take place in and around the main city of Durban and it has good nightlife (above) but the coastline provides great surfing spots.

KwaZulu-Natal is particularly known for its Zulu beadwork, and Durban, Zululand and around the Drakensberg are especially good places to buy jewellery and baskets. Look out for modern twists on traditional items, like baskets woven from telephone wire. This province is also the place to browse for Indian goods, and you can pick up items such as sari silks or spices in Durban. For the ultimate shopping mall experience, head to the Gateway in Umhlanga Rocks, thought to be the largest mall in the southern hemisphere and crammed with hundreds of shops, restaurants and cafés.

There are a couple of good theatres in Durban, including the well-regarded Playhouse, and a several multiscreen cinemas showing the latest international releases. There are numerous 'traditional' villages throughout the province showing Zulu dancing, although few offer an authentic view of Zulu life.

Durban has a good nightlife scene, with one of the country's best nightclubs and a number of bars popular with surfers—Florida Road is lined with trendy bars and restaurants. Pietermaritzburg is perhaps even livelier, thanks to its large student population, with a good selection of noisy bars and clubs, and more relaxed venues frequented by the bohemian set. Elsewhere along the coast, there are a few laid-back bars, used by either the surfing or the scuba diving fraternity, but for the most part entertainment is family-focused and low-key.

North Beach and South Beach in Durban have specially designated surf and boogie board (similar to a surf board, but ridden on your stomach not standing) areas, and there are shark nets to protect swimmers and surfers. Sodwana Bay in KwaZulu-Natal has developed into one of the country's best scuba diving areas. The Drakensberg Mountains are famous for their

superb hiking, and the area is best visited independently; there's a huge variety of hikes available from a range of bases. The province has a number of coastal and inland parks and nature reserves which you can visit as part of a tour or independently.

Most of the child-friendly activities in KwaZulu are nature-based, from beaches to spotting crocodiles or tracking wildlife in a national park. The Gateway at Umhlanga Rocks has activities for older children.

There are not many festivals in this region, but those that exist tend to be based on coastal and beach activities, such as surfing tournaments or family fun days.

KEY TO SYMBOLS	
🛍	Shopping
🎭	Entertainment
🍸	Nightlife
⚽	Sports
✪	Activities
♡	Health and Beauty
✹	For Children

BATTLEFIELDS ROUTE

⭐ DAVID RATTRAY
Fugitives' Drift Lodge
Tel 034-6421843
www.fugitivesdrift.com
The top expert on the region
has counted the UK's Prince
Charles among his clients.
David Rattray leads unforgettable tours of the battlefields,
providing a stirring view of
the area. If you want to take
part in one of these tours, you
must book months in advance.
🚗 Approx 50km (31 miles) south of
Dundee towards Greytown on the R33

DURBAN

🏛 AFRICAN ART CENTRE
1st Floor, Tourist Junction,
160 Pine Street, Durban 4001
Tel 031-3047915
This is one of the best places
in Durban to buy beautiful
Zulu beadwork, baskets and
ceramics. The shop is a non-
profit-making outlet for rural
craftspeople—the choice is
broad and the items on sale
are good value.
🕐 Mon–Sat 9–6

🏛 MUSGRAVE CENTRE
115 Musgrave Road, Berea 4001
Tel 031-2015129
The trendy Musgrave Centre
has 110 shops, with a mix of
chic boutiques and national
chain stores. There are also
elegant restaurants, a cinema
complex and a Sunday craft
and curio market, held on level
five of the parking area.
🕐 Mon–Sat 9–5, Sun 10–2

🏛 THE PAVILION
Westville 3629
Tel 031-2650558
Based in the suburb of
Westville, the Pavilion, with
its 320 shops and restaurants
and multiscreen cinema, is
always busy—an estimated
one million people visit this
mall each month.
🕐 Daily 9–5

🏛 VICTORIA STREET MARKET
Corner of Queen and Victoria streets,
Durban 4001
Tel 031-3064021
The modern, rather dingy
Victorian Street Market is
crammed with more than
170 stalls selling African
curios, leather goods, fabrics
and copper. The main attraction, however, are the spices
and dried beans imported
from India. Upstairs are food
stalls serving up delicious
snacks such as *bunny chow*
(a half-loaf of bread with the
middle scooped out and filled
with curry), samosas and
Durban curries.
🕐 Mon–Sat 6–6, Sun 10–4

*The Isandlwana Battle Memorial,
seen on the Battlefields Route*

🎭 BARTLE ARTS TRUST
(BAT) CENTRE
45 Maritime Place, Small Craft Harbour,
Durban 4001
Tel 031-3320451
A popular arts centre right
on the harbourfront, BAT has
a concert hall, a bar and a
restaurant overlooking the
water. There is live jazz on
most evenings.
🖐 Free; special events from R20

🎭 THE CATALINA THEATRE
18 Boatman's Road, New Wilson's
Wharf, Maydon Wharf, Durban 4001
Tel 031-3056889
www.thecatalina.co.za
The Catalina, a relative newcomer, is an enjoyable little

theatre based at trendy New
Wilson's Wharf. It seats 175
people and puts on contemporary performances, from
flamenco guitar recitals to
Indian plays.
🖐 From R30

🎭 THE PAVILION
Westville 3629
Tel 031-2650001
The Nu Metro multiscreen
in this large shopping mall
shows international releases
in plush, air-conditioned
surrounds.
🕐 9am–11.45pm 🖐 From R37

🎭 THE PLAYHOUSE
231 Smith Street, Durban 4001
Tel 031-3699555
This theatre complex shows
regular performances in five
auditoria: the Opera, Loft,
Drama, Studio and Cellar
Supper Theatre. The eclectic
selection of shows ranges from
Shakespeare to contemporary
political satire and modern
dance.
🖐 From R35

🍸 BEAN BAG BOHEMIA
18 Windermere Road, Greyville 4001
Tel 031-3096019
A vibey bar on the ground
floor of an old converted
Durban town house, Bean
Bag Bohemia is a fun place
and is popular in the evenings
when the bar attracts a well-
to-do crowd. There are good
snacks on offer with a strong
Mediterranean influence—the
shared meze platters go well
with the drinks.
🕐 Daily 11am–late 🖐 Free

🍸 CLUB 3-30
330 Point Road, Durban 4001
Tel 031-3377172
Club 3-30 is one of South
Africa's top clubs with a
number of dance floors. It
plays an assortment of dance
music (techno, house and
R 'n' B) to a young and
fashionable crowd.
🕐 Fri–Sat 10pm–late 🖐 From R20

WHAT TO DO

🍸 JOE KOOLS

North Beach, Durban 4001
Tel 031-3329697
This hugely popular bar and restaurant is right on the beach, opposite one of the more popular surf sites. The outside terraces have great beach views and are lit with strobe lights at night when the surfing fraternity takes over.
🕐 Daily 8am–late 💰 Fri–Sat R10–R20; free rest of week

🏏 KINGSMEAD

Tel 031-3354200
www.sacrickettickets.co.za (for tickets)
Kingsmead cricket ground, home to the KwaZulu-Natal provincial cricket team, is a modern stadium with large grandstands. All of Durban's big matches are played at this popular venue, and it was host to several World Cup cricket matches in 2003. The weather is generally good, but as it's close to the sea there is always a chance of rain or poor visibility.
🕐 Cricket season: Dec–end Mar
💰 From R60

🏌 WINDSOR PARK MUNICIPAL GOLF COURSE

Windsor Park 4001
Tel 031-3122245
This 18-hole course is next to the Umgeni River, just north of Durban. Equipment can be rented here by the day or by the week.
💰 From R50–R60

🤿 DIVE NAUTIQUE

Somerset Park 4320
Tel 082-5532834
www.divenautique.co.za
This dive operator offers both PADI (Professional Association of Dive Instructors) and NAUI (National Association of Underwater Instructors) courses, equipment rental and sales, and runs single dives. It also organizes dolphin-watching boat trips.
💰 Courses from R1,800

🌊 NORTH BEACH SURF SHOP

137 Lower Marine Parade 4001
Tel 031-3684649
You can rent boards at this shop on North Beach, and it also offers coaching, equipment rental and advice.
💰 From R100 for a 1-hour lesson

🌊 SURF ZONE

Ocean Sports Centre, North Beach 4001
Tel 031-3685818
There are several designated surfing and boogie boarding beaches along the seafront. Surf Zone is based on North beach and rents boogie boards and surf boards.
💰 Board rental from R50 per hour

The African Art Centre, Durban

HLUHLUWE-IMFOLOZI

🦓 DINIZULU SAFARIS

89 Zebra Street, Hluhluwe 3960
Tel 035-5620025
www.dinizulu.co.za
This established family outfit has an excellent knowledge of Zululand and its parks. Game drives using 4WD open vehicles are organized in Hluhluwe-Imfolozi and Mkuze game reserves, along with day trips to other places of interest in the area.
💰 Four-hour trip from R245

MARGATE

🤿 AFRICAN DIVE ADVENTURES

Shelly Beach Ski Boat Club, Shelly Beach 4265
Tel 082-4567885
As well as offering a wide range of NAUI diving courses, this operator runs daily dives at the Protea Banks, where schools of hammerhead and Zambezi sharks are regularly to be seen.
💰 Courses from R1,700

ORIBI GORGE

🪂 WILD 5 ADVENTURES

Oribi Gorge Hotel, Oribi Gorge
Tel 039-6870253
www.oribigorge.co.za
Oribi Gorge is the ideal spot for a number of adventure sports. Wild 5, based at the Oribi Gorge Hotel, just outside the reserve on the way to Port Shepstone, offers white-water rafting trips in conventional rafts or large inner tubes on the Umzimkulu River, abseiling (rappelling) from Lehr's Waterfall and a 75m (245ft) freefall gorge swing.
💰 Freefall gorge swing from R160

PIETERMARITZBURG

🎵 CROWDED HOUSE

Commercial Road, Pietermaritzburg 3201
Tel 033-3455977
Pietermaritzburg's main club is very popular with the students from the university. It plays alternative and dance music, with some live bands. Thursday is the biggest night, known as 'Pig Night'—when you pay your entrance, you are given a glass for the night, which is then refilled as often as you like until midnight.
🕐 Mon, Tue, Thu 9.30pm–5am
💰 R5–R10; 'Pig Night' R30

RORKE'S DRIFT

🎨 ELC CRAFT CENTRE

Rorke's Drift 3016
This shop by Rorke's Drift sells locally produced Zulu crafts: baskets, ceramics, dyed cloth and handmade carpets.
🕐 Mon–Fri 8–4.30, Sat 10–3

ST. LUCIA

⭐ ADVANTAGE CHARTERS
Corner of McKenzie Street and Katonkel Avenue, St. Lucia 3936
Tel 035-5901199
www.zululink.co.za
Explore Lake St. Lucia on a two-hour boat ride or try whale-watching in season; trips run from June to November, when humpback, minke and occasional southern right whales travel along the coast heading for the warmer breeding waters of Mozambique. Other tours available from Advantage include day-trips to Cape Vidal and deep-sea fishing.
💵 Day tour to Cape Vidal R375; sunset cruise R100

SODWANA BAY

⭐ CORAL DIVERS
Tel 035-5710290
www.coraldivers.co.za
A good-value place to learn to dive in Sodwana is at this live-in dive centre, which has PADI courses suitable for all levels from beginners to dive masters. The package includes dorm accommodation and equipment. Some of the best sites for diving off Sodwana are Two Mile Reef and Five Mile Reef. The closest snorkelling site to Sodwana is on Quarter Mile Reef, 500m (1,640ft) off Jesser Point.
💵 Open water diver course R1,850

⭐ SODWANA BAY LODGE
Tel 035-5716000
www.sodwanadiving.co.za
A similar but more trendy set-up to Coral Divers (see above) is available at Sodwana Bay Lodge, which offers a number of all-inclusive diving packages, with courses including transport to and from Durban. They also organize day trips to a number of places.
💵 Open water diver course (5-day) from R3,776

UKHAHLAMBA-DRAKENSBERG

🏛 INGKAR ART GALLERY & MG TRADERS
On the R600, just after the junction with the D160 to Monk's Cowl
A couple of curio shops and stalls here promote local ethnic arts and crafts and you will find some unusual pieces for sale, including paintings of the mountains.
🕐 Times erratic

⭐ CATHEDRAL PEAK HOTEL GOLF COURSE
Cathedral Peak
Tel 036-4881888
www.cathedralpeak.co.za
Keen golfers will be pleased to

Learning to dive at Sodwana Bay

know that the northern and central Drakensberg has four golf courses. Cathedral Peak Hotel (▷ 288) has a nine-hole course; in good weather the mountain backdrop takes some beating.
💵 From R80 for 9-hole round
🚗 From the N3 (heading north), turn off at the Winterton/Colenso exit and turn left onto the R74 Winterton/Bergville, followed by a left onto the R600 in Winterton (at the Engen garage). Follow signs for Cathedral Peak until you see signs for the hotel

⭐ KZN WILDLIFE
uKhahlamba-Drakensberg
Tel 033-8451000 (central booking)
www.kznwildlife.com
Trout were introduced into the rivers of the Drakensberg around the turn of the 20th century and over the years fly-fishing for trout has become a popular pastime. Fishing licences are available from KZN Wildlife.
💵 Trout fishing R60–R80 per day

⭐ SANI PASS TOURS
Underberg 3257
Tel 033-7011064
www.sanipasstours.com
Tours go to the top of Sani Pass by 4WD, stopping off at a Basotho village on the way. The road is terrifyingly steep and winding, but the views are outstanding. A picnic lunch in the Black Mountains or lunch at the Sani Top Chalet (▷ 219) is included.
💵 Adult R240, child (under 14) R120

UMHLANGA ROCKS

🏛 GATEWAY SHOPPING MALL
Umhlanga Rocks 4319
Tel 031-5662332
North of Durban is the Gateway Mall, said to be the largest shopping mall in the southern hemisphere. As well as shops and restaurants, there is a range of activities, from cinema to an artificial surf wave.
🕐 Mon–Thu 9–7, Fri–Sat 9–9, Sun 9–6

⭐ GATEWAY SHOPPING MALL
Umhlanga Rocks 4319
Tel 031-5662332
This enormous shopping mall has a variety of activities that will appeal to children of different ages, from an IMAX cinema and an impressive abseiling (rappelling) and climbing wall, to the world's largest artificial surf wave and a popular skateboarding park.
🕐 Mon–Thu 9–7, Fri–Sat 9–9, Sun 9–6

ZULULAND

🎵 SHAKALAND
Tel 035-4600912
www.shakaland.com
This popular Zulu theme park has daily cultural shows, which include Zulu dancing and tours of a 'traditional' village where tribal customs such as spearmaking, the beer ceremony and Sangoma rituals are explained. Although not representative of how the Zulu live today, the food and dancing here are very good.
🕐 3 hour tours at 11 and 12.30
💰 R250 🚗 14km (8.5 miles) north of Eshowe on the R66

🎵 SIMUNYE
Tel 035-4305300
This lodge is a far more authentic and enjoyable introduction to Zulu culture, offering traditional accommodation, trips to local kraals (a traditional African village of huts, usually enclosed by a fence) and a chance to meet local Zulu people. In the evenings guests are treated to Zulu food, dancing and singing beneath the stars.
💰 R963 per night 🚗 On the D256, off the R66 north of Eshowe

⭐ ZULULAND ECO-ADVENTURES
Zululand Backpackers, 38 Main Street, Eshowe 3815
Tel 035-4744919
www.eshowe.com
The ex-mayor of Eshowe, Graham Chennells, is now a registered guide involved in community projects. He runs cultural tours of the surrounding countryside, taking in contemporary Zulu life and visiting projects such as the Eshowe Skills Centre, a paper-making project, and the Rotary Classroom Project (the building of 2,000 classrooms in the region).
💰 Tours from R65

FESTIVALS AND EVENTS

Celebrating beach life at Durban's Summer Splash

FEBRUARY

KAVADI FESTIVAL OF PENANCE
Durban
Shri Siva Subramanium Temple, 122 Sidar Road, Durban
Tel 031-3047144
This Hindu festival is celebrated all over South Africa, but especially in Durban. Ritual piercing is performed by the penitents and you will see processions and floats decorated with flowers.

MARCH

SPLASHY FEN
Tel 033-7011932
www.splashyfen.co.za
This music festival, held on the Splashy Fen farm 19km (12 miles) from Underberg, has developed into one of the country's leading alternative music festivals. The focus is on folk, rock and guitar music. It has been running since 1990 and now attracts more than 12,000 revellers.
🕐 Four days at the end of March

DECEMBER

DURBAN SUMMER SPLASH
www.durban.gov.za
This week-long beach festival includes a number of events, concerts and competitions along Durban's Golden Mile, from the Bay of Plenty Pier to the Snake Park Beach.
🕐 Second week of December

LIMPOPO AND MPUMALANGA

The provinces of Limpopo and Mpumalanga are great places to buy unusual gift items and artwork. The hot springs at Bela-Bela are extremely popular and a good way to relax after the exercise that activities along the Blyde River offer you, such as white-water rafting (above).

There is a good choice of arts and curio shops around the main visitor attractions. Although the VhaVenda people, known for their fine pottery and drums, come from Limpopo, their art is difficult to track down, due mainly to the inaccessibility of the villages where much of it is produced. However, most good art shops around the country stock these items. Nelspruit has a choice of practical shops for stocking up on supplies, while Hoedspruit has two interesting shops offering top-end arts and gifts.

Nelspruit has a handful of bars, but there is little in the way of lively nightlife elsewhere in the provinces.

The Panorama region around the Blyde River Canyon is perfect for activities such as hiking, mountain biking, white-water rafting or kloofing

(canyoning). Rafting is perhaps the most popular activity after hiking: the lower Blyde River and the Sabie River both have mild rapids, while the northern section of the Blyde River and the Olifants River offer fast adrenalin-pumping rapids. Near Graskop are two new and exciting adventure activities: the Big Swing and the Zipliner. Elsewhere, some of the more popular areas have golf courses and cultural tours on offer: those that visit the VhaVenda are among the most interesting. There is good horseback-riding in the Soutpansberg Mountains.

Bela-Bela is one of the country's biggest domestic visitor destinations, attracting two million visitors thanks to its hot springs and a huge resort has grown up around them. For more fashionable

pampering, many of the camps within the private game reserves around Kruger offer beauty therapies and massages to their guests.

The reptile parks of Mpumalanga are big draws for families, and Croc River Reptile Park, just outside Nelspruit, is one of the most enjoyable for children. Some of the adventure activities around the Blyde River Canyon are also popular, especially the easier white-water rafting section of the southern Blyde River.

KEY TO SYMBOLS	
⊕	**Shopping**
🎭	**Entertainment**
🍸	**Nightlife**
⛹	**Sports**
✪	**Activities**
♡	**Health and Beauty**
✸	**For Children**

BELA-BELA

⊘ FOREVER RESORTS AVENTURA
Tel 014-7362200
www.aventura.co.za
This resort contains the main springs of Bela-Bela (once known as Warmbaths) and is so vast guests are required to wear plastic identity bracelets at all times. The 50°C (122°F) springs are rich in sodium chloride, calcium carbonate and are also slightly radioactive. There are mineral pools, a spa with hydrotherapy and a full range of beauty treatments, plus other activities. Day visitors are allowed until 5pm.
🛁 One hour full-body massage R280

BLYDE RIVER CANYON

⊘ OTTER'S DEN WHITE WATER RAFTING
Otter's Den Lodge
Tel 015-7955488
www.ottersden.co.za
This operator organizes trips on the Olifants and Blyde rivers, including overnight trips staying at their camp on the Blyde River.
🛁 Full overnight trips from R1,100
🚌 On the R531, 29km (18 miles) from Hoedspruit

GRASKOP

⊘ BIG SWING AND ZIPLINER
Tel 072-2238155
The newest activities in the region, the Big Swing and the Zipliner, are just north of town, on the lip of the Graskop Gorge. The Big Swing is similar to a bungee jump but with an outward swing on the descent. After jumping the free fall is 68m (223ft), equivalent to a 19-floor building, and lasts around 3 seconds. The Zipliner is a zip wire that runs 130m (425ft) across to the other side of the gorge—you slide across in an attached harness.
🕐 Tue–Sun 9–5 🛁 R235 (Big Swing), R350 (tandem, with complimentary Zipliner), R40 (Zipliner only)

HOEDSPRUIT

⊕ BOMBYX MORI SILK FARM
Tel 015-7955564
The excellent farm shop on South Africa's only silk farm sells a wide range of products; silk scarves, blankets, silk-filled duvets and cushions. There is a kiosk and tea garden.
🕐 Mon–Sat 9–4, Sun 11–2 (summer only) 🚌 23km (14 miles) south of Hoedspruit, on the R531

⊕ MONSOON GALLERY
Tel 015-7955114
www.monsoongallery.com
Next door to the famous Mad Dogz Café (▷ 268), this shop stocks arts and crafts of the highest standards—the owner

Forever Resorts Aventura in Bela-Bela

has been collecting fine African arts and antiques for decades. Packing and shipping can also be arranged.
🕐 Mon–Fri 9–6, Sat–Sun 10–3 🚌 On R527, east of the junction of the R527 and R36

MAKHADO

⊘ KUVONA CULTURAL TOURS
Shilvuari Lakeside Lodge
Tel 015-5563512
This operator specializes in the VhaVenda people, with tours to tribal sacred sites, traditional ceremonies and villages in the Soutpansberg and Venda. The company is active in community development through tourism.

🛁 Tours from R75 🚌 6km (4 miles) west of Makhado on the Levubu Road

⊘ SADDLES HORSE TRAILS
Tel 015-5165455
Horseback riding trails, suitable for novices through to more advanced riders, can be organized in the Soutpansberg Mountains lasting from one to three days. These include overnight stays at bush camps, meals and guides.
🛁 Weekend trip from R450
🚌 Between Polokwane and Makhado

NELSPRUIT

⊕ RIVERSIDE MALL
White River Road, Nelspruit 1200
Tel 013-7570080
This mall proudly claims to be the largest shopping mall in Mpumalanga. It contains the usual mix of shops, restaurants, banks and department stores, and is a good place to stock up on supplies.
🕐 Mon–Sat 9–6, Sun 9–3 🚌 5km (3 miles) out of town, on the White River Road

⊘ RIVERSIDE MALL
White River Road, Nelspruit 1200
Tel 013-7570300
Mpumalanga's largest mall is also home to an eight-screen Nu Metro cinema, showing all the latest international releases.
🕐 Mon–Sat 10–5 🚌 5km (3 miles) out of town, on the White River Road

⊘ O'HAGAN'S
Sunpark Mall, corner of General Dan Pienaar and Piet Retief streets, Nelspruit 1201
Tel 013-7413580
This branch of the South African Irish themed pub chain has a wide selection of imported beers on offer, plus filling pub meals served on an attractive open-air terrace. There is usually some live music at weekends.
🕐 Daily 9am–late 🛁 Free

WHAT TO DO

THE OLD VIC
38 Nel Street, Nelspruit 1201
Tel 013-7527343
The Old Vic occupies a converted church in the middle of town, and opens early for breakfast. The pace picks up in this laid-back pub at the weekends when a DJ plays music until late.
Daily 8am–late Free

CROC RIVER REPTILE PARK
Tel 013-7525511
The Croc River Reptile Park is a relatively new addition to the local sights, and like many other crocodile parks in southern Africa, claims to be the largest of its type in the country. A lot of effort and expense has gone into creating an exciting attraction, especially aimed at children. The reptiles are on show in a variety of houses, each with a different environment. The turtle pond, crocodile pool and fish pond are linked by a cascading waterway, there is a tropical house with a waterfall and an aquarium, and the reptile gallery houses 88 indigenous and exotic species.
Daily 9–5; daily handling demonstrations at 11 and 3 Adult R35, child R15 North of Nelspruit, off the R40 towards White River

PHALABORWA

HANS MERENSKY COUNTRY CLUB
Club Road, Phalaborwa 1390
Tel 015-7813931
This club is based around an 18-hole PGA championship golf course and is a must for golfers who want to enjoy the experience of negotiating wildlife on the greens while they are playing. Watch out for the hippos on the 17th hole. Your caddie's local knowledge is particularly welcome when you encounter wild game during a round; the odd antelope may be okay, but elephants are enough to put most people off their game.
Green fees R350

SABIE

THE BOOKCASE
Main Street, Sabie 1260
Tel 013-7642014
This second-hand book shop is full of interesting volumes and collectors' items. The African section is particularly good, with many books from the late 1800s on the great explorers, titles from the 1950s and 1960s on the rise of apartheid, and atlases from the days when most African countries were still colonies. A number of books banned in South Africa during the apartheid years have appeared in this shop.
Daily 8–5

Pots made by the VhaVenda people, Makhado

THE BIKE DOC
At Sabie Backpackers, Sabie 1260
Tel 013-7642118
Mountain biking is becoming increasingly popular in the forests around Sabie. The Bike Doc rents bicycles and runs tours to the trails in the area, some of which have been used for the national Mountain Bike Championships in recent years.
From R125

TZANEEN

GREEN RHINO
Tourist Information, Shop 13, Oasis Mall, Aqua Park, Tzaneen 0850
Tel 015-3071294
www.tzaneen.com

SEPTEMBER

SPRING CHERRY AND AZALEA BLOSSOM FESTIVAL
Magoebaskloof
Tel 015-2764972
Around Haenertsburg, the Spring Cherry and Azalea Blossom Festival Craft Fair and Orchid Exhibition takes place—this is when the entire valleys transform into a bank of colour.

NOVEMBER

NATIONAL GOLD PANNING CHAMPIONSHIPS
Pilgrim's Rest
Tourist Information Centre, Main Street, Upper Town
Tel 013-7681060
www.pilgrimsrest.co.za
These championships are held in Pilgrim's Rest when the village hosts a festival lasting four to five days. The World Gold Panning Championships took place here in 2005.
End of November

The tourism office at Tzaneen provides a range of activities on the Letaba River and around, including the ever more popular kloofing (canyoning). Other activities include micro-lighting, quad-biking and tubing (riding on water on a large inflated tube).
Kloofing from R135

COACH HOUSE HOTEL AND SPA
Tel 015-3068000
www.coachhouse.co.za
The Coach House Hotel is hidden away in the forests. Its Agatha Spa offers health and beauty therapies, from massages and facials to aromatherapy, mud and seaweed wraps, and reflexology.
Facial R250; full-body massage R300 15km (9 miles) south of Tzaneen, near to Agatha Forest Reserve

GAUTENG AND FREE STATE

WHAT TO DO

Johannesburg leads the way here with a sense of style and fashion rarely seen elsewhere in the country—and you will be able to find a myriad things to do. The suburbs of Jo'burg, such as Melville and Sandton (above), have become safer and more popular with visitors. The region's other major city, Pretoria, is not far behind.

Enormous shopping malls have taken Johannesburg by storm (the city has more than 20) and visiting one is almost inevitable, as they have not only shops but restaurants, pharmacies and cinemas. Pretoria, too, is a city of shopping malls. The small towns of Free State have curio stalls, but Clarens has a number of excellent small galleries and art shops, while Bloemfontein has several malls, including an attractive lakeside one.

Johannesburg has a handful of well-regarded performance venues. The main theatre, the Civic, hosts traditional productions and a number of visiting performances from overseas. The Newtown Cultural Precinct around the Market Theatre Complex is once again making a mark on the city following years of neglect, and puts on a good selection of community and political theatre, as well as hosting arts festivals.

Johannesburg, arguably, has the best nightlife in the country. It has a constantly changing bar and club scene, with new

places springing up and closing down every few months. Jo'burg is also one of the most integrated cities in the country. The Melville area is one of the most popular, and the northern suburbs generally have a good smattering of bars and clubs. Hillbrow and Yeoville are best avoided.

In Pretoria, the liveliest places to go are the student haunts of Hatfield and Brooklyn. At the heart of these two suburbs are large modern developments with countless bars and restaurants. These are safe areas and everything is within walking distance.

Although not yet matching Cape Town, Jo'burg has a lively and liberal gay scene, with an annual gay pride march held every September. The main gay-friendly area is around Braamfontein, known as the Heartland. But don't expect as much integration here as elsewhere.

Johannesburg has several great venues to watch sports. The Ellis Stadium hosts rugby matches and some soccer

games; the main venue for soccer is the FNB Stadium, on the outskirts of Soweto, due a major face-lift in preparation for the 2010 Soccer World Cup. Pretoria and Bloemfontein have large cricket stadiums; the latter with grassy banks to laze on. Elsewhere, the main activity is hiking, but horse-back-riding is also popular in the Maluti Mountains.

Johannesburg's shopping malls are good places for kids; many have cinemas or IMAX. Gold Reef City is one of the most popular, crammed with thrill rides and attractions. More sedate, but no less enjoyable, is the city zoo, which caters mostly for kids and has fun evening walks to see nocturnal animals.

KEY TO SYMBOLS	
⊕	Shopping
⊕	Entertainment
♈	Nightlife
⊗	Sports
✪	Activities
♡	Health and Beauty
✷	For Children

BLOEMFONTEIN

🏛 LOCH LOGAN WATERFRONT
First Avenue, Bloemfontein 9301
Tel 051-4487808
www.lochloganwaterfront.co.za
The attractive Loch Logan outdoor shopping mall sits next
to a lake and dam in Kings
Park. Some of Bloemfontein's
trendiest restaurants and bars
are scattered along the boardwalk on the water's edge. As
well as boutiques and galleries, there is an arts and
crafts market that stocks good
gifts from the region.
🕐 Daily 9am–midnight

🎵 JAZZ TIME CAFÉ
Loch Logan Waterfront 9301
Tel 051-4305727
This is a great place for an
evening out in the company
of Bloemfontein's young and
fashionable. It's a huge cocktail
bar with an outside terrace
and a mix of live music—jazz,
blues and big-band. There's a
Middle Eastern theme, with
interesting snacks like *zivas*,
Yemeni pancakes.
🕐 Daily 8pm–midnight 🎟 Free

♿ GOODYEAR PARK
Bloemfontein 9301
Tel 051-4306365
www.sacrickettickets.co.za
International cricket matches
are played at the Goodyear
Park stadium, to the west of
central Bloemfontein. The
ground is a fun, small stadium
where fans can relax and enjoy
themselves on grass banks.
🕐 Cricket season: Dec–end Mar
🎟 From R40

CLARENS

🏛 JOHAN SMITH ART GALLERY
Clarens Square, Clarens 9707
Tel 058-2561620
www.johansmith.co.za
This is one of a clutch of art
galleries and shops in Clarens.
It sells vibrant oil paintings of
South African rural life by cele-
brated artist Johan Smith, and
stocks fine glass, ceramics and
paintings by other local artists.
🕐 Mon–Fri 10–5, Sat 10–3

⭐ ASHGAR CONNEMARA STUD
Tel 058-2561181
www.bokpoort.co.za
The stables at Bokpoort offer
the most exciting horseback
riding trails in the region. Their
standard route lasts for two
days, spending a night at a
deserted homestead in the
Maluti Mountains. There are
also shorter trails lasting up to
six hours on the surrounding
farmland, during which you
will be able to spot antelope
and zebra.
🎟 From R150 🚩 Signposted 5km
(3 miles) out of Clarens, on the road
to Golden Gate

*An entertainer playing at the
Rosebank Mall*

JOHANNESBURG

🏛 AFRICAN CRAFT MARKET OF ROSEBANK
Cradock Avenue, Rosebank 2196
Tel 011-8802906
The former street traders of
this area have now been
housed in one ethnic-inspired
building in the middle of the
popular Rosebank Mall. Curios
from all over Africa are for sale
at more than 140 stalls. Credit
cards are accepted and shipping can be arranged. It's a
lively spot, with street performers and musicians, and on
Thursday evenings, African
food is served and there's even
a cabaret show.
🕐 Tue–Sun 9–5

🏛 ART AFRICA
62 Tyrone Avenue, Parkview 2193
Tel 011-4862052
This is a great place to pick up
inexpensive gifts, as the shop
has a strong emphasis on recycled art products. Some of
the most interesting pieces
include flowers made from
plastic and baskets woven
from telephone wire. There
are also some rare antiques
from across Africa.
🕐 Mon–Fri 9–6, Sat 9–4

🏛 HYDE PARK MALL
Jan Smuts Avenue, Hyde Park 2196
Tel 011-3254340
For a taste of Johannesburg's
luxurious side, head to Hyde
Park Mall, popular with the
ladies-who-lunch set. There
are a number of stylish (and
expensive) boutiques, cafés
and smart restaurants, and an
outlet of the Exclusive Books
chain, which often hosts book
signings by authors.
🕐 Daily 9–6

🏛 KIM SACKS GALLERY
153 Jan Smuts Avenue, Parkwood 2193
Tel 011-4475804
A selection of quality ethnic art
from all over Africa is for sale
in this gallery, occupying a
lovely old house and regarded
as one of the top galleries in
the city. There is a good range
of contemporary South African
pieces, including sculptures,
prints, beadwork and ceramics.
🕐 Mon–Fri 9–5, Sat–Sun 10–1

🏛 ROSEBANK MALL
Corner of Cradock and Baker streets,
Rosebank 2196
Tel 011-7885530
This mall has one of the most
pleasant eating areas, a large
open air piazza lined with
cafés, making it ideal for sitting
in the sun and watching people go by. It has much more of
a village feel than the average
indoor shopping mall, with
a good selection of clothes
shops and a busy flea market
held on the roof every Sunday
(9–5). Just outside, on Cradock

Avenue, is the hugely popular African Craft Market, a bustling building housing dozens of stalls selling arts and crafts from across the continent (▷ 211).

🕐 Daily 9–6

🎭 SANDTON CITY AND SANDTON SQUARE

Corner of Sandton Drive and Rivonia Road, Sandton 2196
Tel 011-2176000

Sandton City is the biggest of the city's malls, with endless chain stores selling clothes, books, music, art and curios. There are also cinemas, super-markets, restaurants, cafés and bars. Across a walkway is the trendy Sandton Square, with boutiques and a number of smart restaurants.

🕐 Shops: daily 9–9

🎬 CINEMA NOUVEAU ROSEBANK

Rosebank Mall, corner of Cradock and Baker streets, Rosebank 2196
Tel 082-16789 (central reservations)

The city's main arthouse cinema is in the Rosebank Mall, and shows a selection of international (mostly European and some South African) independent films, many with subtitles.

🕐 9.45am–8.30pm 💷 From R37

🎬 CIVIC THEATRE

Loveday Street, Braamfontein 2001
Tel 011-8776800

This modern theatre is an impressive set-up with four auditoria and frequent per-formances of South African plays. There is also a schedule of visiting international musi-cals, ballets and classical orchestras, with a mix of traditional performances and large-scale productions.

💷 From R90

🎬 MARKET THEATRE

56 Miriam Makheba Street, Newtown Cultural Precinct 2001
Tel 011-8321614

The Market Theatre has under-gone revitalization that has

saved it from disappearing from Johannesburg's arts scene. It was once famous for its community theatre and controversial political plays during the 1980s, but the decline of the central city made the theatre less and less popular. The Newtown Cultural Precinct is now once more the hub of Johannesburg's arts scene and the theatre remains one of the best and most established in Gauteng.

💷 From R40

🎬 NU METRO

Hyde Park Shopping Mall, Jan Smuts Avenue, Hyde Park 2196
Tel 011-3254257

Street performers outside the Market Theatre Complex

This is one of a number of multiscreen cinemas in a shopping mall. It shows all the major international releases in comfortable, air-conditioned theatres, and has the usual snacks and drinks on offer.

🕐 Daily 9.45am–10.15pm
💷 From R37

🎬 STER KINEKOR

Sandton City, corner of Sandton Drive and Rivonia Road
Tel 082-16789

The Sandton City multiscreen cinema is a popular place, showing all the major interna-tional releases throughout the day and evening.

🕐 Daily 11–11 💷 From R37

🎵 BLUES ROOM

Village Walk Mall, Sandton 2146
Tel 011-7845527/8
www.bluesroom.co.za

One of the best jazz and blues venues in Gauteng, the Blues Room is a stylish basement bar and restaurant, catering to music lovers who are after a decent meal. There's live music every night and the pace picks up later when diners take to the floor for a dance. The American-style dishes on the menu are named after blues legends.

🕐 Tue–Sat 7pm–late 💷 R50

🎵 CATZ PYJAMAS

Corner of 3rd and Main streets, Melville 2092
Tel 011-7268596

Jo'burg's original 24-hour bistro and cocktail bar has a funky atmosphere, famous nachos and potent sangria. Although it's open throughout the day, the atmosphere really only picks up late in the evening, carrying on until the early hours.

🕐 Open 24 hours 💷 Free

🎵 COOL RUNNINGS

4th Avenue, Melville 2092
Tel 011-4824786

The popular Jamaican-themed chain of bars/clubs comes into its own at this Melville branch. It is one of the most popular bars around, when a young crowd gathers to work its way through the extensive cocktail list. There's loud music every night, and occasional drum-ming sessions are held in the bar.

🕐 Daily 11am–2am 💷 Free

🎵 KULCHA

Northcliff Corner Shopping Centre, Beyers Naude Road, Cresta 2194
Tel 083-3112005
www.kulcha.org.za

This relative newcomer hosts stylish weekly parties and is home to the yearly Gay Pride after-party, held in September. There are two dance floors—the Retro Blue room and the

jungle-themed 'cave'—as well as a cocktail lounge.
🕐 Sat only 9pm–late 💰 R20 before 11pm, R40 after

🍸 MONSOON LAGOON
In Caesar's Casino, next to the airport
Tel 011-9281290
Johannesburg's biggest and brightest club is this huge special events venue, which regularly hosts TV and fashion parties. It's a trendy, mainstream club (over 23s only) covering several levels with a number of dance floors, bars and lounges. It's lavish and totally over the top and makes for a great night out.
🕐 Tue–Sat 8pm–late 💰 From R70 (from R50 for women)

🍸 ROXY'S RHYTHM BAR
20 Main Road, Melville 2092
Tel 011-726 6019
This lively club attracts a student crowd who come here for the dance music—a mix of deep house, garage, hip-hop and drum 'n' bass. There are live acts on some nights, and the feel and theme of a particular evening changes according to the DJ.
🕐 Mon–Sat 8pm–late 💰 R40

🍸 THE STARDUST PALACE
Jorrison Street, Braamfontein 2001
Tel 082-495 2585
The two dance floors at the Stardust, one of the city's most popular gay clubs, get very lively, with weekly cabaret shows and professional (and rather scantily-dressed) dancers setting the tone. There's hard techno on one floor and commercial house and disco on the other, plus seven bars, a snack bar and a pool.
🕐 Wed–Sun 9pm–late 💰 From R20

🏉 ELLIS PARK
Staib Street, Doornfontein 2094
Tel 011-4028644
www.ellispark.co.za
Ellis Park is the home of the Lions rugby team, and matches are played here regularly

during the season (Feb–end May). The stadium seats 50,000 spectators and it can be a lively day out, with fans bringing their *braais* (barbecues) and beers with them. It's also home to the city's Kaizer Chiefs soccer club.
🎫 From R40

🏉 FNB STADIUM
Nasrec Road, Ormonde 2091
Tel 011-494 3522
Johannesburg is, first and foremost, home of the country's greatest soccer teams, and the FNB Stadium, on the outskirts of Soweto, is the best place to see a match. More popularly called Soccer City, it is the

Traditionally dressed women dance at Gold Reef City

largest of Jo'burg's stadiums and home of the South African Football Association. This will be the venue of the opening match and the final of the 2010 Soccer World Cup (following a proposed R300 million face-lift).
🕐 Football season: Feb–end Sep 🎫 From R25; tickets in person from Computicket outlets (South African-issued credit cards only online and by phone), or in person at stadium

⛳ HOUGHTON GOLF CLUB
2nd Avenue, Lower Houghton 2198
Tel 011-7287337
Many major tournaments are held at this important golf course, including the South

African Open. It's one of the oldest courses in Johannesburg and is rated one of the top ten courses in South Africa.
⛳ Green fees from R300

⛳ WANDERERS GOLF CLUB
Rudd Road, Illovo 2196
Tel 011-4473311
Set next to the famous cricket ground (Wanderers' Stadium, see below), this is another of the oldest courses in South Africa. It's a challenging course and hosts the South African PGA Championship.
⛳ Green fees from R275

🏏 WANDERERS' STADIUM
Corlett Drive, Illovo 2196
Tel 011-3401544
www.wanderers.co.za;
www.sacrickettickets.co.za (tickets)
The Wanderers' Stadium is one of South Africa's premier cricket grounds and regular international matches are played here in season. This was a major venue for the 2003 Cricket World Cup.
🎫 From R21 (weekend test match), from R80 (one-day international)

🎢 GOLD REEF CITY
Northern Parkway & Gold Reef Road, Ormonde 2091
Tel 011-2486800
www.goldreefcity.co.za
This large theme park, created around the idea of a 19th-century gold mine, is a big hit. It has a large number of thrilling rides, many based on the rollcoaster idea, and there's a huge Ferris wheel. It has a variety of entertainment aimed specifically at children, with a circus in December. An added bonus is that children under 1.2m (4ft) in height get in free, but you should bear in mind that some rides will have a height restriction.
🕐 Tue–Sun 9.30–5 💰 R80 for entrance to rides

✪ IMAX

Hyde Park Shopping Mall, Jan Smuts Avenue, Hyde Park 2196
Tel 011-3256182
This is the city's only IMAX screen—five floors high with surround sound. A range of short films is shown, usually covering nature and science, with four shows daily during the week, and five at the weekends.
🕐 Daily 10–5 💰 From R30

✪ JOHANNESBURG ZOO

Jan Smuts Avenue, Parktown 2193
Tel 011-6462000
www.jhbzoo.org.za
The city zoo has undergone an upgrade and has a number of child-orientated displays. The night tours to see the nocturnal animals are particularly fun, ending with marshmallows and hot chocolate around a bonfire. There's a small restaurant on site serving light meals and refreshments.
🕐 Daily 8.30–5.30 💰 Adult R30, child R18

PRETORIA

🏬 HATFIELD PLAZA

Burnett Street, Hatfield 0083
This relatively small shopping mall in the lively suburb of Hatfield has a good choice of accommodation and restaurants. The front parking area is transformed into a lively flea market at weekends, selling anything from African crafts to CDs and clothes.
🕐 Mon–Fri 9–6, Sat 9–4

🏬 MENLYN PARK

Atterbury Road, Menlo Park 0181
Tel 012-3488766
Pretoria's premier new mall for 'shoppertainment' is Menlyn Park, which has 300 shops and restaurants, a 15-screen cinema, an IMAX cinema, a bowling alley and an unsual drive-in cinema. Its architectural focal point is its large tent-like roof that can be seen from some distance away.
🕐 Mon–Thu, Sat 9–7, Sun 9–5 💰 From R30

🏛 OEVERZICHT ART VILLAGE

Between Gerard Moerdyk Street, Kotze Street and Van Boeschoten Lane
Tel 012-4402320
This is a delightful small pocket of old Pretoria, with rows of houses dating from between 1895 and 1920, all of which have been perfectly restored. Today, they house galleries, antique shops and restaurants.
🕐 Mon–Fri 10–5, Sat 10–3

🎬 DRIVE-IN

Menlyn Park, Atterbury Road, Menlo Park 0181
Tel 012-3488766
For a slightly different cinema experience, head to this drive-in cinema on the roof of

Goods on sale at the market on Hatfield Plaza, Pretoria

Pretoria's largest shopping mall. If you don't have your own car, you can rent one of four original converted Chevys.
🕐 Mon–Sat screenings at 7.30pm and 8.30pm, Sun screening at 7.30pm
💰 R55 per car, or R30 per person to rent a Chevy

🎬 NU METRO

Hatfield Plaza, Burnett Street, Hatfield 0083
Tel 012-3625899
Housed in the basement of this shopping complex, the Nu Metro has a number of screens showing all the latest international releases.
🕐 Daily 9.45am–10.15pm
💰 From R37

🍵 BOSTON TEA PARTY

Glen Galleries Building, Shop 2, Menlo Park 0181
Tel 012-3653625
A large conference venue during the day, at night the Boston Tea Party transforms into a popular venue with live music, comedy and dancing, with DJs spinning records. It's an impressive place, holding up to a thousand revellers.
🕐 Wed–Sat 6pm–late 💰 From R20

🍹 COOL RUNNINGS

Burnett Street, Hatfield 0083
Tel 012-3620100
Another outlet of this popular chain, the Hatfield branch attracts a trendy young crowd who come for the weirdly named (but excellent) cocktails, cheap filling meals and live reggae music (Sunday evenings). This is currently one of the 'in' places and is always busy at the weekend.
🕐 Daily 9am–late 💰 From R10

🍸 TINGS & TIMES

Just off Burnett Street in Hatfield Galleries, Hatfield 0083
Tel 012-3625537
This little bar has a mix of live music and can get very crowded, so be sure to arrive mid-evening to guarantee a table. It serves great cocktails, and Middle Eastern and vegetarian bites are dished out for late-night snacks.
🕐 Mon–Sat 11am–1am, Sun 6pm–midnight 💰 Free

🍸 UPSTAIRS AT MORGAN'S

Burnett Road, Hatfield 0083
Tel 021-3626610
For a night of dancing with the local student population, this small nightclub offers commercial dance music and disco classics, with live music at weekends. Expect the likes of foam parties and 'pig nights' (the rather messy all-you-can-drink evenings).
🕐 Thu–Sat 7.30pm–late 💰 R25

FESTIVALS AND EVENTS

JANUARY

RUSTLER'S VALLEY FESTIVAL
www.rustlers.co.za
For those in the know, Rustler's Valley has one of South Africa's premier alternative festivals. Each New Year it invites different live bands and DJs to perform their latest material, offering a great opportunity to enjoy some excellent live music in an attractive setting.
🔲 In the Maluti mountain foothills, between Fouriesburg and Ficksburg, about 5km (3 miles) from the Lesotho border

FEBRUARY/MARCH

FNB VITA DANCE UMBRELLA FESTIVAL
Wits Theatre, University of the Witwatersrand, Johannesburg
Tel 011-4428435
www.wits.ac.za/paa
This annual event showcases contemporary dance and choreography, and has become one of the most important dance festival in South Africa.
🕐 Mid-February to mid-March

The Joy of Jazz is celebrated every summer in Johannesburg

EASTER

RAND EASTER SHOW
Johannesburg
Tourist Office, 195 Jan Smuts Avenue, Johannesburg 2001
Tel 011-3278001
www.joburg.org.za
This festival is held for ten days around Easter and is a mixture of exhibitions, events, stalls and funfairs. Contact the tourist office for details.

SEPTEMBER

ARTS ALIVE
Locations around Johannesburg
Tel 011-5492315
Johannesburg's Arts Alive International Festival promotes itself as a cultural celebration of spring. The festival showcases a mixture of activities: concerts, dance, cabaret, art and theatre. Many of the events take place around the Newtown Cultural Precinct (▷ 212).

NOVEMBER/DECEMBER

STANDARD BANK JOY OF JAZZ INTERNATIONAL FESTIVAL
Newtown Cultural Precinct, Johannesburg
www.joyofjazz.co.za
This three-day festival has developed into one of the country's foremost jazz platforms, uniting the finest South African musicians with international jazz stars. Focusing on a variety of jazz styles, it attracts more than 20,000 music fans to the Cultural Precinct every year.

🏃 CENTURION PARK
Tel 012-6631005
www.sacrickettickets.co.za
Centurion Park, the ground where international cricket matches for Pretoria are played, is 23km (14 miles) from the middle of town. Home to the Northern Transvaal provincial cricket team, the Park is a modern, circular stadium dominated by a huge single grandstand. The rest of the boundary is made up of grass banks which are great places for spectators to have picnics and *braais* (barbecues).
🕐 Cricket season: Nov–end Mar
🎟 From R38 🚍 Off the R21, between Pretoria and Johannesburg

🏉 LOFTUS VERSVELD RUGBY STADIUM
Kirkness Street, Sunnyside 0002
Tel 012-4200700
Pretoria is the home of the Northern Transvaal Rugby Union team, and all their matches are played at this stadium in Sunnyside, close to the middle of town. It is also the venue for occasional soccer matches.
🎟 From R35

🎬 IMAX
Menlyn Park Shopping Mall, Atterbury Road, Menlo Park 0181
Tel 012-3681186
Part of the Menlyn Park shopping mall, this giant IMAX screen, with wrap-around sound, shows wildlife films.
🕐 Daily 9–9 🎟 From R35

🐾 PRETORIA ZOO
Corner of Paul Kruger and Boom streets
Tel 012-3283265
This is South Africa's largest and best designed zoo and is surprisingly spacious, with animal enclosures, an aquarium and a reptile park. There's a cableway that stretches right over the zoo, plus electric self-drive buggies to help you get around. The grounds are criss-crossed with 6km (4 miles) of trails with picnic sites.
🕐 Summer 8–5.30; winter 8–5
🎟 Adult R35, child (2–15) R22

NORTHERN CAPE AND NORTH WEST PROVINCE

The Northern provinces provide excellent outdoor activities, many of them based around watersports. There are also several informal markets to be found along the roadside (above). The region is home to Sun City, and while not to everyone's taste, has a vast range of things to do, from golf to concerts.

This is not the region to come to for retail therapy, as the best shops are in the major cities like Cape Town.

The only really popular concert venue for visitors is in the enormous resort of Sun City, which hosts a range of visiting shows, and has a theatre and cinemas.

Kimberley is known for its historic pubs, including one that claims to the oldest in South Africa. History certainly abounds in these old watering holes—one is a drive-in. Cecil Rhodes regularly entered on horseback, as legend has it,

but he didn't like to dismount while enjoying an ale.

One of the best ways to explore the Northern Cape region is by rafting along the Gariep (Orange) River, which for the most part is blissfully deserted and wild. Several companies organize canoe or rafting safaris below the Augrabies Falls into the lower reaches of the river. A popular tour is the Black Eagle Canoe Trail, which covers around 75km (47 miles) over a period of five days; nights are spent camping on the riverbanks under the stars. There are also

shorter one-day trips, where rapids rarely rise above grade 3. Elsewhere, keen golfers flock to the course at Sun City, famous for its annual competition, and you will find good mountain biking trails around the Namakwa region.

KEY TO SYMBOLS	
⊞	Shopping
♪	Entertainment
▽	Nightlife
🏃	Sports
✪	Activities
♡	Health and Beauty
✹	For Children

WHAT TO DO

AUGRABIES FALLS

⭐ KALAHARI ADVENTURE CENTRE
Tel 054-4510177
www.kalahari.co.za
An excellent way to experience the gorge is by rafting its rapids. The most popular stretch is known as the Augrabies Rush, an 8km (5-mile) section pulling out just 300m (985ft) above the falls. Longer two- and five-day trails involve rafting on some impressive rapids as well as calmer stretches.
💰 Half-day rafting from R150 🚗 From Kakamas, turn right off the N14 towards Augrabies Falls. The lodge is 10km (6 miles) before the falls

KIMBERLEY

⭐ HALFWAY HOUSE
Du Toitspan Road, Kimberley 8300
Tel 053-8316324
The historic Halfway House pub is famous for its bizarre drive-in section, which the owners claim was where Cecil Rhodes used to ride in on his horse to sip a quick beer. There's an enjoyable atmosphere here, with cold beer on tap and good, simple pub meals, but it can get very busy at weekends.
🕐 Mon–Sat 11am–2am 💰 Free

⭐ STAR OF THE WEST
North Circular Road, Kimberley 8300
Tel 053-8326463
Close to Kimberley's first diamond mine (▷ 158–159) is what claims to be the oldest pub in South Africa, dating from 1870. While it's a bit of a tourist trap these days it still retains its character, with a long wooden bar and other original features. The tram to the mine museum stops across the road (on request).
🕐 Daily 10am–late 💰 Free

⭐ KIMBERLEY COUNTRY CLUB
Dickenson Avenue, Cassandra, Kimberley, 8300
Tel 053-8323775 (ticket enquiries)
Occasional international cricket matches are played at the Kimberley Country Club. Watching a game here makes a pleasant change from the large stadiums in the cities: the atmosphere is very laid-back and you might meet the players in the hotel bar after the game. During the domestic season, Kimberley is home to Griqualand West, one of the region's teams.
🏏 Cricket season: Dec–end Mar
💰 From R25

⭐ AQUARUSH
Tel 084-8835850
Aquarush organizes trips from Kimberley to the Gariep (Orange) River, with a range of white-water rafting tours from

Sun City is known for its casino

grade 1 to grade 5 rapids. The operator can also organize mountain biking, fishing and abseiling (rappelling).
💰 Day trip from R180

NAMAKWA

⭐ PEDROSKLOOF FARM
Springbok 8240
Tel 027-6721666
There are several mountain biking trails on this private farm ranging in length and difficulty, but you have to bring your own bicycle. Closer to Springbok, there are two cycle routes in the Goegap Nature Reserve. Note that drinking water is scarce, so you should bring your own.

💰 Free, but only available to guests on the farm (R200 dinner, bed and breakfast) 🚗 25km (15.5 miles) from Kamieskroon

⭐ RICHTERSVELD CHALLENGE
Opposite the tourist office on Voortrekker Street, Springbok 8240
Tel 027-7121905
This good-value local operator can organize tours throughout the area, including overland trips, 4WD tours of Ai–Ais/Richtersveld Transfrontier Park, and boat trips on motorized inflatables on the Gariep (Orange) River.
💰 Day river trips from R650

SUN CITY

⭐ SUN CITY
North West Province
Tel 014-5571000
www.suninternational.co.za
This enormous resort has a vast range of entertainment facilities, including cinemas, and a theatre which has hosted a number of big-name stars such as Elton John.

⭐ SUN CITY
North West Province
Tel 014-5571000
www.suninternational.co.za
This ultra-lavish resort has a range of activities, but the most popular is golf. The course is internationally renowned, thanks to the Sun City Million Dollar Golf Challenge, founded in 1980, which over the years has attracted most of the world's top golfers.
💰 Green fees R400 for residents, R475 for non residents

UPINGTON

⭐ KALAHARI TOURS & TRAVEL
12 Mazurkadraai, Upington 8800
Tel 054-3380375
www.kalahari-tours.co.za
Kalahari organizes tours in the region, including river rafting on the Gariep (Orange) River. There are also short day-trips and the longer Black Eagle Canoe Trail.
💰 Three-hour trip R250

LESOTHO AND SWAZILAND

Lesotho and Swaziland are known for their arts and crafts, such as hand-made baskets and bowls (above), which are good value and of a high standard. Adventure sports have become big business, particularly in Swaziland.

The main area to head to for crafts is the Ezulwini Valley. Much of the valley road is lined with stalls selling a superb selection of wood sculptures and carving, bright rugs and weavings, beautiful ceramics and clothes. Mbabane has a lively market.

Crafts from Lesotho include traditional hats, which are conical and made of roughly woven wicker, and woollen and mohair blankets and rugs. These can be bought at a number of casual stalls set up by roadsides in rural areas. Teya-Tayaneng is a well-known handicraft base and prices are cheaper than in the capital, Maseru. Bear in mind that opening times are very flexible and shops may open or shut without warning.

The Why Not Disco in the Ezulwini Valley is a Swazi institution, open for more than 25 years. There are a couple of other long-standing bars, but the only other main attraction is the handful of casinos.

Swaziland has a host of outdoor activities. One tour operator, Swazi Trails, dominates the scene, with a wide range of activities including caving, abseiling (rappelling), hiking and cultural and arts tours around the main craft sites. Perhaps the most popular excursion is white-water rafting on the Great Usutu River, a fun and exhilarating way to experience Swaziland's great outdoors.

In Lesotho, the main activity is pony trekking, an idyllic way of exploring the countryside. The Basotho are renowned as a nation of horsemen, and for generations the strong Basotho pony has been bred as the ideal form of transport in the rugged mountains. Treks range from one hour to six days, with overnight stops in local villages, mountain lodges and campsites. Don't expect mad gallops across open spaces—much of the trekking goes up and down steep and rocky mountainsides, where

the ponies carefully pick out a route. No experience of horse-back riding is needed.

The Ezulwini Valley has one of Swaziland's biggest beauty attractions, the Swazi Spa Health & Beauty Studio, an excellent place to get pampered or go for a swim in the hot springs—and great value.

A highlight in the Swazi social calendar is the Umhlanga Reed Dance, when hundreds of young women dance for the King and the Queen Mother. It's an awe-inspiring sight, and not to be missed if you're here in August. Lesotho holds an arts festival in early October in Morija.

KEY TO SYMBOLS	
⊕	Shopping
⬤	Entertainment
⬤	Nightlife
⬤	Sports
⬤	Activities
♡	Health and Beauty
⬤	For Children

LESOTHO

MALEALEA

⭐ MALEALEA LODGE
Tel 051-4366766 (reservations in South
Africa)/082-5524215 (mobile phone)
www.malealea.co.ls
This is the finest place is
Lesotho for pony trekking
around the local area, with
treks lasting from one hour to
six days. An average of seven
hours are spent in the saddle
each day, although the sure-
footed ponies make it easy
riding. Only local Basotho
guides are used, and Mike and
Di Jones, who own the lodge,
are deeply involved with local
sustainable tourism initiatives.
🚗 10km (6 miles) south of Morija the
B40 turns off from the Main South Road
to the left, and follows through to
Malealea 32km (20 miles) away

MASERU

🏛 BASOTHO HAT
Central Kingsway, next to the
tourist office
Tel 22322523
This craft shop, with its
unmissable large conical
roof shaped like a Basotho
hat, has a good selection of
local crafts—jewellery, leather,
wool, sheepskin and mohair
products—and the hats. But
prices are higher than in
smaller towns and rural areas.
🕐 Mon–Sat 10–5

NORTHERN MOUNTAINS

⭐ NEW OXBOW LODGE
Tel 051-9332247 (reservations
from South Africa)
www.oxbow.co.za
One of the best trout-
fishing locations is on the
Malibamatso River near the
New Oxbow Lodge. The lodge
arranges guided fishing trips to
the river, which are very popular with South Africans, so
make reservations in advance.
🎣 Day's fishing from M130 🚗 Access
from the lodge, just over the Moteng
Pass. From Butha-Buthe, turn left at the
T-junction in town and continue until
you see the signs for the lodge

SANI PASS

🔷 SANI TOP CHALET
Tel 033-7021069 (South Africa)/
082-7151131
www.sanitopchalet.co.za
Intrepid visitors who make it
to the top of the Sani Pass
from South Africa stop here
for a celebratory drink. The
lodge and pub claim to be
the highest in Africa and the
views down the valley to
KwaZulu-Natal are incredible.
🕐 Daily 11am–midnighht

TEYA-TAYANENG

🏛 HELANG BASALI
HANDICRAFTS
Main North Road
This craft centre is run by a

*The Basotho hat can be found
at a number of outlets*

local mission and sells a
number of reasonably priced
rugs, blankets, tapestries and
other handicrafts.
🕐 Mon–Sat 10–5 🚗 Just south of
the town

🏛 SETSHOTO WEAVERS
Main North Road
Visitors can watch craftsmen
weaving here, then buy the
goods that have been made.
There's the usual array of
Basotho rugs and blankets on
sale, for reasonable prices.
🕐 Mon–Sat 10–5 🚗 Opposite Blue
Mountain Inn, signposted off Main
North Road

SWAZILAND

EZULWINI VALLEY

🏛 MANTENGA CRAFT CENTRE
Mantenga Valley
Tel 416-2180
One of the principal attractions
along the Ezulwini Valley road
is its craft stalls, and Mantenga,
part of a self-sufficiency project, stocks an excellent range
of crafts, including clothes,
jewellery, screen prints, leather
goods, ceramics, rugs and
carvings. There is also a coffee
shop, a snack bar and a small
tourist information desk.
🕐 Daily 8–5 🚗 1km (0.5 miles) after
turn-off from Ezulwini Valley

🔷 WHY NOT DISCO AND
IF NOT GO-GO BAR
Happy Valley Hotel, MR103,
Ezulwini Valley
Tel 416-1061
Don't be too put off by the
slightly unusual names—this
disco and bar has become an
institution in Swaziland that
has been going for more than
25 years. On weekends many
top bands and performers
come to put on a show here;
there's usually good entertainment and a lively atmosphere.
🕐 Mon–Sat 10pm–late 💶 E10

🏌 ROYAL SWAZI SUN
Ezulwini Valley
Tel 416-5000
This smart hotel complex
has the country's top 18-hole
golf course, which can be
used by day visitors if they
call in advance.
⛳ Green fees E130 for guests, E245 for
day visitors 🚗 Signposted from the
MR3, Ezulwini Valley

⭐ SWAZI TRAILS
Mantenga Centre, Mantenga Valley
Tel 416-2180
www.swazitrails.co.sz
Swazi Trails is the leading
adventure operator in
Swaziland with the best-
organized range of activities.
Their white-water rafting trips
take place year-round on the
Great Usutu River. Two-man

FESTIVALS AND EVENTS

AUGUST/SEPTEMBER

UMHLANGA REED DANCE
Somhlolo National Stadium,
Lobamba, Ezulwini Valley,
Swaziland
Tel 404-4556
If you're in Swaziland at
the end of August into
September, don't miss the
spectacular Umhlanga Reed
Dance, a highlight on the
Swazi social calendar and an
awe-inspiring sight. The event
involves a huge number of
Swaziland's girls and young

women of marriageable age
congregating at the Queen
Mother's home to repair her
roof with reeds. This is followed by a mass display of
bare-breasted dancing in the
open-air stadium, where the
King gets to pick out his next
wife—an honour she cannot
refuse. Visitors are welcome
to join the Swazi crowds
watching the spectacle.

OCTOBER

**MORIJA ARTS AND CULTURAL
FESTIVAL**
Morija, Lesotho
Tel 22360308
www.morijafest.com
The annual Morija Arts and
Cultural Festival takes place
here in the first week of
October, with concerts, tradi-
tional dance, choirs, horse
racing, and food and craft fairs.
This is Lesotho's only event of
its kind so it's worth making an
effort if you are in the country.

WHAT TO DO

rafts are used, led by guides in
kayaks. With a new stretch of
river opened in the remote
Bulunga Gorge, a couple of
adrenalin-pumping rapids have
been added to the list. Trips
vary in length, depending on
river conditions and ability of
participants. All the guides are
Swazis with superb local
knowledge. Swazi Trails can
also arrange guided walking
and hiking trails, including a
two-hour Rhino Walk in Hlane
Royal National Park. The
Malolotja Nature Reserve Hike
offers guided walks to the 90m
(295ft) Malolotja Falls.
🚣 Day rafting from E450 🚗 1km (0.5
miles) after turn-off from Ezulwini Valley

💗 THE SWAZI SPA HEALTH &
BEAUTY STUDIO
Ezulwini Valley
Tel 416-1164
This popular spa is set around
the intriguingly named Cuddle
Puddle, a swimming pool fed
by a hot natural mineral spring.
Housed in dome-shaped buildings modelled on a Swazi
village, it has two large saunas,
two indoor hot mineral pools,
plunge pools, an aromatherapy
steam-tube and the outdoor
Cuddle Puddle. The cost of the
treatments are a fraction of
what you'd pay in northern
Europe or the US.

*A selection of items from Swazi
Candles, Malkerns*

🚣 Full day's use of saunas and mineral
pools E50 🚗 400m (440 yards) from
the turn off for Royal Swazi Hotel,
MR103, Ezulwini Valley

MALKERNS

🛍 SWAZI CANDLES
Tel 528-3219
www.swazicandles.com
Swazi Candles is well known
throughout the region for its
wide variety of beautiful hand-
made candles. The Gone Rural
shop, a little farther on, stocks
handmade pottery and grass
mats.
🕐 Mon–Fri 10–4.30, Sat 10–3
🚗 1km (0.5 miles) from junction
between M19 and Ezulwini Valley,
towards Malkerns

🍴 MALANDELA'S
Tel 528-2001
There's a lively party scene
at this restaurant-cum-pub
that serves good African and
European food, beer on tap
and a big-screen TV for sports
matches. It's a good place to
meet the locals.
🕐 Daily 10am–late 🎫 Free 🚗 1km
(0.5 miles) from junction between M19
and Ezulwini Valley, towards Malkerns

MBABANE

🛍 AFRICAN FANTASY
The Mall, Mbabane
Tel 404-4556
If you'd rather not haggle for
your souvenirs, head for this
shop, which stocks a good
selection of arts and crafts
from around the country. Look
out for the candles from the
famous Swazi Candles shop in
the Malkerns Valley.
🕐 Mon–Fri 10–5, Sat 10–3

🛍 SWAZI MARKET
Msunduza Road, Mbabane
At the end of Allister Miller
Street is this lively market with
stalls selling curios from all
over the country; you'll have to
haggle for the best bargains.
It's an excellent place to buy
fruit and vegetables—especially
fresh guavas and mangoes.
🕐 Daily dawn–dusk

This chapter describes walks and drives that explore South Africa, as well as Lesotho and Swaziland. The start point of each walk and drive is marked on the map on page 222, where you will also find the key to the individual maps.

Out and About

The map below shows the starting points of the walks and drives in this section.

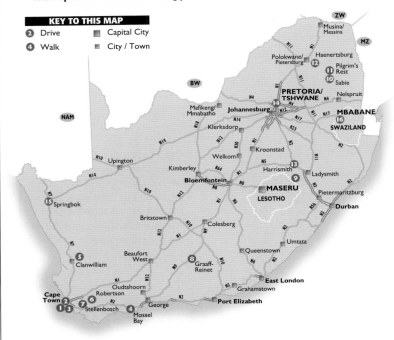

KEY TO THIS MAP

- ❷ Drive
- ❹ Walk
- ▪ Capital City
- ▪ City / Town

KEY TO ROUTE MAPS IN THIS CHAPTER

- ★ Start point
- ▬ Route
- ▪▪ Alternative route
- ▶ Route direction
- ❻ Featured sight along route
- ● Place of interest in Sights section
- ● Other place of interest
- ☀ Viewpoint
- ▲621 Height in metres

WALKS AND DRIVES

1. **Drive** Chapman's Peak (▷ 223)
2. **Walk** The Heart of Cape Town (▷ 224–225)
3. **Walk** Silvermine Nature Reserve (▷ 226–227)
4. **Drive** The Garden Route (▷ 228–229)
5. **Walk** The Sevilla Trail in the Cederberg (▷ 230–231)
6. **Drive** Route 62: From Robertson to the Karoo (▷ 232–233)
7. **Drive** Four Passes Route: The Winelands to the Overberg (▷ 234–235)
8. **Walk** Graaff-Reinet (▷ 236–237)
9. **Walk** The Tugela River (▷ 238–239)
10. **Drive** The Panorama Route: The Mpumalanga Drakensberg (▷ 240–241)
11. **Walk** Pilgrim's Rest (▷ 242–243)
12. **Drive** The Magoebaskloof and Beyond (▷ 244–245)
13. **Drive** The Eastern Highlands (▷ 246–247)
14. **Drive** Magaliesberg Meander (▷ 248–249)
15. **Drive** Northern Namakwa (▷ 250–251)
16. **Drive** Swaziland: The Valley of Heaven (▷ 252–253)

OUT AND ABOUT

CHAPMAN'S PEAK

The most spectacular route on the Cape Peninsula is the famous Chapman's Peak Drive, built early in the 20th century. Viewpoints give you unrivalled views of Cape Town, the coastline and the ocean.

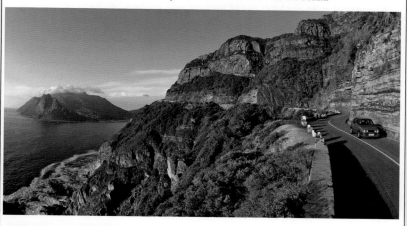

THE DRIVE

Distance: 15km (9 miles)

Allow: 30 minutes

Start at: Hout Bay

End at: Noordhoek

★ **Begin at Hout Bay.** Follow the signs for Chapman's Peak Drive, which will allow you to skirt around the town. On the far side of the bay, the road branches off to the left and begins to climb. Chapman's Peak Drive actually begins just outside Hout Bay at the toll-booth, where you will have to stop and pay R20 (per car). Keep your ticket. Once past the booth, continue straight up the road (there is only one road, so you shouldn't get lost). It hugs the coast, and will eventually rise to 600m (2,000ft) above the ocean. There are viewpoints all along this first stretch.

❶ **Die Josie Lookout,** at around 170m (558ft) above the ocean, is the first viewpoint worth a stop—ignore all the earlier ones. It is on the first headland, reached after about 6km (3.5 miles). Park the car on the right and get out to marvel at the views of Hout Bay. This is one of the most photographed views of Cape Town, with the perfect arc of the beach setting off the blue of the sea, the bulk of the promontories and the green of the surrounding hills.

The road continues around the headland, clinging to a narrow ledge between the stark, yellow-hued rocks and the thrashing ocean below. Look for the giant nets above the road, which catch falling rocks from above.

❷ **Chapman's Point,** a further 2.5km (1.5 miles) along, is the next striking lookout point. This headland juts into the ocean, giving you your first

Endless white sand at Noordhoek Beach

Following the scenic route from Hout Bay

glimpse of the expanse of white sand at Noordhoek beach, shelving steeply into big surf.

Continue along the road, which now begins to slope down towards the seaside village of Noordhoek, until you reach the barriers of the other toll. Show your ticket here and pass through. If you want to visit the beach, take the first road on your right. However, the beach is unsafe for swimming and should be avoided after dark. To get back to Cape Town, you pass back through the toll on the same ticket.

WHEN TO GO

This drive is spectacular at any time of the year; sunset is a particularly popular time of day for it.

WHERE TO EAT

Red Herring

Red Herring Trading Post, Beach Road, Noordhoek

Tel 021-7891783

There's a bar upstairs and à la carte restaurant downstairs. It serves great steaks, plus grilled fish and calamari steak. Sea views make it a great spot for a cocktail.

Ⓣ Daily 10–3, 6–9

OUT AND ABOUT

THE HEART OF CAPE TOWN

This leisurely walk begins at the point where Wale Street meets Adderley Street, Cape Town's busiest thoroughfare, and leads southwards, around and through the spacious Company's Garden. The latter part of the route takes you back into the heart of the city.

THE WALK

Distance: 2.8km (1.7 miles)	
Allow: 2.5 hours	
Start/end at: St. George's Cathedral	

★ **Begin in Wale Street at St. George's Cathedral**
(▷ 69), which in the later apartheid years served as a forum for protest against injustice, both as a political pulpit for Desmond Tutu and as a launch pad for the pivotal peace marches that helped pave the way to full democracy in 1994.

From the Cathedral, turn right and walk a few paces east along Wale Street, then turn first right and make your way north along Government Avenue, a leafy, pedestrian-only road running the length of Company's Garden, where Cape Town began. The tame squirrels that you'll see scurrying among the oaks are an exotic species, introduced by mining tycoon and Cape premier Cecil Rhodes, who imported their ancestors from America a little more than a hundred years ago. The handsome Houses of Parliament are on your left, here seen from the rear.

❶ The Houses of Parliament complex, built of white-trimmed terracotta brick, began life in 1885 and has since been much enlarged—mainly to accommodate the apartheid government's intricate constitutional 'reforms' of the 1980s—into a labyrinthine warren of chambers, offices and corridors.

Continue along Government Avenue for 400m (440 yards). The National Gallery (▷ 68) is the white building on your left.

❷ In front of the Gallery is a series of fountains fronted by a rather austere but striking statue of South African statesman Jan Smuts (1870–1950). A few metres beyond the Gallery is the Old Synagogue, built in 1863 in Egyptian

Wall decoration from the National Gallery

revival style and now incorporated into the complex of the modern Jewish Museum (▷ 67).

Turn back towards the gardens and turn left, walking along the front of the South African Museum and its Planetarium (▷ 69). From here, walk straight ahead between the rose gardens at the start of Company's Garden. Take a moment to turn around and take in the views of Table Mountain behind you, perfectly framed by the boughs of the trees. Continue into Company's Garden proper.

❸ Company's Garden (▷ 67), which the first European colonists planted as a market garden in 1652, was transformed by architect Sir Herbert Baker into an elegant park, with flower beds, trees and shrubs. At the far end of the gardens is Cape Town's oldest statue, that of a grizzled Sir George Grey, Governor of the Cape from 1854 to 1862. Behind the statue stands the South African National Library, the country's oldest reference repository (it dates from 1822) and among the world's earliest free libraries. The building is

based on the Fitzwilliam Museum in Cambridge, England; the entrance lies between Queen Victoria Street and Government Avenue.

Take the right exit from the gardens, turn left onto Government Avenue and walk back to Wale Street. From here, cross the road and head up Adderley Street (▷ 66).

❹ You'll see the old Slave Lodge (▷ 69) on your right, and farther down this busy shopping artery are some handsome old bank buildings interspersed with 1960s shopping malls, such as the Sanlam Golden Acre complex.

Two blocks before the latter—about 300m (330 yards) from Wale Street—turn left into Shortmarket Street, crossing the traffic-free St. George's Mall and leading into Greenmarket Square (▷ 67–68).

❺ Greenmarket Square was built as early as 1710 as a market place, a function it still fulfils nearly 300 years later through its lively daily market. The tree-fringed square is lined with cafés and is a popular meeting place.

Take a stroll around the market before heading to the top (southern) corner of the Square, walking up one block and turning right into Church Street, the heart of the city's trade in antiques and collectibles. A small street market displays a range of antiques and bric-a-brac. At the top of Church Street, turn left onto Long Street.

❻ On Long Street (▷ 67) you can stroll past the cafés, restaurants and quirky shops.

One block on, turn left down Wale Street and you'll see St. George's Cathedral just one block down.

OUT AND ABOUT

WHEN TO GO

You'll get the most out of the walk on a weekday between 9 and 5, when the whole area is bustling. Avoid walking away from Long Street late at night. The summer months are the most pleasant, although it can get intensely hot around midday in December, January and February. Expect lower temperatures and rain in winter.

Lively Greenmarket Square

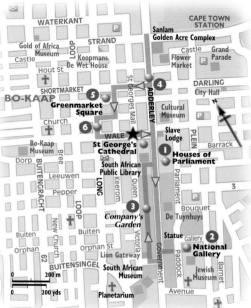

WHERE TO EAT

Primi Piatti
Greenmarket Square, City Centre 8001
Tel 021-4247466
A great lunch spot overlooking Greenmarket Square, serving pizza and pasta.
🕐 Mon–Fri 8–6, Sat 8–3

The classical Houses of Parliament

Company's Garden, with Table Mountain in the background

OUT AND ABOUT

SILVERMINE NATURE RESERVE

More than 2,000ha (5,000 acres) of the Steenberg, the mountain range that straddles the road south from Cape Town, have been set aside as the Silvermine Nature Reserve. It is part of the Cape Floral Kingdom, the smallest but richest of the world's six floral kingdoms. This walk takes in much of the area's indigenous plant life, with the striking backdrop of the peninsula seaboard along the way.

The orange-breasted sunbird is indigenous to the Cape

THE WALK

Distance: 9.5km (6 miles)

Allow: 4 hours

Start/end at: Silvermine Dam

How to get there: From Cape Town take the M64, better known as Ou Kaapseweg ('Old Cape Road'), which bisects the reserve. The way into the reserve's western section is on your right at the top of the pass. Drive straight up to the parking area near the reservoir (2km/1.2 miles)

★ **Set off from the parking area** at the reservoir of the Silvermine Reserve.

❶ The Reserve itself overlooks the narrow 'waist' of the Cape Peninsula, extending from Kalk Bay in the east to Noordhoek in the west. It was given its name in the 1680s by Dutch settlers who believed, too optimistically as it turned out, that a fabulous lode of silver lay somewhere beneath the high ground.

Cross the dam wall and make your way south to the route intersection. Take the left path, and continue up the hill until you reach the vehicle track, bearing right along the ridge to Noordhoek Peak (754m/2,473ft), which is about 2.5km (1.5 miles) from the reservoir.

The views en route take in the sweep of the western seaboard from the Noordhoek Valley below to Kommetjie in the hazy distance. The view, across to Hout Bay in the north, is even better from the top of the peak (the track leads all the way up).

❷ As you head for Noordhoek Peak, don't forget to tear your eyes away from the views and take a minute to look at the plants lining the path and covering the terrain around you. The Cape Peninsula encompasses what is thought to be the world's highest concentration of plant species—nearly 3,000 are crammed into its narrow confines, most belonging to what is known as fynbos ('fine bush'), a heath-like vegetation that includes proteas, ericas, reed-like restios, leucadendrons and various bulbs. Around 200 are indigenous species; more than 900 are to be found in the Silvermine area. Many species are rare and endangered, and most bloom briefly and gloriously after the winter rains have passed, before the hot summer winds begin. Of special note are the golden conebush, a winter-flowering plant, the creamy blackbeard sugarbush and the year-round pagoda tree.

Fynbos attracts a lively complement of birds, among them ground woodpeckers, sugarbirds and the brilliant orange-breasted sunbirds. You may also spot the rock kestrel and, hunting above the slopes, the imperious black eagle.

Once you've taken in the views of the seaboard, retrace your steps and, after about 300m (330 yards), bear left to the Elephant's Eye cave.

❸ Elephant's Eye cave is a dramatic cleft in the landscape, with a fern-festooned interior and wide-reaching views from its mouth of the wine estates of Constantia and the protected Tokai Forest. In good weather, you can see beyond the Southern Suburbs (▷ 72) out to the stretches of the townships on the Cape Flats (▷ 63), with the towering peaks of the Winelands in the hazy distance.

Continue south to rejoin the vehicle track and walk the 2km (1.2 miles) back to the reservoir. Look out for the Prins Kasteel waterfall on your way.

OUT AND ABOUT

The Nature Reserve's rugged scenery, rich with fynbos

WHEN TO GO

The short spring season (usually the end of August to the end of September) is the best time to see the wild flowers blooming on the hillsides. The heat can be intense in summer, so avoid walking in the sun between 11 and 3. Winter days are often wet and chilly.

WHERE TO EAT

There is an attractive picnic spot near the parking area.

PLACE TO VISIT

Silvermine Nature Reserve
☎ 021-7018692
🕐 Sep–end Apr daily 7–6; May–end Aug daily 8–5
💰 Adult R10, child (2–12) R5

A view across the Reserve and out to sea (above)
Cape sunbirds (below) feed on nectar

THE GARDEN ROUTE

Rated among the country's most scenic routes, this drive takes you along the southern maritime terrace from the seaside town of Mossel Bay eastwards to the Tsitsikamma National Park. On your right is the Indian Ocean shoreline; on your left stretches the evergreen grandeur of the Outeniqua and Tsitsikamma mountain ranges.

THE DRIVE

Distance: 210km (130 miles)	
Allow: 2 days	
Start at: Mossel Bay	
End at: Storms River Mouth	

★ **Start in Mossel Bay** (▷ 83) where you pick up the N2. Turn left (northwest) onto the N9 for the last 5km (3 miles) of the run into George (66km/ 41 miles), the town thought of as the gateway to the Garden Route. The seaboard stretch of this part of the drive skirts the pleasant resort villages of Hartenbos, Klein-Brakriver (look out for winter-flowering aloes in the surrounding hills) and Groot-Brakriver, before the route veers inland.

❶ **George** (▷ 80–81), the largest of the region's towns, lies beneath the handsome Outeniqua Mountains, surrounded by fertile countryside. It was named after George III of England, who was the reigning monarch when George became a town in 1811.

Return towards the intersection of the N9 and N2. The inland—and arguably the more rewarding—route is the old Passes Road, which starts 3km (2 miles) outside George and takes you through the well-wooded, rugged foothills of the Outeniqua range for 58km (36 miles): dense forests,

The Outeniqua Choo-Tjoe passenger steam train

tangled patches of fern, wild flowers and dangling creepers all flourish beneath the mountains.

The shorter (40km/25 miles) and more conventional route follows the N2, initially southeast to Wilderness. It then hugs the coast. Reaching Wilderness, the road crests just before the beach, giving you magnificent views across the expanse of sand and sea.

❷ **Wilderness** is an appealingly relaxed seaside village. To get into it, take the first left (signposted 'Wilderness'). The town is rather strung out, but

most of it clusters around the lagoon at the mouth of the Touws River. It is said to go back to 1877, when one George Bennett bought land in the area to start a farm; inspired by the surroundings, he called it Wilderness.

Back on the N2, the road hugs the coast, passing through a forested area, which opens up onto the limpid lagoon stretching for 17km (10.5 miles). Before reaching Knysna, the N2 crosses the northwestern reaches of the lagoon via a long, low road bridge. If you fancy a dip in the sea, take a quick detour: Just before the bridge, you'll see a minor road to your right, which leads along the lagoon's western bank to the little Norman-style Holy Trinity Church at Belvidere. Continue up the slope and then down to the stylish resort village of Brenton-on-Sea and its fine beach. To get back to the N2, return the same way. The N2 then passes along the lagoon before plunging into town.

❸ **Knysna** (▷ 82) acts as the capital of the Garden Route and makes for a pleasant overnight stop. The Outeniqua Choo-Tjoe, southern Africa's last scheduled steam passenger train, runs between George and Knysna. The line, considered one of the most beautiful in the world, opened in 1928.

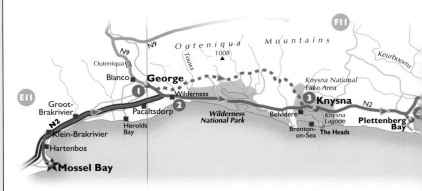

OUT AND ABOUT

Forests stretch along all the next 25km (15.5 miles) of the drive to Plettenberg Bay. A detour into the town (off the N2 to the right) leads to a couple of superb sandy beaches.

④ **Plettenberg Bay** (▷ 86) is possibly the Western Cape's most fashionable resort town. Its glorious position on a mountain-backed bay gave it its original name of Baia Formosa (Beautiful Bay). Its present name is more prosaic, immortalizing an 18th-century governor of the Cape, Joachim van Plettenberg.

If you're not visiting Plettenberg Bay continue along the N2, which passes Keurbooms Lagoon on the right, and the strikingly blue Tsitsikamma Mountains on the left. The N2 crosses over the northern tip of the Keurbooms estuary, climbing and veering to the north. A number of stopping

The view over Lookout Beach, Plettenberg Bay

places en route enable you to look back over the bay, lagoon and sea.

For the final part of the drive you follow the N2 for 65km (40 miles) from Plettenberg Bay along the northern edge of the strip-like Tsitsikamma National Park to Stormsrivier. After 19km (12 miles), a loop road (the R102) takes you down to the sea at enchanting Nature's Valley.

⑤ **Nature's Valley is entered over the high Groot River Pass. There are stupendous views of the sea and surrounding forest from the top. The R102 drops 223m (731ft) to sea level via a narrow gorge, twisting through coastal forest. From the sea, the road turns back up out of the Groot Valley.**

At the top of Groot River Pass, the road crosses the N2 highway and then dips back down along the narrow, forest-fringed road to the Bloukrans River Pass. From the bottom of the pass, look up to the elegantly arched road bridge that spans the immense river gorge—this is the alternative route if you stay on the N2 (and is a popular spot for bungee jumping, ▷ 195). The R102 rejoins the N2 shortly after Coldstream, the next village along this stretch.

A little less than 7km (4 miles) after you reach the intersection of the two routes, turn right for Storms River Mouth and the

Tsitsikamma National Park (▷ 88). The road ends at a restaurant near the entrance.

WHEN TO GO

The Garden Route is pleasant at any time of the year, but while there is year-round rainfall, there is more in winter. Plettenberg Bay enjoys an average annual 320 days of almost uninterrupted sunshine. Avoid high season, from December to February, when the area is at its busiest.

WHERE TO EAT

Knysna Oyster Co.
Long Street, Thesen's Island, Knysna 6571 (across the causeway)
Tel 044-3826942
www.oysters.co.za
A range of seafood, but famous for its Knysna oysters.
🕐 Daily noon–10pm

The Lookout
Lookout Beach, Plettenberg Bay 6600
Tel 044-5331379
Great lunch spot overlooking the beach, serving seafood and grills.
🕐 Daily 9am–11pm

TIP

● For most of the way the Garden Route follows the N2 that connects Cape Town with Port Elizabeth and places far to the east. The drive can be done in a day, but you'll get more out of the area if you take your time, stopping for a night in Knysna (▷ 82).

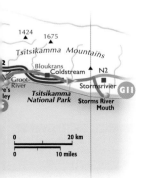

THE SEVILLA TRAIL IN THE CEDERBERG

This is a fairly easy walk along a valley in the Cederberg region, an area inhabited by the San people for thousands of years. It follows a rocky trail in a deserted valley past ten beautifully preserved San rock art sites, most of them some 2,000 years old. The walk is waymarked with painted white footprints on the ground.

THE WALK

Distance: 4km (2.5 miles)
Allow: 2–3 hours
Start/end at: Traveller's Rest farm
How to get there: Traveller's Rest farm is on the Wupperthal Road, 34km (21 miles) from Clanwilliam
Parking: At the farm

The Traveller's Rest farm, where you begin this walk

★ **Start at the Traveller's Rest farm,** where you can park and pick up a map of the trail. Cross the road from the farm and enter through the small gate. The trail winds along a stark, rock-strewn landscape alongside a (usually) dry riverbed. Continue straight ahead and follow the waymarkers veering to the left. You will be walking over weathered rock, with a more or less continuous stretch of rocky overhangs and walls to your left. Look for dassies (rock hyraxes), small, rodent-like mammals looking like overgrown guinea pigs, which inhabit these rocks.

❶ The first rock art site you come to, on your left after 1km (0.5 miles), has a black image of a group of people standing in a circle. This is superimposed over older, more weathered images. Be careful not to touch the paintings as they are exceedingly fragile.

Follow the rock face around to your left for a few paces, and you will come to the second site.

❷ Site 2 has one of the most intriguing paintings, as it shows what looks like long-necked monsters running side by side. The images probably once had a mystical, symbolic significance.

One hundred metres (110 yards) farther on is site 3, again on your left, on top of a rocky ledge over the riverbed. Look for a huge rounded boulder balanced on a couple of other rocks, with a gap underneath: Behind, under and surrounding it are various examples of rock art.

❸ The finest of these is under the boulder (you'll have to lie underneath it to see it properly), and depicts what looks like the hindquarters of antelope—the front parts of the animals may have been painted in a different shade that has faded with age. A short scramble off the ledge is site 4 (look for the waymarkers), which has some clear images of quagga (an extinct zebra) and other zebra.

The next part of the trail leads you, after 500m (550 yards), to a rocky shelf above the river, below which you'll see a pretty patch of indigenous forest including wild olive and almond trees. During August and September, look for the wild flowers on the surrounding hills and valley.

❹ Site 5 is one of the best. It has a fine depiction of a walking archer, and one of a zebra foal that perfectly captures the young creature's first faltering steps. Just a few steps farther on is site 6, with a number of images, including a bright group of dancing women.

Continue around to the left and then straight on down a gully for about 300m (330 yards) until you reach site 7.

❺ Sites 7, 8 and 9 are fairly close together. The images at site 7 are quite faded, but include a couple of faint yellow elephants and two shadowy figures whose faces have eerily faded away. About 250m (273 yards) farther along is site 8, a low cave filled with numerous handprints in various shades. After another 50m (55 yards), site 9 has a multitude of images including some groups of running antelope.

If the riverbed is dry, turn right here (look for the waymarkers) and cross the riverbed, before turning left at the rough road. If the river is flooded, you will have to retrace your steps from here back to Traveller's Rest farm.

❻ Site 10 is just past three cottages, up a gorge, and depicts several processions of people carrying sticks or weapons.

From here, retrace your steps back along the trail to Traveller's Rest farm. For a longer walk you can take the Sevilla Olive Tree Walk, which loops around on the other side of the river and back to the main road.

WHEN TO GO

Summer can be oppressively hot. The best months are May and June, when the weather is cooler and fairly dry, and August and

OUT AND ABOUT

The multi-layered rocks form a dramatic landscape

September, when the wild flowers are in bloom in the Cederberg.

There are well-defined images of quaggas (an extinct South African zebra with a yellowish-brown coat) at a number of sites

WHERE TO EAT

Traveller's Rest serves meals at the Khoisan Kitchen, but you must phone several days ahead to arrange a meal (tel 027-4821824) as it usually opens only if large groups are visiting. Otherwise bring your own picnic, as there are no other restaurants on this route.

WHERE TO STAY

There are 12 cottages and a guesthouse at Traveller's Rest (tel 027-4821824), costing R120 per person per night. You must take food and drink with you.

Horses grazing among the wild flowers at the Traveller's Rest farm

THE SEVILLA TRAIL IN THE CEDERBERG **231**

ROUTE 62: FROM ROBERTSON TO THE KAROO

This drive takes you from the lush countryside of the Cape's Winelands to the dry plains of the Little Karoo, a region hugged by two great mountain ranges. Route 62 is a pleasant, more scenic alternative to the usual highway route from the Cape to the Little Karoo. The drive can comfortably be completed in a day, but if you want to take in some of the wine estates along the route, allow two days, perhaps spending a night in Calitzdorp.

THE DRIVE

Distance: 266km (165 miles)	
Allow: 1 day	
Start at: Robertson	
End at: Oudtshoorn	

★ **Begin the drive just outside the town of Robertson** (▷ 86), heading east on the R60.

The lime-rich soils, kind climate and good pasturage around Robertson combine to make this one of the country's top horse-breeding areas; you'll see some fine thoroughbreds grazing in the fields as you drive past.

This area is the Breede River Valley (▷ 78), flanked here by the high Langeberg range, which you negotiate via Kogmanskloof, a pass, on your way east to Montagu, a distance of 30km (18.5 miles). The pass starts at Ashton; turn left out of the town, off the R60 onto the R62.

❶ **Kogmanskloof** (once known as Cogman's Kloof) is a spectacular pass built by the

Ostrich eggs and feathers are big business in Oudtshoorn

celebrated road engineer John Thomas Baines in the 1870s. It winds for 6km (4 miles) beneath stark rock walls and soaring peaks. En route, the road passes through a rock tunnel, on top of which stand the ruined remains of a fort from the Second Anglo-Boer War (1899–1902). If you feel like a break at this point, stop at the pleasant Keurkloof picnic spot on the Montagu side of the tunnel, where you'll find drinking water and toilets.

The road goes on to the attractive town of Montagu (▷ 83), which lies on the edge of the Little Karoo (▷ 84–85), a broad, flat-bottomed basin wedged between mountains to the north and south. The basin is bisected by the R62—Route 62—which meanders all the way from the Cape Town area to Port Elizabeth, and which takes its inspiration from the famous American Route 66, linking Chicago with Los Angeles. Head out of Montagu on Long Street, which leads onto the R62. The next stretch takes you the 60km (37 miles) to Barrydale.

❷ **Barrydale** is the hub of a prosperous farming district producing apples, peaches, wine and brandy. You can visit the Barrydale Co-operative Cellars, which lay on wine tastings. The landscapes along the way are magnificent. Look out for the wild flowers, especially Livingstone daisies or *mesembryanthemums* (known in South Africa as vygies). The heights of the Langeberg are on your right.

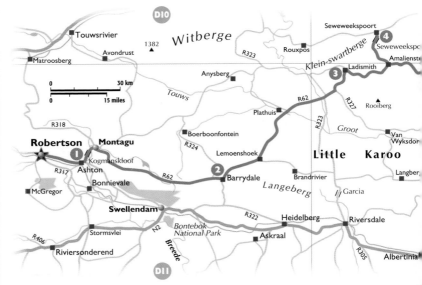

OUT AND ABOUT

After Barrydale the R62 runs northeast for 80km (50 miles) until it reaches Ladismith.

❸ Ladismith is a laid-back little town that nestles beneath the Swartberg's lofty twin Towerkop peaks (2,203m/7,225ft). Like its more famous near-namesake, Ladysmith in KwaZulu-Natal, Ladismith is named after the Spanish wife of Sir Harry Smith, soldier and controversial governor of the Cape Colony in the 19th century. You're now entering ostrich country, though the land here is mainly given over to sheep and fruit.

At the mission station of Amalienstein, 36km (22 miles) beyond Ladismith on the 28km (17-mile) stretch of the R62 leading to Calitzdorp, it's worth taking a diversion onto the little side road leading north into the Swartberg mountains via Seweweekspoort.

❹ Seweweekspoort is a wonderfully scenic river pass. It is said to have got its name either from the fynbos that decorate the hillsides (one species blooms for seven weeks), or from the period needed by the brandy smugglers to complete their route through the uplands.

Back on the R62, continue to Calitzdorp.

Stop along Kogmanskloof for some amazing views

❺ Calitzdorp, with its Victorian buildings, has a rather restful Victorian charm. As you get near the town, you'll begin to notice ostriches roaming the fields on both sides of the road, although the area is better known as the port wine capital of South Africa. The three local wineries, all well signposted from the middle of town, produce some of the country's finest port wines. The most appealing estate perhaps is Die Krans Estate, where there's also a pleasant half-hour vineyard walk. The other two are Boplaas Estate and Calitzdorp Wine Cellars. Calitzdorp holds a Port Festival each July.

From here, the route continues straight to the ostrich capital, Oudtshoorn.

❻ Oudtshoorn lives and breathes ostriches. The approach to the town passes a number of farms and you'll see ostriches wandering around the fields in ever-increasing numbers. You can visit a couple of local show farms (▷ 194) to see how ostriches are bred and to buy ostrich products (anything from eggs and feather dusters to steaks). The wider area's other notable attraction is the remarkable Cango Cave complex (▷ 84–85), 26km (17 miles) north of town.

WHEN TO GO
Any time of the year. Route 62 runs through the transition zone between the relatively lush and well-watered Winelands and the drier, invariably clear-skied Little Karoo. However, spring (October and November) and autumn (February and March) are probably the best touring months.

WHERE TO EAT
Preston's & Thomas Baines Pub
17 Bath Street, Montagu 6720
Tel 023-6143013
Traditional food served in the à la carte restaurant and pub next door, with an attractive open-air terrace.
Ⓒ Daily 10.30–2.30, 5.30–9.45

PLACES TO VISIT
Barrydale Wine Cellar
Route 62 Wine Route, Barrydale
☎ 028-5721012
Ⓒ Mon–Fri 8–5, Sat 9–3

Calitzdorp Wine Estates
Die Krans Estate (tel 044-213 3314; Mon–Fri 9–5, Sat 9–3); Boplaas Estate (tel 044-213 3326; Mon–Sat 9–3); and Calitzdorp Wine Cellars (tel 044-213 3301; Mon–Fri 8–1, 2–5, Sat 8–1).

WHERE TO STAY
Port Wine Guest House
7 Queen Street, Calitzdorp
Tel 044-2133131
www.portwine.net
A pleasant guesthouse dating back to 1830; the five double rooms have four-poster beds and fireplaces.

OUT AND ABOUT

FOUR PASSES ROUTE:
THE WINELANDS TO THE OVERBERG

One of the popular day drives from Cape Town is known as the Four Passes route. This takes you through the heart of the Winelands region to the Overberg in the Western Cape and, as the name suggests, over four mountain passes. The drive can be completed in around three hours, but it's best to take your time and stop off to take in the views en route.

THE DRIVE

Distance: 115km (71 miles)

Allow: 3–4 hours

Start/end at: Stellenbosch

★ **Begin your drive from Stellenbosch,** the heart of the Winelands. From here, take the R310 north towards Franschhoek. Driving up out of Stellenbosch, you cross the first pass.

❶ Helshoogte Pass, despite its unpromising name (it means Hell's Heights), has glorious views of the mountains rolling down to neat rows of vineyards.

From here, the road continues straight and you pass several well-known wine estates, including Boschendal. After 17km (10 miles) you reach an intersection with the R45; a left turn would take you to Paarl (12km/ 7 miles), but the route continues to the right.

This is a pleasant drive up into the Franschhoek Valley, passing several wine estates. The road follows a rail track and part of the Berg River before reaching Franschhoek. Continue straight on through the town until you reach the Huguenot Monument at the end of the main road. Take a left turn here, and follow the road climbing up out of the valley to Franschhoek Pass.

❷ Franschhoek Pass was built along the tracks formed by migrating herds of game centuries ago, and was originally known as the Olifantspad (elephant's path). Pause at the top and look back over the wide views of the valley, with the little town nestling beneath the rugged peaks and surrounded by vineyards.

One of the more surprising aspects of this drive is the change in vegetation once you cross the lip of the pass, 520m (1,700ft) above Franschhoek.

Fynbos produce a number of different coloured flowers

As the road winds down towards Theewaterskloof Dam glittering in the distance, you pass through a dry valley of scrub vegetation and fynbos (the low-lying indigenous vegetation found in the Cape); the fertile fruit farms and vineyards of the earlier part of the drive are no longer to be seen. During spring, watch for flowering fynbos, when they produce bright-hued (and strange-smelling) blooms.

At the bottom of the valley the road reaches the dam and its large expanse of water.

❸ Theewaterskloof Dam is a popular spot for watersports and fishing. The views of the surrounding mountains and the tree plantations stretching up the slopes are particularly striking from here.

Take a right turn across the dam. The road crosses the narrowest part of the dam, and is a good place to look for bird life. Continue on the R321, which passes across the valley towards Grabouw and Elgin, before climbing up to Viljoens Pass, the third of the four passes.

❹ The Hottentots Holland Nature Reserve, a popular hiking region, lies to the right

of the road. Much of the countryside here is given over to orchards. The area is an important apple-growing region, and you'll see people standing at the side of the road selling apples.

The road continues straight on, passing Eikenhof Dam on the right before reaching the undistinguished twin towns of Elgin and Grabouw. Just after the towns, you'll come to the intersection with the N2 highway. Turn right here and continue straight on. Here the road crosses the edge of the Steenbras Dam before climbing up to the fourth and most spectacular pass, Sir Lowry's Pass.

❺ Sir Lowry's Pass cuts over the Hottentots Holland Mountains and, as you come to the top of the road, you are met with astounding views of the entire plain between the Winelands and Cape Town. There is a signposted viewing site at the highest point of the pass from which you can see the vast stretch of coast curving to your left, with Table Mountain looming in the background and the Cape Flats stretching out between.

The N2 winds down the slope of the mountain before reaching the plain. From here, continue straight until you reach the turnoff to Stellenbosch (intersection 38) and turn right onto the R44. This road leads straight back to town.

WHEN TO GO

This drive can be completed at any time, but spring is a particularly good time to visit, as the fruit trees and fynbos will be in bloom. Late summer is also attractive, as the vineyards are busy with workers harvesting the grapes. Expect strong winds in winter.

La Petite Ferme
Franschhoek Pass
Tel 021-8763016
This smart restaurant is well known for its wholesome country cooking and modern fusion dishes like smoked salmon on sweet potato and coconut mash. It has spectacular views of the Franschhoek valley.
🕐 Daily noon–4pm

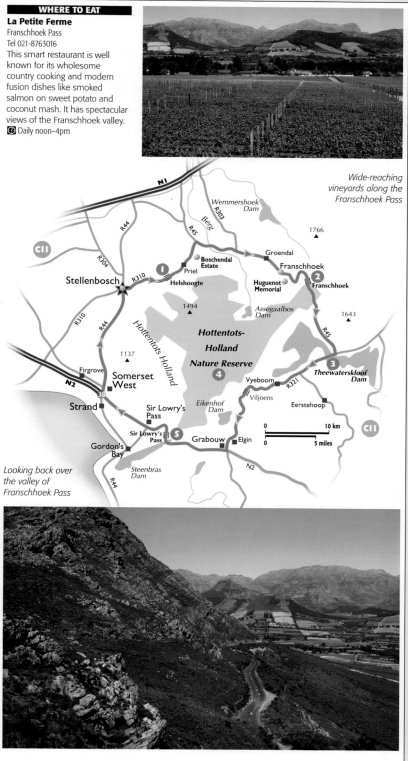

Wide-reaching vineyards along the Franschhoek Pass

Looking back over the valley of Franschhoek Pass

OUT AND ABOUT

GRAAFF-REINET

Graaff-Reinet survived rebellion and rugged frontier life in the arid northern wilderness and is now the neatest and most graceful of the Karoo's towns. While the rest of urban South Africa grew haphazardly, Graaff-Reinet was carefully planned and is full of fine architecture. This walk takes in the best of the town's historical buildings.

THE WALK

Distance: 1.2 km (0.75 miles)	
Allow: 1.5 hours	
Start/end at: Drostdy Hotel	

★ **Begin your stroll at the Drostdy Hotel** on Church Street, the main thoroughfare. From Church Street, smaller roads branch east and west, and it is among these that you'll find most of Graaff-Reinet's historic buildings, museums and restaurants.

❶ The Drostdy hotel itself is a fine building, designed as the court and residence of the local magistrate *(landdrost)* by French architect Louis Thibault and completed in 1806. Take a moment to position yourself at the hotel's handsome front door and gaze down the length of Parsonage Street, with its attractive houses framing the pleasing façade of Reinet House (see below) at the far (eastern) end of the road.

Cross Church Street and walk straight along Parsonage Street, which runs for about 280m (300 yards).

❷ On Parsonage Street you pass the John Rupert Little Theatre on your right (after 100m/109 yards), originally the church of the London Missionary Society but now a small theatre. Also on the right is a row of charming houses built for private occupation but eventually converted for the aged. Perhaps the most appealing of them is number 17, Williams House, which has some especially attractive woodwork.

At the end of Parsonage Street on the right, at its intersection with Murray Street, is the iron-roofed, gabled, Cape Dutch-style Old Residency, which started life as a town house in the early 19th century and now functions

Dutch-style architecture in Church Street

as a small military museum. Cross Murray Street to visit Reinet House.

❸ Reinet House was built in 1812 as the Dutch Reformed Church parsonage. It suffered radical alteration over the years but was carefully restored in the 1950s to its original six-gabled, H-plan elegance. It suffered fire damage in the 1980s but was restored again and is now a museum with period furniture and a collection of antique dolls. Apart from its historical and architectural distinctions, the museum has two unusual claims to fame: It owns the world's largest vine, a monster which, before it was pruned in 1983, had a girth of 3m (10ft) and covered an area of 123sq m (1,323sq ft); and it is the only place in the country permitted to distil a powerful home-made beverage known as Withond (white dog).

Retrace your steps for 100m (109 yards) along the north side of Parsonage Street, which is lined by small 19th-century houses—no. 18 has an interesting stand-alone gable and little windows of very impure glass. Turn right onto Cross Street.

❹ St. James' Anglican church at the corner of Cross and Somerset streets is worth a look. It has some lovely woodwork inside, and the next-door rectory has an eye-catching doll's-house quality about it.

Turn left, then right (north) into cottage-fringed Te Water Street. Look for the imposing Graaff-Reinet Club (1881) on your right. Te Water, which is only some 100m (109 yards) long, ends at Church Square, a pleasant area fronted by the Mayor's Garden.

❺ The Dutch Reformed Church in the square is itself a fine building: Dating from 1887 and built in Gothic Revival style, it was modelled on England's Salisbury Cathedral and contains a splendid collection of ecclesiastical silver.

To return to the Drostdy Hotel, exit the square onto Church Street, where notable buildings include Te Water House from 1818, the Old Library Museum, which dates from 1847, and the Hester Rupert Art Museum, with its collection of contemporary South African art.

❻ The Hester Rupert Art Museum is in the Dutch Reformed Mission church, dating from 1821. Inside is an excellent collection of works by Irma Stern among other modern South African art. Stern (1894–1966) ranks among the country's most innovative painters, although her canvases were dismissed as 'immoral' and 'revolutionary' by the apartheid government; at one point they were actually the subject of police investigation.

From here, continue back to the Drostdy Hotel for a well-deserved cold drink or meal.

OUT AND ABOUT

WHEN TO GO

Any time of the year is good for the walk, but bear in mind that early winter mornings and evenings can be bitterly cold in the Great Karoo. By contrast, the hours in the middle of high summer days are often too hot for walking, and can be uncomfortably dusty.

The Old Library Museum has a diverse collection, such as fossils and 19th-century photographs

WHERE TO EAT

Coral Tree
3 Church Street (opposite the church)
Tel 049-8925947
Karoo lamb is a regional specialty, and the venison (kudu steak) is excellent.
Daily 12–3, 6–10

OUT AND ABOUT

Reinet House has been restored to its former glory and is now home to a collection of period furniture

PLACES TO VISIT

Reinet House (Graaff-Reinet Museum)
Murray Street
049-8923801
Mon–Fri 8–12.30, 2–5, Sat–Sun 9–12

Hester Rupert Art Museum
Church Street
049-8922121 (ask to be put through to museum)
Mon–Fri 9–12.30, 2–5, Sat 9–12, Sun 9–noon

THE TUGELA RIVER

The Royal Natal National Park has some of South Africa's most spectacular scenery, with mountain slopes, thickly forested valleys and rolling grasslands, all watched over by the massive grandeur of the Amphitheatre, one of the best-known features of the northern Drakensberg. This walk, which follows the course of the upper Tugela River, is one of the most rewarding hikes in the park.

THE WALK

Distance: 14km (8.7 miles)

Allow: 6 hours

Start/end at: Thendele Camp

★ **Start the hike at the Thendele Camp parking area.** The walk heads southwest, directly towards the Amphitheatre and its falls, following the river (or riverbed, if the rains have been poor). There are clear signs along the path to the gorge. The path follows the contours of the slope above the river, meandering through protea grassland and patches of yellowwood forest, which provide welcome respite from the sun.

❶ You'll have views of a number of notable northern Drakensberg peaks along the walk. The main peak, Mont-aux-Sources, rises 3,282m (10,765ft) above sea level. Others are the Sentinel (3,165m/10,812ft), the Eastern Buttress (3,048m/ 9,974ft) and Devil's Tooth, a detached peak which was first climbed as recently as 1950 and remains one of the region's most difficult ascents.

The path has a few minor ascents and descents and in due course opens up at the river itself, following its course until you enter the gorge.

❷ The Tugela is the region's largest and, in its upper reaches, most spectacular river. It rises at the western end of the Mont-aux-Sources plateau, finding its way to, and then plunging over, the Amphitheatre's rim in just under 2km (1.2 miles) of cascades, one of which drops a sheer 614m (2,014ft).

As you enter the gorge you have to cross on large stepping stones made of natural boulders—it's a

The sheer size of the Tugela Gorge dwarfs its visitors

good idea to wear shoes with good grip, as the rocks can be slippery (carry some with you, so that you can change from your hiking boots when necessary).

❸ The Tugela Gorge is a scenic and botanic delight. The walk along it takes you to the base of the crescent-shaped Amphitheatre, part of the Mont-aux-Sources ('mountain of springs') massif, which was named for the number of rivers born on its plateau, among them the Tugela (or Thukela).

The path continues on the other side, and at the 6km (3.7 miles) mark the gorge narrows to form the Tugela Tunnel.

❹ The Tugela Tunnel's sandstone walls are moulded into striking shapes, but to pass through here and see them you have to be willing to get wet: There's a certain amount of boulder hopping, and after rain you have to wade along the bottom.

Alternatively, you can climb up the sturdy ladder which is

attached to the rock face on your left. The ladder follows the contours of the face, and at the top you follow the path with the assistance of steel pegs buried in the rock face. At the footpath, turn left and descend again; you'll find yourself at the other end of the Tugela Tunnel.

5 It's from the end of the Tugela Tunnel that you'll have the best views of the waterfall,

region, you may spot the occasional large mammal such as grey rhebok or baboon along the way. You'll certainly see some uncommon birds (more than 230 species have been recorded within the park).

WHEN TO GO
The warmer months from October to March are best for the walk, but bear in mind that the sun will be very strong in

Look out for wildlife along the route, such as baboons

Sentinel Peak (inset) is one of the many peaks in the Drakensberg Mountains (above)

a spectacular sight and well worth the walk. In midwinter the uppermost cascade freezes to a jagged sheet of ice. You can stop for a picnic here and a quick dip in the shallows.

To return to your car, you have to retrace your steps, so make sure you give yourself plenty of time to get back. Look for the Policeman's Helmet—a large freestanding rock formation—on the return walk.

6 Although the route is one of the most popular in the

December and January. There is little shade along the way, so wear a hat and sunscreen, and carry plenty of drinking water with you. You should also be prepared for sudden summer thunderstorms, in which case you should turn back because of the risk of flash flooding. In spring, the area is carpeted with wild flowers. Winters can be extremely cold (though the days are often crisp and sunny), and the peaks and higher slopes are often covered in snow. This is a popular walk, so avoid weekends.

PLACE TO VISIT
Royal Natal Visitor Centre
Tel 036-4386303
The Visitor Centre stocks detailed maps of the area. The number of day visitors is controlled to prevent overcrowding in the park, but this is likely to be a problem only on weekends and holidays.
🕐 Daily 8–4.30
💰 Adult R25, child (3–15) R15
🚌 Well signposted from the N3; 60km (37 miles) from Harrismith, 40km (25 miles) from Bergvill

THE PANORAMA ROUTE: THE MPUMALANGA DRAKENSBERG

This trip along the eastern escarpment, or Mpumalanga Drakensberg, takes you through striking mountain scenery, a landscape of dense evergreen forests, streams and waterfalls, and past the world's third largest gorge—the Blyde River Canyon.

THE DRIVE

Distance:	180km (112 miles) with digressions
Allow:	1 day
Start/end at:	Sabie

★ **Begin the drive in Sabie** (▷ 138). This appealing little upland town began life in 1895 when gold was accidentally discovered in the area. A party of picnickers were amusing themselves by shooting at targets when one of their bullets struck gold-bearing rock. The seam eventually dried up, and Sabie turned its energies to the planting and harvesting of pines. It is now the focus of the country's biggest single block of man-made forest.

Drive north along Main Street, which becomes the R532, and out of town. Cross the Sabie River after 1km (0.6 miles), continue for 200m (220 yards), and turn right on the short road to the Sabie Falls, a cataract falling a dramatic 73m (240ft) into a chasm, spanned by a bridge that serves as a viewing platform. Return to the R532 and proceed for 10km (6 miles) north along the R532, turning right at the signpost to Mac-Mac Pools, which are a little more than 1km (0.6 miles) from the main road.

❶ At Mac-Mac Pools there are picnic spots, superb scenery, and the chance to swim in the clear mountain water (changing-rooms on site). The equally attractive Mac-Mac Falls—twin cascades that plunge into a ravine lined by trees and ferns—are 2km (1.2 miles) farther along the road. The rather odd name for the pools and waterfall relates to the number of Scotsmen who flocked to the early gold diggings.

Follow the signs to Graskop (▷ 125), another, even more attractive forest village, which is 23km (14 miles) from Sabie.

From Graskop follow the signs to God's Window, which is on the scenic R534 loop road that starts on your right a couple of kilometres from the village. There are several viewing points along the 2.7km (1.7 miles) of the loop.

❷ God's Window, on the extreme edge of the escarpment, is one of the most spectacular viewing points on the route. From this dramatic cleft in the mountains memorable vistas unfold—of the Blyde River gorge, the backing mountains and the hot and hazy Lowveld plain that stretches away to the east, across the Kruger National Park (▷ 128–135). The R534 also takes you to Wonder View, 1.3km (0.8 miles) farther on.

Return to the R532. A short distance to the west you'll find two of the Escarpment's most beautiful waterfalls: Lisbon Falls, another twin cascade and, 3km (2 miles) to the north, Berlin Falls. Access to both is on gravel. The next, longish stretch of the R532 takes you to a crossing of two small watercourses known as the Treur and Blyde rivers and to nearby Bourke's Luck Potholes, 37km (23 miles) from Graskop.

❸ Bourke's Luck Potholes (1km/0.6 miles beyond the Blyde) are a water-eroded fantasia of rock shapes carved by the river over thousands of years. The potholes are named after early prospector Tom Bourke, who never did make his fortune from the golden lode (although he predicted its presence). Bourke's Luck Potholes are at one end of the Blyde River Canyon, the immediate area's main attraction (▷ 126–127). Carved from red sandstone, its cliff faces plunge nearly 1km (0.6 miles) to the waters below. Strategically sited

viewing spots include World's End and Lowveld Lookout, easily reached from the road and revealing panoramas that take in the immensity of the low-lying country to the east, the hump-like peaks known as the Three Rondavels and the Mariepskop massif.

Return to the R532 and swing round to the northwest, past the Blydepoort Dam on your right, to the intersection with the R36, 39km (24 miles) from Bourke's Luck. Close to the intersection (follow the signs) are the Echo Caves.

❹ Echo Caves are a system of caverns and tunnels extending 1.3km (0.8 miles) into the mountain. They are named for the echoes produced when the stalactites are tapped. Evidence of Stone Age human habitation has been found in the caves. Present-day inhabitants of the caves are a huge colony of bats.

Back on the R36, drive south for 22km (13.5 miles) to Ohrigstad.

❺ Ohrigstad was founded as Andries-Ohrigstad by the eastern Voortrekkers in 1845 and abandoned after malaria devastated the settlement (who moved to a healthier spot, which the Voortrekkers named Lydenburg). The ruins of the Voortrekker fortifications are signposted to your right, just before you reach town.

Continue south for 23km (14 miles) to the intersection with the R533, which leads you east for 27km (16.5 miles), over Robber's Pass, to Pilgrim's Rest.

❻ The splendidly scenic road known as Robber's Pass was named after a highwayman called Tommy Dennison who, in 1912, held up the Lydenburg coach; he used carved wooden

OUT AND ABOUT

The views from God's Window are awesome

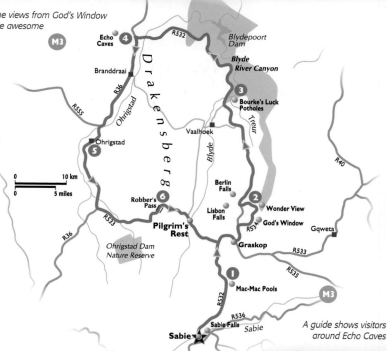

A guide shows visitors around Echo Caves

pistols and put on an American accent, and he spent the money in Pilgrim's Rest the next day.

Drive through Pilgrim's Rest (▷ 137) towards Graskop and then turn south on the R532 for Sabie.

WHEN TO GO
February and March, at the end of the rains, are probably the best months for touring: the air is mild and the countryside lush.

WHERE TO EAT
Country Kitchen
75 Main Street, Sabie
Tel 013-7641901
Traditional South African fare, with seasonally changing menu.
🕐 Tue–Sat 11.30–3, 6–11, Mon 6–11

PLACE TO VISIT
Echo Caves
☎ 013-2380015
🕐 Daily 8.30–4.30
🎟 Adult R30, child (under 12) R15

PILGRIM'S REST

The old mining village of Pilgrim's Rest sits high among the hills of the eastern escarpment. What was once the hub of the early gold mining industry is now an evocative (and much visited) 'living museum'.

THE WALK

Distance: The various venues are within a few steps of each other
Allow: 3 hours
Start at: Diggings Museum
End at: Joubert Bridge

★ **Begin your wander at the open-air Diggings Museum** at the top end of what is known as the village's 'Uptown' section, on the right of the R533. Here you'll get an insight into the working and social lives of the early diggers. Tours, conducted four times a day (at 10, 11, 2 and 3), take in the diggers' huts and include gold-panning demonstrations.

❶ Gold was discovered in the creek of the local stream in 1873, and within days a bustling concourse of hopeful diggers had gathered around the site, their tents and wattle-and-daub huts soon to be replaced by solid little cottages with iron roofs. Traders and canteen owners set up shop; a church, school and newspaper soon appeared, and the Royal Hotel opened its hospitable doors. When alluvial gold grew scarce, syndicates and companies were formed to dig deeper. Plenty of gold was extracted, but the deposits eventually ran out and the last of the mines, the Theta, closed in the 1970s, by which time Pilgrim's Rest had turned its attention to forestry. The then Transvaal provincial government bought the village, in its entirety, in the 1970s, and its buildings were meticulously restored to the condition they were in during the period between 1880 and 1915.

Turn right out of the museum and cross over onto the first road on the left, where you'll see the Anglican Church of St. Mary, built by Cornish miners (from the English county of Cornwall) in 1884 and the oldest of Pilgrim's Rest's surviving brick structures. It's an attractive little building, festooned with bougainvillea.

Panning for gold at the Diggings Museum

Two doors down is the grand-sounding but modest Town Hall, once the hub of village social life, and farther along on your left is Leadley's building, which served as the first hostelry (1885).

The next three venues are also to your left. The Old Print Shop (now a gift shop) and the *Pilgrim's & Sabie News* building tell you something about the turn-of-the-20th-century printing and newspaper-publishing scene. The oddly named European Hotel, the third in the trio, has a charming veranda, today part of a restaurant. A few steps farther along the street (again, on your left) is the Royal Hotel, an evocative place that is still used as a hotel.

❷ The Royal's furnishings and fittings haven't changed much in the past hundred years. Apparently the pub's bar graced a chapel in far-off Lourenço Marques (now Maputo, the capital of Mozambique) until 1893, when an enterprising trader bought it and hauled it all the way across the Lowveld plain and up the escarpment to serve an entirely different kind of congregation.

Set back from the street on your right (east) stands a cottage once

owned by the village hairdresser, stationer and tobacconist. Walk a few paces along and you'll come to the Royal Hotel's old stables, followed by the Tourist Information Centre (inside there's a historical display) and the Miner's House, originally built in 1913 for the local doctor but since re-created as a mine-worker's home complete with period furniture and oddments.

Adjacent buildings include the old Bank House and the Victorian Cottage. Last of the Uptown venues are the Methodist Church and the cemetery (access via the gravel road to your left) and, back on the main street, the general dealer's store once run by Dredzen & Company and now a house museum.

The Downtown part of the village, separated from Uptown by a stretch of open space, is less generously endowed with relics of the past (and consequently less crowded with visitors). To take in the area, continue past the Dredzen & Company museum, past the Roman Catholic church of the Sacred Heart and the Dutch Reformed church, and on to the end of the road, where you'll see the arched, stone-built Joubert Bridge, constructed (over the Blyde River) in 1896. From here, turn back and retrace your steps to the parking area at the Diggings Museum.

WHEN TO GO

Pilgrim's Rest is a pleasant spot at any time of the year, but if you want to miss the biggest crowds of visitors, avoid high season from November to January. Winter nights and mornings can be very cold, and mornings are often misty at any time of year.

WHERE TO EAT

The Vine
Main Street, Downtown, Pilgrim's Rest
Tel 013-7681080
Old-fashioned pub and restaurant with breezy veranda.
Ⓘ Daily noon–late
Ⓦ L R55, D R75, Wine R38

OUT AND ABOUT

Pilgrim's Rest is once again busy with gold prospectors, albeit amateur ones looking for a souvenir

TIPS

• Tickets to museums and sights are not available from individual attractions, and must be bought in advance from the Tourist Information Centre, Main Street, Uptown (tel 013-7681060; daily 9–12.45, 1.15–4.30; www.pilgrimsrest.co.za).
• You can see the sights on a ride in the tractor-driven Zeederberg Omnibus, which regularly drives round the village, but a gentle stroll will allow you to explore at leisure.

The town's general store now sells postcards and other memorabilia

You can see how the miners lived in this reconstructed dwelling

Visit all the sights at Pilgrim's Rest under the cover of the Zeederberg's canopy

OUT AND ABOUT

THE MAGOEBASKLOOF AND BEYOND

This part of Limpopo province is superb touring country. This circular drive leads through the mist-wreathed hills and magical forests at the edge of the northern Drakensberg Escarpment to the realm of the Rain Queen, and then back along the lush Letaba River valley.

THE DRIVE

Distance: 190km (118 miles)
Allow: 2 days (can be done in 1 day)
Start/end at: Haenertsburg

★ **From Haenertsburg**, an attractive village garlanded with azaleas and cherry trees, take the R71 which runs next to the village. Drive northeast for 34km (21 miles) towards Tzaneen Dam Nature Reserve, a route that leads over and down the Magoebaskloof mountains (highest point 1,370m/4,500ft).

❶ The Magoebaskloof (▷ 136) was named after a local 19th-century chieftain called Makgoba, a rebel who refused to pay taxes to the white settler authority and led his people into the then remote reaches of this mountainous region. After a year in hiding he was tracked down by a government-contracted Swazi *impi* (regiment) and then beheaded.

The road passes through countryside that is largely given over to pine plantations but still has some fine stands of natural forest; tree species include giant redwoods, ironwoods and yellowwoods. About 25km (15.5 miles) along the road are the Debegeni Falls.

❷ The crystal-clear pool of the Debegeni Falls, on the Ramadipa River, is believed to be the home of revered spirits. Join them in a swim, or you can walk across the top of the waterfall, but be careful—the rocks are slippery.

Continue on the R71 to the intersection with the R36 and turn north; the short southern stretch would take you into Tzaneen (see below). The nearby Tzaneen Dam reserve is a popular and attractive recreational area, fringed by broad acres of closely packed pine trees. Drive the 14km (8.5 miles) to Modjadjiskloof.

❸ Madjadjiskloof is a hand-some, leafy village. It was known as Duiwelskloof (meaning Devil's cleft) by the Voortrekkers. Its current name is a homage to the legendary Queen Modjadji (see below).

Continue on the same road beyond Madjadjiskloof, and after 30km (18.5 miles) turn right (east), following the signs to Ga-Modjadji (which is 7km/ 4 miles from the R36). You'll find yourself on a rough dirt road; continue until it forks, and head left up the hillside for about 5km (3 miles).

❹ Ga-Modjadji is the domain of the celebrated Rain Queen of the Lobedu people, a mysterious figure, said to be immortal. The English author H. Rider Haggard based the title character of his book *She* (1886) on Modjadji, the runaway princess who was the original Rain Queen; even the great Zulu king Shaka was said to fear her powers. The image is perhaps more romantic than today's reality: The present Rain Queen lives in a modern hillside house in the village. However, in times of drought many farmers—both black and white—still arrive on her doorstep to call on her rain-making powers.

A short way up past the village, on the left, is a forest of cycads. These palm-like plants covered the earth when it was the realm of the dinosaurs. There are pleasant picnic spots, four short walking trails, and (if it's a mist-free day) splendid views towards the Lowveld.

Drive back the way you came and on to Tzaneen (▷ 138).

❺ Tzaneen is the region's largest town, with an attractively tropical feel to it. Tzaneen was the research headquarters of Dr. Siegfried Annecke (1895–1955), the scientist who pioneered research in the field of tropical medicine, and whose work on the 'fever belt' led to the virtual eradication of malaria.

From Tzaneen, take the Agatha Road circuit—signposted from the middle of town—to the south.

❻ The Agatha Road is a scenic route that loops through the New Agatha State Forest for 33km (20.5 miles). A lesser road leading off the main track will bring you to the start of the popular Rooikat Nature Trail, which begins at the plantation's Forest Station, on the right about 1km (0.6 miles) after passing the turning signposted to Granny Dot's Country Spot. Another winds its way to a hotel called the Coach House. This access route has quite a history: It was once used by the old Zeederberg coaches in their rough haul between Polokwane (Pietersburg) and across the Letaba River to the fever-ridden Leydsdorp mining camp in the Lowveld. The original inn was used as a staging post; it's now the only five-star establishment in Limpopo province.

Head back to Tzaneen on the second part of the circular route (which runs north), and then take the open road back to Haenertsburg. This time, however, follow the alternative southern route, the R528, which follows the Great Letaba River valley for 34km (21 miles).

❼ George's Valley, the southernmost extremity of the Letaba River valley is a memorably lovely stretch of the route. The views here are of the Wolfberg massif and the lush, subtropical fruit plantations of the Letaba Valley. Flowering bushes and occasional picnic seats and tables (fashioned from rock) fringe the road.

OUT AND ABOUT

The lush landscape around Tzaneen

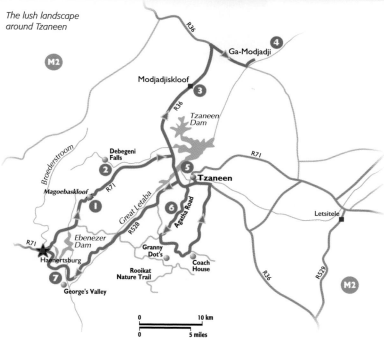

Spring and autumn are probably the best time for the drive. High summer (November through to January) can be hot and humid, and late afternoon is often shattered by violent thunderstorms.

WHERE TO EAT

Picasso's
Haenertsburg 0730
Tel 015-2764724
A good spot for late breakfast or early lunch; try the pancakes.
🕐 Sun–Thu 8.30–4.30, Fri–Sat 8.30am–10.30pm
🚗 Just off the R71

Pekoe View Tea Garden
Pekoe Tea Estate, Magoebaskloof
Tel 015-3054999
Salads, sandwiches and delicious baked goodies, washed down with tea.
🕐 Daily 10–5
🚗 Just out of Haenertsburg, off the R71, 9km (5.5 miles) from Tzaneen

Swimming at the foot of Debegeni Falls

THE EASTERN HIGHLANDS

This trip through the eastern Free State takes in enormous eroded sandstone formations, golden fields of wheat and sunflowers, and fruit orchards (flowering or heavy with fruit, depending on the season), with the lofty Maluti Mountains of Lesotho serving as a backdrop.

THE DRIVE

Distance: 350km (220 miles)	
Allow: 2 days	
Start at: Harrismith	
End at: Ladybrand	

★ **Begin the drive at Harrismith.** The first stretch takes you 52km (32 miles) southwest on the R712 past Phuthaditjhaba.

❶ Phuthaditjhaba is a bustling town, genuinely African in atmosphere. During the apartheid era it served as capital of the Qwa Qwa 'national state', one of the homeland territories (or Bantustans) supposed to give tribal groups a certain degree of independence (this was the territory of the Balokwa and Bakwena tribes). Phuthaditjhaba means 'meeting place of nations' in the Sotho language.

The road takes you on to the rugged spaces of the Qwa Qwa National Park, which you reach via a lesser continuation of the R712. Follow the signs to 'Mountain Resort'.

❷ As you enter Qwa Qwa National Park, magnificent views unfold on your right—of Lesotho's spectacular Maluti Mountains and, in due course, of the gigantic basalt buttress called the Sentinel. Stop at the parking area beneath this massif and walk the 300m (330 yards) to a viewpoint that takes in the grandeur of the Drakensberg's Royal Natal National Park (▷ 120–122),

A weaver demonstrates his skill at Basotho Cultural Village

the Eastern Buttress and Devil's Tooth. As a detour, there's a path that leads from the viewpoint to a sequence of chain ladders that help you climb the Sentinel.

From the Park, return through Phuthaditjhaba and, after 7km (4 miles), turn left on the R712 going west, following the signs to the Golden Gate National Park (the park's eastern entrance is 23km/14 miles from Phuthaditjhaba) and to Clarens.

❸ The Golden Gate National Park is famous for its huge, dramatically sculpted rock formations that vary markedly in coloration: Sandstone and iron oxides have combined to create an eye-catching array of reds, oranges, yellows and golden browns. The Golden Gate itself is the narrow, cliff-flanked valley you drive

through on your way to the reception and information office. Think about breaking your journey here: The park is worth exploring at leisure, and it has two pleasant rest camps (▷ 292). Otherwise, the main road passes right through the middle of the park, and from it you have excellent views of the rock formations.

Continue west towards Clarens. On your left, you'll see the sign to the Basotho Cultural Village (▷ 140), worth visiting for the insight it gives—albeit rather a sanitized one—into Basotho customs, beliefs and lifestyle.

❹ Clarens (▷ 140) is arguably one of South Africa's most attractive villages, especially in autumn when the Lombardy poplars turn a deep gold. A willow-fringed stream runs through it, and it is overlooked by a massive rock feature known as the Titanic.

Drive on along the valley of the Little Caledon River on the R711, following the signs to Fouriesburg (36km/22 miles). Pass through it and continue on the R26 west to Ficksburg (55km/34 miles). On the way to Ficksburg, you'll see signs off the R26 to Rustler's Valley, the venue for one of South Africa's biggest alternative music festivals (▷ 215).

❺ Ficksburg (▷ 141) sits amid lush farmlands. The town is particularly associated with cherries (it hosts an annual Cherry Festival), and in spring

OUT AND ABOUT

the town's streets and surrounding countryside are awash with frothy oceans of cherry blossoms.

The final run (73km/45 miles) takes you to Ladybrand via Clocolan, a tiny town almost overwhelmed by enormous grain silos. You may pass weavers working the local sheep's wool and angora into tapestries.

6 Your final port of call is Ladybrand (▷ 146–147). The town is the last on the main road east into Lesotho, and it has recently enjoyed unusual prosperity, attracting spin-off benefits from

massive investment in the Lesotho Highlands Water Project (▷ 168).

WHEN TO GO
The countryside is especially attractive in the short spring (usually late October) and in autumn (February and March), when the fruit trees and fields are either in blossom or about to be harvested. Golden Gate Park gets large numbers of visitors and is best avoided during local school holidays. Winters can be uncomfortably cold.

The heart of the Golden Gate National Park

WHERE TO EAT
The Posthouse
On the main street, just beyond the square, Clarens
Tel 058-2561534
The town's old post office is now a family restaurant with a mini zoo and an excellent children's menu. For adults there are steaks, quiches and salads.
🕐 Daily 12–3, also Mon–Tue, Thu–Sat 7pm–midnight
🍴 L R55, D R90, Wine R30

This drive takes you right through the Golden Gate National Park

MAGALIESBERG MEANDER

The modest range of hills to the west of Johannesburg and Pretoria is valued by jaded city-dwellers for its tranquillity, the beauty of its landscapes, its secluded hideaways and the lakeside pleasures of a spacious dam. This drive circles the uplands; the main route is in excellent condition, but along the way are some rougher roads that probe their way into the heart of the Magaliesberg.

THE DRIVE	
Distance: 240km (150 miles)	
Allow: 1 day	
Start/end at: Pretoria (Tshwane)	

★ **Set off from Pretoria**, taking the N4 highway that leads along the northern side of the Magaliesberg to Rustenburg, a run of 105km (65 miles). At the time of writing parts of the highway were being upgraded: The first segment is a toll road, but it is possible to use the alternative R27 along some of the route. With the hills on your left, the scenery along this stretch is pleasing. If you feel like a break, you could stop at Buffelspoort Dam—look for the turning about two-thirds of the way along, or 25km (15 miles) before Rustenburg; the resort development, with boating, fishing and picnic areas, is on the reservoir's western shores.

❶ **Rustenburg** (▷ 164) is a medium-sized country town and the hub of a flourishing farming region that produces large crops of wheat, maize, cotton, tobacco, fruit, vegetables and cut flowers. With plenty of rain and an average nine hours of sunshine a day throughout the year, Rustenburg's streets are a blaze of flowering trees and shrubs, including jacaranda,

The striking lilac-blue jacaranda, found in Rustenburg

hibiscus, poinciana and billows of purple bougainvillea. There's industrial wealth too: Nearby are two of the world's biggest platinum mines. Kgaswane Mountain Reserve (▷ 154), in the hills above the town, has good walking opportunities.

Leave Rustenburg on the R24/30, which swings to the southwest around Olifantsnek Dam and then, as the R24, makes its way southeast. There are broad views from Olifantsnek Pass. The 3,000ha (7,400-acre) reservoir irrigates citrus and tobacco plantations, and the dam wall captures the rush of the Hex River as it races through the pass. Just before you reach the tiny village of Maanhaarrand, 30km (18.5 miles) farther along the R24, turn left, and follow the road to the Mountain Sanctuary Park.

❷ The Mountain Sanctuary Park, whose owners are strict conservationists, is a private reserve covering 960ha (2,370 acres). It has picnic spots and a simple rest camp, and from here some attractive walks lead through the hilly countryside. There's a small entrance fee for day visitors.

Return to the R24 for just over 8km (5 miles) and turn left onto the R560 (signposted Hekpoort). After another 7km (4 miles) you'll see, a short distance to your left, a feature named Nooitgedacht, which is the Magaliesberg's highest hill (1,851m/6,071ft above sea level).

❸ Nooitgedacht has its place in the history of the Second Anglo-Boer War. It was on the hill's lower slopes that, in December 1900, a large British force found itself trapped in a gorge by Boer commandos, and lost 637 of its men before making its escape.

Follow the R560 along the valley of the Magalies River, passing the village of Skeerpoort on your right. Just beyond this point the road branches to become the R512. Follow the signs to Hartbeespoort Dam (▷ 154), a major reservoir fed by the Crocodile and Magalies rivers.

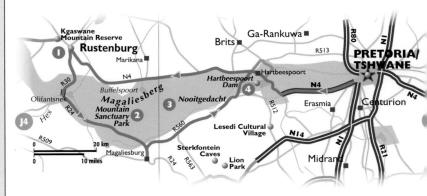

OUT AND ABOUT

4 The Hartbeespoort Dam is a well-developed recreational area, popular for watersports and fishing. Although it can get crowded, it has some peaceful corners and there are pleasant views from the perimeter road. There's a cableway that runs for 1km (0.6 miles) above the dam, from where there are superb views of the surrounding countryside.

The R512 intersects with the R27 11.3km (6 miles) from Skeerpoort. Turn right (east) on the R27, passing through Schoemansville and Hartbeespoort (the area's focal points) to rejoin the N4 highway and head back to Pretoria.

WHEN TO GO

Spring (September and October) and autumn (February and March) are the best months for visiting. Days in the middle of summer can be uncomfortably hot, with afternoon thunderstorms. Avoid this trip on weekends, when the roads are especially busy.

WHERE TO EAT

Ilhanti Country Restaurant and Pub
Buffelspoort Dam
Tel 014-5340056
Family-type steakhouse, also serving seafood. Ttraditional pot cooking in outdoor courtyard on Sundays.
🕐 Tue–Sun 10am–11pm

Taking to the water at Hartbeespoort Dam

PLACES TO VISIT

Mountain Sanctuary Park
Rustenburg
☎ 014-5332050
🕐 Dawn–dusk; book in advance as visitor numbers are strictly controlled

Hartbeespoort Dam Information Shop
Next to the curio market
www.hartbeespoortonline.co.za
☎ 012-2532160
🕐 Tue–Sun 10–5

Tobacco is one of the main crops grown in Rustenburg

OUT AND ABOUT

NORTHERN NAMAKWA

The northern half of Namakwa (Namaqualand) is a region of heat-hazed and often bleak semi-desert. But in parts the rugged terrain is spectacular, with a harsh beauty, and in spring the landscape is transformed by great carpets of wild desert flowers.

THE DRIVE

Distance:	230km (143 miles)
Allow:	1 day
Start/end at:	Springbok

★ **Start the drive at Springbok**, the biggest town and commercial focus for this vast, sparsely populated region. The town sits astride the N7 highway, which leads north all the way from Cape Town to the Namibian border.

❶ Much of Springbok's history is linked to the copper industry. Copper was worked by the Nama folk well before the colonial era, and the first modern mine was sunk in 1852.

Drive east along Voortrekker Street; turn right at the 'Airport' sign, then left just before the airport. Continue for another 6km (3.5 miles), following the 'Goegap' signs, to reach the Goegap Nature Reserve (the total distance from Springbok is 15km/9 miles).

❷ The Goegap Nature Reserve is renowned for its floral wealth (it has almost 600 different plant species) and displays of wild flowers after the brief spring rains. The reserve is an expanse of rough and rugged terrain covering some 15,000ha (37,000 acres) and is distinguished by huge, dome-like granite boulders. Once within the reserve, you can explore the area via a loop road running for 17km (10.5 miles).

Return to Springbok the way you came and drive back down Voortrekker Street, passing under the N7 bridge. You're now on the R64, which takes you through a stretch of rugged countryside. Just 4km (2.5 miles) along, some way to your right, you'll see Van Der Stel's Koperberg ('Copper Mountain'). To get to it, though, you'll have to follow a bit of a diversion. Drive straight on for another 2km (1.2 miles) until

Keeping out of the sun in Namakwa

you get to the crossroads (6km/4 miles from town); turn right, continue for 500m (550 yards), and turn right again onto gravel and continue south past Carolusburg.

❸ Carolusburg was once a lively mining village. About one kilometre (0.6 miles) beyond it is a parking area, and from there a steep path leads up to the old mineshaft, which has splendid views of the surrounding landscape.

Back in the car, go back to the R64 and cross straight over it, following the winding route to Okiep for nearly 10km (6 miles).

❹ Okiep (the name translates as 'big brackish place') was at one time the region's most important copper mine, operated by skilled miners from the English county of Cornwall, a copper and tin mining region for millennia. The old chimneystack is clearly visible, and you can still see some Cornish-style buildings in the town.

Follow the signs back to the N7; turn south after 2.3km (1.4 miles) and, after another 2.3km, branch off west for Nababeep, 10km (6 miles) from the road.

❺ Nababeep is another town of copper workings and slagheaps. Of particular interest are the old locomotive and its rolling stock, which

were pulled by mules until the water supply problems were overcome. These relics are parked in front of the museum.

Head back out of town, turn right at the sign that reads 'Kleinsee via Spektakel', and right again onto the R355, the gravel road that leads west to the Atlantic

seaboard. The distance from Nababeep to the R355 is 11.5km (7 miles).

The countryside on the next (longer, lonelier and untarred) segment of the circular route is classed, botanically, as Namakwa (Namaqualand) Broken Veld. This comprises low shrublands that embrace, among much else, hardy succulents (notably *euphorbias* and *mesembryanthemums*, or 'vygies'). The monotony of the vegetation cover is relieved by taller species such as evergreen resin trees (*ozoroa*) and Namaqua figs. In the few brief weeks of spring, the plains and hill-slopes are dazzling with their bright floral tapestries. You reach the beginning of the Spektakel Pass after 17.5km (11 miles).

OUT AND ABOUT

6 Spektakel Pass was given its name—or so it's said—in 1685 by Cape Governor Simon van der Stel, who took in the spectacle of the vistas as he passed through in 1685.

Pull off at the viewing site, 3.5km (2 miles) farther on, to soak up the desert views, and then, after another 10km (6 miles), turn left for Komaggas. The good gravel road takes you through the hills and then the mountains, their rocks and cliff faces tinged with lichens and copper salts.

Try to visit when the wild flowers are in bloom (right)

7 Komaggas is something of an oasis. Founded by the London Missionary Society in 1829 for its work among the Nama people, it is blessed by a strong-flowing spring and its environs are refreshingly green.

From Komaggas the road runs west, then sweeps south and east to the Messelpad.

8 The Messelpad, or 'masonry road'—a reference to the drystone reinforcing walls that line its trickier stretches—is a tortuous route, corrugated in a few places but perfectly negotiable. It dates back to the 1860s, when it served as the route along which wagonloads of

copper were transported on their way to the sea at Hondeklip Bay.

The driving distance between Komaggas and the road is 34km (21 miles). At the 26km (16 miles) mark you'll begin to negotiate the Wilderperdehoek ('wild horses pass'), from which there are grand views across a vastness of empty plains and low hills. The road is very narrow in places but in generally good condition. It winds through the uplands, eventually emerging into a kindlier countryside of farmlands.

Continue north and then northeast for 25km (15.5 miles) until you rejoin the N7 highway. From here, it's a straight run back to Springbok.

Taking in views of the flower-covered slopes

WHEN TO GO

The flowers bloom for three or perhaps four weeks in the short spring period (September to October). Their appearance and lifespan, and the places where the best displays are to be seen, depend on the volume and distribution of the winter rains, and on whether or not the hot desert breezes (or 'berg winds') blow.

PLACE TO VISIT

Goegap Nature Reserve
☎ 027-7121880
🕐 Daily 7.30–7
🍴 Snack bar

SWAZILAND: THE VALLEY OF HEAVEN

This circular drive takes you from Swaziland's capital, Mbabane, through the popular Ezulwini Valley, where the scenery is undulating savannah. Leaving behind the bustle of Swaziland's tourism hub, the drive continues into a region of farmland and forest and up into the relative cool of the highlands.

THE DRIVE

Distance: 120km (75 miles)
Allow: 1 day
Start/end at: Mbabane

★ **Make your way from central Mbabane** (▷ 172) southwest on the route designated 'Western Distributor Road' and then on the MR3, following the signs to the Ezulwini Valley.

This first steep, short and scenically dramatic stretch was once judged (by the Guinness Book of Records) as the world's most dangerous road, but don't worry—its two lanes make it safe enough today. From the crest of the hill, about 2km (1.2 miles) out of town, you can look down on to and over the valley. At the bottom take the old main road (the MR103, signposted Ezulwini and Malkerns).

❶ The Ezulwini Valley (the Valley of Heaven) is the focus of tourism for Swaziland. Hotels, casinos, restaurants and craft shops line the old Ezulwini road. On your right (12km/7.5 miles from Mbabane), signposted off the road, you can get a taste of local culture at the all-singing, all-dancing Swazi Cultural Village (▷ 172) in the Mantenga Nature Reserve, and at the Mantenga Craft Centre, where carvings, fabrics, pottery and jewellery are all for sale.

A striking natural feature of the valley's skyline is the Lugogo massif, also known as Sheba's Breasts, which dominates the area.

A little farther along you'll see the signposted road that leads to the Mlilwane Wildlife Sanctuary.

❷ The Mlilwane Wildlife Sanctuary (▷ 173) consists of 4,500ha (11,000 acres) of once despoiled land that has been admirably restored and restocked with animals.

Fabrics and other local crafts for sale in Mantenga

Mlilwane began as a private enterprise but was eventually donated to the nation in the 1960s. Its cause was enthusiastically taken up by King Sobhuza after a group of his hunters returned from a four-day foray into the game-rich countryside to the northeast bearing just two impala carcasses. If you have the time, Mlilwane makes for an excellent overnight stay.

Continue to the end of the valley, where you'll pass the National Museum (with exhibits illustrating Swazi life and culture), the country's Parliament, and the King Sobhuza II Memorial, all three of them on your left and set back a little from the road. A short distance beyond and to your right is Lobamba.

❸ Lobamba is the royal village, residence of the king and venue of the annual Incwala, an all-male ceremony in which young men bring special offerings to the king. The Swazi king does not inherit the throne from his father, but is always a member of the royal clan, chosen as a young unmarried man with no children. After he is crowned, he may take as many wives as he likes.

Follow the valley road for a further 5km (3 miles) and turn right on the MR18 to nearby Malkerns ❹, which is signposted. It's a standard Swazi country town largely sustained by the surrounding pineapple plantations. There are a number of craft shops en route worth a look, including the well-known Swazi Candles (▷ 220).

The road from Malkerns continues south and then west, passing through farmland and along the reaches of the Great Usutu River. This road then leads into the town of Bhunya, the focus of the region's forestry and timber industries. There is a giant pulp mill here that has provided much-needed income. Pass through the town and take the MR19 north towards Mhlambanyatsi and Mbabane.

❺ The village of Mhlambanyatsi ('the place of swimming buffalos') is in a delightful part of the country, full of scenic variety and graced by huge and handsome pine plantations. The village itself has nothing special to offer, but there are some rewarding destinations in the wider area, among them the Forester's Arms (▷ 269). This inn, about 12km (7 miles) from Bhunya, stands among the trees in the cool high- lands and is renowned for its sociability (signposted from the MR19).

From here, it's a straight run on the MR19 back to Mbabane, 34km (22 miles) from Bhunya.

WHEN TO GO

Summer days in the Ezulwini Valley can be stifling, and afternoon thunderstorms may spoil your drive, but this is the time that the countryside is at its lush best. It's cooler on the higher ground north of Malkerns. Winter nights and early mornings are often chilly.

OUT AND ABOUT

There is a variety of trails through the Mlilwane Wildlife Sanctuary

WHERE TO EAT

Malandela's
Tel 528-3115/418-3115
Good meals and snacks, including excellent chicken and mushroom pancakes.
🕐 Mon–Sat 12–3, 6–9, Sun 12–3
🚌 On the Malkerns road (MR18), next to the market

Calabash
Tel 416-1187
German and Austrian dishes served in one of the best restaurants in the country.
🕐 Daily 12–3, 6–11
🚌 Close to Timbali Lodge, MR103, Ezulwini Valley

PLACES TO VISIT

Mantenga Craft Centre
🕐 Daily 8–5
🚌 Just off Ezulwini Valley (signposted)

Swazi Candles
www.swazicandles.com
☎ 528-3219
🕐 Daily 8–4.45
🚌 1km (0.6 miles) from intersection between M19 and Ezulwini Valley, towards Malkerns

The Swazi Spa Health & Beauty Studio
☎ 416-1164
🚌 400m (436 yards) from turning for Royal Swazi Hotel, MR103, Ezulwini Valley

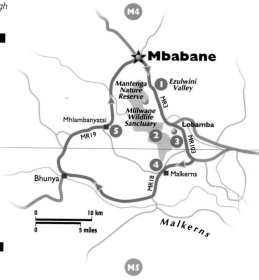

Learning about local culture at the Swazi Cultural Village

OUT AND ABOUT

Many of South Africa's key attractions are often visited as part of a special-interest tour by visitors. While wildlife and culture are the main focuses of the most popular tours, other areas such as wine or adventure sports are becoming increasingly popular.

CULTURE AND HISTORY

DAVID RATTRAY
Tel 034-6421843
www.fugitivesdrift.com
The leading expert on the Battlefields region leads stirring tours of the battlefields, providing a fascinating glimpse of the area's history.

GRASSROUTE TOURS
Tel 021-7061006
www.grassroutetours.com
This Cape Town operator specializes in half- and full-day township tours and visits to District Six. This company works with the communities it visits, with a percentage of its profits going back to the townships.

KARABO TOURS
Tel 011-8805099
karabotours@iafrica.com
Soweto tours lasting four hours, with guides who were active in the anti-apartheid struggle. Historic Pretoria tours and visits to Lesedi Cultural Village also arranged.

SPORTS AND ADVENTURE

DOWNHILL ADVENTURES
Tel 021-4220388
www.downhilladventures.com
Leading Cape Town adventure sports operator Downhill rents out mountain bikes and organizes bike tours, surfing lessons and sand-boarding around the Western Cape.

KALAHARI ADVENTURE CENTRE
Tel 054-4510218
www.kalahari.co.za
Based close to the Augrabies Falls, this operator offers a range of rafting trips along the Gariep (Orange) River and adventure tours to the Kgalagadi Transfrontier Park.

STORMSRIVER ADVENTURES
Tel 042-2811836
www.stormsriver.com
A great many adventure tours are on offer along the Garden Route, from abseiling (rappelling) in Tsitsikamma National Park to scuba diving

Diving can be organized as part of a tour, as can many other adventure sports

off the coast or black-water tubing on Storms River.

SWAZI TRAILS
Tel 268-4162180
www.swazitrails.co.sz
The best-organized adventure operator in Swaziland, offering white-water rafting trips, safari tours around all the national parks, and arts and crafts trails throughout the country.

WILDLIFE

SPURWING
Tel 011-6736197
www.spurwingtourism.com
Top-end safaris specializing in small-group three- to four-day Kruger tours, where guests stay in private lodges and are transported around the park in open 4WD safari vehicles.

STRELITZIA TOURS
Tel 031-2672273/4
www.strelitziatours.com
Wildlife tours around Hluhluwe-Imfolozi Game Reserve and St. Lucia wetlands, as well as a guided drives of the Battlefields.

TRANSFRONTEIRS
Tel 015-793 3816
www.transfrontiers.com
Exhilarating three- or four-day walking safaris, combined with

night-time game drives. Guests sleep in tented wilderness camps, and spend the day tracking game with armed rangers. Tours depart three times a week from Pretoria, Johannesburg or Nelspruit.

WAGON TRAILS
Tel 011-9078063
www.wagontrails.co.za
Budget tours of Kruger National Park by mini-bus from Johannesburg or Pretoria and camping within Kruger. Trips last three or four days.

WINE

EASY RIDER WINE TOURS
Tel 021-8864651
stumble@iafrica.com
Very popular day-long budget wine tours from Stellenbosch. Tours take in five wine estates and include lunch and cheese-tasting.

VINEYARD VENTURES
Tel 021-4348888
www.vineyardventures.co.za
Based in Cape Town, this respected wine tour operator tailor-makes tours around the Winelands (know as 'sipping safaris'), focusing on a handful of top estates and including excellent meals.

OUT AND ABOUT

This chapter lists places to eat and places to stay, broken down by region, then alphabetically by town.

Eating and Staying

EATING OUT IN SOUTH AFRICA

South Africa has an abundance of fresh produce, from the fantastic variety of fish along the coast to the exotic fruit plantations of the northeast. The country—particularly the cities—has undergone something of a culinary revolution and South Africa is emerging as a gastronomic hotspot.

Cooking boerewors *(left); dining alfresco at Selati Lodge, Sabi Sabi (middle); a roast (right)*

WHAT TO EAT AND WHERE

● Cape Malay cooking is found in Cape Town and is the regional cuisine originating from the Cape Malay community, with an interesting blend of spicy curries softened with coconut milk and fruit. Desserts include *malva* pudding, a sticky sponge made with jam. Although there are surprisingly few Cape Malay restaurants, some of the more popular dishes such as *bobotie*, a sweet-spicy dish of minced beef, are hugely popular and served in a number of mainstream restaurants.

● The Indian influence in KwaZulu-Natal means that the best curries are found in Durban. One of the most popular take-out meals is *bunny chow*, a half-loaf of bread with the middle scooped out and filled with curry—the scooped out bread is used as a 'spoon' to soak up the sauce.

● You'll find good seafood along all of South Africa's coasts and game fish such as swordfish and fresh tuna are becoming more popular everywhere. Close to the border with Mozambique look out for delicious Mozambique prawns.

● Afrikaner cooking is much in the mainstream of South African cuisine. Staples throughout the country include *biltong* (dried, salted strips of meat) and *boerewors* (a strong, spicy sausage) usually grilled on a *braai* (barbecue).

● Restaurants vary wildly in quality and service, depending largely on where you are. In most small towns, your choice will be limited to branches of one of the South African steak-house chains, such as Spur or Saddles. Don't be put off, however, as these offer good standards of steak and grills.

A bright menu board outside Mozzarella's in Pretoria

CAFÉS

Many of the places that are called cafés are not the equivalent of a café in Europe or north America. A café in South Africa tends to refer to a small store selling soft drinks, magazines and a selection of food items.

BRAAIS

Braais (barbecues) are the most ubiquitous Afrikaner influence you'll find, and are incredibly popular throughout South Africa. Every picnic

EATING

spot, camping site or rest area has at least one permanent grate, and cooking on a *braai* is seen as something of an art form.

MEAT AND VEGETABLES

- South Africans are big meat-eaters. Meat is almost always of a high standard wherever you are, and you'll be hard pressed to find a menu that doesn't feature steak. Lamb, especially Karoo lamb, is delicious.
- Don't miss trying some of South Africa's game. Ostrich is the most widespread, tasting much like steak (and served similarly), but with a far lower

Black Label, Castle and Windhoek. Maheu, home-brewed beer made from sorghum or maize, is widely drunk by the African population. It has a thick head, is very potent and is not very palatable to the uninitiated. Bitter is harder to come by, although a good local variety is brewed at Mitchell's Brewery in Knysna and Cape Town, and found at good outlets along the Garden Route (▷ 80).

- No liquor may be sold on Sundays except in licensed restaurants with meals. Liquor stores or off-licences are known as bottle stores. These are usually open Monday to Friday 8–6 and

Egg and bacon quiche (left); fish and pasta dishes (middle); a poached pear dessert (right)

fat content. Other game you're likely to come across is springbok, kudu, crocodile and warthog. The big cities have restaurants specializing in exotic game.

- Vegetarians will find their choice greatly limited. South Africa is a meat-loving country and menus rarely include anything but the most basic dishes for vegetarians. Away from the major cities, you'll have to make do with salads, pasta and chips (fries). Cape Town, Pretoria and Johannesburg have a better range for vegetarians, with some trendy meat-free restaurants. Catering for yourself is often an easier option.

ALCOHOLIC DRINKS

- South Africa has made its mark on the international wine scene, and produces a wide range of excellent wines. The Winelands (▷ 90–95) in the Western Cape have the best-known labels, but there are a number of other wine routes dotted around the country.
- John Platter, one of the country's best-known wine critics, has highlighted the following as some of the finest wines on the market (from www.platteronline.com): Cape Point Vineyards Semillon 2003, Hamilton Russell Vineyards Chardonnay 2003 and Jean Daneel Wines Signature Chenin Blanc 2003.
- The prestigious Veritas awards were given in late 2004 to Cloof Crucible Shiraz 2003 and the Boland Cabernet Sauvignon Reserve No. 1 2002.
- South Africa's *Grape* magazine has claimed that Kanonkop Estate, Vergelegen, Neil Ellis Wines, Hamilton-Russell Vineyards and Rustenburg Wines are some of the country's consistently fine estates.
- There is a good range of locally produced beers, as well as imports. Major labels include

Saturday 8.30–2. Supermarkets do not sell beer or spirits; they stop selling wine at 8pm, and don't sell alcohol on Sundays.

NON-ALCOHOLIC DRINKS

- Tap water is chemically treated and safe to drink. Bottled mineral water is available at all restaurants, snack bars and supermarkets, as are international soft drinks such as Coke or Fanta.
- There is also a good range of fruit juices available at most outlets—the Ceres and Liquifruit brands are the best varieties.
- Another popular non-alcoholic drink is rooibos tea, literally red bush tea. This is a caffeine-free tea with a smoky taste, usually served with sugar or honey.

SUPERMARKETS

If you are planning to camp or go self-catering, then you will be able to get most of your supplies at super-markets. They have a similar selection to those in Europe—meat is often cheaper, but fresh fruit and vegetables can be expensive. South Africa is, however, a great source of fresh fruit and local produce such as apples in Ceres or pineapples along the Wild Coast should be good. Main supermarkets include Pick 'n' Pick, OK Bazaars, Woolworths and Shoprite Checkers.

PRICES AND TIMES

● Eating out continues to be very good value, despite the strengthening rand. A three-course meal in a mid-price range restaurant will rarely cost you more than R150 per person, including the wine.

● Service isn't usually included in a bill. If you find the service is good, the standard amount to tip is 10–15 per cent.

● Outside the major tourist places, people eat early and many kitchens close around 9pm, although this is later at the weekend. Some restaurants are often closed on Sunday evenings, when hotel dining rooms or fast food outlets may well be the only choices for eating out. In cities, restaurants are open throughout the day and kitchens shut around 10–11pm.

MORE INFORMATION

A good starting point for choosing a restaurant is buying the latest edition of *Eat Out*, which features South Africa's best choice of restaurants. The magazine costs around R25 and is available in newsagents and tourist offices. There are restaurant listings on the following pages, as well as bars and cafés in What to Do (▷ 175–220).

Pastries to go (left); famous Knysna oysters (middle); fine dining at a luxury game park (right)

MENU READER

atjar mango relish served with Cape Malay curries

biltong air-dried, cured meat, usually made from beef or venison
biryanis rice-based curry
bobotie spiced, minced beef cooked with dried fruit and a savoury custard topping
boerekos Afrikaner country cooking
boerewors spicy beef sausage
braai barbecue
bredie meat and vegetable stew
bunny chow Durban curry served in a hollowed-out loaf of bread

cool drink soft (non-alcoholic) drink

dop drink (alcoholic)

frikkadels meat balls or patties

koeksisters deep-fried plaited doughnuts, soaked in syrup
konfyt candied fruit

malva pudding a sticky sponge made with jam
melktert custard flan dessert
mielie maize

monkey gland sauce piquant sauce of onion, tomato, fruit chutney and Worcestershire sauce, designed for meat (no monkey)

pap (or mieliepap) stiff, savoury maize porridge
peri-peri Portuguese chilli flavouring

potjiekos stew cooked in a cast-iron cauldron over hot coals

rusks dried pieces of bread

sambal spicy relish served with Cape Malay curries
samp mashed maize, usually served with beans
snoek local fish, often served as pâté
sosaties skewered meat; kebab

umqombothi African beer made from maize

waterblommetjie bredie mutton stew made with indigenous water-flowers

EATING

RESTAURANT CHAIN CHART

Name	Description	Website	Price (3 courses)	Kids' menu	Take out
Bimbos	24-hour burgers	www.bimbos.co.za	R30	✔	✔
Nandos	Mozambique-style chicken	www.nandos.co.za	R35	✔	✔
Ocean Basket	High standards of seafood	www.oceanbasket.co.za	R80	✔	✔
Panarottis	Pizza and pasta	www.panarottis.co.za	R60	✔	✔
Primi Piatti	Stylish pizza and pasta	www.primi-piatti.com	R100	–	–
Saddles	American-style steak ranch	www.saddles.co.za	R65	✔	–
Spur	Steak ranch	www.spur.co.za	R110	✔	–
Steers	Flame-grilled burgers	www.steers.co.za	R30	✔	✔

CAPE PENINSULA

This region has experienced a growth in excellent restaurants, strong on Cape Malay and seafood dishes (▷ 256), and all at incredibly good prices. Cape Town in particular likes to eat out, a fact that is reflected in its multitude of restaurants—and the extent to which they get packed out. Summer is obviously the most popular time for this, and the Victoria and Alfred Waterfront, perhaps the city's most popular eating area, gets very busy. Reserving in advance is often a good idea.

PRICES AND SYMBOLS

The restaurants are listed alphabetically (excluding The) by town or area, then by name. The prices given are for a two-course lunch (L) and a three-course dinner (D) for one person, without drinks. The wine price is for the least expensive bottle. See page 2 for a key to the symbols.

CAMPS BAY AND ATLANTIC SEABOARD

BLUES
Victoria Road, Camps Bay 8005
Tel 021-4382040
www.blues.co.za

Blues is one of the most popular restaurants in the Cape, with superb views over Camps Bay and a Californian-style menu. It serves good, stylish food with meat main dishes such as seared duck breast, but the main reason for coming here is the seafood—the oyster platters are famous.
◉ Daily noon–11.30pm
🍴 L R160, D R200, Wine R50

CHARIOTS
107 Main Road, Green Point 8005
Tel 021-4345427
Chariots is an excellent Italian restaurant serving traditional and innovative pasta and risotto dishes, such as curried butternut ravioli. There's also a range of delicate salads and meat dishes. The feel is low-key and relaxed.
◉ Mon–Sat 8am–9.30pm, Sun 8–3
🍴 L R60, D R90, Wine R45

SPECIAL IN CAMPS BAY

THE CODFATHER
Corner of Geneva Drive and The Drive, Camps Bay 8005
Tel 021-4380782
This stylish, laid-back place is a breath of fresh air compared to some of the area's smarter restaurants. The Codfather offers a range of superbly fresh seafood; there's no menu—the waiter takes you to a counter and you pick and choose whatever you like the look of. Everything is served grilled with vegetables, rice or chips. There's also a revolving sushi bar, serving fresh sushi and sashimi.
◉ Daily 2–11
🍴 L R80, D R180, Wine R45

THE NOSE
Cape Quarter, Dixon Street, Green Point 8005
Tel 021-4252200
www.thenose.co.za
This wine bar and restaurant has tables spilling on to the trendy new Waterkant piazza. A wide range of local and international wines is accompanied by excellent seafood (the mussels in white wine and cream are especially good), steaks and handmade burgers. There's an inviting interior, and if you are not feeling too hungry, dishes can be ordered in small portions.
◉ Daily 10.30am–11pm
🍴 L R75, D R112, Wine R52

OCEAN BLUE
Victoria Road
Tel 021-4389838
You're sure to be made welcome at this friendly seafood restaurant, on the road that overlooks the beach. The seafood is excellent, especially the grilled prawns and butterfish kebabs, and the daily specials are well worth trying.
☎ Daily 9.30am–11pm
🍴 L R80, D R100, Wine R48

CAPE TOWN

THE AFRICA CAFÉ
Heritage Square, 108 Shortmarket Street, City Centre 8001
Tel 021-4220221
www.africacafe.co.za
A trendy and tourist-friendly restaurant offering an excellent introduction to the continent's cuisines. The menu is a set 'feast' and includes 10 dishes that rove around Africa, from Kenyan patties to Cape Malay mango chicken curry and Egyptian dips. The price includes the opportunity to order more of the dishes you like, as well as coffee and dessert. Good value if you're hungry, with excellent service.
◉ Mon–Sat 6.30pm–11pm
🍴 D R125, Wine R60

BIESMIELLAH
2 Upper Wale Street, Bo-Kaap 8001
Tel 021-4230850
The Biesmiellah is one of the better known and well established Malay restaurants in the Bo-Kaap area. This family-run place serves a delicious selection of dishes and is the place to come for sweet lamb and chicken curries and sticky puddings. No alcohol is served.
◉ Mon–Sat 12–3, 6–10
🍴 L R70, D R90

CAPE COLONY
Mount Nelson Hotel, 76 Orange Street, Gardens 8001
Tel 021-4831850
One of Cape Town's finest restaurants is in the impressive Mount Nelson (▷ 277), Cape Town's premier colonial-era hotel. The dining room has an old-world charm and the service is impeccable. Dishes are a mix of traditional British (think good roasts) and Cape classics, such as Bo-Kaap chicken and prawn curry, or contemporary seafood dishes. There's live jazz most evenings. Don't miss the gloriously old-school high teas on the outside terrace every afternoon.
◉ Daily 6.30pm–10.30pm
🍴 D R195, Wine R75

EATING

FIVE FLIES

14 Keerom Street, City Centre 8001
Tel 021-4244442
Despite the unappetizing name, this is a long-standing, popular restaurant and is a preferred haunt of lawyers and judges. It has a string of rooms with black-and-white checked floors, high ceilings and crisp white linen. Well-prepared traditional food, such as steak pie or grilled fish, is served.

🕐 Daily 11am–midnight
🍽 L R90, D R150, Wine R45

MAMA AFRICA

178 Long Street, City Centre 8001
Tel 021-4261017
This popular restaurant and bar was one of the first in Cape Town to serve 'traditional' African dishes. It's a big hit with tourists, and the dishes, most of which focus on exotic game (such as crocodile

kebabs, springbok steak and ostrich fillet) are tasty, served with *pap* (maize porridge) and beans. Although it's a little overpriced and service is slow, the lively atmosphere and great live music make it a fun place. The focal point of the restaurant is a bright green carved snake-shaped bar.

🕐 Mon–Sat 7pm–midnight
🍽 D R150, Wine R50

MR. PICKWICKS

158 Long Street, City Centre 8001
Tel 021-4242696
For the best foot-long sandwiches and ice-cream milk shakes in town, head to trendy Mr. Pickwicks. Healthy salads and large pasta portions are popular choices with the young, fashionable clientele, but be prepared for loud techno music, especially in the early evening when an after-work crowd congregates for pre-clubbing drinks. It is also the place to buy tickets

SAIGON

Corner of Camp and Kloof Streets, Gardens 8001
Tel 021-4247669
This Kloof Street eatery serves superb Vietnamese cuisine in a prominent building overlooking the busy street. It's very popular, thanks to its swift and friendly service and delicious fresh dishes—specials include crystal spring rolls, barbecued duck and caramelized pork with black pepper. Be sure that you reserve in advance.

🕐 Daily 12–2.30, 6–10.30
🍽 L R80, D R120, Wine R50

to Cape Town's major club nights and gigs.

🕐 Mon–Sat 8am–late (2 or 3am),
Sun 8–7
🍽 From R40

PRIMI PIATTI

Greenmarket Square, City Centre 8001
Tel 021-4247466
This lively spot overlooks the square from vast windows. The original restaurant of a hugely popular national chain, Prima Piatti serves superb pizzas, bowls of imaginative pasta and a good range of salads. There's a great, bustling atmosphere, and the young fashionable crowd comes here for the huge portions and reasonable prices. You will also find branches in Camps Bay, Claremont and the Victoria and Alfred Waterfront.

🕐 Mon–Fri 8–6, Sat 8–3
🍽 L R50, Wine R32

YINDEE'S

22 Camp Street, Tamboerskloof 8001
Tel 021-4221012
Yindee's is an excellent Thai restaurant serving authentic spicy curries, stir-fries and soups. The setting is appealing, with a string of rooms in a sprawling Victorian house. Diners sit on cushions at traditional low tables. Service can be slow, but it's always popular, so reserve in advance.

🕐 Mon–Fri 12.30–2.30, 6.30–10.30,
Sat 6.30–10.30
🍽 L R75, D R110, Wine R52

CONSTANTIA

THE GREENHOUSE

Cellars-Hohenhort Hotel,
93 Brommersvlei Road,
Constantia 7806
Tel 021-7942137
www.cellars-hohenort.com
One of two highly rated restaurants at this five-star hotel (▷ 278), set in a pretty conservatory with white wicker furniture. The chef produces top-quality food—mostly modern South African, so expect fresh local fish and game—and divine desserts. There's an excellent wine list to match, making this one of the finest restaurants in the area.

🕐 Daily 7.30am–10pm
🍽 L R140, D R220, Wine R60

FALSE BAY

THE BRASS BELL

By the rail station, Kalk Bay 7975
Tel 021-7885455

For a spectacular setting almost in the waves of False Bay, head to this relaxed pub and bistro—the oven-baked pizzas and fish and chips (fries) are the best. Downstairs gets packed with a young crowd, especially around sunset when they congregate on the outside terrace. The more expensive bistro upstairs serves fresh fish and steak.

🕐 Mon–Fri 12–4, 6–11, Sat–Sun
8am–11pm; pub open all day
🍽 L R40, D R70, Wine R43

EATING

OLYMPIA CAFÉ
134 Main Road, Kalk Bay 7975
Tel 021-7886396
A Kalk Bay institution, this laid-back café serves some of the freshest bread in the Peninsula, plus light lunches (sandwiches crammed with delicious fillings, salads and quiche), fabulous cakes and fresh daily specials, often seafood. There's a relaxed, bustling atmosphere and good service, but expect to have to wait on weekends. The bakery at the back turns into a tiny theatre at night.
🕐 Daily 7am–9pm
🍽 L R40, D R75, Wine R35

HOUT BAY

DUNES
Beach Road, Hout Bay 7806
Tel 021-7901876
This sprawling restaurant overlooks the dunes behind Hout Bay Beach, and is very popular with families. The menu is large and the service is quick, but it's best to stick to simple dishes, like grilled calamari or fish and chips (fries). Reserve in advance on weekends or you will be seated in the courtyard instead of the balcony.
🕐 Daily 9am–11pm
🍽 L R75, D R100, Wine R50

FISH ON THE ROCKS
Harbour Road, beyond Snoekies Market
Tel 021-790001
Try the simple and delicious fresh fish and chips (fries) or deep-fried calamari and prawns at this no frills place, which overlooks the harbour.
☎ Daily 10am–9pm
🍽 L R27, D R60, Wine BYO

SOUTHERN SUBURBS

BARRISTERS GRILL
Corner of Kildare and Main streets, Newlands
Tel 021-6741792
Although the mock-Tudor timber interior of the Barristers Grill is traditional, this is a steakhouse that has moved with the times. During the day it is a trendy café and bistro, with plenty of outdoor tables where you can enjoy a leisurely breakfast or a quick lunch. Vegetarians needn't miss out, as there are also meat-free options.
☎ Mon–Sat 8.30am–11.30pm, Sun 5pm–11pm
🍽 L R90, D R120, Wine R40

DON PEDRO'S
113 Roodebloem Road, Woodstock 7925
Tel 021-4474493
Something of an institution, Don Pedro's is an informal, bustling restaurant, serving huge portions of steaks, Malay curries, pasta and pizza at cheap prices. It's a popular spot and the focal point of the Woodstock community, with more of a mixed crowd than you might find elsewhere in town.
🕐 Daily 8am–late (often as late as 5am)
🍽 L R50, D R72, Wine R35

OBZ CAFÉ
115 Lower Main Road, Observatory 7925
Tel 021-4485555
Obz Café is a large, breezy deli-cum-restaurant, with a long bar, deli counter and tables dotted around the parquet floor. This popular place opens all day for light meals, coffee or cocktails. The tapas, salads and tailor-made sandwiches are good, with larger, main meals served in the evenings. The smoking room next door sometimes hosts live music.
🕐 Dec–end Mar Wed–Mon 8am–9pm; Apr–end Nov Wed–Mon 8am–5pm
🍽 L R60, D R90, Wine R43

VICTORIA AND ALFRED WATERFRONT

BAIA
Top Floor, Victoria Wharf, V & A Waterfront 8001
Tel 021-4210935

This fine seafood restaurant is spread over four terraces with moody, stylish decoration and lighting. The venue is very smart (and the meals relatively expensive) and it has become a huge Cape Town success. Expect delicious seafood dishes following a Mozambique theme, such as spicy beer-baked prawns or grilled crayfish. Some tables have striking views of Table Mountain. Service can be erratic, and you need to reserve in advance.
🕐 Daily 12–3, 7–11
🍽 L R120, D R200, Wine R70

BALDUCCI'S
Victoria Wharf, V & A Waterfront 8001
Tel 021-4216002
www.balduccis.co.za
This popular, elegant Italian restaurant has seats overlooking the harbour. It serves a good choice of pasta dishes, and the main meals range from ostrich steaks and luxury lamb burgers to confit de canard and blackened kingklip (eel-like fish). There is also a sushi bar.
☎ Daily 9am–10.30pm
🍽 L R75, D R135, Wine R60

QUAY FOUR
Quay Four, V & A Waterfront 8001
Tel 021-4192008

Quay Four is one of the most enjoyable restaurants on the Waterfront, with a great setting on a huge deck overlooking the water and the hustle and bustle of the harbour. The main deck has a relaxed pub style, offering simple seafood such as fish and chips (fries) served in frying pans. There are some great vegetarian options and good value platters to be shared. Upstairs is a smarter bistro (evenings only), which also specializes in seafood.
🕐 Daily 9am–11.30pm
🍽 L R75, D R100, Wine R40

EATING

WESTERN CAPE

Some of the best restaurants in the country are found in the Winelands region, many of which are part of the wine estates. Franschhoek has a particularly good reputation, with a number of excellent French restaurants. All meals here are, of course, accompanied by delicious local wines. The Garden Route is famous for its seafood: The meeting of the Indian and Atlantic oceans at Cape Agulhas means there is a wide variety available. Local specials include snoek, crayfish and kingclip. Knysna is also well known for its seafood, especially its excellent oysters, which are cultivated in the lagoon. In smaller towns and villages most hotels and hostels offer meals to non-guests.

PRICES AND SYMBOLS

The restaurants are listed alphabetically (excluding The) by town or area, then by name. The prices given are for a two-course lunch (L) and a three-course dinner (D) for one person, without drinks. The wine price is for the least expensive bottle. See page 2 for a key to the symbols.

CITRUSDAL

PATRICK'S
Voortrekker Street, Citrusdal 7340
Tel 022-9213062

Patrick's has an Irish theme, although the meals and wine are rather more local. Some of the best dishes include tender ostrich steaks and grilled line-fish (fish of the day is usually kingclip), and there's a wide range of steaks. It's a good value, friendly place.
- ☺ Tue–Sat 12–2.30, 7–10.30
- 🍴 L R50, D R80, Wine R28

KNYSNA

O'PESCADOR
Brenton Road, Belvidere, Knysna 6571
Tel 044-3860036
The chef from Mozambique here prepares special dishes from his home country. Among them is *caldo verde* (potato and kale soup with chorizo sausage) soup, *bacalhau* (grilled salt cod) and chicken *peri-peri* (a chilli seasoning). More traditional palates can choose the steak (the chilli

SPECIAL IN KNYSNA

KNYSNA OYSTER CO.
Long Street, Thesen Island, across the causeway from the middle of town, Knysna 6571
Tel 044-3826942
www.oysters.co.za

This restaurant is right next to the oyster farm on Thesen Island. There's a range of seafood on offer, but the restaurant is best known for its famous Knysna oysters, usually washed down with a glass of champagne. It's one of the things you must do while in Knysna.
- ☺ Daily noon–10pm
- 🍴 L R55, D R100, Wine R45

sauce with this dish is optional). The atmosphere is relaxed, and while the food isn't cheap, the quality makes up for it. Reserve in advance during holiday season.
- ☺ Mon–Sat 6.30–11
- 🍴 L R90, D R112, Wine R55

PAQUITAS
George Rex Drive, Knysna 6570
Tel 044-3840408
A relaxed family restaurant serving burgers, grilled fish and calamari, along with a wide selection of pizzas and pasta. The food is family-friendly and it's a good place for a laid-back lunch, but the main reason for coming is the stunning views of The Heads, leading to the open sea beyond.

☺ Daily noon–10pm
🍴 From R30, Wine R54

LAMBERT'S BAY

MUISBOSSKERM
On the main beach
Tel 027-4321017
This extremely successful open-air restaurant offers a wide choice of seafood (the crayfish is particularly good) grilled over a barbecue. Meals last about three hours, and while the food is excellent, during peak periods there may be more than 150 people eating here, so it can become a bit of a scrum.
- ☺ Daily 12–3.30, 6–10
- 🍴 R150 (set price), Wine R45
- ⬛ On the beach, 5km (3 miles) out of town towards Elands Bay

LANGEBAAN

STRANDLOPER
On the beach to the north of town
Tel 022-7722490
www.strandloper.co.za
The casual beach-based Strandloper has acquired near-legendary status and shouldn't be missed if you're in the area. The romantic surroundings of the beach at sunset are enhanced by the rickety wooden tables and light guitar music. The food is cooked on a mammoth seafood *braai* (barbecue). The starter is mussels, and the shells then serve as cutlery for the next courses, which are accompanied in the West Coast tradition by home-made bread and apricot jam. The final course is half a crayfish.

Children get a discount according to their height.
- Daily noon–5
- R150 (set price), BYO wine
- Follow signs for Club Mykonos

MONTAGU

PRESTONS & THOMAS BAINES PUB

17 Bath Street, Montagu 6720
Tel 023-6143013

Diners can choose from the smoking section in the pub, the non-smoking main dining room or the small outside courtyard at this à la carte restaurant. Popular choices include the 'Prestons Platter'— a mix of local dishes—or the Karoo lamb, both served with excellent salads. The pub has an intimate wood bar, and stays open after the kitchen closes, perfect for an after-dinner drink on the terrace.
- Daily 10.30–2.30, 5.30–9.45
- L R50, D R120, Wine R35

OUDTSHOORN

DE FIJNE KEUKEN

114 Baron van Rheede Street,
Oudtshoorn 6625
Tel 044-2726403

A fine menu is on offer in this atmospheric, converted town house, with tables in a string of brightly decorated rooms and spilling on to an outside terrace. This is a good place to try a variety of ostrich dishes, from simple steaks or ostrich carpaccio to a good value ostrich stroganoff served with pasta. It's a popular, bustling place with good service.
- Mon–Fri 11.30am–10pm,
Sat–Sun 5.30pm–10pm
- L R54, D R85, Wine R32

PLETTENBERG BAY

THE LOOKOUT

Lookout Beach, Plettenberg Bay 6600
Tel 044-5331379

Surfers and families share the long wooden tables at this beach-side bar and restaurant.

The shady deck, with stunning views of the sand and surf, is popular for its seafood, with daily specials and traditional dishes such as lemon-grilled calamari or shellfish platters, as well as light lunches, including big salads and wholesome soups. You can watch surfers share a wave with a dolphin from the terrace.
- Daily 9am–11pm
- L R45, D R95, Wine R35

ROBERTSON

BRANDEWYNSDRAAI

1 Kromhout Street, Robertson 6705
Tel 023-6263202

Light salads and sandwiches are served here at lunchtime, but the tasty Cape cuisine is popular in the evenings. A local special is *skaapsnek* (sheep's neck), and the wine list, focusing on the Robertson estates, is very good. During the summer months you can sit outside in the neat gardens, and in winter a blazing log fire inside adds to the atmosphere. There's a well stocked wine shop attached.
- Mon–Sat 10–3.30, 7–10,
Sun 11–3.30
- L R40, D R100, Wine R38

TULBAGH

BALLOTINA

43 Church Street, Tulbagh 6820
Tel 023-2301694

Set in a restored Cape Dutch 1817 building, with red-and-white-checked tablecloths and dripping candles, the Ballotina has an Italian edge and caters well for vegetarians and pasta-lovers. The Sunday lunch is very popular for its antipasti, followed by a traditional carvery. The owner and chef is an opera singer, so you may be treated to some impromptu entertainment.
- Tue–Fri noon–3pm,
Fri–Sat 7pm–11pm
- D R60, Wine R30

WHALE COAST

BIENTANG'S CAVE

Left of the Old Harbour,
Hermanus 7200
Tel 028-3123454
www.bientangscave.com

The name doesn't lie—the venue is an actual cave with an extended deck overlooking the waves. Bientang's Cave is known for its excellent seafood buffets, served at simple wood benches and long tables on the rocks overlooking the sea. It's very popular, so reserve in advance on weekends. Access is via steps from the parking area on Marine Drive, left from the Old Harbour; look out for the Bientang Seaworld sign.
- Mon–Thu 11.30–4,
Fri–Sat 11.30–4, 7–9
- L R60, D R110, Wine R38

THE BURGUNDY

16 Harbour Road, Hermanus 7200
Tel 028-3122800

The Burgundy has an attractive setting in a restored rural cottage set back from the Old Harbour. The paved courtyard is the most appealing lunch spot, with tables grouped around a small fountain. This is one of the top restaurants in town, but has a surprisingly relaxed feel, serving good value seafood; the grilled crayfish is especially good.
- Daily 8.30–4.15
- L R70, D R120, Wine R43

EATING

WINELANDS

LE BON VIVANT
22 Dirkie Uys Street,
Franschhoek 7690
Tel 021-8762717

This well kept secret is a real find: a small garden set back from the main tourist drag. Tables are laid out in dappled shade during the day, and dinner is served by candlelight. Light, delicious lunches include smoked trout sandwiches, and there's an excellent value five-course dinner covering a range of local dishes.

🕒 Thu–Tue 12–3, 6.30–10
🍴 L R40, D R120, Wine R40

BOSCHENDAL RESTAURANT
Boschendal Wine Estate, Pniel Road,
Groot Drankenstein 7680
Tel 021-8704274
www.boschendalwines.co.za

The main restaurant on this popular wine estate, set in the old Cape Dutch manor house, offers a great chance to sample a wide range of typical Cape cuisine. The rustic interior is characterized by its sturdy wooden tables. It's only open for lunch, which is a large, set price buffet affair, starting with butternut soup and a range of pâtés, then a selection of main courses—the most popular is traditional roast beef—followed by a choice of local cheeses.

🕒 Daily 12.30–3
🍴 L R195, Wine R55
🚗 From Stellenbosch, follow Adam Tas Road (R310) to Idas Valley and Franschoek. Cross the traffic lights at the bottom of the Helshoogte pass. Continue over the pass, and through Kylemore, Johannesdal and Pniel villages. The main entrance is approximately 1km (0.5 miles) past Pniel on the right-hand side

DE VOLKSKOMBUIS
Aan de Wagen Road,
Stellebosch 7600
Tel 021-8872121
www.volkskombuis.co.za

Well prepared, traditional Cape food is served in this restored Cape Dutch homestead with views across the Eerste River. The menu covers the best of South African cooking, such as *bobotie*, a sweet-spicy minced beef dish, slow-roasted Karoo lamb, springbok loin and smoked *snoek* (fish) wrapped in filo pastry. Standards are very high, the local wine list is excellent and wine-tasting is possible at your table.

🕒 Mon–Sat 12–2.30, 6.30–9.30,
Sun 12–2.30
🍴 L R93, D R126, Wine R50

FISHMONGER
Corner of Plein and Ryneveld streets,
Stellenbosch 7600
Tel 021-8877835

This Portuguese-style seafood restaurant serves a wide choice of fresh, grilled Cape seafood—such as kingclip, calamari and tiger prawns — including taster platters for those who can't decide. There's a relaxed atmosphere, with fishing nets hanging from the ceiling and friendly, professional service. It also has a sushi chef and a reliable menu of various rolls and sashimi, as well as a better choice of vegetarian dishes than many local restaurants. Reservations are essential in the evenings.

🕒 Daily noon–10pm
🍴 L R55, D R100, Wine R45

LORD NEETHLING RESTAURANT
Neethlingshof Estate, Vlottenburg 7604
Tel 021-8838966
www.lordneethling.co.za

The Neethlingshof wine estate has two restaurants on site, including the old-fashioned Lord Neethling, housed in the original Cape Dutch homestead. The food is traditional Cape fare, such as oxtail or ostrich steak with gooseberries, followed by cheese and seasonal desserts (berries with cream) or chocolate pudding.

🕒 Sep–end May Sun, Mon 10–4, Tue–Sat 9am–10pm; Jun–end Aug daily 10–4
🍴 L R76, D R110, Wine R35
🚗 Take exit 33 from the N2 in the direction of Stellenbosch and follow the road until you come to an intersection after approximately 13km (8 miles). At the intersection, turn left; 14 flag poles mark the entrance to the estate

LE QUARTIER FRANÇAIS
16 Huguenot Road, Franschhoek 7690
Tel 021-8762151
www.lequartier.co.za

Le Quartier Français is consistently rated as one of the best restaurants in the region. It has an attractive setting in the fashionable hotel of the same name, with some tables set beneath the trees in the garden courtyard. The menu includes carefully prepared contemporary South African and French dishes, such as salmon with a tapenade crust, but some may find it a little too fussy. Nevertheless, this is *the* place to come for a treat.

🕒 Daily 8am–10pm
🍴 L R120, D R200, Wine R60

WORCESTER

THE PEAR TREE
Corner of Church and Barring streets,
Worcester 6849
Tel 023-3420947

This newcomer promises fine dining and an excellent selection of Breede River wines. The chef prepares French country cooking, including some unusual local dishes, such as rabbit with chilli sauce. This is a good place for a treat and some variation from the standard Cape fare.

🕒 Mon–Sat 8pm–11.30pm,
Sun 9am–3.30pm
🍴 L R80, D R120, Wine R49

EATING

EASTERN CAPE

Port Elizabeth claims to have the highest per capita ratio of restaurants in South Africa, which for visitors means a wide choice without inflated prices. Many of the quality restaurants in Grahamstown are in the main hotels. There are also plenty of inexpensive cafés and takeouts serving the large student population. East London has a fair smattering of good places to eat and thanks to the youthful edge the surfers bring to town, many places double up as restaurants during the early evening and then as lively bars, some with live music, as the night wears on.

EAST LONDON

ERNST'S CHALET SUISSE
Orient Beach, East London 5201
Tel 043-7221840
One of the best restaurants in town, this institution has been in business for over 27 years. The focus is on a mix of local seafood and traditional Swiss dishes. Specials include a Swiss-style pork fillet topped with mushrooms and Gruyère cheese and served with rosti potatoes. There's also a good seafood linguini and a spicy seafood jambalaya. During the day the restaurant has views of the pier and harbour at Orient Beach; at night it takes on a romantic air, with tables overlooking a floodlit tropical garden. Next door, but sharing the same kitchen, is the cheaper Quarterdeck pub.
🍴 Mon–Fri 12–2.30, 6–11, Sat 6–11, Sun 12–2.30
🍷 L R75, D R130, Wine R40

GRAAFF-REINET

DE CAMDEBOO
Drostdy Hotel, 30 Church Street, Graaff-Reinet 6280
Tel 049-8922161
www.drostdy.co.za
The à la carte restaurant in the Drostdy Hotel (▷ 283) is a popular choice for a romantic dinner. The high-ceilinged dining room is furnished with antique wood furniture, and meals are served by candle-light. There are occasional nightly buffets, and the menu has a fine selection of Karoo dishes, including roast Karoo lamb served with vegetables and home-baked bread. The wine list focuses on the Cape.
🍴 Mon–Sat 6.30–10
🍷 D R110, Wine R43

GRAHAMSTOWN

CALABASH
123 High Street, Grahamstown 6139
Tel 046-6222324
The Calabash is a popular traditional South African restaurant in central Grahamstown. The faintly

rustic interior has a fully licensed bar and offers an all-day menu, including cooked breakfasts. Although not quite as traditional South African as the interior might suggest, it also specializes in Xhosa hot-pot (a stew of either chicken, mutton or beef, cooked with potatoes and onions in a rich gravy). The menu offers a standard student-friendly choice of burgers, steaks and filled baked potatoes.

🍴 Daily 7.30am–11pm
🍷 L R65, D R80, Wine R35

JEFFREYS BAY

SUNFLOWER CAFÉ
20 Da Gama Road, Jeffreys Bay 6330
Tel 042-2931682
Vegetarians will appreciate the Sunflower Café, with its great range of meat-free pastas, quiches and bakes. During the day it serves light meals, delicious milk shakes and home-made cakes on a small veranda overlooking the street. There are also simple evening meals, including fresh

local seafood such as lemon-grilled calamari with rice. The walls are hung with local art.
🍴 Daily 8am–11pm
🍷 L R30, D R70

PORT ELIZABETH

BLACKBEARD'S TAVERN
Brookes Hill Pavilion, corner of Marine Drive and Brookes Hill Drive, Summerstrand, Port Elizabeth 6001
Tel 041-5855567

This à la carte restaurant has been run by the same family for three generations. There are great ocean views from the pavilion, and impressive fish tank displays. The menu has an extensive range of seafood (the simple, grilled *kabeljou*, a firm, white, local fish, is popular), as well as steaks, grills and some vegetarian and Italian choices.
🍴 Daily 7am–11pm
🍷 L R48, D R80, Wine R34

ROYAL DELHI
10 Burgess Street, Central 6001
Tel 041-3738216
The Royal Delhi is very popular with locals and students, and has a relaxed atmosphere with a good selection of Indian dishes. Some of the best make good use of fresh local seafood, such as the crab curry or the mild coconut-enriched Goa fish curry. Meat dishes includes a spicy Madras curried oxtail. You can also choose more standard fare (such as lamb chops).
🍴 Mon–Fri noon–11pm, Sat 4pm–midnight
🍷 L R60, D R72, Wine R36

EATING

KWAZULU-NATAL

The Indian influence in KwaZulu-Natal means that the best curries are found in Durban, and the dishes are more authentic than you might expect in some parts of Europe or the US. One of the most popular take-out meals is *bunny chow* (▷ 256). Florida Road in Morningside and Musgrave Road in Berea, in the Durban suburbs, have lots of popular bars and restaurants next to each other making for a convenient night out with plenty of choice. Pietermaritzburg also has a wide choice to suit all budgets. All the large mountain resorts have restaurants and bars on site.

DURBAN

BAANTHAI
138 Florida Road, Morningside 4001
Tel 031-3034270
Well placed on a trendy strip of restaurants and bars, Baanthai is a popular local restaurant serving Thai food. Starters include paper prawns or spicy tom yam soups. There is a large selection of main dishes, mostly stir-fries and Thai curries, but the house specials are worth trying—Sam's crispy blackened chilli fish or the honeyed barbecue spare ribs. The walls are decorated with delicate murals and there's an outdoor balcony.
Ⓒ Mon–Fri 12–3, 7–late, Sat 7–late
L R70, D R100, Wine R35

CHRISTINA'S
134 Florida Road, Morningside
Tel 031-3032111
This is a training restaurant, but that shouldn't put you off. It's still very popular and manages to maintain a good standard of French cuisine. Menus are as varied as the students' curricula, and presentation is a strong point. The breakfast menu is pure luxury, while the regular Saturday lunchtime themed buffet is always popular. In the summer, you can eat outside on the shaded patio.
☎ Tue breakfast, lunch and tea, Wed–Sat all day
L R55, D R100, Wine R40

FAMOUS FISH CO
3–9 King's Battery,
Point Waterfront 4001
Tel 031-3681060/9

Although a little off the usual tourist route, it's worth finding this highly popular outfit with several outlets throughout town. The quirky interior is pleasantly busy with friendly service, and the tables have views out over the ships in the port. The main reason to come is for the seafood. The menu is vast, covering a wide range of grilled local fish, curries and shellfish (and steaks and grills for meat lovers). Special dishes include crayfish thermidor or plain grilled crayfish. There's also an excellent grilled east coast sole, *peri-peri* (chilli sauce) calamari and salads.
Ⓒ Daily 12–4, 6–11
L R67, D R110, Wine R50

GULZAR
39 Umhlana Rocks Drive,
Durban North 4320
Tel 031-5649958
This popular curry house is a good place to sample traditional Natal Indian curries. The menu is extensive, covering north and south Indian dishes, with a selection of chicken, mutton and fish curries, as well as tandoori dishes. Vegetarians are well catered for; it's well-known for its spinach and potato dishes are popular. Other specials include mutton with beans and an excellent prawn curry.
Ⓒ Daily 12–3, 6–10.30
L R65, D R90, Wine R46

JEWEL OF INDIA
Holiday Inn Crowne Plaza,
63 Snell Parade, Durban 4001
Tel 031-3621300

Worth visiting for its exotic side room, with cushions and low tables where you can kick off your shoes, this is one of Durban's finest Indian restaurants, set in the modern five-star Holiday Inn. It specializes in north Indian cuisine, with a full range of rich, spicy curries served with fresh tandoori breads. There is an extensive selection for vegetarians, and Indian musicians provide nightly live music.
Ⓒ Tue–Sun 12–3, 6–11
L R80, D R110, Wine R40

JOE KOOLS
137 Lower Marine Parade, North Beach,
Durban 4001
Tel 031-3329697
For superb views of North Beach while you lunch, head to Joe Kools, a large restaurant and pub with decks overlooking the sand. During the day it's popular with families, and in the evenings it becomes a big surfers' hang-out. The food is standard pub fare, with burgers, pizza, pasta, fried seafood and club sandwiches. It's always a lively spot, and a great place for watching people catching waves from the beach.
Ⓒ Kitchen is open daily 8am–10pm; pub open longer hours
L R54, D R76, Wine R30

ULUNDI

Royal Hotel, 267 Smith Street,
Durban 4000
Tel 031-3040331
www.theroyal.co.za

The Ulundi, one of Durban's best curry restaurants, transports you back to the colonial past. Turbaned waiters dressed all in white serve diners at tables shaded by palms. A wide range of curries is available—the spiciness will be adjusted on request—and you can select up to a dozen condiments from the complementary trolley. On Saturday evenings there is a fixed-price buffet offering masala fresh fish, vegetarian dishes, and chicken and lamb curries.

Ⓒ Mon–Sat noon–3pm, 6pm–midnight
🍴 L R64, D R112, Wine R56

ROMA REVOLVING

John Ross House, Victoria Embankment
Tel 031-3376707
Arrive early for pre-dinner drinks and enjoy the 360-degree view of Durban from this 32nd-floor revolving restaurant. In addition to good value three-course set meals, there's a strong emphasis on seafood and pasta, while the heavily laden dessert trolley has something for everyone.

☎ Mon–Sat 12–2.30, 6–10
🍴 L R50, D R80, Wine R45

LADYSMITH

THE ROYAL HOTEL

140 Murchison Street, Ladysmith 3379
Tel 036-6372176
The main dining room at The Royal Hotel has a range of steaks and pub-style lunches, and a buffet in the form of a carvery. But don't expect much for vegetarians other than salads. The attached pub is

popular with locals in the early evening.
Ⓒ Daily 12–2.30, 6–9
🍴 L R40, D R65, Wine R28

PIETERMARITZBURG

ELS AMICS

380 Longmarket Street,
Pietermaritzburg 3201
Tel 033-3456524
An old-fashioned Spanish restaurant in an attractive Victorian house, Els Amics offers a mix of Catalan, Spanish and South African food, with traditional dishes like gazpacho soup and South African-influenced crab-stuffed artichokes. Seafood includes trout fried with almonds, and there is the usual range of steaks. With six hours' notice you can order paella, and the wine list has some imported options from France and Spain.

Ⓒ Tue–Fri 12–2.30, 6–10, Sat 6–10
🍴 L R55, D R100, Wine R40

ST. LUCIA

QUARTERDECK

McKenzie Street, St. Lucia 3936
Tel 035-5901116
Set at the entrance to the little town of St. Lucia, this friendly local restaurant specializes in seafood. Dishes include simply prepared butter fish, a rich white fish grilled and served with chips (fries), and a platter with a variety of local grilled seafood. You can also get burgers with a range of toppings. It's a good value, laid-back place, but the best feature is the open deck, perfect for watching the world go by while you eat.

Ⓒ Daily 12–3, 6–10
🍴 L R55, D R80, Wine R35

ZULU & I

At the Crocodile Centre
Tel 035-5901144
If you've ever wondered what crocodile tastes like, this restaurant is one of the best places to try it. The setting is appealing, on a shady deck overlooking the wetlands. There are daily specials and a crocodile pasta, as well as a range of seafood dishes for more conventional palates. Traditional breakfasts are served, as are light lunches.

Ⓒ Daily 8am–9pm
🍴 From R25, Wine R25
🚩 Next to the entrance gate to Cape Vidal, just out of town

UKHAHLAMBA-DRAKENSBERG PARK

CATERPILLAR & CATFISH

Top of the Oliviershoek Pass
Tel 036-4386130
www.cookhouse.co.za

The guesthouse (▷ 288) just outside the park is home to one of the best restaurants in the region. It's a popular Sunday lunch venue for people from Gauteng and is fast gaining an excellent reputation. There is an emphasis on fresh local produce; the house special is trout, and there are more than 30 different trout dishes to choose from. Some of the best are spicy Cajun-style, and other dishes concentrate on Mediterranean tastes, such as the grilled cheese and roast vegetables.

Ⓒ Daily 10–3, 6–9
🍴 L R50, D R95, Wine R45

UMHLANGA ROCKS

RAZZMATAZZ

Cabana Beach Hotel, 10 Lagoon Drive,
Umhlanga Rocks 4319
Tel 031-5612371
The Cabana Beach Hotel is home to the resort's best restaurant. The outside terrace has brilliant views over the crashing waves below, making it the best spot for lunch or summertime supper; the interior is decorated in simple terracotta and blues. The menu is dominated by seafood and game dishes—try the crocodile kebabs, venison with red wine and blueberry sauce, or ostrich fillet with Cape gooseberries. It's also well-known for its crème brûlées, and offers good value set menus at lunchtime.

Ⓒ Daily 12.30–3.30, 6.30–10
🍴 L R59 (set menu), D R100, Wine R40

EATING

LIMPOPO AND MPUMALANGA

The largest attraction in this region is the Kruger National Park. If you are staying here, then you will eat at the restaurant at your camp or private game reserve. At the other end of the scale, the small towns around Nelspruit have a number of bars and restaurants and they are well known for their seafood, which arrives daily from Mozambique.

BELA-BELA

O'HAGANS
Waterfront development, Pretoria Road, Bela-Bela 0480
Tel 014-7365068
This outlet of the successful chain has an attractive setting on the Waterfront, with outdoor tables. The interior is filled with mock Irish touches, and the menu includes steaks and schnitzels, along with more traditionally Irish dishes such as steak and ale pie. There's also a good range of local and imported beers.
Ⓒ Daily 10–late
🍴 L R45, D R75, Wine R38

GRASKOP

HARRIE'S
Louis Trichardt Street, Graskop 1270
Tel 013-7671273
Graskop is famous nationwide for its pancakes, and Harrie's started the craze. It's so popular you may have to compete for a table when crowded tour buses arrive at lunchtime. There's a wide selection of delicious sweet and savoury pancakes—try one packed with black cherries and rich vanilla ice-cream. The veranda is a pleasant spot in summer, and there's a fireplace indoors in the winter months.
Ⓒ Daily 7am–6pm
🍴 Pancakes from R20

HAZYVIEW

RISSINGTON INN
White River Road (the R40)
Tel 013-7377700
www.rissington.co.za

The Rissington is best known for its excellent à la carte restaurant, serving delicious food on the outdoor terrace

overlooking gardens. The dinner menu has a fine selection of meat dishes, such as venison stew or stir-fried ostrich. Vegetarian dishes include a rich and creamy aubergine florentine. For dessert, try the chocolate mousse—it's to die for. The wine list has a well chosen South African selection. Reservations are essential.
Ⓒ Daily 12–3, 6–10
🍴 L R60, D R98, Wine R47
🚗 2km (1.2 miles) from Hazyview

HOEDSPRUIT

MAD DOGZ CAFÉ
On the R527
Tel 015-7955425
The food here is some of the best in the region, and this makes for a great lunchtime stop-off en route to Kruger National Park. They serve big, wholesome breakfasts, but the lunches are the best, with a range of fusion meals—using tastes from Asia, Europe and Africa. Dishes include spicy Thai beef salad, Creole chicken and Cape Malay *bobotie* (spiced, minced beef). The setting is lovely, with brightly painted tables clustered under thatched roofs.
Ⓒ Daily 8.30–5
🍴 L R75, Wine R40
🚗 East of junction of the R527 and R36

MAKHADO

SHENANDOAH SPUR
102 Krogh Street, Makhado 0920
Tel 015-5165170
There are surprisingly few places to eat in Makhado, but this family-friendly branch of

the popular chain is probably your best bet. The menu has a wide range of steaks served with a selection of sauces, fries, rice, vegetables or a baked potato. There is also a salad bar, although the standard of this can vary.
Ⓒ Daily noon–10pm
🍴 L R50, D R65, Wine R28

NELSPRUIT

COSTA DO SOL
ABSA Square, Paul Kruger Street, Nelspruit 1201
Tel 013-7526382
This well established restaurant specializes in seafood from Mozambique, brought in fresh from the coast daily. Dishes are a mix of Italian and Portuguese, including good pizza, pasta and veal. It is renowned for its delicious giant Mozambican prawns, simply prepared—grilled with lemon or spicy chilli sauce. The wine list includes some expensive Italian wines.
Ⓒ Mon–Fri 12–2.30, 6.30–9.30, Sat 6.30–9.30
🍴 L R75, D R95, Wine R40

PILGRIM'S REST

THE VINE
Main Street, Downtown, Pilgrim's Rest 1290
Tel 013-7681080
An 'Olde World'-style pub and restaurant, The Vine is a typical small-town establishment serving wholesome meals and beer on tap. It's a popular place, with a small ladies' bar which gets very busy in the early evenings. There's a breezy veranda outside if you'd prefer a quiet meal. The food veers away from the predictable steaks and grills, and offers some well prepared traditional South African dishes, including a rich Cape Malay *bobotie* (a sweet and spicy minced beef dish, cooked with raisins and a savoury custard topping), ostrich neck cooked in a *potje* (a three-legged pot), and braised oxtail and *samp* (mashed maize).
Ⓒ Daily noon–late
🍴 L R55, D R75, Wine R38

EATING

Johannesburg and Pretoria have a wide selection of smart restaurants in the affluent suburbs, such as Melville in Jo'burg, with a choice of traditional South African fare as well as international cuisine, from tapas to sushi. There's also a growing number of 'African' restaurants serving visitors traditional dishes such as stew and *pap* (▷ 258).

SPECIAL IN SABIE

THE WILD FIG TREE
Main Street, Sabie 1260
Tel 013-7642239
One of Sabie's best restaurants, The Wild Fig Tree serves

light lunches and more ambitious meals in the evening. You can choose to dine in the cool interior or on the shaded veranda. The menu is fairly extensive, with delicious local trout, and a wide choice of game such as guinea fowl, crocodile and warthog, usually grilled or served as sausages. This is one of the few places where you'll see impala and gemsbok on the menu. Vegetarians are provided for, although this is essentially a place for meat-eaters. The home-made desserts and pies are very popular, and there's a small curio shop attached to the restaurant.
🕐 Daily 12–3, 6–9
🍷 L R65, D R95, Wine R46

WHITE RIVER

TEN GREEN BOTTLES BISTRO
Casterbridge Farm
Tel 013-7501097
For a pleasant lunch stop, head to this converted farm building. Daily specials are chalked up on the blackboard, with a mix of light lunches, seafood, steaks and sandwiches. Try the famous Maputo sandwich—fresh and juicy Mozambique prawns piled high on home-made bread. The outside terrace is popular, and gets very busy during the day. The farm complex also has a couple of curio shops.
🕐 Daily noon–10pm
🍷 L R60, D R95, Wine R45
🚗 2km (1.2 miles) out of town, between White River and Hazyview

BLOEMFONTEIN

DE OUDE KRAAL
Tel 051-5640636
www.oudekraal.co.za

Despite its remote location, reservations is essential at De Oude Kraal, which is rated the best restaurant in the Free State. Famous for its *boerekos*—typical Afrikaaner farmhouse food—there are various choices. You can have a traditional sheep pit barbecue around the *lapa* (thatched outdoor eating area), or for more formal dinners there are extravagant six-course set menus served in the restored main farmhouse. The wine cellar is a romantic setting for candlelit dinners, and the owners are happy to advise you on which wine to order with your dinner. Various events are held throughout the year, such as a venison festival and wine-tasting events with a formal dinner. Teas are served in the afternoon.
🕐 Mon–Sat 9am–10pm, Sun 12–3
🍷 L R75, D R110, Wine R32
🚗 35km (22 miles) out of town, off the N1 to Cape Town

BEEF BARON
22 Second Avenue,
Westdene 9301
Tel 051-4474290
Locals flock to this established steak house, which offers superb matured steaks in a friendly setting. There's a wooden deck for alfresco dining in the summer. Other dishes on the menu are Karoo lamb, seafood and a selection of vegetarian meals. There's a

decent wine list and a good choice of beers.
🕐 Mon 6–11, Tue–Sat 12–3, 6–11, Sun 12–3
🍷 L R50, D R70, Wine R35

JOHANNESBURG

BLUES ROOM
Village Walk Mall, Sandton 2146
Tel 011-784 5527
www.bluesroom.co.za

The Blues Room is one of the top music venues in South Africa specializing, as its name suggests, in the blues. The venue, all brickwork and dimly lit bohemian chic, has a bar and dining area. The menu includes fresh Knysna oysters or deep-fried Camembert with cranberry sauce for starters. For your main course sample the grilled lamb cutlets, the veal done with paprika, pan-fried calamari or ravioli. Vegetarian dishes are also available. Round off with apple pie or chocolate mousse.
🕐 Tue–Sat 7pm–1am
🍷 R56 entrance charge; D R128, Wine R64

EATING

SPECIAL IN JO'BURG

THE BUTCHER SHOP & GRILL

Sandton Square, corner of Sandton Drive and Rivonia Road, Sandton 2196
Tel 011-7848676/7
www.butchershop.co.za

The sawdust on the floor fools nobody—this award-winning steakhouse is a top-quality restaurant. It's famous for its aged steaks, and although there are a few outlets around the country, this is the original. The menu, understandably, focuses on steaks and other grills; when available there is a specially aged T-bone that is cut to order. There's also a wide selection of seafood, starters and desserts, but nothing for vegetarians other than salad. Visitors can buy cooler bags of vacuum-packed meat to take away with them.
Mon–Sat 12–10.45, Sun 12–9.45
L R95, D R125, Wine R40

CARNIVORE

69 Drift Boulevard, Muldersdrift 1747
Tel 011-9506000
This has become something of an institution and is hugely popular with visitors, who come here for the ultimate 'African' dining experience. The rustic interior, zebra skin chairs and a large central fire pit characterize the inside. Meals are all-the-meat-you-can-eat, with game carved with spears and served on cast-iron plates. There's a choice of at least 10 different types of meat every day, including ostrich, crocodile, warthog, zebra and more conventional meats such as beef and pork, served with a selection of salads and sauces. Vegetarians have a good choice, including *aviyal*, a mix of vegetables cooked in spicy coconut sauce.
Daily 12–4, 6–12
L R100, D R135, Wine R45
30-min drive (approx 30km/18 miles) from central Johannesburg on the N14

DARUMA

6th Floor, Sandton Sun Hotel, 5th Street, Sandton Central, Johannesburg 2196
Tel 011-780 5157

Decorated in traditional Japanese style with natural wood finishes and paper blinds, this seafood, meat, sushi and vegetarian restaurant has a tranquil air about it. If you are bewildered by the very extensive menu, try the seafood platter (for two), which includes lobster, prawns, fresh fish of the day, scallops, calamari and a seasonal vegetable sauté. But if you know your way around Japanese cuisine you can't go wrong with the delicious salmon, mackerel, octopus or tuna on the sushi menu.
Daily noon–10.30pm
L R96, D R176, Wine R64

FOURNO'S BAKERY

Dunkeld West Centre, Jan Smuts Avenue
Tel 011-3252110
Fourno's bakers arrive at midnight to prepare delicious pastries, cakes, croissants, quiches and pies. Locals come here for big breakfasts, trendy coffees or just to hang out. This great value bakery has other branches at the airport's domestic terminal and Fourways Mall.
Daily 7am–6pm
L R45, Wine BYO

GRAMADOELAS

Market Theatre Complex, Bree Steet, Newtown 2001
Tel 011-8386960
One of the best places to get an overview of southern African dishes is at this long-standing, popular venue. Starters include fried mopani worms served in chilli sauce, followed by *sosaties* (spicy kebabs), *bobotie* (sweet and spicy ground beef pie) or dishes from farther afield, such as Morocco or Ethiopia. A delicious dessert is the sticky *malva* (sponge) pudding, or *melktert* (milk tart). This is also the place to try home-brewed sorghum beer or *mageu* (fermented milk). The interior is in appealing Cape Dutch style. Reservations are recommended.
Mon 11.30–3, Tue–Sat 12–3, 6.30–11
L R55, D R95, Wine R35

GRASSROOTS

Village Walk Mall, Sandton 2146
Tel 011-8836020
This is one of the few vegetarian-only restaurants in Johannesburg, and is a good place for non-meat, non-dairy and non-egg dishes. The choice includes pastas, salads, bagels and cakes, which lean towards the fruity, nutty, leafy and grainy type of cuisine. The soups are great, including a delicious pumpkin and leek, or wild mushroom and port. Various herbal teas and smoothies are prepared while you wait for your meal. No alcohol is served.
Daily 8–5
L R40

THE GRILLHOUSE

The Firs, Oxford Road, Rosebank 2196
Tel 011-8803945
South Africa is famous for its quality steaks and this restaurant is hugely popular for its melt-in-the-mouth fillets and succulent sauces. Exposed brick, green leather furnishings, white linen, excellent service and a lively atmosphere add to the experience. Opposite is Katzy's late-night piano bar and cigar lounge, under the same ownership, which has live music most nights and is fast making its way on to Jo'burg's nightlife circuit. You would never know you were in a shopping mall.
Sun–Fri 12–2.30, 5.30–11, Sat 5.30–11
L R105, D R135, Wine R55

WOMBLES

17 3rd Avenue, Parktown North 2193
Tel 011-8802470

A relative new comer, Wombles has fast gained an excellent reputation for its matured steaks. The setting is attractive colonial style, with dark wood tables, high-backed chairs and white linen table-cloths. It has a simple menu, with traditional starters like grilled mushrooms or chicken liver salad, followed by a selection of cuts and sauces. There's also a fair choice of poultry, fish and a couple of vegetarian dishes. Service is friendly and relaxed.

⊙ Mon–Fri noon–11pm, Sat 6pm–11pm

🍽 L R95, D R170, Wine R65

PRETORIA

CAFÉ RICHE

Church Square, City Centre 8881
Tel 012-3283173

The superb Café Riche is the oldest café in the city. The restored art deco building has a real European feel to it, and is perfect for sipping a cappuccino and watching the comings and goings on the square. The large breakfasts are hugely popular, and there is also a light lunch and late-night dinner menu. The café hosts a range of events, such as poetry readings. Don't miss the Sunday brunches, but be prepared for slow service.

⊙ 7am–midnight

🍽 L R40, D R60, BYO wine (corkage R15)

CYNTHIA'S

Maroelana Centre, near Pretoria Country Club, Maroelana 0081
Tel 021-4603220

The atmosphere and food at this popular establishment, set in the southern suburbs off the N1, have a countryside feel to them, with heavy furnishings perhaps more suited to a

colder climate. Dishes are a mix of traditional and modern, with starters such as springbok carpaccio leading on to tender chateaubriand steak. Ask about daily specials—these are often the best choice, especially if they include the Matupo prawns. There's an extensive, good value wine list, and service is swift and friendly.

⊙ Mon–Fri 12–2.30, 6–11.30, Sat 6–11.30, Sun 12–2.30

🍽 L R80, D R120, Wine R36

GERARD MOERDYK

752 Park Street, Pretoria
Tel 012-3444856

Gerard Moerdyk is a delightful African Colonial restaurant, housed in a building dating back to 1920. The cuisine is traditional South African, with specials such as *bobotie* (a spicy mince dish), butternut soup, venison pie and chicken pie, with pineapple relish, onion and tomato relish, and chutney as side dishes. For dessert try the brandy pudding with whipped cream and chocolate ice cream. The restaurant has an extensive list of South African wines.

⊙ Mon–Fri 12–2.30, 6–11, Sat 6–11

🍽 L R80, D R96, Wine R56

Pizza can be found in all varieties across Pretoria

LA MADELEINE

122 Priory Road, Lynnwood 0081
Tel 021-3613667

This French restaurant is regarded as one of the top restaurants in South Africa. The emphasis is on superbly prepared French cuisine, with a changing daily menu dependent on what the markets have to offer. There are no printed menus—instead, the daily offerings are explained by the Belgian proprietor. Expect starters such as oysters or foie gras, followed by langoustines or slow roasted lamb. The wine list is exceptional. Reservations are essential.

⊙ Tue–Thu, Sat 7–11, Fri 12–3, 7–11

🍽 L R190, D R255, Wine R60

MOZZARELLAS

Hatfield Square, Hatfield 0083
Tel 012–3626464

One of a number of alfresco restaurants in lively Hatfield Square, this is a popular choice with local students. It's a good value Italian pizza and pasta place, with tables spilling from the brightly painted interior on to the square outside. The menu is standard Italian, with starters like garlic bread and salad bowls followed by a comprehensive selection of pasta (spaghetti carbonara, penne arrabiatta and more) and pizza with a wide choice of toppings. There's also seafood and steaks, and most people bring their own wine (corkage R15).

⊙ Daily 11.30am–late

🍽 L R50, D R70, Wine R42

EATING

NORTHERN CAPE AND NORTH WEST PROVINCE

Most towns, such as Kimberley, are better served by pubs and bars than by restaurants and there are usually a number of pie and fast food outlets, ideal for picnics. However, there is a handful of good places to eat and, considering the size of Springbok, there are one or two good choices here too. If you are staying in or passing through one of the smaller towns, bear in mind that many guest houses and hotels are open to non-residents.

PRICES AND SYMBOLS

The restaurants are listed alphabetically (excluding The) by town or area, then by name. The prices given are for a two-course lunch (L) and a three-course dinner (D) for one person, without drinks. The wine price is for the least expensive bottle. See page 2 for a key to the symbols.

KIMBERLEY

KALAHARI LODGE RESTAURANT
Corner N12 and Landbou Road,
Kimberley 8300
Tel 053-8315085
Enjoy a cocktail before relaxing in the comfort of this fully licensed à la carte restaurant. Pub meals are served during the day, while Sunday lunch is carvery-style.
☎ Mon–Sat 7am–10pm,
Sun 7am–2.30pm
🍴 L R70, D R90, Wine R40

KEG & FALCON
Du Toitspan Road,
Kimberley 8300
Tel 053-8332075
The popular, English-style Keg & Falcon pub serves decent meals (don't miss their famous foot-long pies). This is part of a chain that is slightly more trendy than most bars, but retains a relaxed feel.
☺ Daily 11am–1am (kitchen closes at 11.30pm)
🍴 L R60, D R60, Wine R30

Pasta dishes are usually of a good standard

UMBERTO'S
Du Toitspan Road,
Kimberley 8300
Tel 053-8325741
This popular, family-run Italian restaurant stands next to the famous Halfway House pub (▷ 217). Red-checked table-cloths and a wood-fired pizza oven set the scene. The food is standard Italian, with good pizza and pasta, salads and slightly more expensive meat and poultry dishes—the steak is good value.
☺ Daily 11–2.30, 5.30–10
🍴 L R45, D R60, Wine R30

RUSTENBURG

KARL'S BAUERNSTUBE
5km (3 miles) from Rustenburg
Tel 014-5372128
A pleasant country pub and restaurant with an Austrian menu, thanks to its Austrian chef and owner. Starters include northern European dishes like marinated herring, and main courses cover a range of hearty schnitzels and goulashes. There are also more South African-themed choices such as steak, fried kingclip and roast duck. The restaurant makes a good stop-off for lunch, and has a shady terrace for alfresco dining.
☺ Tue–Fri 12–2, 6–10, Sat 6.30–10,
Sun 12–2.30
🍴 L R55, D R80, Wine R41
🚗 On the R30; turn off the Pretoria road by the Ultra City

SPECIAL IN UPINGTON

LE MUST
11 Schröder Street, Upington 8801
Tel 054-3323971
www.lemustupington.com

By far the best restaurant in town, and probably one of the best in the Northern Cape, Le Must is a smart set-up in a restored Upington town house. It serves well-prepared fusion dishes accompanied by an interesting local wine list. Some of the most popular choices on the menu are springbok shank with garlic and roast onion mash, followed by delicious coriander ice-cream. The chef travels all over the world for culinary inspiration.
☺ Mon–Fri 12–3, 6–10, Sat 6–10,
Sun 11–3, 6–10
🍴 L R70, D R120, Wine R30

SPRINGBOK

BJ'S STEAKHOUSE
Hospital Street, Springbok 8240
Tel 027-7122701
Locals congregate in this basement restaurant, which is said to serve the best steak in town. The interior has a Spaghetti Western theme and there's a buzzing atmosphere. Food is standard steakhouse fare, including a variety of cuts with different sauces, plus chicken and lamb dishes, and a fisherman's platter. Portions are huge, and the bar gets very lively later in the evening, so expect some dancing.
☺ Daily 12–3, 7–10.30
🍴 L R50, D R100, Wine R30

EATING

LESOTHO AND SWAZILAND

As tourism has yet to really take off in these countries, there are not that many restaurants to choose from. It's more likely you will eat at your game reserve or camp. For those who are self-catering, in every village you'll find a small shop selling basic tinned and dried foods. In most towns, a profusion of street vendors can be found selling a wide variety of goods from home-made fried cakes called *makoenya* to barbecued meat. Outside Maseru most restaurants serve plain but filling meals such as chicken and rice.

LESOTHO

MASERU

LE HAHA GRILL

Lesotho Sun Hotel, Nightingale Road, behind the Queen Elizabeth Hospital, Maseru
Tel 22313111
One of the country's smarter (and better) restaurants is in the Lesotho Sun Hotel, a popular choice with visitors and local businesspeople. At lunchtime there are good value buffets serving a wide choice, from vegetable stir fries to pasta and roasts. There is also a snack menu, and in the evenings an à la carte menu. Reservations are necessary on weekends and during public holidays.
🕐 Daily 7am–10pm
🍽 L M65 (buffet), D M120, Wine M70

STREET VENDORS

Kingsway, Maseru
A good place to pick up a very cheap, filling local meal is one of the many street vendors lining Kingsway in central Maseru, around the taxi station. Be sure to select a vendor who is busy with locals, and where you can see the food is freshly prepared and served piping hot. You can usually choose from deep fried samosas and the staple dish of stiff maize porridge served with a meat stew. A filling meal will rarely cost more than M5. A good on-the-go snack is roasted maize, blackened over coals.

SWAZILAND

EZULWINI VALLEY

BELLA VISTA PIZZERIA

Happy Valley Hotel, MR103, Ezulwini Valley
Tel 416-1061
Bella Vista is well placed for an evening meal before heading to the Why Not club (▷ 219) in the same complex. It serves large portions of Italian fare, including a good vegetarian pizza, pasta dishes and several meat choices. Also here is the Sir Loin restaurant, which serves steaks and grills.
🕐 Mon–Sat noon–2am
🍽 L E50, D E70, Wine E25

CALABASH

Close to Timbali Lodge, MR103, Ezulwini Valley
Tel 416-1187
The Calabash is widely rated as Swaziland's leading à la carte restaurant, and is consistently popular—expect to wait for a table at lunchtime, and be sure to book in the evenings. The menu has a northern European bias, with plenty of German and Austrian dishes. Meals are hearty and meat-heavy (stews and schnitzels are popular choices), but there are also fish and seafood dishes, and several French-style offerings. German beer is available on draught.
🕐 Daily 12–3, 6–11
🍽 L E85, D E100, Wine E77

HIPPO HAUNT

Mlilwane Wildlife Sanctuary, Ezulwini Valley, between Mbabane and Manzini
Tel 416-1591
Besides a snug indoor restaurant with fireplace, the Hippo Haunt comprises two outside wooden deck areas from which the visitor can view hippos, crocodiles and terrapins at close quarters while enjoying meals and drinks from the bar. The food on offer is basic wholesome fare, with lots of meat, including venison. The restaurant serves a range of wines, beers and spirits.

🕐 Daily 12–2, 6–9
🍽 L E64, D E96, Wine E72

MBABANE

FRIAR TUCK

Mountain Inn, Mbabane
Tel 404-2781
www.mountaininn.sz
The smart Mountain Inn on the road out of town also has the area's best restaurant, Friar Tuck. The interior is rather dark, with exposed brick walls, vaulted ceilings and wooden tables. The tables outside overlook the garden and pool, with beautiful views of the Ezulwini Valley. Reliable buffet lunches are served here, and in the evenings there's an à la carte menu with a selection of standard grills, chicken dishes and local specials.
🕐 Daily 11–2.30, 6–10
🍽 L E40, D E60, Wine E30
🚗 4km (2.5 miles) from central Mbabane, on Ezulwini Valley road; look for signs on the left

INDINGILIZI ART GALLERY

112 Johnston Street, Mbabane
Tel 404-6213
This quiet art gallery has a small restaurant in the back garden—a peaceful sanctuary from the noisy city streets outside. You can get wholesome light lunches, some with an African bias, as well as soups, sandwiches and salads. Snacks and cakes are also served throughout the day.
🕐 Mon–Fri 9–5, Sat 9–1
🍽 L E40

EATING

STAYING IN SOUTH AFRICA

South Africa has an excellent range of accommodation options, covering everything from inexpensive backpacker hostels to super-luxurious safari camps. On the whole, rooms are good value, and although prices are rising as the rand gets stronger, you'll be surprised at the degree of comfort your money will buy.

Luxury camping (left); Bay Atlantic Hotel, Cape Town (middle); Island Vibe Hotel, Jeffreys Bay (right)

CAMPING AND CARAVAN PARKS

Camping is the least expensive and most flexible way of staying in South Africa. Every town has a municipal campsite, many with simple self-catering chalets. As camping is very popular with South Africans, sites tend to have excellent facilities, including electric points and lighting, shower blocks and sometimes kitchen blocks. At the most frequented visitor spots, campsites are more like holiday resorts with shops, swimming pools and a restaurant; they can get very busy and are best avoided in peak seasons. Note that sites can often be reserved months in advance, especially in the most popular game reserves and national parks during the school holidays. Some sites do not allow tents during these busy times. For most of the year the weather is ideal for camping, but be prepared for frosts at night in some parts.

Camping fees are either per tent or per person, and on average should be no more than R50 per tent and R60 per person.

If you prefer not to camp, the least expensive alternative to a backpacker hostel is staying in a self-catering chalet, often offered by municipal sites. These vary in quality and facilities, from basic *rondavels* (small, round huts with thatched roofs) with bunks to chalets with a couple of bedrooms and fully equipped kitchens. They can be excellent value, and are often the only budget accommodation available in a town.

BACKPACKER HOSTELS

Backpacker hostels are among the cheapest form of accommodation in South Africa. A bed in a dormitory will cost between R50 and R80 a night, while a double room costs between R120 and R200. Standards can obviously vary, but stiff competition means that most are clean and with good facilities. You can usually expect a self-catering kitchen, hot showers, a TV/video room and internet access. Many hostels also have bars and offer meals or nightly *braais* (barbecues), plus gardens and plunge pools. Most hostels are a good source of travel information and many act as booking agents for bus companies, budget safari tours and car rental.

The Baz Bus (▷ 51) caters to backpackers and links most backpacker hostels along the coast between Cape Town and Johannesburg, including Swaziland. At the last count more than 175 hostels were visited along the route.

Visitors who have a rental car or 4WD should note that the majority of backpacker hostels and cheaper guesthouses do not have secure off-street parking.

● Hostelworld.com has details of international hostels, including a good selection in South Africa.
● Coast to Coast, www.coastingafrica.com, is a free backpackers' guide to hostels across the country.

BED-AND-BREAKFAST

Bed-and-breakfast accommodation is hugely popular in South Africa, and even the smallest town will usually have one private home that rents out rooms. Local tourist offices are the best source of information for finding places. Standards vary, but increasingly some establishments are providing TVs and air-conditioning or fans, and have separate entrances for those who want more privacy away from the owners.

The generous breakfasts that come with the deal are almost always good. They are usually full English breakfasts (such as eggs, bacon, sausages and toast), but it is now common to

STAYING

have a choice of continental breakfast or even traditional South African dishes, such as mince on toast and mealie porridge.

Prices vary according to the facilities, and a bed-and-breakfast in a Victorian house filled with antique furniture will obviously be more expensive than a converted spare bedroom. Prices start at around R90 per person sharing and can go up to as much as R300.

At the top end of the market the luxury bed-and-breakfasts in spectacular locations such as the Winelands in the Western Cape (▷ 90–95) can charge as much as R650.

LUXURY GAME LODGES

The most famous luxury game lodges are on private game reserves adjoining Kruger National Park, although there are others around the country. Their attraction is a combination of exclusive game viewing in South Africa's prime wilderness areas, with top-class accommodation, cordon bleu meals, vintage wines and a spectacular natural setting.

The cost of staying in a luxury game lodge varies from R2,275 to over R6,500 per person each night. This includes all meals, drinks and game-viewing trips. In order to get the most from

A suite at a private lodge comes with an impressive view (left, middle); The Lodge, Fugitives' Drift (right)

GUESTHOUSES

Guesthouses can offer some of the most unusual accommodation in South Africa, with more and more interesting places springing up in cities and small towns all the time. Many are in historic homes, and offering impeccable service; in fact most luxurious rooms outside the major cities tend to be in guesthouses, not hotels. Standards vary enormously; much of what you'll get has to do with the character of the owners and the location of the homes.

Expect to pay from R120 per person for the simplest room, with prices increasing rapidly with quality. Making reservations by phone in advance is always a good idea.
● Guest House Association of Southern Africa, tel 021-7973115, www.ghasa.co.za.
● The Portfolio Collection, tel 021-7620880, www.portfoliocollection.com.

HOTELS

Traditional hotels have generally become a less attractive option, certainly outside the major cities, as the number of boutique hotels and guesthouses increases. Many are either large-scale chain hotels or 1970s hangovers, lacking the character and service found in newer establishments. Nevertheless, in the main cities, hotels often remain a practical option. Note that Cape Town and Johannesburg suffer from a shortage of hotel beds, and you should always reserve well in advance.

Generally, rooms reserved through agents in Europe and the US will be more expensive than if you contact the hotel direct, due to agent booking fees. Many of the more established chain hotels have an online reservation service via their websites.

it, guests tend to stay for at least two nights. The lodges are often isolated and not easily accessible by road, so many reserves have their own airstrips where light aircraft can land.

NATIONAL PARKS

Parks offer a range of accommodation, from basic campsites to functional chalets. If you plan on staying overnight, be sure to reserve ahead through the central reservations office of the relevant authority. All reservations can be made over the telephone, by email or on the website. Most international credit cards are accepted. In high season, it's wise to make reservations a month or two in advance.

SELF-CATERING APARTMENTS

Self-catering apartments are particularly popular with resident South African holidaymakers and there is an enormous choice, especially along the coast. Prices vary with the seasons: unsurprisingly, Christmas is the most expensive time of year, but off-season many resorts are virtually empty and discounts can be negotiated. The quiet season is much of the winter, from May to the end of September.

If you are in a group, an apartment could cost as little as R50 a day per person. Local tourist offices are the best source of information on self-catering accommodation.

PRICES IN THIS BOOK

The prices given in the following listings are the average cost of a double room based on two people sharing in high season, including 14 per cent VAT and breakfast. Prices do not include the one per cent tourist levy charge, unless otherwise stated.

CAPE PENINSULA

You can find just about any type of accommodation that you want in the Cape Peninsula, suiting any budget, and focused around Cape Town. During high season, however, Cape Town struggles to have enough hotel space for all its visitors, so be sure to reserve several months ahead if you're visiting during the summer. Much of the accommodation along the Atlantic seaboard and False Bay is aimed at the self-catering (accommodation with kitchens) market, where families rent houses or flats for a minimum of one week. There are only a few hotels and these are mostly small, family-run establishments.

PRICES AND SYMBOLS

The hotels below are listed alphabetically (excluding The) by town or area, then by name. Prices are for a double room for one night, including breakfast. All the hotels listed accept credit cards unless otherwise stated. See page 2 for a key to the symbols.

CAMPS BAY AND ATLANTIC SEABOARD

AARDVARK BACKPACKERS
319 Main Road, Sea Point 8005
Tel 021-4344172
www.lions-head-lodge.co.za

This trendy backpacker accommodation is close to Sea Point's restaurants, bars and shops. Also known as Lions Head Lodge, it has 37 comfortable hotel rooms with private bathrooms and TV, available at a backpacker's rate. The dorms, each with between 6 and 12 beds, are in former self-catering apartments, and have their own kitchen and bathroom. Facilities include a restaurant, two bars, a beer garden, TV lounge, library and pool. The on-site travel centre is informative, and there's an internet café open daily 8am–8pm.
🛏 From R90 per bed, excluding breakfast
🛏 37, plus dorms

SPECIAL IN CAMPS BAY

HUIJS HAERLEM
25 Main Drive, Sea Point 8005
Tel 021-4346434
www.huijshaerlem.co.za
These two beautifully converted adjacent houses have four rooms in each, connected by well-tended gardens. All rooms have private bathrooms and are extremely comfortable, with solid antique furniture, brass beds (some four-poster), large bathrooms and fabulous sea views. There's a solar-heated salt-water swimming pool in the peaceful garden. Both houses have a breakfast room and lounge—one decorated with Dutch furniture, the other in South African style.
🛏 R850
🛏 8

❓ No children under 14

BAY ATLANTIC
3 Berkley Road, Camps Bay 8005
Tel 021-4384341
www.thebayatlantic.com

The family-run Bay Atlantic guesthouse has some of the best views in the Peninsula. The six light and airy double rooms come with terracotta tiles and white linen, TV and private bathrooms. Some have a private balcony with stunning views of Camps Bay and the Twelve Apostles. There are also two self-catering apartments next door. The quiet garden

has a good-sized pool, and breakfast is served on a balcony overlooking the bay. Parking is available.
🛏 R520
🛏 6
🏊

VILLA ROSA
277 High Level Road, Sea Point 8005
Tel 021-4342768
www.villa-rosa.com
The rose-tinted Victorian villa known as the Villa Rosa sits high above Sea Point. It has eight bright, comfortable rooms, with traditional furnishings, and touches such as fresh flowers and original fireplaces. All rooms have stone-tiled, private bathrooms and TV; some have fridges. Excellent breakfasts are served with breads and jams. This friendly, welcoming and relaxed place also has a pleasant balcony overlooking the sea.
🛏 R520
🛏 8

DE WATERKANT VILLAGE
1 Loader Street, Green Point 8005
Tel 021-4222721
www.villageandlife.com
This is more of a mini-empire than a simple guesthouse: Village and Life owns more than 50 historic Bo-Kaap-style houses and apartments in the trendy Waterkant area, each stylishly and individually decorated, sleeping between one and six. It also owns the Waterkant House, a guest-house with nine comfortable, bright and chic rooms, a splash pool, a beautiful lounge and a terrace (R820 per room). The other main property is House of the Traveller—'luxury' back-packer accommodation with double rooms and a shared bathroom and kitchen. Other properties in stylish and historic buildings are available across Cape Town.
🛏 From R500
🛏 80+
🏊

STAYING

CAPE TOWN

THE BACKPACK

74 New Church Street, City Centre 8001
Tel 021-4234530
www.backpackers.co.za
The Backpack was the first Cape Town hostel and today is one of the best run and most comfortable in town. Occupying several houses, the hostel has large spotless dorms, single and double rooms, and double rooms with private bathrooms. Polished wood floors and African art give it a more trendy feel than many hostels. A tiled courtyard leads to a high-ceilinged bar with a TV. Meals and snacks are served throughout the day, and there are linked gardens with a small pool. A well organized and informative travel office is also on site.
🛏 From R85 per bed
ⓘ 80 beds
🖾

KENSINGTON PLACE

38 Kensington Gardens, Higgovale 8001
Tel 021-4244744
www.kensingtonplace.co.za
This stylish boutique hotel in a quiet, leafy area overlooks the City Bowl. It's small and well run, with excellent and friendly service. The rooms are a good size, each individually styled with a mix of ethnic and ultra-chic furnishings in muted beiges and creams. There's lots of light from the large windows, some with great views over the city. Breakfast is served on a leafy veranda overlooking the small pool and tropical gardens. Parking is available.
🛏 R2,600
ⓘ 8
🖥 🖾

LONG STREET BACKPACKERS

209 Long Street, City Centre 8001
Tel 021-4230615
One of central Cape Town's most sociable hostels is spread around a leafy courtyard, with small dorms and rather cramped doubles, some with their own bathrooms and balconies overlooking Long Street. There's a fully equipped kitchen, TV/video lounge, pool room, internet access, travel office and free pickup from the airport. There's good security with a 24-hour police camera

by the entrance. There's a lively atmosphere, with occasional parties organized and weekly *braais* (barbecues).
🛏 From R70 per bed, excluding breakfast
ⓘ 65 beds

METROPOLE

38 Long Street, City Centre 8001
Tel 021-4247247
www.metropolehotel.co.za

The 45 rooms in the Metropole have understated interiors in mauve and taupe, huge beds, attractive dark-wood furniture and abstract prints on the walls. Some rooms are rather small, but all have beautiful stone bathrooms with bath and shower. The M Bar & Lounge has become a trendy after-work drinks venue, and with its red ostrich-leather chairs and subdued lighting feels more like Manhattan. The elegant restaurant on the first floor serves a mix of Italian and modern South African cuisine. Look out for the art deco elevator. Parking is available.
🛏 R2,650
ⓘ 58
🖥

MOUNT NELSON

76 Orange Street, Gardens 8001
Tel 021-4831000
www.mountnelson.co.za

Cape Town's famous colonial hotel is set in landscaped parkland, with views of Table Mountain. A grand palm-lined

avenue leads to the main building. Rooms are luxurious, with all possible facilities, but some may be rather old-fashioned (expect lots of floral fabrics and chintz). There's a heated swimming pool, tennis courts, squash court and beauty salon, and the celebrated Cape Colony restaurant serves Cape specials and contemporary food, with live jazz performances. Service is impeccable, and the hotel is well worth visiting for the daily cream teas on the veranda. Parking is available.
🛏 R5,125
ⓘ 288
🖥 🖾 🖭

PARK INN

10 Greenmarket Square, City Centre 8001
Tel 021-4232050
www.parkinn.com
The Park Inn is a central hotel set in the historic Shell building, right on bustling Greenmarket Square. The rooms have pleasant neutral interiors and attractive, functional bathrooms (shower only). The small pool deck, with sauna and gym, has beautiful views of Table Mountain. There's a good restaurant—The Famous Butcher's Grill—on the ground floor, with tables overlooking the market, plus a stylish, if rather dark, cigar bar. Service is professional and friendly. Parking is available.
🛏 R620
ⓘ 166
🖥 🖾 🖭

PARKER COTTAGE

3 Carstens Street, Tamboerskloof 8001
Tel 021-4246445
www.parkercottage.co.za
Parker Cottage is a stylish and atmospheric guesthouse in a restored Victorian bungalow in a quiet City Bowl suburb. The eight bedrooms, all with large private bathrooms containing claw-foot baths, have highly polished wood floors and are filled with antiques. There are bright flamboyant touches and a Victorian feel to the furnishing. Breakfast is served in the high-ceilinged breakfast room.
🛏 R750
ⓘ 8

TABLE MOUNTAIN LODGE
10a Tamboerskloof Road,
Tamboerskloof 8001
Tel 021-4230042
www.tablemountainlodge.co.za

Table Mountain Lodge has seven beautifully decorated rooms. They are breezy and very comfortable, with fresh white linen, wooden furniture and floors, huge windows and large bathrooms. There's a small garden and a splash pool, a breakfast room and a tiny bar. The owners are very friendly and welcoming.
🖐 R768
ⓘ 8
🖼

CONSTANTIA
THE CELLARS-HOHENHORT
93 Brommersvlei Road,
Constantia 7806
Tel 021-7942137
www.cellars-hohenort.com
Set in two converted manor houses on a wine estate, this is one of the most luxurious hotels on the Peninsula. The suites and double rooms are individually decorated, with huge beds, antiques and spacious bathrooms. Facilities include two restaurants (▷ 260), a beauty salon, a tennis court, golf course and gardens overlooking False Bay.
🖐 R5,300
ⓘ 46
🔲 🖼

FALSE BAY
BOULDER'S BEACH GUEST HOUSE
4 Boulders Place, Boulder's Beach,
Simon's Town 7975
Tel 021-7861758
www.bouldersbeach.co.za
One of the most relaxing places to stay in the area is a stone's throw from the beach. The rooms in this friendly, well-run guesthouse have a simple, refreshing design, with private bathrooms;

most are arranged around a paved yard without sea views. There are also two self-catering apartments. At night you may see penguins exploring the grounds after everyone has gone home and it's quiet. Parking is available.

🖐 R750
ⓘ 12

BRITISH HOTEL APARTMENTS
90 St. George Street,
Simon's Town 7975
Tel 021-7862214
www.british-hotel.co.za
The great views of the bay from magnificent wrought-iron balconies make this one of the best places to stay in False Bay. The converted Victorian hotel has four elegant, self-catering apartments. Each covers two floors, and has three bedrooms, all with Victorian-style bathrooms. There are polished wood floors throughout, and an attractive mix of maritime antiques, art deco and stylish modern furnishings, with an open-plan kitchen and lounge.
🖐 R300 per person, excluding breakfast
ⓘ 4 apartments

SOUTHERN RIGHT
12–14 Glen Road, Glencairn,
False Bay 7975
Tel 021-7820314
This hotel, set back from the sea, is a fashionable place, but family-friendly. The rooms have private bathrooms, high ceilings, dark polished wood floors and four-poster beds. The stylish bar and restaurant serves pub meals, seafood and grills. Parking is available.
🖐 R765
ⓘ 18

SOUTHERN SUBURBS
KOORNHOOP MANOR HOUSE
24 London Road, Observatory 7925
Tel 021-4480595

This converted Victorian house in a large, peaceful garden has eight rooms with private bathrooms, floral interiors and TV. There's a communal lounge and breakfast room. You will also find two huge and extremely good-value self-catering apartments with three bedrooms and access to a garden. Parking is available.
🖐 R550
ⓘ 8, plus 2 apartments

VICTORIA AND ALFRED WATERFRONT
CAPE GRACE
West Quay Road, V & A
Waterfront 8002
Tel 021-4107100
www.capegrace.com
This luxurious hotel is a large development in a great spot, just a short walk from the main Waterfront shops and restaurants. The large, comfortable rooms are traditionally decorated, with balconies either overlooking the Waterfront or with views of Table Mountain. There's a spa, a stylish bar and the celebrated one.waterfront restaurant, where the service and food are excellent. An attractive swimming pool and deck with a bar opens out from the restaurant. Parking is available.
🖐 R4,400
ⓘ 120
🔲 🖼

VICTORIA & ALFRED
Pierhead, V & A Waterfront 8001
Tel 021-4196677
www.vahotel.co.za
The Victoria & Alfred is a stylishly converted fishing warehouse set in the middle of the V & A Waterfront, with spacious, cool and comfortable rooms. All have king-size beds and TV with DVD player; some have dramatic mountain views. The large marble and stone bathrooms come with a separate WC. The restaurant has a pleasant outdoor deck, also with views of the mountain and serves seafood and steaks. There's a fashionable, airy bar attached. Service is friendly and efficient. Parking is available.
🖐 R1,995, excluding breakfast (R80)
ⓘ 68
🔲

STAYING

WESTERN CAPE

The Cape is such a popular destination that unless you reserve as far in advance as possible you are unlikely to find anywhere to stay in the high season. Fortunately, there are plenty of options and you should consider basing yourself in a smaller town. Many of the wine estates along the Winelands and Garden Route now have accommodation, and the Franschhoek Wine Route has particularly luxurious facilities.

BEAUFORT WEST

MATOPPO INN
Corner of Meintjies and Bird streets, Beaufort West 6970
Tel 023-4151055
Set in a quiet residential street, this was originally the 1834 Drostdy or magistrate's house, now converted into a comfortable guesthouse, with high ceilings and beautiful wood floors. The comfortable rooms are furnished with antiques and brass bed-heads, and all have a private entrance. Traditional Karoo dinners are served by candlelight, and there's a neat garden with a swimming pool. South African statesman Cecil Rhodes spent many a night here on the way to what was then Rhodesia (present-day Zimbabwe and Zambia).
🏨 R390, excluding breakfast (R35)
🛏 9
🅿

THE CEDERBERG

BUSHMAN'S KLOOF
On the Wupperthal Road, over the Pakhuis Pass
Tel 027-4822627
www.bushmanskloof.co.za
This private reserve claims to have the world's largest open-air art gallery—it has one of the best San art sites in South Africa. There are more than 130 sites, dating back 10,000 years. Accommodation is in luxurious cottages or in the main building. All rooms have air-conditioning, private bathrooms, four-poster beds, log fires and wooden decks overlooking a lake. There are four swimming pools, as well as a sauna and a beauty spa where treatments are given outdoors in the shadow of the rocks. The restaurant serves excellent South African fare in an outdoor *boma* (enclosure). Prices include all meals, game drives and tours.
🏨 R3,800
🅿🅿

GEKKO BACKPACKERS
On Arbeidsgenot Farm
Tel 022-9213721

Although this excellent backpacker lodge, set amid orange trees on a citrus farm, is a popular stop with overlander trucks (which means impromptu parties), it's usually a very peaceful spot. There are two dorms and two double rooms. The bathrooms are brightly painted, the large kitchen is fully equipped and there's an honesty bar, a table-tennis room and a small lounge. The surrounding gardens have hammocks strung underneath trees, and guests are free to wander among the orange groves. The farm owner is happy to take guests to swimming holes and San rock art sites.
🏨 From R65
🛏 20 beds
🚗 Drive along the N7 north from Citrusdal; signpost to left after 20km (12.5 miles)

CLANWILLIAM DAM PUBLIC RESORT
Clanwilliam
Tel 027-4828000
The only budget option is in this huge resort, set beside the Clanwilliam dam. It has 180 caravan and tent stands on tiers up the hillside, plus simple, modern, self-catering chalets. There are plenty of trees offering shade, electric

and gas points, and cooking and washing blocks. The resort gets very busy in season, but it's a peaceful area out of the school holidays. There is no restaurant, bar or shop.
🏨 From R35 per person
🛏 180 stands
🚗 1km (0.6 miles) out of town

NOUPOORT FARM
Tel 022-9145754
The Farm is a magnificent mountain retreat with a mix of self-catering and bed-and-breakfast accommodation, providing an excellent base from which to explore the West Coast and the Cederberg region. The fully equipped cottages have kitchens and an outdoor barbecue area, with a mix of double and twin beds. Meals are available on request (full-board rates are available). Some of the cottages are newer than others, with magnificent views and an interesting split-level design.
🏨 R350
🛏 15 cottages
🚗 From the N7, turn off at Piketberg and follow Langstraat into town. At a intersection turn right on to Elands Bay Road. Turn left after 1km (0.5 miles), signposted 'Versfeldpas Drive'. Follow for approximately 13km (8 miles) up the pass to the top of the mountains; look out for a left turning marked 'Langeberg Afdelings pad'; the turning for the farm is 5km (3 miles) along this road

STAYING

KNYSNA

PHANTOM FOREST ECO-RESERVE

Tel 044-3860046
www.phantomforest.com
This superb collection of luxurious tree houses, set in a magnificent forest, offers ultra-stylish accommodation high above the Knysna lagoon. The tree houses are eco-friendly and equipped with huge beds, sisal carpets and African art, and have private terraces. The bathrooms are sumptuous, with views out over the forest. Individual houses are connected by walkway to the excellent restaurant and bar where guests are served sundowner drinks overlooking the lagoon before dining on South African cuisine. There's also a Moroccan-themed restaurant, a beauty spa and pool, and the staff can arrange activities in the area.

🛏 R2,400
🛌 14
🏊
📍 Signposted from Phantom Pass road, on western edge of lagoon

WAYSIDE INN

48 Main Street, Knysna 6571
Tel 044-3826011
www.waysideinn.co.za

The smart Wayside Inn with a Victorian theme is in central Knysna. The bedrooms are stylish, with wrought-iron beds and sisal carpets, ceiling fans (and heating in winter), and a selection of African art, giving them a colonial feel. Each room has a private balcony, and although there's no breakfast room (it's served in your room) or lounge, the veranda is used in fine weather. Hampers can be made to order. Parking is available.

🛏 R480
🛌 15

LANGEBAAN

LANGEBAAN BEACH HOUSE

44 Beach Road, Langebaan 7357
Tel 022-7722625
www.langebaanbeachhouse.com
The small Langebaan Beach House is in an idyllic setting, right on the beach overlooking Langebaan lagoon, and near the West Coast National Park (▷ 87). The sunny bedrooms have terracotta-tiled floors, floral bed covers, TVs and simple, private bathrooms. The lagoon-facing rooms have a veranda overlooking the beach. Cooked or continental breakfasts are served on the terrace, and guests can relax in the small, neat garden with its pool.

🛏 R520
🛌 4
🏊
❓ No children under 12

MOSSEL BAY

OLD POST OFFICE TREE MANOR

Corner of Church and Market streets, Mossel Bay 6506
Tel 044-6913738
www.oldposttree.co.za

The rooms of this hotel are in and around a smart manor house, which is the third oldest building in Mossel Bay. Accommodation is a mix of comfortable, well-styled double rooms, with private bathrooms and beautiful views of the ocean, and larger self-catering suites set around the old manor house. Facilities include a restaurant with an outdoor dining area and fine bay views, a swimming pool, curio shop and cocktail bar. It's a popular place, so reserve ahead in high season. Parking is available.

🛏 R740
🛌 30
🏊

OUDTSHOORN

QUEEN'S

Baron van Rheede Street, Oudtshoorn 6625
Tel 044-2722101
Queen's, set in tidy gardens, is Oudtshoorn's best-known hotel. It's comfortable and friendly, although the guest rooms lack the charm of the public areas, which are stylish and play up to the building's colonial history, with antiques, animal prints and art deco touches. The Colony restaurant serves South African dishes and a buffet lunch on Sundays. The gardens have a swimming pool and tennis courts, and there's a curio shop and secure parking.

🛏 R864
🛌 60
🏊

PLETTENBERG BAY

ABALONE BEACH HOUSE

6km (4 miles) east of Keurboomstrand
Tel 044-5359602
This guesthouse, in a modern house right by a stunning stretch of beach at the other end of the bay from town, also acts as a backpacker hostel. There are three spotless double rooms and a dorm with bunk beds. It is simple and comfortable, with blue carpets and white furniture. Guests can relax in the communal TV area or in hammocks on a terrace around the pool. Self-catering is possible in the shared kitchen, and the owners prepare daily meals on *braais* (barbecues) served on the terrace. A path leads down to the deserted beach.

🛏 From R70
🛌 15 beds
🏊
📍 Follow Keurboomstrand signs from N2, turn in to El Remo and continue to top of hill

STONE COTTAGE

Corner of Harker and Odland streets, Plettenberg Bay 6600
Tel 044-5331331
www.stonecottage.co.za
Stone Cottage is actually two cottages split into four apartments, just five minutes from the main beach and the shops and restaurants in town. The main cottage is a beautifully restored 19th-century building, decorated in neutral beige, grey and white, with high

STAYING

ceilings and gleaming wooden floors, and furnished with antiques and old photographs. The other cottage has two suites and sleeps from two to six people. Both have views over the bay and have private decks overlooking the beach.

🛏 From R700 (depending on number of people and which cottage)
ℹ 4 apartments

SWELLENDAM

ADIN & SHARON'S HIDEAWAY

10 Hermanus Steyn Street, Swellendam 6740
Tel 028-5143316
www.adinbb.co.za

The best place to stay in Swellendam is this award-winning bed-and-breakfast in the middle of town. Hosts Adin and Sharon have put a lot of thought into decorating their three spacious suites, two of which have large four-poster beds, and all have cool terracotta floors, and hand-crafted wooden furniture mixed with antiques. The rooms are set in a neat, shady garden filled with rose bushes. There's a small splash pool and a lounge, and excellent breakfasts are served, including home-made bread and preserves.

🛏 R450
ℹ 3
♿ 🏊

SWELLENDAM BACKPACKERS

5 Lichtenstein Street, Swellendam 6740
Tel 028-5142648
This excellent backpackers' hostel has succeeded in introducing much of the Overberg region to budget visitors. The main house has one small dorm, and the large gardens are dotted with small, individual wooden houses tucked in secluded corners. These have double or twin beds but no electricity—the manager will supply you with a gas lamp

instead. There's lots of camping space, a well-organized kitchen, email access, and home cooked breakfasts and dinners are available. The Baz Bus (▷ 51) calls twice a day.

🛏 From R70 per bed
ℹ 30 beds

WHALE COAST

LIVESEY LODGE

13 Main Road, Hermanus 7200
Tel 028-3130026
www.liveseylodge.co.za
This well run, friendly guesthouse on the outskirts of town has six double rooms set around a leafy garden with a good-sized pool. All have separate entrances and private bathrooms, big beds, TVs and mini-fridges. There are nice touches such as books in all the rooms. Parking is available.

🛏 R700
ℹ 6
🏊

THE MARINE

Marine Drive, Hermanus 7200
Tel 028-3131000
www.collectionmcgrath.com

The historic Marine, part of the Relais & Chateaux group, is one of the finest hotels in the country. The bright white building dominates the cliffs on Marine Drive and offers stunning ocean views. Bedrooms are luxurious with fine furnishings, such as silk curtains, plush carpets, pale suede armchairs and marble bathrooms. There are also thoughtful touches like fresh-cut flowers, and some rooms have four-poster beds and his 'n' her bathrooms. A small spa offers facials and massages, and there are two restaurants; the seafood restaurant has an excellent reputation. Parking is available.

🛏 R2,650
ℹ 42
♿ 🏊

WILDERNESS

MOONTIDE GUEST LODGE

Southside Road, Wilderness 6560
Tel 044-8770361
www.moontide.co.za
Moontide has a wonderful setting right on the edge of Wilderness lagoon, with a deck overlooking the water. Accommodation is in thatched cottages with private bathrooms, set under milkwood trees in a beautiful garden. Each cottage has been decorated with fine furniture, and the rough stone walls give them a rustic feel. There is easy access to the hiking trails in the national park and it's just a short walk from the beach.

🛏 R760
ℹ 7

WINELANDS

AVENUES

32 The Avenue, Stellenbosch 7600
Tel 021-8871843
www.theavenues.co.za
Avenues is a relaxed, family-run guesthouse, just a short walk from the middle of town. All rooms have private bathrooms; some have wooden floors and bright, simple furnishings, others are just as comfortable, but with carpets. The garden-facing room (No. 5) is the nicest, with original fittings in the bathroom. Parking is available.

🛏 R600
ℹ 8
♿

LANZERAC MANOR

2km (1.2 miles) from Stellenbosch
Tel 021-8871132
www.lanzerac.co.za
A very expensive but fittingly luxurious hotel set around an 18th-century Cape Dutch manor house. Bedrooms are decorated with checked fabrics and mellow reds, yellows and blues. Each has a private patio overlooking either the surrounding vineyards or the hotel's gardens, and the bathrooms have a separate shower. Some rooms open on to the swimming pool. The hotel has two restaurants and parking is available.

🛏 R2,700
ℹ 48
♿ 🏊
🚗 Towards Jonkershoek Reserve, Jonkershoek Road

LA FONTAINE
21 Dirkie Uys Street,
Franschhoek 7690
Tel 021-8762112
www.lafontainefranschhoek.co.za
La Fontaine is one of the
finest guesthouses in
Franschhoek. Set in a
central Victorian house, it
is characterized by its stylish
understated decoration,
which includes a mix of
antiques, African art and
fine polished wooden floors.
All bedrooms have large
Victorian-style bathrooms;
some are set in the garden
around a pool and have
more of an ethnic-chic feel.
Breakfast is served on the
vine-shaded courtyard.
R750
12

NANTES-VUE
56 Mill Street, Paarl 7646
Tel 021-8727311
www.nantes-paarl.co.za
This quiet bed-and-breakfast is
set in a central Victorian house.
Its rooms all have high ceilings
and understated interiors—
beds have iron bedheads, the
floor is covered in grass mat-
ting and the bathrooms have
enormous showers and free-
standing baths. The breakfast
room has a country farm feel
to it, and there's a comfortable
lounge with big leather sofas.
In the garden is a one-bed-
room cottage, with an
additional bed downstairs.
R900
5

DE OUDE PAARL
132 Main Street, Paarl 7646
Tel 021-8721002
www.deoudepaarl.com
De Oude Paarl is a smart
new hotel occupying national
monument buildings on the
main road, just before central
Paarl. It has a dark and moody
(but seriously stylish) feel
to it, with its individually
designed rooms decorated
in muted greys and dark reds,
and fine stone bathrooms.
There is an excellent restaurant
downstairs, as well as a wine
boutique, a bar and even a
Belgian chocolate deli. Parking
is available.

R930
25

PLUMWOOD INN
11 Cabriere Street, Franschhoek 7690
Tel 021-8763883
www.plumwoodinn.com
This small guesthouse is in a
quiet residential street. The
bedrooms are individually
styled, with their own private
entrance and bathroom, TV,
country-style furniture and
brightly painted walls. The elegant guest lounge has high
ceilings, a cool tiled floor and
huge leather sofas, ideal for
relaxing with a book. Breakfast
is served in the well-kept garden and dinner is available on
request. Parking is available.
R900
8

? No children allowed

LE QUARTIER FRANÇAIS
16 Hugenot Street, Franschhoek 7690
Tel 021-8762151
www.lequartier.co.za

Le Quartier Français is an
elegant hotel in the middle of
Franschhoek, with enormous
rooms set around a central
courtyard. There is a small
pool and peaceful paths wind
around the property. The
bedrooms have fireplaces and
beautiful stone private bathrooms, plush bright furnishings
and views over the gardens.
The attached restaurant of the

same name (▷ 264) is rated
as one of the best in the
Western Cape.
R2,500, excluding breakfast
14

STUMBLE INN
12 Market Street, Stellenbosch 7600
Tel 021-8874049
The Stumble Inn is set in two
Victorian bungalows. There
are spacious double rooms
and slightly smaller dorms. The
original house has an attractive
rambling garden with shady
cushion banks and hammocks,
a small bar, TV room and a
kitchen. The other house has
a small pool and kitchen. It's
all very relaxed and friendly.
Guests can also rent bicycles.
From R60 per bed
60 beds

THE VILLAGE AT SPIER
Spier Wine Estate, South of
Stellenbosch on the R44
Tel 021-8091100
www.spier.co.za
Probably the Winelands' most
commercial wine estate, but a
thoroughly enjoyable place to
stay. The Village is a series of
condo-style buildings arranged
around courtyards, with private
pools for each section. Rooms
are enormous with stylish
decoration, polished concrete
floors and large windows
which let in plenty of light.
All have satellite TV, mini-bar,
and beautiful bathrooms.
There are four restaurants,
two bars, a spa and a cheetah
park. Parking is available.
R1,382 (includes tourism levy)
155

WORCESTER
CHURCH STREET LODGE
36 Church Street, Worcester 6850
Tel 023-3425194
www.churchst.co.za
The Lodge has pleasant rooms
with a country feel, antique
wood furniture and bright
patchwork quilts on the beds.
All have little extras such as
coffee facilities and mini-fridge.
The building is modern, with a
breakfast room and a Roman-
style pool set in peaceful
grounds. Meals are available at
an attached café and self-
catering is also on offer.
R620
21

EASTERN CAPE

During the last few years Port Elizabeth has experienced a rapid expansion in visitor accommodation and if you're looking for something close to the beach, it's perfect. As the best-known surfing spot in South Africa, Jeffreys Bay attracts large numbers of surfers from all over the world. Consequently, there is a good range of budget accommodation here.

PRICES AND SYMBOLS

The hotels below are listed alphabetically (excluding The) by town or area, then by name. Prices are for a double room for one night, including breakfast. All the hotels listed accept credit cards unless otherwise stated. See page 2 for a key to the symbols.

GRAAFF-REINET

DROSTDY
30 Church Street, Graaff-Reinet 6280
Tel 049-8922161
www.drostdy.co.za

The Drostdy was designed by acclaimed architect Louis Thibault in 1804, and today is a beautifully restored hotel. The bedrooms are at the back of the main house in an appealing complex of 19th-century cottages known as Stretch's Court, originally the homes of emancipated slaves. The bedrooms have a slightly outdated feel (expect a surplus of ruffles and floral fabrics), but the public areas are appealing, with antiques and historical paintings. The Camdeboo Restaurant has a good reputation (▷ 265) and the attached Kromm's Inn serves snacks throughout the day. There's a lovely secluded garden where you can have pre-dinner drinks, as well as a pool and secure off-street parking for your car.
🏨 R730
🛏 51
♿ ☰

SPECIAL IN CRADOCK

DIE TUISHUISE
36 Market Street, Cradock 5880
Tel 048-8811322
www.tuishuise.co.za

It is worth visiting Cradock for Die Tuishuise alone. This guesthouse occupies a series of historical buildings on Market Street, each restored and decorated to reflect the British and Dutch settlers' lifestyles more than a century ago. The bedrooms have beautiful antiques, four-poster beds, private bathrooms and original features such as Victorian fireplaces and polished hardwood floors. Every house has a fully equipped kitchen and lounge and is ideal for families or two couples. Huge breakfasts are served in the Victorian dining room, and dinner is in the Manor House on the corner of the street. The staff are very friendly and helpful.
🏨 R500
🛏 25

GRAHAMSTOWN

THE COCK HOUSE
10 Market Street, Grahamstown 6139
Tel 046-6361287
www.cockhouse.co.za

This beautifully restored 1820s national monument has nine double rooms with private bathrooms, each individually decorated with fine fabrics, antiques and original wood floors. A lovely first-floor veranda overlooks the street, and there's a comfortable lounge and library where author Andre Brink penned four of his novels. Attached is a highly rated à la carte restaurant. Past guests at the Cock House include former South African president Nelson Mandela and President Thabo Mbeki.
🏨 R735
🛏 9

GREATER ADDO ELEPHANT NATIONAL PARK

GORAH ELEPHANT CAMP
PO Box 454, Plettenberg Bay 6600
Tel 044-5327818 (central reservations)
www.gorah.com

This camp has a private concession covering 4,500ha (11,120 acres), but gives access to the rest of the park. Accommodation is in huge, luxurious tents with a colonial theme, complete with four-poster beds, private bathrooms and terraces with views of the park. A relaxing *boma* (enclosed outdoor area) has a free-form rock swimming pool. Meals are served in a renovated coach house, overlooking a waterhole frequented by elephant, buffalo and antelope. The price includes all meals, guided game drives and night drives. The camp comes highly recommended and offers a similar experience to the luxury camps around Kruger (▷ 291); the only drawback is that the service is rather over-attentive.
🏨 R7,700
🛏 10
☰
🚗 Drive east on N2 from Port Elizabeth, through Colchester, then take N10 (north) onto Addo Heights Road (gravel). After 9km (5.5 miles), Gorah is on your left

HOGSBACK

AWAY WITH THE FAIRIES
Signposted from Main Road,
Hogsback 5721
Tel 045-9621031
www.awaywiththefairies.co.za
Away with the Fairies is one of
the best backpacker establishments in the country—friendly,
relaxed and well run. There are
brightly painted dorms and
double rooms, plus one caravan, which sleeps two. There is
a well equipped kitchen, clean
bathrooms and a comfortable
lounge with a fireplace. The
surrounding gardens are beautiful, with plenty of camping
space and a gate that leads to
forest trails. A lively bar serves
big breakfasts and evening
meals, and staff can organize
daily guided walks and sundowner trips.
🛏 R65 per bed
🛏 20 beds

JEFFREYS BAY

ISLAND VIBE
10 Dageraad Street, Jeffreys Bay 6330
Tel 042-2931625

Island Vibe hostel is in an
excellent position at the top
end of Jeffreys Bay, perched
high on a promontory with
views of, and access to, two
beaches. There are large
dorms, doubles and camping
space, with a kitchen, and a
popular bar serving good
breakfasts and set evening
meals. The place has a big
surfer scene, so it can get
noisy. Quieter visitors will
appreciate the beach house,
which has double rooms with
private bathrooms, great sea
views and a more peaceful
atmosphere. The hostel rents
out bicycles, canoes, fishing
rods and surf boards.
🛏 From R60
🛏 Around 40 beds

PORT ELIZABETH

HACKLEWOOD HILL COUNTRY HOUSE
152 Prospect Road, Walmer,
Port Elizabeth 6070
Tel 041-5811300
www.pehotels.co.za
In a late-Victorian manor
house, this luxurious place
has enormous bathrooms. The
bedrooms, some with striking
red walls, are filled with attractive antiques and original
paintings. There are also beautiful mature gardens with a
tennis court. The elegant
dining room has some special
touches—for example, guests
are encouraged to select their
wine from the impressive
cellar. Advanced reservations
are essential during the high
season. Parking is available.
🛏 R2,700
🛏 8
♿
👶 No children under 16

MILLBROOK HOUSE
2 Havelock Square, Central,
Port Elizabeth 6001
Tel 041-5853080
The delightful Millbrook House
bed-and-breakfast is in a leafy
square. The early 20th-century
house has attractive wrought-
iron balconies and a low-key,
peaceful atmosphere. It's a
good-value, family-run place,
with four bright and airy rooms
with private bathrooms, pretty
furnishings, ceiling fans and
satellite TV. There's a small
garden with a splash pool,
and a comfortable lounge.
🛏 R300
🛏 5

SHAMWARI GAME RESERVE

LONG LEE MANOR
Tel 042-2031111 (central reservations)
www.shamwari.com
Long Lee Manor is the largest
of six luxury camps within this
private reserve. It feels like a
smart country hotel that has
been dropped in the middle of
the African bush. All the rooms
are very chic, with plush fabrics
and four-poster beds, under-
floor heating and satellite TV.
Other facilities include a curio
shop, an excellent restaurant
and a floodlit tennis court. At
the nearby Bushman's River is
an outdoor eating area where
guests can watch the animals
drink while they enjoy a meal.

Prices include all meals and
game drives.
🛏 R8,650
♿ 🚗
🚗 From Port Elizabeth, follow signs
for the N2, Grahamstown. After 65km
(40 miles), the park is signposted off
to the left

WILD COAST

BUCCANEER'S
Cintsa 5273
Tel 043-7343012

This superb lodge, set in
forests overlooking Cintsa
lagoon and the beach, has a
wide choice of accommoda-
tion. A 2km (1.2-mile) dirt
track leads to the secluded
site, with a choice of backpacker dorms, double rooms,
fully equipped self-catering
cottages and camping. A lively
bar serves evening meals and
snacks, and there are verandas
with ocean views. The lodge
stretches down towards the
beach, and has a path leading
straight to the lagoon. Other
facilities include free canoes
and surfboards, and a range
of free daily activities such as
guided walks.
🛏 From R70 a bed; from R260 for
a double
🛏 84 beds

THE KRAAL
Mpande 5121
Tel 043-6832384
The Kraal is on a hill above a
beach and lagoon. It is made
up of traditional thatched
Xhosa *rondavels* (thatched
huts) with dormitory beds, no
electricity, 'eco-loos' and hot
showers. It's a simple set-up in
an isolated corner of the Wild
Coast. You can buy supplies at
the kitchen, but the owners
also prepare superb meals.
🛏 R70 per bed
🛏 12 beds
🚗 Signposted from the road to
Port St. Johns; follow signs for 20km
(12.5 miles)

STAYING

KWAZULU-NATAL

Central Durban and the beachfront have an ample selection of accommodation to suit every kind of budget, but in terms of safety and nightlife, things have shifted from downtown to the suburbs of Morningside and Berea. If you choose to stay in central Durban, you will have access to the sights in the city and the beach, but will need a car (and parking at your hotel) to drive to the suburbs and enjoy the nightlife. Alternatively you can choose accommodation in the suburbs or outlying coastal resorts but again you will need transport back into Durban for sightseeing during the day. The attraction of staying in the suburbs is that they are at a higher altitude and therefore cooler and less humid. Accommodation here tends to be in hotels aimed more towards the business person or luxury B&Bs.

PRICES AND SYMBOLS

The hotels below are listed alphabetically (excluding The) by town or area, then by name. Prices are for a double room for one night, including breakfast. All the hotels listed accept credit cards unless otherwise stated. See page 2 for a key to the symbols.

BATTLEFIELDS ROUTE

BULLERS REST LODGE

61 Cove Crescent, Ladysmith 3370
Tel 036-6376154
www.bullersrestlodge.co.za

The family-run Bullers Rest Lodge is a delightful thatched house with fine views of the mountains. The bedrooms are spacious and extremely comfortable, with country-style decoration, beige and cream furnishings and African art on the walls. There is a tiny pub, filled with Boer War memorabilia, and the gardens have a swimming pool and sun deck overlooking Ladysmith. Meals are available (dinner must be reserved in advance and costs R75 per person), and the owners have a great knowledge about the surrounding area.

🛏 R440
🛌 10
🏊

FUGITIVES' DRIFT LODGE

Tel 034-6421843
www.fugitives-drift-lodge.com
Home to famous battlefields guide David Rattray, this is the leading lodge in the region (▷ 106–107), offering stylish accommodation. A night's stay includes a trip to Rorke's Drift in the afternoon, followed by a tour to Isandlwana the following morning. Bedrooms are smart and modern, with cream and beige fabrics, huge beds and well-appointed bathrooms with free-standing baths, and all have private verandas. There are also rooms in an annexe cottage. The lounge and dining room—which serves excellent traditional food—is filled with Battlefields memorabilia. Staying here is a real highlight for anyone with even the slightest interest in history: few story-tellers can evoke the past of a region quite like David Rattray.

🛏 R3,700
🛌 8
🏡 50km (31 miles) south of Dundee, towards Greytown on the R33

ISANDLWANA LODGE

Isandlwana
Tel 034-2718301
www.isandlwana.co.za
This luxury lodge opened in 1999 beneath the rock upon which the Zulu commander stood at the start of the Isandlwana battle (▷ 106). A stunning wood, thatch and stone two-floor building, it blends well with its surroundings. The rooms have private bathrooms and a mix of modern and rustic furnishings, but the highlight is the private balconies with commanding views over the valley and battle site. The swimming pool, also with valley views, is carved out of the rock. Well prepared South African fare is served in the high-ceilinged

stone restaurants, and guests can take a variety of guided historical tours of the area.
🛏 R2,640 (including bed, breakfast and dinner)
🛌 13
🏊 🏡
🏡 Off the R68, between Babanango and Melmoth

DURBAN

BALI ON THE RIDGE

268 South Ridge Road, Glenwood, Durban 4001
Tel 031-2619574
www.baliridge.co.za

A beautifully restored house on the Berea ridge overlooking the city of Durban is home to this small elegant bed-and-breakfast with high-ceilinged rooms and wooden floors. The owner is an importer of Indonesian furniture, which she has used to decorate her establishment. Bali on the Ridge offers its guests excellent value for money, with a comfortable lounge, or sun lounge in cooler weather, private bathrooms and satellite TV in each room, and secure off-street parking.
🛏 R288–R336
🛌 4
🏊 🏡

STAYING

HIPPO HIDE LODGE

2 Jesmond Road, Berea, Durban 4001
Tel 031-2074366

This lodge and backpackers' establishment manages to combine an ethnic, African feel with clean, comfortable accommodation at budget prices. Take the edge off Durban's subtropical heat in the rock pool outside, enjoy a drink at the poolside bar, or go out to eat at one of the many restaurants within walking distance of the Hippo Hide.

🛏 R176–R280, excluding breakfast
🛌 2 singles, 4 doubles, shared dormitory accommodation
🖼

THE ROYAL

267 Smith Street, Durban 4000
Tel 031-3336000
www.theroyal.co.za
The Royal started life 150 years ago as a thatched wattle-and-daub hostelry. Today this sophisticated luxury hotel right in the heart of the city of Durban is distinguished by its indigenous wood finishes and royal blue colour scheme, offering extras such as squash courts, a sauna and valet service. Most rooms have superb panoramic views of Durban. The hotel counts among its guests over the years Mark Twain, H. G. Wells and Marlene Dietrich.

🛏 R1,840–R3,200
🛌 251 (two non-smoking floors)
🖼 🖼 Rooftop 🖼

TEKWENI BACKPACKERS

169 Ninth Avenue, Morningside 4000
Tel 031-3031433
This popular hostel is close to bars and restaurants and about a 30-minute walk from the beach. Dorms and double rooms are available, with some quieter doubles in the house next door. There's a bar showing sports, internet access, laundry and a kitchen.

QUARTERS HOTEL

101 Florida Road, Berea 4001
Tel 031-3103333
www.quarters.co.za

Four historic homes in the suburb of Berea have been converted to create this boutique hotel. There's a refreshingly modern feel to it: The bedrooms have simple white walls and dark red fabrics, with black and white photographs on the walls. Other facilities include a popular on-site brasserie serving meals throughout the day, a shaded courtyard and a modern bar. Most of the rooms have a small veranda overlooking palm-shaded gardens. Parking is available.

🛏 R1,100
🛌 24
🖼

🛏 R80 per dorm bed, R210 for a double
🛌 48 beds
🖼

HIBISCUS COAST

KENILWORTH-ON-SEA

Marine Drive, Margate 4275
Tel 039-3120342
www.kenilworthonsea.co.za
A popular guest lodge and dive resort, set in tropical gardens, Kenilworth-on-Sea is right by the beach. Accommodation is in a string of cottages; all are functional and comfortable, with satellite TV and simple furnishings, plus small outside terraces. Rates include a cooked breakfast and three-course dinner. Scuba diving courses are also offered, and there is a pool on site. Parking is available.

🛏 R220 per person
🛌 28 units
🖼

HLUHLUWE-IMFOLOZI GAME RESERVE

HILLTOP CAMP

Tel 033-8451000
www.kznwildlife.com
Hilltop is the largest of the camps in the park, with the most spectacular location and sweeping views over much of the park and parts of Swaziland. There are various types of accommodation, covering a wide price range. At the top end are comfortable four-bed chalets with fully equipped kitchens. At the budget end are two-bed rest-huts with a communal kitchen and shower block. Although this doesn't have the exclusivity of the smaller bush camps, the central lounge, restaurant, bar, pool and veranda make for a relaxing end to the day. Game drives and guided walks can be arranged from here.

🛏 From R290 (per person for resthut); from R424 (per person for chalet)
🛌 69
🚗 Turning at Mtubatuba leads west on the R618 (50km/31 miles) to Hluhluwe village, which leads (14km/8.5 miles) to the northern Memorial Gate entrance

KOSI BAY

KOSI FOREST LODGE

Tel 035-4741473
www.zulunet.co.za
Kosi Bay is the only private lodge within the reserve, part of the Greater St. Lucia Wetland Park. Its thatched bush suites are hidden in the sand forest, shaded by the forest canopy. There is a restaurant and bar on a wooden terrace surrounding a giant forest tree. The bedrooms have low wooden walls with mosquito netting and roll-up canvas blinds, allowing full views of the surroundings. All have private bathrooms, with open-air baths and showers enclosed by reeds. It's a small and exclusive place; a great way to experience the lakes in luxury.

🛏 R3,170
🛌 16
🚗 From the N2 head north, passing Richard's Bay, Empangeni and Mkuze. About 10km (6 miles) after Mkuze turn right at signs for Jozini and follow signs to the lodge. You will have to arrange transfers by 4WD to the accommodation before you arrive

STAYING

ORIBI GORGE

ORIBI GORGE HOTEL
Tel 039-6870253
www.oribigorge.co.za
This small family hotel is in an 1870s colonial building circled by a veranda and feels like an African country house. There are spectacular views of the gorge from various points around this private estate. The rooms are bright and airy, with fresh white walls and green-and-cream fabrics, light wooden furniture and wooden floors. The attached restaurant serves burgers, steaks and light meals; there is also a country pub, a swimming pool, pool table, gym and curio shop. The pleasant beer garden is a good lunch spot. Activities can be arranged from here with Wild 5 Adventures (▷ 204). Backpackers have cheaper accommodation in a cottage.
🛏 R740
🛏 8
🏊 🐎
🚗 Follow the scenic route through the gorge; on leaving the reserve head towards Port Shepstone. The hotel is on the northern side of the gorge, clearly signposted. An alternative route from the N2 is to take the turning on the road signposted to Oribi Flats; continue along this road and the turning to the hotel is signposted down a dirt road next to a coffee estate

PIETERMARITZBURG

CITY ROYAL
301 Burger Street,
Pietermaritzburg 3201
Tel 033-3947072
www.cityroyalhotel.co.za
The City Royal is a typical small South African town hotel, with slightly old-fashioned but spacious double rooms. All are air-conditioned with private bathrooms, floral fabrics, TV, tea and coffee-making facilities, and there's a restaurant on-site and two bars. It's just a couple of minutes' walk from the middle of town, and the staff are friendly and welcoming. Parking is available.
🛏 R400
🛏 52
♿

REDLANDS HOTEL AND LODGE
1 George Macfarlane Lane, Wembley,
Pietermaritzburg 3209
Tel 033-3143333

The Redlands offers an unusual combination of hotel and self-catering apartments. Set in a large parkland estate in the suburbs, within easy driving distance of the heart of the city, the Redlands is small enough to provide an atmosphere of home, but with hotel facilities, such as a private lounge, tennis court and fine restaurant (available also to guests in the self-catering accommodation). The hotel is very secure, with controlled access to the property and lock-up basement parking.
🛏 R680–R880, excluding breakfast
🛏 12, plus 8 self-catering apartments
🏊

ST. LUCIA

SEASANDS GARDEN COTTAGES
135 Hornbill Street, St. Lucia 3936
Tel 035-5901082
www.seasands.co.za
These attractive tropical-style lodges just outside central St. Lucia are a peaceful place to stay. They have double rooms with a cool white theme and wicker furniture, large beds with mosquito nets and a private balcony; those at the front have sweeping views of the wetlands. The lodges are surrounded by lush tropical gardens, with a pool. There is a restaurant and bar, and all rooms have air conditioning, satellite TV, french windows and spotless bathrooms.
🛏 R750
🛏 56
♿ 🏊

WETLANDS GUEST HOUSE
20 Kingfisher Street, St. Lucia 3936
Tel 035-5901098
Perfectly placed for safaris into the Greater St. Lucia Wetland Park and the Hluhluwe-Imfolozi Game Reserve, this family bed-and-breakfast provides three large luxury double rooms, one twin room with double bed and three-quarter bed, and a sizable family suite with its own kitchenette. Rooms have either bath and shower or shower only. Guests may do their own barbecuing out on the patio or beside the swimming pool. The guesthouse provides secure parking for visitors' vehicles.

🛏 R528–R576
🛏 5
🏊

SODWANA BAY

SODWANA BAY LODGE
Tel 035-5716000
www.sodwanadivelodge.co.za
This is a good choice for scuba divers as it can provide for all their needs. The lodge has attractive twin-bed, reed and thatch chalets built on stilts overlooking woodland. All have a private shower, ceiling fan, mosquito nets and veranda. There is also a volley-ball court, the Leatherback restaurant, a swimming pool and bar. But the main reason for coming here is to learn to dive: There is a fully equipped diving shop, a purpose-built learning pool and a full range of courses from PADI-qualified instructors. Packages are available which include accommodation and diving (starting from around R800 for two nights and 3 dives for certified divers).
🛏 R1,240 (including bed, breakfast and dinner)
🛏 21
🏊

UKHAHLAMBA-DRAKENSBERG PARK

CATERPILLAR & CATFISH
At the top of Oliviershoek Pass,
outside the park
Tel 036-4386130
www.cookhouse.co.za
The quirky Caterpillar & Catfish
guesthouse is a great place to
stay on the Oliviershoek Pass.
It's a pine-panelled mountain
lodge set in a restored trading
post, tucked under large pine
trees. The bedrooms are
brightly decorated with African
artwork, stripped pine and
handmade furniture. There is
also a set of 10 self-catering
units in the gardens sleeping
two to three people. The huge
buffet breakfasts will set you
up for a day's walking, and the
massage room is ideal for
weary hikers. Guided hikes to
fascinating rock art sites are
available, and fishing is possible in the well-stocked trout
dam nearby. In the evenings,
guests congregate in the
beautifully decorated piano
bar and restaurant (▷ 267).
🍴 R440
ℹ️ 8 bedrooms, 10 self-catering units
🚗 From the N3 (heading north)
turn off at the Winterton/Colenso
exit and turn left on to the R74
Winterton/Bergville. Follow the road,
past Winterton and Bergville, for around
80km (50 miles). The lodge is just
before Sterkfontein dam on the left

CATHEDRAL PEAK HOTEL
Cathedral Peak
Tel 036-4881888
www.cathedralpeak.co.za

The Cathedral Peak Hotel has
always been popular with
hikers and climbers because
of its stunning location close
to the high peaks of the
Drakensberg. These days it has
expanded and offers a wide
range of activities, attracting
large numbers of visitors, so
always reserve in advance. It's
a big place, with 90 luxurious
double rooms, several
restaurants and bars, three
swimming pools, and offers
a nine-hole floodlit golf course,
horseback riding, squash, a
mountain bike trail, a climbing
tower, gym, beauty spa and
tennis courts.
🍴 R1,190 (including bed and breakfast,
afternoon tea and dinner)
ℹ️ 90
🏊 ♿
🚗 From the N3 (heading north)
turn off at the Winterton/Colenso
exit and turn left on to the R74
Winterton/Bergville, followed by a
left on to the R600 in Winterton (at
the Engen garage). Follow signs for
Cathedral Peak until you see signs
for the hotel

DIDIMA CAMP
Cathedral Peak
Tel 033-8451000 (reservations)
www.kznwildlife.com

The theme of this KZN Wildlife
resort, close to the Cathedral
Peak Hotel, is the art of the
San people, and the chalets
are designed to look like caves.
Each is thatched and very comfortable, with stylishly rustic
interiors, satellite TV and fireplaces. The self-catering
accommodation sleeps two
people; as these sit back to
back with each other, they can
be converted into four-bed
family units using an inter-
leading door. There's a central
restaurant, a bar and a small
curio shop, as well as displays
of San rock art, with guided
tours to local sites.
🍴 R594 (R640 for self-catering units)
ℹ️ 63
🚗 From the N3 (heading north)
turn off at the Winterton/Colenso
exit and turn left on to the R74
Winterton/Bergville, followed by a
left on to the R600 in Winterton
(at the Engen garage). Follow signs
for Cathedral Peak until you see signs
for the camp

INKOSANA LODGE
Monk's Cowl
Tel 036-4681202
www.inkosana.co.za
Serious hikers will appreciate
this good value lodge and
backpacker accommodation,
with fine views towards the
mountains. There are four
small dormitories, and a
couple of double rooms—some
with private bathroom—as well
as plenty of shaded camping
space. The large dining area
serves big breakfasts and
evening meals (vegetarian
food is available) and the
staff can arrange a variety of
walks and tours in the area.
The lodge is set in a large garden and is a short stroll from
nearby shops and restaurants.
🍴 R60 (camping), from R80 (dorm
bed), R240 (double room)
ℹ️ 28 beds
🏊
🚗 7km (4 miles) from Monk's Cowl.
From the N3 (heading north) turn off
at the Winterton/Colenso exit and turn
left on to the R74 Winterton/Bergville,
followed by a left on to the R600
in Winterton (at the Engen garage).
Ikosana is 25km (15.5 miles) along
this road

ZULULAND

KWABHEKITHUNGA/
STEWARTS FARM
Tel 035-4600644
www.stewartsfarm.com
This is recommended to get
a real feel of Zulu life. The
village is the home of Chief
Mbhangucuza Fakude, his four
brothers and their extended
families. They earn their living
by making traditional Zulu
beads, baskets and shields,
and have now branched out
into the hospitality industry.
Accommodation is purpose-
built and very comfortable, in
12 Zulu beehive-shaped huts,
all with private bathrooms
and bright interiors. There is
also a bar and a swimming
pool. For an extra R165 per
person visitors are treated to
Zulu dancing and singing, and
a taste of Zulu food and home-
brewed beer. Reservations
are essential.
🍴 R800
ℹ️ 12
🏊
🚗 36km (22 miles) from Eshowe on
the R34 towards Empangeni

STAYING

LIMPOPO AND MPUMALANGA

Many of the smaller towns, such as Hoedspruit, have an excellent range of accommodation. But if you are coming to this area, you are probably coming to the Kruger. The park has 12 main rest camps, five bushveld camps, two bush lodges and four satellite camps, owned and managed by South African National Parks (SANParks). All the room rates are very reasonable when one considers where you are and what you are getting. If you are looking for luxury, however, then stay at one of the private game reserves.

PRICES AND SYMBOLS

The hotels below are listed alphabetically (excluding The) by town or area, then by name. Prices are for a double room for one night, including breakfast. All the hotels listed accept credit cards unless otherwise stated. See page 2 for a key to the symbols.

BELA-BELA

CHÂTEAU ANNIQUE
Swanepoel Street extension, Bela-Bela 0480
Tel 014-7362847
www.kloofhuis.co.za
Set in landscaped gardens, this smart guesthouse was originally a country house, built by two Italian prisoners of war. A grand old wooden staircase leads to the bedrooms, all of which are decorated in white and cream, with slightly over-the-top furnishings (lots of drapes and frills) but very comfortable. There are views over the immaculate gardens and guests can use the library.
R400
6
2km (1.2 miles) from town

HAZYVIEW

KRUGER PARK BACKPACKERS
Main Road, Hazyview 1242
Tel 013-7377224
www.krugerparkbackpackers.com
The accommodation here is in beehive-shaped huts (with private bathrooms), decorated with bright tribal designs. The lodge has a lounge and a bar with a pool table. Nightly meals are offered, using home-grown organic produce. Tours can be organized from here, as well as trips into the Kruger.
R75 (dorm bed), R190 (hut)
52
At the junction of the R40 and the road leading to Numbi Gate, 200m (220 yards) past the Caltex garage

SPECIAL IN GRASKOP

THE GRASKOP HOTEL
Corner of Louis Trichardt Street and Main Road, Graskop 1270
Tel 013-7671244
www.graskophotel.co.za
This is one of the best places to stay in the region, and an

ideal base from which to explore the Blyde River Canyon. The Graskop has beautiful public spaces that combine sleek art deco furniture with modern African art and traditional Zulu baskets and weavings. Large Swazi ceramic bowls stand on tables along the corridors, and the bedrooms have dark wood furniture and prints on the walls. There is an à la carte restaurant with an excellent reputation, and the lounge and bar are attractive and relaxing.
R500
34

HOEDSPRUIT

BLYDE RIVER CANYON LODGE
At the foot of the Canyon
Tel 015-7955305
www.blyderivercanyonlodge.com
A very intimate and individual lodge, consisting of six double-thatched rooms with verandas, representing excellent value for money. The whole building is constructed from natural materials and set in beautiful grounds—the owners have gone to great lengths to keep the wildlife totally indigenous, and zebras, warthogs and blue

wildebeest can often be seen wandering across the lawns and through the parking area. There's a bar and a swimming pool, and meals are available on request. You can arrange activities such as mountain biking, kayaking and hiking.
R820
8

Turn off the R531 on to the road signposted to the bottom of the Blyde River Canyon Nature Reserve and Aventura Swadini

FOREVER RESORTS AVENTURA SWADINI
At the foot of the Blyde River Canyon
Tel 015-7955141
www.foreverresorts-sa.co.za
In the middle of a nature reserve, on the banks of the Blyde River, among the peaks of the Drakensberg Mountains, this resort is an outdoor-lover's delight. The Orpen Gate of Kruger National Park is only 80km (50 miles) away. The resort itself has hiking trails and boat trips on the adjacent dam where you can view a spectacular waterfall and hippo and crocodile. Accommodation is in four- to six-person chalets, or in the caravan and camping park. The excellent Billy's Diner provides meals.

R712–R816, excluding breakfast
70 chalets

Turn off the R531 on to the road signposted to the bottom of the Blyde River Canyon Nature Reserve and Aventura Swadini

KRUGER NATIONAL PARK

SANParks central reservations is on 012-4289111, or at www.sanparks.org. Reservations need to be 48 hours in advance. There's an additional daily conservation fee of R120 per adult, R60 per child. Prices are per unit, sleeping between one and six people.

SOUTHERN KRUGER PUBLIC CAMPS

BERG-EN-DAL
Tel 013-7356107
This modern camp's cottages are slightly larger than at the other camps and are more comfortable for three or four people. It has an environmental centre showing wildlife films, a petrol (gas) station, camp shop, restaurant, telephones and launderette. Day walks and day and night game drives are available.

🏕 R100 (camping), R460 (bungalow), R850 (family cottage), R1,700 (guest cottage)

🚐

🏠 Malelane Gate; 92km (57 miles) from Pretoriuskop

PRETORIUSKOP
Tel 013-7355128
This is the oldest and third-largest camp in Kruger. Facilities include a restaurant and cafeteria, a pool made from natural rock, a petrol (gas) station and launderette. Day walks and night drives can be arranged at reception.

🏕 R100 (camping), R160–R850 (hut/bungalow), R1,500 (guesthouse)

🚐

🏠 Numbi Gate; 92km (57 miles) from Berg-en-Dal

SKUKUZA
Tel 013-7354030
Kruger's largest camp has room for more than 1,000 people, and has a vast range of facilities, including a golf course, supermarket, library, restaurant, bank, post office and doctor. There is also an open-air cinema showing wildlife videos in the evenings. Day walks and night drives can be arranged at reception.

🏕 R100 (camping), R230 (safari tent with shared facilities), R460–R770 (bungalow sleeping 1–2), R850 (cottage sleeping 1–4), R1,600 (guest house)

🏠 49km (30 miles) from Pretoriuskop

CENTRAL KRUGER PUBLIC CAMPS

LETABA
Tel 013-7356636
The restaurant here is in a magnificent setting for watching the game come down to drink. Facilities include a mini supermarket, restaurant, launderette, petrol (gas) station and a museum with exhibits on Kruger's elephants. There's a short nature trail around the camp, and day walks and night drives can be arranged at reception.

🏕 R100 (camping), R230 (safari tent with shared facilities), R420–R495 (bungalow), R860 (cottage), R1,600 (guesthouse)

🏠 51km (31 miles) from Phalaborwa Gate

MAROELA
A large campsite with basic cooking and washing facilities. There's a shop at Orpen Gate where you check in and where you can arrange day walks and night drives.

🏕 R100 (camping)

🏠 4km (2.5 miles) from Orpen Gate

MOPANI
Tel 013-7356536

Mopani is one of Kruger's largest and newest public camps, set on a rocky hill overlooking the Pioneer Dam. The chalets have been made from natural materials and are more spacious and pleasant than some of the older camps. Facilities include a swimming pool, nature trail, petrol (gas) station, shop, restaurant, bar, cafeteria and launderette. Night drives can be arranged at reception.

🏕 R460 (bungalow), R490 (cottage), R860–R1,600 (guest cottage)

🚐

🏠 74km (46 miles) to Phalaborwa Gate

OLIFANTS
Tel 013-7356606

Olifants is a peaceful camp overlooking the Olifants River and is one of Kruger's most attractive camps. The thatched chalets blend into the surrounding woodland and facilities include a restaurant, shop, information office, petrol (gas) station and launderette. Night drives can be arranged through reception.

🏕 R420–R600 (bungalow), R1,600 (guest house)

🏠 83km (51 miles) from Phalaborwa Gate; 102km (63 miles) from Orpen Gate

SATARA
Tel 013-7356306
Satara is the second largest camp in Kruger. Facilities include Kruger Emergency Road Service, a car wash, a petrol (gas) station, camp shop, cafeteria and restaurant. Day walks and night drives can be arranged at reception.

🏕 R100 (camping), R460–R690 (bungalow), R870 (cottage), R1,500 (guest house)

🏠 48km (30 miles) from Orpen Gate; 104km (65 miles) from Paul Kruger Gate

NORTHERN KRUGER PUBLIC CAMPS

BATELEUR
Tel 013-7356843
Bateleur is an isolated bushveld camp, where visitors have exclusive access to two nearby dams. The solar-powered camp accommodates up to 34 visitors, and offers day and night game drives.

🏕 R850 (cottage)

🏠 37km (23 miles) to Shingwedzi

PUNDA MARIA
Tel 013-7356873
This peaceful rest camp is hidden by dense woodland. Facilities include a restaurant, bar, shop and petrol (gas)

STAYING

station. Meals must be ordered in advance. The short Paradise Flycatcher nature trail wanders around the camp.

💷 R100 (camping), R415 (bungalow), R850 (cottage)

🚗 8km (5 miles) from the Punda Maria Gate

SIRHENI
Tel 013-7356806

This bushveld camp overlooks Sirheni Dam and is popular with birdwatchers. The camp accommodates up to 80 visitors and offers day and night bush drives.

💷 R725–R850 (cottage)

🚗 28km (17 miles) to Shingwezi; 48km (30 miles) to Punda Maria

KRUGER PRIVATE RESERVES
KWA MBILI GAME LODGE
Thornybush Game Reserve
Tel 015-7932773
www.kwambili.com

The accommodation at this small lodge is comparatively inexpensive for the reserve, and given that the game viewing and service are as good as the other lodges, it represents excellent value. You can stay in thatched chalets or safari tents (all with private bathrooms), decorated with African art. Meals are served around a camp fire or on the open veranda. There is also a bar, lounge, curio shop, bar and lounge area. Game drives, bush walks and all meals are included in the price.

💷 R2,390

ℹ️ 5

🏊

🚗 The main entrance to Thornybush is 9km (5.5 miles) north of Klaserie off the R40; look for signs for Kapama and the Hoedspruit Cheetah project

NGALA
Timbavati Game Reserve
Tel 011-8094300
www.ccafrica.com

Ngala is one of the most opulent of the private lodges in Timbavati and is a member of the Small Luxury Hotels of the World. The lodge is on the Timbavati Flood Plain, a region known for its elephants and lions, and guests have exclusive access to the 14,780ha (36,520-acre) reserve. There's a choice of air-conditioned cottages furnished with antiques, or luxurious fully furnished

SPECIAL IN KRUGER
EARTH LODGE
Sabi Sands Private Game Reserve
Tel 011-4833939
www.sabisabi.com

The innovative Earth Lodge feels like an ultra-trendy boutique hotel set deep in the African bush. Its design cuts into the earth, which means that the lodge is virtually invisible, with smooth stone and grass-covered roofs blending into the surroundings. The camp is set in a cool patch of riverine forest. Suites are super-stylish, with muted tones, natural materials and huge beds. The enormous bathrooms have open-air showers and carved stone baths, and all suites have a private plunge pool. The bar area is made out of the roots of trees, and meals are served in an open-air enclosure cut into the ground. This is a very unusual place to stay. Game drives and walks are conducted with a ranger and tracker.

💷 R11,200

ℹ️ 13

🚗 Accessed by following the R536 from Hazyview to Skukuza; turn off at Glano

safari tents in a satellite camp. The cottages have a smart dining area overlooking a water hole, where silver-service meals are served, while the safari tent camp has a chic and contemporary guest area. Prices include all meals and two game drives a day.

💷 R6,840 (cottage), R9,590 (safari tent)

ℹ️ 20

😊

🚗 Accessed from the turning 9km (5.5 miles) north of Klaserie at Kapama, off the R40

MAKHADO
INN ON LOUIS TRICHARDT
Makhado 0920
Tel 015-5177020

The tranquil setting of this guesthouse makes it a popular choice. There are excellent views of the Soutpansberg Mountains from the thatched *rondavels* (huts) dotted around the beautiful gardens. The furnishings came from the Carlton Hotel in Johannesburg when it closed down and have brought a five-star touch to this country inn. The huts have enormous beds, private bathrooms, TV and phone. Meals are served on the terrace, and guests can relax in the bar or the tea rooms.

💷 R600 (including dinner and breakfast)

ℹ️ 18

🏊

🚗 11km (7 miles) north of Makhado, on the N1 towards Musina

NELSPRUIT
THE ROOST
21c Koraalboom Street, Nelspruit 1201
Tel 013-7411419

This spacious house is just a short walk from the middle of town. The rooms have heavy drapes and pine furniture, but have comfortable beds, armchairs, tea- and coffee-making facilities and a laundry service. All have separate entrances, and some overlook the attractive tropical gardens with a pool. There's also a country-style breakfast room with a small bar and secure parking on-site.

💷 R560

ℹ️ 8

🏊

PILGRIM'S REST
DISTRICT SIX MINERS' COTTAGES
Pilgrim's Rest 1290
Tel 013-7681211

The best value place to stay in Pilgrim's Rest is this set of miners' cottages from the 1920s, on the hill above the town. They are decorated in a style that recalls the gold rush, with brass bedheads and period furniture. Each cottage has a kitchen and a private veranda with views over the valley and mountains. Resere in advance.

💷 R210

ℹ️ 7

STAYING

GAUTENG AND FREE STATE

Johannesburg and Pretoria (Tshwane) have fallen behind in the accommodation stakes, mostly as a result of growth in visitor numbers to the Cape Peninsula. Standards are fine, but most accommodation is in expensive chain-style hotels. The best places to stay are in the suburbs, such as Sandton and Rosebank in Johannesburg, and Hatfield, Brooklyn and Lynnwood in Pretoria. This makes it a little confusing for first-time visitors, who find themselves staying in a district they have never heard of. As Bloemfontein is an overnight stop between Johannesburg and Cape Town, there is lots of accommodation here.

BLOEMFONTEIN

HOBBIT HOUSE
19 President Steyn Avenue, Bloemfontein 9301
Tel 051-4470663
www.hobbit.co.za
Fans of author J. R. R. Tolkien, born in the town, will like this aptly named guesthouse, dating from 1925 and set in secluded gardens, filled with hidden benches and water features. The bedrooms are traditional, with a Victorian feel. The walls are covered in blue-and-white-patterned wallpaper, and the furniture is a mix of antique and country-style. Some rooms have fireplaces; all have large private bathrooms. Breakfast and other meals are served in a rustic breakfast room.
R720
12

CLARENS

MALUTI MOUNTAIN LODGE
Steil Street, Clarens 9707
Tel 058-2561422
www.malutilodge.co.za
This popular family weekend retreat has a fine setting with striking views of the mountains. Accommodation is a mix of double rooms with private bathrooms, traditional *rondavels* (small, round thatched huts) and family suites. All have simple, country interiors, balconies and heating for the cold winter months. There are neat gardens, two restaurants, a swimming pool and a popular pub.

R770 (including dinner and breakfast)
24

GOLDEN GATE NATIONAL PARK

GLEN REENEN CAMP
Tel 012-3431991 (reservations from SANParks); tel 058-2550012 (last-minute reservations)
www.sanparks.org
Glen Reenen has two types of self-catering *rondavels* (huts), each with a shower, fridge and cooking facilities. Some have a TV, two single beds and a double bed in the loft; others have three single beds in one room. Across the road is the campsite, with plenty of shade, set beside a mountain stream, with a communal kitchen and shower blocks and electric points. It's a peaceful setting in a narrow, steep-sided valley, and several good walks start from here (pick up maps in the shop). Be warned that it can be too cold for camping in the winter.
R75–R100 (camping), R380 (*rondavel*), R660 (farmhouse)
On the main road through the park

JOHANNESBURG

BACKPACKERS RITZ
1A North Road, Dunkeld West 2196
Tel 011-3257125
www.backpackinafrica.com
One of Johannesburg's best established hostels, the Ritz has a garden and swimming pool and is set in a secure district. A mix of dorms and double rooms is available, and there's a pub and an internet 'corner', and breakfast and other meals are served. Knowledgeable staff offer tours in Soweto and around the city. There's a free pick-up service from the airport (reserve in advance).
R85 (dorm beds), R260 (double room)

MERCURE INN
Corner of Republic and Randburg Waterfront roads, Randburg 2125
Tel 011-3263300
www.mercure.co.za
The Mercure Inn is a good choice if you're passing through. It's a large-scale hotel and although the rooms are narrow with small bathrooms, they are comfortable. The interiors nods toward ethnic-chic, and all rooms have satellite TV, minibar and modem connections. The public areas are fairly grand, with a mix of marble, African art and chunky furniture. Breakfast is the only meal offered, although there's an arrangement with some of the restaurants in the adjacent Randburg Waterfront mall which means you can charge meals to your hotel account. Parking is available.
R528, excluding breakfast
104

THE MICHELANGELO
135 West Street, Sandton, Johannesburg 2146
Tel 011-2827000
www.legacyhotels.co.za

This is a large, international luxury hotel in the upmarket suburb of Sandton, about 30 minutes' drive from the heart of Johannesburg. The Michelangelo, fitted with plenty of marble in faux Renaissance style, has everything you would expect of a quality hotel: executive suites, several restaurants, its own health spa, a great variety of sporting facilities, pay-TV and

STAYING

fax and internet connections in each room. On your doorstep are all the luxury theatres, shops and cinemas of the area.

💷 R2,544, excluding breakfast

🛈 218

[icons]

SANDTON SUN & TOWERS INTER-CONTINENTAL

Corner of 5th and Alice streets, Sandton 2146
Tel 011-7805000
www.ichotelsgroup.com

This high-rise luxury hotel, part of the InterContinental chain, is popular with tour groups and businesspeople, as well as shoppers—it's next to the enormous Sandton City shopping mall. The rooms occupy 26 floors (those at the top have exceptional views), and are predictably comfortable with marble-effect bathrooms, air-conditioning and satellite TV. There's a good range of facilities, including a swimming pool, gym and sauna, beauty salon, cocktail lounge and four restaurants—Italian, African, Portuguese and Japanese. Service is professional and brisk. Parking is available.

💷 R1,375

🛈 564

[icons]

VERGELEGEN

6 Tottenham Avenue, Melrose Estate 2196
Tel 011-4473434
www.vergelegen-guesthouse.co.za

For a taste of colonial Africa, head to this small guesthouse set in beautiful gardens, close to the popular Rosebank Mall. Each of the nine individually decorated rooms has french windows leading out onto a private terrace, antiques, carved wooden bedheads and interesting tapestries and art on the walls, with welcome under-floor heating in the winter. There are several comfortable lounges decked out in a 1930s colonial theme, and the art deco conservatory has a bar. The friendly, family atmosphere makes it a pleasant change from the chain hotels that dominate the city.

💷 R660

🛈 9

SPECIAL IN JO'BURG

SAXON

36 Saxon Road, Sandhurst 2196
Tel 011-2926000
www.thesaxon.com

One of South Africa's leading hotels is this small boutique hotel in the suburb of Sandhurst. Nelson Mandela spent seven months here editing his book, *The Long Walk to Freedom*, and the presidential suite is named after him. The Saxon is set in 2.5ha (6 acres) of beautifully tended grounds with a huge heated swimming pool, gym and spa. The suites have large four-poster beds and a strong emphasis on African art, while the rooms have African textiles, bathrooms, polished wooden floors and large bay windows looking into the garden. All have DVD and VCR players. The restaurant has high ceilings and two wine cellars. Parking is available.

💷 R5,000

🛈 26

[icons]

LADYBRAND

CRANBERRY COTTAGE

37 Beaton Street, Ladybrand 5745
Tel 051-9242290
www.cranberrycottage.co.za

This converted sandstone Victorian house has 18 rooms, varying in style from Victorian (with four-poster beds and antiques) to modern (neutral and stylish furniture), with private bathrooms. There are also garden suites with a more rustic theme, and the house is surrounded by English-style gardens with a swimming pool. Additional rooms are housed in the original ticket office and waiting rooms of Ladybrand Railway Station, and are decorated

with railway memorabilia and antiques.

💷 R470

🛈 26

[icon]

PRETORIA

BATTISS-ZEEDERBERG GUEST HOUSE

3 Fook Island, 92 20th Street, Menlo Park 0081
Tel 012-4607318
www.battiss.co.za

The original home of the artist Walter Battiss is one of the more unusual guesthouses in South Africa. The house was renovated in the 1980s and Battiss's works remain on the walls and the floors. The bedrooms have high ceilings, shiny wood floors, large french windows opening on to a leafy courtyard, private bathrooms, TVs, fans and a daily serviced kitchenette. You will need your own transport to get into town, but it is close to Menlyn Park shopping mall.

💷 R460

🛈 4

LA MAISON

235 Hilda Street, Hatfield 0083
Tel 012-4304341
www.lamaison.co.za

This comfortable and quirky guesthouse is close to a good choice of restaurants and shops. It's a grand white Victorian mansion, with six individually decorated rooms with attractive antiques, brass beds and private balconies with views of the lush gardens and swimming pool. The restaurant serves excellent cuisine, and has interesting murals on the walls. Breakfast is served here or on the roof terrace. The comfortable guest lounge has deep red cushions and animal print fabrics.

💷 R700

🛈 6

[icon]

STAYING

WHISTLETREE LODGE

1267 Whistletree Drive,
Queenswood 0186
Tel 012-3339915/6
www.whistletree.co.za
The smart Whistletree Lodge is
on a hillside in Queenswood,
close to the Union Buildings.
The rooms are elegantly and
traditionally decorated with
warm tones, sturdy antiques
and silk bedspreads and
cushions; all have private
bathrooms and balconies. The
airy lounge has stylish furniture
and high ceilings, and opens
out to the landscaped garden
with its heart-shaped pool.
There are also floodlit tennis
courts, a sauna and a cocktail
bar; meals are available on
request. Parking is available.
📷 R1,200
🛏 12
📷 📷
❓ No children under 12

RUSTLER'S VALLEY

RUSTLER'S VALLEY
MOUNTAIN LODGE

Tel 051-9333939
www.rustlers.co.za

This mountain lodge is in
the valley that hosts South
Africa's biggest alternative
music festival. It offers a mix
of accommodation, with
rooms in the main building—
the *kraal*—looking in on a
courtyard filled with trees and
painted with traditional southern African designs, as well as
thatched *rondavels* (huts),
sleeping between two and
eight people, and a backpackers' dorm with bunk beds.
The whole complex has a
hippy vibe, which continues
in the restaurant, called
Saucery, where you can get
some of the best vegetarian
food in the country. Camping
is also possible in summer.
📷 R60 (camping) from R28 (cottages),
from R200 (rooms in the *kraal*) 🛏 15

NORTHERN CAPE AND
NORTH WEST PROVINCE

The parks and game reserves have a range of accommodation.
Madikwe, in particular, has excellent luxury lodges. The
Magaliesberg Mountains also has a number of holiday resorts
that are equipped with a complete range of sports facilities,
including golf courses, tennis courts and gyms. If you want
to visit Namakwa during the flower season, then you should
reserve your room as far in advance as possible. As with many
of South Africa's popular destinations, the domestic market
reserves the best value rooms up to a year in advance.

PRICES AND SYMBOLS

The hotels below are listed
alphabetically (excluding
The) by town or area, then
by name. Prices are for a
double room for one night,
including breakfast. All the
hotels listed accept credit
cards unless otherwise
stated. See page 2 for a key
to the symbols.

AUGRABIES

AUGRABIES FALLS
BACKPACKERS

Augrabies 8874
Tel 054-4510177
www.kalahari.co.za
This claims to be one of the
most remote backpackers'
lodges in South Africa, and it
certainly feels off the beaten
track. Some 10km (6 miles)
from the Augrabies Falls
National Park, it provides an
excellent base for exploring
the area. There are some comfortable double rooms with
shared facilities, making it a
good choice for couples on a
budget, as well as backpackers. It has a lounge, kitchen
and large bar with a pool table,
leading out on to an open area
which sometimes hosts parties. The Kalahari Adventure
Centre is based here, with a
wide range of river rafting and
desert trips (▷ 217).
📷 R75 (dorm bed), R150 (double)
📷 From Kakamas, turn right off the
N14 towards Augrabies Falls. The lodge
is 10km (6 miles) before the falls

KGALAGADI
TRANSFRONTIER PARK

MATA MATA

Tel 012-4289111 (reservations)
www.sanparks.org
There are five camps in the
park, but Mata Mata is one
of the most pleasant, lying at
the end of a beautiful road,

with some of the best game
viewing opportunities.
Accommodation is in chalets
which sleep up to six people
and have a bathroom, kitchen
and barbecue area. Huts are
also available, with three beds
in one room and a communal
kitchen and shower block;
the campsite has sandy plots
in front of the chalets. There's
little shade but the setting is
fantastic, very close to a viewpoint. The camp has a small
shop selling basic groceries
and firewood. Electricity is
generated from 5am for two
hours, and again from 5pm
to 11pm.
📷 R85 (camping), R365–R600
(huts and chalets)
📷 118km (73 miles) from entrance
gate; allow at least 2.5 hours to get
there. Maps are available from the
entrance gate

KIMBERLEY

CECIL JOHN RHODES
GUEST HOUSE

138 Du Toitspan Road, Kimberley 8301
Tel 053-8302500
www.ceciljohnrhodes.co.za
This luxurious old-fashioned
guesthouse is set in a converted Victorian house, now
a national monument. The
bedrooms are individually
decorated with antiques and
pale fabrics, and white linen
on the four-poster beds. The
floors are pale wood, and
some rooms have original
features such as fireplaces. All
have small private bathrooms
(with attractive claw-foot
baths), air-conditioning and
TVs. The tea room has tables
under vines outside, and
serves breakfast, light snacks
and tea and cakes throughout
the day.
📷 R550
🛏 7
📷

MILNER HOUSE

31 Milner Street, Kimberley 8301
Tel 053-8316405
www.milnerhouse.co.za
You will find this friendly, family-run guesthouse in the attractive Victorian district of Belgravia. The house has been converted into five rooms, each decorated with hand-made pine furniture and brightly printed bedspreads and curtains, with private bathroom, TV, fans and heaters. There is an open-plan kitchen, lounge and dining room, with log fires in the winter, and breakfast is served on the outdoor patio when the weather is fine. The lush gardens have a good-sized swimming pool.

R380
6

MADIKWE GAME RESERVE

JACI'S LODGES

Tel 014-7789900/1
www.madikwe.com
There are several luxury lodges to choose from within the Madikwe reserve; this one is split into the Safari Lodge and the Tree Lodge. The Safari Lodge takes just 16 guests in individual thatched suites with canvas walls, beautiful hand-made furniture, handcrafted stone baths and an outside 'bush' shower, plus a private viewing deck. Prices include a personal safari guide for all game drives and walks. The Tree Lodge comprises eight tree houses built on stilts in the arms of giant leadwood or tambotie trees. The tree houses are linked by raised boardwalks, and meals are served in a central area. Rates include all meals, two game drives per day and most alcoholic drinks.

R6,580
16

MAGALIESBERG

MOUNTAIN SANCTUARY PARK

Tel 014-5340114
www.mountain-sanctuary.co.za
This farm in the mountains has the best that the area has to offer. The number of visitors is controlled and there are strict regulations designed to preserve and maintain the mountain wilderness, so reserve as early as possible. The accommodation consists of fully equipped, self-catering log cabins and chalets (visitors must provide bedding, towels and food). A stunning pool has been built from natural stone on the lip of the valley offering fantastic views. This sanctuary is an excellent place to explore the mountains, and guests have access to more than 1,000ha (2,470 acres of hiking country.

R60 (camping), R170 (chalets per person), R220 (log cabins per person)

35km (22 miles) from Rustenburg, off the R560

MOUNT GRACE SPA

Old Rustenburg Road
Tel 014-5771350
htttp://mount.grace.co.za

Guests at this spa can choose to stay in one of four 'villages': Mountain, Grace, Thatchstone or Treetop Village. Each has its own atmosphere and theme, offering guests something different. Natural stone has been used for the buildings, and the sound of constantly running water lulls and relaxes the visitor. Facilities at the spa include hydrotherapy, an Elixir Liquid Sound Flotation Pool, mudpacks and steam rooms. The Spa Café has a detoxifying course (on request), as well as salads, soups and sandwiches, fresh juice and wine.

R900–R2,000
50

Take the R24, approaching Magaliesberg village from Johannesburg

ORION SAFARI LODGE

Tel 014-5941040
www.oriongroup.co.za
In the foothills of the Magaliesberg range, very near to the beautiful Rustenburg Kloof nature reserve, this lodge is ideal for outdoor enthusiasts. It offers a wide range of activities including squash, swimming, volleyball and trampolining on the premises; hiking, ballooning, golf, mountain biking, fishing and abseiling (rappelling) nearby. A striking feature of this resort is the Coach Restaurant, housed in a converted 1926 railway carriage. Game viewing at the Pilanesberg National Park or gambling at Sun City are a short drive away.

R800–R1,000, excluding breakfast
131

Just outside Rustenburg on the R27, going towards Mafikeng

SPRINGBOK

SPRINGBOK LODGE

Voortrekker Street, Springbok 8240
Tel 027-7121321
The Springbok Lodge, run by Jopie Kotze, occupies a number of houses that have been converted into a series of double rooms and self-catering flats. Although the rooms are nothing special, they are good value and have a prime central location. The reception area of the main building also acts as an information desk, newsagent and curio shop, with an interesting semi-precious stone display and some old photographs of historic Springbok. There is a very popular restaurant and bar here, which gets busy with visitors who come to hear Kotze's yarns about the town.

R240, excluding breakfast
R70

STAYING

LESOTHO AND SWAZILAND

Lesotho and Swaziland have a number of well-run lodges in the mountains and foothills that provide excellent value accommodation, such as Semonkong Lodge and the superb Malealea Lodge. Otherwise choices are rather few on the ground, but camping is an option.

PRICES AND SYMBOLS

The hotels below are listed alphabetically (excluding The) by town or area, then by name. Prices are for a double room for one night, including breakfast. All the hotels listed accept credit cards unless otherwise stated. See page 2 for a key to the symbols.

LESOTHO

MASERU

LANCER'S INN
Central Kingsway
Tel 22312114
This sandstone building has a good level of comfort but without the large-scale feel of other town hotels. The bedrooms have pretty furnishings and there are a few chalets with private bathrooms in the garden. The hotel has two popular bars, a gym, an African-themed restaurant with an alfresco area, a bakery and a bottle store. Credit cards are not accepted.
🐾 M550
🛏 21
🏊 🍴

SEMONKONG

SEMONKONG LODGE
Tel 051-9333106 (South Africa)
www.placeofsmoke.co.ls
The Semonkong Lodge makes an excellent base for exploring the Lesotho countryside on foot or horseback. There's a mix of rooms in attractive Basotho-style thatched huts, some with private bathrooms. Each of these has its own bathroom and fireplace. There is an à la carte restaurant and bar, as well as a communal kitchen, and fire pits which can be used for cooking. Credit cards are accepted.
🐾 M40 (camping), M80 (dorm bed), M380 (hut)
🛏 13
🚗 Turn right at the end of the main road in central Semonkong, past the soccer pitch, then right again at the bar with a satellite dish on the roof

SPECIAL IN LESOTHO

MALEALEA LODGE
Tel 051-4366766 (South Africa)
www.malealea.co.ls
Owners Mike and Di Jones, both born in Lesotho, are passionate about the country and have done much to direct money from tourism back into local communities. Their lodge is a collection of rooms with private bathrooms, self-catering huts and dorms in an old farmhouse, close to a charming Basotho village. Activities are offered, and proceeds are fed back into community projects. There are three communal kitchens, and home-cooked meals are also available, plus there is an honesty bar, tennis court and general store. This is a great place to meet and learn more about the Basotho people, in beautiful surroundings.
🐾 M220
🛏 110 beds

SWAZILAND

BHUNYA

FORESTER'S ARMS
Tel 467-4377
www.forestersarms.co.za
Forester's Arms is surrounded by forests dotted with waterfalls and the hotel can organize activities in the region. Bedrooms are bright, with yellow walls, blue carpets and pale pine furniture. All have private bathrooms and TVs, and some open out on to the garden. There is a good restaurant serving set menus, with an attractive outdoor terrace where lunch is served. The pub has a blazing log fire, and there are occasional Swazi dancing performances in the evenings. There's a nearby golf course.
🐾 E550 (including breakfast and dinner)
🛏 30
🍴
🚗 12km (7.5 miles) north of Bhunya; on the MR19 between Bhunya and Mbabane

MBABANE

MOUNTAIN INN
Tel 404-2781
www.mountaininn.sz
The Mountain Inn is bright and modern, with comfortable rooms decorated with blue and green European-style furnishings. Some have balconies with beautiful views over the Ezulwini Valley; all have private bathrooms, TVs and telephones. The garden has a pool, and there is a good restaurant (▷ 273).
🐾 E740
🛏 50
🏊
🚗 4km (2.5 miles) from central Mbabane, on Ezulwini Valley road; look out for signs on the left

MLILWANE WILDLIFE SANCTUARY

MAIN CAMP
Tel 528-3944/3
www.biggameparks.org

The Mlilwane Wildlife Sanctuary is a delightful place to stay. There are various choices, from the backpacker lodge to the top-end guest lodge, but the most enjoyable is the original main camp, which has a mix of traditional Swazi beehive grass huts and wood-and-thatch huts (both with private bathrooms). The camp is unfenced, so expect to see impala, warthog and ostriches wandering around—beware of hippos at night. There is a central seating area around a large log fire, a bar with a deck overlooking a hippo pool, and an open-sided restaurant, also with views of the hippos.
🐾 E340
🛏 16

Planning

BEFORE YOU GO

CLIMATE AND WHEN TO GO
- South Africa has a great variety of climates, ranging from the harsh dryness of the Kalahari desert to the lush tropical heat of KwaZulu-Natal.
- **Winter** is from June to the end of September. It is often sunny and mild during the day, although temperatures can drop below freezing at night in the Cape and the Karoo, and snow falls on higher mountain peaks.
- **Summer** is from November to the end of March. It tends to be hot, particularly between December and February, and often humid, depending on where you are in the country. Temperatures can reach upwards of 30°C (86°F), although the Western and Eastern Capes are rarely hotter than 30°C. Gauteng and KwaZulu-Natal become very humid.
- Expect rainfall along the Garden Route all year round. As a general rule it becomes progressively wetter the farther

TIME ZONES
South Africa is 2 hours ahead of Greenwich Mean Time (GMT). There is no daylight saving time. Compared to noon in Johannesburg, the time differences in other major cities are as follows:

CITY	TIME DIFFERENCE	NOON IN JO'BURG
Amsterdam	-1	11am
Auckland	+11	11pm
Berlin	-1	11am
Brussels	-1	11am
Chicago	-8	4am
Dublin	-2	10am
London	-2	10am
Madrid	-1	11am
New York	-7	5am
Paris	-1	11am
Perth	+6	6pm
Rome	-1	11am
San Francisco	-10	2am
Sydney	+9	9pm
Tokyo	+7	7pm

WEATHER STATIONS

PRETORIA/ TSHWANE
1299m
4262ft

Durban
7m
23ft

Cape Town
42m
138ft

desert areas around Upington and the Kalahari, although temperatures at night can drop below freezing.
- The best time of year for game viewing is June to September, when vegetation is low and a lack of water forces animals to congregate around waterholes. Winter is also the best time for hiking, avoiding the high temperatures and frequent thunderstorms of summer.

WEATHER REPORTS
- The best sources of weather information are the international news websites, such as www.bbc.co.uk or www.cnn.com.
- Alternatively, visit one of the specialist websites such as www.weather.com, or the South African Weather Service website at www.weathersa.co.za.

WHAT TO TAKE
- Items such as medicines, contact lens solution, insect repellent and sunscreen are widely available from pharmacies, usually at lower prices than you'll pay at home.
- Summers are hot, so bring loose-fitting natural-fibre clothes, a wide-brimmed hat, sunglasses and high-factor sunscreen.
- South Africans are casual, so shorts and T-shirts are fine during the day. Men may need long trousers (pants) and a shirt, and women a skirt, for evenings.

east you travel. Most of the rain falls in summer, although the Cape can remain dry for most of the summer. In the interior, the summers are hot and dusty, with intermittent heavy rainfall; winters are cool with sunny days.
- Northern Cape summers have temperatures in the region of 45°C (113°F)—too hot, and unsafe, for hiking. Winter is the best time to visit the northern

PLANNING

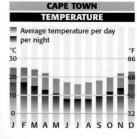

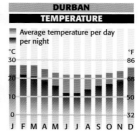

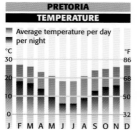

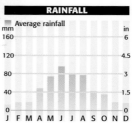

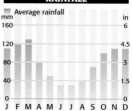

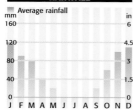

- If you plan to go on safari, bring lightweight clothes in beiges and browns (anything bright might disturb the animals) and a good pair of binoculars. You can buy camera film around the country.
- Footwear should be as airy as possible in the hot weather; sandals or canvas shoes are ideal. Bring boots for longer hikes—lightweight water-repellent synthetic fabric boots are best in summer; leather in winter.
- Mosquito nets are useful in wilderness areas, depending on the season.
- In winter, from June to the end of September, bring a sweater and jacket (and note that most guesthouses do not have any heating).
- Bring photocopies of all important documents (passport, travel tickets, driver's licence) and keep these separate from the original documents.

WILDLIFE

- The export of wildlife souvenirs from rare and endangered species may either be illegal or require a special permit. Before you make any purchase, check

Summer in South Africa is from November to March

CUSTOMS ALLOWANCES

200 cigarettes
250g of tobacco
50 cigars
1 litre of spirits
2 litres of wine
50ml of perfume
250ml of eau de toilette
Gifts and souvenirs to the value of R500

Further information:
Customs and Excise, Johannesburg International Airport, tel 011-9232400; Cape Town International Airport, tel 021-9340221

customs regulations in South Africa and your home country.

PASSPORTS AND VISAS

- All visitors must carry a valid passport. All passports must have one clear blank page, otherwise visitors will be denied entry.
- EU nationals and citizens from the US, Canada, Australia and New Zealand do not need visas to enter South Africa, but always check the latest information before you travel.

- On arrival, you will be granted a temporary visitor's permit, lasting up to 90 days.
- You must have a valid return ticket to get a permit.
- It is possible to apply for an extension to the permit at one of the Home Affairs offices in the major cities (see below). This can take up to 3 weeks and costs around R400. Note that going to Lesotho or Swaziland and returning to South Africa is not a way to extend your holiday visa: When you re-enter, South African immigration will scan your original South African entry stamp, on which the given date of departure is still valid.
- Home Affairs offices include: Cape Town: tel 021-4624970 Durban: tel 031-3087900 Johannesburg: tel 011-6394000 Port Elizabeth: tel 041-4871026 Pretoria: tel 012-3241860.
- For more information visit the Department of Home Affairs at www.home-affairs.gov.za.

TRAVEL INSURANCE

- It is vital to take out full travel insurance before departure, including cover for medical evacuation by air ambulance to your own country. At the very least, make sure you have medical insurance and coverage for personal effects.
- Check that your policy covers all activities that you may do, such as trekking or diving.
- Report stolen goods to the police to obtain a signed, dated and stamped statement for your insurer.

PLAN AHEAD

- Before you set off, have a dental inspection and get some spare glasses (also make sure you have the prescription).
- If you have a longstanding medical condition, arrange a check-up with your doctor.
- For more health information, see pages 304–305.

SOUTH AFRICAN EMBASSIES AND CONSULATES ABROAD		
COUNTRY	**ADDRESS AND TELEPHONE NUMBERS**	**WEBSITE**
Australia	Corner Rhodes Place and State Circle, Canberra, tel 02-6273 2424	www.rsa.emb.gov.au
Canada	15 Sussex Drive, Ottawa K1M 1M8, tel 613-7440330	www.southafrica-canada.ca
Republic of Ireland	Alexander House, Earlsford Centre, Earlsford Terrace, Dublin 2, tel 1-6615553	
UK	South Africa House, Trafalgar Square, London, WC2N 5DP, tel 020-7451 7299	www.southafricahouse.com
US	3051 Massachusetts Avenue NW, Washington, DC 20008, tel 202/232 4400 (Also consulates in Los Angeles and New York)	www.saembassy.org

PRACTICALITIES

CLOTHING
● During the day, the general attitude towards clothes is a relaxed one (▷ 298). However, in the evening, a smarter style is appreciated (such as long trousers or skirts), particularly if you are going to a club, bar or restaurant. Women may want to be more covered up in conservative rural areas.

ELECTRICITY
● Current is 220/240 volts at 50 cycles per second.
● Plugs have three round pins. US visitors should bring a transformer. Adaptors are widely available in South Africa.
● Bring a torch (flashlight) for more rural areas.

LAUNDRY
● Towns and cities have self-service launderettes, with coin-operated washers and dryers. Most also have a service where you can drop off laundry and have it cleaned by staff.
● Almost all hotels, guesthouses, bed-and-breakfasts and hostels have laundry services.
● The larger camps in national parks have launderettes; all have sinks where you can hand wash items.

MEASUREMENTS
● South Africa uses the metric system.
● Distances are measured in kilometres, petrol (gas) is priced by the litre, and food is sold in grams and kilograms.
● Temperatures are given in degrees Celsius (centigrade).

PUBLIC TOILETS
● There are few public toilets in towns and cities, although all the

CONVERSION CHART		
FROM	**TO**	**MULTIPLY BY**
Inches	Centimetres	2.54
Centimetres	Inches	0.3937
Feet	Metres	0.3048
Metres	Feet	3.2810
Yards	Metres	0.9144
Metres	Yards	1.0940
Miles	Kilometres	1.6090
Kilometres	Miles	0.6214
Acres	Hectares	0.4047
Hectares	Acres	2.4710
Gallons	Litres	4.5460
Litres	Gallons	0.2200
Ounces	Grams	28.35
Grams	Ounces	0.0353
Pounds	Grams	453.6
Grams	Pounds	0.0022
Pounds	Kilograms	0.4536
Kilograms	Pounds	2.205
Tons	Tonnes	1.0160
Tonnes	Tons	0.9842

main visitor sights, museums and galleries have them, as do department stores and shopping malls.
● The busier public beaches in the Western Cape and KwaZulu-Natal have toilets and shower facilities.
● National parks and reserves have toilets near main parking areas (maps provided on entry will mark these).

SMOKING
Most restaurants have designated non-smoking areas, although this is less common in rural areas. Smoking is prohibited in many public areas, such as shopping malls, and is restricted on public transport—keep a look out for signs. Bars and nightclubs allow smoking, although the bar areas are sometimes smoke free.

GAY AND LESBIAN VISITORS
The South African constitution is one of the most progressive in the world—and Cape Town is the self proclaimed 'Gay Capital' of Africa. The city has a number of big festivals and events aimed at the gay population, such as the annual Mother City Queer Project (▷ 190). However, the picture is not the same across the entire country, and away from the cities

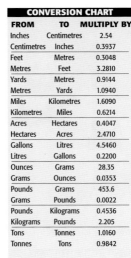

CLOTHING SIZES		
Use the chart below to convert the size you use at home.		
UK	**Metric**	**US**
36	46	36
38	48	38
40	50	40
42	52	42
44	54	44
46	56	46
48	58	48
7	41	8
7.5	42	8.5
8.5	43	9.5
9.5	44	10.5
10.5	45	11.5
11	46	12
14.5	37	14.5
15	38	15
15.5	39/40	15.5
16	41	16
16.5	42	16.5
17	43	17
8	36	6
10	38	8
12	40	10
14	42	12
16	44	14
18	46	16
20	46	18
4.5	37.5	6
5	38	6.5
5.5	38.5	7
6	39	7.5
6.5	40	8
7	41	8.5

(SUITS, SHOES, SHIRTS, DRESSES, SHOES)

South Africa is a conservative place, so be prepared for at least some disapproval.
● For more information, contact: Gay, Lesbian and Bisexual Helpline in Cape Town (tel 021-4222250; Mon–Fri 1–5, Sat–Sun 1–9).
● If you want advice on a range of issues, as well as listings, visit www.gaynetcapetown.co.za.
● *Exit* (www.exit.co.za) is a gay and lesbian newspaper, found online and at bookstores and newsagents in larger cities.

VISITING WITH CHILDREN
● As an outdoors destination, South Africa is a great place for children. South African families like to holiday in their own country, generally in high season—from December to February—so you'll find plenty

of family-friendly hotels, guesthouses and restaurants. Family rooms, with four to six beds, are common.
● Most sights, museums, galleries, aquariums and theme parks have substantial discounts for children (defined as 'learners', meaning under-18s). Children's entry fees mentioned in this book apply to under-18s unless otherwise stated.
● Local tourist offices often have lists of attractions for children. The larger offices have booklets outlining things for families to do.

VISITORS WITH A DISABILITY

● Although the situation regarding people with disabilities was for many years neglected, things have markedly improved in recent years.
● Large hotels in the main cities usually have wheelchair access and rooms adapted for guests with disabilities. The better-known museums, galleries and sights are also often wheelchair friendly, although the farther you are from the cities, the less likely you are to find disabled access.
● National parks are improving their act, with increasingly accessible accommodation, and the introduction of amenities such as 'Braille Trails' or wheelchair trails.
● Transport is variable. The national train system has trains with wide doors and aisles, and ramps are available. Domestic

flights can usually accommodate wheelchair users, although the airline needs prior warning. The larger car rental firms rent out automatic cars with hand controls. See page 58 for more information on getting around with a disability.
● The Association for the Physically Disabled (tel 011-6468331) can provide information about facilities and outdoor activities for those with disabilities.
● The SA National Council for the Blind (tel 012-3461171) has a directory of services for the visually impaired.
● The National Council for Persons with Physical Disabilities in South Africa (tel 011-7268040; www.ncppdsa.co.za) has advice on renting wheelchairs and other services for people with disabilities.
● Disabled People South Africa, (tel 021-4220357;

Children playing at the water's edge at Mossel Bay

www.dpsa.org.za), a national body representing people with disabilities, has contact details on transport and accessibility.

PLACES OF WORSHIP

● The majority of South Africa's population is Christian, but this congregation is by no means homogeneous. There are three main Christian denominations: indigenous African churches; Dutch Reformed Church; and Church of England.
● There are also significant Muslim and Hindu populations, and a small Jewish community.
● Local tourist offices will provide you with details of local places of worship and service times.

Members of the congregation at St. John's Church, Maseru

MONEY MATTERS

BEFORE YOU GO
• It is a good idea to carry your funds in several forms, including traveller's cheques, rands, credit cards and US dollars, euros or sterling. Check what fee your bank will charge for using your credit card in South African ATMs.

LOCAL CURRENCY
• The South African currency is the Rand (R), which is divided into 100 cents (c). Notes available are: R10, R20, R50, R100 and R200. Coins available are: 1c, 2c, 5c, 10c, 20c, 50c, R1, R2 and R5
• Visitors are restricted to bringing in R5,000 cash in person. Change any surplus rand back into your own currency before leaving South Africa. This is most easily done at the airport; banks usually require proof of initial transactions.

NEARBY COUNTRIES
• The currency of Lesotho is the Maloti (M) and in Swaziland it is the Emalangeni (E). They are dependent on the rand and the exchange rate is identical. The currencies are interchangeable within each country, but this is not the case in South Africa. You will need to change your Maloti or Emalangeni into rand.

A bank sign at Port Elizabeth

• Most currencies can be purchased only from within South Africa and not before you leave home. However, rand can easily be exchanged in neighbouring countries on arrival.

BANKS AND BUREAUX DE CHANGE
• Normal banking hours are Monday to Friday 9–3.30; Saturday 9–10.30 or 11.
• All main banks provide foreign exchange services for a fee.
• You can also change money at branches of Rennies Travel

(www.rennies.co.za), which acts as an agent for Thomas Cook. You will find branches of Rennies in all regional and visitor hubs and in nearly all of the country's shopping malls.
• American Express Foreign Exchange Service has offices in the larger cities and offers a *poste restante* service to card holders. Visit their website at www.americanexpress.co.za.
• Larger hotels will change money for you, but they often charge huge fees.

EXCHANGE RATES
• The exchange rate is subject to daily fluctuation. At the time of writing, exchange rates were approximately:
$1 = R6
€1 = R8
£1 = R11
For up-to-the-minute exchange rates, go to www.xe.com.

ATMS
• Using an ATM (Automatic Teller Machine) is the most convenient and cheapest way of obtaining funds.
• ATMs are widely available and use the Plus and/or the Cirrus systems. Visa, MasterCard, American Express and Diners Club are also accepted.

SOUTH AFRICAN BANKNOTES

South African banknotes are in denominations of 10, 20, 50, 100 and 200 rand. The 1, 2 and 5 cent coins are round and copper-coloured (note that 1c and 2c are no longer minted, but are still in circulation); the 10, 20 and 50 cent coins are yellow with shaped sides. The R1, R2 and R5 coins are a silver colour.

The eye-catching façade of a bank in Koffiefontein

- The amount you can withdraw varies between systems and cards, but you should be able to take out up to R1,000 per day.
- Be aware of the risks of theft during or immediately after a withdrawal. Never accept a stranger's help with an ATM. Take note of your surroundings and use ATMs in banks or shopping malls, where guards are often on duty.

CREDIT CARDS

- Credit cards are a convenient way of covering major expenses, and also offer some of the most competitive exchange rates when withdrawing cash from ATMs.
- Cards are particularly useful when renting a car: Many companies will rent out a car to foreign visitors only if they have a credit card.
- Credit cards are not usually accepted as payment for fuel.

TRAVELLER'S CHEQUES

- These can be exchanged at banks in most main towns.
- There is an efficient system of replacement if cheques are lost or stolen.
- Make sure you keep a full record of the numbers and value of your cheques, and always keep the receipts separate from the cheques.
- The disadvantages of traveller's cheques are the time it takes to cash them, and the commission charged by banks, which can be high.
- The most widely recognized traveller's cheques are American Express, Thomas Cook and Visa.
- Traveller's cheques in US dollars, British sterling and euros can be exchanged at banks throughout the country.
- Thomas Cook issues South African rand traveller's cheques, which are sometimes accepted as payment in shops and hotels.

VAT REFUNDS

- Value Added Tax (VAT) of 14 per cent is levied on goods and services, but foreign visitors can get a refund on goods costing more than R250. You can do this at the airport before checking in when departing, or at the Victoria and Alfred Waterfront in Cape Town.
- To get the refund, present a full receipt, a non-South African passport and the goods that you have purchased.
- The procedure is simple at the airport but allow plenty of time, especially if your flight is at night.

PRICES OF EVERYDAY ITEMS	
50cl bottle of water	R12
Sandwich for eating out	R15
Cup of tea/coffee	R10
Pint of beer	R12
Glass of wine	R10–R14
Daily newspaper	R3.80
Roll of camera film	R45
20 cigarettes	R11.50
Ice cream	R10
Litre of petrol	R4.30

TIPPING	
Restaurants	10–15 per cent (service is included)
Bar service	loose change
Tour guides	optional, but can be up to 10 per cent of total cost of tour
Hairdressers	5–10 per cent
Taxis	5–10 per cent
Chambermaids	R10 per day
Porters	R3–R5
Petrol station attendants	R2–R5

- At border crossings such as Beitbridge (Zimbabwe) or Ramotswa (Botswana) the procedure is painfully slow, as there are few customs officials to check goods against receipts. Expect a lengthy wait.

TIPPING

- Tipping is common but not compulsory. If you don't feel you've had good service, you don't have to leave anything. But remember that exchange rates mean that you, as a visitor, are likely to be able to spare the tip.
- See the Tipping box above for a guide to amounts to leave.

ATMs are widely available in South Africa's towns and cities

HEALTH SERVICES

● South Africa has a well-developed health service, but it suffers from being overused and underfunded.

● In the cities, hospitals tend to be fairly well maintained. However, you may prefer to follow the example of wealthy South Africans and opt for private medi-clinics, which are numerous in the cities and rival those of Europe and the US.

BEFORE YOU GO

● See your doctor or travel clinic at least six weeks before your departure in case you need anti-malaria tablets or vaccinations. Your doctor can also give advice on travel risks.

● Make sure you have full travel insurance (▷ 299).

● Have a dental check, especially if you are going to be away for more than a month.

● Obtain a spare set of glasses, and take a prescription with you in case you break your glasses.

● Make sure you know your blood group.

● If you suffer from a long-term condition, make sure that you have a Medic Alert bracelet/necklace with this information on it. See your doctor for a check-up before you leave.

HEALTH HAZARDS

● The commonest hazards facing visitors are diarrhoea, sunstroke and sunburn.

● The main parasitic disease is malaria (▷ 305), and the key viral disease is dengue fever; both are transmitted by mosquitoes (malaria is transmitted at night and dengue fever in the day, so insect repellent should be worn at all times).

● Bacterial diseases include tuberculosis (TB).

● Bilharzia is a water-borne parasite found in some areas: Don't swim or paddle in natural water without checking that the water is not infected. Beware that hippos and crocodiles may be lurking in the water.

● Rabies is a risk in rural areas; dogs and monkeys are particularly common carriers.

Avoid swimming or wading in water infected with Bilharzia

HEALTHY FLYING

● Visitors to South Africa from as far as the UK or US may be concerned about the effect of long-haul flights on their health. The most widely publicized concern is deep vein thrombosis, or DVT. Misleadingly called 'economy class syndrome', DVT is the forming of a blood clot in the body's deep veins, particularly in the legs. The clot can move around the bloodstream and could be fatal.

● Those most at risk include the elderly, pregnant women and those using the contraceptive pill, smokers and the overweight. If you are at increased risk of DVT see your doctor before departing. Flying increases the likelihood of DVT because passengers are often seated in a cramped position for long periods of time and may become dehydrated.

To minimize risk:
Drink water (not alcohol)
Don't stay immobile for hours at a time
Stretch and exercise your legs periodically
Do wear elastic flight socks, which support veins and reduce the chances of a clot forming

EXERCISES

1 ANKLE ROTATIONS   **2 CALF STRETCHES**   **3 KNEE LIFTS**

Lift feet off the floor. Draw a circle with the toes, moving one foot clockwise and the other counterclockwise

Start with heel on the floor and point foot upward as high as you can. Then lift heels high, keeping balls of feet on the floor

Lift leg with knee bent while contracting your thigh muscle. Then straighten leg, pressing foot flat to the floor

Other health hazards for flyers are airborne diseases and bugs spread by the plane's air-conditioning system. These are largely unavoidable but if you have a serious medical condition seek advice from a doctor before flying.

GUIDE TO VACCINATIONS

	All vaccinations should be organized six weeks before departure
BCG (anti-TB)	Required, if staying for more than 1 month
Hepatitis A	Required; the disease can be caught easily from food/water
Polio	Required, if last vaccination was at least 10 years ago
Rabies	Advisable for rural areas
Tetanus	Required, if last vaccination was at least 10 years ago (but after 5 doses you've had enough for life)
Typhoid	Required, if last vaccination was at least 3 years ago
Yellow fever	South Africa is not regarded as a risk area for this disease but other African countries, to the north, are. If you are likely to use South Africa as a base for more extensive African travel then it's wise to get vaccinated.

• HIV/AIDS is a huge problem in South Africa, but remember that you're likely to be infected only through unprotected sex or intravenous drug use.

• Check with a doctor if you are bitten by a snake, spider or scorpion or an animal that might be carrying rabies, or if you stand on any creature in the ocean.

• Treat even minor grazes with caution, as there are parasites and poisonous plants to which you will have no immunity.

WHAT TO TAKE
Anti-malarials

• Most of South Africa is malaria-free, but if you visit some areas, you must take anti-malaria pills.

• Malaria occurs in northern and eastern Mpumalanga, eastern Limpopo province, northern KwaZulu-Natal and Swaziland, particularly in the Lowveld region in and around the Kruger National Park.

• You should consult your doctor six weeks before departure for full advice.

• The start times for anti-malarials vary. If you have never taken Lariam (Mefloquine) before, it is advised to start it at least two to three weeks before entering the malarial zone. Chloroquine and Paludrine are often started a week before arrival, but Doxycycline and Malarone should be started only one to two days before entry to a malarial area.

• You should always check with your doctor, but general guidelines are that all except Malarone should be continued for four weeks after leaving the malarial area.

• Malarone needs to be continued for only seven days afterwards (if a tablet is missed or vomited you should seek specialist advice).

Diarrhoea treatments

• Ciproxin (Ciprofloxacin) is a useful antibiotic for some forms of diarrhoea. Over-the-counter treatments are a great standby for awkward times (such as before a long bus/train journey or on a trek), although it is not a cure for any underlying causes.

Mosquito repellents

• DEET (Diethyltoluamide) is about the best you can buy. Apply the repellent every four to six hours, but more often if you are sweating heavily. If you want to use natural repellents like citronella remember that it must be applied very frequently (ideally hourly) to be effective.

WATER AND FOOD SAFETY

• Tap water is safe to drink, but check before drinking in bush camps.

• During treks, avoid drinking from streams; the best rule to follow is to boil water for ten minutes before drinking it. Do not drink from rivers or lakes.

• Food safety is not usually a problem in South Africa, although it's always a good idea to stick to restaurants and food stands that are busy.

SUMMER HAZARDS

• Do not underestimate the strength of the African sun.

• Wear loose-fitting, lightweight clothing, cover your head with a wide-brimmed hat and wear a good pair of sunglasses.

• The absolute minimum sun screen protection factor you should use is 15, but higher factors are recommended.

• Stay out of the sun between 11am and 3pm.

• Drink at least 2 litres (4 pints) of water per day.

EMERGENCIES

• Dial 10177 for an ambulance in the case of an emergency. Otherwise, drive to the casualty department (ER) of the nearest hospital. Note that you will have to pay for medical treatment.

FINDING A HOSPITAL, DOCTOR OR DENTIST

• The best source for finding these is the *Yellow Pages*, listed under 'Medical Practitioners'.

• Local pharmacies have a list of doctors and dentists. It's also worth asking at your hotel.

• There are two leading private hospital companies in South Africa. The largest is Netcare (tel 011-3010000 or 082-911 for emergencies; www.netcare.co.za). The other company is Medi-Clinic (tel 021-8096500; www.mediclinic.co.za).

• www.travelclinic.co.za lists travel clinics around the country.

PHARMACIES

• Pharmacies can be found in all towns and cities in South Africa, usually providing excellent over-the-counter advice.

• The drugs that they stock often have different brand names from those you may be used to. Make sure you know the chemical name of the drug you require.

• Some drugs that require a prescription in Europe or the US can be bought without one in South Africa.

• Towns and cities always have at least one pharmacy open for 24 hours. Check with local tourist offices.

CASUALTY DEPARTMENTS

Netcare private hospitals	tel 082-911 for emergencies; www.netcare.co.za
Medi-Clinic private hospitals	tel 021-8096500; www.mediclinic.co.za

Major state hospitals	
Cape Town	Groote Schuur, Main Road, Observatory, tel 021-4049111
Johannesburg	Johannesburg General Hospital, Jubilee Road, Parktown, tel 011-4884911
Pretoria	Academic Hospital, Dr Savage Road, Prinshof, Pretoria 0001, tel 012-3541000

FINDING HELP/SAFETY

EMERGENCY NUMBERS
Police
10111
Fire
10111
Ambulance
10177

EMBASSIES/CONSULATES	
Australian Embassy	292 Orient Street, Arcadia, Pretoria, tel 012-3423781 or 0800-993511 (24 hours)
Canada	1103 Arcadia Street, Pretoria 0028, tel 012-4223000
Irish Embassy	1st Floor, Southern Life Plaza, 1059 Schoeman Street, Arcadia, Pretoria, tel 012-3425062
New Zealand Embassy	Block C (2nd floor), Hatfield Gardens, 1110 Arcadia Street, Hatfield, Pretoria, tel 012-3428656
UK Embassy	255 Hill Street, Arcadia, Pretoria, tel 012-4217500
US Embassy	877 Pretorius Street, Arcadia, Pretoria, tel 012-4314000

There are many stories and rumours about the crime rate in South Africa, but while some areas certainly have a high incidence of violent crime, visitors are rarely affected. As for visits to any country, safety is mostly an issue of common sense. If you take sensible precautions, it is highly unlikely that you'll become a victim.

PERSONAL SECURITY

● Never carry more cash than you need, and place valuables in your hotel safe.

● Avoid looking like a tourist, so do not sling your camera around your neck.

● Expensive jewellery should be left at home and keep all valuables out of sight.

● Carry a bag that can be hung diagonally across the body (rather than a shoulder bag or rucksack).

● Keep belongings close to you in public areas. If you're sitting in a crowded restaurant or bar, it's good practice to loop a strap of your bag around your leg, or use bag clips when available.

● Follow local advice on where it is safe to walk. In general, walk around towns and cities in daylight only; take a taxi at night. Some areas should be avoided altogether (such as Hillbrow in Johannesburg).

● Even in a safe area like the Victoria and Alfred Waterfront in Cape Town, it is still advisable to stick to well-lit, busy areas at night.

● You should not visit townships without a guide or on an organized tour.

● Avoid beaches at night.

● Plan your route before you leave your hotel—standing at a street corner peering at a map will only attract attention.

● If you feel unsafe or threatened in any situation, don't hang around: Make as swift an exit as possible.

A police officer rests on his motorbike at Mbabane

● Be cautious of anyone invading your personal space, and watch for ploys to distract your attention, particularly at cash machines.

● Take your mobile (cell) phone with you, or rent one at the airport. It can be useful in an emergency, but keep it out of sight.

● Don't give spare change, sweets (candy) or pens to begging children. Instead, consider making a donation to a local charity.

● Beware of tricksters, such as people in the street with clipboards asking for sponsorship for their studies.

● If you are unfortunate enough to be a victim of a mugging or bag snatching, do not resist. There is a high incidence of gun crime in South Africa and assailants may use weapons if they feel threatened.

● See page 57 for car and driving safety advice.

FEMALE VISITORS

If you observe the advice on personal security, then there is no reason for you to be at greater risk than male visitors. However, make sure you don't travel alone at night and never hitchhike. You might also want to consider dressing more conservatively in quieter, rural areas. This will help protect you against any unwanted attention.

LOST PROPERTY
If you lose your passport

● Always keep a separate note of your passport number and a photocopy of the page that carries your photo, and visitor's permit. Keep the copy separate from your passport, and leave another copy with someone reliable at home. Alternatively, scan the relevant pages and email them to yourself at a web-based email address (such as www.hotmail.com or www.yahoo.com).

● Report the loss or theft of a passport as soon as possible to the police, and then contact your embassy or consulate (see box for contact details).

● The Tourist Assistance Unit of the South African police will help you with processing reports as quickly as possible, but cutting through bureaucratic red tape may still take some time.

● For more information call the Tourism Information and Safety Call Line (tel 083-1232345).

PLANNING

If you lose money or other valuables

- Inform your travel insurance company as soon as possible.
- In the case of theft, inform the police and make sure you get a copy of your written, signed, dated and stamped statement for your insurance claim.
- If you have lost your traveller's cheques, or they've been stolen, notify the issuing company. Always keep a record of the numbers and denominations of your cheques, and keep receipts separate from cheques (if receipts are also lost, the issuing company may not replace the cheques).
- Given the amount of time it takes to process a complaint, it is usually not worth the trouble for inexpensive items.

POLICE

- In an emergency, you should call 10111. If necessary, a flying squad can be deployed to assist you.
- To report a minor crime or theft, visit the local police station (for their address, look in the *Yellow Pages* or ask at the local tourist office or at your hotel).
- All towns have local police stations, and cities have several.

To call the police in an emergency, dial 10111

- The South African government has given high priority to protecting visitors: Recent initiatives include the deployment of tourist police in some large towns.
- There is a nationwide Tourist Assistance Unit to help visitors process reports and complaints more swiftly.
- If you are arrested, remain calm and contact your embassy or consular service as soon as you can.

GAME VIEWING

It is not just in urban areas that you need to be aware of your surroundings. Game viewing here has become an increasingly independent activity and you have the opportunity to drive on an extensive network of roads—and there are times when you will find yourself on your own. There are also rules and regulations to protect the wildlife and the landscape.

- It is strictly forbidden to feed the animals.
- Never get out of your car unless it is a designated area. You will be liable to be prosecuted—and you may well be seriously injured or even killed.

Make sure that you heed warnings given in game parks

- Don't leave your car in search of help if it breaks down while in a game park or reserve. Stay inside the car until a park ranger comes to help you.
- Pass a message to other visitors in their own vehicles for them to relay to the park authorities.
- If night falls, remember that there will be a record of your car entering the park, but not leaving. This will alert the park rangers and they will organize a search party.
- Keep your litter inside the car and dispose of it when you reach a camp.
- There are speed limits around the parks, which need to be adhered to. If you don't, you could be fined, and you are likely to miss the wildlife.
- If you decide to go bush walking, make sure you let someone know where you are going and at what time you plan to return.
- Shake your sleeping bag out before settling down for the night and hang shoes upside down.
- Make sure you have enough supplies for the day, and in particular enough water, whether you are driving or hiking.
- For more information contact South African National Parks (www.sanparks.org) or KZN Wildlife (www.kznwildlife.com). Between them they run the majority of parks you are likely to visit.

COMMUNICATION

South Africa has a good telephone system, an easy-to-use (if slow) mail service, and a large number of internet cafés, all making it easy for you to stay in touch with home during your visit.

TELEPHONES
The telephone service is very efficient, although numbers tend to change every couple of years.
● When telephoning within South Africa, you need to dial the full area code for every number, even if you are calling from within that area.
● When dialling a number in South Africa from abroad, drop the first 0 in the area code.
● Card and coin phones are widespread and work well; even in remote national parks there are usually card phones from which you can direct dial to anywhere in the world.
● Blue public phone booths are coin-operated, but these are becoming rare as green card phones take over.
● Phonecards are sold for R10, R20, R50 and R100. They are available from larger super-markets, newspaper stores, some pharmacies and Telkom vending machines. A R50 card is sufficient to make an international call to Europe or the US for at least 10 minutes.
● Phone booths in backpacker hostels, shops and bars are known as 'chatterboxes' and are usually charged at a higher rate.
● Hotels often double the normal rates, and even a short international call can become very expensive.
● There are a number of private companies that offer fax and mail services, but these also tend to charge about double the usual rate for calls.

● Cheaper calls, known as 'Callmore Time', are available between 7pm and 7am on weekdays and from 7pm on Friday until 7am on Monday. Discounts apply only to national calls. You can usually speak for up to 50 per cent longer than at standard rate times for the same charge.
● 'Worldcall' cards are available at newspaper stores and post offices. You can use them from any phone by dialling the access number and following the voice prompts, and then the international number. They cost R50 and offer slightly cheaper rates than regular phonecards. There is a tollfree number on the back of the card if you need assistance.

MOBILE PHONES (CELL PHONES)
● South Africa uses the GSM system for mobile phones. You should be able to use your mobile, as long as you have

Card phones are green and coin-operated phones are blue

arranged to do so with your service provider before you left your home country.
● Mobile phone numbers in South Africa start with 082, 083, 084 or 072.
● It's a good idea to replace your SIM card with a South African one on arrival. These can be rented at the international airports (▷ 42–44), as can complete phones, at a cost of about R15 per day, and R3 for a minute-long local call. You can also buy a pay-as-you-go SIM card for around R140.
● If you are not bringing your own mobile phone and you are driving yourself, it is essential to rent one for emergencies.

ROADSIDE PHONES
There are telephones at regular intervals along all major roads. They are directly linked to the emergency services, so should only be used in a genuine emergency. However, the best advice is still to carry your own mobile phone.

MAIL
The internal mail service is notoriously slow, but the international service is generally reliable if you use airmail.
● Letters to Europe and the United States should generally take no more than a week, although over the busy Christmas season it can take up to a month.

A public phone in Butha-Buthe, Lesotho

PLANNING

COUNTRY CODES FROM SOUTH AFRICA

International access code	09 +
Australia	61
Belgium	32
Canada	1
France	33
Germany	49
Greece	30
Ireland	353
Netherlands	31
New Zealand	64
Spain	34
Sweden	46
UK	44
USA	1

To call home from South Africa, dial 09, then the country's access code. To call South Africa from home, the country code is 27.

AREA CODES

Cape Town	021
Bloemfontein	051
Durban	031
East London	043
Kimberley	053
Johannesburg	011
Mafikeng/Mmabatho	018
Pietersburg/ Polokwane	015
Port Elizabeth	041
Pretoria	012

POSTAGE RATES

Domestic stamps:	R17 for book of 10 stamps
Postcard sent by airmail to anywhere in the world:	R3.45
Letter (maximum weight 50g)	
sent by airmail to anywhere in the world:	R4

- Stamps can be bought at post offices and at stationers.
- Mailboxes are usually just outside post offices and are bright red.
- Opening times for post offices are Mon–Fri 8.30–4, Sat 8–12.
- Parcels have been known to disappear en route, so it's a good idea to send valuable items as registered mail.
- Postnet (www.postnet.co.za) is a private mail company with outlets all over South Africa, providing mail services, fax, telephone service and internet access, as well as a *poste restante* service. Although their charges are slightly higher, they are generally regarded as more reliable than the national mail system.

LAPTOPS

If you intend to bring your own laptop to South Africa, remember to bring a power converter to

Red mailboxes were inherited from British colonial rule

recharge it and a plug socket adaptor. A surge protector is also a good idea. To connect to the internet you need an adaptor for the phone socket.

If you use an international internet service provider, such as AOL or Compuserve, it's cheaper to dial up a local node rather than the number at home. Dial-tone frequencies vary from country to country, so set your modem to ignore dial tones.

INTERNET

South Africa is well served by the internet, and most companies, tourist offices, hotels and guesthouses have email addresses and websites. There are plenty of internet cafés in all major towns and cities (usually costing around R5 for 10 minutes). Many hotels, guesthouses and backpacker hostels offer email access as a service, although rates are higher than in internet cafés. You can also check emails at Vodacom and Postnet shops, and the Post Office has started introducing internet access. In the more remote regions, you are unlikely to see internet cafés unless the town is served by a university or college.

You are shaded from the sun as you make your call from these public phones in Thohyandou

PLANNING

OPENING TIMES AND TICKETS

BANKS
Banks are usually open Mon–Fri 9–3.30, Sat 8.30 or 9–10.30 or 11.

BARS
Bars open mid-morning and close around 11pm, but much later in the big cities.

CAFÉS
Expect most cafés to open at around 7am and to close in the late afternoon (5–6). Cities and main towns always have a few 24-hour cafés.

DOCTORS AND PHARMACIES
These function under normal business hours (usually 8.30–5 or 6), but most towns have 24-hour doctors and pharmacies providing a service in rotation. Ask at the local tourist office.

GOVERNMENT OFFICES
These are open only on weekdays and usually close for lunch (8.30–1, 2–4.30).

MUSEUMS AND GALLERIES
Opening times vary around the country. In the cities, most are open from around 9 or 10 until 5. Some museums close on Sundays or Mondays. Rural museums often close for lunch. See individual entries in The Sights section for details.

OFFICES
Businesses are usually open Mon–Fri 8.30–5, Sat 8.30–2.

PLACES OF WORSHIP
Many places of worship are kept locked and can be visited only during services. Times are usually posted at entrances, or check with the local tourist office.

POST OFFICES
Post offices in towns and cities are open Mon–Fri 8.30–4, Sat 8–12. These times are shorter in more rural areas.

RESTAURANTS
Many restaurants open for breakfast from around 8am. Lunch is usually served between 12 and 3. Many kitchens close until 6, then staying open until 10 or 11.

SHOPS
Opening times vary widely depending on where the shop is. As a general guide, shops are open Mon–Fri 8–6, Sat 8 or 9–2 or 3, Sun 9–1. Malls in cities are often open until 10pm, but note that even in Jo'burg or Cape Town, shops usually close on Saturday afternoons. Larger supermarkets usually stay open until around 8pm. In rural areas, shops are closed on Sundays.

DISCOUNTS AND CONCESSIONS
● Children under the age of 18 can sometimes get discounts of up to 50 per cent on entry to museums, galleries and other attractions.
● Children under 5 often get in for free.

NATIONAL HOLIDAYS	
1 Jan	New Year's Day
21 Mar	Human Rights Day
Friday before Easter Sunday	Good Friday
Monday after Easter Sunday	Family Day
27 Apr	Freedom Day
1 May	Workers' Day
16 Jun	Youth Day
9 Aug	National Women's Day
24 Sep	Heritage Day
16 Dec	Day of Reconciliation
25 Dec	Christmas Day
26 Dec	Day of Goodwill

● Seniors receive discounts on most admission charges, but may need to present ID.
● International Student Identity Card (ISIC) carriers will receive discounts on admission to most museums and galleries. The cards are issued by student travel agencies across the world, and give special rates on all forms of transportation, as well as other discounts and services.
● Youth Hostel Association (YHA) card carriers are eligible for discounts. The cards themselves can be bought from some South African backpackers' hostels for considerably less than in other countries. Card holders get 10 per cent off at YHA affiliated backpackers' hostels and 5 per cent off the price of Baz Bus tickets (▷ 51).
● Resident South Africans sometimes qualify for a discount on entry to national parks, but need to prove their identity.

TOURIST OFFICES

South Africa has an excellent infrastructure of tourist offices, and even the smallest town has some sort of visitor information bureau. The cities have particularly good services: Expect a wealth of free information and advice on what to do, special events, where to eat and stay, what's available for families, access to sights for people with disabilities and nightlife. Some also offer internet access and have gift shops.

If you're touring the country, it's an excellent idea to visit the main tourist office whenever you arrive in a city or the main town of a region, to pick up vital information on activities, and to stock up on maps.

Most offices have regional information, and leaflets about national parks and game reserves. You can usually expect to find an accommodation reservation service (either by phone or in person; some offices have online reservations as well), for which you will have to pay a small fee. This is usually in the form of slightly inflated room rates. In addition to the tourist offices, there is a great deal of visitor information available on the internet.

TOURIST OFFICES

City Tourist Offices

Bloemfontein Tourist Centre, 60 Park Road, Bloemfontein 9301, tel 051-4058490/8489, www.mangaung.co.za

Cape Town Tourism, The Pinnacle, corner of Burg and Castle streets, tel 021-4264260, www.cape-town.org

Ceres Tourism, in the town library on Owen Street, Ceres 6835, tel 023-3161287, www.ceres.org.za

Citrusdal Tourist Office, 39 Voortrekker Street, Citrusdal 7340, tel 022-9213210, www.citrusdal.com

Durban Tourist Junction, Station Building, 160 Pine Street, Durban 4001, tel 031-3044934, www.durbanexperience.co.za

Gansbaai Tourism Bureau, corner of Berg and Main streets, Gansbaai 7220, tel 028-3841439, www.gansbaaiinfo.com

George Tourism Bureau, 124 York Street, George 6529, tel 044-8019295/7, www.georgetourism.co.za

Greater Hermanus Tourism Bureau, Old Station Building, Mitchell Street, tel 028-3122629, www.hermanus.co.za

Graaff-Reinet Publicity Association, 13a Church Street, Graaff-Reinet 6280, tel 049-8924248, www.graaffreinet.co.za

Graskop, Panorama Tourist Association, Louis Trichardt Street, Graskop 1270, tel 013-7671377, www.panoramainfo.co.za

Hogsback Tourism, Main Road, in Nina's Deli, Hogsback 57212, tel 045-9621326, www.hogsbackinfo.co.za

Jeffreys Bay Tourism, corner Da Gama and Drommedaris roads, Jeffreys Bay 6330, tel 042-2932323, www.jeffreysbay.com

Johannesburg Tourism, 195 Jan Smuts Avenue, Johannesburg 2001,tel 011-3278001, www.joburg.org.za

Kimberley, Diamond Fields Tourist Information Centre, corner of Bultfontein and Lyndhurst streets, Kimberley 8300, tel 053-8327298

Knysna Tourism, 40 Main Street, Knysna 6571, tel 044-3825510, www.tourismknysna.co.za

Makana (Grahamstown) Tourism, 63 High Street, Grahamstown 6139, tel 046-6223241, www.grahamstown.co.za

Nelspruit, Lowveld Tourism Association, Crossing Centre, Nelspruit 1201, tel 013-7551988, www.lowveldinfo.com

Oudtshoorn Tourist Bureau, Baron van Reede Street, Oudtshoorn 6625, tel 044-2792532, www.oudtshoorn.com

Pietermaritzburg Tourism, Publicity House, 177 Commercial Road, Pietermaritzburg 3201, tel 033-3451348, www.pmbtourism.co.za

Pilgrim's Rest Tourist Information Centre, Main Street, Upper Town, tel 013-7681060, www.pilgrimsrest.co.za

Plettenberg Bay Tourism, Melville's Corner shopping mall, Main Street, Plettenberg Bay 6600, tel 044-5334065, www.plettenbergbay.co.za

Port Elizabeth, Nelson Mandela Bay Tourism, Donkin Lighthouse Building, Belmont Terrace, Port Elizabeth 6001, tel 041-5858884, www.nelsonmandelatourism.co.za

Pretoria (Tshwane) Tourism Information Bureau, Old Netherlands Bank Building, Church Square, City Centre 0002, tel 012-3581340, www.tshwane.gov.za

Springbok, Namakwa Tourism Information, Voortrekker Street, Springbok 8240, tel 027-7128035, www.northerncape.org.za

Stellenbosch Tourist Office, 36 Market St, tel 021-8833584, www.stellenboschtourism.co.za

Tulbagh Tourist Information Office, 4 Church Street, Tulbagh 6820, tel 023-2301348, www.tulbaghtourism.org.za

Upington Tourist Office, in the Kalahari Oranje Museum, Schröder Street, Upington 8801, tel 054-3326064, www.upington.co.za

Regional Tourist Offices

Eastern Cape Tourism, tel 043-7019600, www.ectourism.co.za

Gauteng Tourism Authority, tel 011-3409000, www.gauteng.net

Lesotho Tourist Board Office, central Kingsway, Maseru, tel 22312896, www.lesotho.gov.ls/lstourism.htm

Limpopo Province Tourism Board, tel 015-2907300, www.limpopotourism.org.za

Mpumalanga Tourism Authority, tel 013-7527001, www.mpumalanga.com

Northern Cape Tourism Authority, tel 053-8322657, www.northerncape.org.za

North West Province, tel 018-3861225, www.tourismnorthwest.co.za

Swaziland Information Office, Swazi Plaza, Mbabane, tel 404-2531, www.mintour.gov.sz

Tourism KwaZulu-Natal, tel 031-3667500, www.zulu.org.za

Western Cape Tourism, tel 021-4265639, www.capetourism.org

MEDIA

NEWSPAPERS

The *Sunday Times* and *Sunday Independent* are weekly English-language papers. They have national coverage, although several editions are produced for different areas. The excellent weekly *Mail & Guardian* (which has close links to the British *Guardian*) provides the most objective reporting on South African issues, and has in-depth coverage of international news.

Daily English-language newspapers include: *The Star* and *The Citizen* (Johannesburg); *The Daily News* and *The Natal Mercury* (Durban); *The Argus* and *The Cape Times* (Cape Town). *The Sowetan* provides a less white-orientated view of South African news and has the best coverage of international soccer. There are also a number of papers published in Afrikaans, Zulu and Xhosa.

MAGAZINES

There are a number of South African publications that visitors will find useful. The yearly *Eat Out* magazine lists reviews of the best restaurants in the country, but it tends to concentrate on rather smart and expensive eateries. *Time Out Cape Town* is another useful annual magazine with good nightlife and culture listings. The monthly *Getaway* is aimed at the South African love of the outdoors, but has

excellent travel features and ideas, as well as reviews of different accommodation and activities throughout the whole of southern Africa.

RADIO

Radio is the most popular medium in the country, and even the most remote corners are reached by broadcasters. The South African Broadcasting Corporation (SABC) has numerous national stations catering to speakers of the country's 11 official languages. The corporation has an agreement with the UK's BBC, which means that listeners can hear BBC news and other broadcasts at certain times of day. 5FM is the SABC national

Papers are published in English, Afrikaans, Zulu and Xhosa

A bookstore at the Bridge Mall, Port Elizabeth

pop music station, while Metro FM offers R 'n' B, hip-hop and kwaito (▷ 19). There is also an abundance of local commercial and community radio stations, such as Good Hope FM in Cape Town or Radio Zulu in Johannesburg.

TELEVISION

The SABC—the state broadcaster—has significantly restructured its service in the last decade to accommodate all official languages. The majority of the output is in English, followed by Afrikaans, Zulu and Xhosa.

There are now four free channels available: SABC 1, 2 and 3, and the newer e channel. The last is the most popular and tends to have better news and entertainment broadcasts; SABC 3 has a link with CNN, however, and provides live CNN broadcasts in the afternoon.

The paying channel M-Net is available in most hotels, guesthouses and backpacker hostels, and shows a range of sports, sit-coms and movies. It is available free from 5pm to 7pm ('open time'). Many hotels also have satellite TV, known as DSTV, with a variety of sport, movie and news channels.

BOOKS, MAPS AND FILMS

BOOKS

South Africa has produced a number of internationally recognized novelists including Nadine Gordimer, André Brink and J. M. Coetzee. The following are some of the best-known books to come out of South Africa, and will provide you with valuable and entertaining insight into the culture and history of the country.

Fiction

● *Disgrace* by J. M. Coetzee, about a Cape Town academic's fall from grace.
● *July's People* by Nadine Gordimer, the story of a white family rescued from revolution by its gardener.
● *Dry White Season* by André Brink, the moving tale of a teacher's attempt to uncover politically motivated murders in the 1980s.
● *Indecent Exposure* by Tom Sharpe, a riotous, slapstick South African-based tale.
● *Down Second Avenue* by Eskia Mpahalele, a story of the trials and tribulation of growing up in a Johannesburg township in the 1940s.
● *Cry the Beloved Country*, Alan Paton's poignant view of black urban migrants in 1940s South Africa.
● *The Story of an African Farm* by Olive Schreiner, one of the earliest South African novels, about two women living on a Karoo farm.
● *King Solomon's Mines* by H. Rider Haggard, a tale of swashbuckling heroism against an African background.
● *Alexandra Tales*, short stories by Isaac Mogosti, about family life in Alexandra township.

Autobiography and Non-Fiction

● *Long Walk to Freedom* by Nelson Mandela, the most important autobiography to come out of South Africa.
● *No Future Without Forgiveness*, former Archbishop Desmond Tutu's account of his experience of the Truth and Reconciliation Committee.
● *Country of My Skull* by Antjie Krog, a disturbing but gripping account of the Truth and Reconciliation Committee.

● *The Lost World of the Kalahari*, Laurens van der Post's famous 1958 travelogue about the San is considered to be rather fanciful, but it is still an entertaining read.
● *The Bang-Bang Club* by Greg Marinovich and Joao Silva, a harrowing account of two photo-journalists' experiences in the township wars of the early 1990s (▷ 38).
● *A Field Guide to the Larger Mammals of Africa*, Jean Dorst and Pierre Dandelot.
● *Birds of South Africa*, Gordon Maclean Roberts.

MAPS

The Automobile Association of South Africa (www.aa.co.za) has shops in all major cities selling national, regional and touring maps. Tourist offices are also a good source of local maps.

The Map Studio (tel 0860-105050; www.mapstudio.co.za) produces a wide range of maps covering much of Africa.

This book contains an atlas of South Africa on pages 320–331. There is a plan of Cape Town's City Bowl on page 66 and an area map of the Winelands on page 92.

FILMS

South Africa's film industry is small, but growing. Leon Schuster is South Africa's best-known director and actor. His slapstick films are the highest earning and most watched films

Cinema Nouveau, in Cape Town

in the country. Director and producer Anant Singh is the force behind a new film studio being built in Cape Town, although this will be used in the main by foreign companies. But South Africa is booming as a film location thanks to its terrific landscapes and value for money.
● *Yesterday*, directed by Darryl James Roodt, is the first feature film to be shot in the Zulu language and was nominated for Best Foreign Language Film at the 2005 Oscars. It follows the story of a woman who discovers she is HIV Positive.
● *Forgiveness*, directed by Ian Gabriel, deals with issues of forgiveness in the light of confessions from an ex-apartheid policeman.
● A reworking of the opera *Carmen*, set in a South African township, won the 2004 Golden Bear Best Film Award at the Berlin film festival. *U-Carmen e-Khayelitsha* has all its lyrics in the Xhosa language.
● The South African-English co-production *Hotel Rwanda* (2004) was nominated for three Oscars in 2005 and was shot in Johannesburg.
● Samuel L. Jackson stars in a screen version of the book *Country of My Skull* (see Autobiography and Non-Fiction), called *In My Country* (2004) in the US.

USEFUL WEBSITES

Logging on at an internet café in Cape Town

BACKPACKERS
www.hihostels.com
Advice and information from
Hostelling International.
www.coastingafrica.com
Useful hostel reviews from Coast
to Coast, which publishes a free
annual backpackers' guide to
hostels across the country.
www.btsa.co.za
Hostel information from BTSA
(Backpacking Tourism South
Africa).

DOCUMENTATION
www.fco.gov.uk
Comprehensive travel advice
from the UK Foreign and
Commonwealth office.
www.travel.state.gov
US Department of State
travel advice.

DRIVING
www.aa.co.za
The Automobile Association of
South Africa, with road safety
advice and emergency
breakdown information.
www.nra.co.za
Road information from the South
African National Road Agency.

HEALTH
www.cdc.gov
US government website with
excellent advice on travel health.
www.doh.gov.uk
Useful UK government website
with advice on vaccinations.
www.tmb.ie
Irish-based website with a good
collection of tropical travel health
information.

www.who.int
Website of the World Health
Organization, with lists of
diseases and vaccines.

MUSEUMS
www.museums.org.za
Museums Online South Africa
provides a number of links to
museums around the country.
www.samaweb.org.za
Regional events at museums,
from South African Museums
Association.

MUSIC
www.putumayo.com
Lively website with interesting
articles on the music scene.

NATIONAL PARKS AND
GAME RESERVES
www.sanparks.org
Comprehensive details of all the
national parks, including prices,
news and online reservations.
www.capenature.org.za
Official data on the game
reserves in the Western Cape.
www.kznwildlife.com
Outline of all the game reserves
in KwaZulu-Natal.

NEWS
www.iol.co.za
Nationwide website for the main
daily and weekly newspapers.
www.sabc.co.za
Daily news from the state
broadcaster, SABC.
www.mg.co.za
In-depth news articles from the
Mail & Guardian, the leading
weekly paper.

RESPONSIBLE TRAVEL
www.fairtourismsa.org.za
Information on fair trade in
tourism in South Africa.
www.responsibletravel.com
UK-based portal for alternative,
responsible holidays.
www.tourismconcern.org.uk
Details of this UK charity's work
with communities.

TOURIST INFORMATION
www.southafrica.net
Comprehensive country
information from SATOUR,
the national tourism board.
www.overberginfo.com
Wide-ranging information on
the Overberg region of the
Western Cape.
www.gardenroute.co.za
Useful travel tips covering one
of the most popular regions in
South Africa.
www.go2africa.com
Full accommodation and holiday
reservation service for Southern
Africa, with useful practical
information and links to
overland companies.

For websites of city and regional
tourist offices, see page 311.

WINE ROUTES
www.wine.co.za
Details of all the routes available
in South Africa, plus articles on
wines.

LANGUAGE GUIDE

South Africa has 11 official languages, and scores of other, 'unofficial' African languages are spoken. Most people understand and speak English, which tends to dominate much of the cultural and political scene.

However, English is actually the mother tongue of a relative minority—just 9 per cent of the population. isiZulu, the language of the Zulus, is the largest, at around 28 per cent of the population and Afrikaans is the mother tongue of over 14 per cent. Most Afrikaans-speakers are not white, but 'coloured' (▷ 5–6). The other official languages in South Africa are:

- Sesotho sa Leboa
- Sesotho
- Setswana
- SiSwati
- Tshivenda
- Xitsonga
- isiNdebele
- isiXhosa.

With such a wide variety of languages, you will hardly have time to learn more than a smattering of even one or two. However, you'll find that learning a few phrases of whichever language dominates the area you are going through will be worthwhile.

It's worth noting that the English spoken in South Africa uses British English rather than American terms. For example, South Africans refer to the 'boot' of a car (not the trunk), 'lift' (instead of elevator), and 'petrol' (instead of gas). The influence of American television and films is being felt, however. You will hear 'cell phone' and 'movie', for example, rather than 'mobile phone' and 'film'.

ENGLISH
South African English has a huge and interesting vocabulary, borrowing a wide range of terms, phrases and words from Afrikaans and various African languages. See box for a list of common colloquialisms.

AFRIKAANS
Afrikaans is the language of around 60 per cent of the white population, and 90 per cent of 'coloured' people. It is probably the language, aside from English, which you will come across most

SOUTH AFRICAN/ENGLISH COLLOQUIALISMS	
Most of these are derived from Afrikaans, but are widely used in South African English.	
Ag	pronounced like the German 'ach'. Used at the beginning of a sentence, often to indicate irritation
Babelas	hangover
Bakkie	small pick-up van
Bergie	homeless person/tramp
Biltong	dried, cured meat
Bob	money
Boet	brother/guy/dude
Braai	barbecue
Bru	brother/guy (affectionate term between men)
Cooldrink	soft (non-alcoholic) drink
Dingus	thing (used when the speaker does not know the word for something, as in 'thingy' or 'whatchamacallit')
Doff	stupid/idiot
Dop	drink (alcoholic)
Frikkadel	meatball
Gatvol	fed up
Hap	bite (as in 'bite to eat')
Howzit	hello/how are you?
Izzit	used widely in conversation, meaning 'really?', or 'is that so?'
Jawelnofine	how about that?
Jol	party
Just now	soon (this implies someone will do something in the near future, but not immediately)
Koppie	small hill
Kos	food
Larny	well-dressed, smart
Lekker	good/nice/tasty/fun
Madiba	Nelson Mandela's clan name, used widely as a term of endearment (including in the press), also meaning 'grandfather'
Nooit	no/never
Now now	in a little while (as in 'I'll be with you now now')
Oke	guy/man
Padkos	food for the road
Platteland	flatlands, rural areas
Robot	traffic lights
Shame	used to denote sympathy
Skrik	fright
Slip-slops	flip-flop or thong shoes
Stoep	veranda
Tackies	sports shoes/sneakers
Yebo	hello/yes

often as a visitor. Many Afrikaans words are used in South African English (see South African/English Colloquialisms box). It is widely spoken in the Western and Northern Capes, where it is the first language of much of the population. Derived from Dutch, it also incorporates words from English, East Africa, Indonesia and from the indigenous Khoi and San languages. While most Afrikaans-speakers understand

English, many do not, so it's worth learning a few phrases.

THE NGUNI LANGUAGES
isiZulu, isiXhosa, SiSwati and isiNdebele are collectively referred to as the Nguni languages, and have a lot of similarities in syntax and grammar. isiZulu is the most widely spoken. It is the first language of much of KwaZulu-Natal's population, and is spoken

USEFUL WORDS AND PHRASES

ENGLISH	AFRIKAANS	ISIZULU	ISIXHOSA	SETSWANA	SESOTHO	SISWATI
Hello	Hallo	Sawubona	Molo (good morning) Rhoananai (good evening)	Dumela	Dumela	Sawubona
Goodbye	Totsiens	Sala kahle	Sala sentle	Sala sentle	Sala Hantle	Salakahle
How are you?	Hoe gaan dit?	Ninjani?	Kunjani?	O tsogile jang?	O kae?	Ninjani?
Fine, thank you	Goed, dankie	Ngisaphila	Ndiphilile, enkosi	Ke tsogile sentle	Ke phela hantle	Kulungile
Please	Asseblief	Uxolo	Nceda	Tsweetswee	(Ka kopo) hle	Ngicela
Thank you	Dankie	Ngiyabonga	Enkosi	Ke a leboga	Ke a leboha	Ngiyabonga
Yes	Ja	Yebo	Ewe	Ee	E	Yebo
No	Nee	Cha	Hayi	Nnyaa	The	Cha
Excuse me	Verskooon my	Uxolo	Uxolo	Intshwarele	Ntshwaerele	

by many in Gauteng, Free State and Mpumalanga.

SiSwati, spoken in Swaziland, is very similar to isiZulu, as is isiNdebele, which is spoken in North West Province and part of Gauteng. isiXhosa is the language of the Eastern Cape (and Nelson Mandela's mother tongue), as well as in the townships of Cape Town.

THE SOTHO LANGUAGES

This group of languages includes Setswana, Sesotho sa Leboa and Sesotho, and all three are again very similar. Sesotho is the language of the Lesotho people, and is also spoken in Free State. Sesotho sa Leboa (also known as Northern Sotho) is concentrated in the northeast of South Africa. Setswana is the main African language of Botswana, and is also spoken south of the border, in parts of the Northern Cape and North West Province.

EMERGING LANGUAGES

A lingua franca of the urban townships is Tsotsi taal, widely spoken by young males. This is a hybrid of Afrikaans, English and African languages, which evolved as a result of linguistically diverse populations living side by side. It is a dynamic language, with new words and phrases regularly being created.

USEFUL WORDS IN AFRIKAANS

For translations of Afrikaans road signs, see page 56.

Airplane	Vliegtuig	**Good/nice**	Lekker
Airport	Lughawe	**Information**	Inligting
Arrival	Aankoms	**Left**	Links
Bank	Bank	**Low-lying lake**	
Barbecue	Braai	**or swamp**	Vlei
Bed and		**Lunch**	Middagete
breakfast	Bed en ontbyt	**Market**	Mark
Beach	Strand	**Mountain**	Berg
Bill	Rekening	**Petrol**	Brandstoff
Border	Grens	**Pharmacy**	Apteek
Borough	Burg	**Police**	Polisie
Breakfast	Ontbyt	**Post Office**	Poskantoor
Cheap	Goedkoop	**Pub/bar**	Kroeg
Cheque	Tjek	**Right**	Regs
Church	Kerk	**Station**	Stasie
City	Stad	**Ticket**	Kaartjie
Credit card	Kredietkaart	**Town centre**	Middestad
Departure	Vertrek	**Traveller's**	
Dinner	Aandete	**cheque**	Reisigerstjek
Expensive	Duur	**Village**	Dorp
Exit	Uitgang	**Wine**	Wyn
Field	Veld		

CAPE DUTCH ARCHITECTURE

This architectural style is found only in the Western Cape, appearing in the mid-18th century and heavily influenced by European architecture. The style is identifiable by its symmetrical designs and prominent gables. Other strong features, especially of early designs, are thatched roofs and sash windows. Good examples are the estate at Vergelegen (▷ 93), the homesteads in the Hex River Valley (▷ 81) and in Tulbagh (▷ 87).

GLOSSARY FOR US VISITORS

anticlockwise	counterclockwise	level crossing	grade crossing
aubergine	eggplant	lorry	truck
bank holiday	public holiday	licensed	a café or restaurant that has
bill	check (at restaurant)		a license to serve alcohol
biscuit	cookie		(beer and wine only unless
bonnet	hood (car)		it's 'fully' licensed)
boot	trunk (car)	lift	elevator
busker	street musician	nappy	diaper
caravan	house trailer or RV	note	paper money
car park	parking lot	off-licence	liquor store
carriage	car (on a train)	pants	underpants
casualty	emergency room (hospital	pavement	sidewalk
	department)	petrol	gas
chemist	pharmacy	plaster	Band-Aid or bandage
chips	french fries	post	mail
coach	long-distance bus	public school	private school
concessions	reduced fees for tickets,	pudding	dessert
	often available to	purse	change purse
	students, children and	pushchair	stroller
	elderly people	return ticket	roundtrip ticket
courgette	zucchini	rocket	arugula
crèche	day care	roundabout	traffic circle or rotary
crisps	potato chips	self-catering	accommodation including a
directory enquiries	directory assistance		kitchen
dual carriageway	two-lane highway	single ticket	one-way ticket
en suite	a bedroom with its own	stalls	orchestra seats (in theater)
	private bathroom; may also	surgery	doctor's office
	just refer to the bathroom	tailback	traffic jam
football	soccer	takeaway	takeout
full board	a hotel tariff that includes	taxi rank	taxi stand
	all meals	ten-pin bowling	bowling
garage	gas station	tights	panty-hose
garden	yard (residential)	T-junction	an intersection where one
GP	doctor		road meets another at
half board	hotel tariff that includes		right angles (making a T
	breakfast and either lunch		shape)
	or dinner	toilets	restrooms
handbag	purse	torch	flashlight
high street	main street	trolley	cart
hire	rent	trousers	pants
jelly	Jello™	underpass	subway
jumper, jersey	sweater	way out	exit
junction	intersection	windscreen	windshield (car)
layby	rest stop, pull-off		

SIGNIFICANT DATES

40,000BC	Country inhabited by the San people
26,000BC	Earliest recorded San rock art
1488	Bartholomeu Dias, the Portuguese navigator, rounds the Cape of Good Hope
1580	Sir Francis Drake rounds the Cape
1652	The Dutch establish a supply station under the command of Jan van Riebeeck
1795	The British occupy the Cape
1835–54	Afrikaner Voortrekkers leave the Cape to establish their own rule in other regions
1838	Boer-Zulu War
1866	Diamonds are discovered near the Vaal River
1886	Gold is discovered in present-day Johannesburg
1879	Anglo-Zulu War
1880–81	First Anglo-Boer War
1899–1902	Second Anglo-Boer War
1912	The South African Native National Congress is founded, later becoming the ANC
1948	The implementation of apartheid begins
1990	President F. W. de Klerk lifts the ban of the ANC
1994	ANC wins the first democratic elections with Nelson Mandela becoming president

SOUTH AFRICAN AIRWAYS

Voted **'Best Airline to Africa'** by the travel industry for 14 consecutive years, South African Airways offers the most connections to destinations in Southern Africa ensuring unbeatable flexibility when booking your holiday.

By booking online at **www.flysaa.com**, you can access fantastic flight specials to South Africa and save 10% on international flights and domestic flights.

FREQUENT SERVICES
SAA fly direct to South Africa from many cities around the world, including London, New York, Atlanta and Perth.

CHOICE OF CLASSES
- First class   180° lie flat bed on all flights
- Business class   180° lie flat bed on all flights
  Dedicated Departure and Arrival lounges for our premium passengers
- Economy class Personal seat back video entertainment and audio system
                 Complimentary food and beverages throughout the flight

From the moment you step on board,
let us share our passion and knowledge of our homeland with you

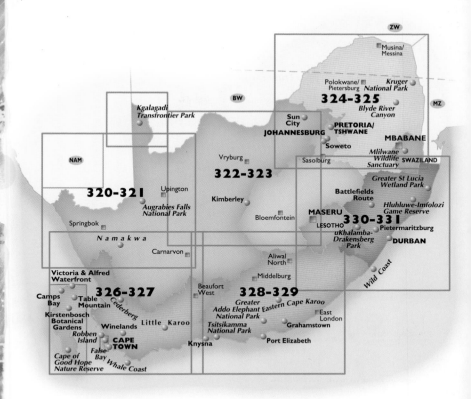

ZW

Musina/
Messina

Polokwane/
Pietersburg   *Kruger*
               National Park

324-325

Kgalagadi
Transfrontier Park

BW   Blyde River
                      Canyon

MZ

Sun
City   **PRETORIA/**
JOHANNESBURG   **TSHWANE**
                                    MBABANE
               Soweto
                      Mlilwane
Vryburg   Wildlife   SWAZILAND
               Sasolburg Sanctuary
322-323

NAM   Greater St Lucia
                                 Wetland Park
Upington   Battlefields
                  Route   Hluhluwe-Imfolozi
Kimberley   Game Reserve
320-321
       Augrabies Falls Bloemfontein **MASERU**
       National Park   **330-331**
Springbok   LESOTHO   Pietermaritzburg
                                 uKhalamba-
    N a m a k w a   MASERU Drakensberg   **DURBAN**
                                 Park
       Carnarvon
                  Aliwal
                  North   Wild Coast
Victoria & Alfred   Middelburg
Waterfront   Beaufort
326-327   West   **328-329**
Camps   East
Bay   Table   Greater   Eastern Cape Karoo London
      Mountain   Addo Elephant
Kirstenbosch   National Park   Grahamstown
Botanical Winelands Little Karoo
Gardens   Little Karoo
Robben   Tsitsikamma
Island   **CAPE**   National Park Port Elizabeth
Cape of   **TOWN** Knysna
Good Hope False
Nature Reserve Bay Whale Coast

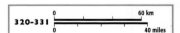

320-331   0   60 km
           0   40 miles

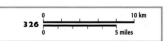

326   0   10 km
           0   5 miles

Maps

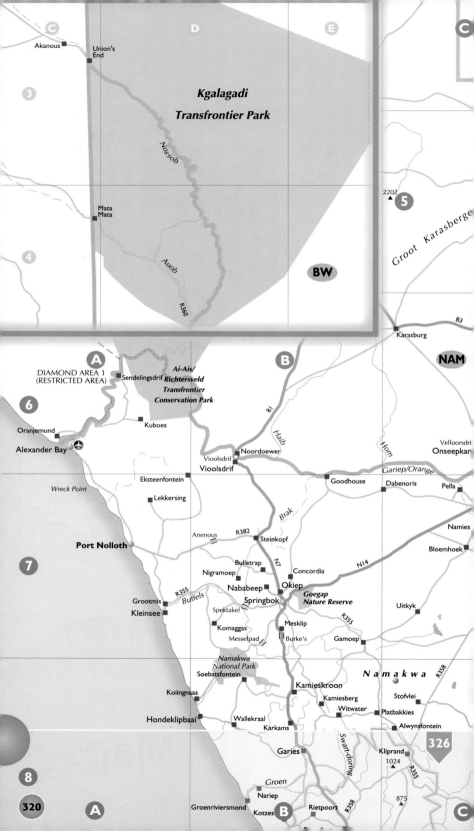

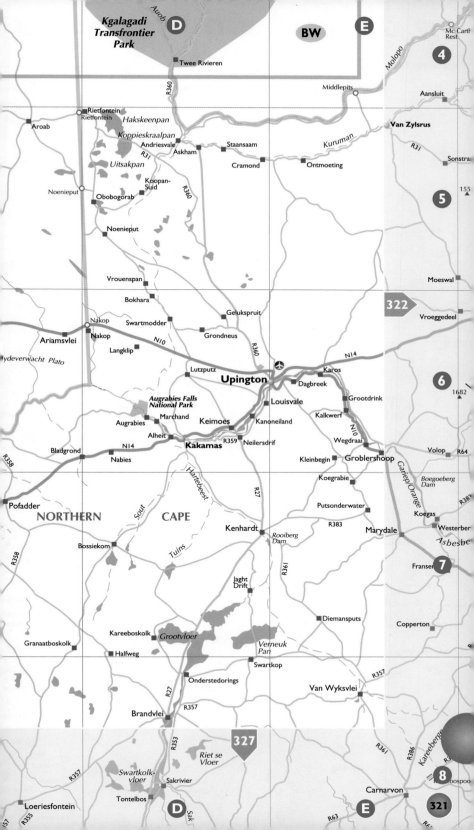

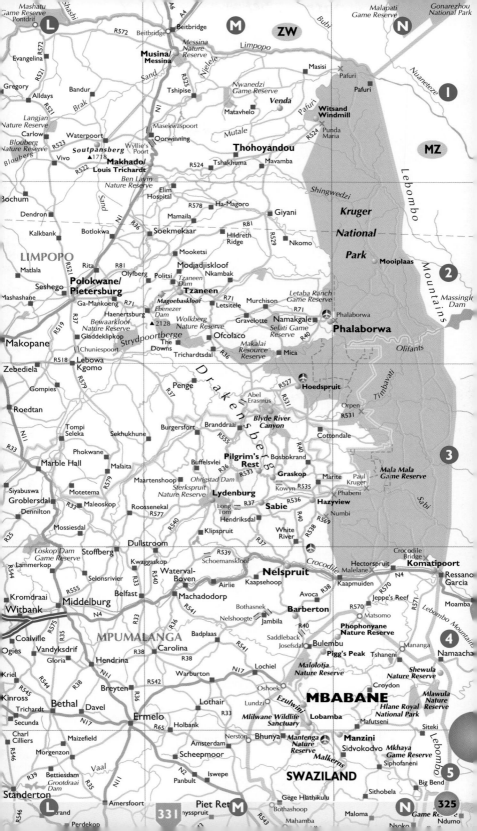

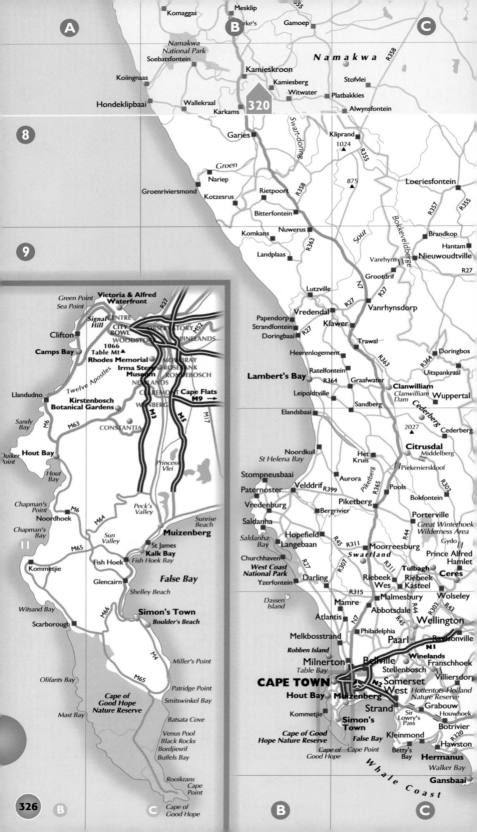

Namakwa

Komaggas
Mesklip
Burke's
Gamoep
R355
R358

Namakwa National Park
Soebatsfontein
Kamieskroon
Kamiesberg
Stofvlei
Koiingnaas
Witwater
Platbakkies
Hondeklipbaai
Wallekraal
Karkams
320
Alwynsfontein
R358

8

Garies
Kliprand
1024 ▲
R355
Groen
R358
Swart-doring
875 ▲
Loeriesfontein
Nariep
Rietpoort
R357
R355
Groenriviersmond
Kotzesrus
Bitterfontein
Sout
Bokkeveldberge
Brandkop
Komkans
Nuwerus
Hantam
Landplaas
R363
Vanrhyns
Nieuwoudtville
R27

9

Lutzville
Grootdrif
N7
R27
Vredendal
Doringbos
Papendorp
Strandfontein
Klawer
R364
Uitspankraal
Doringbaai
R27
Heerenlogement
Trawal
Cederberg
Lambert's Bay
Ratelfontein
Graafwater
Clanwilliam
Wuppertal
Leipoldtville
R364
Clanwilliam Dam
Sandberg
Elandsbaai
2027 ▲
Cederberg
Citrusdal
Noordkuil
St Helena Bay
Het Kruis
Middelberg
Piekenierspas
Stompneusbaai
Aurora
Pikelberg
Pools
Bokfontein
Paternoster
Velddrif
R399
Piketberg
R365
R303
Vredenburg
Bergrivier
Porterville
Saldanha
Hopefield
Moorreesburg
Great Winterhoek Wilderness Area
Gydo
Saldanha Bay
Langebaan
R45
R311
Prince Alfred Hamlet
Churchhaven
Swartland
Tulbagh
Ceres
West Coast National Park
Darling
R307
R311
Riebeek Wes
Riebeek Kasteel
Wolseley
Yzerfontein
R315
Malmesbury
R303
R43
Dassen Island
Mamre
Abbotsdale
R44
Wellington
Atlantis
N7
Philadelphia
Paarl
Klapmuts
Melkbosstrand
Robben Island
Milnerton
Belville
Winelands
Franschhoek
Table Bay
Stellenbosch
Villiersdorp
CAPE TOWN
Somerset West
Hottentots-Holland Nature Reserve
Hout Bay
Muizenberg
Grabouw
Houwhoek
Kommetjie
Strand
Sir Lowry's Pass
Botrivier
Simon's Town
Kleinmond
R320
Cape of Good Hope Nature Reserve
False Bay
Betty's Bay
Hawston
Cape Point
Hermanus
Cape of Good Hope
Walker Bay
Whale Coast
Gansbaai

(Cape Peninsula inset map)

Green Point
Sea Point
Victoria & Alfred Waterfront
Signal Hill
CENTRE
CITY BOWL
OBSERVATORY
N7
Clifton
WOODSTOCK
PINELANDS
Camps Bay
1066
Table Mt ▲
MOWBRAY
ROSEBANK
Rhodes Memorial
Irma Stern Museum
RONDEBOSCH
NEWLANDS
Llandudno
Twelve Apostles
Kirstenbosch Botanical Gardens
CLAREMONT
WYNBERG
Cape Flats
M9 →
Sandy Bay
M6
M63
CONSTANTIA
M3
M5
M17
Hout Bay
Princess Vlei
Duiker Point
Hout Bay
Peck's Valley
Sunrise Beach
Chapman's Point
M6
M64
Muizenberg
Noordhoek
Chapman's Bay
Sun Valley
St James
Kalk Bay
Fish Hoek Bay
Kommetjie
M65
Fish Hoek
Glencairn
False Bay
Witsand Bay
M66
Shelley Beach
Scarborough
Simon's Town
Boulder's Beach
M4
Olifants Bay
Miller's Point
M65
Mast Bay
Patridge Point
Smitswinkel Bay
Cape of Good Hope Nature Reserve
Batsata Cove
Venus Pool
Black Rocks
Bordjiesrif
Buffels Bay
Rooikrans
Cape Point
Cape of Good Hope

Munyu	330 K9	Okiep	320 B7	Piet Retief	331 M5
Murchison	325 M2	Old Bunting	330 L9	Pieter Meintjies	327 D10
Murraysburg	328 F9	Old Morley	330 K9	Pietermaritzburg	331 M7
Musina (Messina)	325 M1	Olifantshoek	322 F6	Pigg's Peak	325 M4
Mynfontein	328 G8	Olyfberg	325 M2	Piketberg	326 C10
		Omdraaisvlei	322 F7	Pilgrim's Rest	325 M3

N

		Onderstedorings	321 D8	Platbakkies	320 B8
Nababeep	320 B7	Ons Hoop	324 K2	Plathuis	327 D11
Nabies	321 D6	Onseepkans	320 C6	Platrand	330 L5
Naboomspruit	324 K3	Ontmoeting	321 E5	Plettenberg Bay	328 F11
Nakop	321 D6	Oorwinning	325 M1	Plooysburg	322 G7
Namakgale	325 M2	Oostermoed	324 J3	Pofadder	321 C7
Namies	320 C7	Orania	322 G7	Politsi	325 M2
Napier	327 D11	Oranjefontein	324 K2	Polokwane/	
Nariep	326 B8	Oranjerivier	322 G7	Pietersburg	325 L2
Ndumo	331 N5	Oranjeville	324 K5	Pomeroy	331 M6
Neilersdrif	321 D6	Orkney	323 J5	Pongola	331 N5
Nelspoort	328 F9	Osizweni	331 M6	Pools	326 C10
Nelspruit	325 M4	Ottosdal	323 H5	Port Alfred	329 J11
New England	329 J8	Oudtshoorn	327 E11	Port Edward	330 L8
New Hanover	331 M7	Ouplaas	327 D11	Port Elizabeth	328 H11
New Machavie	324 J5	Oviston	329 H8	Port Grosvenor	330 L9
Newcastle	330 L6	Owendale	322 F6	Port Nolloth	320 A7
Ngobeni	331 M6	Oxbow	330 K6	Port Shepstone	331 M8
Ngome	331 M6	Oyster Bay	328 G11	Port St Johns	330 L9
Ngqeleni	330 K9			Porterville	326 C10
Ngqungu	330 K9			Postmasburg	322 F6
Nhlangano	331 M5	**P**		Potchefstroom	324 J5
Niekerkshoop	322 F7	Paarl	326 C11	Potfontein	328 G8
Nietverdiend	324 H3	Pacaltsdorp	327 E11	Poupan	322 G7
Nieu-Bethesda	328 G9	Paddock	330 L8	Pretoria/Tshwane	324 K4
Nieuwoudtville	326 C9	Pafuri	325 N1	Prieska	322 F7
Nigel	324 K4	Palala	324 K2	Prince Albert Road	327 E10
Nigramoep	320 B7	Palmerton	330 L9	Prince Albert	327 E10
Nkambak	325 M2	Palmietfontein	329 J8	Prince Alfred	
Nkau	330 K7	Pampierstad	323 G5	Hamlet	326 C10
Nkomo	325 M2	Pampoenpoort	328 F8	Priors	328 H8
Nkwalini	331 N6	Panbult	325 M5	Pudimoe	323 G5
Nobokwe	329 K9	Papendorp	326 B9	Putsonderwater	321 E7
Noenieput	321 D5	Papkuil	322 F6		
Noll	328 F11	Park Rynie	331 M8	**Q**	
Nondweni	331 M6	Parys	324 J5	Qacha's Nek	330 K8
Nongoma	331 N6	Patensie	328 G11	Qamata	329 J9
Noordhoek	326 B11	Paternoster	326 B10	Qiba	329 J9
Noordkuil	326 B10	Paterson	329 H10	Qoboqobo	329 K10
Normandien	330 L6	Paul Roux	330 K6	Qolora Mouth	329 K10
Northam	324 J3	Paulpietersburg	331 M5	Qoqodala	329 J9
Nottingham Road	330 L7	Pearly Beach	327 C12	Qora Mouth	329 K10
Noupoort	328 G8	Pearston	328 H10	Queensburgh	331 M7
Nqabara	329 K10	Peddie	329 J10	Queenstown	329 J9
Nqamakwe	329 K9	Peka	330 K7	Qumbu	330 K9
Nqutu	331 M6	Pella	320 C7		
Nsoko	331 N5	Penge	325 M3	**R**	
Ntseshe	329 K9	Perdekop	330 L5	Radium	324 K3
Ntshilini	330 L9	Petersburg	328 G9	Ramabanta	330 K7
Ntywenke	330 K8	Petrus Steyn	330 K5	Ramatlhabama	323 H4
Nutfield	324 L3	Petrusburg	323 H7	Ramotswa	324 H3
Nuwerus	326 B9	Petrusville	322 G7	Ramsgate	330 L8
Nyokana	329 K10	Phalaborwa	325 M2	Randalhurst	331 M6
		Philadelphia	326 C11	Randburg	324 K4
O		Philippolis Road	328 H8	Randfontein	324 K4
Oatlands	328 G10	Philippolis	328 H8	Ratelfontein	326 C9
Obobogorab	321 D5	Philipstown	328 G8	Rawsonville	326 C11
Odendaalsrus	323 J6	Phokwane	325 L3	Reddersburg	323 H7
Ofcolaco	325 M2	Phuthaditjhaba	330 K6	Reebokrand	323 G7
Ogies	324 L4	Pienaarsrivier	324 K3	Reitz	330 K6
		Piet Plessis	322 G4		

Reitzburg	324 J5
Reivilo	322 G5
Renosterkop	328 F9
Renosterspruit	323 J5
Rhodes	329 K8
Richards Bay	331 N7
Richmond	328 G9
Richmond	330 L7
Riebeeckstad	323 J6
Riebeek Kasteel	326 C10
Riebeek Oos	329 H10
Riebeek Wes	326 C10
Rietbron	328 F10
Rietfontein	321 D5
Rietkuil	330 L5
Rietpoel	327 D11
Rietpoort	326 B8
Rietvlei	331 M7
Rita	325 L2
Ritchie	322 G7
River View	331 N6
Riversdale	327 E11
Riviersonderend	327 D11
Roamer's Rest	330 K8
Robert's Drift	324 L5
Robertson	327 D11
Rode	330 L8
Roedtan	325 L3
Roodebank	324 L5
Rooiberg	324 K3
Rooibokkraal	324 J2
Rooibosbult	324 J2
Rooiwal	330 J5
Roosboom	330 L6
Roossenekal	325 L3
Rosebank	331 L8
Rosedene	327 E9
Rosendal	330 K6
Rosmead	328 H9
Rostrataville	323 H5
Rouxpos	327 D10
Rouxville	329 J8
Rust de Winter	324 K3
Rustenburg	324 J4
Rustig	323 J5
Rusverby	323 J4

S

Saaifontein	327 E9
Sabie	325 M3
Sada	329 J9
St Faith's	330 L8
St James	326 C11
St Lucia	331 N6
St Marks	329 J9
Sakrivier	327 D8
Saldanha	326 B10
Salem	329 H10
Salt Lake	322 G7
Sandberg	326 C10
Sandvlakte	328 G11
Sannaspos	323 J7
Sannieshof	323 H4
Sasolburg	324 K5
Scarborough	326 B11
Scheepersnek	331 M6

Weenen	331 L7
Wegdraai	321 E6
Welgeleë	323 J6
Welkom	323 J6
Wellington	326 C11
Wepener	323 J7
Wesley	329 J10
Wesselsbron	323 J6
Wesselsvlei	322 F5
Westerberg	322 E7
Westleigh	323 J5
Westonaria	324 K4
White River	325 M3
Whites	323 J6
Whitmore	330 K9
Whittlesea	329 J9
Wiegnaarspoort	328 F10
Wilderness	327 F11
Williston	327 D9
Willowmore	328 F10
Willowvale	329 K9
Winburg	323 J6
Wincanton	322 F5
Windsorton Road	323 G6
Windsorton	323 G6
Winkelpos	323 J5
Witbank	325 L4
Witkop	329 J8
Witmos	328 H10
Witpoort	323 H5
Witput	322 G7
Witsand	327 D11
Witteklip	328 H11
Witwater	320 B8
Wolmaransstad	323 H5
Wolseley	326 C10
Wolwehoek	324 K5
Wolwespruit	323 H6
Wonderkop	330 J6
Wondermere	323 J4
Woodlands	328 G11
Worcester	327 C11
Wuppertal	326 C9

X

Xolobe	329 J9

Y

Yzerfontein	326 B10

Z

Zaaimansdal	328 F11
Zastron	329 J8
Zebediela	325 L3
Zeerust	323 H3
Zunckels	330 L7
Zwelitsha	329 J10
Zwingli	324 H3

ACKNOWLEDGMENTS

Abbreviations for the credits are as follows:
AA = AA World Travel Library, t (top), b (bottom), c (centre), l (left), r (right), bg (background)

UNDERSTANDING SOUTH AFRICA

4 South African Tourism; 5l AA/C Sawyer; 5c, 5r South African Tourism; 6l AA/C Sawyer; 6c, 6r South African Tourism; 6bl AA/S McBride; 8tl South African Tourism; 8tr AA/P Kenward; 8rct, 8cr AA/C Sawyer; 8cbr, 8br South African Tourism; 9tl South African Tourism; 9lct AA/S McBride; 9cl, 9lcb South African Tourism; 9bl AA/S McBride; 9br AA/S McBride; 10 Mala Mala Game Reserve; 11(1), 11(2), 11(3), 11(4), 11(5), 11(6) South African Tourism; 11(7) AA/S McBride; 11(8) South African Tourism; 12(9), 12(10), 12(11), 12(12), 12(13), 12(14), 12(15), 12(16) South African Tourism; 13(17), 13(18), 13(19), 13(20), 13(21), 13(22), 13(23), 13(24) South African Tourism; 14(25), 14(26), 14(27), 14(28), 14(29), 14(30), 14(31), 14(32), 14(33) South African Tourism.

LIVING SOUTH AFRICA

15 South African Tourism; 16/17bg AA/C Sawyer; 16tl AA/S McBride; 16tc AA/C Sawyer; 16tr AA/S McBride; 16c AA/P Kenward; 16bl AA/C Sawyer; 16cr Home Coming Revolution; 17tl AA/C Sawyer; 17tr South African Tourism; 17c AA/C Sawyer; 17cr AA/C Sawyer; 18/19bg AA/S McBride; 18tl Spier Wine Estate; 18tr South African Tourism; 18cl AA/C Hampton; 18cr AA/C Sawyer; 18b AFP/Getty Images; 19t Time Life Pictures/Getty Images; 19cl South African Tourism; 19ct AA/S McBride; 19c AA/C Sawyer; 19cr South African Tourism; 19r South African Tourism; 20/1bg South African Tourism; 20tl Mala Mala Game Reserve; 20cl AA/S McBride; 20c AA/C Sawyer; 20cr AA/S McBride; 20bl South African Tourism; 20/1t South African Tourism; 20/1c AA/S McBride; 21tc AA/C Hampton; 21cl David Mabunda; 21c AA/S McBride; 21r AA/S McBride; 22/3bg AA/S McBride; 22tl Getty Images; 22tc AA/P Kenward; 22c Getty Images; 22cr Para-Pax; 22cl AA/C Sawyer; 22/3t South African Tourism; 23c AFP/Getty Images; 23tr Rex Features; 23cr Getty Images; 24/5bg South African Tourism; 24tl South African Tourism; 24t AA/P Kenward; 24cr South African Tourism; 24cl South African Tourism; 24/5t South African Airways; 25cl Gorah Elephant Camp; 25c AA/C Sawyer; 25r South African Tourism; 26bg AA/P Kenward; 26tl Penguin Group (USA); 26tc AA/C Sawyer; 26ct AA/S McBride; 26cb AA/C Sawyer; 26cl AA/M Birkitt; 26r Rex Features.

THE STORY OF SOUTH AFRICA

27 AA/C Sawyer; 27l AA/S McBride; 28/9bg Courtesy of the University of Pretoria Mapaungubwe Museum; 28t South African Tourism; 28b AA/C Sawyer; 28/9c AA/S McBride; 29c Courtesy of the University of Pretoria Mapungubwe Museum; 29bl South African Tourism; 29br South African Tourism; 30/1bg AA/C Sawyer; 30tl AA/C Sawyer; 30bl Dave Bartruff/Corbis; 30c Mary Evans Picture Library; 30b Mary Evans Picture Library; 30br AA/C Sawyer; 31cr Rex Features; 31c Mary Evans Picture Library; 31b AA/S McBride; 31br AA/P Kenward; 32/3bg AA/C Sawyer; 32tl South African Tourism; 32bl South African Tourism; 32c AA; 32cr Rex Features; 32/3b Mary Evans Picture Library; 33cl AA; 33c AA; 33bl National Army Museum, London, UK/Bridgeman Art Library; 33bc AA/C Sawyer; 33br Africana Museum, Johannesburg, South Africa/Bridgeman Art Library; 34/5bg South African Tourism; 34tl Bettmann/Corbis; 34bl Mary Evans Picture Library; 34/5b The Art Archive; 34/5c AA/C Sawyer;

35bl Mary Evans Picture Library; 35br AA/C Sawyer; 36/7bg AA/C Sawyer; 36tl AA/C Sawyer; 36bl Time Life Pictures/Getty Images; 36/7b Rex Features; 37cl AA/C Sawyer; 37cr Hulton Archive/Getty Images; 37bl AA/C Sawyer; 37c Time Life Pictures/Getty Images; 37br Contemporary African Art Collection Limited/Corbis; 38/9bg AA/P Kenward; 38tl Rex Features; 38bl Random House Archive & Library; 38/9b Time Life Pictures/Getty Images; 39c Time Life Pictures/Getty Images; 39cr AA/P Kenward; 39b Time Life Pictures/Getty Images; 40bg South African Tourism; 40cl AFP/Getty Images; 40bl Truth & Reconciliation Commission; 40cr AFP/Getty Images; 40bl Louise Gubb/Corbis; 40br Rex Features.

ON THE MOVE

41 AA/P Kenward; 42/3t Digital Vision; 42b AA/C Sawyer; 44/5t Digital Vision; 44b AA/C Sawyer; 45b AA/C Sawyer; 46/7t South African Tourism; 46b AA/S McBride; 48 AA/P Kenward; 49t AA/C Sawyer; 49c South African Tourism; 49b AA/C Sawyer; 50t AA/C Sawyer; 50b AA/C Sawyer; 51 AA/C Sawyer; 52/3t Ethos Marketing/Blue Train; 54/5t AA/C Sawyer; 54c AA/C Sawyer; 56/7t AA/C Sawyer; 56c AA/S McBride; 56b AA/S McBride; 57c AA/S McBride; 58t AA/C Sawyer; 58b AA/C Sawyer.

THE SIGHTS

59 South African Tourism; 61t, 61c, 61r AA/C Sawyer; 62t, 62l AA/C Sawyer; 63tl, 63tr, 63b AA/C Sawyer; 64t, 64cl, 64cc, 64cr AA/C Sawyer; 65 AA/C Sawyer; 67cl, 67cc, 67cr AA/C Sawyer; 68r, 68l AA/C Sawyer; 69cl, 69c, 69cr AA/C Sawyer; 70t, 70cl, 70cr, 70b AA/C Sawyer; 71t, 71b AA/C Sawyer; 72tl, 72tr AA/C Sawyer; 73t AA/C Sawyer; 73b Rex Features; 75r, 75l AA/C Sawyer; 76t, 76l AA/C Sawyer; 78tl, 78tc, 78tr AA/C Sawyer; 79t, 79r AA/C Sawyer; 80tl, 80bl South African Tourism; 80tr AA/C Sawyer; 81tl, 81tc, 81tr AA/C Sawyer; 82t, 82c, 82b AA/C Sawyer; 83tl, 83tc, 83tr AA/C Sawyer; 84t, 84cl, 84b AA/C Sawyer; 85t, 85r AA/C Sawyer; 86tl, 86tc, 86tr AA/C Sawyer; 87tl, 87tc, 87tr AA/C Sawyer; 88t South African Tourism; 88l AA/C Sawyer; 89t South African Tourism; 89b AA/C Sawyer; 90t, 90cl, 90cc, 90cr, 90b AA/C Sawyer; 91 South African Tourism; 92 AA/C Sawyer; 93 AA/C Sawyer; 94cl, 94cc, 94cr AA/C Sawyer; 95cl, 95cc, 95cr, 95b AA/C Sawyer; 97tl, 97tc, 97tr, 97b AA/C Sawyer; 98t 98cl, 98cc, 98cr AA/C Sawyer; 98b AA/P Kenward; 99 AA/C Sawyer; 100t, 100l, 100b AA/C Sawyer; 101 South African Tourism; 102tl, 102tr AA/C Sawyer; 103t, 103r AA/C Sawyer; 104t, 104l AA/C Sawyer; 106t, 106b AA/S McBride; 106cl AA/C Sawyer; 107t, 107r South African Tourism; 107b AA/C Sawyer; 108t AA/C Sawyer; 108cl, 108b AA/P Kenward; 108cc, 108cr AA/S McBride; 109 AA/P Kenward; 110cl, 110bl AA/S McBride; 111t South African Tourism; 111b AA/S McBride; 112t, 112l AA/S McBride; 113t, 113cl, 113c AA/S McBride; 113r AA/R Strange; 113b South African Tourism; 114tl, 114tr, 114c South African Tourism; 115t South African Tourism; 115r AA/C Sawyer; 116tl, 116c South African Tourism; 116tr AA/S McBride; 117tl, 117b South African Tourism; 117tr KZN Wildlife; 118t, 118l AA/S McBride; 119tl, 119tr AA/S McBride; 120t AA/P Kenward; 120bl South African Tourism; 121 South African Tourism; 122 South African Tourism; 123t, 123cr AA/S McBride; 123b South African Tourism; 125tl, 125tc AA/S McBride; 125tr AA/C Hampton;

126 AA/S McBride; 127t AA/C Sawyer; 127r AA/C Hampton; 128/9 South African Tourism; 130 AA/S McBride; 130/1 South African Tourism; 131r AA/S McBride; 132cl, 132b South African Tourism; 133t, 133cr, 133b AA/S McBride; 133cl, 133cc AA/C Sawyer; 134t, 134cl, 134cbl South African Tourism; 134cc AA/C Hampton; 134cr, 134b AA/S McBride; 135t South African Tourism; 135b AA/S McBride; 136tl, 136tr AA/S McBride; 137tl, 137tc AA/S McBride; 137tr South Africa Tourism; 138tl AA/C Hampton; 138tc, 138tr, 138b AA/S McBride; 140tl, 140tr AA/S McBride; 140tc AA/C Sawyer; 141tl, 141tr, 141b AA/S McBride; 142t, 142cl, 142b AA/S McBride; 142cc AA/P Kenward; 142cr AA/C Sawyer; 143 South African Tourism; 144/5 South African Tourism; 144 AA/S McBride; 145r Apartheid Museum; 146tl, 146tc, 146tr, 146b AA/S McBride; 147tl AA/S McBride; 147tr South African Tourism; 148 South African Tourism; 149t, 149cc AA/C Sawyer; 149cl South African Tourism; 149cr AA/S McBride; 150l, 150c AA/S McBride; 151c AA/C Sawyer; 151r, 151b AA/S McBride; 153t South African Tourism; 153b AA/C Hampton; 154tl AA/S McBride; 154tr South African Tourism; 155tl, 155tr AA/S McBride; 156t, 156cl, 156cc, 156cr, 156b AA/C Sawyer; 157 AA/C Sawyer; 158t South African Tourism; 158cl AA/P Kenward; 158/9, 159t, 159b AA/C Sawyer; 159cr AA/S McBride; 160t, 160cl, 160c South African Tourism; 160cr AA/C Hampton; 161t, 161b South African Tourism; 162/3 South African Tourism; 163 AA/C Hampton; 164tl, 164tr, 164b AA/S McBride; 165t, 165b AA/S McBride; 165c AA/C Sawyer; 166tl, 166tr, 166b Images of Africa; 168tl, 168tr AA/S McBride; 169tl, 169tr AA/S McBride; 170t AA/S McBride; 171t, 171b AA/S McBride; 172tl, 172tr, 172b AA/S McBride; 173t, 173c, 173b AA/S McBride; 174tl, 174tr AA/S McBride.

WHAT TO DO

175 South African Tourism; 176/7t AA/S McBride; 176 AA/C Sawyer; 177 AA/C Sawyer; 178t South African Tourism; 178l AA/C Sawyer; 178r Spier Wine Estate; 179t, 179r AA/C Sawyer; 180/1t AA/C Hampton; 180l, 180/1c, 181r South African Tourism; 182t AA/C Hampton; 182c South African Tourism; 183t, 183r AA/P Kenward; 184/5t, 184c AA/C Sawyer; 185c Para-Pax; 186/7t, 186, 187 AA/C Sawyer; 188/9t, 188, 189 AA/C Sawyer; 190t AA/C Sawyer; 190c South African Tourism; 191t, 191c AA/C Sawyer; 192/3t, 192, 193 AA/C Sawyer; 194/5t, 194, 195 AA/C Sawyer; 196/7t, 196 AA/C Sawyer; 197 South African Tourism; 198/9t AA/P Kenward; 198 South African Tourism; 199 AA/C Sawyer; 200/1t AA/P Kenward; 200 AA/C Sawyer; 201 South African Tourism; 202/3t AA/C Sawyer; 202 South African Tourism; 203 Fugitves' Drift Lodge; 204/5t AA/C Sawyer; 204 AA/S McBride; 205 AA/S McBride; 206t AA/C Sawyer; 206b AA/S McBride; 207t AA/S McBride; 207c Photodisc; 208/9t, 208, 209 AA/S McBride; 210/1t, 211 AA/S McBride; 210 South African Tourism; 212/3t AA/S McBride; 212 AA/C Sawyer; 213 AA/P Kenward; 214/5t, 214 AA/S McBride; 215 Digitalvision; 216/7t, 216, 217 AA/S McBride; 218/9t AA/P Kenward; 218, 219 AA/S McBride; 220t AA/P Kenward; 220c AA/S McBride.

OUT AND ABOUT

221 South African Tourism; 223t South African Tourism; 223b AA/C Sawyer; 224 AA/C Sawyer; 225t, 225c, 225b AA/C Sawyer; 226 South African Tourism; 227t, 227c AA/C Sawyer; 227b South African Tourism; 228 AA/P Kenward;

229 AA/C Sawyer; 230, 231t, 231c, 231b Traveller's Rest Farm; 232 AA/C Sawyer; 233 South African Tourism; 234 South African Tourism; 235t, 235b AA/C Sawyer; 236 AA/C Sawyer; 237t, 237b AA/C Sawyer; 238 AA/S McBride; 239tr South African Tourism; 239l, 239b AA/S McBride; 241t South African Tourism; 241b AA/S McBride; 242 AA/S McBride; 243t, 243c, 243bl, 243br AA/S McBride; 245t AA/S McBride; 245b South African Tourism; 246 AA/S McBride; 247t, 247b AA/S McBride; 248 South African Tourism; 249t, 249b South African Tourism; 250 South African Tourism; 251t, 250/1 South African Tourism; 252 AA/S McBride; 253t, 253b AA/S McBride; 254 South African Tourism.

EATING AND STAYING

255 South African Tourism; 256cl, 256cr South African Tourism; 256c Sabi Sabi; 257cl, 257c South African Tourism; 256bl AA/S McBride; 257cr Bushmans Kloof Wilderness Reserve; 257b AA/S McBride; 258cl AA/S McBride; 258c AA/C Sawyer; 258cr Sabi Sabi; 259 AA/C Sawyer; 260l South African Tourism; 260cr, 260br AA/C Sawyer; 261b, 261r AA/C Sawyer; 262l, 262c, 262r AA/C Sawyer; 263bl, 263c, 263cr AA/C Sawyer; 264c, 264r AA/C Sawyer; 265c, 265r AA/C Sawyer; 266l, 266tr AA/S McBride; 267tl, 267tr AA/S McBride; 268bl Rissington Inn; 269tl The Wild Fig Tree; 269c De Oude Kraal; 269r AA/S McBride; 270tl, 270c AA/S McBride; 271c, 271bl AA/S McBride; 271br Photodisc; 272tr Le Must; 272bl Photodisc; 273tr AA/S McBride; 274l Gorah Elephant Camp; 274c, 274r AA/C Sawyer; 275l, 275c Sabi Sabi; 275r Fugitives' Drift Lodge; 276l, 276c AA/C Sawyer: 277t, 277b AA/C Sawyer; 278l, 278c AA/C Sawyer; 279 AA/C Sawyer; 280l, 280c AA/C Sawyer; 281l, 281c AA/C Sawyer; 282t, 282b AA/C Sawyer; 283l AA/C Sawyer; 283r Gorah Elephant Camp; 284l, 284r AA/C Sawyer; 285l, 285r AA/S McBride; 286l, 286c AA/S McBride; 287tc, 287r AA/S McBride; 288l, 288c AA/S McBride; 289c, 289r AA/S McBride; 290c, 290tr AA/S McBride; 291 Sabi Sabi; 292 AA/S McBride; 293tc, 293r AA/S McBride; 294 AA/S McBride; 295 AA/S McBride; 296 AA/S McBride.

PLANNING

297 AA/C Sawyer; 299 AA/C Sawyer; 300 AA/S McBride; 301t AA/P Kenward; 301b AA/S McBride; 302t AA/C Sawyer; 302b Currency information courtesy of MRI Bankers Guide to Foreign Currency; 303t, 303b AA/C Sawyer; 304b AA/S McBride; 306 AA/S McBride; 307t AA/S McBride; 307b AA/R Whittaker; 308t AA/C Sawyer; 308b AA/S McBride; 309t AA/C Sawyer; 309b AA/S McBride; 310 AA/S McBride; 311 AA/C Sawyer; 312t AA/C Sawyer; 312b AA/S McBride; 313 AA/C Sawyer; 314 AA/C Sawyer.

Project editor
Clare Garcia

Design work
Bob Johnson, Jo Tapper

Picture research
Carol Walker

Internal repro work
Susan Crowhurst, Ian Little, Michael Moody

Production
Lyn Kirby, Helen Sweeney

Mapping
Maps produced by the Cartography Department of AA Publishing

Main contributors
Matthew Buckland, Peter Joyce, Francisca Kellet, Richard Whitaker, Lizzie Williams

Copy editor
Audrey Horne

Published by AA Publishing, a trading name of Automobile Association Developments Limited, whose registered office is Fanum House, Basing View, Basingstoke, Hampshire RG21 4EA. Registered number 1878835.

A CIP catalogue record for this book is available from the British Library.

ISBN-10: 0-7495-4631-X
ISBN-13: 978-0-7495-4631-1

Selected text supplied by Footprint Handbooks Limited © 2004

Key Guide is a registered trademark in Australia and is used under license.
Binding style with plastic section dividers by permission of AA Publishing.

Colour separation by Keenes
Printed and bound by Leo, China

Find out more about AA Publishing and the wide range of travel publications and services the AA provides by visiting our website at www.theAA.com/bookshop

A01619
Maps in this title produced from map data:
© New Holland Publishing (South Africa) (PTY) Limited 2004
and © Footprint Handbooks Limited 2004

Relief map images supplied by Mountain High Maps® Copyright © 1993 Digital Wisdom, Inc
Weather chart statistics supplied by Weatherbase © Copyright 2004 Canty and Associates, LLC
Communicarta assistance with time chart gratefully acknowledged

We believe the contents of this book are correct at the time of printing. However, some details, particularly prices, opening times and telephone numbers do change. We do not accept responsibility for any consequences arising from the use of this book. This does not affect your statutory rights. We would be grateful if readers would advise us of any inaccuracies they may encounter, or any suggestions they might like to make to improve the book. There is a form provided at the back of the book for this purpose, or you can email us at Keyguides@theaa.com

COVER PICTURE CREDITS
Front cover and spine: South African Tourism
Back cover, top to bottom: AA/E Meacher, AA/P Kenward, AA/C Sawyer, AA/C Sawyer

Dear Key Guide Reader

———————●———————

Thank you for buying this Key Guide. Your comments and opinions are very important to us, so please help us to improve our travel guides by taking a few minutes to complete this questionnaire.

You do not need a stamp (unless posted outside the UK). If you do not want to cut this page from your guide, then photocopy it or write your answers on a plain sheet of paper.

Send to: **Key Guide Editor, AA World Travel Guides FREEPOST SCE 4598, Basingstoke RG21 4GY**

Find out more about AA Publishing and the wide range of travel publications the AA provides by visiting our website at www.theAA.com/bookshop

ABOUT THIS GUIDE

Which Key Guide did you buy? _____

Where did you buy it?_____

When? _ _ month/ _ _ year

Why did you choose this AA Key Guide?
❏ Price ❏ AA Publication
❏ Used this series before; title _____
❏ Cover ❏ Other (please state) _____

Please let us know how helpful the following features of the guide were to you by circling the appropriate category: very helpful (**VH**), helpful (**H**) or little help (**LH**)

Size	**VH**	**H**	**LH**
Layout	**VH**	**H**	**LH**
Photos	**VH**	**H**	**LH**
Excursions	**VH**	**H**	**LH**
Entertainment	**VH**	**H**	**LH**
Hotels	**VH**	**H**	**LH**
Maps	**VH**	**H**	**LH**
Practical info	**VH**	**H**	**LH**
Restaurants	**VH**	**H**	**LH**
Shopping	**VH**	**H**	**LH**
Walks	**VH**	**H**	**LH**
Sights	**VH**	**H**	**LH**
Transport info	**VH**	**H**	**LH**

What was your favourite sight, attraction or feature listed in the guide?

Page _____ Please give your reason _____

_____

Which features in the guide could be changed or improved? Or are there any other comments you would like to make?

_____

_____